HANDBOOK OF WORK AND ORGANIZATIONAL PSYCHOLOGY

Volume 4: Organizational Psychology

HANDBOOK OF WORK AND ORGANIZATIONAL PSYCHOLOGY

(Second Edition)
Volume 4: Organizational Psychology

Edited by

Pieter J.D. Drenth

Vrije Universiteit,
Amsterdam,
The Netherlands

Henk Thierry

Tilburg University,
The Netherlands

Charles J. de Wolff

Catholic University,
Nijmegen,
The Netherlands

Psychology Press
a member of the Taylor & Francis group

Psychology Press Ltd
27 Church Road
Hove
East Sussex, BN3 2FA, UK

British Library Cataloguing in Publication Data
A catalogue record for this title is available from the British Library

Volume 4
ISBN 0–86377–526–8 (Hbk)

10017 27 44

Cover illustration by Clive Goodyer
Cover design by Rachael Adams
Typeset by Mendip Communications Ltd, Frome, Somerset
Printed and bound in the United Kingdom by Redwood Books Ltd,
Trowbridge, Wilts, UK

0863775284

Contents

Contributors to Volume 4

Jen A. Algera, Technische Universiteit Eindhoven, Faculteit Technische Bedrijfskunde, Postbus 513, 5600 MB Eindhoven, The Netherlands.

J.H. Erik Andriessen, Technische Universiteit Delft, Faculteit Wijsbegeerte en Technische Maatschappij Wetenschappen, Kanaalweg 2b, 2628 SB Delft, The Netherlands.

Stanisława Borkowska, University of Lodz, Katedra Pracy I Polityki Społecznej, ul POW 3/5, 90-255 Lodz, Poland.

Jan Willem Broekhuijsen, A. Mauvelaan 12, 1401 CK Hilversum, The Netherlands.

Gaston de Cock, Katholieke Universiteit Leuven, Faculteit Psychologie en Pedagogiek, Tiensestraat 102, B 3000 Leuven, Belgium.

Pieter J.D. Drenth, Vrije Universiteit, Faculteit Psychologie en Pedagogiek, Van der Boechorststraat 1, 1081 BT Amsterdam, The Netherlands.

Frans M. van Eijnatten, Technische Universiteit Eindhoven, Faculteit Technologie en Management, Postbus 513, 5600 MB Eindhoven, The Netherlands.

Dick de Gilder, Universiteit van Amsterdam, Faculteit der Psychologie, Roetersstraat 15, 1018 WB Amsterdam, The Netherlands.

Maarten R. van Gils, Rijksuniversiteit Groningen, Faculteit Bedrijfskunde, Postbus 800, 9700 AV Groningen, The Netherlands.

Ben Groenendijk, Sonderholm 76, 2133 JG Hoofddorp, The Netherlands.

Frank Heller, The Tavistock Institute, Centre for Decision Making Studies, 30 Tabernacle Street, London EC2A 4DE, UK.

Paul L. Koopman, Vrije Universiteit, Faculteit Psychologie en Pedagogiek, Van der Boechorststraat 1, 1081 BT Amsterdam, The Netherlands.

Ton Korver, Katholieke Universiteit Brabant, Faculteit Sociale Wetenschappen, Postbus 90153, 5000 LE Tilburg, The Netherlands.

Jolanta Kulpińska, University of Lodz, Faculty of Economics and Sociology, ul. POW 3/5, 90-255 Lodz, Poland.

Jaap J. van Muijen, Vrije Universiteit, Faculteit Psychologie en Pedagogiek, Van der Boechorststraat 1, 1081 BT Amsterdam, The Netherlands.

Stef van Nieuwkerke, Zuid Leeuwstraat 37, 3404 Neerlanden, Belgium.

Johannes M. Pennings, University of Pennsylvania, The Wharton School, 2000 Steinberg Hall, Philadelphia, PA 19104, USA.

Henk Thierry, Katholieke Universiteit Brabant, Faculteit Sociale Weternschappen, Postbus 90153, 5000 LE Tilburg, The Netherlands.

Peter Veen, Rijnseweg 5, 3984 NG Odijk, The Netherlands.

René van der Vlist, Rijksuniversiteit Leiden, Faculteit Sociale en Gedragswetenschappen, Postbus 9555, 2300 RB Leiden, The Netherlands.

André F.M. Wierdsma, Universiteit Nijenrode, Straatweg 25, 3621 AG Breukelen, The Netherlands.

Karel De Witte, Katholieke Universiteit Leuven, Faculteit Psychologie en Paedagogiek, Tiensestraat 102, B 3000 Leuven, Belgium.

1

Interaction of Person/Group–Organization–Environment

Henk Thierry

The chapters in this fourth volume of the *Handbook* bear upon the behaviour of individuals or groups in work organizations. This behaviour is not only related to features of organizations but also to those of the organizational environment and the links between them. Organizational characteristics concern, e.g., the organization structure (such as the degree of centralization or formalization) and its strategy and culture. Environmental characteristics include such things as legislation and regulations, political decision making, investment climate, and industrial relations (e.g. between employers and trade unions). A first question is the extent to which the behaviour of individuals and groups is determined by organizational and environmental features. For example, it appears that under uncertain conditions people are motivated by slightly different aspects of their work than in situations where the circumstances are predictable. A second question that links up with this is to what extent such features are in turn influenced by the behaviour of people in groups or organizational units. An example of this is the phenomenon that the more highly educated people there are in an organization who perform quite complex tasks, the less

specific the rules often are. We see, moreover, that a number of subjects at the organization and environment levels can also be considered as independent themes, including such things as organization culture, democratization in companies, and interorganizational networks.

The subjects addressed in this volume are characteristic of organizational psychology. Often it is not only the behaviour of groups of people *in* an organization that is at issue, but also the behaviour *of* an organization, for example, of particular sections or company units. Furthermore, various levels of analysis play a continual role; and in almost every chapter, contributions from other disciplines are discussed in greater or lesser detail. Yet it is the "psychological" explanation, the predicting and the influencing of behavior (of individuals, groups, and other "sets" of people) that constitute the key theme of this volume. The reader will also repeatedly come across references to chapters from earlier volumes. Thus we emphasize, as we did in the Introduction ("What is Work and Organization Psychology?") to this new handbook, that, although a distinction can be made between organizational psychology, work psychology, and personnel psychology, they should certainly not be separated from each other.

The first four chapters in this volume bear upon the theme *Organization theories* or, what is perhaps a more appropriate term, *Perspectives on organizations*. Remarkably, virtually all the other chapters in this fourth volume regularly hark back to this theme. For organization theories are nearly always (also) about how people's behaviour—in organizations or in a part of them—can be interpreted, and subsequently regulated and predicted. This occurs, depending on the "school" to which an author belongs, by means of very wide-ranging concepts. Such concepts often form the poles of one dimension. The following are some such examples (which are not always completely independent of each other):

- *Development ... Design*: the learning capacity and the growth of a social system versus the experts' plan for the solution to a particular problem.
- *Control ... Involvement*: the steering of behavior through "control" and hierarchy versus through the development of staff "commitment" to work and organization.
- *Stable structure ... "Negotiated order"*: the view that features of an organization lead an "objective" existence versus the view that those features are based on social exchange processes, a shared value structure, and negotiation.
- *Short term ... Long term*: criteria for success (and survival) bear upon efficiency in the short term versus effectiveness in the long term.

In their chapter on "Organization Theories", Veen and Korver focus primarily on the behaviour *of* an organization whereby the question of what an organization actually is (a building?, a collection of people?, a differentiated social structure? etc.) regularly crops up. More than 10 organization theories or perspectives are discussed, more or less chronologically: In addition to such conceptions as "scientific management" and "integration—motivation", contingency theory is also addressed.

Pennings keeps the focus on this last-mentioned subject in his chapter on "Structural Contingency Theory". He calls this theory an empirical reaction to a whole range of ideological management theories (a number of examples of which are discussed by Veen and Korver) that believe that there is one best way of organizing. A distinctive feature of structural contingency theory is rather the view that the effectiveness of an organization depends on the congruency between the organizational structure and the environment (a congruency that must be re-established each time changes occur). He discusses this theory vis-à-vis deterministic definitions of organizational structure among others, and those that conceive of the organization as a socially constructed reality.

Van Eijnatten describes the "Developments in Socio-Technical Systems Design" by means of four phases. Certainly, in its first decades, socio-technical design was seen as a typically European development. Its point of departure was that technological and social conditions must be seen as having equal value and that, by redesigning technology and the requirements of the job, both the human being and the organization would function better. It all started with the famous study carried out in English coal mines in the late 1940s and early 1950s. Van Eijnatten clearly illustrates that countries such as England, Sweden, Norway, and The Netherlands have different emphases.

The environment of organizations forms the subject of Van Gils' chapter on "Interorganizational Networks". The environment can also be seen as a limitation on the organization, as a collection of interacting organizations, as a social system, and as a network (whereby two or more organizations join forces). Remarkably, a number of organization theories mentioned in earlier chapters can also shed light on the nature and the meaning of networks. Finally, the hybrid organization, e.g. a "joint venture", is discussed.

The next five chapters share *Organizational culture and change* as a common theme. In "Organizational Culture", Van Muijen points out that interest in a subject such as culture has existed for quite some time, but that in anthropology and social sciences this has shown a sharp increase over recent decades. Very different approaches to, and thus also definitions of, culture have resulted from this. Thus, culture can, for example, be considered as a feature of an organization (an organization "has" a culture), but also as a metaphor: What is meant by this is that organization structures and processes have a symbolic meaning. After a discussion of the work of Schein, this author addresses the functions of (sub)culture, the concept of organization climate, and the competing-values model of organizational culture.

In their chapter "Organizational Psychology in Cross-cultural Perspective", Drenth and Groenendijk address the question of whether cultural factors can account for differences in organizational characteristics or for those in attitude and behaviour, as well as whether culture might be a contingency factor in the relationship between organization and human behaviour. They provide a detailed discussion of methodological problems that occur in cross-cultural research (including equivalence and aggregation), followed by an examination of the results of cross-cultural research. Finally, they pose the question: To what extent will cultural differences converge in the future?

Van der Vlist, in "Planned Change in Organizations and Organizational Development in the 1990s", describes how both main streams (development or planned change) have gradually lost some of their exclusive character and partly flow into one another as far as such concepts as the "design" and "development" of organizations are concerned. Furthermore, both streams are approached increasingly from the perspective of organizational theories, namely from contingency theory. Van der Vlist elaborates on the role of participation and involvement, on resistance and barriers to changes.

The diagnosis and assessment of changes, partly so that decisions by interested parties (for example, administrators) can be more effectively made, are the main themes of "Assessment of Organizational Change" by Thierry, Koopman, and De Gilder. A number of concepts and variables are discussed by means of a system model. After a discussion of methods and instruments for "assessment", various phases are addressed with regard to the relationship between principal, clients, and researcher/consultant.

Then Heller analyzes the backgrounds to successful organizational changes as well as the causes of failure in such change projects. The latter may well occur rather more often than one might think; it is very likely that the literature available tends to be selective in favour of "success stories". With regard to the contribution of the social sciences to important change processes, the author comes to the conclusion that this is not only modest, but has also been made with a somewhat varying degree of success.

The subject of the next chapter, "Motivation and Satisfaction", might also have been included in the volume on Work Psychology or that on Personnel Psychology. Characteristically, theories on (work) motivation relate to features of the individual person, aspects of the nature of work, and organization characteristics. Thierry reviews 10 motivation theories, categorized according to two dimensions: reinforcement–cognition, and content–process. Then various (work) satisfaction models are discussed, jointly with an overview of some returning measurement problems. Satisfaction is conceived as a construct that usually operates rather independently in empirical research, although it is conceptually closely related to the cycle of motivated behaviour.

In the chapter that follows Thierry examines the subject of "Compensating Work". First, various pay theories are discussed, most of which were designed with different intentions (often to explain individual motivation). After an account of the recent reflection theory, Thierry focuses on various systems and forms of pay, as well as the main points of empirical research. Finally, because this subject is playing an increasing role in "strategic" company policy, a number of themes for future research (e.g. on "strategic" pay) are addressed.

Three chapters relate to "Leadership", "Decision-making" and "Participation". In the first chapter Andriessen and Drenth analyze the theory and research about leadership in general terms. They show that concepts of the leader's functions are heavily dependent upon the view of the organization as a whole. They are different in a strongly economically-oriented, Taylorist organization than they are in one in which human and social factors are acknowledged as making an important contribution, or in a concept which considers organizations as complex systems or as political arenas. A discussion of the wealth of research into the meaning and influence of the personality factors, behavioural styles, expectations and attitudes of the leader him- or herself, and of members of the group, culminates in the presentation of a complex leadership model which attempts to integrate the essential elements of the leader, the group, and the situation.

In "Complex Decision-making in Organizations", Koopman, Broekhuysen, and Wierdsma demonstrate that there is often a close relationship between decision-making theories and organization theories. After a discussion of four models, which differ from each other in the outcomes that they consider to be acceptable, a number of process approaches are sketched, including Mintzberg's phase model. Furthermore, the context in which the decision making takes place is examined, including the newness of a problem and its environment. Subsequently, the focus is on the individual manager and the factors that determine how his or her decision making is structured.

Andriessen provides in "Industrial Democratization and Industrial Relations" an overview of a number of different forms of participation, at various levels in a work organization, which are found in a range of countries with highly diverse systems of labour relations. After an account of the goals of participation, the author examines structures in the United Kingdom, and in southern and northern Europe. There follows a discussion of examples in The Netherlands (including the works council), after which the results of (inter)national research are addressed.

It is not possible to classify the following chapters under one umbrella theme; they are, however, all linked to one or more of the preceding themes. De Cock, de Witte, and Nieuwkerke begin their chapter on "Effective Communication within the Organization" with a discussion of the components of the communication process. Then they turn to main determinants of effectiveness, one of which is constituted by the nature of feedback. An important role is attributed to organizational climate, that is differentiated into four distinct types of climate. Communication processes are clearly affected by the dominant organizational climate type.

Koopman and Algera examine in "Automation: Social-organizational Aspects" first various forms of automation. After a discussion of the effects of automation on employment and the extent to which automation is a part of strategic company policy, they draw attention to various problems that regularly crop up between designers, principals and the future users of equipment. This leads to a discussion of two models, after which two strategies are addressed: the incremental-iterative and the linear-integral strategies.

The final chapter presents an interesting case study: the transition from a centralized, socialist-led society to a free market economic system, and the effects of this upon work organizations, and the attitudes and behaviour of employees. Describing this transformation in Poland, Borkowska and Kulpińska argue that, despite a number of circumstances that are unique to Poland, many problems and social reactions which they note, also apply to other central European nations which have passed through a similar transition.

2

Theories of Organization

Peter Veen and Ton Korver

1 INTRODUCTION

An organization is a complex and multi-faceted phenomenon. It is therefore virtually impossible to provide a satisfactory all-encompassing definition. Listing its characteristics is usually felt to be sufficient. In this vein, organizations are often described as associations:

- of individuals, whose aim is to achieve *goals*;
- in which the work is split up into different tasks (specialisation and *differentiation*);
- in which the *integration* of activities takes place by means of formalized rules and a hierarchical structure (management structure);
- with a certain *permanence* in time.

(For comparable description see Hall, 1972, p.9; Katz & Kahn, 1978 ch. 3; Miller & Friesen, 1984; Mintzberg, 1979; Pfeffer, 1982; Robbins, 1987.)

The problems of definition already indicate that it is unclear what organization theories are seeking to explain exactly: how goals are formulated, how differentiation and integration develop, how permanence is achieved? In dealing with organization theories it is necessary continually to ask what an organization actually is, and what aspects the theories are trying to explain in consequence. Consideration of the different approaches to organizations is therefore at the same time a consideration of the question as to which are the most important problems for organization. To illuminate this, the theories will be dealt with, more or less, in order of their historical occurrence. The emphasis in this analysis will be placed on the behaviour *of* organizations rather than on behaviour *in* organizations, although in the course of the analysis it will become clear that these two approaches are difficult to separate from one another. This means, for example, that traditional theories of motivation, satisfaction, roles, conflicts, communication, and so forth will only be taken into consideration in so far as they play a role in more general organizational theories.

2 FOUR TRADITIONAL APPROACHES

2.1 Introduction

In this section a description is given of the four traditional approaches to "organization": scientific management, the bureaucratic tradition, the human relations school, and scientific administration.

2.2 Scientific management

The scientific management school (Taylor, 1911) is primarily known for its time-and-motion studies. The theory proceeds from a conception of organization in which goals are well known, the selling of goods or services is no problem, and the availability of the means of production is guaranteed (Sofer, 1972, p.38). The approach is characterized by a concentration on repetitive tasks. Using methods of rational analysis, tasks are analyzed and measured as accurately as possible. Based upon this analysis, the task is broken down into its component parts, and then regrouped in such a way that the highest possible level of productivity (ratio: benefits/costs) is achieved. In this way the task-related behaviour of individuals is directed toward very specific and specialized goals (March & Simon, 1958, p.13). An important aspect of this approach is that it links remuneration to performance. Taylor proceeded from the assumption that the interests of employer and employee ran parallel. His method enabled managers "to give the workman what he most wants—high wages—and the employer what he wants—a low labour cost—for his manufactures" (Taylor, 1911, p.10).

The techniques developed by Taylor have had a longer life than his general points of departure. He offers four principles by which "scientific management" distinguishes itself from regular management practice:

1. The manager systematically gathers knowledge (science) about each aspect of the employees' work. This knowledge replaces the guesswork used until then in structuring the work.
2. The manager "heartily" works together with his or her subordinates to make sure that the work is done in accordance with the acquired knowledge and insights.
3. Work and responsibility are almost equally divided between management and workers. The manager takes over all the work which he or she is most qualified to carry out. Previously, almost all the work and the largest share of the responsibility were allotted to the workers.
4. The emphasis is on an intensive and harmonious relationship between the boss and his or her subordinates; the "objective" techniques which have been developed facilitate in achieving this relationship, primarily because they offer protection from arbitrary measures taken by management.

Taylor's view of work organizations is, of course, in some aspects rather dated. Take, for instance, his interpretation of one of the more important problems of an organization: a worker does not work to his or her full capacity. According to Taylor, this is partly because the worker fears a spiral of increasing demands, and partly because management lacks the necessary knowledge. Supported by his conviction that knowing is the same as doing and his belief in unlimited growth, Taylor has developed a view that in his day was a very modern one, and whose basic assumptions still deserve our attention. In particular, his focus on the integration of employer and employee and his insights about the organization of the task and its workplace environment have led to techniques of great practical significance.

A recent illustration of the actuality of scientific management can be found in the *lean production approach* (Berggren, 1993; Womack, Jones, & Roos, 1990). Like scientific management, lean production is an attempt to optimize the process of organizational throughput. The concept was developed originally in the Toyota company in post-war Japan, in a situation of a large pent-up demand confronted with a shortage of means. Lean production is the conscious attempt to make the most of scarce resources: resources that are in great demand for a host of products—leading to stiff competition—and that have to be used in the most economical—or lean—manner devisable. It is the latter aspect that has received most attention. Lean production has sometimes been dubbed "flexible Taylorism" or "democratic Taylorism", or even "Toyotism".

Lean production shares with scientific management, e.g. the emphasis on the design of cooperative management–employee relations. The instrument used in the context of the Japanese economy is "lifetime employment", a job guarantee for a restricted segment in the labour market. Security of employment, not pay, is the prime mover in designing the employment relation.

Focusing more narrowly on the system of production, we see, next to similarity (the emphasis on standards and standardization) and continuity (the emphasis on logistics leading to the "just-in-time" method in lean production), a few significant changes. Two among those deserve mentioning; both of them pertain to a comparatively sober assessment of the possibilities of exhaustive production planning. Foremost among the changes is the existence of teams, of team production. Second, there is the role of the team and its members in quality control, maintenance, and improvement.

Planning of work and production in scientific management is predicated on the successful isolation of the direct worker from all external disturbances. This lead is followed in lean production but not to its extremes. It is recognized that all workers need some discretion to correct minor flaws and to help colleagues if need be. The idea of teamwork is directly related to this. Teamwork means in the first place that every worker bears responsibility for his or her own work and for that of his or her colleagues, since all participate in the realization of the company's objectives. The "team" actually is coterminous with the company. It is not the elementary building block of the work organization design; rather, it signals the co-operative spirit that all jobs in the company exist for one and the same reason.

The role of the worker in teamwork is especially prominent in quality control. Whenever something substandard is noticed, all the workers are supposed to assume responsibility for restoring the standard. For achieving the standard the active participation and intervention of the worker is needed and acknowledged. That is rather a difference from scientific management, where active and autonomous intervention of workers, as a general rule, is discouraged. But there is a second difference as well, relating to the improvement of all standards as a day-to-day assignment for all workers: a standard, in the world of lean production, is never perfect or finished; it can always be improved upon, and improving upon it is not the exclusive task of the engineer. Rather, it is the responsibility of all. Part of everybody's daily routine is suggesting improvements, however small, however incremental.

Both scientific management and its most recent offshoot of lean production focus very much on the microcosms of the work group and pay little attention to the structural and administrative aspects of the organization as a whole, which are more or less taken for granted.

2.3 The bureaucratic tradition

The structural aspect of organizations is one of the themes which is emphasized in the bureaucratic tradition. Max Weber is the originator of this approach toward organizations (1946, 1947). According to Weber (in the summary of Blau, 1956, pp.28ff.), the bureaucratic organization exhibits the following characteristics:

1. The activities which take place in the organization are grouped in tasks. These tasks are grouped in positions (office). The tasks grouped together in a certain position constitute the required activities for the individual who holds the position (job). Everyone does a part of the total work.

2. The positions are organized hierarchically. Each position is supervised by a higher position. The head of a department is responsible to his or her boss both for his or her own behaviour and for the behaviour of his or her subordinates. In executing this responsibility, the head of department possesses legitimate power (authority) over his or her subordinates. This authority is precisely and carefully described.

3. The activities are guided by a cohesive system of rules (standardization and formalization). The system of standards is aimed at guaranteeing uniformity in the performance of the task, and it has a coordinating function in the sense that it regulates the harmonization of activities with one another.

4. The behaviour of individuals is formal and impersonal, *"sine ira et studio, without hatred or passion, and hence without affection or enthusiasm"* (Weber, 1947, p.340). This ensures that individuals are treated fairly and equitably.

5. Work in a bureaucracy is based on technical and *professional* qualifications. There are

rules for hiring and firing. Organizational loyalty is encouraged by the opportunity of promotion.

The pure bureaucratic form of administrative organization is "from a purely technical point of view, capable of attaining the highest degree of efficiency and is in this sense formally the most rational known means of carrying out imperative control over human beings" (Weber, 1947, p.337). Bureaucracy is described elsewhere by Weber (1946, p.214) as "The fully developed bureaucratic mechanism compares with other organisations exactly as does the machine with non-mechanical modes of production." The bureaucratic organization owes its superiority to the fact that the organization is protected, according to the above principles, against disruptive influences. As a result, internal processes are stabilized and made into routines, and consequently efficiency is increased (Perrow, 1970, p.59).

Merton (1957, pp.197ff.) has pointed out that carrying bureaucratic principles to extremes can lead to dysfunctional results. Because rules come to be their own justification, rigidity is promoted. Organizational behaviour is directed toward the maintenance of the status quo, even when this is not the best line of behaviour for the organization. What was a good rule under circumstance A, does not have to be a good rule under circumstance B (Perrow, 1979, p.29).

Selznick (1943) has stated that an informal structure exists in the organization parallel to the formal one. This informal structure, which contributes to the realization of a gradual change in goals, is based on the different interests of the various participants in the organization. Particularly when the organizational goals are not operational a diffuse struggle for control of the organization takes place. This will lead to the further crystallization of partial and partisan interests, thus forming a threat to organizational efficiency.

Gouldner (1954) demonstrates that bureaucratic rules make clear the minimally acceptable contribution to the members of an organization. This has the dysfunctional result that less is achieved than is possible, which in turn leads to closer supervision. Power, which becomes less visible through the use of rules, now becomes again more visible; tensions within the organization increase as a result. This analysis of dysfunctional results shows that there are two implications contained in the bureaucratic model:

1. the individuals in an organization identify themselves with the organization, and that their interests are identical to those of the organization;
2. the conditions under which the organization functions remain reasonably stable.

As soon as these implications no longer hold, the traditional stereotype of the bureaucracy, in which the rigidity of the organization and the lack of room for manoeuvring predominate, comes to the fore.

Perrow (1979, p.6) states, however "bureaucracy is a form of organization superior to all others we know or can hope to afford in the foreseeable future". This conclusion is justified primarily for the organization of routine tasks. Perrow counters the allegation of a lack of freedom for individuals in an organization by pointing out that the rules also provide protection from arbitrariness (compare the function of objective techniques in Taylor; see 2.2).

We see one of the essential problems of organizations appear in the course of the analysis of dysfunctional outcomes: *How uncertainty can be reduced without sacrificing flexibility,* or how efficiency *now* can be combined with effectiveness in the *long run.* The bureaucratic theory explains how organizations can achieve the efficiency, but not how they can also remain flexible in the process.

2.4   The human relations approach

The bureaucratic approach presents a picture of how an organization seeks to protect itself from the needs and motives brought along by the individuals who form part of it. The dysfunctional outcomes show this never to be completely successful. Moreover, individuals in an organization must cooperate with one another, which entails additional problems. "For the larger and more complex the institution, the more dependent is it upon the whole-hearted co-operation of every member of the group" (Mayo, 1975, p.62).

The series of investigations carried out in the Hawthorne factory of the Western Electric Company, Chicago, in the 1920s and 1930s directed attention to this factor, and to the human factor in general (Homans, 1951, ch. 3–4; Mayo, 1975; Roethlisberger & Dickson, 1939).

Commencing with the typical scientific management approach concerning the relationship between physical working conditions and work performance, the investigators were slowly but surely compelled to acknowledge the importance of the motivation of the individuals involved in the work process (see especially, Roethlisberger, 1952, ch. 2: "The road back to sanity"). In the so-called "relay assembly test room" where small telephone relays were assembled by hand (about 500 units per day, per person) the following characteristics were registered for five girls over five years: performance (quality, quantity), working conditions (humidity, hours worked, and so forth), personal circumstances (hours of sleep, meals, physical condition). During the first one and a half years of the experiment, performance improved continually. This result was initially attributed by the investigators to the experimental changes—until they reintroduced the old (less favourable) working conditions as a control measure. To their—and our—amazement, however, performance remained at the same high level. An analysis of exactly what the investigators had done yielded the insight that they had fundamentally changed the work situation along completely different lines than intended. The "operators" were consulted about changes, which would not have been effectuated if the operators had serious objections to them. They were asked about their reactions to and feelings about the changes. Their health and sense of well-being were a topic of considerable interest. In short, the normal leadership style was suddenly drastically changed. This made the investigators realize that the determining factor was the significance accorded to events in the organization by those involved, and the feelings which were developed by the participants concerning these events.

The image of the economic man who operates logically and rationally in his own interest, must

apparently be supplemented by an image of the individual who also has feelings and emotions with respect to his or her work situation. Other investigations in the Hawthorne series have illuminated other elements (the role of norms, for example; see Homans, 1951, chs. 3–6). The conclusions from these investigations can be summarized as follows:

1. An organization is a system. A change in one element cannot take place in isolation. When the element in question changes, the whole organization changes.
2. The organization not only produces goods or services, but it also distributes outputs and revenues (both material and non-material) among its members, who attach a certain significance to this distribution.
3. A continuous process of social evaluation takes place within the organization. Changes in the organization are evaluated for their social consequences, and in particular for their consequences for the status of the individual and the group.
4. The behaviour of individuals in organizations is not guided by economic motives alone. Values, opinions, and emotions all play an important role.
5. The personal relationships in an organization cause an informal structure alongside the formal structure; this informal structure has considerable impact upon the behaviour of individuals.

The Hawthorne investigations have been subjected to a great deal of criticism. Carey's article "The Hawthorne studies: a radical criticism" (1967), for example, is a devastating attack upon the various analyses upon which the conclusions of the Hawthorne studies are based. Carey makes it plausible that the production results of the relay assembly room were not achieved as a result of participation, consultation, and so forth, but were rather due to a new system of compensation. He also makes it plausible that a high level of performance, exacted by means of discipline, has probably led to a new form of leadership, rather than the reverse.

Despite this criticism it remains important that

the Hawthorne studies have focused attention on the motives and values that people import into the organization. Actually, the (faulty) interpretation of the Hawthorne studies has stimulated a fruitful research tradition that has somewhat validated and enriched the insights originally formulated by the Hawthorne researchers (see section 3.4, "The integration–motivation approach").

An aspect that is nearly totally absent in the Hawthorne studies is the consideration of task and work content, an aspect upon which the scientific management school, for example, places so much emphasis. A related criticism from a sociologist's standpoint is that although the Hawthorne investigations did succeed in bringing into focus the human aspects of organizations, they unfortunately succeeded at the same time in totally neglecting the institutional and structural components (Silverman, 1970, pp.73–77). The human relations approach has been unable to provide any significant insight into the organization as such (Perrow, 1979, ch. 3). The approach does succeed in bringing to the surface the problem of the *integration of individual and organization,* but provides hardly any tools for finding a solution.

2.5   The scientific administration approach

The scientific administration approach is characterized by its emphasis on the problem of grouping tasks into jobs, jobs into departments, and departments into the total organization, and by the search for principles that will guide the management of the organization resulting from this process. The approach confines itself to the pragmatic description of the formal relationships within organizations. It makes virtually no use of "theory" in the true sense of the word. It consists largely in summing up organizational activities and points that deserve the attention of the manager of an organization. Gulick (Gulick & Urwick, 1973, p.13), for example, delineates the seven functions of the manager as: "planning, organising, staffing, directing, co-ordinating, reporting and budgeting (POSDCORB)". The most important prescriptive principles of the scientific administration approach are as follows (see Massie, 1965, pp.396ff., Simon, 1957, ch. 2):

1. Scalar principle: authority relationships must run in a continuous hierarchical line from the top to the bottom levels of the organization.
2. Unity of command: each member of an organization must receive instructions and orders from only one other member of the organization.
3. Exception principle: all routine decisions must be reduced to procedures and then delegated. Only exceptions are referred back to the direct superior.
d. Span-of-control: the number of subordinates for each boss must be limited because individuals have a limited capacity for handling complicated relationships.
e. Specialization and departmentalization: distribution of work is a basic principle. The distributed work must be regrouped in departments. This grouping can take place on the basis of (a) goal, (b) process, (c) customer, market, or material, and (d) location. The underlying idea is to combine homogeneous units and to separate heterogeneous units.

These principles comprise, as it were, a pragmatic complement to the abstract principles formulated by Weber. The assumptions upon which these principles are founded can be summarized as follows (Massie, 1965, p.404):

1. Efficiency is measured in terms of productivity. Individuals are primarily motivated by material needs (loyalty for remuneration).
2. Human beings act rationally. To make this possible, tasks and competencies must be circumscribed as precisely as possible, and relationships must be laid down in a fixed pattern (Weber's rules and regulations).
3. People prefer the predictability and safety of a task that is described in detail; they prefer not to have to solve problems themselves. Simple tasks also lead to greater productivity (Weber's specialization and differentiation principle).

4. People often have an aversion to work, and they must therefore work within a framework of clearly determined responsibilities and under strict supervision. Management should be objective and impersonal (Weber's "*sine ira et studio*").

5. Authority originates at the top of the organization and is delegated downwards (Weber's principle of the hierarchical superstructure).

6. The manager's task has universal features—which means that it can be carried out in the same way, no matter what the particular circumstances (Weber's principle of interchangeability and exchangeability; the issue that management is a profession for which one is educated, implies that a manager can function at any location).

The "theory" attempts mainly to solve the problem of *how the work can be split up and then reintegrated*. The system of requirements and suppositions is primarily descriptive and prescriptive, and therefore virtually untestable (March & Simon, 1958, pp.30ff.; Simon, 1957, pp.20ff.). When practical applications of the principles are attempted, irreconcilable contradictions often appear, unless it can clearly be indicated which criteria are considered most important (see Simon, 1957, pp.41ff.). Implicit in this approach, as in the burcaucratic theories, is that the situation is more or less stable, and that the means–goals relationships are known. In this approach an even more pronounced emphasis than in the bureaucratic one has been placed on structuring the organization internally in the interest of efficiency.

For an organization operating in a more or less stable environment, and consequently being more or less stable itself, the prescriptions emanating from the "scientific administration" school are still a very practical tool in structuring organizations (Carroll & Gillen, 1987). However, like the other approaches already discussed, one can hardly speak about a theory from which hypotheses can be derived to be tested empirically.

2.6 Summary and conclusions

The four classical approaches highlight a number of problems which any organization must solve, and for which the approaches also propose some quite specific solutions.

- The "scientific management" approach emphasizes the problem of how the individual's working capacity can be utilized in the most efficient way possible, and how people can themselves be allowed to reap the benefits of this efficiency. The solution for this problem is sought in maximizing the structuredness and the instrumentality of the task, and in remuneration in accordance with work done.

- The bureaucratic approach puts forward the problem of how the organization can be protected against internal and external disturbances. Control and coordination of organizational operations is realized by means of a hierarchical structure and a system of rules.

- The human relations approach directs its attention to how the needs of people can be reconciled with organizational goals.

- The scientific administration approach consists primarily of a pragmatic development of the bureaucratic ideas, and gives directions for how to manage an organization efficiently. As in the bureaucratic approach, the emphasis is upon internal efficiency.

Gaining a sufficient degree of efficiency, control, stability, structure, and motivation is the complex problem of understanding and managing the area that defines the locus of and the tension within the many relationships of individuals–organizations–environments. The various approaches show that the organization must navigate among a number of obstacles to arrive at a solution for this problem. It should control the behaviour of its members, and guide it in the direction preferred by the organization. At the same time, it ought to guarantee that these individuals remain sufficiently motivated. The organization must combine internal efficiency with flexibility and a capacity to adapt to changing circumstances. More generally, the most basic problem for an organization is to meet the demands of both its members and its environment, while maintaining its own identity and cohesion.

3 AN AREA OF TENSION: RELATIONSHIPS AMONG INDIVIDUAL– ORGANIZATION–ENVIRONMENT

3.1 Introduction

The four classical approaches focus upon the tension between individual and organization. Usually, just one aspect of the tension area is highlighted and solutions are proposed, based on implicit assumptions and theories. The notion that a number of contradictory demands should be satisfied simultaneously in the search for solutions is often present somewhere in the background, but it rarely receives the attention it deserves. In the following, several other approaches are considered, in which some of these contradictions are a prominent theme. Also, a modest attempt will be made to bridge the contradictory currents in the theories considered.

3.2 The structural-functionalist approach

The structural-functionalist approach builds upon both the bureaucratic and the scientific administration approaches. The functionalists proceed from the assumption that organizations have a function in their environment—for example, an electricity company that provides electricity for homes and industry. As long as this function is fulfilled adequately, the organization retains its right of existence. It then receives the necessary support and contributions. One of the criteria for adequately fulfilling function is that it takes place at an acceptable cost. A good structure can help to control these costs. Thus a form of organization that makes it possible to act quickly without unnecessary controls, can help to cut costs.

The function that is fulfilled is the goal of the organization, and the "*primacy of orientation to the attainment of a specific goal* is used as the defining characteristic of an organisation which distinguishes it from other types of social systems" (Parsons, 1969, p.33; original italics). In Parsons' view, an organization derives its cohesion from its value system, which is part of the more comprehensive value system of the environment within which the organization functions. For the organization to be able to function, it is

necessary that individuals and groups share the value system of the organization; this is made possible by the fact that they in turn are part of the broader society. By fulfilling its functions within the framework of existing norms and values, the organization legitimizes its existence with regard to both the society as a whole and the individuals who comprise that society. According to Parsons' view of organizations, the existence and mainten- ance of shared norms and values is a necessary condition for the social system's ability to main- tain an orderly and cohesive existence.

The core of the functionalist view of organiza- tions is the conception that they can be regarded as natural systems, which seek to survive through adaptation. This means that changes can only be explained in terms of adaptations of the organiza- tion to internal and external disruptions. It is inherent in this approach that the theory can give a plausible account in retrospect of why some organizations adapt successfully and others do not, but it can make no predictions of success or failure. In addition, such a theory cannot explain *why* some organizations manage to adapt and others do not. To provide such an explanation, the theory must be able to incorporate the idea that an organization actively designs and influences its own structure *and* environment.

Another point of criticism is that this approach devotes little attention to the opposing interests that can exist between the organization, on the one hand, and its members, on the other, and between the organization and the society in which it functions. The structural-functionalists proceed from the assumption that an "unseen hand of nature" ensures that power is distributed in corre- spondence with the importance of the function fulfilled by individuals within the organization, and by the organization in society as a whole (see Silverman, 1970, pp.59ff.).

The hand is blind, as well as unseen, and is therefore just. The winner has adapted, the loser has not. Dysfunctions are by definition temporary. Such an approach fails to take into account that members of organizations, unlike natural organ- isms, are not specially programmed to function within organizations, and therefore are not likely to succumb to their fate without a struggle. By asking for whom the dysfunctions are dysfunctional, it becomes clear what kind of problems the theory entails. The strongest is always right—in retrospect. It is impossible to predict who will win and how a conflict will be resolved. It is not surprising that the theory is chiefly illustrated with case studies (Clark, 1969; Messinger, 1955; Selznick, 1949). Yet, the structural functionalists deserve merit for having introduced the concept of equilibrium into organization theory. They have tried to explain why social order and continuity exist in organizations despite fluctuations in circumstances and actors. Disturbances of the equilibrium can equally be the result of tensions within the organization, and of tensions between the organization and its environment. The tensions within the organization are primarily due to too great an emphasis on efficiency and/or stability resulting in over-coordination and trying to maintain the status quo for too long. This inevitably leads to a disruption of the internal exchange equilibrium, because, for example, the employees lose the motivation to strive towards a good performance. Tensions will also occur when external exchange relationships are disrupted, e.g. products become too expensive or of poor quality, and consequently customers drop away. In these cases the structural-functionalists have directed our attention to the general phenomenon that organizations will try to re-establish an equilibrium (Parsons, 1967). How and at what level remains unclear, as already indicated. What also remains unclear is to what degree organizations can exist with unresolved problems and conflicts because of a less-than-perfect equilibrium, internally or externally.

Structural-functionalism as such is no longer a unified doctrine within the field of organization studies. We find elements of structural-functionalism in a whole series of other approaches, however. The emphasis on adaptation, for example, is as common a feature in "natural" systems theories as it is in the "open systems" concept as such. Also, the idea that it is impossible to speak of organizational goals or needs as if these were developed in isolation from the environment, is now integrated into most theories and concepts of the organization (Luhmann, 1964; Naschold, 1969). The stress on "balance" or "equilibrium", although emanating from several sources, is an important aspect of this idea. So is the insight that organizations do more than simply adapt to environmental demands and conditions. Indeed, structural-functionalism has been accompanied, from its very inception, by a part of institutional theory in which the *reciprocal* influence of environments on systems and vice versa is highlighted. Originally, this took the form of a critique on conceptions in which the organization was equated with its formal aspects only. The criticism, simply, was that organizations are not so much "rational" as "natural" systems (Scott, 1981). In itself, that was no more than one of the lessons structural-functionalism as such taught and therefore is not new at all. But in the institutional criticism the "lesson" took a distinct form that, in contrast to the structural-functional template it came from, has survived until the present day.

The institutionalists focused on the "latent", not the "manifest" functions of the organization. "Manifest", in this perspective, simply means that we have to evaluate the organization in its explicit functions: to provide goods or services, for example. Latency, in the institutional perspective, means that an organization has far more, and far more complex, links with its environments than the mere provision of goods or services. Accordingly, the institutionalists stressed within the organization the *in*formal aspects of the organization where others had stressed its formal aspects. In so far as the external relationships of the organization were concerned, they stressed the criteria of organizational legitimacy, relative to organizational performance in a narrow sense (Perrow, 1986; Scott, 1990). In doing so, the institutionalists have enriched our understanding of the "environment", transforming it from a rather residual category into a concrete and detailed landscape of networks, cultures, histories, and backgrounds of activities and persons, up to and including role sets and role ambiguities.

Although the structural-functionalistic approach in its more modern form has created a much more detailed picture of the internal organizational functions and processes, on the one hand, and of the complexities of the external environment, on the other, it still fails to tackle the central issue of how these two complex sets of interdependencies interact, how they mutually influence each other. Another conceptual framework is necessary to tackle these questions. The open-system theory, with its emphasis on mutual exchange processes, tries to develop such a framework.

3.3   Open-system theory

A system can be defined as a collection of elements, distinguishable within reality taken as a whole. The elements within the system are related: the relations form the structure of the system. These relations do not preclude relationships with elements beyond the system, i.e. relationships with the environment of the system (in't Veld, 1975, p.10).

The first part of this definition provides a static picture of the organization, consisting of people, positions, and tasks, along with their interrelationships, as it is often presented in organization schemes. Without further additions this is a *closed*, independently operating system. With the addition that the system can have relationships with elements outside the system, *open systems*, interacting with their environment, also come to be included in the definition. As a result, the system takes on a *dynamic* character. Organizations are open systems which on the surface appear reasonably stable. This stability is not achieved because all the elements and their interrelationships remain unchanged, but because changes in one element, or in a relationship among elements, are compensated for by changes somewhere else in the organization.

The open system maintains a dynamic equilibrium. If two department heads have an argument, but it is in the vital interest of the organization that their two departments work in harmony with one another, then either the individuals in the two departments will find a way of bringing about some degree of coordination, or cooperation will be imposed from a higher position in the organizational hierarchy.

The open-system theory originated in an attempt to develop a science which would be able to explain the principles of systems in general. The theory is a generalization from the principles of closed systems (kinetics, thermodynamics) de-

veloped in physics, and is therefore also known as "general systems theory" (GST) (see von Bertalanffy, 1950; Berrien, 1968, ch.1.).

The open-system theory attempts to develop principles for describing systems that are valid for every level of analysis (see Berrien, 1968, p.11; Miller, 1978). This means that the system boundary can be arbitrarily defined, depending on the perspective chosen. A change in perspective does not mean that other insights are needed to explain relationships. If an organization is defined as a system (and with it, individuals as subsystems and the environment as a supra-system), virtually the same insights are needed as when the group is defined as a system (with individuals as subsystems and the organization as a supra-system). It is characteristic of the open-system theory, as applied to organization, that, in a single coherent approach, it attempts to deal with the problem of harmonization of the relationship among individual–organization–environment (see especially Katz & Kahn, 1978). In this approach, the following assumptions are made concerning the organization as a system (see Silverman, 1970, p.27):

1. The subunits of an organization are dependent on one another and contribute to the whole, in exchange for which they receive a contribution from the organization. The system model is an *exchange model*. How the subunits are linked to one another (the structure comes into being) is one of the most important questions.

2. Organizations are guided by their needs. If these needs are not satisfied, the organization ceases to exist. Goals are articulated on the basis of these needs. If goals are not achieved, or if there is too great a discrepancy between needs and goals, the viability of the organization is diminished.

3. Organizations behave as a coherent whole. It is of course true that this organizational behaviour is shaped by the human elements (subsystems) in the organization. Yet the only way of understanding the processes involved is to regard the individuals in terms

of their relationships (structures). A mere summing up of the behaviour of the component elements yields insufficient insight into the whole.

4. The organization as a system is in its turn part of a supra-system. The exchange relationships with this supra-system must fulfil the needs of both the organization and the supra-system.

A number of questions are raised by this approach:

- What different types of relationship exist among the elements, subsystems, and systems?
- What contributions do the various structures (different relationship patterns) make towards satisfying the system needs? Two criteria in particular are employed in this connection (Etzioni, 1960): the criterion of survival and the criterion of effectiveness (the extent to which goals are achieved).
- How do changes take place? One answer to this question proceeds from the supposition that the system will gradually grow towards a situation in which the degree of internal consistency is so high that it is optimally suited to fulfil the needs existing in and outside the organization. As these needs change, in this view, the system adapts itself automatically. We have already seen in the structural-functionalist approach that this makes it very difficult to predict differences among organizations. Thus, the system model is primarily descriptive in character.

For our subject, theories of organization, the post-war developments in *systems thinking* have been of major importance. First, it is firmly established that organizations and systems are not identical. An organization may be considered as host to a whole series of systems: of mechanical, biological, psychological, and social character. Moreover, these system types are usually hierarchical or complex. They can be decomposed into ever simpler units, as a factory can be decomposed into a series of departments, departments into a series of offices, offices into a series of jobs, jobs into a series of tasks, each smaller unit being a

subsystem of a large system, each larger system being the environment of the smaller system. Smaller systems can be tightly and loosely coupled to other systems (at least until the very elementary units are reached); all systems maintain relations between elements, which in their turn can be loosely and tightly coupled too. Indeed, the idea of describing organizations along the axes of coupling and complexity or hierarchy has received considerable attention since the late 1950s.

Organizations are many things to many people; they are also many systems to many other systems. The systems concept as such has an immense generality and can be applied to practically everything, from simple organisms, through machines, to the psyche, to organizations, and even to whole societies. Common to all applications, however, is the *systems/environments* distinction and the insight that dependent on problem and/or analytical level, every entity can be both system and environment. This is the major rule of the game: it is not possible to talk about a system and its environments if it is impossible to specify the boundaries spanning (bridging and maintaining) system and environments. Membership in organizations is an excellent proxy for a boundary. It hardly makes sense to discuss any organization at all if it is not known who is a member and who is not. A person would hardly be interested in a discussion on the advantages of being employed if he or she would not be able to distinguish the employed from the unemployed.

All systems, then, are systems within an environment. Purely self-contained systems are artificial products, never to be mistaken for the real thing. Real systems always exist in environments and cannot be described or explained apart from them. It may be decided not to focus on the environment—for example, because it is expected that the major sources of variation will be found within the system rather than in its environment. That is what Taylor is supposed to have done: to have focused on organization as systems of throughput to the relative neglect of, especially, the output relations of the organizational system. That emphasis gained Taylor the reputation of being a proponent of a "closed" systems view, looking at the inside of systems only and forgetting their environments. That is wrong on two accounts, however. The first of these is that Taylor devoted much time and attention to input variation (due to the labour market and to the suppliers, generally, of an organization) and the possibilities of controlling such variation. The "one best way" of scientific management was never intended to be so irrespective of input conditions. That is, the relative neglect of the output environment is more than compensated for by Taylor's relative emphasis on input as a crucial and variable environment.

The second correction is more pertinent in the present context. If, as we assert, modern systems theories are predicated on the distinction of systems/environments, then there is strictly speaking no such thing as a closed system. All systems are open, i.e. interact with and within environments. The distinction between "open" and "closed" systems does not, therefore, refer to system properties. What the distinction refers to is where the original source of variation of the systems/environment *relationship* must be sought. The easiest way to grasp this is by posing the question whether—in the problem one is trying to solve—the environment is treated as the independent variable (and the organization as the dependent one), or vice versa, or something in between. This leads to the acceptance of the idea of a continuum with the environment as the independent variable on one extreme and the organization as the independent variable on the other extreme. Most positions, of course, are not on the extremes but somewhere in between.

Note that this is a continuum of open systems. The idea has to be rejected that the positions on the continuum are "paradigms", i.e. conceptual systems that cannot be translated into one another, as they are by definition incommensurable or incompatible. Rather, positions differ because they set out to answer different research questions. The differences, therefore, relate to research programmes, not to different and incompatible paradigms (Grandori, 1987).

Different approaches try to rephrase, complement, and redirect the questions posed. Indeed, although historically the concept of open systems in organizational theory was developed as a criticism of structural-functionalism, it was recognised at the time that characteristic concepts of structural functionalism, like "needs", "reproduction"; and "adaptation" testified to its open-systems slant. Structural-functionalism in this respect was incomplete, rather than wrong.

After this brief meta-theoretical detour it becomes easier to see what the specific merits of the systems approach are in handling some of the most tenacious problems organizational theorists have wrestled with. One of these problems is the three-level interaction between person, organization, and environment. In a systems approach it becomes abundantly clear that the exchange relationships between individuals and the organization, and between the organization and its environment, are developing simultaneously, and that therefore the different criteria of effectiveness must be met simultaneously for both the environment and the individuals in the organization. The environment will only make new input available to the organization as long as the organization offers goods and services at a socially acceptable cost. The individual will only make his or her labour available as long as the balance between costs and benefits continues to tip in his or her favour (Katz & Kahn, 1978, p.38).

The most important characteristic of open-system theory is that, contrary to the strict structural-functionalist approach, it does not assume that the organization one-sidedly adapts itself to the environment. Central in the approach is a continuous and active process of mutual adaptation between person, organization, and the organizational environment. By abandoning the idea of automatic and passive adaptation, the open-systems theory can start to provide suggestions of why some organizations survive (positive balance) and others do not. In this sense the system approach offers a descriptive-analytical potential. To be able to predict which organizations will survive and which will not, however, it is necessary to gain knowledge of the processes and factors that play a role in survival. It is, therefore, necessary to elaborate further the descriptive framework, in such a way that indications can be given of which structures contribute under which conditions to the effectiveness of the organization and its capacity for adaptation. The theory should also be elaborated to increase the understanding of the role played in that balancing process by the actively interacting elements, subsystems, and systems, each having their own interests. The picture of an organization as a passive entity is replaced by an interaction perspective in which the meanings attached to these processes by human actors play a central role. This last point brings with it special problems, which are the focus of the integration–motivation approach.

3.4 The integration–motivation approach

Unlike ants, people are not pre-programmed to fulfil specialized tasks in the social structures called organizations. This makes it necessary for organizations to make special efforts to integrate and motivate the human components that in the end make up its living tissue. This is the central theme of the integration–motivation approach, with a strong emphasis on the positive contributions that well motivated people are able to make towards the performance of the organization. For this reason the approach is also often designated as the "human resources" approach or, pointing towards some of its roots, the "neo-human relations" approach.

Argyris (1957, 1959, 1964), in particular, has laid the groundwork for this approach. He emphasizes the fact that the formal bureaucratic organization demands passive, dependent behaviour of individuals, especially those who function at the lower levels of the organization. This is extremely frustrating for the individuals, who will react in a number of ways (e.g. with aggression, apathy) that constitute a threat to the desired gains in organizational efficiency because of the diminished motivation of the organization's members. Thus it is important for the organization to strive for greater congruence between the needs of its members and the various task and organization structures. Argyris seeks the solution for this problem in giving persons the highest degree of autonomy possible, combined with clear task requirements (1964, chs. 7 and 9). He also recognizes that structure, style of leadership, etc., can change along with the situation (1964, p.211).

Likert's (1959, 1961) central concern is how individuals can be motivated in such a way that they perform optimally for the organization (1959, p.186). Likert proposed as the organization's

guiding principle that its structure should ensure that the members of the organization experience all their interactions as supportive and as contributing to their sense of personal worth (1959, p.191). For this to be realized, every member of the organization must be part of one or more "well-knit, effectively functioning work groups" (p.191). The coordination of these groups takes place by means of "linking pins". These are individuals who belong to two groups. They function as a superior for one group, and represent this group at the next higher level. At this higher level they themselves then function in a subordinate position. Likert's linking-pin structure is, in this sense, no different from classical organization structures. The difference bears primarily upon Likert's idea that the superior does not interact with each individual separately, but with the whole group as a "team". The reciprocal trust and loyalty that develop as a result help to make conflicts about goals and interests manageable. A necessary condition for this process is the presence of opportunities for exerting influence on both sides of the relationship; the influence of the supervisor of a particular group on his superior plays an essential role (1961, p.114).

Both Argyris and Likert work with a more complex image of man than is usual in the classical theories. The needs they ascribe to organization members are very similar to the need hierarchy postulated by Maslow (1954): physiological needs, needs for safety and security, need for social contact, need for respect (self-respect and respect of others, often acquired by means of work performance) and the need for self-realization or self-expression. These needs are actualized in the order given in the sense that first the physiological needs must be satisfied to a certain basic level before the need for economic security, for example, starts playing a role. McGregor (1960) has pointed out that the conventional management conception assumes that people in organizations are only motivated by the needs at the lower level of Maslow's hierarchy, and that for the rest they are lazy and recalcitrant, so that they must be kept under strict supervision (theory X). When, however, it is assumed that needs higher in the hierarchy also play a role (McGregor's theory Y; 1960) and the organization takes this into account, then there is a possibility that individuals and the organization can become better attuned to one another.

The integration–motivation approach is, in a number of aspects, an improvement over both the classical management approach and the human relations approach. It uses a considerably more differentiated image of man than the rational-economic one prevailing in the classical management approach. There is clearly a greater emphasis on structural solutions for problems than in the human relations approach. Yet the integration–motivation approach can also be criticised on a number of counts:

1. It has already been pointed out that the goals of organizations and the relationship to the environment are considered as a given in the integration–motivation approach. Schein (1965, chs. 6 and 7) has attempted to close this gap by making use of functionalist insights. He suggests that an organization is effective if it adapts itself to the demands of the environment and manages to grow, thus increasing its chances of survival. The organization accomplishes this by means of "adaptive-coping cycles" (pp.98ff.) aimed at observing and interpreting changes in the environment followed by the adaptation of activities. The criteria of effectiveness are further specified in terms of this cycle as (1) the capability of obtaining valid and reliable information, and communicating it; (2) possessing the necessary creativity and flexibility for introducing changes; (3) members' integration and involvement with the goals of the organization; (4) the presence of a psychological climate of support and freedom (p.103).

2. This group of organizational psychologists proceeds from the assumption (as do the structural-functionalists) that all organizations are basically the same. This leads to Likert's developing "one best way" for organizations to function—the participative method (1961, pp.222ff; called system 4 in his later work, 1967)—and that there are specific translations of the theory appropriate to each specific situation (1961, p.24),

the prevailing idea remains that "the description of the forest is valid, even though many of the trees are not, perhaps, where they should be" (1961, pp.89ff; see also the so-called "contingency theories" of leadership, Fiedler, 1978). His final position is that the participative systems exhibits the "operating characteristics" that *every* organization in general must have (p.236).

3. The integration–motivation approach also assumes that an organization is, in principle, populated by emotionally mature individuals, who will identify themselves with the organization (Likert, 1961, p.236). The possibility that individuals may exist with an abiding divergent orientation from the organization is not seriously considered (see Goldthorpe, Lockwood, Bechhofer, & Platt, 1968; Silverman, 1970, p.55).

4. A fundamental problem for the integration–motivation approach is the lack of a well-founded theory of needs. Several attempts to formulate such a theory and to underpin it with theoretical data have been undertaken (e.g. Alderfer, 1972; Foa & Foa, 1980; Wahba & Bridwell, 1976), none of them very satisfactory. Because of the fundamental nature that such a theory must necessarily have, the chances of great strides towards one are generally considered to be slim (e.g. Salancik & Pfeffer, 1977, p.43).

5. The empirical support for the ideas propagated in the integration–motivation approach is extensive. In particular, Likert and his group of collaborators have collected a wealth of data. It cannot be denied though that the interpretation of these data by this group tends to be somewhat optimistic on occasion. Perrow (1979, ch. 3), for example, demonstrates that in the investigation by Marrow, Bowers, and Seashore (1967) in the Weldon Company, where a dramatic increase in production took place following the introduction of Likert's participative system, this effect was primarily the result of classical management and efficiency measures.

Reviews taking into account, e.g., the relation

between participation and motivation, also convincingly demonstrate that the supposed relations are not as unambiguous as Likert (1967) would have us believe (Cotton, Vollrath, Frogatt, Lengnick-Hall, & Jennings, 1988; Lowin, 1968; Veen, 1973; Wagner & Gooding, 1987).

One of the key problems of the integration–motivation approach is that it considers the person as an element that has to be integrated into the organization more or less lock, stock, and barrel. A different approach, going back to Chester Barnard (1938) and worked out in more detail by Simon (1945, 1961) and March and Simon (1958), focuses on the balance of inducements and contributions. Central in this approach stands the notion of an organization as an environmentally conditioned system of activities. It must be stressed that the system consists of activities and *not* of persons, machines, buildings, etc. Persons belong to the environment of the organization, not to the organization itself (of course, they belong to many environments in many systems of organized activities; one and the same person may be a mother, a volunteer in the fire brigade, a soccer player, a member of the local PTA (parent–teachers association), a spouse, a friend of friends, and so on). Persons are nearly always (at least in modern society) only partially involved in organizational membership (the situation where people are totally immersed in one organization is known as one of the "total institutions": imprisonment is an example, as is psychiatric hospitalization). From the perspective of the organization, the fact that it refers to activities enacted by persons, but not to the persons themselves, is also significant. Persons may disappear, be sacked, move on or resign, but the organization will stay in operation. The fact that organizations do not depend on the specific skills of a specific individual is not accidental to the definition of the organizational phenomenon. In the view of Barnard this is an essential characteristic. Organizations are in an important sense impersonal (Barnard, 1938, pp.72–73) and have to induce their members to contribute to the goals of the organization. The objective in balancing inducements and contributions is to devise a scheme of incentives that will attract those contributors the organization is interested in, and scare off

unwanted ("undesirable" in the words of Barnard) contributors. Incentives, then, and the selectivity of organizational recruitment are but two sides of the same coin (pp.159–160). It will be obvious that the selective nature of recruitment must be accompanied by differential rewards and sanctions, and thus by hierarchy and authority (Barnard, 1938). This idea has proved basic in conceptualizing the employment relationship as a relationship of authority (in contrast to a pure exchange relationship) (Barnard, 1938; Simon, 1961; March and Simon, 1958; Stinchcombe, 1990).

Organizations cannot and do not assume that the mere fact of people participating in the organization will suffice to elicit the needed contributions. The decision to participate in an organization differs from the decision to contribute to the goals of the organization, in the same manner that the decision not to leave the organization can vary independently of the decision to do one's very best (in the same vein, much research shows that being satisfied with work is very different from being motivated to contribute to the maximum of one's abilities). Participation is continued only when, from the point of view of the participant, inducements at least balance contributions. Again, the notion of balance is crucial. Whether the organization succeeds in achieving this balance depends on the combined effect of four factors (Barnard, 1938, p.155):

1. the state of the environment (for example, whether business conditions are favourable or not, whether competition is fierce or not, etc.);
2. the effectiveness of the organization (can it deliver what the market is asking for?);
3. its efficiency (can it deliver at competitive costs?);
4. the right level of inducements (if too high, comparatively, inefficiency threatens, if too low, comparatively, contributions may be withdrawn).

All four factors refer to systems/environment balances: between the organization under consideration and other organizations in a market or other environment. It is a typical "open systems"

view, without using the concept itself, that Barnard has proposed. No wonder, then, that many
elements of Barnard's reasoning can be found in
other approaches (see section 4). The environmental emphasis figures strongly in the population
ecology school; the emphasis on overall effectiveness is shared with the contingency approach; the
efficiency emphasis returns in many of the
approaches by economists; and the emphasis on
inducements is a key element in the resource
dependence and institutionalist approaches (cf.
Williamson, 1990). Many of the more prominent
new approaches in the study of organizations,
accordingly, "return" to Barnard. Many of his
insights were incorporated in the view of
organizations as decision-making and information-processing entities as developed in the
early classics of March and Simon (1958), Cyert
and March (1963), and Thompson (1967).

3.5   Summary and conclusions

In discussing the classical approaches, it was
observed that efficiency, control, and motivation
are the problems existing in the field of tension
between the organization, the individual, and the
environment, for which the organization must find
a solution. The structural-functionalist approach,
which concentrates on the relationship organization–environment, assumes that the parts are
automatically subordinate to the whole system
(the organization). The motivation of individuals
and the achievement of a sufficient degree of
efficiency are not problems that this approach
addresses. They are, at most, constraints within
which the actual problem unfolds: the adaptation
of the organization (by means of its structure) to
the environment. The approach provides no explanation for why some organizations succeed in
adapting and others do not.

The integration–motivation approach makes
exactly this adaptation of individual and organization its main concern. It concentrates on the
problem of how individual needs can be combined
with an organization's need for a high degree of
efficiency (ratio of standard costs/actual costs) and
a high productivity level (ratio of results/costs).
The adaptation of an organization to the environment is the marginal condition within which this
problem unfolds.

Both the structural-functionalist and the integration–motivation approaches proceed from the
assumption that organizations are comparable and
that, under certain given conditions, there is one
best way of organizing. The structural-functionalists emphasise the relationship between an
organization and its environment, whereas the
relationship individual–organization is taken as
given. Just the opposite is the case in the integration–motivation approach: the relationship
individual–organization is emphasized, whereas
the relationship organization–environment is
treated as a constant. This contrast graphically
demonstrates that the two approaches aim at
explanations at two different system levels.

In the open-system theory it is made clear that
the boundary between subsystem (group or individual), system (organization), and the supra-
system (environment), is an arbitrary one, and that
the problems at each boundary are in fact the same.
Not only must the organization be alert to changes
in the environment—which, for example, lead to
setting new requirements for production—the
individuals functioning within the organization
must also adapt to the changing requirements of
the organization (for example, a different type of
or more highly developed expertise). But the
reverse is also true: an organization must take into
account the desires of individuals in the same way
that the environment cannot afford to ignore the
desires of organizations (support, protection from
competition). We are looking here at two sides of
the same coin: to influence and being influenced.
Individuals and groups will try to influence the
organization just as the organization will try to
influence them. The same mutual influencing
process takes place between the organization and
its environment.

The open-system approach makes clear that
both at the boundary individual–organization, and
at the boundary organization–environment, the
same kind of problems must be solved. It also
demonstrates that the structural-functionalist
and the integration–motivation approaches supplement one another in this problem area. The
problem of maintaining the status quo versus
flexibility and adaptation must be solved at both
levels. The same exchange relationship exists
between individuals and organizations as between

organizations and environment. In its structure, the organization tries to coordinate the various individual subgoals with the goals it has with respect to the environment. The structure also fulfils a function in the control and harmonization of the elements of the organization. Because the stability acquired in this way is too rigid to guarantee survival in a changing environment, continuous adaptation to internal and external conditions is effectuated through the necessary decision-making processes, in which the different contradictory demands must be weighed against one another in an attempt to achieve a balance between stability and flexibility.

4 CONTROL AND DECISION MAKING

4.1 Control and structure

The structure of the organization can be considered as the result of the actions and reactions of the organization in trying to achieve its objectives in a continuously changing environment. Important determinants of the structure are: technology (Blau, McHugh Falbe, McKinley, & Tracey, 1976; Perrow, 1967; Hickson, Pugh, & Pheysey, 1969), the degree of uncertainty in the environment (Aldrich, 1979; Hannan & Freeman, 1977; Lawrence & Lorsch, 1967), the size of the organization (Child, 1972; Hall, 1972), and the power relationships (Mintzberg, 1983).

The organization will not only passively try to protect itself against internal and external disturbances, it will also actively try to get as much control as possible over foreseeable contingencies in the environment in order to eliminate these wherever practicable. In particular, contingencies that are essential for survival are a target for this strategy. The most extreme form of control is, of course, incorporation of the vital contingency areas into the organization. For example, if an oil company comes to the conclusion that access to distribution channels is essential and that this access may be threatened, it may decide on a strategy of developing or buying its own distribution network. Another way of trying to control contingencies in the environment is to build up coalition networks (Aldrich, 1979, chs. 9–13).

Successful attempts to incorporate or otherwise controlling uncertainties will lead to new hierarchically ordered processes and more complex internal and external relationships. Because of these new developments specialist functions and coordination mechanisms become necessary. A well-known example of this is the formation of specialist departments directed at homogeneous segments of the environment, e.g. separate service functions for professional customers and general consumers. By separating these boundary spanning functions, the organization is better able to fine tune its behaviour towards the different requirements of different environmental segments.

The focus on organizational boundaries implies a theory of choice that, in effect, is not so much about choice as about attention and search. Attention, search, choice, and decision making are the concepts that most aptly describe the information-processing theory of organizational behaviour.

Crucial in this context is the concept of attention. No system (for reasons of bounded rationality) can attend to everything, and the things it does attend to cannot all be dealt with at the same time. What gets attention and what role search plays, is what this branch of theories of organization is all about. Systems do not automatically discover the things that need to be attended to, and quite often the "things" are not simply out there but have first to be named, described, and prepared for organizational processing. Quite often, again, the way attention is focused is more rule bound than it is intentional, more history-constrained than future oriented (Cyert & March, 1992, pp.214ff). What gets decided may be determined by what is already there (a series of competencies, a way of procedurally going through the motions, etc.), rather than by the "objective" characteristics and demands of the task to be accomplished. Against this background, taking a decision has been likened to rummaging in the contents of a garbage can. Something is bound to be found, although it may differ from the solution the system or the environment had expected to find (March, 1994, pp.198–206; see also section 4.3).

In this connection, the relevance of "satisfying" (as opposed to "maximizing") criteria in allocating organizational attention, search efforts, and actually taking the decision is critical (Cyert & March, 1992; March & Simon, 1993, pp.3–4). Satisfying is not just a limit on the system's "intended" rationality, it is also a useful approach in discovering what organization members actually attend to in situations of ambiguity and confusion (Weick, 1995). More generally, what rationality means in ambiguous situations, what the impact is of rules and routines relatively to intentions in ambiguous situations, and what the weight of organizational structure relative to strategy is, are among the more exciting questions spelled out and debated in the frontier area of economics and psychology (Hogarth & Reder, 1986; and later, section 5.2).

Organizational structure and system–environment boundary characteristics, like degree and type of interdependence, boundary maintenance and boundary-spanning activities, are closely and intricately linked. If the technological components and boundary-spanning components can be clearly separated the organization will tend to develop a centralized structure. If such a separation is not possible, configurations will be formed that are relatively autonomous, like organizational divisions.

To summarize, the primary function of the organizational structure can be stated as the accomplishment of the coalignment of people, tasks, and positions in a way that reduces and makes more manageable the uncertainties caused by internal and external factors against acceptable costs, while maintaining the necessary flexibility. In the classic bureaucratic approach we saw that the view of the organization essentially remained one of an autonomous system that manages to protect to a large degree its internal functioning from the disturbances and fluctuations in the environment, while in the process achieving substantial efficiency improvements.

4.2   The contingency approach

The contingency approach (Child, 1977; Galbraith, 1977, ch. 3; Lawrence & Lorsch, 1967), in which the link between structure and uncertainty takes centre stage, goes one step further than the classical bureaucratic ideas. It leaves behind the idea that the organization can be protected against uncertainty in the environment and actually postulates that such protection is undesirable.

The central tenet of the contingency theory is that the organization will be more effective the more its structure is adapted to cope with the demands that internal and external uncertainty put on it. The structure is considered to be adaptive if it reflects the uncertainties confronting it (congruency principle). Given different kinds of complexity and different degrees of uncertainty, each requiring different reactions, the organizational structure has to be differentiated in a way that enables it to match these requirements through specific parts and specific processes. Such a differentiation in its turn puts new integration requirements on the organization to safeguard an adequate degree of coordination. The more effective organization will be the one that not only successfully adapts itself through this differentiation and integration process to its environment, but also manages to handle the ensuing internal tension between differentiation and integration effectively.

The general statement that the structure should reflect the uncertainties of the environment is in itself insufficient to form a theory with specific hypotheses. Several authors have tried to develop a coherent set of hypotheses in order to build a testable theory (e.g. Lawrence & Lorsch, 1967; Thompson, 1967; Schoonhoven, 1981), but all these authors have come up against some fundamental problems that characterize the contingency approach.

A first problem is formed by the fact that the two key concepts of the theory, structure and uncertainty, are both multi-dimensional (James & Jones, 1976; Downey, Hellriegel, & Slocum, 1975; Tosi, Aldag, & Storey, 1973). It can be argued that this a problem of definition and measurement, and not strictly a problem of the theory. Even if we accept this argument, it is certainly a formidable obstacle to testing the theory properly.

A much more central problem of the theory is that it is far from clear exactly what congruency between structure and environment means. The typical organization is confronted with a multitude of uncertainties, often putting conflicting demands on the organization, towards which a multitude of structural and other solutions are possible (Child, 1972, 1973; Aldrich & Pfeffer, 1976), nearly all of them compromises. Unless the theory is able to indicate which solutions to which uncertainties will lead to greater effectiveness, it will remain seriously flawed.

Weick, in accordance with Ashby's law of "requisite variety", assumes that a large measure of uncertainty outside the organization must be met with a large measure of variability within the organization. This means that, when an organization is faced with a great deal of uncertainty, the criteria determining which behaviour the organization should select must be such that a wide array of behavioural possibilities can be taken into consideration. The chance will then be greater that one of the approaches is successful. In Weick's theory, this is achieved by assuming that, when the level of uncertainty is high, very few criteria will be used to select behaviour, so that many possibilities will be considered.

The theory does not answer the question of how an organization can determine when the uncertainty is pronounced enough to make it worth the cost of investigating many possibilities. This problem is intertwined with another problem, which has been lucidly formulated by Weick (1979 p.135): "Under what conditions does adaptation preclude adaptability?" Each time an organization succeeds in reducing uncertainty this experience, precisely because it has been successful, could thwart adaptations in the future, which may call for entirely different behaviour. This clearly raises the issue of what criteria the organization must use to arrive at a choice between the manifold possibilities for action it has evoked.

In addition, whenever the equilibrium is disturbed, the organization is faced with the dilemma noted earlier of short-term efficiency versus long-term effectiveness. A characteristic of this dilemma is that it is often clear enough what the costs are of certain actions in the short run, but not what the benefits are in the long run. Thus the choice will usually be made for "efficiency in the short run". This may not such a bad choice, as there are a number of indications in the literature that organizations that opt for a strict limitation of internal inconsistencies, even when it involves sacrificing the variability that makes long-term adaptation possible, can still be extremely suc-

cessful (Khandwalla, 1973; Pennings, 1975). A possible explanation for this phenomenon is that short-term efficiency creates "slack resources" (reserves) with which information systems can be set up, which can help in making better predictions of uncertainties and provide a measure of "survival time" in case of a radical change, thus allowing for the effectuation of the necessary adaptations.

Another reason to opt for short-term efficiency and the maintenance of internal consistency is that in an extremely turbulent environment it prevents the organization from reacting to every fluctuation that comes along. While busy devising a tactical response to one change the next one might come along, one that the organization might not even notice. Holding fire might be a perfect adaptive device under the circumstances. Even if this means that in the longer term a organization might miss out on the main chance, there is the distinct chance that it will find a niche opportunity where its fossilized status will offer it an advantage over the competitors that have moved with the times. Either the organization is selected by the environment, e.g. customers looking for old-fashioned quality, or it actively looks for niche opportunities itself, e.g. by looking for new markets for its old products. This line of reasoning is very much part of the so-called "population-ecological" approach (Aldrich, 1979; Astley & Van de Ven, 1983; Hannan & Freeman, 1977).

In this perspective it is not really the firm that chooses or selects an organizational form. There is no adaptation between an individual organization and its environment, for the adaptation that does take place is not situated at the level of an individual organization at all. Instead, adaptation occurs at the level of the population of organizations and its composition: less fit specimens are replaced by better fit specimens, and under certain environmental conditions the population as such becomes extinct. Like natural selection: if certain food supplies disappear organisms must vanish; if supply conditions change, the size and composition of the original population will have to change along with them. How fast such change will occur and how complete the process will be also depends, of course, on the richness of supplies and on the dependence of the organisms. Competition for scarce resource is not always, as we know, cut-throat, and many organisms (or, for that matter, organizations) have some slack or redundancy: a reserve that can be mobilized in the face of shortages and that can be mobilized to claim a fighting position in the distribution of what is left. Even in this approach, then, the environment is not completely a given. Partly, at least, the environment is negotiable.

A perspective that stresses the negotiability of the environment is the so-called "resource-dependence" approach (Pfeffer & Salancik, 1978). This approach has shown particular relevance in the analysis of *inter*-organization relation*s*. Its point of departure lies, as in the population-ecological approach, in the environment. But where in the population-ecological approach the unit of analysis is the complete population in a certain environment (for example, all the organizations serving a given market), in the resource dependence approach it is a particular network of organizations or the individual organization within such a network that constitutes the unit of analysis. An organization is, as an open system, dependent on externally generated but scarce and contested resources. These resources can be classified along two axes. Resources may be more or less *critical* for the survival of the organization, and they may be more or less *controlled* by other organizations in the environment.

The implication is that, through the establishment of forms of inter-organization relationships (from vertical integration through mergers and joint ventures to value adding partnerships), the resources on which the organization is dependent can be brought into the sphere of influence of the individual organization. In doing that, the state of uncertainty within any given environment will change as will the number of organizations involved in any given series of transactions. An explicit concern with the problem of information selecting and handling is inherent in the approach (Aldrich, 1979). One advantage of this is, of course, that it opens the way to highlighting the options the firm has, not so much in adapting to the given environment but in choosing a new one (for example a new market or niche). Recently, Pfeffer incorporated human resource dependence in this

perspective, arguing that sustainable competitive advantage and developing committed and selectively recruited human resources are two sides of the one success coin (Pfeffer, 1994).

The perspective may be made more dynamic by applying it to the network of relations within an individual organization. This is considered to be a set of subunits that may and will form coalitions, and thus attract and reject partners in a game conditioned by the attempts of subunits to reduce their dependence on others or, in reverse, to enlarge their control over other subunits. In this way resource dependence becomes closely connected to the sociology of power relationships in organizations and organizational networks (Crozier & Friedberg, 1977; Pfeffer, 1982; Nohria & Eccles, 1992), and to the sociology of strategic-choice approaches (Child, 1982).

Resource dependence can also be considered as the sociological twin sister of the economic markets and hierarchies approach in organization theory (Grandiori, 1987). This approach, which may be called paradigmatic for the renewed interest within the economic discipline for a theory of organization, tries to explain, like the resource-dependence approach, which boundaries organizations are likely to choose in the face of uncertainty and competition. Starting from the usual economic assumption of market transactions as the normal economic form of coordinating activities and exchange, the question, then, is under what circumstances transactions are "taken out" of the market and made subject to organization or "hierarchy" as Williamson (1975, 1985) puts it. These circumstances are seen to depend mainly on environmental uncertainty and on "small numbers", i.e. the condition of having only a few effective trading partners. Moreover, these circumstances are seen to be present in rather a large number of cases and, because, in the face of uncertainty and a small number of players, hierarchy often turns out to be more profitable than direct market exchange. Consequently organizations following this route flourish. The similarity between this perspective and the resource-dependence approach is striking. This includes the extension of the original approach to intra-organizational boundaries, for example, by explicitly focusing on the employment relationship and the differential form this will assume under different transaction conditions, specified in terms of measurability of output and specificity of human capital (Williamson, 1975, 1985).

The approach outlined here clearly puts a big question mark against the central assumption of the contingency theory, i.e. that the structure will closely follow the demands of the environmental circumstances. Obviously, this is by no means an automatic occurrence, and internal consistency might prevail over adaptation without necessarily having a negative influence on the effectiveness of the organization. As indicated, this might mean that the organization will have to migrate to a different environment or that a different environment will seek out the organization.

The addition of the population-ecological and the resource-dependency approaches has added some tantalizing pointers to which direction the contingency theory might be developed, but still leaves unsolved the central problem of the theory: how to specify which reaction is most effective under which circumstances. The insights that have been formulated are mostly of a very general nature and are quite often prescriptive rather than predictive (Mintzberg, 1983, p.153).

One of the factors left out of the theory is the role played by the decision-making actors in determining the, in theory, highly abstract interactions between the organization and its environment. Like the (neo-)Darwinian explanations of evolution, the contingency family of theories is good at explaining post hoc why certain organization–environment combinations are successful survivors (for the time being); and, as for the Darwinian theories, the deterministic concept of the Blind Watchmaker as invoked by Dawkins (1991) is lurking somewhere in the shadows.

It is perhaps no accident that it is a business historian, Alfred Chandler (1962, 1977, 1990), who has tried to explain why, beginning around the turn of the last century, many of the larger companies changed their organizational form from a functional one to a divisional one. In his view, strategic considerations by the key actors have been a prominent driving force in the process of change in which structure was shaped to follow the strategic considerations. Strategy in the cases highlighted by Chandler was strongly related to the product mix the company was producing, and in particular to the product–market combinations the company was concentrating on (see also Ansoff, 1987, p.24). A market, in Chandler's perspective, is nothing but an information problem, the source of which lies outside the organization. Different markets constitute, consequently, different information problems. What a company needs, therefore, is the capacity to construct different structures relating the company to these different problems. Divisions are just that: administrative structures linking the organization to its markets; that is, linking decision and informational problems to demands (Stinchcombe, 1990).

This is simple and straightforward enough. Yet, one of the most remarkable novelties in Chandler's writings is the insistence we find there on the *conscious* managerial efforts to "invent" new organization structures and to "innovate" existing organizations accordingly. His approach is not deterministic, in that environmental variation would "prescribe" the organizational track to be followed. It is not the "situation" that drives toward new organizational form. His approach, or rather the historic examples from which his approach is derived, is activist and intentional, not deterministic and functional.

Clearly Chandler's approach leads to the next question organizational theorists need to address: which factors influence the perception of internal and external circumstances, particularly of the most influential decision makers in the organization; and, consequently how are the key decisions influencing the shape and eventually the fate of the organization taken?

In decision-making theories we see the focus on efficiency and effectiveness returning, now combined with the perspective of the motivation and (partial) involvement and interest of the human actors in the organization.

4.3 Decision-making theories

As indicated earlier, the weighing of alternatives in an organization is done by individual decision makers: they decide what eventually is going to happen. The organizational structure is the result of a series of such choices. Yet there is always considerable latitude for interpretation left in the structure, even in highly bureaucratized organizations. Also, changing circumstances will compel adaptations and readjustments. An equilibrium at one point will by definition be temporary and potentially unstable. The decision-making process has a continuous influence on the fragile equilibrium of organizational processes and the ensuing structure. Explanations of this process may contribute to a better understanding of the phenomenon of the organization.

The classical decision-making theories proceed from the assumption that decisions are made rationally. Rationality is generally defined as choosing among alternatives in such a way that the expected outcomes represent the maximizing of the values held by the decision maker, be it individual, group, or organization (March & Olsen, 1976, p.69; Simon, 1957, p.75). Rationality in this approach has to be understood from the perspective of the actor making the decision. This perspective is not necessarily the same for other actors, individuals, or groups, inside or outside the organization; only when other actors share the same value system and have access to the same information will the definition of rationality be a shared one. This is one of the reasons why organizations expend considerable effort on socializing and indoctrinating their members.

Another aspect of the rationality concept as already defined is the assumption that the decision-making actor is fully informed, has an unequivocal sequence of preferences for available alternatives, and consequently is able to maximize outcomes in the way the theory predicts (March & Simon, 1958, p.138). These conditions are seldom satisfied. Often, situations are so complex that the decision makers can only pay attention to a limited amount of the information, as indicated earlier. Not only may they choose a satisfying strategy in selecting information, they may also, rather than trying to achieve maximum or even optimum outcomes, just aim for satisfactory outcomes (satisfying vs maximizing; March & Simon, 1958, pp.140ff).

Yet another aspect of the classical rationality concept is that the impression is given that the decision-making actor is just a cool, calculating machine in no way hindered by emotions. This

obviously is not the case. Apart from the fact that people in the organization do not always share the same values, which in itself is a source of emotional conflicts (March & Olsen, 1976, pp.82ff), they also perceive events coloured by emotions and feelings. In this context, Janis and Mann (1977, p.45) introduce the concept of hot cognitions, which induce the supposedly cool decision maker to inject a fair amount of subjectivity in his or her judgements. This is the main reason for the coloured and selective handling of information that is such an important part of organizational life, and that often is reflected in learned rules of interpretation of events. These rules can be of individual or organizational origin, but have in common that they lead to subjective biases and filtering in the perception of events.

Based on social cognition and perception theories, Kiesler and Sproul (1982) list the following common biases and mistakes that managers suffer from in judging interpreting events:

> illusory correlation: the assumption that events are related to each other because they resemble each other; illusory causation: the assumption that an event causes another event because they happen to be the focus of attention at the same time; gap creation: the unjustified assumption that events did not take place because they did not fit into accepted cognitive schemes; gap filling: the unjustified assumption that events did take place because they fitted into the expectations generated by accepted cognitive schemes; ignoring discrepant information: neglecting to take account of certain information because it is extremely surprising; preference for ambiguous information: enabling to interpret information in such a way that that self-deprecatory learning can be avoided; preference for self-enhancing information: failing to code or store self-deprecatory information. (see also Janis & Mann, 1977, ch. 8)

Not only is the perception and interpretation of events coloured by these mechanisms, organizational learning in general suffers from these biases, consolidating them into accepted wisdom in the organization. This is illustrated in a series of studies about the interpretation of success and failure in the annual reports of organizations, which show a clear self-serving bias (Bettman & Weitz, 1983; Salancik & Meindl, 1984; Staw, McKechnie, & Puffer, 1983). This bias can be a conscious choice; for example, to convey a certain image to stockbrokers and analysts. Often, though, the bias will be an unconscious act originating in a need to protect cherished interpretations of reality or in a strong commitment to the achievement of certain goals (see Janis & Mann, 1977, ch. 10).

March and Feldman (1981) have pointed out yet another phenomenon that plays a role in the perceptions of members of the organization. According to their insights, information quite often acquires a symbolic and value-loaded significance. The behaviour elicited by these symbols and values is aimed at validating and reinforcing them. In this vision, the search for information by the organization is led not so much by the need to arrive at certain decisions, as by the need to make sure that the environment still provides support for the organizational symbols and values. In the words of March and Feldman: much of the information is gathered and treated in a surveillance mode rather than a decision-making mode (p.182).

Based on the insights outlined earlier, it is difficult to escape the conclusion that rational decision making in the sense of coming to a decision on the basis of the unbiased perception and objective interpretation of events is the exception rather than the rule. This is confirmed by the studies of strategic decision making in organizations (see Koopman, Broekhuysen, & Wierdsma in this Volume of the *Handbook*; Mintzberg, Raisinghani, & Theorêt, 1976; Quinn, 1988). Theories of decision making clearly will have to take account of a different rationality concept or even a reasoned irrationality concept.

In an attempt to start talking about the irrational in a rational way a whole raft of new metaphors has been invented. Cohen, March, and Olsen (1972) have described decision making as a garbage can process in which answers are looking for a problem. March and Olsen (1976, pp.69ff) talk about the technology of foolishness and draw

up a set of rules to make this manageable. Hedberg, Nystrom, and Starbuck (1976) recommend looking at organizational structures in terms of camping on a seesaw. Weick (1977b, pp.193ff) suggests that effective organizations be defined as garrulous, clumsy, superstitious, hypocritical, octopoid, organized anarchy, wandering, and grouchy.

These metaphors have led to amusing descriptions and to new categories and ways of understanding organizations. They primarily emphasize that organizing is a process that attempts to reconcile the irreconcilable. This leads to the question of whether this means that a theory of organizational behaviour and decision making is impossible. Although we would be loath to embrace such a conclusion, it has to be acknowledged that the metaphors offered here hardly form theories that lead to testable hypotheses. It is probably more fruitful to consider them as a first step towards formulating a meta-theory, a way of looking at problems organizations have to cope with rather than as systematic attempts to construct a theory of organizations (Weick, 1979, p.235). Morgan (1986) has developed this approach systematically and analyzes organizations with the aid of nine metaphors, or images, varying from the well known image of the organization as a machine via the organization as a culture to the organization as a prison and an instrument to exercise power.

Despite the lack of coherent overall theories of decision making in organizations, considerable progress has been made towards a better understanding of the underlying dynamics of decision-making behaviour. Empirical research has made it clear that the reality organizations have to cope with is unclear, complex, and continuously changing. Consequently, the decision-making processes reflect all this. From social psychology and other disciplines, a number of promising theories have been formulated to help understand important aspects of the complex interplay of the factors determining the decision-making processes.

4.4 Summary and conclusions

The control and decision-making approaches mainly focused on trying to understand the determinants and effect of the organizational *structure*.

It was concluded that the most important function of structure is the reduction of uncertainty. This reduction of a particular uncertainty inevitably led to the creation of new uncertainties.

The theories of decision making, then, demonstrated that this web of shifting uncertainties is so complicated that explanatory models based on classical assumptions of rationality had to be stripped of these assumptions step by step in order to preserve the connection with the empirical data available. Under these circumstances, the construction of a coherent theory of organizational structure and control becomes an attempt that seems doomed to failure: trying to navigate between the Scylla of rationality and the Charybdis of empirical reality on the way to the promised land of understanding how organizations control the achievement of their goals and objectives. The question that raises its head in this context is whether the concept of organizations as goal-directed systems is a tenable one.

5   GOALS AND DIALECTICS

5.1   Goals

The most salient characteristic in the definition of organizations is the achievement of goals. "Few discussions of organisation theory manage to get along without introducing some concept of organisational goal" (Simon, 1964, p.1). Two approaches may be discerned (see, e.g., Campbell, 1977, pp.20ff; Etzioni, 1960; Georgiou, 1973; Gouldner, 1959):

1. the so-called "goal-centred" approach, based on the assumption that the organization is controlled by rational decision makers, trying to realize their vision of a set of goals;
2. the natural-systems approach, based on the assumption that "survival" is the overarching goal of the organization.

The latter approach assumes that, because of the very variety and complexity of the demands an organization has to face, it is actually impossible to pin-point a relatively small number of well-defined organizational goals. That is why the organization can only be described as being oriented towards the assurance of survival as its goal. Survival is assured, as long as the organization (at acceptable costs) fulfils a function in its environment, and as long as the organization manages not to deplete its vital environmental input components (such as raw materials). The problems inherent in this approach have already been indicated here in the subsections on systems theory and on structural-functionalist theories.

In the goal-centred approach the concept of rationality returns. The various aspects of and perspectives on this concept were dealt with in the discussion of decision theories. We indicated in particular that as rationality does not mean the same thing for everybody, a plurality of different and even conflicting goals may come about.

It is generally accepted in most organizational theories that the concept of the organizational goal in not a very fruitful one. In accepting a multitude of goals as the more promising approach, the problem arises, though, of how to determine what the goals in question are. Perrow (1961) proposed a pragmatic solution to this problem, i.e. to consider as goals the established policy guidelines of an organization, its so-called "operative goals". This approach elicits several questions: Such as how these goals come about, and how the different individual perspectives get clustered in a meaningful and workable way?

Cyert and March (1959, 1963, ch. 3) conceptualize the organization as a coalition consisting of several subcoalitions (for example, manufacturing versus marketing; subordinate staff versus senior staff). In this view, the following assumptions are made: (a) the organization consists of individuals with potentially conflicting interests and preferences; (b) through a negotiating process coalitions are formed with a shared preference order for certain outcomes, the objectives; (c) consequently, the coalition can conceptually be considered as one factor in the organizational force field (1959, p.78). This last point does not mean that the goals of an organization have become unequivocal. At most, agreement can be found on vague goals (for example, more internationalization), coupled with a large degree of uncertainty on subgoals, for example, whether it is feasible to open one's own subsidiary in France or advisable to employ an agent.

Determining the side-payments offered to the members in a coalition is the most important process through which goals get specified. By means of this process the value of the personal contributions relative to a specified goal is indicated. This implies that, in order to entice participation in the coalition, some minimal consensus on goals must exist. Someone considering joining an organization must balance contributions to be made against rewards to be achieved. A person will accept responsibility for the subsidiary in France if he or she considers him or herself suitable for the job, likes the job and gets paid adequately. On the other hand, the organization will make the offer only if it is reasonable certain about the contribution of a person as a member of the coalition. Coalitions formed in this way are, as a rule, not stable. Owing to the complexities of the forces at work in the organizational context, small adaptations are introduced continuously.

The underlying model in this approach is a mixture of negotiating and decision making. The results of negotiating feed into organizational decisions. In their turn, the results of these decisions feed the process of negotiating. This conceptualization seems to allow for an answer to the problem of how to combine individual goals into organizational ones. Looking closer, however, we can see that little new understanding has emerged. In particular, the process in which balances between conflicting interests must be found and priorities set, remains unclear.

Simon (1964) reformulated the problem in the sense that the organization (persons in the organization) must simultaneously satisfy a large number of constraints. Sometimes one particular constraint gets emphasized and acquires the status of *goal*. It is evident, for example, that an organization will want to use the best qualified employees at the lowest cost possible. When, however, minimalization of cost is accorded the status of *goal* there might be a danger that the quality constraint will not be satisfied.

The quality requirement is a constraint for the efficiency goal of achieving the lowest possible cost. When the quality requirement is transformed into a *goal* then the factor of cost becomes a constraint for that goal. If we add to this equation that a high-quality labour force is effective only in a context of challenging and motivating work, a new constraint emerges, i.e. the necessity of creating a work environment that offers such challenges. If successful, the motivational environment can of course become a side-payment in itself, potentially ameliorating the pressure on the cost factor in the process.

The foregoing illustrates clearly that each decision on one of the relevant factors in the situation is a constraint for other decisions. In other words, the whole of constraints and/or goals behaves like a system. Certain decisions and the consequent actions are determined predominantly by systemic requirements emanating from the relationships between elements in the system. In order to understand the emergence of organizational goals from the set of constraints, we need to understand their mutual relationships. Accordingly, Simon claims (1964, p.21): "In view of the hierarchical structure that is typical of most formal organisations, it is a reasonable use of language to employ organisational goal to refer particularly to the constraint sets and criteria of search that define roles at the upper levels." An unsolved problem, remaining with this approach, is how to forecast what will happen in a situation in which different subcoalitions express mutually exclusive combinations of constraints as their goals.

Pennings and Goodman (1977, pp.152ff) use Thompson's (1967, p.128ff) concept of "dominant coalition" to indicate that in such circumstances the coalition with the greatest power has the greater leverage in establishing the criteria for choosing goals. Its negotiating position is stronger. The demands it puts forward determine the frontiers of what is organizationally possible more than the demands of other coalitions do. Its demands acquire *goal*-status prior to the demands voiced by others. Following Simon, Pennings and Goodman define organization goals as "desired end-states specified by the dominant coalition" (1977, p.161). Constraints differ from goals in the sense that they are defined as minimum conditions or base levels that the organization has to satisfy in order to survive. Again in the vein of Simon, Pennings and Goodman situate the dominant coalition at the top levels of the organization.

The role of the dominant coalition in establishing the goals of the organization is a specific form of the more general phenomenon of "power" in organizations as described by several authors (Bacharach & Lawler, 1980; Mintzberg, 1983; Pfeffer, 1981; Veen, 1982, ch. 6). Formally, the most detailed approach is the one by Bacharach and Lawler, modelled on coalition-theoretical views. They take the organization to be a *network* of coalitions. The dominant coalition is part of this network. The network or set of coalitions is in a continuous process of being (re-)constituted, and does not always coincide with the groupings as defined by the formal structure of the organization. On the other hand, the formal structure does create the framework for the formation of coalitions based on the interests and power relations as reflected in the structure. The underlying power structure in particular determines the emergence of coalitions (Wilke, 1983).

Relations of power are determined by the dependencies in achieving desired outcomes (Emerson, 1972; Veen, 1983). In its turn, this hinges on the degree to which one person can procure valuable outcomes for another person and the degree to which alternatives are available. Hickson, Hinings, Lee, Schneck, & Pennings (1971) operationalized this notion of dependency in the organizational context as the degree to which uncertainty is reduced and the degree of substitutability of outcomes. Important factors influencing this are, for example, the degree of centrality of the position of the person in the organization, and the degree to which his or her task consists of routine activities.

It is not only members of the organization who have interests at stake. External "stakeholders" (owners, trade unions, customers) may play a role as well, and will influence the goals and constraints of the organization (Mintzberg, 1983, chs. 4–7). In this perspective the organization becomes "an arena within which participants can engage in behaviour they perceive as instrumental to their goals" (Cummings, 1977, pp.59–60). This vision on the nature of organizational goals is intimately related to interactionist perspectives on organization (see later). One of its corollaries is that organizational goals are not considered as clearly defined and stable. Rather, they are regarded as the continually shifting result of implicit and explicit processes of negotiating, given the more or less stable collection of tasks and activities in the organization. This implies that the definition of rationality shifts continually, in line with the outcomes of those negotiations.

5.2   The dialectic of organizing versus organization (process and structure)

Karl Weick (*The social psychology of organizing,* 1979) puts forward the thesis that every organization is the product of the process of organizing, described as a: "consensually validated grammar for reducing equivocality by means of sensible interlocked behaviours". For the behaviour of people in organizations a reality is seen to be created, in which agreements will be construed to make it manageable and, in terms of outcomes for the participants, acceptable. For most actors, of course, the organization is not a newly created reality but a reality that already exists and that they will experience as such. Nevertheless, this does not mean that they accept the situation as a given; rather, they try to influence and shape it (Veen & Van Haren, 1980). In combination with external influences, we get the picture of an organization as a phenomenon in perennial flux. Although some parts of the organization may at times be static, other parts will at the same time show dynamic movement: "Any changes that infringe upon this order, whether something ordinary like a new staff member, a disrupting event, a betrayed contract; or whether something unusual, like the introduction of a new technology or a new theory, will call for re-negotiation or re-appraisal, with consequent changes in the organizational order" (Strauss, Schatzman, Bucher, Ehrlich, & Sabshin, 1963, p.165).

The structure of the organization, consequently, may be regarded as an order, developed through explicit and implicit negotiating, defined as any interaction between persons or groups in which mutual influencing occurs (Veen, 1983).

This so-called "negotiated order" perspective (Day & Day, 1977) underscores the active role of the individual in shaping the organizational reality. The approach emphasizes the constantly changing network of interactions. This stands in strong contrast to the previous approaches in which either the stability of the structure was emphasized (structural-functionalism, rational-bureaucratic approach) or the character of goals at the organizational or the given individual level (decision making, integration-motivation approach). In the "negotiated order" approach the accent is on the dialectical relationship between (temporarily) stable relations (structure) and the actions of persons and groups within or outside that structure (see also Benson, 1977).

Rationality is in this perspective the end product of a process of rationalizing, i.e. it is making sense *ex post* of behaviour that would appear as senseless and chaotic when seen from the perspective of an external frame of reference (Brown, 1978).

According to Weick (1979, p.152): "People in organisations need to find out what they have done" and: "people act out and realise their ideas" (Weick, 1977a, p.187). In a recent publication Weick (1995) emphasizes even more strongly the extent to which the organizing process is construed by the participants themselves and made rational only later on. "Sense-making" is the concept used by Weick to characterize the process of organizing, and he stresses that sense-making should be taken literally; it is not a metaphor. It is not a way of just "reading" reality. At the same time as the situation is read its interpretation is "authorised" by the actor. Sense-making is, even more so than in the earlier concept of "enactment", a process through which organization members try to reduce equivocality and eliminate confusion. Indeed, Weick now strongly contrasts uncertainty and equivocality with on the one hand ignorance and on the other with confusion. His thesis is that the problem for members of the organization is not so much uncertainty as equivocality, not so much ignorance as confusion. The primary function of sense-making becomes not so much information gathering as the setting and maintaining of an orderly set of *priorities*. The orientations and opinions that people bring with them into the organization, and the ensuing interactions of these which each other, determine what is perceived as the organizational reality. In so far as this reality is shared and has stable traits it can be described with the concept of *culture*, defined as: "the continuous creation of shared meanings" (Jellinek, Smircich, & Hirsch, 1983, p.335). Linking this definition

with the coalition approach of Bacharach and Lawler (1980), the culture of the organization can be considered as the outcome of negotiations on interests and positions of power (Pruitt & Rubin, 1986; Rahim, 1989). The ensuing expectations, norms and values express the rights and the duties of the members of the organization. Comparable with other cultures, the culture of organizations is constantly changing, and subcultures may exist (Morgan, 1986, pp.120ff).

The interest in the phenomenon of organizational culture (see reviews in Jellinek et al., 1983; Smircich & Calás, 1987; also Ch. 7, Vol. 4 this *Handbook*) reflects the need to get a theoretical grip on the process of organizing that is fundamental to the development and functioning of organization structures. In this approach it is highlighted that too much of a discrepancy between the norms and values of the organizational culture, on the one hand, and the codes of conduct and the structures of the organization, on the other, jeopardizes the continuity of the organization from within. In the same way the continuity is threatened from the outside in the case of too wide a discrepancy between environmental demands and the products or services offered by the organization (compare the concept of *incongruence* as used by Nightingale & Toulouse, 1977).

The "negotiated order" perspective is a dialectical approach in which it is argued that from interactive areas of tension new organizational syntheses emerge. Benson (1977) makes clear that this implies that the organization must be studied as a unified whole. To do justice to the complexity of the organizational phenomenon it needs to be viewed from complementary levels: the morphological level and the level of substructures.

The morphological level refers to the form of the organization as it can be abstracted from the concrete organizational reality (for example, the charted organization structure). Classical organization approaches are targeted at this level, classifying the different organizational forms and measuring its aspects and effects. The dialectical approach on this morphological level is focused on the processes through which the organization form has come into being and on the processes that maintain this form.

The analysis at the substructural level is more

focused on the undercurrent of emotions and feelings, leading to tensions and conflicts in the organization. In contrast to the classical and rationally inclined morphological organization theories, these tensions are not ignored. Instead they are recognised as a fundamental characteristic of social processes (Gagliardi, 1986). As conflicts arise continually, opportunities for reconstructing the organizational reality emerge permanently as well (Weick, 1979, pp.147ff). The most fundamental and general contradiction in this context is that between the existing social structure and the ongoing process of social structuration (Benson, 1977, p.16).

In this view the contradiction between rationality and irrationality is not cancelled out. Rather, the contradiction is an essential element in organizational life, which must be reflected in the theories trying to make sense out of the complexities the study of organizations throws up. Theories focusing one-sidedly on one or other aspect only, are by definition limited in their explanatory value. This does not imply that partial theories are always incorrect. What it does imply is that they have to be complemented with their relevant counterparts (Benson, 1983).

When viewed from the rational (morphological) aspect this means, for example, that it must be clarified what the irrational organizational aspects of rational solutions consist of. The accent, then, will be on the link between interests at stake and solutions arrived at. Consequently, processes of influencing and power will be central in analyzing the organization phenomenon (Brown, 1978; Veen & Van Haren, 1980). The complicated processes of intra-organizational influencing lead to structural solutions and the construction of rules of the organizational game, which will as a matter of definition be classified as "rational" by the winner. Those participants, however, whose interests are less well served will not give up their struggle for a larger future share. In so far as they succeed in this, the definition of rationality and effectivity will get modified. The fundamental problem for the organization, therefore, consists in finding workable solutions for managing these fields of opposing forces and interests. These solutions, by definition, are a multitude of quasi-stable equilibria: construed and constantly debated rationalities.

5.3 Summary and conclusions

In the discussion of the development of the concept of goal, it was concluded that the organization is faced with a constantly shifting reality, as a consequence of which new approaches continuously have to be developed. One implication of this was that the organizational definition of rationality changes all the time. The ensuing discussion of the "negotiated order" perspective resulted in a dialectical point of view, accentuating power relationships and processes of influencing and implying that "rationality" and "irrationality" must be considered as labels for the ideas of the winner and losers, respectively, of these processes of influencing. As such, both concepts should be part of theories or organization. Such theories are at present not available.

6   CONCLUSION

We started out with the observation, based on the classical approaches to theories of organizations, that the organization is trying to solve a series of problems, characterized by the fact that solving one partial problem renders the solution of other problems more complex. We finished with the observation that this is inevitable and inherent in the phenomenon of the organization as an arena of interests. We ended, consequently, with a way of looking at organization through the perspective of negotiated order and sense-making rather than with a theoretical model, making predictions about organizational behaviour.

This lack of firm theory could be attributed to the fact that the dialectical perspective only recently started to attract attention. This is a somewhat improbable idea, though, once it is realized that the intellectual roots of this perspective go back a long way without, however, having led to theories with testable prediction.

The real question therefore is whether it is fruitful to try and develop an all-encompassing theory of organization, as such an attempt is practically the same as developing a general theory of social order, which—at least for the time being—seems to be out of reach. It is tempting, against this background, to return to Merton's (1957) assessment of the state of affairs on grand theory and to aim—for the time being—for theories of the "middle range". We might actually be well advised to omit the phrase "for the time being". Once we stop and look into the question of what needs explaining in the phenomenon of the organization, it will become clear directly that there is such a huge number of partial aspects to be explained that a theory that attempts to explain all of them will be too abstract and general to allow for the deduction of concrete and testable predictions. In this sense, it is more useful to construct valid partial theories, and it may be a consolation for those addicted to grand theory that the position taken here does not exclude the eventual future ordering of partial theories in the framework of an encompassing descriptive mode. The reflection on a fruitful perspective for the observation of organizations may help, then, to choose the most productive partial theories and to pinpoint the key processes that deserve further study.

REFERENCES

Alderfer, C.P. (1972). *Existence, relatedness and growth: Human needs in organizational settings.* New York: Free Press.

Aldrich, H.E. (1979). *Organizations and environments.* Englewood Cliffs, NJ: Prentice-Hall.

Aldrich, H.E., & Pfeffer, J. (1976). Environments of Organizations. In A. Inkeles (Ed.), *Annual review of Sociology* (vol. 2, pp.79–105). Greenwich, CT: JAI Press.

Ansoff, H.I. (1987). *Corporate strategy.* Harmondsworth: Penguin Books.

Argyris, C. (1957). *Personality and organization.* New York: Harper.

Argyris, C. (1959). Understanding human behavior in organizations: One viewpoint. In M. Haire (Ed.), *Modern organization theory* (pp.115–154). New York: Wiley.

Argyris, C. (1964). *Integrating the individual and the organization.* New York: Wiley.

Astley, W.G., & Van de Ven, A. (1983). Central perspectives and debates in organization theory. *Administrative Science Quarterly, 28,* 245–273.

Bacharach, S.B. & Lawler, E.J. (1980). *Power and politics in organizations.* San Francisco: Jossey-Bass.

Barnard, C. (1938). *The functions of the executive.* Cambridge, MA.: Harvard University Press.

Benson, J.K. (1977). Organizations: A dialectical view. *Administrative Science Quarterly, 22,* 1–21.

Benson, J.K. (1983). A dialectical method for the study of organizations. In G. Morgan (Ed.), *Beyond method* (pp.331–346). Beverly Hills, CA: Sage.

Berggren, C. (1993). *Alternatives to lean production: Work organization in the Swedish auto industry.* Ithaca, NY: ILR Press.

Berrien, F.K. (1968). *General and social systems.* New Brunswick, NJ: Rutgers University Press.

Bertalanffy, L. von (1950). The theory of opens systems in physics and biology. *Science, 111,* 23–29.

Bettman, J.R., & Weitz, B.A. (1983). Attributions in the board room: Causal reasoning in corporate annual reports. *Administrative Science Quarterly, 28,* 165–183.

Blau, P.M. (1956). *Bureaucracy in modern society.* New York: Random House.

Blau, P.M., McHugh Falbe, C., McKinley, W., & Tracey, P.K. (1976). Technology and Organization in Manufacturing. *Administrative Science Quarterly, 21,* 20–40.

Brown, R.H. (1978). Bureaucracy as praxis: Toward a political phenomenology of formal organizations. *Administrative Science Quarterly, 23,* 365–382.

Campbell, J.P. (1977). On the nature of organizational effectiveness. In P.S. Goodman, J.M. Pennings, & associates (Eds.), *New perspectives on organizational effectiveness* (pp.13–55). San Francisco: Jossey-Bass.

Carey, A. (1967). The Hawthorne Studies: A radical criticism. *American Sociological Review, 32(3),* 403–416.

Carroll, S.J., & Gillen, D.J. (1987). Are the classical management functions useful in describing managerial work? *Academy of Management Review, 12,* 38–51.

Chandler, A.D., Jr (1962). *Strategy and structure: Chapters in the history of the American industrial enterprise.* Cambridge, MA: MIT Press.

Chandler, A.D., Jr. (1977). *The visible hand: The managerial revolution in American business.* Cambridge, MA: The Belknap Press.

Chandler, A.D., Jr (1990). *Scale and scope: The dynamics of industrial capitalism.* Cambridge, MA: The Belknap Press.

Child, J. (1972). Organization structure and strategies of control. *Administrative Science Quarterly, 17,* 163–177.

Child, J. (1973). Strategies of control and organization behavior. *Administrative Science Quarterly, 18,* 163–177.

Child, J. (1977). *Organization: A guide to prob' practice.* London: Harper & Row.   72). A

Clark, B.R. (1969). *The open do study.* New York: McGraw-H

Cohen, M.D., March, J.G.

garbage can model of organizational choice. *Administrative Science Quarterly, 17,* 1–25.

Cotton, J.L., Vollrath, D.A., Frogatt, K.L., Lengnick-Hall, M.L., & Jennings, K.R. (1988). Employee participation: Diverse forms and different outcomes. *Academy of Management Review, 13,* 8–22.

Crozier, M., & Friedberg, E. (1977). *L'Acteur et le système.* Paris: Seuil.

Cummings, L.L. (1977). Emergence of the instrumental organization. In P.S. Goodman, J.M. Pennings, & associates (Eds.), *New perspectives on organization effectiveness* (pp.56–62). San Francisco: Jossey-Bass.

Cyert, R.M., & March, J.G. (1959). A behavioral theory of organization objectives. In M. Haire (Ed.), *Modern organization theory* (pp.76–90). New York: Wiley.

Cyert, R.M. & March, J.G. (1963). *A behavioral theory of the firm.* Englewood Cliffs, NJ: Prentice-Hall.

Cyert, R.M., & March, J.G. (1992). *A behavioral theory of the firm.* (2nd Edn). Cambridge, MA and Oxford, UK: Blackwell.

Dawkins, R. (1991). *The blind watchmaker.* London: Penguin Books.

Day, R., & Day, J.V. (1977). A review of the current state of negotiated order theory: An appreciation and critique. In J.K. Benson (Ed.), *Organizational analyses: Critique and innovation* (pp.128–144). Beverly Hills, CA: Sage.

Downey, H.K., Hellriegel, D.H., & Slocum Jr, J.W. (1975). Environmental uncertainty: The construct and its application. *Administrative Science Quarterly, 20,* 613–629.

Emerson, R.M. (1972). Exchange theory, Part II: Exchange relations and network structures. In J. Berger, M. Zelditch, & B. Anderson (Eds.), *Sociological studies in progress* (Vol. 2). Boston: Houghton Mifflin.

Etzioni, A. (1960). Two approaches to organizational analysis: A critique and a suggestion. *Administrative Science Quarterly, 5,* 257–278.

Fiedler, F.E. (1978). The contingency model and the dynamics of the leadership process. In L. Berkowitz (Ed.), *Advances in experimental social psychology* (Vol. 2, pp.60–112). New York: Academic Press.

Foa, E.B., & Foa, U.G. (1980). Resource theory. Interpersonal behavior as exchange. In K.J. Gergen, M.S. Greenberg, & R.H. Willis (Eds.), *Social exchange: Advances in theory and research* (pp.77–94). New York: Plenum Press.

Gagliardi, P. (1986). The creation and change of organizational cultures: A conceptual framework. *Organization Studies, 7,* 117–134.

Galbraith, J.R. (1977). *Organization design.* Reading, MA: Addison-Wesley.

ou, P. (1973). The goal paradigm and notes counter paradigm. *Administrative Science* 291–310.

Goldthorpe, J.H., Lockwood, D., Bechhofer, F., & Platt, J. (1968). *The affluent worker: Industrial attitude and behaviour.* Cambridge: Cambridge University Press.

Gouldner, A.W. (1954). *Patterns of industrial bureaucracy.* Glencoe, IL: Free Press.

Gouldner, A.W. (1959). Organizational analysis. In R.K. Merton, L. Broom, & L.S. Cottrell Jr (Eds.), *Sociology today.* New York: Basic Books.

Grandori, A. (1984). A prescriptive contingency view of organizational decision making. *Administrative Science Quarterly, 29,* 192–209.

Grandori, A. (1987). *Perspectives on organization theory.* Cambridge, MA: Ballinger.

Gulick, L., & Urwick, L. (Eds.) (1973). *Papers on the science of administration.* New York: Columbia University, Institute of Public Administration.

Hall, R.H. (1972). *Organizations: structure and process.* Englewood Cliffs, NJ: Prentice-Hall.

Hannan, M.T., & Freeman, J. (1977). The population ecology of organizations. *American Journal of Sociology, 82,* 929–964.

Hedberg, B.L.T., Nystrom, P., & Starbuck, W.H. (1976). Camping on seesaws: Prescription for a self-designing organization. *Administrative Science Quarterly, 21,* 41–65.

Hickson, D.J., Hinings, C.R., Lee, A.C., Schneck, R.E., & Pennings, J.M. (1971). A strategic contingency theory of intra-organizational power. *Administrative Science Quarterly, 16,* 216–229.

Hickson, D.J., Pugh, D.S., & Pheysey, D.C. (1969). Operations technology and organization structure: An empirical reappraisal. *Administrative Science Quarterly, 14,* 378–397.

Hogarth, R.M., & Reder, M.W. (Eds.) (1986). *Rational choice: The contrast between economics and psychology.* Chicago: University of Chicago Press.

Homans, G.G. (1951). *The human group.* London: Routledge & Kegan Paul.

James, L.R., & Jones, A.P. (1976). Organizational structure: A review of structural dimensions and their conceptual relationship with individual attitudes and behavior. *Organizational Behavior and Human Performance, 16,* 74–113.

Janis, I.L., & Mann, L. (1977). *Decision making: A psychological analysis of conflict, choice and commitment.* New York: Free Press.

Jellinek, M., Smircich, L., & Hirsch, P. (Eds.) (1983). Organization culture. *Administrative Science Quarterly, 28,* 331–449.

Katz, D., & Kahn, R.L. (1978). *The social psychology of organizations.* (2nd Edn). New York: Wiley.

Khandwalla, P.N. (1973). Viable and effective organization design of firms. *Academy of Management Journal, 16,* 481–495.

Kiesler, S., & Sproul, L. (1982). Managerial response to changing environments: Perspectives on problem sensing from social cognition. *Administrative Science Quarterly, 27,* 548–570.

Lawrence, P.R., & Lorsch, J.W. (1967). *Organization*

and environment: Managing differentiation and integration. Boston: Harvard Business School.

Likert, R. (1959). A motivation approach to a modified theory of organization and management. In M. Haire (Ed.), *Modern organization theory* (pp.184–217). New York: Wiley.

Likert, R. (1961). *New patterns of management.* New York: McGraw-Hill.

Likert, R. (1967). *The human organization: Its management and values.* New York: McGraw-Hill.

Lowin, A. (1968). Participative decision making: A model, literature, critique and prescriptions for research. *Organization Behavior and Human Performance, 3,* 68–106.

Luhmann, N. (1964). *Funktionen und Folgen formaler Organizationen.* Berlin: Duncker & Humblot

McGregor, D. (1960). *The human side of enterprise.* New York: McGraw-Hill.

March, J.G. (1994). *A primer on decision making.* New York: Free Press.

March, J.G., & Feldman, M.S. (1981). Information in organizations as signal and symbol. *Administrative Science Quarterly, 26,* 171–186.

March, J.G., & Olsen, J.P. (1976). *Ambiguity and choice in organizations.* Bergen: Universitetsforlaget.

March, J.G., & Simon, H.A. (1958). *Organizations.* New York: Wiley.

March, J.G., & Simon, H.A. (1993). *Organizations* (2nd Edn). Cambridge, MA and Oxford, UK: Blackwell.

Marrow, A.J., Bowers, D.G., & Seashore, S.E. (1967). *Management by participation: Creating a climate for personal and organizational development.* New York: Harper & Row.

Maslow, A. (1954). *Motivation and personality.* New York: Harper & Row.

Massie, J.L. (1965). Management theory. In J.G. March (Ed.), *Handbook of Organizations* (pp.387–422). Chicago: Rand McNally.

Mayo, E. (1975). *The social problems of an industrial civilization.* London: Routledge & Kegan Paul.

Merton, R.K. (1957). *Social theory and social structure* (2nd Edn). Glencoe, IL: Free Press.

Messinger, S.L. (1955). Organizations transformation: A case study of declining social movement. *American Sociological Review, 20,* 3–10.

Miller, D. & Friesen, P.H. (1984). *Organizations: A quantum view.* Englewood Cliffs, NJ: Prentice-Hall.

Miller, J.G. (1978). *Living systems.* New York: McGraw-Hill.

Mintzberg, H. (1979). *The structuring of organizations: A synthesis of the research.* Englewood Cliffs, NJ: Prentice-Hall.

Mintzberg, H. (1983). *Power in and around organizations.* Englewood Cliffs, NJ: Prentice-Hall.

Mintzberg, H., Raisinghani, D., & Theorêt, A. (1976). The structure of "unstructured" decision processes. *Administrative Science Quarterly, 21,* 246–275.

Morgan, G. (1986). *Images of organization.* Beverly Hills, CA: Sage.

Naschold, F. (1969). *Organization und Demokratie.* Stuttgart: W. Kohlhammer Verlag.

Nightingale, D.V., & Toulouse, J.M. (1977). Toward a multi-level congruence theory of organization. *Administrative Science Quarterly, 22,* 264–280.

Nohria, N., & Eccles, R.G. (Eds.) (1992). *Networks and organizations: structure, form, and action.* Boston: Harvard Business School Press.

Parsons, T. (1967). A paradigm for the analyses of social systems and change. In N.J. Demerath & R.A. Peterson (Eds.), *System, change and conflict* (pp.189–212). New York: Free Press.

Parsons, T. (1969). Suggestions for a sociological approach to the theory of organizations. In A. Etzioni (Ed.), *A sociological reader on complex organizations* (2nd Edn, pp.32–46). New York: Holt, Rinehart & Winston.

Pennings, J.M. (1975). The relevance of the structural contingency model for organizational effectiveness. *Administrative Science Quarterly, 20,* 393–410.

Pennings, J.M., & Goodman, P.S. (1977). Toward a workable framework. In P.S. Goodman, J.M. Pennings, & associates (Eds). *New perspectives on organizational effectiveness* (pp.146–184). San Francisco: Jossey-Bass.

Perrow, C. (1961). The analysis of goals in complex organizations. *American Sociological Review, 26,* 854–865.

Perrow, C. (1967). A framework for the comparative analysis of organizations. *American Sociological Review, 32,* 194–208.

Perrow, C. (1970). *Organizational analysis: A sociological view.* Belmont, CA: Brooks-Cole.

Perrow, C. (1979). *Complex organizations: A critical essay.* (2nd Edn). New York: Random House.

Perrow, C. (1986). *Complex organizations: A critical essay.* (3rd Edn). New York: Random House.

Pfeffer, J. (1981). *Power in organizations.* Boston: Pitman.

Pfeffer, J. (1982). *Organizations and organization theory.* Marshfield, MA: Pitman.

Pfeffer, J. (1994). *Competitive advantage through people: Unleashing the power of the work force.* Boston: Harvard Business School Press.

Pfeffer, J., & Salancik, G.R. (1978). *The external control of organizations: A resource dependence perspective.* New York: Harper & Row.

Pruitt, D.G., & Rubin, J.Z. (1986). *Social conflict: Escalation, stalemate and settlement.* New York: Random House.

Quinn, J.B. (1988). Managing strategies incrementally. In J.B. Quinn, H. Mintzberg, & R.M. James (Eds), *The strategy process: Concepts, contexts and* Englewood Cliffs, NJ: Prentice-Hall.

Rahim, M.A. (1989). *Managing confl disciplinary approach.* New York: P

Robbins, S.P. (1987). *Organizations*

design and applications. Englewood Cliffs, NJ: Prentice-Hall.

Roethlisberger, F.J. (1952). *Management and morale.* Cambridge, MA: Harvard University Press.

Roethlisberger, F.J., & Dickson, W.J. (1939). *Management and the worker.* Cambridge, MA: Harvard University Press.

Salancik, G.R., & Meindl, J.R. (1984). Corporate attributions as strategic illusions of management control. *Administrative Science Quarterly, 29,* 238–254.

Salancik, G.R., & Pfeffer, J. (1977). An examination of need-satisfaction models of job-attitudes. *Administrative Science Quarterly, 22,* 427–456.

Schein, E.H. (1965). *Organizational psychology.* Englewood Cliffs, NJ: Prentice-Hall.

Schoonhoven, C.B. (1981). Problems with contingency theory: Testing assumptions hidden within the language of contingency "theory". *Administrative Science Quarterly, 26,* 349–377.

Scott, W.R. (1981). *Organizations: Rational, natural, and open systems.* Englewood Cliffs, NJ: Prentice-Hall.

Scott, W.R. (1990). Symbols and organizations: From Barnard to the institutionalists. In O.E. Williamson (Ed.), *Organization theory: From Chester Barnard to the present and beyond* (pp.38–55). New York & Oxford: Oxford University Press.

Selznick, P. (1943). An approach to a theory of bureaucracy. *American Sociological Review, 8,* 47–54.

Selznick, P. (1949). *TVA and the grass roots.* Berkeley: University of California Press.

Silverman, D. (1970). *The theory of organizations.* London: Heinemann.

Simon, H.A. (1945). *Administrative behavior.* New York: Free Press.

Simon, H.A. (1957). *Administrative behavior* (2nd Edn). New York: MacMillan.

Simon, H.A. (1961). A formal theory of the employment relation. In H.A. Simon, *Models of man: Social and rational* (pp.183–195). New York: John Wiley.

Simon, H.A. (1964). On the concept of organizational goal. *Administrative Science Quarterly, 9,* 1–22.

Smircich, L., & Calás, M.B. (1987). Organizational culture: A critical assessment. In F.M. Jabbin, L.L. Putnam, K.H. Roverts, & L.W. Porter (Eds.), *Handbook of organizational communication: An interdisciplinary perspective.* Newbury Park, CA: Sage.

Sofer, C. (1972). *Organizations in theory and practice.* New York: Basic Books.

Staw, B.M., McKechnie, P.I., & Puffer, S.M. (1983). The justification of organizational performance. *Administrative Science Quarterly, 28,* 582–600.

Stinchcombe, A.L. (1990). *Information and organizations.* Berkeley: University of California Press.

~s, A., Schatzman, L., Bucher, R., Ehrlich, D., &

Sabshin, M. (1963). The hospital and its negotiated order. In E. Freidson (Ed.), *The hospital in modern society.* (pp.147–169). New York: Free Press.

Taylor, F.W. (1911). *The principles of scientific management.* New York: Harper.

Thompson, J.D. (1967). *Organizations in action.* New York: McGraw-Hill.

Tosi, H., Aldag, R., & Storey, R. (1973). On the measurement of the environment: An assessment of the Lawrence and Lorsch environmental uncertainty subscale. *Administrative Science Quarterly, 18,* 27–36.

Veen, P. (1973). Participatie: Een poging tot synthese. In P.J.D. Drenth, P.J. Willems, & Ch.J. de Wolff (Eds.), *Arbeids-en Organisatiepsychologie.* Deventer: Kluwer.

Veen, P. (1982). *Mensen in organisaties.* Deventer: Van Loghum Slaterus.

Veen, P. (1983). Macht en beïnvloeding: een overzicht. In P. Veen & H.A.M. Wilke (Eds.), *Zicht op macht* (pp.3–17). Assen: Van Gorcum.

Veen, P., & Haren, T. van (1980). Gedrag in organisaties. In J. Jaspers & R. van de Vlist (Eds.), *Sociale Psychologie in Nederland III.* Deventer: Van Loghum Slaterus.

Veld, J. in 't (1975). *Analyse van organisatieproblemen.* Amsterdam: Agon/Elsevier.

Wagner, J.A., & Gooding, R.Z. (1987). Shared influence and organizational behavior: A meta-analysis of situational variables expected to moderate participation. *Academy of Management Journal, 30,* 524–541.

Wahba, M.A., & Bridwell, L.G. (1976). Maslow reconsidered: A review of research on the need hierarchy theory. *Organizational Behavior and Human Performance, 15,* 212–240.

Weber, M. (1946). Types of Authority. In H.H. Gerth & C. Wright Mills (Eds.), *From Max Weber: Essays in Sociology* (pp.224–229). New York: Oxford University Press.

Weber, M. (1947). *The theory of social and economic organization.* Transl. A.M. Henderson & T. Parsons. Glencoe, IL: Free Press.

Weick, K.E. (1977a). Enactment processes in organizations. In B.M. Staw & G.R. Salancik (Eds.), *New directions in organizational behavior.* Chicago: St Clair Press, pp.267–300.

Weick, K.E. (1977b). Re-punctuating the problem. In P.S. Goodman, J.M. Pennings, & associates (Eds.), *New perspectives on organizational effectiveness* (pp.193–225). San Francisco: Jossey-Bass.

Weick, K.E. (1979). *The social psychology of organizing* (2nd Edn). Reading, MA: Addison-Wesley.

Weick, K.E. (1995). *Sensemaking in organizations.* Thousand Oaks, CA: Sage.

Wilke, H.A.M. (1983). Coalitieformatie: macht en controle. In P. Veen & H.A.M. Wilke (Eds.), *Zicht op Macht* (pp.47–58). Assen: Van Gorcum.

Williamson, O.E. (1975). *Markets and hierarchies:*

Analysis and antitrust implications. New York: The Free Press.

Williamson, O.E. (1985). *The economic institutions of capitalism.* New York: The Free Press.

Williamson, O.E. (Ed.) (1990). *Organization theory:* *From Chester Barnard to the present and beyond.* New York and Oxford: Oxford University Press.

Womack, J.P., Jones, D.T., & Roos, D. (1990). *The machine that changed the world: The story of lean production.* New York: Macmillan.

3

Structural Contingency Theory

Johannes M. Pennings

INTRODUCTION

Ever since the fifties, management research has shown a growing interest in explaining differences in organizational structure. The idea that there was more than one method of organizing has been widely held since the day and age of authors such as Burns and Stalker (1961) and Dill (1958). It was believed that organizations may be either decentralized or centralized in their decision-making processes, structured in highly formal or more informal ways, or chaotic while still exhibiting a high degree of effectiveness. Consequently, it was held that several organizational forms might accomplish the same goals, that is, there were several ways of making organizations "tick" as effectively as possible. However, views stating that certain organizational types were superior to others remained prevalent. Nevertheless, normative views had firmly established themselves.

In addition, the ideas developed by people such as Frederick Winslow Taylor (1911), Fayol (1949), Urwick (1943), and even Weber (1947) —some in semi-abridged forms—had not only

obtained a widespread following, they were also gradually applied more frequently in business. In these authors' views, there was one specific type of organization that was better than any other—the organization that had embraced labor efficiency promoting techniques. Thus, labor ergonomics in the form of "Taylorism" was at its height. Hand and arm movements were observed meticulously in order to arrive at the most efficient task and work structure. Job profiles were established to eliminate ambiguity. The need for delegating decisions to the executive staff was eradicated with the simplification of work, division of labor and strict hierarchy, monocratic management with clear authority, etc. Although there are still companies today that persist in following the bible written by Taylor & Co., it is now widely accepted that these structures are rigid and often have shortcomings in the organizational process (see Chapter 2, Volume 4, however).

There have, of course, been other reactions to Taylor and his following prior to the emergence of structural contingency theory, and the entire history of industrial and organizational psychology as well as in organization theory generally presents a reliable catalogue of these reactions. They comprise, for example, the so-called "human relations school", the socio-technical school, and the concept of restructuring (Van Assen & Den Hertog, 1984). More recently, also Peters and Waterman (1982) and Peters' subsequent string of books have been vocal critics in their opposition to these earlier schools. In their controversial *In Search of Excellence*, they propagate a 180-degree turn towards a "new theory" within which decentralization, freedom, and indeed, lawlessness was tolerated as promoting creativity, entrepreneurship, devotion, and even work motivation.

Ironically, still more recently, we have witnessed a resurgence of some Taylor-like ideas—for example, the current fad around *business process re-engineering* (Hammer & Champy, 1993). Here too, the emphasis is on a singular template aimed at removing slack and waste from the organizations" operations, by eliminating functions that appear to be redundant, and stressing a bare-bone design of a sequence of operations that is well engineered. Perhaps this currently accepted one cause–one consequence approach to organization design, with its slant toward restructuring and downsizing signals the reincarnation of Taylorism, albeit in different packaging.

There remains an important difference between the more ideologically biased reactions and the fairly "neutral" or "value free" contingency theory. Structural contingency theory is basically non-normative, keeps its applicability in perspective, presupposes a complex (rather than a simple) perception of reality and has a more academic, empirical basis. Thus it may be viewed as a positivist rather than an ideological response to the missionary management schools.

In passing it may be noted that there are interesting "contingency-based parallels" to motivational and leadership studies, in which we have been able to observe a similar scientific undermining of dated, normative views. In these studies, contingency views developed by House (1971), Fiedler (1978) and Hackman and Lawler (1971) also became empirical substitutes for dated views.

In this chapter, the main aspects of *structural* contingency theory (as distinct from leadership contingency or motivational contingency) will be illustrated. First, a brief overview of the current

theories will be given in order to pinpoint its position. This is also relevant when a review of the theory is provided at the end. Following a brief description of its origin and background, the theory will be described extensively. Next, two important derived problems will be treated: the methodological pitfalls existing even now, and the practical implications for organization advisers and managers. Finally, in the conclusion, the current and future position of contingency in organization theory will be evaluated.

1   NICHE IN CURRENT ORGANIZATION THEORY

Structural contingency theory holds a prominent place in the current field of organization theory. That field has been crowded, however, with various other theories or schools of thought, each vying for legitimacy and popularity. At present, structural contingency theory competes with these theories, but all of them also complement one another to some degree. Contingency theory belongs to a cluster of theories that embody some rational calculus in that they stress some optimizing adaptive approach to conditions in the organization's environment. This approach recognizes that differences among organizations reflect more or less deliberate changes in strategy and structure in response to threats, transformations, and jolts in their environment. The central view is that the organization is capable of adapting to the environment and that its managers have discretion or elbowroom to ensure that this adaptation takes place in the best possible way. This view includes the idea that organizations and their leaders are rational and that they are both prepared and able to do whatever enables their organization to function as well as possible.

While structural contingency considers the entire organizational social architecture, the "resource dependence" view (cf. Pfeffer & Salancik, 1978), often referred to as exchange theory, is limited to the architecture of boundary arrangements. The emphasis is on managing and controlling business relationships with suppliers, clients, unions, etc. The organization is in constant contact with the environment in order to obtain raw materials and labor, but also extra-mural know-how. The organization is not autarchic and, in various respects, it has to integrate in the organizational process persons and organizations that are critical components in its environment. Particularly, much attention is paid to the degree of tension that exists between the organization and its environment. Research within this school of thought has disclosed that organizations develop boundary structures. Such boundary structures are established to regulate border traffic (e.g., information and other resources entering or exiting the organization) and to obtain the best possible negotiated position for the organization, in relation to important external institutions and persons. Hence, the main focus of research has been on so-called boundary structures, such as interlocking directorates, strategic alliances, "joint ventures", employer's organizations, coordination networks and "gatekeepers". Examples of "gatekeepers" and their departments include public relations officers, legal advisers, purchase officers and commissioners. The formation of boundary structures is contingent upon the presence of critical external dependencies, which stabilizes the relationship between organizations and their environment, whereas the remaining parts of the organization are shielded by it. For example, the aircraft manufacturer Boeing outsources the construction of the aircraft's body to external subcontractors, while retaining the design and construction of the cockpit and wings, which reflect the core skills, and consequently its core activities. Being embedded in a value chain, it becomes crucial for Boeing to position itself such that reverberations in that chain do not become disruptive. Thus, the creation of long-term contracts with suppliers, the formation of joint task forces, and the exchange of engineers all serve to shield the firm's core operations from jolts and other unforeseen events.

Structural contingency theory places more emphasis on integral organization design, including that which covers boundary arrangements. We have called both resource dependence and structural contingency theory intentional-rationalistic elsewhere (Pennings, 1984, 1985). The underlying idea is analogous to the one in economics, on the

understanding that rationalism in its pure form is not attainable, a view that is firmly rooted in the work carried out by Simon (March & Simon, 1958).

These theories stand in sharp contrast with deterministic theories, of which the so-called ecological theories are definitely the most salient (Hannan & Freeman, 1984; Nelson & Winter, 1982; Singh, House & Tucker, 1986). Differences in organizational structures are evident from new organizations with their alternative "blueprints" or when existing organizations whose blueprints (or genetic profiles) are no longer adequate, go bankrupt. This is sometimes expressed in terms of the well-known Darwinian slogan "survival of the fittest". According to this movement, the optimum relationship between organization and environment develops by means of selection: specifically *those* organizations which have a structure that is optimally congruent to a particular environment will survive and negative selection will ensure that the best members of the species will continue. While structural contingency would argue that organizations might change their design to adapt to a changing environment, organizational ecologists believe that they are substantially inmutatable entities.

Once founded, organizations become quickly sluggish, rigid and practically unchangeable; their managers possess little leeway to apply structural changes. There are obligations to various groups of subcontractors, suppliers, clients, government institutions and unions. Decisions made in the initial stages of the organizational process lead lives of their own. Norms, customs, rules of thumb, symbols and rituals have taken hold and they are very difficult to change. The genetic code of the organization is embedded in each one of these elements. Lamarckian interventions aimed at obtaining evolutionary short-circuits, as it were, are doomed to fail. (In biology, Darwin's counterpart, Lamarck, has claimed that one can intervene in the evolutionary process to change its course or rate.) In the same way as surgical interventions will not change the genetic profile of an organism, a reorganization will not transform the fundamental nature of the organization either, unless a reorganization is considered to be the establishment of a new organization. The transformed organization exhibits the same vulnerability as its newer counterparts and, to further the analogy, is therefore equally susceptible to children's diseases and high infant mortality (Hannan & Freeman, 1984). In brief, organizations reflect a high degree of continuity and resistance to change.

One only has to compare the laborious efforts taken by educational institutions to change their course programs, or to compare the tremendous obstacles accountant companies face in the process of becoming general firms of consultants. Or, traditional small grocery stores fighting a losing battle against supermarket chains, even when they converted into minisupermarkets. According to population ecologists, the rationality does not reside in individual firms, but in the population or industry, which allows only the fittest organizations to survive whereas the less fit languish and decline. This is sometimes referred to as ecological rationality, because the level of analysis is the population of organizations rather than the single organization. The disappearance of the regular grocery shop should not be explained therefore in terms of a shopkeeper's narrow-mindedness, but from the viewpoint of all populations of stores and their relative birth and death rates. In turn, these are associated with the extent to which structure and environment are congruent.

A more recent example is the demise of manufacturers of mechanical watches and weighscales, brought about by the micro-electronic sweep. The Swiss watch industry has been swept from the earth, first by Timex and next by Japanese firms such as Seiko. The Dutch firm Van Berkel which was an industry leader of mechanical weigh-scales has likewise been victimized by the replacement of electronic weigh-scales. One might say that the skills for designing and producing mechanical watches and weigh-scales conferred no longer a competitive advantage, and in fact became obsolete. The firms were incapable of shedding their old skills while acquiring new skills, so that their markets selected them out of existence.

Finally, there exists a whole range of phenomenological constructs in which organizations are interpreted as ideal realities (cf. Berger & Luckman, 1966; March & Olson, 1976; Weick, 1979). Berger and Luckman (1966) and their European predecessors (e.g., Mannheim, 1957) are at the cradle of this conception. They view reality as being intersubjective, socially constructed, and inseparable from the factors themselves. Weick (1979) takes organizations to be collectively formed cognitive structures that provide the members of the organization with meaning. In fact, nothing exists apart from their socially created organization and environment.

March and Olsen (1976) are the creators of the so-called garbage-can model (Cohen, March & Olsen, 1972), in which organizations are described as a set of sanitation bins. The contents consist of solutions (awaiting problems), individuals, and problems, which have been piled up during the organization's existence. The chance processes in the garbage-cans may be rationalized to form something meaningful and orderly after the event, but this is "speaking in hindsight" or retroactive justification (see Chapter 14, Vol. 4, this manual for more details). In this model, differences in organizational structures are hardly connected with internal attempts towards (re)organization, nor do they have a great deal to do with selection processes; they have become detached and chiefly fulfil a symbolic function. The organization is nothing other than a set of collective views shared by the members of the organization, and maintained, put in order, and strengthened by daily interactions.

In this tradition, the contrast between organization and environment is suspended. The environment is just as much a creation of the organization as the organization is itself a social construction. It is also important to note that the individual as a social agent is central in this tradition. Social structures disassociated from his or her (construction of) meaning are not interesting and provide little insight.

Compared to sense-making treatments of organization, contingency theory assumes organizational structure and the environment to be objectified and analyzed as an autonomous reality. This reality is ontologically unequivocal and methodologically quantifiable.

The above-mentioned phenomenological authors holds that no social reality exists over and above the individual. Researchers belonging to this camp are therefore often anthropologically trained and attempt to describe the essence of an organization by the researcher's observation. These are often colorful case studies in which the here and now is narrated vividly. Examples are Van Maanen's studies of a police station or of fishermen (1975, 1988), Weick's analysis of firemen perishing during a forest fire (1993), and March and Olsen's account of the political frictions and messy developments surrounding the appointment of a Dean at a university (1976). In these cases, the analysis is based on the garbage-can model; however, this type of study probes deeper-lying social phenomena while ignoring the more or less formal structure of the organization (the surface!).

Structural contingency theory is undoubtedly one of the older theories that emphasizes objectified social structures. It addresses the question of how various structures can eliminate garbage-can-like states, or, should this not be possible, how certain structures can keep these under control (Thompson, 1967). It has lost some of its popularity, mainly as a result of the strong appeal of alternative views.[1] There are, however, signs that indicate that the later views contain many elements also to be found in contingency theory and that in this way they prove to be old wine in new bottles. In order to explain all this, it is now appropriate to take a closer look at contingency theory.

2 BACKGROUND

In its general form, contingency theory can be formulated relatively easily. The theory claims that the effectiveness of an organization depends on the degree of congruence between its social structure and its environment. "Goodness of fit" is a term often mentioned in the Anglo-Saxon specialist literature.

Organizational structure comprises the choice of a social architecture or role configurations. The choice involves two aspects: grouping individuals (or their positions) in departments (divisions), and forming a coordination system to allow those departments to cooperate. Metaphors such as Roman Catholic hierarchy, machine and computer may be used to illustrate such architecture.

In this sense the computer, for example, is made up of many components each fulfilling certain tasks, whereas some components hierarchically control the performance of other components. Organizations are essentially systems of positions that have been combined into departments by division of labor. This subdivision leads to inter-dependencies requiring coordination. Various kinds of subdivisions are possible, and comprise, for instance, those based on function and skills, or on "purpose", such as market, geographic area, and product. Functional differentiation often leads to the highest interdependence with considerable integration costs; it burdens management most heavily. The traditional company with a department for sales, production, development, and administration serves as an example. The mutual dependence often gives rise to conflicts.

Differentiation based on purpose is best illustrated by the so-called M-form, where "M" refers to multi-divisional; where more precisely the design is based on product lines, technology, or markets. Generally speaking, this type of organization is more decentralized and decisions are made at lower levels. Being relatively more "uncoupled" systems (Weick, 1979), these organizations are more strongly focused on the external environment and they exhibit more pluriformity or chaos, even. Conflicts among divisions are infrequent.

The most important coordination mechanism (according to Williamson, 1975) in organizations is "hierarchy". This author even equates hierarchy with organization, witness the title of his well-known publication *Markets and Hierarchies*! Other coordination forms are lateral relations, organizational culture, reward systems, normalization, and standardization of tasks (Thompson, 1967).

The situational determinants of the organizational structure are mainly related to the environment. The definition of the environment and the identification of relevant dimensions show a great deal of variation in the organizational literature. The environment has been compared to a "cloud" enveloping the organization; as the market or the branch of industry in which it competes for customers, suppliers or other relations; as a set of external factors with which it has relations; as a network of organizations in which it is embedded; as a population of organizations of which it is a member; or as a cognitive construct that is interpreted, created, and maintained by the members (cf. "enacted", Weick, 1979). It is not feasible within the context of this chapter to provide a full account of all these views. Generally, most researchers of structural contingency theory either compare the environment to a "cloud" or view it as a geographically, technologically, or commercially defined "relevant" environment (Emery & Trist, 1970). Complexity and uncertainty are among the most frequent attributes to describe and measure it. Examples are: the changeability of consumer behavior, the intensity of competition, the degree of technological innovation and predictability of public policy, and the homogeneity of customers or staff. We may claim that it is easier to assess the environment *ipso facto* if the customers of an organization are homogeneous. For example, a hospital may develop specialisms for certain types of patients, for children or for cancer patients, or it may be a "general hospital", or a firm of solicitors may concentrate on cases of divorce, contracts, liability and real estate; or it may provide legal services in each one of these sectors. In the latter case, the environment is considerably more complicated.

The organization and its management (including designers, advisers, etc.) are limited by environmental conditions in adopting certain structural "blueprints" or templates. The nature of the environment narrows the range of options that managers and other designers of the organizational structure have when considering structural changes. The range of options is limited, since an "organic", decentralized and informal structure must have the upper hand in an uncertain and complicated environment. A simple and predictable environment, on the other hand, requires a more "mechanical", centralized, and even bureaucratic structure. A lack of congruence between environment and structure will affect effectiveness adversely and, therefore, is an important consideration in the (re)organization process.

By way of dovetailing as a metaphor, the designers must bring the firm's design in line with aspects of the environment, as it were. A certain level of environmental uncertainty, for example, must coincide with a certain level of centralization—in which case the level of performance of the organization will be high.

This train of thought is fairly old. Its first advocates were Dill (1958) and Burns and Stalker (1961), who introduced the terms "mechanical" and "organic" to the organization literature. Burns and Stalker (1961) have described a number of cases from the English electronics industry. This industry, having been an important supplier for the British government during the Second World War, discovered after the war that changing over from a market chiefly consisting of the government to a market of private investors was a precarious undertaking for many companies. The authors demonstrated that the market was becoming considerably more complicated and less predictable. Various companies adapted structurally, for example, by replacing an organization based on function by one based on product, by consequently decentralizing many decisions, by allowing more lateral communication between departments, and by forcing members of staff into a particular task description less often. These companies gained considerably better achievements and managed to forestall bankruptcy.

The implication was that the mechanical regime that had proved suitable during the Second World War had now become an impediment and was making it difficult for the companies to judge the customers to their true merits, to develop new products, and to stand up to competition.

A true flood of publications has been published since the study conducted by Burns and Stalker (e.g., Armour & Teece, 1978; Dewar & Werbel, 1979; Donaldson, 1995; Drazin & Van de Ven, 1985; Gresov & Drazin, 1987; Khandwalla, 1977; Lawrence & Lorsch, 1967; Pennings, 1975, 1987; Schoonhoven, 1981). These organization-theoretical studies have been succeeded by a long stream of experimental studies on group communication structures (e.g., Bavelas, 1950) and also studies on organizational strategy (e.g., Chandler, 1962; Rumelt, 1974). The empirical support for the theory is not as robust as that brought forward by Burns and Stalker. Notably Scott (1981) and Pfeffer (1982) brought conflicting results to attention. Many textbooks have assumed the theory to be true and correct, nonetheless, and they have referred to it in making normative claims for the design of organizational structures (cf. Galbraith, 1977; Nadler, Hackman & Lawler, 1979).

3 THE THEORY

In order to uncover the underlying problems and contradictory results, we first need to dwell on the theory at some length. Figure 3.1 shows a schematic representation to which the above idea of dovetailing is central.

On the left-hand side, Figure 3.1 shows a set of structural and environmental dimensions which may or may not be combined in types. The dimensions or types describe the structure of the topic of organizations or their components, such as departments, divisions, project groups, etc. Social structure and organization design are often considered synonymous. Both relate to the social architecture of positional configurations, as illustrated by means of organization diagrams. A social structure may, however, develop spontaneously from the interaction of individuals and then become more or less durable. Design, on the other hand, is associated with the use of a blueprint, constructed by management and staff, which imposes a pattern on the position holders of the organization.

Congruence can be determined by comparing or dovetailing structural dimensions or types, such as centralization and complexity, two by two. From a static point of view, a correlation between a structural and environmental dimension illustrates this congruence in the same way as discriminant analysis exposes the overlap between an environmental and an organizational type.[2] As complexity increases, the decision-making process requires more decentralizing. The basis for this claim can be found in so-called information theories. The experimental research on communication networks in group context and the conceptual work done by Thompson (1967) and Galbraith (1977), among organization theoreticians, are important contributions in this connection. An interesting comparison can be made between organizations

and computers. Like computers, organizations deal with a given quantity of information, which can be expressed in "bits". The information varies, depending on the degrees of turbulence, complexity, homogeneity and changeability. Factors increasing the quantity of information that organizations have to deal with are, for example, demographic differences among bank customers, changes in the course programs of secondary schools, modifications in the tax codes, etc.

The quantity of information can result in cognitive stress in the organization in the same way that computers can be overburdened. The difference between the quantity of information and the capacity of the system and/or organization leads to "uncertainty". The more uncertainty, the higher the odds that things will go wrong and that the organization will become overburdened. Overburdening will lead to lower achievements, because the system may crash unless it can enlarge its information processing capacity. In the ideal case, there is a perfect correspondence between quantity of information and information processing capacity.

The "computer" or "cybernetics" metaphor is extremely useful in illustrating the organization as an information processing unit. For that matter, there is a metaphor or "image" (Morgan, 1987) behind every theory on organizations. We conceptualize the organization as an information processing system which either does or does not have the capacity required to run smoothly. The organizational dimensions may therefore be interpreted as information-reducing or capacity-enhancing. The types of mechanical and organic structures can therefore be interpreted in terms of information processing and capacity; organic regimes have a larger capacity.

The many experimental studies on communication networks illustrate this idea. Experimental social psychologists have simulated structures that tend towards the "wheel" and the "circle". A channel of communication is created in an artificial group of five subjects, allowing the members to communicate directly with a limited number of fellow members. The remaining members can only be made contact with indirectly. In the wheel, four members can have contact with each other only by passing a fifth; the fifth member is usually

FIGURE 3.1

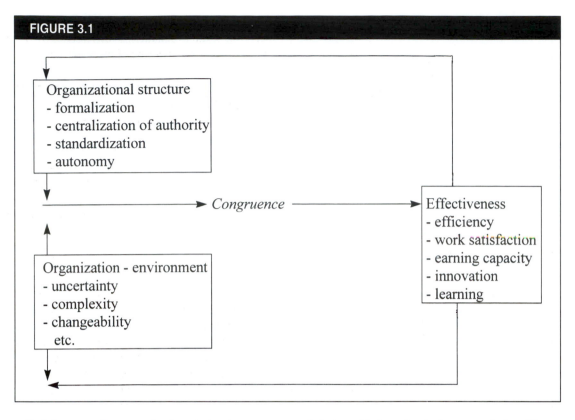

called the central person. In the circle, the members have contact with their neighbors only. Interaction with further members therefore calls for the involvement of some intermediaries. The studies conducted by Bavelas (1950) and Leavitt (1951) showed that wheel structures work faster and that the groups make fewer errors. However, Leavitt (1951) discovered that this is solely the case if the task is simple. The circle produces better results if the tasks are complex. A typical example of a simple task is finding a shared symbol from a set of six symbols that differ for each member in all other respects. A difficult task would entail the planning for the removal of office furniture with either a minimum number of rides or with the smallest possible number of trucks.

These studies illustrate structural contingency theory in a nutshell. There are differences in the environment (task complexity, etc.) that correspond with differences in organizational structure. Compared to the wheel, the circle is more decentralized, less hierarchical, and probably also more chaotic. This structure does not match simple tasks. Somewhat audaciously, these structures

might be called mechanical or organic (see Figure 3.2).

An interesting epilogue is formed by the study conducted by Mulder (1960). Whereas the communication networks were being manipulated by the experimental researcher, the subjects were shown to develop an alternative social architecture in the process, during the execution of such an experiment. Mulder terms this architecture "decision structure". It originates within the communication structure and may or may not be centralized.

The analogy between network experiments and computers also comes to mind easily. The wheel does not function properly if the tasks require a large quantity of cognitive energy, unless, as Mulder states, the members of the network are attuned to each other by means of their decision structure. Otherwise the central person will probably suffer "role overload" because he or she cannot keep track of it all and becomes overworked! A discrepancy exists between that person's information capacity and the number of data that he or she receives, processes, and transmits.

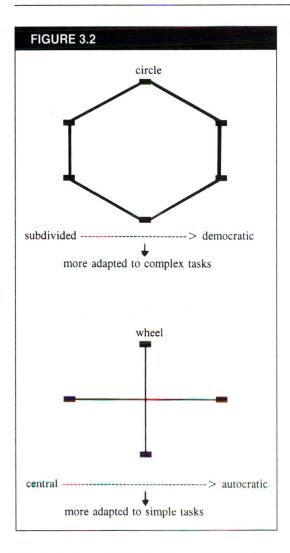

FIGURE 3.2

circle

subdivided - > democratic

more adapted to complex tasks

wheel

central - > autocratic

more adapted to simple tasks

Thanks to the work done by Simon (1960), Miller (1956), and Tversky and Kahneman (1974), we know that the individual has limited potential for information processing, that he or she chooses to be guided by rules of thumb and misleading mnemonic devices, or shows signs of "satisficing" (contenting oneself with a "satisfactory" way out) in order to resist cognitive stress. Such adaptational and transformational tendencies lead to incorrect or incomplete decisions. As a consequence, the central person in the wheel degenerates into a bottleneck, whereas the brain capacity of the peripheral members remains quite underutilized. In the circle, a linking of the brain capacity of the members takes place, so the total capacity employed is considerably larger. It is this infor-

mation-theoretical reasoning that implicitly lies at the root of the explanation of differences between wheel and circle in terms of performance.

4 GALBRAITH

An explicit reference to computer metaphors is made by Galbraith (1977), whose work cannot be imagined without the highly influential *Organizations in Action* by Thompson (1967). Thompson's book is not only one of the standard works in organization theory, it is also an important document for contingency theory. The book, however, is highly abstract. Fortunately, Galbraith has given us a popularized version.

Within his Thompsonian frame of reference, Galbraith points out four alternative ways to arrive at an optimum relation between information quantity and capacity. These are redundancy or "slack", the creation of independent groups or departments, vertical information systems, and lateral relations. The former two have an information-reducing effect, whereas the latter two provide the organization with more capacity.

There is redundancy when the organization allows more means or reduces the levels of achievement. Slack reduces the quantity of information, because the same tasks (e.g., the Rubik cube, the queue of customers at the bank, aid in case of a natural disaster, etc.) are allotted more time or other means. An organization can, for example, set up larger stocks, extend the time allotted, and tolerate a wider margin of errors. Compared to their Japanese competitors, American automobile manufacturers set up considerably larger stocks, so they are less vulnerable in case of unforeseen circumstances. Additionally, they make use of relatively more redundancies, which is not free of expense, of course. As with the other three options, the organization has to pay a particular price for the reduction in terms of information stress.

Independent units reduce information because this leads to a lower degree of interdependence, and communication and coordination activities associated with it. Gaining independence reduces the lateral contribution made by other departments or other employees, so the total information is less. The formation of autonomous units is also often linked to a relatively homogeneous environment. Examples may be found in the work done by Thompson (1967) and Williamson (1975). Companies changing over from a functional (U-form) to a divisional (M-form) structure often subdivide their environment into sub-environments, which are further subdivided into various component markets, segments, geographical areas, or categories of customers. For example, banks now have a consumers' division, a commercial division, an international division and a capital market division. Each one of these divisions deals with a fairly homogeneous clientele, whereas in the older days when banks used to be organized on a functional basis a banker had to be "a jack-of-all-trades"! Goal specialization now enables the banker to focus on a market and he or she deals with a specific type of customer.

The other two options have a capacity-enhancing effect. Vertical information systems such as electronic networks with access to continually upgraded data bases, expand the information processing capacity of organizations. Examples include the reservation systems used by airlines, Microsoft's system of maintaining and updating customer communication interfaces (Cusumano & Selby, 1995), and the elaborate electronic networking between departments, suppliers and clients as in Kao. Kao, a Japanese cosmetics firm, furnishes one of the best illustrations of the organization as a "hypertext" in that the various information sharing units can navigate between data sources such that employees have access to information regardless of where the information originates (compare Nonaka, 1994). More recently, Kaplan (Kaplan & Norton, 1993) has advocated a system of balanced scorecards in which organizations maintain a data bank on financial, customer, process, and innovative aspects of performance. Galbraith (1977) distinguishes between four types appearing in a two × two table whose dimensions are *periodicity* (periodic or continuous) and *range* (local or global). Information can be updated every now and then (e.g., every pupil's academic achievements) or continuously (e.g., seat reservations of an airline company). The information may relate to a department or the total of all mutually dependent departments. For example, the airline reservation system does not involve one route but all routes worldwide. In computer jargon, these vertical information systems are termed "on line, real time".

Finally, Galbraith mentions the lateral relations that comprise both the intermediaries, the coordinating committees, working groups, project management, and the matrix. We have encountered the lateral relations in our discussion of communication networks. The circle is, in fact, a lateral system of information storage and processing! Following Thompson (1967), Mintzberg (1983) points to "mutual adjustment", in particular. It is mutual attuning which is central to the circle structure. It is also an essential element of the coordinating activities in a matrix organization. These structures are characterized by Lawrence and Lorsch (1967) as "integrative mechanisms", because they join differentiated systems, as it were, and gear the departments to one another and provide conditions for the solution of conflicts between mutually dependent departments.

Whereas "traditional" vertical integration systems may have a centralizing effect, such lateral arrangements generally show a decentralizing effect and they reflect the communication circle in real organizations, as it were. These relations replace the hierarchy in the coordination of activities and consequently relieve the top management team. This not only contributes towards a higher degree of participation, but also promotes a greater amenability towards the public being served: customers, patients, students or tax payers. Of course, the inevitable demise of the mainframe computer, and its gradual replacement by electronic networking, together with e-mail and internet, suggests that the vertical information system is becoming increasingly horizontal, and can thus be construed as becoming more and more an integrative mechanism.

Galbraith's (1977) framework is useful at illustrating the metaphor of the organization as a (mainframe)computer or cybernetic system. Like other system approaches of organizations (cf. Emery & Trist, 1970), empirical verification is hard to come by. It should also be stressed that Galbraith's publication predates the "discovery" of organization culture, which is currently viewed as a key ingredient of organization design. Furthermore, his view of contingency theory is apolitical with little regard for power shifts that could be brought about by major changes in the vertical information systems—for example, the creation of elaborate electronic networks giving many employees access to a multitude of data on organizational performance. In fact, the rise of Local Area Networks, servers, Intranet or specific software such as SAP, and of course the Internet have led to an information technology sweep. The term vertical information system is rather antiquated now, and it would be preferable to refer to "horizontal information systems". A Japanese cosmetic firm like KAO has fully institutionalized a horizontal information system, in which everybody can navigate between various information contexts such as sales territories, production departments, etc. The Japanese writer Nonaka (1993) has shown that information flow through elaborate networks becomes a more viable way to represent organization structure. This information technology sweep is drastically altering the organizational landscape and has led to a reduction of organizational levels, and increased empowerment, networking (e.g. Kanter, 1989) and decentralization. These new developments can be readily included in a refashioning of contingency theory as we will show later.

We may nonetheless view Galbraith's frame of reference as an ordering method for gaining insight into the essence of contingency theory. The four ingredients have equifinality, because they are alternative means to harmonize information and capacity in such a manner that effectiveness is guaranteed.

5 OPERATIONAL DEFINITION OF CONCEPTS

The abstract concepts have to be translated into measurable, observable variables. Variables representing the concepts can be combined into factors or dimensions. We can also use the variables to find clusters, that is, relatively homogeneous organization types.

In more general terms, on the one hand, we see both the environment and the organizational structure as a whole (or a Gestalt) consisting of attributes. In this manner, we may interpret these attributes as environmental information or organizational capacity, respectively. Dimensions of the environment such as complexity, diversity, variability, unexpected trends or changes and rapid growth of supply and demand, can all be related to information.

On the other hand, organizational attributes (or dimensions) such as horizontal and vertical differentiation, formalization, and decentralization of decision-making processes can be interpreted as alternative means to enhance capacity. As indicated in Figure 3.1, the congruence between structure and environment results in higher levels of effectiveness. The effectiveness itself can also be described with a variety of indicators, both economic (cf. earning-capacity) and non-economic (cf. work satisfaction) (Campbell, 1977).

A highly centralized organization will have less capacity and will consequently be more rigid in its reactions towards the environment. A concise hypothesis may run as follows: "organizations will have a better earning-capacity if they decentralize their decision-making in a rapidly changing environment." Claims, such as the one formulated above, have formed the basis for a long tradition of empirical studies.

6 EMPIRICAL VERIFICATION

Publications by Pfeffer (1982) and Scott (1981), for example, have presented an extensive inventory of all the empirical research. However, in this chapter, we will limit ourselves to the most important studies.

Although effectiveness is an important variable in structural contingency theory, most studies have limited their scope mainly to calculating correlations between environmental and organizational dimensions. Naturally, the occurrence of correlations is a primitive method to validate contingency theory and a very large number of studies fall under this domain of contingency research. Organization size in particular is a much employed "contingency variable": the larger the organization, the stronger the formalization of behavior or centralization of decisions, and so on, and so on (cf. Huber, 1988; Kieser & Kubicek, 1978).

For a full verification of contingency theory we need to consider variables such as earning-capacity, productivity, work satisfaction, or quality of service in the studies. All things considered, there can be suboptimal organizations that have not taken the implications of contingency theory seriously! The attempts of authors to link up correlations to effectiveness criteria are more useful. Regrettably, these studies are scarce. They comprise classic studies such as the one conducted by Woodward (1965), and more recent publications such as Dewar and Werbel (1979), Drazin and Van de Ven (1985), Schoonhoven (1981), Pennings (1975, 1987), Gresov and Drazin (1987), Van de Ven (1976), Van de Ven and Drazin (1984), Miller and Friessen (1980), Miller (1988), Armour and Teece (1982), and Ferry (1979).

Whereas the earlier studies (e.g., Dewar & Werbel, 1979; Pennings, 1975) employed a two-variables approach, an interest for multivariable attempts has developed more recently. Both environment and organizational structure are multidimensional. We also know that various organizational dimensions are not independent of one another; a variable such as centralization correlates with standardization. In addition, it has been noted earlier that contingency theory presupposes equifinality, hence alternative organizational dimensions can produce the same adaptational advantage. This style of thinking is manifest in the studies done by Drazin and Van de Ven (1985) and Pennings (1987). In these studies, a number of environmental dimensions are related to organization dimensions simultaneously, and this kind of analysis is also carried out with a simultaneous search of differences in effectiveness. Whereas previous studies (e.g., Pennings, 1975) were negative, these new studies provide some support for contingency theory. Drazin and Van de Ven (1985), in their study on job centers, found that the level of work satisfaction is higher as these centers organize themselves in accordance with contingency norms. Pennings (1987) found that bank offices have larger profit margins

or smaller expenses if they show an optimum relation between environment and structure.

Most of the contingency studies have pursued a dimensional research strategy. In the light of the mutual correlations between environmental and organization variables, however, there have also been authors who combined groups of variables into configurations or Gestalts. Actually, we have already seen this in Burns and Stalker's (1961) construction of the mechanical and the organic organization and the type of market in which they function best.

A distinction can be made between a priori typologies and empirical typologies, otherwise called taxonomies. At present, typological approaches are not yet suited for unequivocal contingency verifications because the development of the methodologies and techniques for the construction of organizational and environmental types is incomplete. We do not know, moreover, what attributes would have to be part of this kind of typology. As in personality theory, organization theory has a very high number of variables that have also often been defined operationally in a variety of ways by various researchers. There are scales of structure dimensions based on data originating from records (Pugh & Hickson, 1976), from interviews (Hage & Aiken, 1969), and from questionnaires (Hall, 1963). In some cases, their converging and discriminating validity remains in doubt (Pennings, 1973). Miller and Mintzberg's argument(1983) in favor of a typological research strategy therefore seems premature. It is not known yet what variables can replace each other within an equifinality frame of reference, either. If different structure dimensions are functionally equivalent (they can have the same effect each by themselves and, therefore, can substitute each other), we do not need to classify all dimensions in every type. A great deal of further research will be necessary.

7 METHODOLOGICAL PROBLEMS

Besides the issue of dimensional versus typological research strategies, structural contingency researchers face two other problems: the level of analysis and statistical interaction.

The level of analysis may vary greatly. Researchers have focused on small groups and business units (e.g., Drazin & Van de Ven, 1985), departments (e.g., Lawrence & Lorsch, 1967) and large companies (e.g., Rumelt, 1974). The hypotheses were supported most convincingly in research regarding small units. Rumelt (1974) found no connection at all between structural and environmental dimensions (divisionalization and strategic diversity), but one was found between divisionalization and earning-capacity. The level of analysis may have a connection with the kind of variables that are included in the analysis. Rumelt emphasized global configurations, such as functional versus divisional structures. Drazin and Van de Ven (1985), on the other hand, focused on the patterns of interaction, communication and influence between individuals who keep constant contact with each other.

The distinction between primary and secondary structures has been made before (Pennings, 1987). Primary structures are expressions of social architecture, such as those we see reflected in organization diagrams and which can only be represented on a higher level of analysis. Primary structures delimit the important departments and divisions of the total organization. They are subsequently subdivided into smaller units. Mulder (1960) calls this the "meso level", because it lies between the macro-organizational and micro-individual levels. Secondary structures are discerned in these smaller units. They comprise the local, durable patterns of behavior such as those which have spontaneously evolved. They include relations of authority between the manager and his or her subordinates, power and communication structures, climate and differences in status. Formerly, such phenomena were sometimes summed up in the term "informal organization" (cf. Homans, 1951). It might be argued, in keeping with Mulder's study on the circle and the wheel, that the experimental channels of communication are primary, whereas the decision structure is secondary. Studies have shown that these secondary structures are more likely to be adapted to task-specific or environmental aspects, probably because they can be influenced more easily by the participants, whereas the imposed primary structures are rather inert. Thus, it may be argued that contingency

ideas are more applicable to these secondary structures. These levels of analysis must therefore remain strictly separated. Research within these levels will promote insights about structural contingencies, if only because we are led to expect more continuity within each of these levels.

This train of thought is also present in Kieser and Kubicek (1978). They provide an exhaustive overview of the situational determinants of organizational structure, making a distinction between internal and external contingencies with the inclusion of environment or context and age, size, technology, and form of property. These authors feel that the organization is not a holistic phenomenon; it is really a conglomerate of several components such as groups, departments, branches, etc. Each of these components often displays a structure of its own, which may or may not be in keeping with the partial environment. This may especially be expected in organizations with divisional structures (Lincoln & Zeitz, 1981). The consequence is that contingency hypotheses have to be verified at an appropriate level. An attractive advantage of lower aggregations is the higher number of observations that the researcher can attain, and the robustness of the associated statistical tests. It is considerably simpler to have a large number of observations if the level of analysis is shifted from, for example, banks to bank offices, or from hospitals to clinical departments, or from city councils to local authority services.

A second problem relates to interaction. Several authors have argued that the tension between situational determinants and the choice of structures renders a conventional causal analysis inappropriate. Such an analysis divides variables into independent and dependent variables with an arrow from the former to the latter. A large difference exists between a causal and a functional (or mutual causality) analysis, because the former presupposes a uni-directional and the latter presupposes a bi-directional relationship. The problem becomes even more complicated if the idea of functional equivalence is added to these problems. The organization may have various structural alternatives to achieve the same result. All of this involves tricky methodological pitfalls.

Complicated patterns of interaction between

variables have to be discovered. When contingency researchers say that there is a relationship between environmental and organizational variables which explains the effectiveness, they are in fact suggesting that there is an interaction between those two categories of independent variables. This is recognized emphatically by Lazarsfeld (1958) who puts contingency on a par with interaction, and by Schoonhoven (1981, p.351) who holds that "explicit recognition should be given to the fact that contingency arguments produce interactive propositions."

Two interaction variants can be distinguished: multiplicative and fitting. Multiplication can be represented mathematically as

$$y = a + bx_1 + bx_2 + b(x_1*x_2).$$

In our case, y can stand for effectiveness, x_1 uncertainty, and x_2 centralization of another structural dimension. The addition of the multiplicative term makes it possible to study whether the effect of centralization on effectiveness depends on the degree of environmental uncertainty or complexity. In other words, it is assumed that the effectiveness is high if high levels of both environmental dimensions $x_{1...i}$ and structural dimensions $x_{2...j}$ are observed. Effectiveness is lower if one of the dimensions has a low scale value.

In the second variant, there are certain environmental and structural values that agree with each other. The degree of agreement is critical, but can be qualified, for example, by claiming that within a certain interval of x_1 there can be a certain range of x_2 values without effectiveness suffering. Naturally, the contingency idea implicates that such "fitting" must take place stringently, because otherwise the theory would lose its explanatory force. All kinds of organizational structures would otherwise be adequate, irrespective of the degree of uncertainty of the environment (Donaldson, 1985).

The possibility of studying this has been illustrated by Drazin and Van de Ven (1985) and Pennings (1987). In these studies, a structure profile of effective departments was made within a set of five categories of environments. This profile is the "ideal" configuration, so to speak. Next, differences in structure profile between these departments and the other units were correlated with effectiveness. The more the department

deviated from the ideal profile, the smaller its effectiveness. These kinds of results also create the impression that contingency research has important practical consequences.

8 NEW DEVELOPMENTS

As was indicated before, the field of management and organization theory has witnessed an emergence of new schools of thought, with population ecology, institutional theory, organizational economics (including transaction economics and agency theory) and the resource-based view of the firm among the most prominent. In this crowded field, contingency theory has been able to hold its own position. On the one hand, researchers continue to explore new implications while empirically refining existing ones, while other have argued that competing schools borrow heavily from contingency theory, and in fact are often a form of contingency theory-in-disguise.

A recent publication by Donaldson (1995) belabors the latter point. He is concerned about the crowded field in which structural contingency theory shares the space with competing theories, some of which we briefly reviewed in an earlier part of this chapter. Donaldson believes that institutional, ecological, resource dependence and economic theories of organizations are typically anti-managerial since they rule out discretion in the choice of organizations and their environment. These schools are said to be deterministic in that they allow little room for managers to dismantle or to alter the design of their organization. Empirical studies often provide a glimpse of contingency factors, but these are either carefully assumed away, or the empirical findings are distorted to nullify contingency-driven inferences.

For example, institutional studies purport to claim that an organization's structures, practices, and beliefs mirror the conditions of the environment in which it is "chartered". Additionally, organizations mimic each other and tend to take their social reality for granted. For example, the adoption of multi-functional teams, the implementation of an incentive compensation plan, the installation of total quality systems, and/or the staffing of boards of directors with women and other "tokens" have become standard practice in many organizations. Non-adoption of such arrangements precludes to obtainment of a seal of approval. Such design choices are divorced from the organization's functioning and any reference to a goodness of fit between such structures and organizational environments is misplaced. We should not view them as tools for efficiently producing outputs, but rather recognize that they reflect the norms and values of their environment. Non-conformity with widely held, taken-for-granted standards endangers an organization's status, prestige and goodwill.

Thus, the mimicry of structures and other design elements confer legitimacy, safeguarding the organization's existence. Donaldson shows convincingly, that what seem to be purely mimicry-induced structural changes, are in fact brought about by contingent conditions. Furthermore, he claims that data are misrepresented in order to advance the conclusion that organizations become increasingly alike (homogenization due to institutional or legitimacy producing pressures) so that contingent factors are negligible (Donaldson, 1995, pp.85–89). Consistent with structural contingency theory, he then proceeds to show that substantial variations in structural arrangements in samples of institutional studies of organizations remain, variations which contingent factors such as size can explain.

Similarly, Donaldson claims that Pfeffer and Salancik (1978) distort data in order to sustain their political view of organization which adopt those structures that maximize a favorable negotiation relationship with external actors such as governmental bureaucracies, suppliers, and clients. Recall that these authors were mostly concerned with boundary arrangements such as boards of directors and public relations departments. Likewise, population ecology has produced many findings which do not require us to borrow Darwinistically inspired propositions.

Ecologists assume that structure is the result of a never ending quest of organizations to become more reliable and more consistent, such that they end up in an inertial trap from which they cannot easily escape. Different organizational designs should not be attributed to the unique ways in which managers implement design decisions. These differences are instead due to negative selection, which leads eventually to the retention of those designs with superior survival value. The fittest structures are the structures associated with the best survival value. Reorganization of an unfit design in order to establish an environmental fit are doomed to fail, because in the very least this exposes the firm to the same risks that confront new organizations who have to weather the liability of newness.

Donaldson is right in critiquing authors such as Hannan and Freeman (1977, 1984) for disregarding "unobserved heterogeneity" (1995, p.61). These authors treat organizations as black boxes; each organization counts as one unit, and what happens inside that unit is irrelevant. Because their theory deals with markets, rather than with organizations, theirs is not really an organizational theory, but a theory of markets, whose elements are examined with the vital statistics of organizational birth and death. When the inquiry moves towards organizational issues, for example by examining "core" [e.g., functional versus multidivisional design] and "peripheral" [e.g., job titles, number of authority levels] parts of the organization design, the theory loses some of its parsimony, and the integrity of its paradigm falls apart.

In the space of these pages, it would go too far to provide full coverage to these and other components of Donaldson's survey of American "antimanagement theories". His monograph is an impressive testimony to the claim that contingency theory has not quite superceded other, newer theories.

On the other hand, we have also witnessed new attempts on elaborating and revising contingency theory. New developments that might be expressions of proliferating paradigms in organization theory include the concept of culture, the notion of the networking organization (Burt, 1997; Kanter, 1989), the learning organization (Senge, 1990), and the mean and lean organization (Pil & MacDuffie, 1996).

Culture as part of design

The concept of organizational culture became prominent after contingency theory had established itself fully, but before elements, other than structure were considered key elements of the organization's design. Culture can be defined as the shared values, beliefs, and assumptions members express about their organizations, or the set of practices that have become established among them. Research by Hofstede, Nuyen, Ohayv, and Sanders (1990) and O'Reilly, Chatman, and Caldwell (1991) suggests that culture can be readily added to an organization's profile. Hofstede et al. (1990) consider four dimensions of organizational culture such as whether it gravitates towards a *results* or a *process* orientation. They find, for example, that cultural differences that are associated with whether an organization operates in the manufacturing or in a Research and Development (R & D) setting affects the likelihood that it will have a process-oriented or results-oriented culture respectively. Labor-intensive versus capital-intensive firms, while controlling for size, likewise tend more towards process- versus results-oriented cultures. Flat organizations manifest also more results-oriented expressions of organizational reality. The task and market environment are said to clearly affect the scores on the four cultural dimensions which these authors operationalized in their study. More importantly, as Hofstede et al. write "within the twenty participating units, we found idiosyncratic components of organizational cultures within limits *set by the task and the systems*" (1990, p.311; italics added).

The research by O'Reilly et al. can also be construed as a study that eventually should become part of the body of work on contingent organizational culture. In their study, the link deals with culture and the organization's human resources. The fit between employees and culture varies by the personality dimensions of the employees, thus suggesting the need to match human resources to the prevailing values of the organization. Conversely, the culture might be adapted to accommodate the personality characteristics of a new wave of hirings.

New views of organizations

Concurrent with the rise of organizational culture, we have seen the emergence of some new conceptualizations, which render the distinction between the earlier mentioned primary and secondary structures more relevant and valid. This is most evident in the notion of the *networking* and *lean*

and mean organization. While distinct, these two images of organizations overlap considerably. In a networking organization we encounter a preponderance of micro-electronic linkages, but also numerous teams with overlapping membership and densely developed ties with suppliers, customers, and other external actors (e.g., Nonaka, 1994). The role of the manager alters drastically, and in fact gives rise to an elimination or erosion of many, traditionally defined, managerial activities such as planning, coordination, and communication. It is therefore not surprising that the so-called "delayering", downsizing, and restructuring lead not only to a reduction of the ranks of management, but also in a growth of horizontal linkages within and across organizational units. Such organizations might also become lean and mean.

The concept has a Japanese provenance. In the lean and mean organization there exist very little slack, such as buffer inventories, waiting time and surplus repair personnel. To compensate for the increased vulnerability, firms such as Toyota and Nissan invest heavily in human resource training and the cultivation of autonomous, self-policing, multifunctional teams. Such arrangements make the firm a very flexible organization with speedy, smooth communication and a sharing of the responsibility to get a high quality product or service out of the door.

It should also be obvious that the networking and lean and mean organization allows their membership a wide latitude to write their own design. Given the requirements of procurement, quality assurance, and customer responsiveness, each unit will establish a set of routines that have optimum adaptive value. While "kanban", just-in-time and other features of a lean and mean organization might look the same for each and every adopting organization, we should not interpret them as a one-page description on how to install such coordination tools. While each unit might vicariously learn from other units, each will arrive at its own unique set of capabilities to deal with its contingencies. Pil and MacDuffie (1996) showed, for example, that the mimicry of the lean and mean blueprint by non-Japanese automobile manufacturers has led to major advancements in efficiency and effectiveness, but also that

European car makers still lag behind their Japanese counterparts.

We should expect here an interesting opening up of new lines of inquiries in which contingency arguments are an important ingredient: in what way will the design of the 21st century organization design benefit from the elements of contingency thinking that crystallized in the 20th century? This question will be particularly important if and when we treat organizational design not as fixed in stone, but as evolving and constantly calibrating its fit with a changing landscape; in short as a learning organization. The 21st century organization will be a learning organization to the extent that it will constantly re-examine the appropriateness of its design, question its functioning and seek improvements accordingly.

The learning organization is nicely illustrated in the case study of Microsoft (Cusumano & Selby, 1995). Initially, Microsoft was one of numerous computer software start-ups. Over time, it began to make significant investments in design, processes and external relationships. Five elements constitute the key ingredients of Microsoft as a learning organization: (1) learn systematically from old and current products and processes, (2) stimulate feedback with quantitative information, (3) view the customer as an integral part of the product or service, (4) treat the suppliers as a key element in the value chain, and (5), most important, encourage linkages between projects, functions and divisions. In other words, Microsoft encourages its employees to constantly re-examine the way they perform their jobs, to question the processes which they have instituted, and to perform "post-mortems" on the projects and their teams such that the firm will always display those designs that optimize innovation, customer responsiveness and efficiency. Each project is thus an opportunity to better approximate the goodness of fit between the firm and its environment. These latter statements bring us also to the practical significance of structural contingency theory.

9 PRACTICAL ASPECTS

Virtually all American organization textbooks dwell on contingency theory extensively and attach important practical regulations to it. This is remarkable, really, because a great deal of empirical work still needs to be conducted before specific recipes can be presented. Some interesting remarks can be made in spite of this fact.

The normative message of structural contingency theory is particularly clear for managers and their advisers, because effectiveness is becoming a consideration of paramount importance. Effectiveness imposes constraints on managers in their freedom of choice. If optimal earning-capacity is required, managers will be deprived of a great deal of leeway. They can choose only from a limited number of designs. From a strategic point of view, managers have a short menu of blueprints at their disposal in which to design their organization.

This is an extremely important implication, particularly because Child (1972), in his classic article, argued that contingency researchers have made a reactive, passive, and helpless caricature of the organization! His concept of "strategic choice" will, therefore, require further investigation.

According to Child's (1972) famous concept, organizations have a broad margin in selecting (and of course leaving) their relevant environments. They can alter their range of products and services; transfer production facilities, for example, from an EU country to a Third World country; and reduce their dependence towards suppliers or customers, for example, by vertical integration and the forging of strategic alliances with firms in their value chain.

Organizations can also afford much internal freedom. The existing social architecture can be altered or even demolished. In other words, Child ascribes a large amount of potential action to organizations and vehemently opposes a deterministic view on the role of the environment.

The difference with structural contingency thinking is, however, not as great as it seems. It is indeed true that its thinking is abstracted from individuals, their motivations and their variabilities. Thus a fear exists that scholars fall into the trap of reification; we only need to refer to the above problem of the level of analysis. Furthermore, at the level of the organization we are susceptible to other sorts of phenomena beyond the meso or micro level of analysis.

We could draw a comparison between the social reality of Hong Kong, as viewed from a helicopter, compared to a pedestrian in its streets. From the helicopter, we see all kinds of durable regularities from which we can easily deduce structures. We see that traffic keeps to the right, that people halt at junctions, etc. We need not introduce any motivation or social action theories in this situation. How different our pedestrian's view is. We see that some people cross at junctions without any apparent reason, and we need to know their motives before we are able to say anything meaningful about it. Viewed from the helicopter, traffic infractions are not so relevant in order to describe or explain structural patterns; they are at most unexplained deviations, "noise" or, to use a statistical metaphor, unexplained sums of squares. If we wish to explain global regulations, we do not have to get involved in the level of the individual. If, however, we wish to explain "noise", for example, non-conformity, innovation or sabotage, our research problem is quite different and naturally we have to get involved in the motives, attitudes, and beliefs of individual persons.

As has been stated, structural contingency theory is limited to the level of the organization or its components. The individual actions and the freedom of choice of the members are not so salient in this account. At the meso level, there is a greater interaction between social structures and the individual actions of the members. Their interests and preferences are manifest in the evolution of social relations and connections. In other words, the theory is sufficiently flexible to view the social architecture not as a fossil, but rather as an organic reality that is constantly subject to the influences of individual persons and groups.

The freedom of choice is constrained by the limits to action that result from considerations of effectiveness. The above idea of fitting interaction and functional equivalence, however, especially creates the impression that the freedom of choice can be extremely wide. The menu from which one can choose is not yet fully known, but we do know at present that it can be fairly extensive. The scope of this freedom is not only subject to empirical but also to philosophical difficulties. Dahrendorf (1979) has pointed this out once again.

Naturally, the argument could be used that particular combinations of environmental and structural variables occur more often than other combinations. In this sense, there are not only limitations of choice that we can ascribe to mathematical limitedness (because we relate a limited number of environmental and structural variables to effectiveness)—there will also be empirical and hermeneutic constraints. We have stated earlier that authors such as Miller and Mintzberg (1983) view certain Gestalts or archetypes as dominant. Other authors have pointed towards cognitive or cultural constraints.

Most persons use an *implicit organization theory* (Downey & Brief, 1983). This term is a play on the implicit theory of personality, which refers to the tendency of individuals to view certain personality characteristics as correlated. These are amateurish theories that often surface when people "talk hot air". Although they have not been studied rigorously, they have a large influence on the attitude one adopts and the behavior that one displays. The consequences perceived, in turn, amplify the "theory" again. For example: fat people are candid, of good cheer and humorous.

Individuals in general, and managers and entrepreneurs in particular, also subscribe to primitive, not empirically founded theories on organizations. Governmental bureaucracies and numerous Fortune 500 firms are held to be rigid, conservative and inefficient; start-ups and small companies in the micro-electronic field in Silicon Valley and new biotechnology firms are flexible, innovative, and daring. Many people imagine a ladder or a hierarchy with a management of one person, possibly with a staff that provides the line with organization counseling or support. A flat organization is hard to imagine and it will therefore not be chosen from a menu of designs for the organizational structure. In many cases, these "theories" also affect the choice, and the legitimization of blueprints that people would prefer to see in use in organizations. They impose supplementary constraints on the freedom of choice which structural contingency theory, as described above, postulates.

Contingency theory has also had the primary merit of proposing certain structural innovations, such as the matrix (cf. Davis & Lawrence, 1977) or networking arrangement (Nonaka, 1994) and causing these to be well received, even when these do not square with the stereotypes that are commonplace in a society (Hofstede, 1980). In his pioneering work on cultural differences and their implications, Hofstede demonstrates that there are various implicit (and explicit!) organization theories in various societies. These not only legitimize particular structures, but can also frustrate the introduction and the actual institutionalization of alternative structures.

By way of example, the matrix structure that has become widely diffused in the United States has not been well received in France, possibly because French culture (with its high "power distance") is incompatible with a decentralized, dual leadership structure. Whereas such considerations do not form a central component of structural contingency theory, they provide a good frame of reference for the practical attainability of various organization designs in different societies. Note that in Hofstede's frame of mind, organizational culture represents practices that vary from firm to firm, while national culture embodies deep-seated values and beliefs that are discernible in any of the organizations that reside in that country. Those deep-seated values vary not much from organization to organization, while practices (such as results- versus process-oriented behaviors) do vary. What Hofstede also tells us is that such practices vary within the limits set by national culture. National culture "programs" each and every member of our society and, therefore, saddles our mind with a distinct software. His observations alert us to the limits that managers face when they seek to redesign their organization, or when they attempt to export their design principles to other cultures; as might be the case with multinational corporations who diversify to other countries having divergent values (compare Pennings, Barkema & Douma, 1994).

10 CONCLUSION AND DISCUSSION

At the outset of this chapter a brief plan of organization theory was presented. It was stated that structural contingency theory, together with other intentional-rationalistic theories, contrasts sharply with population ecology and the interpretative theories.

There is no doubt that structural contingency has lost some of its centrality, that other paradigms of research traditions have become more visible, and that fads in this field make it hard to indicate where this theory will eventually find its "niche".

The theory has lost some of its public appeal, because mainly the phenomenological schools have provided new insights and, more importantly, have also laid bare a social reality to which older accounts of the organization paid hardly any attention or indeed none at all. The introduction of anthropological and literary methods and techniques in organization theory has made many researchers sensitive to a social reality to which structural contingency theory paid no attention.

Furthermore, there exists a widespread aversion towards "design" among organizational theorists. The design implications of structural contingency theory connote engineering and consultancy. While consultants like McKinsey and Hammer and Champy engage in research and enjoy considerable success in disseminating their findings, most organization theorists remain aloof, particularly those who seek to model the conduct of firms. The aversion is oriented to both social (functional boundaries), electronic (inclusion or exclusion of networks) and even physical barriers such as architecturally designed encumbrances and bridges (Darley & Gilbert, 1985). Barriers have profound influence on where, how and with whom we interact. They shape the diffusion of knowledge in organizations and determine therefore their potential for learning, for expanding their knowledge base and for deploying that knowledge to those locations where it can be exploited. If we continue to resist engineering-like inputs in our thinking regarding organizations, we will become increasingly distant to those who recognize that the social and physical design of organizations needs to be addressed in order for them learn, to change and to redesign themselves.

The 21st century will undoubtedly reveal many innovations in the design of organizations. It is difficult to predict what those innovations will entail. Structural contingency theory is sufficiently broad to accommodate an explanation of their adoption. Even the arrival of chaos theory into our field is compatible with the tenets of contingency thinking. After all, in the end each and every organization is self-designing and will look for ways to outperform itself and its competitors. It follows that our challenge remains to link theory to practice, to provide a framework for examining organizations that produces knowledge having both practical and theoretical utility.

NOTES

1. Additional "rationalists" paradigms have emerged. Much attention has been attracted by the so-called transaction cost economy (Williamson, 1975) and the internal labor market theory. Reasons of space do not allow us to examine these here.
2. In organization theory, as in various social sciences, the methodology with regard to dimensions, variables or attributes, has developed strongly. Our knowledge concerning types, Gestalts, and configurations is considerably more limited.

REFERENCES

Armour, H., & Teece, D. (1978). Organizational structure and economic performance. *The Bell Journal of Economics, 9*, 106–122.

Assen, A. van, & Hertog, F.J. den (1984). Werkstructurering. Van taakroulatie tot organisatie-ontwerp. In P. J. D. Drenth, Hk. Thierry, P. J. Willems, Ch. J. de Wolff (Eds.), *Handboek Arbeids- en Organisatiepsychologie*. Deventer: Van Loghum Slaterus.

Baum, J.A.C., & Singh, J.V. (1994). Organizational hierarchies and evolutionary processes: Some reflections on a theory of organizational evolution. In J.A.C. Baum & J.V. Singh (Eds.), *Evolutionary dynamics of organizations*. Oxford: Oxford University Press.

Bavelas, A. (1950). Communication patterns in task-oriented groups. *Journal of Acoustical Society of America, 22*, 725–736.

Berger, T., & Luckman, T. (1966). *The social construction of reality*. New York: Doubleday.

Burns, T., & Stalker, G.M. (1961). *The management of innovation*. London: Tavistock.

Burt, R.S. (1997). The contingent value of social capital. *Administrative Science Quarterly, 42*, 339–365.

Campbell, J.P. (1977). On the nature of organizational effectiveness. In J.M. Pennings and Associates. *New perspectives on organizational effectiveness*. San Francisco: Jossey-Bass.

Chandler, A. (1962). *Strategy and structure*. Cambridge, MA: MIT Press.

Child, J. (1972). Organizational structure, environment and performance; the role of strategic choice. *Sociology, 6*, 2–22.

Cohen, M.D., March, J.G., & Olsen, J.P. (1972). A garbage-can model of organizational choice. *Administrative Science Quarterly, 17*, 1–25.

Cusumano, M.A., & Selby, R.W. (1995). *Microsoft secrets*. New York: The Free Press.

Dahrendorf, R. (1979). *Life Chances: approaches to social and political theory*. Chicago: University of Chicago Press.

Darley, J.M., & Gilbert, D.T. (1985). Social psychological aspects of environmental psychology. In G. Lindzey & E. Aronson (Eds.), *Handbook of social psychology* (3rd Edn.), pp.949–991. New York: Random House.

Davis, S.M., & Lawrence, P.R. (1977). *Matrix*. Reading, MA: Addison Wesley.

Dewar, R., & Werbel, J. (1979). Universalistic and contingency predictions of employee satisfaction and conflict. *Administrative Science Quarterly, 24*, 426–448.

Dill, W.R. (1958). Environment as an influence on managerial autonomy. *Administrative Science Quarterly, 2*, 409–443.

Doeringer, P., & Piore, M. (1971). *Internal labor markets and manpower analysis*. Lexington, MA: Heath.

Donaldson, L. (1985). *In defence of organization theory*. Cambridge: Cambridge University Press.

Donaldson, L. (1995). *American anti-management theories of organization*. Cambridge: Cambridge University Press.

Downey, K., & Brief, A.P. (1983). Cognitive and organizational structures: a conceptual analysis of implied organizational theories. *Human Relations, 36*, 1065–1089.

Drazin, R., & Ven, A.H. van de (1985). Alternative forms of fit in contingency theory. *Administrative Science Quarterly, 30*, 514–539.

Emery, F.E., & Trist, E.L. (1970). The causal texture of organizational environments. In F.E. Emery (Ed.), *Systems thinking*. London: Penguin Books.

Fayol, H. (1949). *General and industrial management*. London: Pittman.

Ferry, D.L. (1979). *A test of a task contingency model of unit structure and efficiency*. Dissertation. Philadelphia: The Wharton School.

Fiedler, F.E. (1978). The contingency model and the dynamics of the leadership process. In L. Berkowitz (Ed.), *Advances in experimental social psychology*, Volume II. New York: Academic Press.

Galbraith, J.W. (1977). *Organization Design*. Reading, MA: Addison-Wesley.

Gresov, C., & Drazin, R. (1987). A multivariate test of the contingency model. *Academy of Management Proceedings*. New Orleans.

Hackman, J.R., & Lawyer, E.E. (1971). Employee reactions to job characteristics. *Journal of Applied Psychology Monograph*, 55, 259–286.

Hage, J., & Aiken, M. (1969). Routine technology, social structure, and organizational goals, *Administrative Science Quarterly*, 14, 366–376.

Hall, R.H. (1963). The concept of bureaucracy: an empirical assessment. *American Journal of Sociology*, 69, 32–40.

Hammer, M., & Champy, J. (1993). *Re-engineering the corporation.* New York: Harper.

Hannan, M.T., & Freeman, J.H. (1977). Population ecology of organizations, *American Journal of Sociology*, 82, 929–964.

Hannan, M.T., & Freeman, J.H. (1984). Structural inertia and organizational change. *American Sociological Review*, 49, 149–164.

Hofstede, G. (1980). *Culture's consequences: International differences in work related values.* Beverly Hills: Sage.

Hofstede, G.H.B., Nuyen, D.D., Ohayv, & Sanders, G. (1990). Measuring organizational cultures: A qualitative and quantitative study across twenty cases. *Administrative Science Quarterly*, 35, 286–316.

Homans, G. C. (1951). *The human group.* London: Routledge & Kegan Paul.

House, R.J. (1971). A path-goal theory in leadership. *Administrative Science Quarterly*, 16, 312–328.

Huber, G.P. (1988). *Developing more encompassing theories about the relationship between organizational design and organizational effectiveness.* Working paper, Austin: University of Texas.

Kanter, R.M. (1989). The new managerial work. *Harvard Business Review*, 67, 86–94.

Kaplan, R.S., & Norton, D.P. (1993). Putting the balanced scorecard to work. *Harvard Business Review*, 71, 134–142.

Khandwalla, P.N. (1977). *The design of organizations.* New York: Harcourt, Brace, Jovanovich.

Kieser, A., & Kubicek, H. (1978). *Organisationstheorieen.* Stuttgart: Kohlhammer.

Lawrence, P.R., & Lorsch, J.W. (1967). *Organization and environment: Managing differentiation and integration.* Boston: Division of Research, Graduate School of Business and Administration, Harvard University.

Lazarsfeld, P.F. (1958). Evidence and inference in social research. *Daedalus*, 87, 99–130.

Leavitt, H.J. (1951). Some effects of certain communication patterns on group performance. *Journal of abnormal and social psychology*, 46, 38–50.

Likert, R.E. (1967). *The human organization.* New York: McGraw-Hill.

Lincoln, J.R., & Zeitz, G. (1981). Organizational properties from aggregate date: Separating individual from structural effects. *American Sociological Review*, 45, 391–408.

Maanen, J. van (1975). Police socialization. *Administrative Science Quarterly*, 20, 207–228.

March, J.G., & Simon, H.A. (1958). *Organizations.* Englewood Cliffs: Prentice Hall.

March, J.G., & Olsen, J.P. (1976). *Ambiguity and choice in organizations.* Oslo: Universitetsforlaget.

Miller, D. (1988). Relating Porter's business strategies to environment and structure: Analysis and performance implications. *Academy of Management Journal*, 31, 280–308.

Miller, D., & Friessen, P.H. (1980). Archetypes of organizational transition. *Administrative Science Quarterly*, 25, 268–299.

Miller, D., & Mintzberg, H. (1983). The case for configuration. In G. Morgan (Ed.), *Beyond method.* Beverly Hills: Sage.

Miller, G.A. (1956). The magical number seven, plus or minus two: Some limits on our capacity for processing information. *Psychological Review*, 63, 81–97.

Mintzberg, H. (1983). *Structures in five.* Englewood Cliffs: Prentice Hall.

Morgan, G. (1987). *Images of organizations.* Beverly Hills: Sage.

Mulder, M. (1960). Communication structure, decision structure and group performance. *Sociometry*, 23, 1–14.

Nadler, D.A., Hackman, R.J., & Lawler, E.E. (1979). *Managing organizational behavior.* Cambridge: Harvard University Press.

Nelson, R.R., & Winter, S.G. (1982). *An evolutionary theory of economic change.* Cambridge: Harvard University Press.

Nonaka, I. (1990). Redundant, overlapping organization: A Japanese approach to managing the innovation process. *California Management Review*, 32, 27–38.

Nonaka, I. (1994). A dynamic theory of organizational knowledge creation. *Organization Science*, 5, 14–37.

O'Reilly, C.A., Chatman, J., & Caldwell, D. (1991). People and organizational culture. A profile comparison approach to assessing person–organization fit. *Academy of Management Journal*, 34, 487–516.

Pennings, J.M. (1973). Measures of organizational structure. *American Journal of Sociology*, 73, 686–704.

Pennings, J.M. (1975). The relevance of the structural contingency model for organizational effectiveness. *Administrative Science Quarterly*, 20, 393–410.

Pennings, J.M. (1984). Organisatietheorie in de VS. *Mens en onderneming*, 38, 339–350.

Pennings, J.M. (1985). *Organizational strategy and change.* San Francisco: Jossey Bass.

Pennings, J.M. (1987). Structural contingency theory: A multivariate test. *Organization Studies*, 8, 223–240.

Pennings, J.M., Barkema, H., & Douma, S. (1994). Organizational learning and diversification. *Academy of Management Journal*, 37, 608–640.

Peters, T.J., & Waterman, R.H. (1982). *In search of excellence.* New York: Harper & Row.

Pfeffer, J. (1982). *Organizations and organization theory*. Marshfield: Pitman.

Pfeffer, J., & Salancik, G.R. (1978). *The external control of organizations*. New York, Harper & Row.

Pil, F.K., & MacDuffie, J.P. (1996). The adoption of high involvement practices, *Industrial Relations, 35*, 423–455.

Pugh, D.S., & Hickson, D.J. (1976). *Organizational structure in its context: The Ashton programme III*. Westmead: Saxon House.

Rumelt, R.P. (1974). *Strategy, structure and economic performance*. Cambridge, MA: Harvard University Press.

Schoonhoven, C.B. (1981). Problems with contingency theory: testing assumptions hidden within the language of contingency theory. *Administrative Science Quarterly, 26*, 349–377.

Scott, W.R. (1981). *Organizations: rational, natural and open systems*. Englewood Cliffs: Prentice Hall.

Senge, P. (1990). *The fifth discipline*. Boston: Harvard Business School Press.

Simon, H.A. (1960). *The new science of management decision*. New York: Harper & Row.

Singh, J., House, R.J., & Tucker, D.J. (1986). Organizational change and organizational mortality. *Administrative Science Quarterly, 31*, 587–611.

Taylor, F.W. (1911). *The principles of scientific management*. New York: Harper & Row.

Thompson, J. (1967). *Organizations in action*. New York: McGraw-Hill.

Tversky, A., & Kahneman, D. (1974). Judgment under uncertainty: Heuristics and bias. *Science, 185*, 1124–1131.

Urwick, L.F. (1943). *The elements of administration*. New York: Harper & Row.

Van Maanen, J. (1988). *Tales of the field: On writing ethnography*. Chicago: University of Chicago Press.

Ven, A.H. van de (1976). A task contingent model of work-unit structure. *Administrative Science Quarterly, 19*, 183–197.

Ven, A.H. van de, & Drazin, R. (1984). The concept of fit in organization theory. In L.L. Cummings & B.M. Staw (Eds.), *Research in organizational behavior, 7*. Greenwich, JAI Press.

Weber, M. (1947). *The theory of social and economic organization*. New York: Oxford University Press.

Weber, M. (1978). *Economy and society*. Berkeley: University of California Press.

Weick, K.E. (1979). *The social psychology of organizing*. Reading, MA: Addison Wesley.

Weick, K.E. (1993). The collapse of sensemaking in organizations: The Mann Gulch disaster. *Administrative Science Quarterly, 38*, 628–652.

Williamson, O.E. (1975). *Markets and hierarchies*. New York: The Free Press.

4

Developments in Socio-Technical Systems Design (STSD)

Frans M. van Eijnatten

INTRODUCTION

Since its inception in the 1950s, the socio-technical design paradigm of organizations has never left the scene of socio-scientific and management literature. Socio-Technical Systems Design (STSD) plays an important role in giving shape to factories, offices, and government institutions that follow modern patterns. Socio-technical systems design is an applied science that aims to improve the functioning of both the worker and the organization through adaptation or fundamental redesign of contents and organization of technology and human labour tasks. Many authors, not least psychologists, have contributed to the development of this broad approach in the past four decades, oriented to both management and staff.

In socio-technical systems design, social and technical aspects are considered and fine-tuned to one another with respect to their mutuality. Nowadays, such an orientation is referred to by the term "integral". To give a historic overview that does some justice to the total range of ideas and elaborations in this area would take us far beyond the available space and intentions of this volume. We have therefore opted for a selection of essentials. For a more extensive introduction to Socio-Technical Systems Design as an integral design method, we refer the reader to Van Eijnatten (1993a).

In this chapter we give a broad outline of the history of Socio-Technical Systems Design. Instead of striving for completeness, we choose to typify the phases distinguished anecdotally. In addition, we characterize the episodes by giving short descriptions, and we sketch the dissemination of Socio-Technical Systems Design for time and location. We will concentrate on countries where a substantial development of the paradigm has taken place. Special attention therefore is paid to the relevant Dutch representatives and developments.

Before we explain the actual development of Socio-Technical Systems Design (STSD) using a division based on phases, we will first give a general delineation of methodological points of departure and aspects regarding content.

METHODOLOGICAL STARTING-POINTS

For a long time, STSD in its striving for integration—with the structure of the organization as its object of study and integral (re)design as its objective—was a scientific outsider. Such a holistic, design-oriented science was not very suitable for the academic disciplines found at the universities. STSD was not only new as a design theory in terms of its contents, but it also implied a clearly different paradigm in terms of methodology. To gain a notion of the actual meaning of STSD, scientists and staff officials had to take a different attitude in various respects. First, they had to learn to think about new schemes, and, besides that, to do their work differently.

This new line of thought implied a move from the "machine" approach to the "system" approach (Eyzenga, 1975). The main features of the former approach are: stressing reduction (converting wholes into parts, disaggregation); stressing analytical thinking (explaining the behaviour of wholes from the sum of the behaviour of the parts); and stressing mechanistic thinking (concerning the unicausal cause/effect relationships). Here, the object of the study is viewed as a machine. The main features of the systems approach include stressing expansion (the parts are included in ever-expanding wholes; aggregation); stressing synthetic thinking (explaining behaviour from the role of the parts in the larger whole); and stressing teleological thinking (determining and changing objectives, adaptation; cause is essential, though not sufficient, for a certain result). The object of the study is looked upon here as an "open system" that interacts with its environment.

The other way of working meant moving away from the use of a predictive model cycle towards a regulatory cycle, on the one hand, and a different stance of the researcher, on the other; from being distant to being of influence. The empirical or predictive cycle (De Groot, 1980) accentuates the testing of hypotheses derived from an a priori formulated theory by means of the following steps: observation, induction (generalizing general connections from observed connections), deduction (formulating ideal types/hypotheses), tests (verifying/falsifying), and evaluation. The regulatory or design cycle (Van Strien, 1986) underlines actual designing and, by that, developing a theory for practice carrying out the following actions: problem definition, diagnosis, plan, action, evaluation. The role of the researcher is no longer distantly observant, but more involved and in fact influential. The relevant technique is called "action research".

ASPECTS REGARDING CONTENT

The contents of the socio-technical approach can be characterized as a reaction to the unilateral stress of previous paradigms (scientific management; bureaucracy; human relations; see elsewhere in this volume) on the technical or the social aspects of the organisation. In the new viewpoint, both factors are moulded together as components of the same "socio-technical whole".

In an attempt to illustrate STSD briefly and concisely, Van Beinum (1990a) lists nine features of substance of what he calls "the new organisational paradigm", and defines them with the features of the "old paradigm": the Tayloristic bureaucracy. He makes the following comparisons (p.3):

- Redundancy of functions versus redundancy of parts. Rather than maximizing the labour division, STSD suggests a minimal work division. Everybody has to be capable of carrying out different tasks, which leads to the enhanced usability of personnel.
- Internal versus external coordination and control. Self-regulation rather than step-wise supervision is considered of paramount importance in the socio-technical paradigm. An emphasis is placed on small organisation units with internal coordination and semi-autonomous control.
- Democracy versus autocracy. STSD designers strive for direct participation of workers

in decision-making. Democracy in the workplace is the foundation of this approach.

- Joint optimization versus fragmentation. STSD prefers an integral to a partial approach, which implies optimization of various aspects rather than maximizing one's own field-specific aspect.
- People as a resource versus a commodity. The socio-technical paradigm considers the worker to be complementary to the machine, and not as its useful extension. People are the most valuable asset an organization has, and they should be invested in.
- Minimum critical versus total specification. STSD designers make sure they do not design an organisation down to the last detail. The idea is that designers need only figure out the contours; the rest is filled in by the users according to their own insights and needs. To an important extent the current situation is conditional to the actual organisation of work.
- Maximum task breakdown versus optimal task grouping (narrow versus broad skills). The socio-technical paradigm strives for complex tasks in a simple organization instead of simple jobs in a complex organization. This means that workers must have various kinds of skills.
- Individual versus group. In STSD, the smallest organizational unit is the group, not the individual. In this way it is possible for individuals to take the organization of work into their own hands.
- Alienation versus involvement and commitment. Job erosion leads to alienation. Socio-technically redesigned labour systems are characterized by "whole tasks". It is meaningful work, thus promoting personnel commitment.

TOWARDS A DIVISION BASED ON PHASES

STSD is a series of major and minor discoveries, projects, conceptualizations, and developments of methodologies. On top of this, the literature about

it is very splintered. Nevertheless, an attempt has been made to record the history of the socio-technical organization paradigm. Thus, Merrelyn Emery (1989) distinguishes several important turning-points:

- As a first important fact—no more than a starter—she mentions Lewin's leadership experiments just before the Second World War (cf. Lippit & White, 1939). These laboratory studies pointed to three basic types for organizational structures: the autocracy (bureaucracy), the democracy, and the "laissez-faire" type (variant without structure).
- The first actual turning-point of STSD is the set of British mine studies (cf. Trist & Bamforth, 1951; Trist, Higgin, Murray, & Pollock, 1963). In these field studies, researchers discovered an alternative form of work organization (the so-called "semi-autonomous work group"), and applied it on a limited scale.
- The second actual turning-point of STSD is the Norwegian "Industrial Democracy Project" (cf. Emery, F. & Thorsrud, 1964). Here, employers, employees, and the government jointly carried out research into and improved the democratic content of industrial sectors for the first time.
- The third actual turning-point of STSD covers the development of the so-called "participative design" methodology in Australia (cf. Emery, F. & Emery, M., 1974). As a result, workers themselves carried out the whole trajectory of socio-technical analysis and redesign by means of "participative design workshops" and "search conferences".
- Van Beinum (1990a) points out a fourth actual turning-point in the development of STSD: "large-scale and broadly based organizational change process with democratic dialogue as the leading element on the conceptual as well as on the operational level" (cf. Gustavsen, 1985), as has been brought into practice on a national scale in Sweden. Eventually, the Dutch approach to Integral Organization Renewal (De Sitter, Den Hertog, & Van Eijnatten, 1990) may

become a competitor. This approach not only combines a structure and process option, but looks for the happy medium between the expert and participative approach.

The four turning-points form sequential steps in a democratization of the workplace.

Grounded in a bibliometrical analysis of the literature (cf. Van Eijnatten, 1990a,b), we have sought to split the historical line of STSD into phases (cf. Van Eijnatten, 1993a). We distinguish three development trajectories:

1. Phase I (1949–1959+): the period of the Socio-Technical Pioneering Work.
2. Phase II (1959–1971+): the period of Classical STSD.
3. Phase III (1971–): the period of Modern STSD.

The latter phase can be subdivided further into the following:

- Type A (1971–): Participative Design.
- Type B (1973–): Integral Organizational Renewal.
- Type C (1979–): Democratic Dialogue.

- Type D (1971–): North American Consultancy.

Figure 4.1 gives a representation of the phases thus defined, combined with the turning-points previously mentioned. What immediately strikes us is that the trajectories cover each other to a certain extent in time. One could almost talk of parallel flows. Two main reasons can be given for this. First, the inventors/developers of the paradigm regroup to discuss new ideas from time to time, while the implementors/consultants continue to follow the course taken for a limited period. Secondly, the development of STSD does not coincide in the different countries and continents: one country is already in the next phase while the other has yet to start the previous one. It also happens (in the United States, for example) that the entire development only begins to pick up after a couple of years.

Now Classical STSD and Modern STSD approaches of all kinds can be found in different locations all over the globe, each equally professional. Unfortunately, this does nothing to help people new to this field, who have difficulties discussing matters with colleagues because of the

FIGURE 4.1

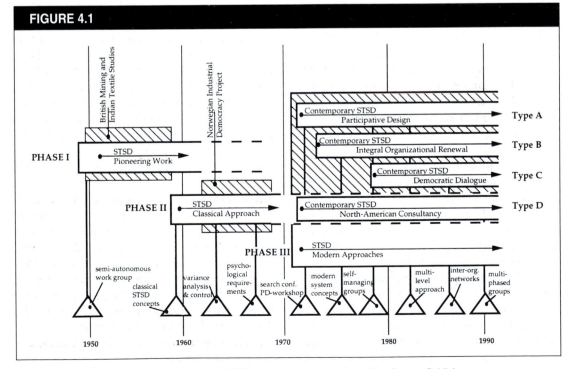

The phases and milestones in the development of STSD. Reprinted by permission of Van Gorcum Publishers.

epistemological and conceptual differences. Concrete end-dates cannot be given to the various stages as it is unclear whether they will cease to exist.

HIGHLIGHTS IN THE DEVELOPMENT OF STSD

To typify the development of STSD, each phase will be described by means of anecdotes. We will discuss the discovery of the Semi-Autonomous Work Group (Phase I), the Industrial Democratization Project (Phase II) and Participative Design, and Democratic Dialogue and Integral Organizational Renewal (Phase III), respectively.

THE TAVISTOCK EPISODE

STSD's beginnings are found in post-war British coal mines. The early 1950s brought about a new form of work organization that we now look upon as "self-managing groups". The British coal industry, which has always had its ups and downs, suffered frequent labour conflicts. It was nationalized and further mechanized after the Second World War. As a field of work, it was not that easy for social scientists to penetrate. However, Ken Bamforth, a new researcher from the Tavistock Institute of Human Relations in London, managed to get into the field in a way many others did not. The advantage of being an ex-miner was that he could visit the Elsecar mine in South Yorkshire without too much trouble. One of his stops led to a discovery: he noticed an aberrant form of work organization in a new coal seam, called "the Haighmoor". The "longwall" mechanization method normally used, would not work, because of a short coal front. The local mine management allowed him to carry out descriptive research with Eric Trist, because of his former employment. Things became a bit harder, however, when they wanted to publish their findings. After some commotion, the mine management eventually agreed to a strongly censored version of their work.

In their article, now widely renowned, which was carefully included in an elaborate description of the mechanized coal-mining process unravelled in small subtasks, Trist and Bamforth (1951) present, in guarded terms, a unique underground alternative work organization built up of so-called "composite work groups". These were small, relatively autonomous work groups consisting of eight miners, who were responsible as a group for a full cycle in the coal-mining process. This "new" form of work organization had similarities to the manual situation that had existed up to the introduction of mechanization. What appeared in Haighmoor was that there were other, even better, ways of modelling the way work was carried out at the same mine. This was diametrically opposed to the prevailing practice of "one best way of organizing that fused Weber's description of bureaucracy with Frederic Taylor's concept of scientific management" (Trist, 1981, p.9). It was a grand success and led to the introduction of a new scientific paradigm: Socio-Technical Systems Design. As Trist later recalled in his correspondence with Emery, the beginnings of the socio-technical paradigm were not exactly plain sailing. In fact, the pioneering phase came about erratically.

Real tests with autonomous groups were carried out in the Bolsover mines in the East Midlands coal field. When Fred Emery stayed at this mine, during his sabbatical leave from Australia in 1952, he found autonomous groups in seven locations. However, here too, the National Coal Board was terrified of what might happen and cancelled a proposal for further diffusion. From January 1955 until March 1958, Trist and associates did a series of graphic case studies and field experiments with semi-autonomous work groups in the mines of North-West Durham. The reason for this was the "discovery" of "the working of a conventional, semi-mechanized, three-shift longwall cycle by a set of autonomous work groups" (Trist, 1981, p. 16). Trist ardently states how groups consisting of 40 to 50 miners worked here, exchanging their various tasks and drawing up the shift schedules themselves. They had defined an adapted "fair" rewarding system among themselves. Compared to identical circumstances with a traditional work organization, however, the output here was 25%

higher, the costs were lower, and absenteeism was cut by half! A flood of reports was published about this Bolsover case. A collected survey of these mine studies can be found in Trist et al. (1963).

Analogous to this, two field experiments were undertaken in the textile industry (the Jubilee and Calico Mills in Ahmedabad, India; cf. Rice, 1958) from the Tavistock base. Both in an automated and a non-automated weaving mill a system of semi-autonomous groups was introduced, and with lasting success in the latter (Miller, 1975).

Trist (1977) says that in the 1950s autonomous groups could be found in both the London harbour and British retail trade, but that attempts to study them all failed. Another early socio-technical reorganization is known from Scandinavia. In Sweden, autonomous groups were introduced in the Stockholm telephone exchange (cf. Westerlund, 1952).

The pioneering phase of STSD is characterized by notional vagueness. The lack of both time and resources at "The Tavistock" made systematic concept development impossible. From the very beginning the workers were encouraged in their observations by the emergence of open-systems thinking, which was initially derived from biology, but later stemmed from cybernetics too. They eagerly took on the new concepts and tried them out in practice.

The well known "Gestalt" notion, later renamed the "holistic system" (Angyal, 1941), allows for a closer inspection of the coal-mining situation in its entirety, i.e. both social and technical aspects and their mutual connection.

By means of the "open system" concept (Von Bertalanffy, 1950), the environment is considered. Thus, the unpredictable work situation in mines, hostile to workers, can become explicitly involved in study. The researchers make the concept of "self-regulation" the footing of the semi-autonomous group (Sommerhoff, 1950). Self-regulation of all steps in the coal-mining process is most effective in an unpredictable environment, and "requisite variety" (Ashby, 1956)—that is, all-round miners in the semi-autonomous group—is needed. Trist and Bamforth recorded this fact in the Elsecar mine in South Yorkshire: small semi-autonomous work groups made up of eight miners, all receiving equal reward, who took on a complete production cycle in the coal-mining process as a group. The continuing labour division, typical of early 20th-century mechanization of the industry, was rigorously done away with. Actual practice provided all the necessary ingredients for a new theory of organization. However, the exact conceptual elaboration only took place from the early 1960s onwards.

CLASSICAL STSD IN EUROPE

The further development of STSD was foreshadowed by Fred Emery's arrival at the Tavistock in 1958, while director Wilson left. Trist eventually managed to find financial support for Socio-Technical Concept Development, so that Emery, aided by Herbst and Miller, could start on the difficult task of tying up the many loose ends from the pioneering phase. The transition from the pioneering phase to that of classical STSD is demarcated by three documents (Emery, 1959; Herbst, 1959; Tavistock 526–528: cf. Miller, 1959). Following Emery (1959), the start of the idea of open systems in the production organization results in the evolution of a "socio-technical system". Both social and technical components are part of a socio-technical system, i.e. people and machines. The technical component is taken to be the "internal environment" of the organization. In his review, Trist (1981) says that the technical and social systems are independent of one another; the former follows the laws of natural sciences, and the latter those of social sciences. However, the two do not operate independently of each other. They rely on each other to fulfil the production function. We are dealing with a connection of heterogeneities. The economic aspect is not a separate third system in Emery's view (1959), as previously suggested by Rice (1958), but may be seen as a means to measure the effectiveness of the socio-technical whole.

In the years that followed, Emery also went to work on the formalization and methodological foundation of STSD as an open systems approach (cf. Emery, 1967). Jordan's message (1963) that people are supplementary to, and not an extension of machines, was motivation enough to further explore the design precept of "joint optimisation". The social and technical systems were no longer to be maximized as independent bodies, but to be optimised at the same time instead. The point was to reach the "best match" between technical instrumentation and social work organization. In 1963 Emery wrote of "the ideal of joint optimisation of coupled, but independently based, social and technical systems". In the early sixties, Emery did pioneering work in the field of science theory and methodology too. He further developed Von Bertalanffy's (1950) "open systems" concept, for example, so that a definition of the process of "active adaptation" was simplified, and he based STSD on Sommerhoff's (1950) methodology of "directive correlation" "as a rigorous framework for contextualism" (Emery, personal communication, 1990). The methodology of "directive correlation" offered by Emery lies at the heart of the socio-technical paradigm, and encompassed in brief the symbiotic relationship between an open system and its environment. The way in which the two are a result of one another while determining one another, was and still is difficult for many people to comprehend, and it was Emery who often pointed this out.

The epistemological and methodological documents mentioned earlier, though hard to get to, were the key to the foundation of STSD as a scientific paradigm, because they laid the facts bare. We shall not go into this subject in detail any further here, except for one theme. The well-known environment typology can be viewed as a direct consequence of the establishment of STSD. From the study by Tolman and Brunswik (1935) and using Sommerhoff's (1950) "directive correlation" methodology, and Ashby's (1952) concept of "joint environment", Emery and Trist (1965) generated an environment typology that takes "causal texture" as its base. The terms point to the "degree of organization" of the environment, in which systems originally non-related become interwoven to an increasing extent. The division consists of four classes of increasing complexity and unpredictability: (1) placid, randomized environment; (2) placid, clustered environment; (3) disturbed-reactive environment; (4) turbulent field. With this typology, the next logical step in socio-technical conceptualization, one can better understand the increase in (changeable) demands affecting the organization, which are heading for the organization from increasingly rapidly changing markets. Successful interaction between the organization and the increasingly complex environment greatly influences the chances of survival. This typology was expanded by the hyper-turbulent "vortex" variant by Babüroglu (1988): (5) vortical environment.

The Norwegian "Industrial Democracy" (ID) programme, which ran from 1962 to 1969, was a historic part of the Classical STSD period. The mine studies in the United Kingdom made it difficult to do action research there. However, in the early 1960s opportunities arose for larger-scale experiments in Norway. A joint committee was formed between employer and employee organizations at the beginning of 1962 to take a closer look at matters of industrial democracy. The government decided to become part of this committee at a later stage. At first, research in this area was subcontracted to the Trondheim Institute for Industrial Social Research (IFIM), which in turn called in the Tavistock Institute. Eric Trist was the original contact, but Fred Emery from "The Tavistock" with Einar Thorsrud of the Norwegian Work Research Institutes (WRI) in Oslo were the ones who embodied and led the ID project (cf. Thorsrud & Emery, 1964). The most important feature from the research programme was formulated as "a study of the roots of industrial democracy under the condition of personal participation in the work place" (Emery & Thorsrud, 1976, p.10). The programme dealt, in particular, with sequential field experiments in which alternative forms of work organization (primarily centred on semi-autonomous work groups) were set up and tested. Next, the effects on employee participation for each layer within an organization were investigated.

The companies allowed to participate in these projects were carefully chosen by the experts of the "Joint Committee". The most important sectors in Norway were represented, being the metal, paper, and chemical industries. The choice was based on an elementary diffusion theory (Emery et al., 1958, see also the section on Modern STSD). We will now give a brief description of the four main projects:

1. The first project started in 1964 in Christiania Spigerverk, a wire-draw plant in Oslo (cf. Marek, Lange, & Engelstad, 1964). Group work was introduced by the investigators with little difficulty, but the reward system instantly posed all kinds of problems. The whole process of change was not supervised properly in this project. Local unionists and management did not really empathize with the project, so it was cancelled when the research team left the factory, having been there more than a year.

2. The second project took place in February 1965 after prudent familiarization and sustained sessions with unions and management at the chemical-pulp department of the Hunsfos paper mill located in Vennesla, Kristiansand (cf. Engelstad, Emery, & Thorsrud, 1969). Here, they managed to get a firmer hold on the change process: the introduction and formation of "extended groups" was accompanied step-by-step by project and work groups composed of employees' spokespeople, and lower and upper management. However, the project really got under way when the research team withdrew into the background and the (upper) management committed itself more pronouncedly. In 1966, the new work organization thrived and the effects of group work and multi-skilled personnel were finally proved. However, early in 1967, the project ran aground because of a crisis in the paper industry and the associated priority changes in management. In the 1970s the Hunsfos employees took over the project for themselves and gave it a new lease of life (cf. Elden, 1979).

3. The Industrial Democratization programme met with greater hold-ups. After an initial refusal by the management to join the programme because of politically sensitive issues within the company, the third ID project finally started—more than two years after the first application—in December 1965 at NOB household appliances/metalware in the Hommelvik division near Trondheim (cf. Thorsrud, 1972). Here too, an experiment with semi-autonomous groups took place, carefully set in the organization, specifically for a new production line for electric radiator heaters. This project became the spearhead of the ID programme, which attracted many interested parties from Norway and Sweden. Later, when a new factory had to be put into use, in connection with higher production, the employees succeeded in maintaining the new organization.

4. The fourth ID project was launched in 1967—at the request of the firm itself—in the chemical concern Norsk Hydro, more specifically in the rearrangement of the old and the design of a new fertilizer factory in Heröya, Porsgrun (cf. Bregard et al., 1968). This project, which also involved Louis Davis, was one of the many variants to the introduction of a group structure supported by a training programme and a reward system adapted to group work. It was a resounding success: the two factories showed a good performance well into the 1970s with this socio-technical work organization.

The four demonstration projects just described were the basis for considerable study (cf. Emery & Thorsrud, 1964, 1976; Engelstad, 1972; Gustavsen & Hunnius, 1981). They were meant to explain the functionality in practice of the new socio-technical organization principles, but unfortunately these examples initially had little following. Though the experiments were successful (cf. Gustavsen & Hunnius, 1981), they were largely limited to the department or the factory where they had started. In turn, the "experimental gardens" were separated from the rest of the organization and thus it started to resist such a change. This phenomenon was referred to by Merrelyn Emery (1989) as "paradoxical inhibition". Although various diffusion programmes were set up, the programme came to a halt in Norway around 1970.

The situation for the neighbouring country Sweden, however, was the opposite. A cooperative project carried by employers and unions similar to that in Norway was set up. Soon employers wanted to start their own programme in more than 500 companies (cf. Jenkins, 1975) as a result of slow progress. They also promoted a socio-technical programme when new plants were built (cf. Agurén & Edgren, 1980). Apart from Saab-Scania, where parallel production groups were already formed in 1972, Volvo in particular has a reputation for having developed a whole range of pioneering new forms of work organization, Kalmar being the most well known (cf. Agurén, Hansson, & Karlsson, 1976; Agurén et al., 1984). For a more extensive overview of the Volvo projects, see Auer and Riegler (1990).

From 1965 on, the Industrial Democracy programme was redone in the United Kingdom. The Norwegian example was "copied", as best they could, at Avon Rubber, Shell, and RTZ (personal communication of Emery, 1990). However, one important element was lacking: a steering committee composed of employers and employees. "The Shell Philosophy programme was an innovation but not a change in trajectory. It was developed because we could not get a sanctioning body of the union and employer leaders in the UK, as we had in Norway" (Emery, 1990).

The Norwegian ID programme and its variants are characteristic of the Classical STSD period, in which the expert approach prospered. While the ID programme was moulded and elaborated on in Norway, a major emphasis was placed on a systematic explication of the project approach— among other things, because this functioned as a demonstration of the new approach. This led to important "breakthroughs" in the field of method and concept development. In the ID project approach, the whole process of change was defined and monitored in phases and steps. The starting point was a thorough socio-technical analysis of the in situ business situation. The notions of "variance" and "variance control" (cf. Engelstad, 1970; Hill, 1971) were essential here. Based on Herbst's (1959) concept of "disturbance control", the principle of "signalling occurring disturbances and their control by the employees themselves as close to the source as possible" was operationalized through projects. The implementation of this principle came about through use of the so-called "variance control matrix": a table with both specific disturbance sources and (factual) disturbance controls. This procedure became the first formal socio-technical method. The so-called "traditional variance analysis" technique

was first used at the Hunsfos paper mill (Engelstad et al., 1969). The steps are as follows:

1. Identifying key success criteria.
2. Drawing the layout of the system.
3. Listing the steps in the process in order.
4. Identifying unit operations.
5. Identifying variances.
6. Constructing a variance matrix.
7. Identifying key variances.
8. Constructing key variance and control tables.
9. Suggesting technical changes.
10. Suggesting social system changes.

The technique was then used at the Stanlow oil refinery of Shell-UK (cf. Emery, Foster, & Woollard, 1967; Foster, 1967; Hill, 1971) working from the Tavistock. Emery and Thorsrud developed a series of job redesign principles to be used for the actual experiments with Industrial Democratization based on the work of Louis Davis from the United States (cf. Emery & Thorsrud, 1964, pp.103–105). These so-called "structural propositions" for joint optimization acted as criteria for the assessment of the existing and newly created work situations. Afterwards, they were often repeated in the literature in various publications (e.g. Emery & Thorsrud, 1976).

CLASSICAL STSD DEVELOPMENTS IN THE NETHERLANDS

From the very beginning, the Netherlands has held an important place in the history of STSD. Dutch researchers have been involved in the development and application of the paradigm from the outset.

From 1957 to 1959, Hans van Beinum was the first in the Netherlands to carry out a kind of socio-technical field experiment. This was done at the Department of Transfers of the then Post Cheque and Giro Services (PCGD) in the Hague (Van Beinum, 1963a). At the main Current Account department, which employed 1700 personnel, he examined the effects of the introduction of "stable table groups", of another method of management ("business discussions"), and of delegating power. He found no differences in productivity between experimental and control groups. However, Van Beinum did conclude that the experimental groups clearly expressed a more positive judgement of their working situation after the introduction of the organizational changes (Van Beinum, 1963b, p.112). In the 1960s, Van Beinum undertook several other projects, both from the Tavistock (Van Beinum, 1968) and in the Netherlands (Van Beinum, Van Gils, & Van Verhage, 1968). In connection with this, we have to mention Van der Vlist, who—like Van Beinum—did Tavistock research in Dublin. He subsequently carried out a socio-technically influenced dissertation research, under the guidance of Mulder and following Van Gils' tracks, to study the group performance of ships' crews in Dutch offshore fishing (Van der Vlist, 1970). Following this, the effects of naval fishing were examined by Herman Kuipers (1969) through simulation, and reported in a dissertation (Kuipers, 1980).

Allegro started a socio-technical project subsidized by the Social Economic Council (SER) in 1969 at the cotton-spinning mill Bamshoeve in Enschede (Allegro, 1973a,b). This analysis is a textbook example of a classical socio-technical analysis, with much emphasis being placed on the variance control matrix.

In the late 1970s, Allegro and De Vries (1979a,b) did a socio-technically-inspired experiment at the Centraal Beheer insurance company in Apeldoorn. The immediate cause was the development and introduction of the "Effective Life Insurance Information System" (ELVIS) initiated from technology. The project consisted of the re-introduction of work consultation in 25 groups at the life insurance department and experimentation with a contract (client)-oriented approach. A test with three contract control groups was a success. In contrast with the Bamshoeve, more emphasis was placed on the training of group supervisors in a different type of guidance and leadership. The researchers spoke of an integration of a task-structural and a group-dynamic approach, and of structure and culture.

Parallel with these projects, pioneering work was done in the 1960s and 1970s at Philips in the area of work structuring (see elsewhere in this volume).

Walravens (1977) carried out a series of field experiments with what he calls "Industrial Democracy". These projects were concerned with work consultation and task structuring at the Worsted and Ironing Spinning Mill Swagemakers-Bogaerts in Tilburg, and at the packaging company Thomassen & Drijver-Verblifa in Oss. The total organization including all its policy levels and its relevant environment was the express object of research. The projects show a clear resemblance with the Norwegian ID projects described earlier. Walravens (1977, p.247) opted for:

> a development and institutionalisation of bottom-up participation, where all levels are continuously involved in the changes, in order to guarantee success and continuity. Characteristic ... is the attention given to the relationships of the enterprise with the organisations or parts of organisations that are relevant to its functioning, such as works councils, unions, employers' organisations, ... and the government.

Walravens actually carried out two projects and concluded that the success and permanence of the organizational change depended on the extent to which employees were personally responsible. At the same time, however, he remarked that there was little enthusiasm in Dutch companies in 1977 to experiment with enlarging participation. The study contributed to the insight that the exclusive application of a micro-approach concerning humanization of work is too limited to achieve structural improvements in the area of Industrial Democratization.

Looking back on the projects portrayed in this section so far, we must conclude that various applications of Classical STSD can be recognized in the Netherlands. Remarkably, the same shortcomings of this "expert-driven" approach have come to the fore, namely little acceptance, disappointing diffusion, and the hedging in of projects.

MODERN STSD IN DIFFERENT CONTINENTS

The results from the Classical STSD period were a disappointment. A time of introspection followed, which led to extensive thought on the strategy being developed. This took place in various places in Europe, North America, and Australia without much tuning between the groups. Thus, separate approaches came into existence that have many common features on closer inspection. An emphasis on the diffusion process rather than on the changes of content themselves is a main characteristic of the Modern STSD period. In this context, one speaks of a "figure-ground reversal" (cf. Emery, M., 1986; Emery, M. & Emery, F., 1978; Herbst, 1976) as a contrast to the previous phase. The "figures" refer to our factual structures (the factories, offices, institutions), the "ground" to our lifestyles and values. The object of change is reversed, so a change in attitude is the focus: learning to participate.

Elden (1979a, pp.250–251) outlined the features of Modern STSD in sequence:

1. A design-team representative of (if not elected by) the employees: At the very least, employees agree to a change effort, and union representatives are usually redesign-team members.
2. Employees receive some training in work-design concepts and techniques.
3. Participatory search processes initiate the change effort and are not necessarily limited to the design team.
4. The design team develops its own criteria and alternatives (little reliance on installing some pre-designed package).
5. All employees concerned participate, at least in evaluating alternatives.
6. There is a high degree of participation in all phases of the redesign process (planning, developing alternatives, evaluating, etc.) which is focused and paced by the people affected (not primarily by management or change experts).
7. Outside experts have a shared learning role that changes over time (from some teaching to learning with the participants and eventually to learning from them).
8. There is a supportive network of co-operative relations between design teams from different organizations who learn from each other's experience (they are not entirely dependent on experts for the necessary learning).

MODERN STSD DEVELOPMENTS IN AUSTRALIA

Fred Emery, who had spent over ten years in Europe, went back to Australia in 1969. Once there the petitions came pouring in for projects analogous to those he had worked on in the United Kingdom and Norway. He found himself having to allow companies to set up and realize their own design projects. The "vertical project group" (top-down cross-section of the hierarchy) tried out at Hunsfos was the basis for the so-called "vertical slice approach" that Emery later formulated. The approach meant having to improve "Industrial Democracy" for the entire organization by means of "self-managing design groups". The groups were made up of employees, supervisors, and managers who ranked differently in the organization, but who expected to work together as equals.

The ID diffusion process in Norway has been a failure that Emery was not ready to repeat. He attributed the poor results mainly to the expert approach advocated by the researchers. The projects had never managed to gain a proper footing within the companies, because there was a lack of involvement. The expert approach was no longer a viable option in view of the changed spirit of the times (the student demonstrations in Paris had only recently taken place).

Emery gradually realized, from the perspective of STSD research, that an entirely new democratic value system lay hidden beneath the semi-autonomous work group in the UK and the principles for task redesign developed in Norway. Emery and Thorsrud (1964, p.105) started by describing "a limited number of general psychological requirements", but Emery (1977, p.68) later goes on to describe "a set of workable and relevant values . . ., things ... valued in work regardless of sex, nationality or race". He outlines these values as follows (Emery, 1977, p.68):

1. Freedom to participate in decisions directly affecting their work activity.
2. A chance to learn on the job, and go on learning.
3. Optimal variety.
4. Mutual support and respect of their work colleagues.
5. A socially meaningful task.
6. Leading to some desirable future.

Trist (1976) also talks of new values that enable us to cope with the increasing complexity of the environment, mentioning things like self-actualization, self-expression, and "capacity for joy".

In 1971 Emery produced a technique called the "deep slice" method of Participative Design. This method allows employees, (middle) management, and union representatives to work on task and organization design together when the project starts. The idea behind this was to get rid of any opposition to change. The South Australian Meat Corporation SAMCOR (Yearling Hall), the Royal Australian Air Force, and Imperial Chemical Industries (ICI) were the experimental breeding grounds for this technique. Even before the famous 14-page "little golden book" was published (cf. Emery, F. & Emery, M., 1974, 1975) the method had been transferred to India (cf. Nilakant & Rao, 1976), the Netherlands, and Norway. By 1972 things started to look up in Norway as diffusion was given a new boost. This was the result of companies assuming control of the development themselves following the departure of the researchers.

"Participative Design" (PD) is described by Merrelyn Emery as "an environment for conceptual and experiential learning about democratic learning organizations" (cf. Emery, M., 1989, p.114). During the 1970s, two such environments were further worked out: the Participative Design Workshop (Emery & Emery, 1975) and the Search Conference (Emery & Emery, 1978).

The Participative Design Workshop (PDW) is a gathering that lasts between one-and-a-half and three days. Four to ten members are chosen from all layers of the organization ("deep slice") and come together as equals in a total design group to map, assess, and redesign the working situation with the counsel of a so-called "facilitator". The fundamental substance of the self-managing design group can be found in Part I of the "little golden book" (Emery & Emery, 1975). This places the six psychological requirements mentioned earlier next to the "genotypes" of the bureaucratic ("redundancy of parts") and the democratic ("redundancy of functions") structures, and gives a concise description of the advantages of the latter. The methodical basis that underpins the workings of the total design team, is reflected in Part II of the book. The different jobs of staff are assessed using the six psychological job requirements, and the process flow is analyzed. Also, training requirements are obtained from a so-called "multi-skilling table", which helps evaluate skills per person for every (group) task. The aim of the PD workshop is to accomplish structural organizational change by those involved. The complete framework is "anti-expert-oriented", and works on the hypothesis that "the most adequate and effective designs come from those whose jobs are under review" (Emery & Emery, 1975). Content is not the focus here, but the participative process where the members of the organization devise their own evolutionary learning process. The Search Conference (SC) is a non-hierarchical meeting for policy preparation, based on the principle of "redundancy of functions", involving a maximum of 35 persons who cooperate in isolation for two to three days. It is their task to work out plans for the future as a group of equals. The socio-technical search conference makes use of the indirect or "Broad Front" approach, and is aimed at the joint development of "desirable and probable future scenarios". Special care is paid to the opportunities and limitations provided by the environment, without neglecting the history of the company. This participative form of pro-active planning assumes that people are pragmatic and strive for meta-objectives (ideals); that they are willing to learn and wish to decide their own future. The distinct goals are: deciding policy, planning, and learning in a non-dominant democratic structure. According to Merrelyn Emery (1993), both PD tools have their own function: SC is primarily a participative planning methodology; whereas PDW is the actual organization redesign instrument.

An explicit diffusion strategy underlies Participative Design. The point of departure for this strategy was the diffusion model constructed by Emery, Oeser, and Tully (1958) for an agricultural renewal programme in South-East Australia. Qvale (1976, p.459) made a brief abstract of the findings of Emery et al. (1958):

a. Diffusion of new principles must start within the existing structure and in a way flow from one level of leaders to the next.

b. Generally, external scientific advisors will only influence the diffusion process through the leaders.

c. Oral and written communication is rarely enough to lead to change, except on the level of leaders.

d. Outside the level of leaders diffusion depends upon the force of the example. To be effective the demonstration must be such that everyone can see the similarity with his own condition.

e. A well-respected person or group must be behind the example.

To explain the (Norwegian) democracy experiments, Philip Herbst (1976) further developed this diffusion theory. The network concept is central to Herbst's theory. According to him (1976, p.33), a network group should be portrayed as the reverse of an autonomous group. It is a transient organization of similar thinkers in separate locations, who periodically meet for consultation. Such a meeting is sometimes referred to in the literature as a "flocking session" (cf. Davis & Cherns, 1975). Flocking is a phenomenon that involves different people with collective interests coming together for a few days to confer intensely, without arranging another meeting. According to Herbst (1976), flocking by members of a network is exactly what keeps them together, and it supports a network's objective, namely maintaining "long-term directive correlations". The process chiefly involves stimulating one another to reach a common, though not (fully) specified objective. The primary function is the collective learning process.

Emery & Emery (1978) ground their Participative Design paradigm on an open-system model, which they believe to be pertinent to the diffusion process. The "system" has the members of a PD workshop, search conference, or network of companies, whereas the "environment" includes "the extended social field of directive correlations" (Emery & Trist, 1981), together forming a changed society in its totality.

They call the input function "learning" and the output function "planning". In general, both Merrelyn and Fred Emery state that the level of the environment complexity decides the form assumed by the learning and planning functions in practice. In a competitive "type III" environment ("disturbed, reactive") the learning function assumes the form of "problem solving", and the planning function that of "optimizing, utilising technical and economic standards only". In a turbulent "type IV" environment (rapid, unpredictable changes, disturbed ecological chains) learning occurs through "puzzling" (Angyal, 1965), and planning through the active and adaptive formation of "desirable future scenarios" (Emery, 1977).

Puzzling is a kind of learning—in the literature it is also looked upon as "double loop learning" (cf. Argyris, 1976)—in which individuals try to trace the more vital basic questions in a non-hierarchical, friendly atmosphere. They try to find trends in an excess of data, filtering out "the leading part" (Emery, 1967). Planning subsequently occurs by plotting, evaluating, and adapting a strategy in sequence, which consists of jointly formulated "desirable future scenarios". Thorsrud (1972) feels this type of policy-making is a form of active, adaptive planning, which is essentially a continuous learning process. The real drive behind PD is the pleasure experienced during this learning process. Instead of assuming an expectant attitude, people are willing to get to work. In the PD workshop, they work as a group, by themselves, to adapt the working situation (in their own company); in the search conference, participants develop future scenarios.

As a kind of Modern STSD, PD is still not as prevalent as its classical antecedent. Presumably this is because of the anti-expert character of the new approach, which sets consultancy agencies on a sidetrack. In the 1970s, PD workshop projects were mainly confined to Scandinavia, India, the United Kingdom, and the Netherlands. Moreover, only a few of these projects have been recorded in the literature. In North America and Canada, the application of Participative Design has only recently started to emerge (see the section on STSD developments in the United States).

MODERN STSD DEVELOPMENTS IN SCANDINAVIA

In Scandinavia, STSD went off at a slightly different tangent after 1970. We are referring here to the initiation of a "large-scale change process in a broadly based societal context with democratic dialogue as vanguard" (Gustavsen, 1985). In essence, it is a response to the Participative Design approach, emphasizing the formation of networks and the development of local theories. According to Gustavsen and Engelstad (1986), the Democratic Dialogue (DD) approach assumes that all interested parties can and should participate. To promote DD, these authors defined the circumstances under which a democratic dialogue may come about.

A democratic dialogue should especially be formed at organized network meetings. Therefore, conferences functioning like springboards are central to this. The DD network philosophy should be set against a background of years of experience with democratization in the working situation. More specifically, it is a reaction to the moderate outcome of PD. In Scandinavia, PD was only brought into practice in (some) large companies during the 1970s. In small and medium-sized companies it never really caught on. This was attributed, among other things, to the lack of adequate joint networks. People are trying to change this by means of DD, both in Norway and in Sweden.

In Norway, a national basis emerged for the development of local networks in 1982, when employers and employees jointly agreed to strengthen network-oriented activities both professionally and financially. Based on the regional experiences gained in this context, the so-called "Development Organization" (DO) approach matured steadily (Engelstad, 1990). This is a more indirect approach to PD, aimed at creating a suitable platform for bilateral exchange—also for SMEs (small and medium-sized enterprises)—and enhancing the quality of the mutual dialogue. The DO approach rests on five pillars: (1) the strategy forum; (2) company-wide conferences; (3) supra-departmental project groups; (4) basic groups within departments; (5) socio-technical changes in the daily work organization.

The first two pillars demand further explanation. The strategy forum is not so much a steering group in the traditional sense, but rather a semi-open conditioning body of the network that also allows external experts in at the body's request. The strategy forum conceives general aims, brings together (groups from) the participating centres in the organization network, stimulates productive dialogues, and supports contacts with the whole "broad field" of activities.

As for the conferences, it can be said that originally these were largely built up in the same manner as those in the PD tradition. However, they gradually became more fixed. From the experiences gained with branch projects, the Dialogue Conference (DC) method was developed. It is a type of PD workshop or search conference for network development. It works on the assumption that the quality of the dialogue is a major medium for the change process. The DC method can be separated into three successive stages: entry into the branch network; business development projects; augmentation of the (supporting) network. In phase one, the demonstration conference is held, the strategy forum is chosen, and regional promotion conferences are formed. In phase two, a "whole-company" conference is arranged, and a supporting expert is let in to the company part-time as a "scholarship holder", paid and supported by the national programme. In phase three, a "network development" conference is begun to enlarge the number of firms taking part and supporting institutions. The strategy forum acts as an initiator and coordinator in all these activities. The content of the conferences is mostly the concern of the groups participating. However, the order of the sessions and constitution of the groups are carefully planned beforehand.

As pointed out previously, the national, tripartite stimulation programmes in Scandinavia are highly important in realizing an infrastructure for a democratic dialogue. In Norway, this is the HABUT programme, which translates into "The Basic Agreement's Enterprise Development Measures". In Sweden, it is the LOM programme, initiated by the Swedish Work Environment Fund. Here, the acronym stands for "Leadership, Organization and Codetermination". LOM is the most comprehensive of the two programmes in its content and size. Gustavsen (1989) reports there are more than 100 firms and institutions taking part in this programme, begun in 1985. For a broad evaluation of the LOM programme see Naschold (1992, 1993).

The results of DD are without doubt imposing. However, whether the Democratic Dialogue described here will actually encompass a subsequent qualitative leap forward in the development of STSD, or is just a further broadening, development and expansion of Participative Design, cannot be convincingly concluded at this time. Fred Emery (1990, personal communication) reports that a real fourth phase would feature the development of "organizational forms for the management of self-managing work groups". The Dutch approach to "Integral Organisational Renewal" (IOR) would then be more eligible for the designation of "fourth phase turning-point" (see also the section on STSD in the Netherlands).

STSD DEVELOPMENTS IN THE UNITED STATES AND CANADA

STSD only really managed to gain a firm footing in North America after the return of Louis Davis in 1967. He had been to the Tavistock and from there had been participating in the Norwegian "Industrial Democracy" experiments. Katz and Kahn had just published their "Social Psychology of Organizations" at the time (1966). Davis had convinced Eric Trist to temporarily give up his position at the Tavistock for a seat at an American university. Later this proved to be his last time in Europe. Davis and Trist established themselves at

the University of California in Los Angeles (UCLA), where they developed a complete STSD programme together. UCLA became the breeding ground for a whole generation of American socio-technologists. UCLA's graduates spread out across various other North American universities (e.g. Pennsylvania State, Case Western Reserve, Texas Tech, Harvard, Loyola, and Toronto), or worked as advisers in companies and institutions (e.g. Alcan, Proctor & Gamble, General Motors, General Foods, Digital, US Army, Labour Canada; cf. Taylor & Felten, 1993).

An important feature of the North American STSD approach is that, under the influence of Trist right up to his death in 1993, it remained a faithful copy of the original classical Tavistock approach described earlier (cf. Taylor & Felten, 1993). The socio-technical approach, which was renamed "Quality of Working Life" in the United States, was used in many American companies as an application of participative redesign in the 1970s (cf. Davis & Cherns, 1975; Taylor, 1990). Lately, it seems that Participative Design is gaining more advocates in the United States because of Merrelyn Emery. Modern STSD in North America is therefore clearly becoming more pluralistic.

STSD DEVELOPMENTS IN THE NETHERLANDS

A conceptual addition to the development of STSD that broke new ground was provided by Ulbo de Sitter. He was the first to oppose the original paradigmatic elaboration of Classical STSD, concerning both content and methodology. Among other things, De Sitter's opposition centres on the obsolete system-theoretical foundation of the paradigm and with its partial and static elaboration as a socio-scientific approach in the area of the quality of work. Also, Ad van der Zwaan (1973) points to the lack and insufficient specificity of the definitions used. In view of the inadequate accessibility of many conceptual "Tavvi" documents in which Fred Emery in particular did much significant conceptual digging, one may wonder whether all this criticism is warranted. In our judgement, even after having read these development papers and considering the directive correlation methodology, these points of criticism do actually have some value. In brief, the most relevant theoretical and method-ological objections, presented by Van der Zwaan (1975) to the international forum, are as follows: insufficiently precise definition of basic concepts, inadequate attention for the system–environment relationship, the incorrect system–theoretical dis-tinction between a social and technical subsystem, too great a reduction of the social system into a mainly psychological entity, and the inadequate separation of the analytical and the design models. The latter point focuses on the improper use of the Variance Control Matrix (cf. the section on Classi-cal STSD in Europe) for redesign purposes. As De Sitter et al. (1990) underline, an analysis of disturbance sources coupled with disturbance controllers only provides information on the oper-ation of the existing architecture of the production system. It is completely inappropriate for the moulding of a renewed structure, because it is organized dissimilarly.

These objections prompted the development of a fresh theoretical base. For the purposes of analysis and redesign, STSD is broadly described as the study and explanation of the way in which technical instrumentation and the division of work determine [system behaviour, capacity and func-tions] in their mutual connection and in relation to given environmental conditions, and also the

application of this knowledge in (re)designing production systems (De Sitter, 1974a, p.76). In 1989, he replaces the text between square brackets in the previous sentence by "the possibilities for the production of internal and external functions" (De Sitter, 1989b, p.232). For a graphic represen-tation of the central factors from this intricate explanation and their relationships, see Figure 4.2.

Technical instrumentation is defined here as the technical *accoutrements* of people and abilities concerning potential. Work division is taken to be the grouping, allocation, and coupling of execu-tive and regulative functions. This concerns the segregation of executive and regulative tasks, on the one hand, and the disjoining or dividing of executive and regulative tasks in suboperations and subregulations respectively, on the other.

In this characterization of STSD, it is repeated that the nature of the interdependence, in particu-lar between technical instrumentation and work division, biases the behaviour of the system. This occurs through internal (directed towards pur-chase, preparation, manufacturing, and sales) and external system functions (directed towards various "markets"). In essence, De Sitter develops a process theory of change, which he labels with the term "Model of Balance", in which the dynamics of cyclic interdependencies (both cause and effect, compare the principle of the servo-controlled mechanism) are central.

The structure of the selective labour process is

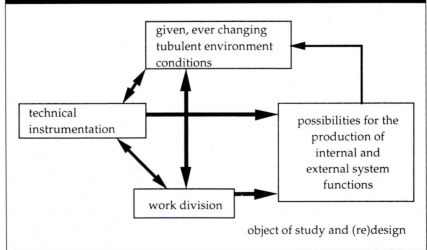

FIGURE 4.2

STSD; a graphic representation. Reprinted by permission of Van Gorcum Publishers.

explicitly looked at in the Model of Balance. The quantitative aspect of the labour process is the quantity of goods and services exchanged, the qualitative aspect is the permanence, and growth of work relationships. The labour process is seen as a crossroads for various institutional and private exchange processes; needs and values are considered changeable social processes fostered by society and introduced into the work situation by individuals and groups. Signification is a function that is inherent in selective social processes, and is closely connected to the regulation of the labour process: "What structural conditions do my labour processes have to comply with in general, so that I can solve numbers and kinds of problems that change in time and participate while giving meaning?" (De Sitter, 1978, p.9). Where there is a lack of regulative elements in work alienation occurs, but regulations provide involvement in work. Stress occurs when someone faces difficulties and cannot get rid of them.

The Balance Model, which in principle is applicable to all kinds of social systems, including companies, can describe the dynamic process simply and economically, in which open system and environment continuously follow from the alteration in the other, in ever-changing ways. From this perspective the design is a different system-theoretical option to Emery's directive correlation methodology. In his elaboration, De Sitter predominately focuses on interaction conditions, i.e. upon conditions of structure. The operational problems in production control are the explicit starting-points in this.

In 1973, a well defined and coherent system concept framework was published, including the "empty cartridge" concept of "aspect-system" that Tavistock did not know about (cf. De Sitter, 1973). In the same article, one finds much work is poured into an attempt to fit the "mould" of the systems approach as to its content, by means of "a scheme of interaction strategy" (p.138). After 1973, this scheme was changed into a more verbal model. What lies at the heart of the Balance Model is the so-called "interference" phenomenon. This happens in a situation where one process operation is disturbed or possibly obstructed entirely by another. One notion of interference (De Sitter, 1978, p.15) is:

the chance that two or more interaction processes meet each other in the labour process, and as a result of their normative and/or material incompatibility, cause a disturbance which tends to affect the possibilities for interaction which come into being through the labour process.

The crux of the new process model for classical STSD is to prevent or cure interference, and to stop it spreading in the system. This can be achieved through regulation. Regulation can be broadly defined as the maintaining of balance in processes fine-tuned to different functions in a system. The Balance Model utilizes the feedback loop as a basic model of the labour process. It is better not to separate and divide use (realizing connections) and regulation (selecting connections) in the feedback loop, but rather to combine them (principle of minimum division of labour).

The Balance Model, like classical STSD, departs from the so-called "latitude premise". The premise is an assumption regarding the scope of control founded on the axiomatic cybernetic "Law of Requisite Variety" (Ashby, 1956). This law generally implies that the external variability of the environment (turbulence) as information can be only compensated for or cancelled by a proportional internal variability of the open system (unprogrammed production control/latitude). De Sitter (1978) interprets the variability of the information as the need for control, and the potential open-systems variability as opportunities for control. The balance between the need and opportunities for control is interpreted as the quality of work.

A fundamental notion in the Balance Model is control capacity. De Sitter (1978) reports that this notion does "not refer to authority but to control opportunities resulting from the objective nature of the labour process" (pp.20–21). In 1980, he succinctly described control capacity as the problem-solving or disturbance reduction capacity: "In actual practice the control capacity present manifests itself in the process' sensitivity to disturbance, and thus the degree to which a disturbance ripples onwards without the possibility to reduce it through regulative action" (p.69).

In the past few decades, measuring instruments

for control capacity (and latitude) have been made by De Sitter and Heij (1975), Egmond and Thissen (1975), Van Eijnatten (1985), Pot et al. (1989a,b), and De Sitter (1989c).

Towards the end of the 1970s, the Dutch approach to STSD was expanded considerably, eventually to become the method of "Integral Organizational Renewal" (IOR). In the early 1980s, new opportunities arose for STSD, because the quality of work was no longer viewed as social extravagance, but as a vital base for a flexible production organization. Themes like the quality of working life, efficiency, and effectiveness, as well as social cohesiveness and cooperation, are set within a model for the first time. In line with this there is a call for "new factories and offices" based on modern STSD (De Sitter, 1981a). The way is made clear for more policy-based integration of the following areas of attention: the quality of work (with stress and alienation as problems), the quality of the organization (with flexibility and controllability as bottlenecks), and the quality of the internal industrial relations (with employee turnover, absenteeism, and labour conflicts as central issues). The issue of industrial democracy has traditionally been spread across the preceding problem areas, which have been individually studied by psychologists, sociologists, economists, and organization scientists. The essential thing is the interaction between these aspects, although the focus is the dynamic whole. In a cyclical movement the quality of work, organization, and industrial relations should mutually reinforce each other (upwards spiral) instead of weakening each other (downwards spiral), as often happens. Getting away from the downward spiral of the division of labour in the production organization, however, is the first condition for this. De Sitter (1980) feels these qualities are each other's counterparts in the proper production structure and that they "maintain each other as a pattern of characteristics" (p.25). The functional importance of participation in decision-making is acknowledged as a medium for industrial democracy, to have a synergetic effect on these problem areas (De Sitter, 1981b). Thus, Modern STSD became a reality in the Netherlands as well.

Integral design is the central element in the IOR approach (De Sitter, 1994). The fundamental issue is the flexibility of the complete production system. The aim of STSD for now is to enhance the controllability and the quality of work through alterations in structure. An integral approach is a structural approach by definition, where "structure" means being part of a process that does not change a lot over a period (nature of the operations, norms). The gist of an integral approach is "that on the basis of a strategic orientation, external function demands are determined. ... Problems in the business management are evaluated in the light of the function demands ..." (De Sitter, 1989a, p.36). Getting rid of bottlenecks that can be solved independently of each other is called "improvement" (partial structural alteration), whereas settling interdependent problems is called "renewal" (integral structural alteration). In essence, renewal means reordering process functions with respect to order flows. De Sitter (1989a, 1994) characterizes IOR as a clean break from the old functional production concept to the new flow-oriented production concept. The Balance Model we have already looked at acts as the centre of IOR concerning content; interference and control capacity are its central concepts. The IOR approach entails making an inventory of market demands and performance criteria (Bolwijn, 1988). In addition, one needs to identify, analyze and set structural parameters, which collectively reduce the chance of and sensitivity to disturbance of the production system (adapted from De Sitter, 1989b, p.234):

1. Functional (de)concentration: Grouping and coupling performance functions with respect to order flows (transformations). There are two extremes: All order types are potentially coupled to all subsystems (concentration), or each order type is produced in its own corresponding subsystem (deconcentration in parallel flows).

2. Performance differentiation: Separating the preparation, supporting and manufacturing functions into specialized subsystems.

3. Performance specialization: Dividing a performance function into a number of performance subfunctions and allocating them in separate subsystems.

4. Separation of performance and control functions: Allocating a performance and corresponding control function to different elements or subsystems.

5. Control specialization: Allocating the control of functional aspects to separated aspect-systems (quality, maintenance, logistics, personnel, etc.).

6. Control differentiation: Splitting feedback loops into separate control levels (strategic, structural, and operational).

7. Division of control functions in the feedback loop: Allocating "sensing", "judging", and "action selection" functions to separate elements or subsystems.

Performance and control are the primary functions here. At first, two primary aspect-systems were discerned: the Production Structure (P), as a grouping and coupling of executive functions, and the Control Structure (C), as a grouping and coupling of regulative functions. Subsequently, the Information Structure (I) was included as a technical elaboration of P and C. Many design principles were formulated in the 1980s (see Table 4.1).

What drew special attention was the shaping of the production structure through parallelization and segmentation. One can really speak of a method to fundamentally change the organization of the technical processes, which is an explicit objective of the socio-technical paradigm. The IOR approach has done much to realize the parallelization of order flows. For an elaborate study on the opportunities provided by Product Flow Analysis (Burbidge, 1975) as a technique for parallelization, see Hoevenaars (1991). Besides this, the formation of the control structure has also been worked out in detail (Landré, 1990; Van Amelsvoort, 1989, 1992). Also, the exploration of the information aspect has been given attention (Van Eijnatten & Loeffen, 1990).

The IOR approach also discerns distinct design-sequence rules (De Sitter, 1994; De Sitter et al., 1986). Therefore, the production structure has to precede the control structure and the design of process technology in its formation, and the design of control circles should follow allocation, selection, and coupling in that order. Besides the content of the (re)design, the mechanism with which change comes about also receives full attention. A renewal trajectory of two to four years is proposed (Den Hertog & Dankbaar, 1989), including a strategic exploration, on-the-job-training, and training for self-design, as well as project phasing and management. De Sitter (1993) states that "within the boundaries of what is feasible a socio-technical agent of change strives for: a) commitment; b) a well-balanced design according to his/her own professional conviction and judgment; c) self design by knowledge transfer" (p.176). This approach attempts to be a fusion between the expert and the participative

TABLE 4.1

A selection of design principles from the IOR approach (adapted from De Sitter, 1989b, pp.237–249).

Design strategy	Structure	Level	Parameter
a. Parallelization	P	macro	1
b. Segmentation	P	meso	2 + 3
c. Unity of time, place and action	B	micro	4 t/m 7
d. Bottom-up allocation of feedback loops	B	micro, meso	4
e. Uncoupling of feedback loops in time	B	meso	6
f. Building in feedback loops in each task	B	micro	1 t/m 7

approaches. To make things clearer, the terms from IOR are compared with those of a more traditional STSD in Table 4.2.

In 1981, the Dutch Institute for the Promotion of the Quality of Work and Organization (NKWO) was established. The aim of this foundation is to train business executives of all levels in socio-technical principles, so that they can take control of the redesign in their own company (compare the approach of Participative Design).

Various teams are working on the development of (parts of) the IOR approach in the Netherlands:

- Until 1988, the research team "Quality of Work and Organization" (KWO) at the University of Nijmegen worked on a follow-up to the Socio-Technical Task Analysis (STTA): the conceptualization and application of the Flexible Labour Systems Approach (BFA) (cf. Koopman-Iwema, 1986; Van Eijnatten, 1987). A practical approach was involved that would give shape to the task structure at the micro-level (building in steering capacity, control capacity and latitude in labour tasks). It was based on a design philosophy, in which social perspectives in mutual interaction with business administration and other aspects are discussed. It concentrated on a bottom-up approach and on the function demand quality of work.
- From 1985 on, NIPG/TNO in Leiden in cooperation with NIA Amsterdam and IVA Tilburg have been working on the development of the WEBA methodology (cf. Projectgroep WEBA, 1989a,b; Pot et al., 1989a,b). This methodology is used by the Dutch Labour Inspectorate as an instrument to test application of the Law on Working Conditions, section on welfare (Arbeidsinspectie, 1991).
- The STSD Group at Eindhoven University of Technology worked on the conceptualization and application of the Flexible Company Approach (BFB) until 1986 (cf. De Sitter et al., 1986). It concerned a design paradigm involving the top-down redesign of the production structure and the bottom-up redesign of the control structure. This approach encompasses all levels and aspects, but

emphasises the macro- and meso-levels, using controllability in particular as a function demand, and specifically stresses the logistic aspect.

- From 1988 on research teams at Eindhoven University of Technology have been working on the methodological development of IOR (cf. Van Eijnatten & Hoevenaars, 1989), the integration of BFA and BFB into the Flexible Organizations Approach (BFO) (cf. Van Eijnatten, Hoevenaars, & Rutte, 1988, 1990), and on the documentation of its content (Van Eijnatten 1990a,b, 1993a,b, 1994a,b; Van Eijnatten et al., 1992; Kuipers & Van Amelsfoort, 1990).

Since its foundation, NKWO/Koers has been working on the use and practical application of IOR and the development and implementation of a socio-technical training programme for business executives (cf. the journal *Richtingwijzer* and Ligteringen, 1989). Now there are various other STSD-oriented consultancies besides Koers (e.g. ST-groep, Oss; Rubicon, Vessem; Intueri, Boxtel) that lend support to companies in the actual implementation of IOR by means of projects, courses and publications related to working practice (cf. the journal *Panta Rhei*, and Van Amelsvoort & Scholtes, 1993).

- Those most actively involved in the development and extension of socio-technical thought through research and education are the universities of Eindhoven, Groningen, Leiden, Rotterdam, Nijmegen, and Maastricht. Several dissertations have been published in recent years (Van Amelsvoort, 1992; Benders, 1993; Boonstra, 1991; Deetman, 1994; Fruytier, 1994; Haak, 1994; Ten Have, 1993; Heming, 1992; Hoevenaars, 1997; Roberts, 1993). In 1994, the Dutch Foundation for STSD (SSTN) was established (Van Eijnatten, 1994c). All Dutch full professors involved in the field of STSD are members of the foundation.
- The Technology, Work and Organization (TAO) research network prompted research involving IOR in the period 1988–1994. The Maastricht Economic Research institute on

TABLE 4.2

Pertinent contrasts in content between the mainstream approach and the Dutch variant of STSD (De Sitter et al., 1990, p.27).

	Some conceptual differences	
	Traditional STSD	Dutch STSD
definition of system components (aspect-systems)	social system (S) technical system (T)	production structure (P) control structure (C) information structure (I)
main (re)design objective(s)	quality of work (partial improvements)	flexibility, controllability quality of work (integral renewal)
(re)design scope/ aggregation level of intervention	work groups micro	total organization micro–meso
basic concepts	open system responsible autonomy self-regulation	integral design controllability interference control capacity
main (re)design principles	minimum critical specification redundancy of functions requisite variety incompletion human values	parallelization of P segmentation of P unity of time, location and action (C) uncoupled control cycles whenever possible (C) control capacity built in every task
main (re)design strategies	reaching the "best match" between technology and organization (ideal of joint optimization) by using: • search conference • 9-step method (variance control) • participant design	reduction of complexity by obtaining a balance between required variation and available opportunities for process variation, both brought back to acceptable minimum levels, advocating informed self-design: • including all aspects • at all levels • with all parties
form of work organization (self-regulating units)	semi-autonomous work group discretionary coalitions	whole-task group semi-autonomous work group operational group result-responsible unit business unit

Innovation and Technology (MERIT) coordinated these activities through links with international networks (cf. Den Hertog, 1988a,b; Den Hertog & Schröder, 1989).

STSD AT THE END OF THE 20TH CENTURY

The socio-technical approach has been evolving for over four decades now. In this time the paradigm has developed from a chance rediscovery of an adaptable kind of work organization in a British coal mine, to an integral option to Taylorism dating from the beginning of the Industrial Revolution. The open system and self-regulation are its chief ideas. Throughout its evolution, the socio-technical approach has continued to revitalize and revive itself.

- In the pioneering phase of Tavistock, the mine studies were built on theoretical terms on the whole, with a mixture of notions originating from the speedily arising revolutionary system thinking.
- These notions were further extended in the Classical STSD period, and also adjusted for content in more detail, made logically consistent, and founded in method(olog)ical terms.
- During Modern STSD, models and methods were attuned to advancements in systems theory and the paradigm was enriched by an elegant and necessary "do-it-yourself" method. The emphasis was increasingly being placed on the formation of interorganizational networks and integral production renewal.

Yet, disregarding all the surface changes, the ultimate aim of STSD has always been kept in mind: the integration of aspects was and still is of capital import. Integrative thinking will go on to be popular in the period to come. In this context, Van Beinum (1990b) speculates on a shift from socio-technical to socio-ecological design. The organization plus its environment will both be object and objective of change. In Sweden, the LOM programme is almost a forerunner of this kind of approach.

With the onset of the 1990s, and particularly within the car industry, which was facing a crisis, discussions again arose about the pros and cons of STSD. These particularly concerned other approaches based on the Tayloristic model, like the Toyota Production System. In the Western world this extremely successful method of production has been dubbed Lean Production. The discussions on effectivity have been set in a different light now that the Volvo management has decided to close the brand new factory in Uddevalla, where socio-technical experiments were being carried out with complete parallelization of the final assembly process of the Volvo 740 (cf. Janse, 1989). For the moment, it seems that the Tayloristic concept will only hold in sectors that produce relatively large batches of products. Outside these sectors there is a gradual transfer to the new flow-oriented production concept. In advocating integral organization renewal, modern STSD gained unexpected support from an American approach that is rapidly growing in importance: Business Process Reengineering. Also, in the United States, people are showing increased interest in a more integral and participative STSD approach. Japan has come up with the innovative concept of "Holonic Production Systems", i.e. decentralized adaptive assembly systems with autonomous cells, involving "Human Integrated Manufacturing" (HIM). What this entails is that the worker takes part in one or more holons, supplies the creativity and makes decisions, while the equipment supplies the accommodating instrumentation (Sol, 1990). In the Netherlands, the STSD organization-renewal model has been applied to the process of product creation (Simonse & Van Eijnatten, 1993; De Sitter, 1994).

These and other developments will play an important role in shaping the new face of STSD into the next century. Its main focus will remain the same, whatever shape STSD takes on.

ACKNOWLEDGEMENTS

The author would like to extend special thanks to Fred Emery, Hans van Beinum, Friso den Hertog, and Ulbo de Sitter for their valuable suggestions and additions to earlier versions and variants of this chapter, and to Steven Ralston for the English translation.

This theoretical study was partly supported through a contribution from the TAO research stimulation programme (industry cluster).

ABOUT THE AUTHOR

Dr. Frans M. van Eijnatten is an associate professor (UHD) at the Graduate School of Industrial Engineering and Management Science, Eindhoven University of Technology, the Netherlands

REFERENCES

Agurén, S., & Edgren, J. (1980). *New factories: Job design through factory planning in Sweden.* Stockholm: Swedish Employers' Confideration SAF.

Agurén, S., Hansson, R., & Karlsson, K.G. (1976). *The Volvo Kalmar plant: The impact of new design on work organization.* Stockholm: The Rationalization Council, SAF-LO.

Agurén, S., Bredbacka, C., Hansson, R., Ihregren, K., & Karlsson, K.G. (1984). *Volvo Kalmar revisited: Ten years of experience.* Stockholm: Trykert Balder.

Allegro, J.T. (1973a). *Organisatie-ontwikkeling van onderaf: Naar een grotere betrokkenheid in de werksituatie.* Leiden: Stenfert Kroese; COP/SER.

Allegro, J.T. (1973b). *Socio-technische organisatie-ontwikkeling.* Leiden: Stenfert Kroese, proefschrift Erasmus Universiteit Rotterdam (Dutch language).

Allegro, J.T., & Vries, E. de (1979a). *Project human-isering en medezeggenschap bij Centraal Beheer te Apeldoorn: Verslag van een veranderingsproject bij een onderneming werkzaam op het gebied van levens-en pensioenverzekeringen, schadeverzekeringen, financieringen en computerdiensten.* Den Haag: COB/SER (Dutch language).

Allegro, J.T., & Vries, E. de (1979b). Project "Humanization and participation" in Centraal Beheer. In A. Alioth, J. Blake, M. Butteriss, M. Elden, O. Ortsman & R. van der Vlist (Eds.), *Working on the quality of working life: Developments in Europe* (pp.223–237). Boston: Nijhoff.

Amelsvoort, P.J. van (1989). Een model voor de moderne besturingsstructuur volgens de sociotechnische theorie. *Gedrag en Organisatie, 2,* (4/5), 253–267.

Amelsvoort, P.J. van (1992). *Het vergroten van de bestuurbaarheid van produktieorganisaties.* Eindhoven: Technische Universiteit, proefschrift (Dutch language).

Amelsvoort, P.J. van, & Scholtes, G.H. (1993). *Zelfsturende teams: ontwerpen, invoeren en begeleiden.* Oss: ST-Groep (Dutch language).

Angyal, A. (1941). *Foundations for a science of personality.* Cambridge, MA: Harvard University Press, pp.243–261. [Also published in New York: The Viking Press. Also published in 1958 (revised). Also abridged in F.E. Emery (Ed.) (1969), *Systems thinking: Selected readings* (pp.17–29). Harmondsworth, UK: Penguin Books.]

Angyal, A. (1965). *Neurosis and treatment: A holistic theory.* New York: Wiley.

Arbeidsinspectie (1991). *Functie-inhoud analyseren en beoordelen; de WEBA-methode.* Den Haag: Arbeidsinspectie (Dutch language).

Argyris, C. (1976). Single-loop and double-loop models in research on decision making. *Administrative Science Quarterly, 21,* 363–375.

Ashby, W.R. (1952). *Design for a brain.* London: Chapman & Hall. [2nd Edn., (1960). New York: Wiley.]

Ashby, W.R. (1956). Selfregulation and requisite variety. In F.E. Emery (Ed.) (1969), *Systems thinking: Selected readings* (pp.105–124). Harmondsworth, UK: Penguin Books.

Auer, P., & Riegler, C. (1990). *Post-Taylorism: The enterprise as a place of learning organizational change. A comprehensive study on work organization changes and its context at Volvo.* Stockholm/Berlin: The Swedish Work Environment Fund/Wissenschaftszentrum für Sozialforschung.

Babüroglu, O.N. (1988). The vortical environment: The fifth in the Emery-Trist levels of organizational environments. *Human Relations, 41,* 181–210.

Beinum, H.J.J. van (1963a). Veldexperimentele ervaringen in een bedrijfssituatie. In M. Mulder (Ed.), *Mensen, groepen, organisaties.* Assen: Van Gorcum (Dutch language).

Beinum, H.J.J. van (1963b). *Een organisatie in beweging: Een sociaal-psychologisch veldexperiment bij de postcheque-en girodienst.* Leiden: Stenfert Kroese, proefschrift Rijksuniversiteit Groningen (Dutch language).

Beinum, H.J.J. van (1968). *The design of a new radial tyre factory as an open sociotechnical system.* London: Tavistock Document 150.

Beinum, H.J.J. van (1990a). *Observations on the development of a new organizational paradigm.* Stockholm: The Swedish Centre for Working Life. [Paper presented at the seminar on "Industrial Democracy in Western Europe", Cologne, March.]

Beinum, H.J.J. van (1990b). *Over participatieve demo-cratie.* Leiden: Rijksuniversiteit (tweede) intreerede (Dutch language).

Beinum, H.J.J. van, Gils, M.R. van, & Verhagen, E.J. (1968). *Taakontwerp en werkorganisatie: Een socio-technisch veldexperiment.* Den Haag: Commissie Opvoering Produktiviteit, COP/SER. [Also in P.J.D. Drenth (Ed.) (1970), *Bedrijfspsychologie* (pp.458–472). Deventer: Van Loghum Slaterus.]

Benders, J.G.J.M. (1993). *Jobs around automated machines.* Nijmegen: Katholieke Universiteit, Ph.D. thesis.

Bertalanffy, L. von (1950). The theory of open systems in physics and biology. *Science, III,* 23–29. [Also in F.E. Emery (Ed.) (1969), *Systems thinking: Selected readings* (pp.70–85). Harmondsworth, UK: Penguin Books.]

Bolwijn, P.T. (1988). *Continuïteit en vernieuwing van produktiebedrijven.* Enschede: Universiteit Twente, Faculteit Bedrijfskunde, intreerede (Dutch language).

Boonstra, J.J. (1991). *Integrale organisatie-ontwik-keling: Vormgeven aan fundamentele verandering-sprocessen.* Culemborg: Lemma (Dutch language).

Bregard, A., Gulowsen, J., Haug, O., Hangen, F., Solstad, E., Thorsrud, E., & Tysland, T. (1968). *Norsk Hydro: Experiment in the fertilizer factories.* Oslo: Work Research Institute.

Burbridge, J.L. (1975). *Final report: A study of the effects of group production methods on the human-ization of work.* Turin: International Centre for Advanced Technical and Vocational Training.

Davis, L.E., & Cherns, A.B. (1975). *The quality of work life: Problems, prospects and state of the art,* Vols. I and II. New York: Free Press. Also published in London: Collier McMillan.

Deetman, G. (1994). *Het ontwerp van taakgroepen.* Eindhoven: Technische Universiteit, proefschrift (Dutch language).

Egmond, C., & Thissen, P. (1975). *Een onderzoek ten behoeve van het ontwikkelen van regelprofielen, uitgevoerd op de shop-floor.* Eindhoven: Technische Universiteit, Faculteit Bedrijfskunde (Dutch language).

Eijnatten, F.M. van (1985). *STTA: naar een nieuw werkstruktureringsparadigma.* Nijmegen: Katho-lieke Universiteit, proefschrift, druk: Nederlandse Philips Bedrijven, Eindhoven (Dutch language).

Eijnatten, F.M. van (1987). Benadering van flexibele arbeidssystemen (BFA): Ontwerpfilosofie. In A.L.M. Knaapen, W.J.M. Meekel, R.J. Tissen, & R.H.W. Vinke (Eds.), *Handboek methoden, technieken en analyses voor personeelsmanagement, aflevering 5* (pp.101–112). Deventer: Kluwer Bedrijfsweten-schappelijke Uitgaven (Dutch language).

Eijnatten, F.M. van (1990a). *Classical socio-technical systems design: The sociotechnical design paradigm of organizations.* Eindhoven/Maastricht (Nether-lands): TUE/MERIT, TUE Monograph BDK/T&A 001—Merit Research Memorandum 90-005.

Eijnatten, F.M. van (1990b). *A bibliography of the classical sociotechnical systems paradigm.* Eind-hoven (Netherlands): University of Technology, Department of Industrial Engineering and Manage-ment Science, Report EUT/BDK/39.

Eijnatten, F.M. van (1993a). *The paradigm that changed the workplace.* Assen: Van Gorcum.

Eijnatten, F.M. van (1993b). *The socio-technical systems design (STSD) paradigm: A full bibliography of 2685 English-language literature references, Rel-ease FBEL 04T.* Eindhoven (Netherlands): Eind-hoven University of Technology, Graduate School of Industrial Engineering and Management Science, Report EUT/BDK/59. [Also on IBM-compatible micro floppy disk.]

Eijnatten, F.M. van (1994a). *Het sociotechnisch ontw-erp paradigma van organisaties: een volledige bibliografie van 1145 Nederlandstalige literatuurre-ferenties, Release FBNL 02T.* Eindhoven: Tech-nische Universiteit, Faculteit Technische Bedrijfskunde, Vakgroep Technologie & Arbeid, rapport BDK/T&A 016, Juli. [Also on IBM-compat-ible micro floppy disk (Dutch language).]

Eijnatten, F.M. van (1994b). *The socio-technical systems design (STSD) paradigm: A full bibliography of 3082 English-language literature references, Rel-ease FBEL 05T.* Eindhoven (Netherlands): Eind-hoven University of Technology, Graduate School of Industrial Engineering and Management Science, BDK/T&A 009, August. [Also on IBM-compatible micro floppy disk.]

Eijnatten, F.M. van (Ed.) (1994c). *Presentatie stichting sociotechniek Nederland (SSTN).* Nijmegen: Sticht-ing Sociotechniek Nederland, druk: Reproduktie en Fotografie van de CTD, Technische Universiteit Eindhoven (Dutch language).

Eijnatten, F.M. van, & Hoevenaars, A.M. (1989). Moderne Sociotechniek in Nederland: Recente ont-wikkelingen in aanpak en methode ten behoeve van integraal organisatie(her)ontwerp. *Gedrag en Organ-isatie, 2,* 289–304 (Dutch language).

Eijnatten, F.M. van, & Loeffen, J.M.J. (1990). *Some comments about information systems design for production control from the perspective of an inte-gral sociotechnical organization philosophy.* Eind-hoven (Netherlands): Eindhoven University of Technology, Graduate School of Industrial Engineer-ing and Management Science, Department of Tech-nology and Work, BDK/T&A 003. [Paper presented at the International Conference "Computer, Man and Organization", Nivelles, Belgium, 9–11 May.]

Eijnatten, F.M. van, Hoevenaars, A.M., & Rutte, C.G. (1988). *Integraal (her-)ontwerpen: De benadering van flexibele organisaties.* Eindhoven: Technische Universiteit, Faculteit Bedrijfskunde, intern rapport (Dutch language)

Eijnatten, F.M. van, Hoevenaars, A.M., & Rutte C.G. (1990). Integraal ontwerpen van organisaties rond nieuwe technologieën. In J. F. den Hertog & F. M. van Eijnatten (Eds.), *Management van technologische vernieuwing* (pp.85–108). Assen: Van Gorcum (Dutch language).

Eijnatten, F.M. van, Hoevenaars, A.M., & Rutte, C.G. (1992). Holistic and participative (re)-design: STSD modelling in the Netherlands. In D. Hosking & N. Anderson (Eds.), *Organizing changes and innovations: European psychological perspectives* (pp.184–207). London: Routledge.

Elden, J.M. (1979a). Three generations of work-democracy research in Norway: Beyond classical sociotechnical systems analysis. In R. Cooper & E. Mumford (Eds.), *The quality of working life in Europe* (pp.226–257). London: Associated Business Press.

Emery, F.E. (1959). *Characteristics of socio-technical systems.* London: Tavistock Institute Document No. 527. Also in L. E. Davis & J. C. Taylor (Eds.) (1972), *Design of jobs* (pp.177–198). Harmondsworth, UK: Penguin Books. Also in F.E. Emery (Ed.) (1978), *The emergence of a new paradigm of work* (pp.38–86). Canberra: Australian National University, Centre for Continuing Education.

Emery, F.E. (1967). The next thirty years: Concepts, methods and anticipations. *Human Relations, 20,* 199–237. [Also in F.E. Emery (Ed.) (1981), *Systems thinking: Selected readings.* Harmondsworth, UK: Penguin Books.]

Emery, F.E. (1977). *Futures we are in.* Leiden (Netherlands): Martinus Nijhoff.

Emery, F.E. (1990). *Socio-technical theory: Its history.* Canberra: Australian National University, this author's private correspondence, 1907–1990.

Emery, F.E., & Emery, M. (1974). *Responsibility and social change.* Canberra: Australian National University, Centre for Continuing Education.

Emery, F.E., & Emery, M. (1975). Guts and guidelines for raising the quality of working life. In D. Gunzburg (Ed.), *Bringing work to life: The Australian experience* (pp.28–54). Melbourne: Cheshire/Productivity Promotion Council of Australia.

Emery, F.E., & Thorsrud, E. (1964). *Form and content of Industrial Democracy. Some experiments from Norway and other European countries.* Oslo: Oslo University Press. [Also published in London: Tavistock (1969), and in Assen: Van Gorcum (1969).]

Emery, F.E., & Thorsrud, E. (1976). *Democracy at work: The report of the Norwegian industrial democracy program.* Leiden (Netherlands): Martinus Nijhoff. [Also published in Canberra: Australian National University, Centre for Continuing Education (1975).]

Emery, F.E., & Trist, E.L. (1965). The causal texture of organizational environments. *Human Relations, 18,* 21–32. [Also in F.E. Emery (Ed.) (1969), *Systems thinking: Selected readings* (pp.241–269). Har-

mondsworth, UK: Penguin Books. Also in W.A. Pasmore, & J.J. Sherwood (Eds.) (1978), *Sociotechnical systems: A sourcebook* (pp.13–27). La Jolla, CA: University Associates.]

Emery, F.E., & Trist, E.L. (1981). The causal texture of organizational environments. In F. E. Emery (Ed.), *Systems thinking* (Vol. 1). London: Penguin Books.

Emery, F.E., Oeser, O.A., & Tully, J. (1958). *Information, decision and action.* Melbourne: Cambridge University Press.

Emery, F.E., Foster, M., & Woollard, W. (1967). Analytical model for sociotechnical systems. In F. E. Emery (Ed.) (1978), *The emergence of a new paradigm of work* (pp.95–112). Canberra: The Australian National University, Centre for Continuing Education.

Emery, M. (1986). Toward an heuristic theory of diffusion. *Human Relations, 39,* 411–432.

Emery, M. (Ed.) (1989). *Participative design for participative democracy.* Canberra: Australian National University, Centre for Continuing Education.

Emery, M. (Ed.) (1993). *Participative design for participative democracy.* Canberra: Australian National University, Centre for Continuing Education, revised edition.

Emery, M., & Emery, F.E. (1978). Searching: For new directions, in new ways, for new times. In J.W. Sutherland (Ed.), *Management handbook for public administrators* (pp.257–301). New York: Van Nostrand Reinhold.

Engelstad, P.H. (1970). Socio-technical approach to problems of process control. In F. Bolam (Ed.), *Papermaking systems and their control.* British Paper and Boardmakers' Association.

Engelstad, P.H. (1972). Socio-technical approach to problems of process control. In L.E. Davis, & J.C. Taylor (Eds.), *Design of jobs* (pp.328–356). Harmondsworth, UK: Penguin Books.

Engelstad, P.H. (1990). *The evolution of network strategies in action research supported socio-technical redesign programs in Scandinavia.* Oslo: Work Research Institutes. [Paper presented at the 1990 National Academy of Management Meeting, San Francisco, August 12–15.]

Engelstad, P.H., Emery, F.E., & Thorsrud, E. (1969). *The Hunsfos experiment.* Oslo: Work Research Institute.

Eyzenga, G.R. (1975). *Organisatie en systeem: Inleiding in het gebruik van de systeembenadering bij de analyse en de synthese van bedrijfskundige problemen.* Amsterdam: Agon Elsevier (Dutch language).

Foster, M. (1967). *Developing an analytical model for socio-technical analysis.* London: Tavistock Document No. HRC7 en HRC15.

Fruytier, B.G.M. (1994). *Organisatieverandering en het probleem van de baron van Münchhausen: Een systeemtheoretische analyse van de overgang van het*

Tayloristisch produktieconcept naar het nieuwe pro-duktieconcept. Delft: Eburon, proefschrift Katholieke Universiteit Nijmegen (Dutch language).

Groot, A.D. de (1980). *Methodologie: Grondslagen van onderzoek en denken in de gedragswetenschappen.* Den Haag: Mouton, 7e druk (1e druk 1961), (Dutch language).

Gustavsen, B. (1985). *Workplace reform and democratic dialogue: Economic and industrial democracy,* Vol. 6. London: Sage.

Gustavsen, B. (1989). *Creating broad change in working life, the LOM programme.* Toronto: Ontario Quality of Working Life Center.

Gustavsen, B., & Engelstad, P.H. (1986). The design of conferences and the evolving role of democratic dialogue in changing working life. *Human Relations, 39,* 101–116.

Gustavsen, B., & Hunnius, G. (1981). *New patterns of work reforms. The case of Norway.* Oslo: Norwegian University Press.

Haak, A.T. (1994). *Dutch sociotechnical design in practice: An empirical study of the concept of the whole taskgroup.* Assen: Van Gorcum, PhD thesis State University Groningen.

Have, K. ten (1993). *Markt, organisatie en personeel in de industrie: Een empirisch onderzoek naar produktieregimes als configuraties van arbeidsdeling en arbeidsrelaties.* Tilburg: Tilburg University Press, proefschrift Katholieke Universiteit Brabant (Dutch language).

Heming, B.H.J. (1992). *Kwaliteit van de arbeid, geautomatiseerd ...: Studie naar kwaliteit van arbeid en de relatie tussen automatisering, arbeid en organisatie.* Delft: Technische Universiteit, proefschrift (Dutch language).

Herbst, P.G. (1959). *Task structure and work relations.* London: Tavistock Document 528. Also in Herbst, P.G. (1974), *Sociotechnical design: Strategies in multidisciplinary research.* London: Tavistock Publications.

Herbst, P.G. (1976). *Alternatieves to hierarchies.* Leiden: Martinus Nijhoff.

Hertog, J.F. den (1988a). *Technologie, arbeid en organisatie in de industrie: Plan voor ontwerpgericht onderzoek.* Maastricht: MERIT (Dutch language).

Hertog, J.F. den (1988b). *Technologie en organisatie: Mythe en missie.* Maastricht, Rijksuniversiteit Limburg, oratie, juni (Dutch language).

Hertog, J.F. den, & Dankbaar, B. (1989). De sociotechniek bijgesteld. *Gedrag en Organisatie, 2,* (4/5), 269–287 (Dutch language).

Hertog, J.F. den, & Schröder, P. (1989). *Social research for technological change: Lessons from national programmes in Europe and North America.* Maastricht: University of Limburg, Maastricht Economic Research Institute on Innovation and Technology, MERIT 89-028.

Hill, C.P. (1971). *Towards a new philosophy of management.* London: Gower Press. [Also published in Kent, UK: Tonbridge, and in New York: Barnes & Noble.]

Hoevenaars, A.M. (1991). *Productie-structuur en organisatievernieuwing: De mogelijkheid tot paralleliseren nader onderzocht.* Eindhoven: Technische Universiteit, proefschrift (Dutch language).

Janse, F. (1989). *Werkplaats voor de nieuwe mens: Volvo sticht assemblage-kliniek aan het Karregat.* In CAD/CAM in Bedrijf, augustus, 26-30 (Dutch language).

Jenkins, D. (1975). *Job reform in Sweden.* Stockholm: Swedish Employers' Confederation SAF.

Jordan, N. (1963). Allocation of functions between man and machines in automated systems. *Journal of Applied Psychology, 47,* 161–165. [Also in L.E. Davis & J.C. Taylor (Eds.) (1979), *Design of jobs* (pp. 6–11). Santa Monica, CA: Goodyear.]

Katz, D., & Kahn, R.L. (1966). *The social psychology of organizations.* New York: Wiley.

Koopman-Iwema, A.M. (Ed.) (1986) *Automatiseren is reorganiseren: richtlijnen voor personeelsmanagement.* Deventer: Kluwer (Dutch language).

Kuipers, H. (1969). *Simulatie van de samenwerking tussen vissersschepen van de grote zeevisserij.* Leiden: NIPG/TNO (Dutch language).

Kuipers, H. (1980). *Van concurrentie naar samenwerking.* Leiden: Rijksuniversiteit, proefschrift (Dutch language).

Kuipers, H., & Amelsvoort, P.J. van (1990). *Slagvaardig organiseren: Een inleiding in de sociotechniek als integrale ontwerpleer.* Deventer: Kluwer (Dutch language).

Kuipers, H., & Bagchus, P.M. (1983). Bemanningsstructuren in de scheepvaart. *Mens en Onderneming, 37,* 228–251.

Landré, C.J.W. (1990). *Een methode voor het inrichten van de besturing van de produktie met behulp van sociotechnische principes: Van ontwerptheorie naar een concrete (her)ontwerpmethode.* Eindhoven/Den Bosch: Technische Universiteit, Faculteit Bedrijfskunde, vakgroep Technologie en Arbeid/NKWO-Koers (Dutch language).

Ligteringen, B.H. (1989). *Op weg naar betere dienstverlening: Kwaliteit van werk en organisatie in administratieve en informatieverwerkende organizaties.* Den Haag/Den Bosch: COB/SER 89-62/NKWO (Dutch language).

Lippit, R., & White, R.K. (1939). The "social" climate of children's groups. In R.G. Barker, J.S. Kounin, & H.F. Wright (Eds.) (1943), *Child behaviours and development.* London: McGraw-Hill.

Marek, J., Lange, K., & Engelstad, P.H. (1964). *Report I, industrial democracy project. The wire drawing mill of Christiania Spigerverk.* Trondheim: IFIM, Institute for Industrial Social Research.

Miller, E.J. (1959). Technology, territory and time: The internal differentiation of complex production systems. *Human Relations, 12,* 243–272. [Also in W.A. Pasmore, & J.J. Sherwood (Eds.) (1978),

Sociotechnical systems: A sourcebook (pp.96–119). La Jolla, CA: University Associates.]

Miller, E.J. (1975). Sociotechnical systems in weaving, 1953–1970: A follow-up study. *Human Relations, 28*, 349–386. [Also in W.A. Pasmore, & J.J. Sherwood (Eds.) (1978), *Sociotechnical systems: A sourcebook*. La Jolla, CA: University Associates.]

Naschold, F. (1992). *Evaluation report commissioned by the board of the LOM programme.* Stockholm: The Work Environment Fund.

Naschold, F. (1993). Organization development: National programmes in the context of international competition. In F. Naschold, R.E. Cole, B. Gustavsen, & H.J.J. van Beinum (Eds.), *Constructing the new industrial society* (pp.3–120). Stockholm/Assen: The Swedish Center for Working Life/Van Gorcum.

Nilakant, V., & Rao, V.R. (1976). Participative Design: The Hardwar experience. *National Labour Institute Bulletin, 2*, 277–287.

Pot, F.D., Christis, J., Fruytier, B.G.M., Kommers, H., Middendorp, J., Peeters, M.H.H., & Vaas, S. (1989a,b) [see Projectgroep Welzijn bij de Arbeid (WEBA).]

Projectgroep Welzijn bij de Arbeid (WEBA) (Pot, F.D. et al.) (1989a). Functieverbetering en Arbowet. *Gedrag en Organisatie, 2*, 361–382 (Dutch language).

Projectgroep Welzijn bij de Arbeid (WEBA) (Pot, F.D. et al.) (1989b). *Functieverbetering en organisatie van de Arbeid.* Voorburg: Ministerie SoZaWe, DGA/AI S71 (Dutch language).

Qvale, T.U. (1976). A Norwegian strategy for democratization of industry. *Human Relations, 29*, 453–469.

Rice, A.K. (1958). *Productivity and social organization: The Ahmedabad experiment.* London: Tavistock Publications.

Roberts, H.J.E. (1993). *Accountability and responsibility: The influence of organizational design on management accounting.* Maastricht (Netherlands): University of Limburg, University Press, PhD thesis.

Simonse, L.W.L., & Eijnatten, F.M. van (1993). *Sociotechnical product creation: An exploratory study concerning the improvement of the cooperation of professionals in the product creation process.* Eindhoven (Netherlands): University of Technology, Graduate School of Industrial Engineering and Management Science, BDK/T&A 015.

Sitter, L.U. de (1973). A system-theoretical paradigm of social interaction: Towards a new approach to qualitative system dynamics. *Annals of System Research, 3*, 109–140.

Sitter, L.U. de (1974a). Sociotechniek. *Mens en Onderneming, 28*, 65–83 (Dutch language).

Sitter, L.U. de (1978). *Kenmerken en funkties van de kwaliteit van de arbeid.* Eindhoven: Technische Universiteit, afdeling Bedrijfskunde. [Also in J.J.J. van Dijck, J.A.P. van Hoof, A.L. Mok, & W.F. de

Nijs (Red.) (1980), *Kwaliteit van de arbeid; een sociologische verkenning.* Leiden: Stenfert Kroese (Dutch language).]

Sitter, L.U. de (1980). *Produktie-organisatie en arbeidsorganisatie in sociaal-economisch perspectief: Kanttekeningen rondom het vraagstuk van de kwaliteit van de arbeid en organisatie.* Eindhoven: Technische Universiteit, Afdeling Bedrijfskunde, vakgroep Organisatie-sociologie, diktaat no. 1.160 (Dutch language).

Sitter, L.U. de (1981a). *Op weg naar nieuwe fabrieken en kantoren.* Deventer: Kluwer (Dutch language).

Sitter, L.U. de (1981b). *The functional significance of participation.* Eindhoven (Netherlands): University of Technology, Department of Industrial Engineering, internal report.

Sitter, L.U. de (1989a). *Integrale produktievernieuwing: Sociale en economische achtergronden van het TAO-programma.* Maastricht: MERIT (Dutch language).

Sitter, L.U. de (1989b). Moderne Sociotechniek. *Gedrag en Organisatie, 2*, 222–252 (Dutch language).

Sitter, L.U. de (1989c). *Kwaliteit van de arbeid: Uitgangspunten, gevolgen, meten, beoordelen.* Den Bosch: Adviesgroep Koers, intern rapport, januari (Dutch language).

Sitter, L.U. de (1993). A sociotechnical perspective. In F.M. van Eijnatten (Ed.), *The paradigm that changed the workplace* (pp.158–184). Assen: Van Gorcum.

Sitter, L.U. de (1994). *Synergetisch produceren. Human resources mobilisation in de produktie: Een inleiding in structuurbouw.* Assen: Van Gorcum (Dutch language).

Sitter, L.U. de, & Heij, P. (1975). Sociotechniek 6; een sociotechnische analyse van arbeidstaken. *Mens en Onderneming, 29*, 133–155 (Dutch language).

Sitter, L.U. de, Hertog, J.F. den, & Eijnatten, F.M. van (1990). *Simple organizations, complex jobs: The Dutch sociotechnical approach.* Paper presented at the Annual Conference of the American Academy of Management, San Francisco, 12–15 August.

Sitter, L.U. de, Vermeulen, A.A.M., Amelsvoort, P.J. van, Geffen, L. van, Troost, P., & Verschuur, F.O. (Groep Sociotechniek) (1986). *Het flexibele bedrijf: Integrale aanpak van flexibiliteit, beheersbaarheid, kwaliteit van de arbeid en produktie-automatisering.* Deventer: Kluwer (Dutch language).

Sol, E.J. (1990). *Holonic production systems: Systeemkeuze, opbouw en eigenschappen.* Eindhoven: Technische Universiteit, Faculteit Technische Bedrijfskunde, notitie (Dutch language).

Sommerhoff, G. (1950). *Analytical biology.* London: Oxford University Press.

Strien, P.J. van (1986). *Praktijk als wetenschap: Methodologie van het sociaal-wetenschappelijk handelen.* Assen: Van Gorcum (Dutch language).

Taylor, J.C. (1990). *Two decades of socio-technical systems in North America.* Los Angeles, CA: University of Southern California, Institute of Safety and Systems Management. [Paper presented at the 1990 National Academy of Management Meeting, San Francisco, 12–15 August.

Taylor, J.C., & Felten, D.F. (1993). *Performance by design: Sociotechnical systems in North America.* Englewood Cliffs, NJ: Prentice-Hall.

Thorsrud, E. (1972). *Workers' participation in management in Norway.* Geneva: Institute for Labour Studies.

Thorsrud, E., & Emery, F.E. (1964). *Industrial conflict and industrial democracy.* Paper presented at the Operational Research Society Conference, Cambridge, September. London: Tavistock Document T 358.

Tolman, E.C., & Brunswik, E. (1935). The organism and the causal texture of the environment. *Psychological Review, 42,* 43–77.

Trist, E.L. (1976). Toward a post-industrial culture. In R. Dublin (Ed.), *Handbook of work, organization and society* (pp.1011–1033). Chicago: Rand McNally.

Trist, E.L. (1977). Private communication to Fred Emery. In. F.E. Emery (Ed.) (1978), *The emergence of a new paradigm of work* (pp.5–10). Canberra: Australian National University, Center for Continuing Education.

Trist, E.L. (1981). *The evolution of socio-technical systems. A conceptual framework and an action research program.* Toronto: Ontario Quality of Working Life Centre. Also in A.H. van de Ven, & W.F. Joyce (Eds.) (1981), *Perspectives on organization design and behaviour* (pp.19–75). New York: Wiley.

Trist, E.L., & Bamforth, K.W. (1951). Some social and psychological consequences of the longwall method of coal-getting. *Human Relations, 4,* 3–38.

Trist, E.L., Higgin, G.W., Murray, H., & Pollock, A.B. (1963). *Organizational choice: Capabilities of groups at the coal face under changing technologies; the loss, rediscovery and transformation of a work tradition.* London: Tavistock Publications.

Vlist, R. van der (1970). *Verschillen in groepsprestaties in de Nederlandse zeevisserij.* Groningen: Wolters-Noordhoff, proefschrift Rijksuniversiteit Utrecht (Dutch language).

Walravens, A. (1977). *Veldexperimenten met industriële democratie.* Assen: Van Gorcum, proefschrift Technische Universiteit Twente (Dutch language).

Westerlund, G. (1952). *Group leadership: A field experiment.* Stockholm: Nordisk Rotogravyre.

Zwaan, A.H. van der (1973). Een kritische evaluatie van het socio-technisch systeemonderzoek. In P.J.D. Drenth, P.J. Willems, & Ch.J. de Wolff (Eds.), *Arbeids-en Organisatiepsychologie.* Deventer: Kluwer (Dutch language).

Zwaan, A.H. van der (1975). The sociotechnical systems approach; a critical evaluation. *International Journal of Production Research, 13,* 149–163.

5

Interorganizational Networks

Maarten R. Van Gils

1 INTRODUCTION

In the Netherlands at the end of the 1970s and in the early 1980s, a growing interest in the field of interorganizational relations and networks began to develop. This interest manifested itself in a stream of publications (Breuer, 1978, 1982; Edelman Bos, 1980; Van Gils, 1978; Godfroy, 1991; Hartman, 1980, 1982; Luscuere, 1978; Wassenberg, 1980). In 1982, the *Handbook of Labour and Organizational Psychology* published a summary of the status of the field at that time (Van Gils, 1982), and highlighted a number of topics which were then of particular interest in the Netherlands.

At that time, interorganizational analysis was mostly approached by means of a four-dimensional classification of the environment and of the way in which organizations in that environment functioned and interacted with each other (Van de Ven, Emmett, & Koenig, 1974). Distinctions were made between:

1. The environment as an external constraining phenomenon, within which the organization has to function. This perspective has been further elaborated by the contingency approach in particular (Burns & Stalker, 1961; Lawrence & Lorsch, 1967). The main

aspects are: (a) the characteristics of the environment; (b) the effects that it has on the structure of the organization; and (c) the strategies and tactics used by organizations to influence the environment.

2. The environment as a set of interacting organizations (Evan, 1976), also called a network of interactions or of interorganizational relations. The emphasis in this is on the exchange relations between organizations with the aim of realizing objectives.

Dimensions have been developed to compare the nature of the interactions and exchange relations of the organizations within a network. The following dimensions can be distinguished:

a. Homogeneity: The functional and structural similarity of organizations;
b. Domain consensus: The extent to which the objectives of an organization are disputed, compatible or commensurable;
c. Stability: The stability of the network of relations in terms of turnover and new members;
d. The distribution of resources: The quantity and kind of resources that organizations have at their disposal, as

well as the quantity and kind of resources that other organizations need. Central to this is the power balance between organizations;

e. Participation in multiple networks: The number of actors that represent a multitude of organizations.

In addition to the relational characteristics of the interorganizational network, interorganizational analysis also involves research into the way in which the interaction between organizations is coordinated. The key variables for this coordination are (a) formalization; (b) intensity; (c) reciprocity; and (d) standardization.

3. The environment as a social system. The focal point of view here is the behaviour in and between sets of organizations that function as social systems. The characteristics of the set of interacting organizations are a point of departure for analysis.

4. Van de Ven et al. (1974) have added a fourth dimension to the three listed earlier, oriented towards a further elaboration of the aforementioned third dimension: interorganizational collectivity. In interorganizational collectivity two or more organizations combine their forces in order to achieve specific goals. Interorganizational collectivity can act as a unity and take decisions designed to realize the objectives and goals of the collectivity. If these organizations decide to transfer or delegate responsibilities to a joint body the word "network organization" is often used. Godfroy (1991) defines a network organization as "a structural provision that with a limited independence can act in the name of the whole network".

For a long time, the literature on interorganizational relations and interorganizational networks has been dominated by the social sciences. It is remarkable that in the Netherlands the focus has long been primarily oriented towards the non-profit-making and public sectors, exceptions notwithstanding (Wassenberg, 1980). Interest in interorganizational analysis on the part of the industrial sector has been somewhat neglected, and it has not been an important object of study in economics either. Spencer (1992) points out that the reason for this lack of interest on the part of the economic sciences in industrial networks might lie in the dominance of the traditional market model, where markets are viewed as atomized, composed of homogeneous, independent and easily replaceable actors, who are controlled by the price mechanism.

In the second half of the 1980s, interest in interorganizational questions revived, with the emphasis on interfirm networking in particular. An important reason for this renewed interest lies in changes in the industrial structures under the influence of (a) technological developments; (b) internationalization of markets; and (c) the increasing speed with which (technological) innovations have followed on from each other (Huyzer et al., 1990).

Van der Zwan (1989, p.1177) mentions three important factors, which, as a result of these developments, have led to strategic cooperation between organizations:

1. to obtain an entrée into markets that have entrance restrictions;
2. the obtaining of important knowledge that a partner can supply;
3. agreements about the commercialization of the technology in order to reduce the risks and the high costs of the development of new products, as well as increasing the possibilities of making flexible use of new technologies.

The development of strategic forms of cooperation between organizations under circumstances of uncertainty has a high priority owing to the vital importance of these three factors. Obviously, existing forms of organization are not considered adequate to answer the necessity of having to go along with these new developments, and to acquire and to develop the necessary knowledge for this process, and thus reach a more developed state.

Reed and Hughes (1992) also point to the importance of new forms of organization and talk about the transfer of the rational-bureaucratic model, with its universal principles, to networks with a larger spectrum of structural options. The question they ask is whether this involves a fundamental transformation, or the further development of old, already fixed, organizational forms into a more advanced state.

Organizations confronted with developments caused by the availability of new technologies, the internationalization of markets, and changing demands and requirements see themselves as obliged to develop new structures that can take advantage of the new opportunities.

Mayntz (1991, p.4) is quite outspoken about these developments, when she speaks about "the ascendence of networks" and states that "the structure of the economy may in fact have become increasingly network-like", by which she means the interactive relations between enterprises.

The concept of strategic cooperation implies mutual relations between organizations, which can be complementary as well as competitive, and are experienced as a viable pattern of organization. Strategic cooperation manifests itself in organizational forms such as joint ventures, comakership (the collaboration between the contracting body and the supplier), minority participation in other organizations, cooperation in specific areas such as distribution, R&D, marketing, etc. As a result of their strategic character, these developments have received a lot of attention from the press. Examples of these are:

- Cap Volmac, a consultancy firm operating in the field of information technology, starts joint ventures with its clients in order to develop solutions. In these ventures Cap Volmac is a risk-bearing shareholder, which implies that the company has become a risk-bearing entrepreneur instead of an executor of assignments given by others.
- British Telecom pays $4.3 billion for an interest in MCI Communications. In addition, the two concerns have founded a joint venture with a capital of $1 billion for the transfer of speech and data on behalf of international companies (*Het Financieele Dagblad*, 4 June 1993).
- Dasa is holding talks with the Spanish CASA

about collaboration with regard to participation in an European consortium for regional airplanes (*Het Financieele Dagblad*, 3 June 1993).

- The alliance between KLM and Northwest Airlines, and the failed alliances between KLM and British Airways, and KLM, SAS, Swiss Airlines, and Austrian Airlines.

Alliances are often founded for offensive purposes; offensive in the sense of increasing market share, penetrating new markets that might require cooperation with other organizations, and investment in expensive new technology. The interest that Krupp has taken in Hoesch is an example of a defensive alliance. Here, cooperation is deliberately used to keep foreign competitors at bay and to prevent hostile takeovers.

New concepts such as technology networks (Mulder, 1992; Pennings, 1992), industrial networks (Spencer, 1992), and industrial marketing networks, characterize specific areas of application such as distribution, product innovation, and product development. Reasons for participation in these networks can be risk-sharing, and thus a reduction in uncertainty, cost reduction, an increase in control over the environment (offensive and defensive), the complexity of developments that require high investments and risks, etc.

This chapter will focus on coordination between organizations, as the most important developments are taking place in this area. Before this theme is developed, section 2 will elaborate the concepts of interorganizational relations and interorganizational networks. Section 3 will pay attention to a number of dominant theories that are applied to interorganizational analysis. The following points will be briefly discussed:

a. the ecological model;
b. the dependence model;
c. the institutional model;
d. the transaction-cost model.

After this theoretical review, section 4 will discuss designs of and conditions for strategic interorganizational cooperation, focusing on joint ventures, which are sometimes labelled "hybrid organizations".

2 INTERORGANIZATIONAL RELATIONS AND INTERORGANIZATIONAL NETWORKS

Interorganizational relations can be described as the relations among, and the ensuing interactions of, the focal organization, or a population of organizations, with other organizations in their environment, such as suppliers, buyers, unions, and banks. Evan (1976) uses the concept of "organization set" here. Evan uses a systems perspective. A distinction is drawn between a population of organizations that take care of the input for an organization and a population of organizations that receive goods and/or services. In both cases this can generate feedback processes. In both the input and the output processes, factors such as power and dependency play an important role. It is important, therefore, to analyze which of the variables create power and dependency, and how organizations deal with these dependencies, as well as the structural aspects of the interaction processes (Aldrich, 1979).

An interorganizational network also consists of legally independent, autonomous, interdependent organizations, with converging, but also diverging, interests and characteristics, which are connected with each other through interactive, reciprocal exchange relations. Here, however, the object of analysis is not so much the behaviour of individual organizations but the network itself. The network is therefore a system that is more than the individual characteristics of the constituting elements, and its attributes should be studied as phenomena in themselves (Berkowitz, 1982).

The attention paid by the social sciences to the network concept increased in the 1970s. Berkowitz points out that the majority of social scientists in and before that time made use of concepts such as input, output, feedback, system, and boundary, which were borrowed from cybernetics and information theory and were applied to socio-cultural systems. Gradually, interest in network processes has grown, as well as the underlying notion that a system is more than the sum of its parts.

Benson (1978, p.71) also focuses on the importance of treating networks as a developing phenomenon requiring an analytical framework

that is attuned to it. Aldrich (1979, p.281) emphasizes that a network is not a "corporate body" and therefore cannot act as an organization. According to Aldrich, the assumption with network analysis is that networks can restrain as well as foster the activities of an organization that can be identified at the aggregate level.

Mayntz (1991, p.10) describes a network as a structure with several nodal points, each of which consists of loosely coupled parts. She sees the rise of interorganizational networks as a qualitatively distinguished social structure characterized by a combination of elements belonging to two basic governance forms; on the one hand—characteristic of markets—a multitude of autonomous actors, and, on the other hand, the capability—characteristic of hierarchies—of selecting goals on the basis of coordinated action.

In this description the interorganizational network is a synthesis of the dialectical process between two extremes: market and hierarchy; on the basis of interaction and in spite of the divergent interests of the participants, it is capable of producing intentional collective outcomes.

Mayntz describes the dominant logic of interorganizational networks from this point of view as negotiation, which presumes a willingness to compromise on an intentional and voluntary basis. This involves taking the objectives and the interests of the interaction partner into consideration.

The importance of negotiation is also emphasised by Mulder (1992). Mulder focuses on one particular interorganizational network, namely the technology network. His premise is that economic theories cannot explain the differences in the outcomes of choices that organizations make with regard to technology. The technology network is defined in this study as the set of relations that are useful for the objective of the development, maintenance and application of new technology. His definition of the concept of relation is very important for this. A relation exists between individuals or groups with regard to the development of a technology if they have reached agreement about the roles each is willing to fulfil in relation to their own technology. This is based on the principle that all relations, and in particular the agreement about the roles to be fulfilled, are renegotiable in the course of time.

This renegotiation might involve the introduction of new partners into the network, but also the renegotiation of mutual roles and agreement about it. The presupposition in network analysis, therefore, is that interorganizational networks can facilitate as well as restrain the activities of the organizations that are a part of them: activities that can be identified at the level of the network. This involves two supplementary meanings being added to the concept of a network: networks as a stream of exchange relations, and networks that function as negotiating systems.

The interdependencies between the actors in the network can be labelled as symbiotic and competitive (Aldrich, 1979; Van der Zwaan, 1990). Symbiotic interdependence implies reciprocal dependence between heterogeneous organizations that are complementary to each other. Competitive interdependence concerns homogeneous organizations that compete with each other for scarce resources. Van der Zwaan (1990) discusses a regional healthcare network, which is trying to coordinate the activities of the front line care organizations, general hospitals, and mental health organizations, as an example of symbiotic interdependence. It is a structure which intends to conduct concerted decision-making but which involves both cooperation and negotiation. Negotiation is more likely to be expected when the decision-making process deals with the distribution of scarce resources or with questions of identity.

Interorganizational networks characterized by symbiotic interdependence can be based on forms of cooperation that can vary in intensity, degree of formalization and reciprocity. The stronger the need for the coordination of activities, the more likely it is that the stronger parties in the network will opt for a tight structure. Some general forms of coordination are:

1. adjustment of behaviour;
2. incidental cooperation;
3. formalized cooperation on the basis of procedures;
4. the creation of coalitions or federal alliances;
5. the founding of intermediary organizations (often labelled as network organizations);
6. merger.

The autonomy of the participating organizations, or their view of that autonomy, will diminish as the cooperation intensifies.

The intermediary organization as a form of cooperation can be characterized as a structural provenance that can act with limited responsibility in the name of the whole network (Godfroy, 1991). Lammers (1988) describes intermediary organizations as a type of organization "that is designed and maintained by one or more organizational mandataries to interlink (sets of) organizations". According to Lammers, intermediary organizations can have a representative function that is mandated from the bottom up, but can also be created as a control function mandated by a higher organ (i.e. the government). Examples of network or intermediary organizations can be found in many sectors of society, such as the health and welfare sectors, employers' federations, trade unions, the Association of Dutch Universities, etc. These intermediary organizations often play the role of linchpin between their constituents and the government.

A merger is the most far-reaching form of collaboration. In fact, the organizations legally dissolve themselves in order to form a new organization with its own judicial structure. Network or intermediary organizations can sometimes be founded for temporal objectives, as well as for an indeterminate time, in order to fulfil functions for affiliated organizations.

3 THEORETICAL DIRECTIONS

The increased interest in interorganizational relations and interorganizational networks in organization theory is also a reaction to the dominant structural-functionalist contingency models in organization studies, in which changes in an organization are the result of environmental factors or of strategic choices (Sandelands & Drazin, 1989).

The contingency perspective addresses itself to:

● the situational aspects of the organization–environment interface;

- the design and the functioning of the organization in relation to the specific interface configuration with the environment;
- the strategies that organizations can use to influence that environment, in order to create certainty and unequivocalness over that environment (Van de Ven et al., 1974).

The environment is characterized in abstract terms such as hostile/friendly; homogeneous/heterogeneous; dynamic/stable; permissive/inaccessible, and the characteristics of these environmental factors are input for the design of the organization. In contingency theory, the process aspect with regard to the question of how environments influence organizations and how organizations cope with environmental constraints is neglected.

With the growing interest in the problems of interorganizational relations and interorganizational networks, the relational characteristics between organizations have gradually become increasingly recognized, with the result that the environment, as an interorganizational field of organizations, has become an object for analysis. The focus was initially on the relations and the related processes between a focal organization and other organizations ("organization set"), but has gradually shifted towards the interorganizational interdependencies between organizations in a specific population of organizations.

A number of theoretical perspectives have paid attention to the phenomenon of interorganizational relations and networks. The most dominant are:

1. The ecological model. The "population-ecology" model is based on the premise that changes in a population of organizations can be partly explained by the selection processes that operate on organizations, enforced by the internal and external constraints on the adaptability of organizations.
2. The dependence model. The "resource dependence" model also focuses on the external constraints on organizations, but its major emphasis is on the internal organizational-political decision-making processes, and the way in which organizations manage the processes of adjustment to the environment.

3. The institutional model. In this model the environment is conceptualized as a set of rules and regulations which organizations or a set of organizations have to follow or to satisfy in order to get external support and legitimation.
4. The transaction-costs economics model. In this model the emphasis is on the way in which transactions can be controlled in a continuum with hierarchies at one end and markets at the other.

The first two perspectives are based on what Pfeffer calls "external control of organization behavior" (Pfeffer, 1982). The basic premise here is that organizations strive to adjust to their environments. To comprehend and explain the behaviour of organizations, it is not only necessary but probably also sufficient to only take the characteristics and the restraints of the environment into account. The third perspective has its origins in sociology and accentuates the explicit or implicit rules and regulations which the organization has to satisfy in order to gain external legitimacy and support. Pfeffer puts the last perspective among the "theories of organizational-level rational action" and it is considered to be an economic theory of organization. From this perspective, organizations are seen as rational and prospective actors with the aim of realizing collective goals.

Distinctions are not drawn between interorganizational relations and interorganizational networks in the further elaboration of these theoretical models.

3.1   The ecological model

Since the 1970s, the "population-ecology model" in interorganizational relations has attracted much interest. The model was developed from the theory of natural selection in biology. Organizations can flourish or perish under certain environmental conditions. An ecological approach, therefore, implies a search for the conditions under which this can happen.

In organization theory, the ecological model is also a reaction to more traditional approaches, in which the social relations within an organization are the central point of view. The ecological model puts the emphasis on the relations between organizations. Organizations are clustered in populations which share a common fate with regard to the resources that define "niches" in the market. A niche consists of a combination of resources and constraints yet to be distinguished that are sufficient to support a specific type of organization (Astley, 1984, p.529).

Organizations within a common environment compete with each other and have a relationship of competitive interdependence with each other. This "win–lose" situation can be turned into a "win–win" situation. All the interdependencies together have an influence on the survival or failure of organizations and result in a division of organizational forms adapted to the specific environmental configuration (Aldrich, 1992).

Organizational change is explained on the basis of the analysis of the characteristics and the distribution of the resources of organizations. From this point of view, the behaviour of organizations is externally controlled and restrained. The ecological model focuses on the explanation of processes that manifest themselves in a population of organizations and are the determining factors for changes within organizations.

According to this model, change is achieved on the basis of three stages: (1) variation, (2) natural selection, and (3) retention (Aldrich, 1979).

1. Variation. Over the course of time, planned and unplanned, systematic, and random variations manifest themselves within and among a population of organizations. These can be variations in organizational form (bureaucratic/non-bureaucratic, capital intensive/labour intensive), in performance levels, in products and services that organizations supply, in the configuration of the network as a result of the entry of new organizations within the same population, etc.

2. Selection. In the second phase a differential selection takes place, which eliminates certain non-viable variations. The importance of selection is derived from the fact that there are internal and external restraints on the adaptability of organizations. The internal restraints can be the result of an internal power struggle, tradition, etc. The

external restraints can be related to "sunk costs", the costs that have already been made and cannot be recouped, the availability of information, or questions of legitimacy that can limit the flexibility of an organization. Organizations that cannot adjust themselves to environmental characteristics cannot survive, whereas others that cannot or will not satisfy those requirements, will fail (Pfeffer, 1982; Perrow, 1986).

3. Retention. A selection of variations takes place; the remaining variations are anchored in the organization, which makes it possible for certain behaviour to be continued. The change process in the ecological model characterizes itself by "punctuated disequilibrium" situations, periods of stability in populations of organizations are disturbed by short outbursts of innovation and creativity. In such a period new organizations enter the network and those organizations that cannot adapt themselves to the developments are pushed out.

Aldrich (1992, p.19) points out that not only are the internal decision-making processes in the ecological approach neglected, but also the individual in the organization, and in addition that relatively little attention is paid to the microprocesses that connect an organization with the environment, and in which individual actors with their interpretations occupy a central place.

Of the total number of articles on interorganizational relations published in the *Administrative Science Quarterly* from 1988 on, the majority are based on the system characteristics of the population-ecology model. Miner, Amburgey, and Stearns (1990) investigated a population of a thousand Finnish newspapers over a period of 200 years. The research is based on two central questions:

1. Is there evidence for the existence of interorganizational relations that function as a buffer and therefore protect the organization from environmental disturbances?

2   What is the effect of interorganizational relations on the success or the failure of internal organizational changes in periods of external turbulence?

The research results support the prediction that interorganizational linkages (for instance, with external shareholders) function as buffer organizations protecting organizations against failure, and also contribute to an increase in the attention paid to internal organizational change, even in periods of relative stability. The discovery that the presence of interorganizational relations increases rather than reduces the chances of failure in internal organizational processes is striking.

Other examples of interorganizational research based on the ecological model are Oliver (1988), Levinthal (1991), Ranger-Moore and Banaszak-Holl (1991).

3.2   The resource-dependence model

The dependence model is also based on the premise of external constraints, but emphasizes the importance of political-economic forces in a interorganizational network or in interorganizational relations. In order to survive, organizations need scarce resources from the environment in which it conducts transactions.

The two forms of interdependence already mentioned—symbiotic or co-operative interdependence and competitive interdependence—play an important role in this model. Symbiotic interdependence is based on reciprocal dependence between organizations that are in principle unequal, and that in respect to each other possess similar scarce resources. An example of symbiotic interdependence is co-makership, the long-standing cooperation between the contractor and a limited number of suppliers on the basis of mutual professional trust. Broersma (1991) lists the following advantages of this organizational form of symbiotic interdependency:

1. the acquisition of technology that an organization cannot develop either fast enough or in an economically accountable way by itself;
2. the securing of entry into markets and distribution channels where the cost price for the coalition is lower;
3. a decrease in commercial risks with respect to competitors;
4. the attainment of economies of scale in production.

Competitive interdependence concerns similar organizations that compete with each other in, for instance, industrial or consumer markets. The interorganizational analysis focuses on the nature of the dependencies of one organization or an interorganizational network. The dependencies can be related to the availability of scarce resources such as finance, authority, legitimacy, and information (Benson, 1978; Pfeffer, 1982).

Pfeffer summarizes the dependence model as follows:

1. Organizations are the fundamental units for comprehending both interorganizational relations and society.
2. These organizations are not autonomous, but are instead constrained by a network of interdependencies with other organizations.
3. Interdependence, linked to uncertainty about the behaviour of others, leads to a situation in which survival and continued success are uncertain.
4. Organizations try to control external dependencies, although these controlling acts can never be fully successful and in themselves again lead to new patterns of dependence and interdependence.
5. These patterns of dependence produce both inter- as well as intra-organizational power, which has its effect on the behaviour of the organization.

Benson (1978) has elaborated certain aspects of the dependence model by concentrating on those factors that contribute to the equilibrium in the interorganizational network. He distinguishes four dimensions:

1. Domain consensus: The agreement between participants in the organizations involved concerning their roles and the domain involved.
2. Ideological consensus: The agreement about task characteristics and the ways to deal with the tasks;
3. Positive evaluation: The positive judgment of the employees of the organizations involved about the value and significance of the work done in the other organizations.
4. Coordination of activities: Patterns of cooperation and coordination between organizations. Work is coordinated as the

programmes and activities in two or more organizations are increasingly attuned to each other with maximum effectiveness and efficiency.

Benson has so far focused on the balance within the network, which can be influenced by one or more of the above-mentioned factors. A second aspect that Benson pays attention to is the influence of the environment on the network. This environment is important if it influences scarce resources such as money and authority, as well as the division of power in the network. Important dimensions for this are the concentration/dispersal of scarce resources that are at the disposal of the network, and are in the hands of a few or many participants in the network; power concentration/dispersal in the environment of the network; network autonomy/dependence; the amount of control that forces in the environment have over the network and the question of what constitutes these forces (i.e. trade unions, consumer organizations, government offices, etc.); the scarcity/abundance of sources that the environment has available; the control mechanisms that the environment can use in relation to the network (sanctions, stimulative measures on behalf of the network).

Benson distinguishes four strategies that can be used by actors within the network, or by actors outside the network, with the aim of bringing about changes in the network:

1. Cooperative strategies. The actors can coordinate their actions by agreement and compromise. This presupposes that there is not much of a power gulf between the actors.
2. Disruptive strategies. Undermining one or more actors in the network, for example by influencing money streams, or by not complying with agreements.
3. Manipulative strategies. The conscious changing of conditions and structures that can lead to the requirement of scarce resources.
4. Authority strategies. Organizations that occupy a dominant position (on the basis of money and/or authority) in the network.

Walton (1972), in his treatise on interorgan-izational decision-making and identity conflict, agrees with Benson's aforementioned dimensions and strategic options. With regard to interorganizational interaction, Walton differentiates between the instrumental and the expressive significance that interaction can have for actors.

Instrumental interests are, for instance, expressed by the professional involvement of the various actors in the objectives, strategies, and policies of the organization, as well as by the kind of control instruments and the responsibilities involved. Instrumental interests between actors can be compatible or incompatible. The amount of incompatibility between the the instrumental stakes influences the character of the decision-making process, for instance, problem-solving versus negotiation. Expressive interests are closely related to the question of identity, and therefore with the creating of significance and meaning: what kind of organization are we, what do we stand for, what unites us, and what makes us unique? Expressive interests characterize themselves by their emotional values and influence the way in which other organizations and the way they operate are regarded. Expressive interests can be compatible or incompatible. Compatibility implies mutual reinforcement; incompatability can lead to conflicts of identity. The amount of complementariness between instrumental and expressive interests and preferences substantially influences the ways in which processes of interorganizational decision-making take shape.

Attention to expressive interests and their related processes is what particularly distinguishes the work of Walton from the work of other authors who make use of the dependence model. Expressive interests with regard to emotions are not in themselves new, but their significance has been underexposed in studies about interorganizational relations, probably due to the dominance of research into decision-making based on the "tradition" of bounded rationality (March & Simon, 1958). In bounded rationality, the emphasis lies primarily on instrumental rationality as the organizing principle and thus neglects or marginalizes expressive factors.

A practical example

In the Netherlands, the restructuring of the intermediate organizations ("umbrella organizations") in the welfare and front-line health sector is an example of a process of interorganizational decision-making. A hundred government-subsidized autonomous organizations were involved in this process. These organizations fulfil a function between the government and the operational organizations. Each umbrella organization is related to a specific activity, for example, care of the disabled, the elderly, social work, juvenile work, family care, adult education, etc. In many of these fields the umbrella organizations were created along denominational lines, i.e. Roman Catholic, Protestant, or neutral. There was considerable overlap in the tasks and functions fulfilled by the organizations involved in the key activities. Co-ordination among the various umbrella organizations hardly existed and was difficult to implement. Many of these umbrella organizations were members of the National Council for Social Welfare, a super-umbrella organization for its members, and had close relations with the various Dutch political parties. Both the super-organization and its member organizations exercised great influence on the government bodies related to these different fields. This tangle of intermediary organizations, various political parties, and government departments is described by Van Doorn (1978) as an "iron band around the government".

The increasing threat of restructuring put the two major scarce resources of these intermediate organizations, money and legitimacy, under pressure. The main threat was that the umbrella organizations would lose control over these resources as a result of the restructuring of their tasks, which was of course perceived by them as inadmissible. The first effect was already noticeable: the power base of the National Council for Social Welfare was diminishing rapidly. As its legitimacy eroded, the super-organization was no longer able to satisfy the divergent interests of its members; in the eyes of the political parties, it had become too powerful.

The process of the restructuring of the intermediary organizations was fought tooth and nail. Each organization tried to keep itself outside the process by all the means at its disposal. The consequences for the Department of Social Welfare and Health Care in this process were far-

reaching. Many of the civil servants working there had a one-to-one relationship with an intermediary organization. The relationship between an intermediary organization and civil servants in the ministry can be characterized as one of mutual dependency. For the civil servants, this relationship was a legitimation of their work, as well as a position of power because of their knowledge of the decision-making processes within the Department, and because of their influence on those decision-making processes. For the intermediary organization, the relationship with civil servants gave them access to the decision-making processes, as well as the reassuring thought that the continued survival of the organizations was important to the civil servants too.

The political parties, who strongly supported the process of restructuring, also contributed to the chaotic situation. On the one hand, there was a strong feeling that restructuring was necessary, but on the other hand they were under great pressure from the intermediary organizations with their well-organized lobbies and representatives in parliament. Instrumental stakes and expressive interests both played an important role in the whole process.

The expressive nature of these interests was conveyed by underlining the fact that it was important not to affect the identity of the various work sorts. The instrumental interests were revealed with regard to the material interests necessary to fulfil the various service functions that organizations had built up over time. The model for restructuring these social-welfare organizations took approximately 15 years.

Walton's model can be used in relation to concerted decision-making between organizations to locate the key factors that foster or frustrate those processes.

3.3   The institutional model

Just as the dependency model puts the emphasis on the importance of scarce resources to explain interorganizational transactions, the institutional model emphasizes other environmental variables, in particular the existence of institutions. Institutions are described by Baum and Oliver (1991, p.187) as government and community organizations (i.e. churches, public, private, and religious schools, professional associations, etc.) in the task environment of an organization with an indisputable social acceptance.

The process of institutionalization implies that organizations will conform to an institutionalized pattern in their structures and values, as a consequence of, for instance, political pressure and social expectations with regard to their behavioural patterns. Organizations not only compete for scarce resources, but also for legitimacy, political power, and social acceptance.

From a theoretical point of view, the process of institutionalization means relinquishing the idea that an organization can be considered as an actor acting in a rational way (Pfeffer, 1982). Institutionalization is rooted in conformity. Conformist behaviour often arises through an acceptance of external rules and expectations with regard to the way in which it functions (Meyer & Rowan, 1977). The displacement of the goals can be a consequence of this, which implies that the goals of an organization are not so much derived from its own mission, but are a reflection of what the shareholders controlling the scarce resources consider desirable. Organizations change their structures and processes to conform to an institutionalized pattern and thus acquire support and legitimacy.

Just as the dependence model of the "rational actor" takes as its point of departure the adjustment in a strategic sense to the characteristics of the environment, the institutional approach implies that the organization incorporates the characteristics of its task environment. Given the institutional pressure on organizations to conform to the specific requirements of regulations, values, and norms, which cannot be ignored, this means that organizations in a specific population will conform more and more to institutional pressure, which in itself enlarges the power of these institutions. The process of adaptation and conformity to institutional pressure results in organizations in a specific population beginning to resemble each other (isomorphism). This tendency towards isomorphism was strongly present in the above-mentioned intermediate organizations in the welfare and front-line health sector. Such populations characterize themselves by a high level of interaction between the organizations with

the objective of obtaining countervailing power. This power can also be obtained by creating alliances with established institutions, showing behaviour that is in line with their expectations and in that way safeguarding scarce resources and thus increasing their own chances of survival.

Selznick (1965), in his study of the Tennesee Valley (TVA), gives a famous example of an institutional approach. This programme from the end of the 1930s was unique in the United States: an economic aid programme modelled on socialist principles, with the doctrine of involvement and control coming from within society itself. Gradually the TVA-organization was taken over by local organizations and politicians, who placed their own representatives in key positions in the TVA-organization. This enabled them to control the policies. The takeover was legitimized by the doctrine that cooptation was desirable and therefore necessary.

Baum and Oliver (1991) investigated the effects of institutional linkages on the failure of child care service organizations in Toronto during the period 1971–1978. Institutional linkage is defined by the authors as "a direct and regularized relationship between an organization and an institution in the organization environment". The research showed that institutional relations played an important role in increasing the survival chances of the organization through greater access to scarce resources, more stability, legitimacy, and social support.

Another example of research from this theoretical perspective, in which use is also made of the dependence model, is given by Fennell, Ross, and Warnecke (1987). The study dealt with the support programmes of the National Cancer Institute in the United States. This institute financially supports experiments, evaluations, and demonstrations of new knowledge, and technologies and methods that can contribute to a decrease in the effects of cancer. So-called "network programmes" were created, which linked hospitals that specialized in cancer with other hospitals, clinics, and doctors with the aim of improving the quality of the fight against specific kinds of cancer in a geographical area.

From this institutional perspective, in which the importance of non-market-oriented scarce resources is central, it was postulated that this would result in an increase in the density of the network and a higher homogeneity between the organizations in that network. It was hypothesized that the organizations would look increasingly similar as a result of their efforts to adapt themselves more to the environment. Although not all the hypotheses were confirmed, the importance of non-economic, non-market factors for explaining interorganizational relations could be demonstrated, and thus the significance of the institutional theory.

3.4   The transaction-cost model

The transaction-cost model occupies an important place in economic theories of organization. The crux of the theory is a manner of organization by which economic transactions can be steered. Williamson (1975, 1985), who built upon the work of the economist Coase, is the originator of this theory. The essence of his model is that two important organizational forms, namely market and hierarchy (organizations), are alternative possibilities for coordinating transactions that are part of an exchange process. By this he means an answer can be found to the question of how the changeover in the 20th century from a quantity of small enterprises (market) to a limited number of large enterprises (hierarchy) can have taken place.

The theory is important for the discussion of interorganizational networks, as these are often placed in the middle of the continuum market–hierarchy, and are seen as an intermediate form of organization that embraces not only elements of the market but also of the hierarchy.

A market involves parties that are more or less equal, that are complementary to each other, and where the transactions among parties are characterized by their non-repetitive nature and do not require transaction specific investments. Coordination by the market also has disadvantages. For instance:

- Uncertainty. Changes in the environment that the entrepreneur either cannot control or are difficult to foresee can occur.
- Repeat transactions. Long-term contracts with clients or suppliers render the entrepreneur vulnerable. The breaking-up of the relationship can be expensive.
- Limited rationality. Information is limited as not everything can be taken into account. This can lead to opportunistic behaviour on the part of some of those involved.

As an organizational form for realizing coordination, the hierarchy manifests itself when (a) efficiency is important; (b) transaction-specific investments in terms of time, energy, and money cannot easily be transferred to others; and (c) certainty about the outcome of transactions is important. In other words, the hierarchy is an organizational form that absorbs the imperfections of the market in terms of uncertainty, opportunistic behaviour, and limited rationality. Not only can transactions be transferred from the market to the hierarchy, but also the significance of the hierarchy can be diminished by making more use of coordination through the market.

Williamson's first studies, when he based his theory on the developments in the United States, also take as a point of departure a market–hierarchy continuum, and he suggests that the market is the origin of elementary forms of economic exchange and that the hierarchy as organizational form embodies the evolutionary omega of economic developments. This implies, however, that the meaning of hierarchy as structure exists only because it is constituted after the event.

Perrow (1986, p.236) accentuates this by stating that "transaction-costs economics is an efficiency argument for the present state of affairs, as most mainstream economic theories are". Perrow refers here to Williamson's arguments that the presence of giant organizations in certain branches of industry offers the most efficient manner to produce goods in an industrial society.

With the increasing interest in interorganizational networks, the question of how these can be fitted in the market–hierarchy continuum can be raised.

Van der Zwaan (1990) places interorganizational networks, which he also calls structured markets, in the middle of the market–hierarchy continuum. The poles are characterized by strong bonding towards the hierarchy and by structurelessness towards the market.

Astley and Brahm (1989) follow this intermediate positioning of interorganizational networks and emphasize that its increased significance has to be seen as a structural answer to the need for intermediary forms of coordination between market and hierarchy—intermediary in the sense that they will deal with the exchange of scarce resources between organizations, as well as market relations.

The importance of this interorganizational coordination, also labelled a hybrid form of coordination, can, according to the authors, be ascribed to three developments:

1. the increased significance of high technology in the economy;
2. the acceleration in technological developments and their organizational consequences, such as shorter product life cycles;
3. the increased technological interdependence between organizations (blurring of boundaries), which requires, for instance, flexibility, exchange of scarce resources, sharing of risks, and which at the same time places high demands upon coordination of cooperation among organizations.

This concept of interorganizational network is notable because of the paradox of the two poles of market and hierarchy, both of which are needed in order to solve the question of coordination in an acceptable way. On the one hand, there is the need for flexibility, which might make it necessary for organizations to contract out activities which could be done by partners with whom forms of long term cooperation could be established. On the other hand, there is a greater need for the integration and coordination of activities in interdependent markets, industries, and countries, which requires the management of exchange relations based on organizational forms that enhance and stabilize these relations.

Mayntz (1991) and Powell (1990) disagree with the view that networks are a "half-way post" between market and hierarchy. Mayntz considers networks to be a qualitatively distinguishable type of social structure that is characterized by a combination of two basic governance forms. These are, on the one hand, a multitude of autonomous units (markets) and, on the other hand, the ability to give shape to the chosen objectives and goals by means of concerted action (hierarchy). The network therefore presents itself

as a synthesis, and is the result of a dialectical process. In the field of economic activities, for instance, the rise and growth of economic organizations transforms atomistic markets into oligopolies and monopolies. With the expansion of "corporations", however, these become more and more internally decentralized and are transformed into relatively loosely coupled systems (see also Bartlett & Goshal, 1989, on the transnational organization, which they characterize as an integrated network).

Mayntz points out that both hierarchies and markets have dysfunctional consequences: the hierarchy, because it subordinates, and the market because it is not capable of controlling the production of negative consequences (i.e. environmental problems). Mayntz is of the opinion that the network at least has the power to avoid both of the above-mentioned dysfunctions by combining the individual autonomy of the participants in the market with the capacity of the hierarchy consciously to pursue goals and to control their actions with regard to unanticipated consequences.

Boisot and Child (1988) have applied the basic ideas of the transaction-cost theory to the economic reforms that have taken place in the People's Republic of China since 1978. These economic reforms are characterized by a shift from the hierarchy towards coordination through the market. The authors, however, point out that Williamson's model needs enlargement. The fact that there are more possibilities for transaction-cost control in agreement with social preferences, which result from a traditional culture, and which are connected with the limited infrastructure of an economically less-developed country, should be taken into account.

The authors emphasize the importance of the information aspect, which is inherent in the transaction of goods and services, and a prerequisite for their initiation and completion. Transactions of goods and services not only require their production and exchange, but also the exchange of information. The structures that govern transactions can differ in the ways in that the diffusion and distribution of information is realized.

Boisot and Child point out that Williamson departs too much from the simple dichotomy of market versus hierarchy, and therefore does not sufficiently take into account the social embeddedness of economic transactions and the different ways in which information codification takes place in, for instance, rules, procedures, and diffusion.

Williamson's theory is based on the premise of economic rationality and efficiency for explaining the choice of certain transaction modes. As a result, Williamson neglects the ways in which the social relations in a country, both behavioural and structural, as an expression of the culture, either damage or support the efficient execution of different transaction modes.

For China, taking the transactional continuum market versus hierarchy as the point of departure would theoretically mean a massive disinvestment in the hierarchy (bureaucracy), which should lead to coordination by the market. A similar development, however, manifests itself only slightly in certain areas. Boisot and Child point out that the markets in China primarily compete with "fiefs", with regard to the control of necessary uncommitted transactions. In the urban industrial sectors the dynamics of the economic reforms push in the direction of the fiefs as the dominant way of coordinating transactions.

Fiefs accentuate the significance of personal relations as well as the importance of shared values and convictions, the submission to higher goals, and hierarchically structured face-to-face, personalized power relations. The legitimation of this kind of leadership is often based on charisma, which makes networks of personalized hierarchical relations important.

The absence of a physical economic infrastructure making national information accessible, and which should thus lead to lower transaction costs, is an important factor influencing the present situation. For the time being, the building up of personal relations, and thus the importance of face-to-face relations, remains the dominant transaction form.

Powell (1990) is also of the opinion that the premise of a continuum on which economic exchange relations can be arranged is too mechanical and static. According to him, the logic of transaction costs cannot explain the existence of a broad spectrum of other organizational forms. In his view, the premise of a continuum unjustly postulates the supposition that the market is the departure point for elementary forms of economic exchange, and that the hierarchy embodies the evolutionary destination of economic development.

Powell (1990) cites Moses Finley, who, on the basis of historical analysis, demonstrates that in the classical world there was no market in the modern sense of the word. It is equally true that developed markets did not originate with the arrival of the Industrial Revolution. Economic units arose from the dense networks of political, religious, and social bonds (guilds) that have controlled economic activities through the ages.

For Powell, the interorganization network is an independent form of coordination, and therefore not a hybrid between market and hierarchy. In this view, networks are particularly suited to circumstances where there is a need for reliable and efficient information. A basic assumption about networks is that units in the network are dependent on scarce resources and that profit can be achieved by pooling scarce resources. This pooling of resources points towards the significance of complementarity between actors in the network as a normative base for acting, as well as the importance of norms of reciprocity and relations as a means of communication for conflict handling. Society's present interest in strategic alliances illustrates this.

4   INTERORGANIZATIONAL COOPERATION

4.1   Increase in the significance of networks

Since the beginning of the 1980s in particular, the market sector in the USA, Europe, and Japan has characterized itself by the proliferation of all sorts of (inter)national forms of cooperation among organizations. The resulting variety of network forms are often labelled as strategic alliances, strategic partnerships, or strategic cooperation. These concepts are collective terms for interorganizational cooperation with regard to the exchange of technologies, collective use of distribution channels, cooperation in the field of R&D,

marketing, and production. The major goal is the reduction of risks and the creation of economies of scale (Van der Zwan, 1989; Huyzer et al., 1990; Guggler, 1992).

As the concepts alliance, partnership, cooperation, strategic networks, etc., all have the same significance in the international literature, only the terms strategic alliances and interorganizational cooperation will be used here. Strategic alliances can be described as voluntary interrelationships among two or more organizations, in which the partners maintain their independence and identity and which focus on the stabilization or improvement of their competitive position in the long term (Huyzer et al., 1990).

Different factors have led to the rise of different forms of interorganizational cooperation. The most common are:

- internationalization of markets and global competition;
- increasing complexity of technology and the possibilities offered by strategic cooperation for gaining access to these new technologies or markets;
- the increasing rapidity with which products succeed each other, which in turn leads to a shorter life cycle for products and increases the importance of cooperation in the field of product development (Mattson, 1987; Huyzer et al, 1992);
- the spreading of risk where costly investments are involved (Broersma, 1991);
- the need for standardization; clients do not want each producer to develop his own version of the product, but are in favour of general industrial standards (Biemans, 1989);
- the placing of obstacles in the paths of newcomers to the market (Harrigan, 1987).

In order to be able to make use of the strategic possibilities created by market and technological developments, information is required. An important advantage of interorganizational cooperation is the emphasis placed on the dispersal and interpretation of new information. Seen in this way, organizational networks are complicated communication networks in which information plays a vital part.

The advantage of this diffusion of information is clear when networks are contrasted with markets and hierarchies (Powell, 1990, p.325). In the market information has to be bought, with the risk of being confronted with opportunism and high costs.

In the hierarchy, information is codified, that is to say, formalized in terminology with specific meanings. The advantage of controlling information streams as the essence of codification is that uncertainty can be reduced and that conceptual unequivocality and thus stability can be created (Boisot & Child, 1988). The disadvantage, however, is that the daily routine in the organization neglects the importance of variety, of the unusual. Much of the potential information is undervalued or becomes embedded in the daily routine, into existing patterns of action, which can lead to the confirmation of what already exists. Much of the information dispersed through an organization has no semantic value in the sense that it has changed the receiver.

The interest in forms of interorganizational cooperation is expressed by concepts such as industrial networks, technology networks (Pennings, 1992; Mulder, 1992), industrial marketing networks (Spencer, 1992), innovation networks (Biemans, 1989), strategic alliances, etc. These concepts indicate certain fields of application in which the network occupies an important place. The emphasis is on long-term relations that make the transfer of scarce resources between organizations possible, and recognizing that each is dependent on the other concerning competencies such as knowledge, access to distribution channels, etc., as well as that the risks of new developments with their high costs can be shared. These strategic developments make specific demands on management and the related control structures.

Strategic alliances are often created because of offensive considerations, with the aim of strengthening their position in the market. Defensive considerations, however, are not uncommon either, for example the creation of entry restrictions for newcomers to the market. The concept of an industrial network is generally seen as an umbrella under which different network applications can be brought together. Spencer points out the difference between the network approach of industrial markets and the traditional market model. In the latter model the market is seen as a set of atomized, homogeneous, independent and exchangeable actors, governed by the price mechanism, rational planning, and the optimal use of available resources. The network approach sees markets in the industrial sector as a set of heterogeneous actors that perform activities and make use of heterogeneous resources. Furthermore, exchanges take place between the actors, which result in the simultaneous development of adaptation and mutual interdependence, which take the form of relational patterns between the actors.

Network analysis can involve:

1. the different links in the network and the explanation of their origins;
2. the location of actors in the network;
3. the way in which relational structures and positions in the network influence the behaviour and perception of the actors, and the way that they look at the network configuration.

In addition to an analysis of interorganizational networks, it is important to investigate the effects of networks. What are the factors which contribute to the success of cooperation, how does one deal with conflicts, how do networks develop over time? These are some examples of questions that have not yet received sufficient attention. The emphasis in research is more on the question of why networks based on cooperation are created, on the structure of the network, and on the factors that influence the structure, rather than on the factors that can explain the success or failure of cooperation between organizations.

The COB/SER research (1984) in the field of industrial innovation, and Biemans' project (1989) on the development of new medical technology, are two Dutch research projects investigating the question of the factors influencing the success or failure of cooperation between organizations. The COB/SER research project concentrated on 15 companies. The aim was to clarify:

- how cooperation between organizations with regard to innovation is established;

- which circumstances necessitate which types and processes of cooperation;
- what conditions have to be fulfilled to increase the possibility of a successful cooperation. One unexpected result of this research project was that partners with a complementary relationship towards each other fared no better than competing partners.

With regard to the basic conditions for successful concerted action, the following points can be mentioned:

- the importance of isolating the innovation project in one's own organization;
- an expected result, which will be profitable for all participating organizations;
- the participants should be willing to learn from the cooperation;
- the search for additional knowledge and/or possibilities should be a motive for cooperation.

The following can be mentioned as positive factors influencing the success of the cooperation:

- the involvement of key figures in the organization at important moments of decision;
- project management;
- the acceptability of the financing of the innovation project and of the amount of time taken up by each partner.

The following negative factors with regard to success emerged:

- changes in the composition of the project team;
- differences in organizational cultures between partners that cannot be handled adequately;
- having support or finance companies that work slowly and try to guarantee an impossible level of security by means of complicated regulations.

Biemans (1989) has done research in the field of medical-technology networks. In this network a number of stakeholders are involved: patients, the community, government bodies, industry, the medical profession, research centres, insurance companies, and the media. Biemans points out that in a network with so many players the chances of misunderstandings, problems, and frustrations are manifold. He emphasizes the importance of open communication, taking into account the fact that expectations, demands, wishes, and possibilities should be clarified as far as possible at the beginning of the project. A second aspect with regard to successful cooperation concerns the fact that the parties involved should realize that the establishment of a network is also the creation of a long-term relationship, and that cooperation, therefore, is more than just placing a certain amount of money at the disposal of the partners in the network and approving a research programme. Cooperation between partners requires flexibility. This flexibility has to be expressed in contracts that leave the possibility of adapting to changing circumstances open.

In both of these examples, the COB/SER project on cooperation in innovation, and Biemans' medical-technology project, the choice of partners in the cooperation, the management of the relationship, and the communication between the participating organizations emerge as the critical factors for success. Cooperation in a network of organizations is influenced by the presence of both converging and diverging interests, there is both cooperation and competition, or, to put it another way, there is cooperative competition. It is the balancing of these two opposites that is vital for the success of the strategic alliance between organizations.

Kneppers-Heynert (1992, p.28) points out that cooperative relationships form the legal basis for the coordination of economic activities between legal autonomous organizations. She observes that entrepreneurs often do not make clear formal arrangements, and states that "businessmen who sign agreements on the backs of matchboxes are not unusual".

In the literature about strategic alliances, relatively little attention has been paid to the processes that enhance or block cooperation. This is in line with Sandelands and Drazin's (1989) criticisms. With regard to the theories on environment, strategy, and organization as the contingency theory, and the transaction-cost theory, they conclude that a structural-functionalist tradition

dominates, but that the factual processes, the way in which processes are enacted, stay underexposed.

An example of a structural-functional approach with regard to industrial marketing networks ("market-as-networks") can be found in the research programme of the so-called "Swedish school" (Mattson, 1987). In this programme, use is made of structural network theories developed within the social sciences. The dependence perspective is central to Mattson's approach. Organizations are dependent on other organizations for scarce resources. This requires long-term relations that can contribute to the reduction of costs connected to exchange relations and production, which in turn can lead to a complex network of relations between organizations.

To describe a network structure, four dimensions are distinguished:

1. network structure: the amount of interdependence between the positions;
2. homogeneity: the amount of similarity between the positions;
3. hierarchy: the partition of influence between organizations;
4. exclusivity: the amount of interdependence between positions in the network and positions in other networks.

Mattson subsequently distinguishes three strategic dimensions from the network perspective:

1. emphasis on adjustment to the existing network, or emphasis on changing the network;
2. emphasis on homogeneity in the relations between the partners or emphasis on heterogeneity;
3. emphasis on internal resources or emphasis on external resources, both of which can be divided into homogeneous and heterogeneous.

These three strategic dimensions lead in theory to different strategic possibilities.

So far, Mattson has followed the traditional description of networks. The "surprise" comes when Mattson wants to draw the strategic change consequences with regard to these strategic possibilities. For instance, the questions then asked are:

1. How do managers think and act in accordance with the existing ideas about networks?
2. How do managers in different parts of the organization perceive and interpret networks and changes in networks?
3. How do managers in different interdependent organizations perceive and interpret the networks they are involved in?
4. To what extent are changes in one or more network positions dependent on other positions?
5. How do managers deal with the estimation of the amount of time and the timing of strategic changes in a network (overestimation/ underestimation)?

In the first part of his approach, Mattson departs from a reality that can be objectively structured and from which strategic possibilities can be deducted. These possibilities require change and the management of change. His five questions with regard to the perceptions of managers make clear the importance of the subjective dimensions. The consequences of this approach, however, the duality of and the interaction between the subjective and objective dimensions of social reality, remain undiscussed. The subjective dimension is expressed by the processes through which meaning is created and the power, norms, and values that are related to it, and over the course of time can acquire an institutionalized character. Meanings become institutionalized and can be experienced as an "objective" reality, which in itself influences the structuring of processes. In this sense there is a continuous play of interpenetration between the objective and the subjective.

This duality is central to Orlikowski's conception of technology (1992, p.404; see also Gergen, 1992). Orlikowski follows Giddens' "theory of structuration" with regard to the interplay between the subjective and the objective dimensions of reality. A "theory of structuration" involves the recognition that human behaviour can be enhanced or restrained by structures, but these structures are nevertheless the result of previous acts. Structural characteristics exist in the rules and means that actors develop and employ in their daily lives. These rules and means structure human interaction, and they are at the same time reconfirmed by their use.

Paraphrasing Orlikowski's concept of the duality of technology, we can speak of the duality of networks. Networks are created and changed by human acts, but at the same time are used to give body to actions. In accentuating this duality, it should be emphasized that the duality is not a dichotomy, but the reciprocal relationship between objectivism and relativism, and as a result a bridge can be created between reality as a representation and reality as a social construction.

The tension between objectivism and relativism has hardly received any systematic attention in research into interorganizational networks. It is a field that is dominated by what Pfeffer (1982, p.121) calls "theories of organization-level rational action" and "theories of the external control of organizational behavior" (see also section 3 of this chapter), but which neglects the processes that enable the creation and change of networks.

Figure 5.1 is an example of the strategic alliances of the multinational corporation DASA AEROSPACE.

The figure does not show the kinds of relations, but rather the multitude of strategic alliances, that the organizations maintain with each other. The nature of these alliances can vary from majority/ minority participations, licences, markets and distribution agreements, cooperation in the field of R&D, co-makership, joint ventures, etc.

The building up of these alliances in an international context is a complex process, which is carried out in phases and places high demands on the qualities of the management.

Important prerequisites are, for instance:

- intercultural human resource and organization development; breaking through monocultures;
- the facilitation of structural and cultural changes; the building up of international teams;
- the ability to deal with different organizational identities;
- good knowledge of macro-economic interdependencies.

These are obvious points of attention in themselves, but it is very time-consuming and problematical to realize them in practice. In general, the main problems are:

FIGURE 5.1

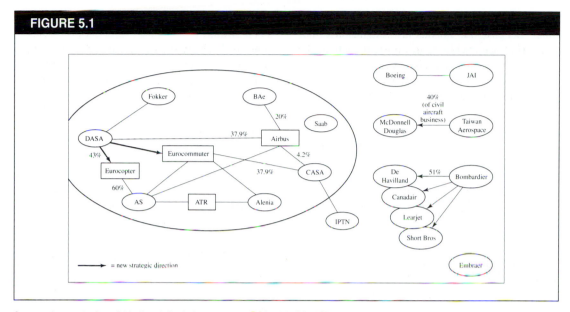

Cooperation strategies within the civil aviation company DASA AEROSPACE.

- domain battles; the absence of a common vision;
- lack of transparent information and communication on the part of management;
- the mutual motives for collaboration between partners are unclear and can lead to mistrust;
- the absence of reliable control mechanisms (hard and soft) for developing the alliance further.

4.2 Hybrid organizations

Strategic alliances are characterized by what is generally referred to as their hybrid character. Borys and Jemison (1989, p.235) define "hybrids" as organizational arrangements that make use of the resources or governance structures of one of the participating organizations. The clearest example of a hybrid is the joint venture, an organization form often characterized as cooperative competition: competition and cooperation.

A joint venture is a strategic alliance in which two or more owners create a separate organization for the execution of a common, sometimes new, activity, whereby the resulting losses/profits will be shared in an agreed manner (Harrigan, 1987; Huyzer et al., 1990). The motives for the creation of a joint venture include, for instance, a reduction

in uncertainty, the increase of internal power, risk-sharing, access to other markets, and inhibiting the entry of new competitors into the market.

The joint venture attracts great interest both in practice and in the literature on organization and management. This is also reflected by the fast growth of the number of joint ventures. Guggler (1992) remarks that in the European Community until 1982, only 46 joint ventures were announced. In the year 1989 alone, 129 joint ventures were founded. In the USA, the number of joint ventures increased sixfold in the period 1976–1987.

Van der Geest (1989) concludes that research on joint ventures has found that 70% did not fulfil their expectations, and many of the joint ventures had a rather short life, owing to disagreements between the partners.

In the literature on strategic alliances, in accordance with the transaction-cost theory, the hybrid is generally treated as an organizational form that absorbs the disadvantages of both the market and the hierarchy, or which combines the advantages of both. From this perspective, the hybrid is regarded as being in the middle of the market–hierarchy continuum.

Different environments are brought together in the hybrid. First, the various environments which the owners of the hybrid have; each with their own markets, in which they can compete with each other. Second, the various task environments of the hybrid itself with regard to the objectives for which it was founded; and third, the organizations that participate in the joint venture (the owners of the hybrid) are also a task environment for the hybrid.

A hybrid is very vulnerable to conflicts if:

1. the interests of the mother organizations towards the hybrid diverge, which can lead to mutual distrust;
2. the interests of the hybrid towards the mother organizations diverge.

If the interests between the mother organizations, and those of the hybrid towards the mother organizations, diverge, this can mean a continuous threat to the stability and the continuity of the hybrid. It is, therefore, not only a question of which organizations will become partners, but also which part of each partner belongs to the hybrid.

The potential instability of hybrids has been pointed out by Van der Klugt (1989, p.1180), among others, who compares the joint venture to a marriage that is based on inadequate grounds. It is, therefore, not surprising that all joint ventures are in principle unstable; in founding a joint venture, the partners of the hybrid have different objectives.

Strategic alliances are definitely not risk free. Poor communication between the partners, the holding back of information, lack of trust between partners, insufficient commitment to the alliance, the career interests of managers, etc., are factors which can result in the envisioned cooperation eventually turning into a conflict between the partners with all the accompanying consequences, usually legal and thus also financial.

Pennington (1992) emphasizes the importance of a clear communication strategy on the part of top management with regard to cooperation with other organizations, and the need to identify key areas which might be vulnerable to tension and conflicts and therefore need attention early on.

Borys and Jemison (1989, p.236) are of the opinion that a theory that can identify the qualities that contribute to the success or failure of a hybrid is necessary. They suggest a research agenda in which attention is paid to:

- the goals of the partners with regard to the hybrid;
- the defining of its boundaries;
- the increased value ;
- the stability of hybrids.

According to Borys and Jemison, interest in the objectives for establishing joint ventures, as well as the way in which objectives are formulated (i.e. global versus precise), has usually been neglected.

With regard to the defining of the boundaries of the hybrid, not only is it necessary to pay attention to the boundaries between the hybrid and its environment, but also to the boundaries between the hybrid and its partners. Partners can impose claims on the hybrid that can be mutually conflicting and not in fact desired by either partner.

In hybrids where the increased value process is unclear, different visions can arise with regard to the way in which the production and development processes have to be executed, and the organizational conditions necessary.

Finally, it is important to maintain stability in the joint venture, and to develop mechanisms, for instance contracts, which will enhance this stability.

Parkhe (1993), in line with Borys and Jemison (1989), emphasizes the importance of a research agenda and theory development with regard to hybrid organization forms. Parkhe focuses in particular on four key concepts that can be the basis for an integrated approach to joint ventures. These four key concepts are:

1. trust, with the emphasis on the selection and characteristics of the partners;
2. reciprocity, in particular the motives that lie at the heart of the formation of a joint venture;
3. opportunism, the control of the process of cooperation and possible conflicts;
4. tolerance, with regard to the stability and the achievements of the joint venture; the prevention of opportunism.

Reich and Mankin (1986) give an example of opportunism in Japanese–American joint ventures that has the potential for conflict. The Japanese partners have succeeded in keeping the functions with a high increased value in Japan, and thus the capabilities and knowledge in areas, such as project engineering and manufacturing processes, which lie at the heart of competitive positions. This is a conflict-prone situation.

In practice, conflicts that have to be judicially fought manifest themselves regularly. Guggler (1992) gives the example of an organization that is accused of taking the partner's technology, or technology that has been jointly developed, and eventually using it against the partner in the joint venture by forming an alliance with an another organization. Guggler says that these abuses can be prevented by managing alliances with the aim of:

1. imposing restrictions and exclusivity conditions on each of the partners;
2. restricting the transfer of key technologies;
3. increasing control over the partner's operations;
4. getting a better view of the implications of the cooperation and creating clarity of objectives;
5. building relationships of trust and commitment on the basis of a win–win situation.

5 EPILOGUE

It is undeniable that in the past different forms of strategic alliances have been developed and that the boundaries between organizations have become more diffuse. The problems of strategic alliances encompass a great number of questions, and the impression remains that research into this topic is still in its infancy, although there is great public interest in it. Key questions for further research are:

- Which factors determine the choice for or against a strategic alliance?
- Which factors determine the choice of partners in the strategic alliance, and how can the motivation of potential partners for the alliance be ascertained (Parkhe, 1993)?
- What are the requirements of alliances for the management and organization of the organizations involved?

- Which factors determine the success or failure of the cooperation strategies (Harrigan, 1987)?
- To what extent do strategic alliances create structural changes in the competitive environment of an organization (Harrigan, 1987)?
- How durable are hybrids, and what are the factors which influence this (Powell, 1990)?

With the increasing significance of and interest in strategic alliances, the theme of interorganizational networks has experienced a fast development. The developments in technology and the globalization of markets have certainly contributed to this. To what extent these developments lead or have led to a world of "disorganized capitalism" (Lash & Urry, 1987) or to a shift from "organization to disorganization" has yet to be seen.

In research, the field of interorganizational relations is approached from different theoretical perspectives. Some authors, such as Parkhe (1993), argue for a more integrated approach with regard to the problems of "voluntary interfirm cooperation". This, likewise, requires a clear underlying theoretical structure, which should contribute to a better understanding of this relatively new phenomenon.

What becomes clear is that these developments have led to a critical review of existing organizational theories, and authors such as Gergen, Cooper, Burrell, and others have contributed significantly to this (see Reed & Hughes, 1992). It is only to be expected that the theme of interorganizational networks, and in particular interorganizational cooperation, will play an important role with regard to future research and theory development in the field of Organization Studies.

I shall end with a citation from Gergen (1992, p.209):

The tendency to view organization as an autonomous, self-contained system will recede, and instead, the organization's outcomes will become inseparable from those of the broader community. The misleading distinction between inside and outside the organization will blur.

REFERENCES

Aldrich, H.E. (1979). *Organizations and environments.* Englewood Cliffs, NJ: Prentice-Hall.

Aldrich, N.E. (1992). Incommensurable paradigms? Vital signs from three perspectives. In M. Reed & M. Hughes (Eds.), *Rethinking organization: New directions in organization theory and analysis.* London: Sage.

Astley, W.G. (1984). Toward an appreciation of collective strategy. *Academy of Management Review, 9,* 526–535.

Astley, W.G., & Brahm, A. (1989). Organizational designs for post-industrial strategies: The role of interorganizational collaboration. In Ch.C. Snow (Ed.), *Strategy, organization design and human resource management.* London: Jai Press.

Bartlett, Chr.A., & Ghoshal S. (1989). *Managing across borders. The transnational solution.* London: Hutchinson.

Baum, J.A.C., & Oliver, Chr. (1991). Institutional linkages and organizational mortality. *Administrative Science Quarterly, 36;* 187–218.

Benson, J.K. (1978). The interorganizational network as a political economy. In L. Karpik (Ed), *Organization and environment.* London: Sage.

Berkowitz, S.D. (1982). *An introduction to structural analysis: The network approach to social research.* Toronto: Butterworths.

Biemans, W. (1989). *Developing innovations in networks.* Dissertation, Universiteit Groningen.

Boisot, M., & Child, J. (1988). The iron law of fiefs: Bureaucratic failure and the problem of governance in the Chinese Economic Reform. *Administrative Science Quarterly, 33;* 507–527.

Borys, B., & Jemison, D.B. (1989). Hybrid arrangements as strategic alliances: theoretical issues in organizational combinations. *Academy of Management Review, 14,* 234–249.

Breuer, F. (1978). De interorganisationele analyse. *Tijdschrift M & O, 32,* 32–45.

Breuer, F. (1982). *De organisatie-adviseur en zijn netwerk.* Alphen a.d. Rijn, Netherlands: Samsom.

Broersma, H. (1991). *Co-makership. Trend voor de jaren negentig.* Dissertation, Universiteit Groningen.

Burns, T. & Stalker, G.M. (1961). *The management of innovation.* London: Tavistock.

COB/SER (1984). *Samenwerken bij Innovatie. 's-Gravenhage.* Netherlands: COB/SER.

Doorn, J.A.A. van (1978). *De verzorgingsstaat in de practijk.* In J.A.A. van Doorn, en C.J.M. Schuyt, (Eds.), *De stagnerende verzorgingsstaat.* Meppel, Netherlands: Boom.

Edelman Bos, J.B.M. (1980). In breder verband . . . over netwerken en netwerkadvisering. *Tijdschrift M & O, 34,* 215–224.

Evan, W.M. (1976). An organization set model of interorganizational relations. In W.M. Evan (Ed.), *Interorganizational relations.* Harmondsworth, UK: Penguin Books.

Fennell, M.L., Ross, Chr.O., & Warnecke, R.B. (1987). Organizational environment and network structure. In N. Ditimaso & S.B. Bacharach, (Eds.), *Research in the sociology of organizations.* Greenwich, CT: Jai Press.

Geest, L. van der (1989). Concurrentie en Samenwerking. *Economisch Statistische Berichten, 74, 3735,* 1173.

Gergen, K.J. (1992). Organization theory in the post modern era'. In M. Reed, & M. Hughes, (Eds.), *Rethinking organization: New directions in organization theory and analysis.* London: Sage.

Gils, M.R. van (1978). De organisatie van organisaties: aspecten van interorganisationele samenwerking. *Tijdschrift M. en O., 32,* 9–31.

Gils, M.R. van (1982) Interorganisationele relaties en netwerken. In P.J. Drenth, H. Thierry, P.J. Willems, & Ch.J de Wolf (Eds.), *Handboek A&O-Psychologie.* Arnhem, Netherlands: Van Loghem Slaterus.

Godfroy, A.J.A. (1991). Netwerken van Organisaties. In *Handboek Organisatie, BC 25.100:1–34.* Alphen aan den Rijn: Samson.

Guggler, P. (1992). Building transnational alliances to create competitive advantage. *Long Range Planning, 25,* 90–99.

Harrigan, K.R. (1987). Joint ventures: A mechanism for creating strategic change. In A. Pettigrew, (Ed.). *The management of strategic change.* Oxford: Basil Blackwell.

Hartman, C. (1980) Netwerkadvisering: strategische positie als invalshoek. *Tijdschrift M & O, 34,* 367–383.

Hartman, C. (1982). Het netwerk Oosterschelde. I. Inleiding: naar een procesanalyse van netwerken. *Tijdschrift M & O, 36,* 7–12.

Huyzer, S.E., Lutmes, W., Spitholt, M.G.M., Slagter, W.J. van Wijk, A.H., Leest, D.J. van der, & Croese, D. (1990). *Strategische Samenwerking.* Alphen aan de Rijn: Samsom.

Klugt, C.J. van der (1989). Practische aspecten van strategische hergroepering. *Economisch Statistische Berichten, 74,* 3735; 1179–1182.

Kneppers-Heynert, E.M. (1992). *Over grenzen.* Groningen: Wolters Noordhof.

Lammers, C.J. (1988). The interorganizational control of an occupied country. *Administrative Science Quarterly, 33:* 438–457.

Lash, S., & Urry, J. (1987). *The end of organized capitalism.* Cambridge: Polity Press.

Lawrence, P. & Lorsch, J. (1967). *Organization and environment.* Boston: Harvard School of Business Administration Press.

Levinthal, D.A. (1991). Random walks and organizational mortality. *Administrative Science Quarterly, 36,* 397–420.

Luscuere, C. (1978). Samenwerking tussen organisaties: ideologieën en dilemma's. *Tijdschrift M & O, 32*, 49–61.

March, J.G. & Simon, H.A. (1958). *Organizations*. New York: John Wiley.

Mattson, L.G. (1987). Management of strategic change in a "Markets-as-networks" perspective. In A. Pettigrew (Ed.), *The management of strategic change*. Oxford: Basil Blackwell.

Mayntz, R. (1991). *Modernization and the logic of interorganizational networks*. Discussion paper. Max-Planck-Institut für Gesellschaftsforschung. Lothringerstrasse 78. D.5000 Köln 1. Germany.

Meyer, J.W. & Rowan, B. (1977). Institutionalized organizations: Formal structure as myth and ceremony. *American Journal of Sociology, 83*, 440–463.

Miner, A.S., Amburgey, T.L., & Stearns, T.M. (1990). Interorganizational linkages and population dynamics: Buffering and Transformational Shields. *Administrative Science Quarterly, 35*, 689–713.

Mulder, K. (1992). *Choosing the corporate future*. Dissertation: Universiteit Groningen.

Oliver, Chr. (1988). The collective strategy framework: An application to competing predictions of isomorphism. *Administrative Science Quarterly, 33*, 543–561.

Orlikowski, W.J. (1992). The duality of technology: Rethinking the concept of technology in organizations. *Organization Science, 3*, 398–427.

Parkhe, A. (1993). "Messy" research, methodological predispositions, and theory development in international joint ventures. *Academy of Management Review, 18*, 227–269.

Pennings, J.M. (1992). Technological Networking and innovation implementation. *Organization Science, 3*, 356–383.

Pennington, A. (1992). Managing technology partnerships. *Journal of General Management, 17*, 46–55.

Perrow, Ch. (1986). *Complex organizations: A critical essay*. New York: Random House.

Pfeffer, J. (1982). *Organizations and organization theory*. London: Pitman.

Powell, W.W. (1990). Neither market nor hierarchy: Network forms of organization. In B.M. Staw & L.L. Cummings, (Eds.), *Research in organizational behavior*. London: Jai Press.

Ranger-Moore, J., & Banaszak-Holl, J. (1991). Density dependent dynamics in regulated industries: Founding rates of banks and life insurance companies. *Administrative Science Quarterly, 36*, 36–65.

Reed, M., & Hughes, M. (1992). *Rethinking organizations: New directions in organization theory and analysis*. London: Sage.

Reich, R., & Mankin, E.D. (1986). Joint ventures with Japan give away our future. *Harvard Business Review*, March/April, 78–86.

Sandelands, L. & Drazin, R. (1989). On the language of organization theory. *Organizational Studies, 10*, 457–478.

Selznick, P. (1965). *TVA and the grass roots*. New York: McGraw-Hill.

Spencer, R. (1992). Positions in networks: worth a second look. In J.J.J. Van Dijck, & A.A.L.G., Wentink, (Eds.), *Transnational business in Europe*. Tilburg University.

Ven, Van de, A.H., Emmett, D.C., & Koenig, R. Jr (1974). Frameworks for Interorganizational analysis. *Organization and Administrative Sciences, 5*, 113–130

Walker, G., & Poppo, L. (1991). Profit centers, single source suppliers and transaction costs. *Administrative Science Quarterly, 36*, 66–87.

Walton, R.L. (1972). Interorganizational decision making and identity conflict. In M. Tuite, R. Chisholm, & M. Radner (Eds), *Interorganizational decision making*. Chicago, Aldine.

Wassenberg, A. (1980). *Netwerken: Organisatie en Strategie*. Boom: Meppel.

Williamson, O.E. (1975). *Markets and hierarchy: analysis and anti-trust implications*. New York: Free Press.

Williamson, O.E. (1985). *The economic institutions of capitalism: firms, markets, relational contracting*. New York/London: Free Press/Collier Macmillan.

Zwaan, A.H. van der (1990). Netwerken: Samenhang en samenwerking in de gezondheidszorg. In J.A.M. Maarse & J.M. Mur-Veeman, (Eds.), *Beleid en Beheer in de Gezondheidszorg, Problemen, Structuren, Processen en Effecten*. Assen: Van Gorcum.

Zwan, A. van der (1989). Strategische samenwerking. *Economisch Statistische Berichten, 74, 3735*, 1176–1179.

6

Organizational Culture

Jaap J. van Muijen

1 INTRODUCTION

In the past few decades organizations have been confronted with increasing economic competition and international cooperation. In fact, there is more international competition then ever before. For instance, the growing single European market pressures companies in and outside the European Union countries to search for partners. Mergers and acquisitions are common practice in almost every industry. An example is the cooperation of Volvo Car Netherlands, Volvo Sweden, and the Japanese company Mitsubishi in a new automobile company NedCar in the Netherlands. The increasing international competition and cooperation, and the emerging of free-trade zones, like NAFTA (North American Free Trade Area) and the European market, emphasizes the importance of understanding cultural aspects in a particular organizational context. Understanding of the influence of organizational culture, in interaction with national culture (i.e. dominant values in a society) on organizational processes, is considered crucial for success or failure.

Kilmann, Saxton, and Serpa (1985) explain why organizational culture is so important in acquisitions and mergers. They use the metaphor of an iceberg. The mass below the surface of the water represents the organizational culture. As two icebergs approach one another, the danger lies in the invisible mass below the surface. Like the mass of an iceberg, organizational culture must be made visible, that is, must be articulated, before two or more organizations can be integrated. In other words, in a merger of organizations, not only the financial and economical aspects but also the cultural characteristics of the firms should be taken into consideration.

"The problems associated with integration of firms often lead to a lower level of post-merger performance" (Denison, 1990, p.17). These problems are often related to the cultural characteristics of the integrating firms. For example, organization A treats the employees as expenses and management will try to reduce these costs, whereas in organization B employees are viewed as resources and management will invest in them.

Organizational culture does not only play a critical role in mergers and acquisitions but also in organizational diagnosis, organizational development, and Human Resource Management (see Table 6.1). In the case of organizational diagnosis one is interested in the strong and weak aspects of the current strategy and their relation to organizational culture. This could lead to questions such as: Are negative results caused by the organizational

TABLE 6.1

The Different Roles of Organizational Culture in Organizational Research.

Organizational diagnosis	Thermometer: What is the culture of the organization?
Organizational development	Starting point: Which aspect of the culture must be changed before implementing strategic changes successfully?
Mergers/acquisitions/joint-ventures	Is there a fit between the cultures of the involved organizations?
Human Resource Management	Commitment to the organization and motivation

culture or by, for instance, management? For example, Philips, the troubled Dutch electronics group, started operation Centurion. This new Philips catechism was supposed to lead to a culture shock. According to the CEO (Chief Executive Officer), Timmer, the only purpose of this operation is to whittle away bureaucracy and enhance profitability through changing the organizational culture (*Financial Times*, 1990).

Organizational diagnosis is often related to organizational development. In the case of operation Centurion, the intention is to change the organizational culture and other elements of the organization, such as structure and management style, in order to enhance profitability. After implementing of changes, one could diagnose culture again and determine how successful those changes are. For example, is the culture of Philips indeed less bureaucratic after Centurion?

An assumption underlying operation Centurion was that, for good performance, organizations depend more and more on their members' commitment to and involvement in both their work and the organization. "Effectiveness is, to a greater extent than before, a result of teamwork, sharing information, willingness to cooperate, staying up-to-date with developments in one's occupation or field, and, the capacity to adjust to the changing environment" (Van Muijen & Koopman, 1994, p.368). Here we find the link with Human Recource Management (HRM). HRM is a "distinctive approach to employment management, which seeks to achieve competitive advantage through the strategic development of a highly commited and capable workforce using an integrated array of cultural, structural, and personnel techniques" (Storey, 1995, p.5). Organizational culture either facilitates or inhibits the role of HRM.

What is organizational culture? Traditionally, culture has been studied by anthropologists. In general, organizational researchers have conceptualized organizational culture as analogous to the general cultural concept (Rousseau, 1990). Therefore, in the next section, five perspectives of organizational culture, based on five theoretical trends or research programs in cultural anthropology, will be described.

2   PERSPECTIVES OF ORGANIZATIONAL CULTURE

There is no consensus among anthropologists on "what culture is, what it means, what its characteristics are, what it is composed of, what it does, or how it should be studied" (Sackmann, 1991, p.8). For example, in 1952, Kroeber and Kluckhorn listed 164 definitions of culture. It is not suprising that there is also a large variety of definitions of organizational culture. According to Sackmann, there are "almost as many definitions and understandings of culture as there are people writing about it" (1991, p.2).

Although there is no consensus on the nature of

culture, there are several classifications of theories of culture. An important classification is made by Smircich (1983). She describes five perspectives of organizational culture. These perspectives relate to five theoretical culture mainstreams in anthropology: cross-cultural management; corporate culture; organization cognition; organizational symbolism; and unconscious processes and organization. In the first two perspectives, culture is a variable, that is, culture is seen as an aspect of the organization: culture is something an organization has. In the other three, culture is a root metaphor, that is, the organization is a culture (see also section 3).

Researchers within the _cross-cultural_ perspective study, among other things, the cross-country variation in organizational variables, such as structure (Tayeb, 1988), leadership (Bass, Burger, Doktor, & Barett, 1979; Smith et al., 1994), decision making (Heller, Drenth, Koopman, & Rus, 1988; IDE, 1981, 1993), and organizational culture (Van Muijen & Koopman, 1994). Within this perspective, culture is a background (independent) variable. Culture almost becomes synonymous with country.

In the second perspective, _corporate culture_, the culture of the organization, is studied. Organizational culture then becomes a topic for research like other organizational variables, such as leadership (Den Hartog, Van Muijen, & Koopman, 1996; Roberts, 1986; Schein, 1992), structure (Hofstede, Neuijen, Ohayv, & Sanders, 1990; Pennings & Gresov, 1986), reward systems (Kerr & Slocum, 1987; Pennings, 1986) and effectiveness (Denison, 1990; Quinn & Cameron, 1988). Culture is seen as an aspect of the organization and one is interested in understanding the interdependence of several parts of the organization (or system) in relationship with environmental variables. In other words, the study is about contingent relationships among context variables and organizational variables. Organizational culture can be considered as the normative glue that holds an organization together (Tichy, 1982). The implication is "that the symbolic cultural dimension in some way contributes to the overall systemic balance and effectiveness of an organization" (Smircich, 1983, p.344).

In the _cognitive perspective_, culture is regarded as a system of shared cognitions or a system of knowledge and beliefs. "The human mind generates culture by means of a finite number of rules" (Smircich, 1983, p.342). Organizations are viewed as systems of knowledge. According to Argyris and Schön (1978), organizations can be described as cognitive enterprises. "Individual members are continually engaged in attempting to know the organization, and to know themselves in the context of the organization" (p.16). And "all deliberate action had a cognitive basis, that is reflected norms, strategies, and assumptions or models of the world which had claims to general validity" (Argyris & Schön, 1978, p.10). Experiences of Individual organizational members are stored in organizational memory maps. These maps are guidelines for how to act in certain situations. Weick's social-construction theory (1979) is an another example of this perspective. Weick's concept-cause maps correspond with Argyris and Schön's memory maps. In this perspective researchers are interested in finding the rules or scripts guiding action or the structure of knowledge (e.g. Weick's grammar rules).

In the _symbolic perspective_, an organization is conceived of as a pattern of symbolic discourse. The organization needs reading, deciphering, and interpreting of symbols in order to be understood. Events and patterns of action have a deeper symbolic meaning than their direct instrumental intention. A good example is the work by the anthropologist Geertz (1973). He searches for the meaning of symbols. "Believing with Max Weber, that man is an animal suspended in webs of significance he himself has spun. I take culture to be those webs, and the analysis of it to be therefore not an experimental science in search of law but an interpretative one in search of meaning" (Geertz, 1973, p.5). Geertz is an opponent of the cognitive perspective. He speaks of the cognitive fallacy. According to Geertz, cognitive anthropology makes a fundamental mistake in assuming that culture consists of mental phenomena, which can be analyzed by mathematical or formal philosophical methods. Searching for grammar rules (Weick, 1979), which underlie meaningful behavior, like organizing, is useless. Such rules exclude the context of the symbol. Within the symbolic perspective, the focus of organizational researchers is on how organizational members interpret and understand their work-related experiences, and how these interpretations and understandings are related to action.

The fifth perspective Smircich distinguishes is the *structural and psychodynamic* view. Culture is seen as the manifestation or expression of unconscious psychological processes. "From this point of view, organizational forms and practices are understood as projections of unconscious processes and are analyzed with reference to the dynamic interplay between out-of-awareness processes and their conscious manifestations" (Smircich, 1983, p.351). The organizational analyst searches for objective foundations of social expressions or arrangements of human beings. An example of such research is the work by Mitroff (1982). The intention of his study was to discover structural patterns underlying the manifestations of social arrangements using Jung's work on archetypes as a basis. Structuralism has a direct link to the French anthropologist Lévi-Strauss. In his theory, culture is the reflection of universal, unconscious, and immanent structures of the human mind. Cultural expressions are keys to universal codes. As each culture is a product of the human mind and its fundamental mental processes, there are universal characteristics common to all cultures. According to Lévi-Strauss, the universal characteristics can be found in the unconscious structure of cultures (see Smircich, 1983).

Both in cross-cultural and in corporate culture, perspective culture is regarded as a variable. In the cross-cultural perspective, culture is a part of the environment and will function like an independent variable. In the corporate-culture perspective, culture is part of the organization and is seen as a result of organizational activities. Organizational culture can be an independent variable, a dependent variable or a moderator. In both perspectives, organizational analysts search for patterns of relationships between organizational variables and context variables. An organization is viewed as an organism striving to surviving in an uncertain environment.

In the organization cognition, the organizational symbolism, and the unconscious processes and organization perspectives there is a common vision or mode of thought, which differs from the instrumental-elementary vision of organizations of the cross-cultural and corporate-culture perspectives. This mode of thought implies that organizations are cultures, and therefore they are constructed social realities, meaningful for their members. Organizational analysts are interested in the meaning of organizing and not in the effectiveness or outcomes of organizations.

3   STRUCTURAL FUNCTIONALISM

The difference between variable and root metaphor runs parallel with the difference between structural functionalism and holism. Czarniawska-Joerges (1992) discusses why organization theory and anthropology parted. In 1961, Waldo had written a review essay entitled "Organization Theory: An Elephantine Problem". The Elephantine problem tells us about blind men (i.e. researchers) meeting an elephant. "It was six men of Indostan, to learning much inclined, who went to see the elephant, (though all of them were blind), that each by observation, might satisfy his mind" (Saxe, in Mirvis & Sales, 1990, p.345). Each researcher investigates a certain part of the elephant. The foot is a tree trunk, the muscular trunk seems to be a liana, and nobody sees the elephant. Waldo discusses why organization theory has adapted the methodology and positivist paradigm of behaviorism. He argues that, in contrast with his own preference, that is, holism, the behaviorist revolution has succeeded. "The general goal is a value-free generalization about how the subject phenomena behave, given specified conditions" (Waldo, 1961, p.217). Organizational sociologists have also adapted this objectivistic-reductionistic research methodology. Czarniawska-Joerges describes the victory of structural functionalism within organization theory using the studies of Selznick (1949/1966), Rice (1958), and Crozier (1964) as examples. According to Leach (1976), "the essence of structural-functional research is to understand the interdependence of several parts of the system as it exists at the present time" (p.3). Organizational culture, like structure, is a part of the system.

Within the structural-functionalistic paradigm researchers assume that a subsystem arises, functions, and grows as a result of the functional meaning it has in a system (Lammers, 1984). Other assumptions are that a subsystem can be designed in a rational way and that only those subsystems functional for the system will survive (survival of the fittest).

As mentioned, within the corporate-culture perspective, organizational culture is a subsystem. Within this perspective, researchers are interested in the functional meanings of organizational culture related to other organizational variables as leadership and performance. Organizational culture as an aspect of an organization is "the next attempt to explain the E in Lewin's famous $B = f(P,E)$ equation" (Reiches & Schneider, 1990, p.28); that is, behavior is a function of person and environment.

The research methodology of structural functionalism emphasizes the adage that only the measurable is researchable. This methodology can be contrasted with ethnography, the core methodological approach in holism. Although some anthropologists went with the mainstream in organization theory (structural functionalism), most stayed with a holistic perspective.

4 ETHNOGRAPHY

According to Cohen (1974), the essence of ethnography is the study of the social impact of symbols in a culture over a long period of time; that is, to observe and describe behavior of group members in its relation to cultural symbols in different situations. "The key to understanding cultures lies in a portrayal and analysis of how members of the culture structure the meanings of their world" (Barley, 1983, p.395). Ethnography is both a method and a product (Neuijen, 1992). Ethnography as method refers to the study of the social influence of symbols (including symbolic behavior) in a certain culture. The researcher can be observing outsider (for example, Mead, 1949) or observing participator (for example, Buraway, 1981; in this case, the researcher was active as an employee in a factory). In both cases, the researcher observes the subject-matter over a long period of time. Ethnography as product refers to the result of the study. That is, in how much depth does a researcher want to analyze the portrait of symbols and behavioral patterns? Is his or her aim to describe underlying taken-for-granted assumptions (cf. Schein, 1992, see section 5.1 in this chapter); or does the researcher want to read a manuscript, like Geertz (1973)? "Doing ethnography is like trying to read (in the sense of construct a reading of) a foreign manuscript, faded, full of ellipses, incoherencies, suspicious emendations, and tendentious commentaries, and written not in conventional graphs of sound, but in transient examples of shaped behavior" (Geertz, 1973, p.10). Data are collected through observing behavior of members of a certain culture in several situations, and by interviewing informants.

Geertz distinguishes between thick and thin descriptions. "Thin" means that only the action is written. "Thick" refers to the context in which the action takes place. He paraphrases Ryle's description of a boy with a twinkling eye. His wink could mean he has something in the eye, a tic, or it could be an intentional movement indicating a certain message: a message for someone else who will react, etc. The meaning of the twinkling eye, that is, the interpretation of a symbol, will only be clear in the whole context. Geertz (1973) emphasizes "that cultural analysis is intrinsically incomplete. And, worse than that, the more deeply it goes the less complete it is" (p.29). The meaning of symbols is anchored in a painted landscape, and the search for underlying structures runs the risk of isolating the symbols from the landscape, like political, economical, and physical circumstances.

In short, organizational culture as root metaphor is based on phenomenological and hermeneutical assumptions. The organization can be understood as a culture. The organization should be understood and interpreted by analyzing the artifacts, behavioral patterns, and other visible characteristics, and their symbolic implications. The organizational analyst focuses on how organization members interpret their experiences, how these interpretations influence their behavior, and, how they arrive at shared interpretations, meanings, and knowledge.

5   ORGANIZATIONAL CULTURE

Pettigrew (1979) introduces the culture concept into the field of organizational behavior and theory. He argues the importance of rituals, myths, and symbols in understanding organizations. In the 1980s, organizational culture became a very popular concept. Many books on organizational culture were published (for example, Deal & Kennedy, 1982; Frost, Moore, Louis, Lundberg, & Martin, 1985; Handy, 1985; Martin, 1992; Peters & Waterman, 1982; Pondy, Frost, Morgan, & Dandridge, 1982; Schein, 1985; Schneider, 1990; Trice & Beyer, 1993). For an excellent overview of the development of the organizational-culture concept and its definitions we refer the reader to Reiches and Schneider (1990). An influential psychologist who has studied organizational culture is Edgar Schein. As a social psychologist, Schein propagates an evolutionary perspective on organizations. His view on culture is part of the corporate-culture perspective. He defines culture as rooted in social psychology and group dynamics rather than treating culture as an antropological concept. Therefore, symbolic concepts like rituals, ceremonies, myths, etc. are not explicitly studied by Schein, who prefers to emphasize psychological concepts like problem solving, learning, values, and basic assumptions.

5.1   Edgar H. Schein

In his book on organizational culture, Schein (1992) presents a dynamic definition of culture and a related model. He defines the culture of a group as "a pattern of shared basic assumptions that the group learned as it solved its problems of external adaption and internal integration, that has worked well enough to be considered valid and, therefore, to be taught to new members as the correct way to perceive, think, and feel in relation to those problems" (p.12). There are at least three important aspects in this defintion. In the first place, culture concerns critical assumptions determining how group members perceive, think about, and feel about things, and it does not include overt behavior patterns. Secondly, culture belongs to a group; and, thirdly, culture is learned. The definition includes two basic functions of culture: to solve problems of internal integration and of external adaption.

The basic assumptions Schein mentions in his definition of culture are unconscious taken-for-granted beliefs, perceptions, thoughts, and feelings about, for example, the environment, reality, truth, time, human nature, and relationships. These assumptions tend to be non-confrontable, non-debatable, and hence very powerful determinants of human behavior. An excellent example of the influence of such basic assumptions on the life of organizational members is provided by Morgan (1986, p.125). He describes the situation at ITT under the tough and uncompromising leadership of Harold Geneen. Harold Geneen created a corporate culture based on intimidation and confrontation. His policy-review meetings could be "so grueling that many executives were known to break down and cry under pressure." The culture was characterized as a jungle. The underlying basic assumption about human relationships was, "do it to them, before they do it to us". In the terms of McGregor (1960), the basic assumption about human nature was theory X.

Culture is developed through learning processes in a group as it solves problems of internal integration and external adaption. From an evolutionary perspective, an organization either survives or disappears in a certain environment as a function of its ability to adapt to or to cope with its changing environment. Therefore, in cultural analysis we need to understand how leaders or founders define the environment of their organization. What is the function of an organization in the environment, that is, what is the core mission and what are the main goals of the organization? How has the organization accomplished its tasks? From a group-member view, it is about matters such as: how do we deal with our environment?; which environmental information is necessary?; what are the environmental demands?; how do we evaluate these demands and information?; what is our mission?; which means need to be used to attain the goals?; and which criteria should be used in evaluating performance, that is, what is success, when are we satisfied, and when do we have to be worried?

In order to survive in the external environment an organization must also be able to develop and maintain a set of internal relationships among its members. In order to accomplish organizational goals there is a need for division and coordination of departmental and individual tasks. The organization has to solve problems such as creating a common language and conceptual categories, proper (behavioral) manners, power distribution, and allocation of reward and punishment.

Internal integration and external adaption are inextricably intertwined processes. First and foremost, the environment determines the prospects and opportunities for an organization to divide and coordinate several tasks in order to realize its goals. Eventually, organizational members are shaped by the way the organization has successfully solved internal and external probems. This process results in a pattern of shared perceptions, cognitions, and emotions (i.e. culture). On the basis of this pattern, organizational members perceive and define the environment in terms familiar and meaningful for all of them. The organizational culture provides an affective, cognitive, and perceptual acculturation program, through which organizational members learn to deal with all kinds of problems related to internal integration and external adaption. Organizational members learn to filter environmental stimuli and act in accordance with certain standard coping mechanisms or problem-solving techniques.

According to Schein, the process of culture formation is, in a sense, identical to the process of group formation. Both processes are the outcome of leadership activities and shared experiences. During the entrepreneurial stage, the leader or founder provides solutions for problems related to internal integration and external adaption. This process leads to shared patterns of beliefs, feelings and values, and group membership. Schein calls these patterns the culture of the group. In the early stages, culture is the result of leadership activities, that is, culture is a dependent variable. But, once a culture exists, it is the directing and sense-making factor in a group or organization. For example, culture will determine the criteria for leadership, that is, determine who will or will not be a leader.

Culture is formed by a group. Schein does not specify the size of the social unit to which culture can be applied. Some authors (e.g. Schermerhorn,

Hunt, & Osborn, 1994) define a group as a system or collection of two or more people working together in order to achieve one or more common goals. From a cultural perspective, others define a group by emphasizing a common set of norms (Steers & Black, 1994). In general, a cultural group consists of two or more people sharing some basic assumptions and values. This implies that within an organization there can be several subcultures, for example, departmental cultures (see also section 5.2 in this chapter).

As mentioned before, Schein suggests several levels of organizational culture. In his model he distinguishes three different levels (see Table 6.2). These levels could be seen as the layers of an onion. The outer layer contains the most visible level of culture, that is the artifacts, technology, and behavioral patterns. Here we find visible behavior of group members, status system, logos, material outputs, and language. Schein argues that overt patterns of behavior and artifacts are easy to observe, but hard to decipher. That is, it is difficult to unravel the meaning of artifacts in a given group. He continues to argue that behavior is always determined by cultural disposition and environmental factors. Therefore, to understand culture, a culture analyst must go beyond overt group behavior. "Only after we have discovered the deeper layers (...) of culture can we specify what is and what is not an artifact that reflects culture" (Schein, 1992, p.14).

The next layer of the onion contains the values of the group. Values function as normative and moral anchors that guide the behavior of group members in certain situations. Values reflect assumptions about what is right and wrong. "Values are broad tendencies to prefer certain states of affairs over others" (Hofstede, 1991, p.8). Schein makes a distinction between values based on prior cultural learning and values not based on prior cultural learning, the so-called espoused values. Espoused values (Argyris & Schön, 1978) are based on ideological assumptions. They reflect the ethics of what is right and what is wrong. The difference between these kinds of values is analogous to the difference between the verbs "to do" and "to say". An organization might state that one of its important values is not to cheat competitors or clients. This might, however, contradict the actual actions. In most societies cheating clients is viewed as wrong; however, in some organizations this might be the norm.

Norms are anchored in values and directives for action. The distinction between norms and values is not absolute, but smooth. According to Bennis and Nanus (1985), managers do things right, and leaders do the right things. To do the right things is related to the values, and to do things right is related to norms. Norms are embedded in values.

The difference between values based on prior learning and espoused values is reflected in the nature of the norms. In the case of espoused values the norm is absolute, that is, everybody should behave in a certain way. In our example, people should not cheat their customers. In the case of values based on prior learning, the norm is statistical (Hofstede, 1991). That is, the norms are descriptions of choices actually made by the group reflecting certain values.

The third layer consists of the basic assumptions. The unconscious assumptions are taken for granted and are therefore difficult to change. These implicit assumptions guide behavior. The assumptions direct group members in an organization to perceive, interpret and restore events. The assumptions form the foundations of perceptual training. "Basic assumptions are so taken for granted that someone who does not hold them is viewed as crazy and automatically dismissed" (Schein, 1992, p.16). A manager of a Western company who attributes low sales to an angry forest god, is regarded as a lunatic by his colleagues.

In summary: the elements of culture are formed during the process of solving actual problems encountered by a group. An organization in the entrepreneurial stage has to solve some internal problems, but mostly external problems. In this case, the first solution proposal comes from the leader (most of the time, this is the founder of the organization), who has beliefs about reality and how to act. If the proposed solution works well and the group has a shared perception of success, the values involved undergo a cognitive transformation process (validation), by which they become taken for granted. This validation can be social (if the solutions reduce anxiety and uncertainty) or physical (for example, financial). Values that remain conscious and are articulated in official documents and in the organizational philosophy will act as moral guidelines to organization members. If the values involved are not based on prior learning, we have to take into account that these values may be incongruent with the actual behavior of the organization.

5.2 Subcultures

Louis (1985) claims that within a single organization there are several sites where a culture may develop. These sites are referred to as the intraorganizational loci of culture. Such loci of culture can also be interorganizational. Guest, Peccei, and Thomas (1994) refer to these sites as organizational subcultures. In addition, subcultures may reflect certain cultures beyond organizational boundaries, namely interorganizational subcultures. An example of such a locus of culture is a professional culture. Finance departments from several banks and assurance companies might have the same kind of subculture because of the same professional training of the accountants at universities. The corporate cultures of each of these organizations might be quite distinctive, however.

Within an organization there can be several

TABLE 6.2	
Three Levels of Organizational Culture (after Schein, 1985).	
Artifacts, technology, behavioral patterns	Visible, but hard to decipher
Values	Not visible
Basic assumptions	Unconscious and taken for granted

subcultures (Louis, 1985; Martin, 1992). Louis (1985) states that culture develops around the top of an organization. There may be a for-your-eyes-only culture among the ruling elite. Also, there may be a for-public-consumption culture at the top, deliberately designed by the ruling elite to be passed down through the organization. As soon as this type of culture spreads through the organization, one can speak of the corporate culture. Schein (1992) also emphasizes the importance of leaders in developing a corporate culture.

Culture might also develop in a vertical slice of the organization, such as a division. The division might distinguish itself through unique social interactions, for example a publisher might have a division for newspapers, a division for scientific journals and books, and a division for literature. Each division might have its own culture. A horizontal slice of an organization, such as particular type of job or hierarchical level, can also be a potential locus of culture. For example, system engineers at a computer company may have develop a set of shared understandings (Louis, 1985).

Subculture can also refer to a distinctive local culture, local in geographical sense, which could be different from the dominant organizational culture (Guest et al., 1994). For example, a unit located in a rural area might have a culture differing from a similar unit in a urban area. Such cultural differences might be caused by differences in environmental conditions (e.g. infrastructure), cultural context (for example, in The Netherlands there are regional differences in the attitude concerning absenteeism), management styles, etc.

Finally, subculture could also refer to a specific issue, such as service, quality, or safety. In this sense, one can speak about the safety culture of an organization (Guest et al., 1994; Wilpert, 1996). This kind of subculture ideally exists throughout the entire organization. Table 6.3 shows the possible subcultures within an organization.

When discovering subcultures it is interesting to take a closer look at Dansereau and Alluto's (1990) discussion of levels of analysis. They describe four levels of analysis. Here, the third and fourth level are of interest, that is, the group and collective level. In general, the group level corresponds with a department, unit, or division and the collective level with the entire organization. Besides the level of analysis the authors distinguish between wholes and parts. The wholes view implies that, given a certain level analysis, the focus is on differences between the units of analysis. For example, the research question concerns differences between departmental subcultures. The focus is on similarities (shared meanings) within departments and differences between departments. When there are no signifi-

TABLE 6.3	
Possible Subcultures Within an Organization (after Jansen, 1994).	
Élite culture/corporate culture	"For-your-eyes-only" or "for-public-consumption"
Departmental culture	Horizontal slice, for example, sales department
Divisional culture	Vertical slice, for example, a division
Local culture	Within a geographical location/unit
Issue-related culture	Metaphorical, related to an important issue throughout the organization, for example, safety culture or quality culture
Professional culture	On basis of professional background and training

cant differences between the departments one can not speak of departmental subcultures. The parts view focuses on similarities between units of analysis. A group, for example, organization or department, "is viewed as a differentiated (hetero-geneous) unit of analysis where each group shows a similar (common) differentiation" (Danserau & Alutto, 1990, p.200); for instance, the accountants example. The part perspective emphasizes the universal validity of a given principle within a population (for example, a certain industry), whereas the whole perspective emphasizes the uniqueness of a certain unit.

5.3 The functions of organizational culture for its members

Schein (1992) describes the two main functions of organizational culture: external adaptation and internal integration. As mentioned, external adap-tation is the process of reaching goals and dealing with outsiders. "Internal integration concerns the creating of a collective identity and the means of matching methods of working and living together" (Schermerhorn et al., 1994, pp.430–1). The organizational culture socializes organizational members by providing a cognitive, emotional, and perceptual program. Organizational members learn how to handle problems related to coordi-nation and cooperation, and problems related to external adaptation and surviving in a certain environment. The acculturation process leads to uncertainty or anxiety reduction. It helps organiza-tional members to filter environmental stimuli and enact the filtered stimuli into their schemata, to interpret these stimuli, and to act on basis of this interpretation. The world would be overwhelming and a constant threat if people could not filter stimuli. The phenomenon of culture shock is a an example of inadequate acculturation in solving problems in a new environment.

Other authors (Morgan, 1986; Reiches & Schneider, 1990; Weick, 1985) conclude that the function of culture is to provide a shared meaning of organizational and environmental processes and events. Shared meaning is, of course, related to the idea of a cognitive, emotional, and percep-tual acculturation program. Culture can also be described as the social and normative glue in an organization or group (Tichy, 1982). Culture is normative glue in the sense that it is a source of strength and identity (Schein, 1992). Organiza-tional members take pride in their membership, because it gives them an identity. For example, I work for Shell. Because of this glue, organiza-tional members can communicate and cooperate in a way incomprehensible to outsiders. In a first meeting in a company, a visitor or researcher might feel like a fish out of water, because of the frequent use by organization members of organization-specific language, idioms, and abbreviations. However, these natural expressions facilitate group cohesion and cooperation.

Organizational culture provides a cognitive, emotional, and perceptual program, through which organizational and environmental pro-cesses and events are interpreted (shared meaning) and through problems of internal integration and external adaptation could be solved. The outcome of these processes is reduction of anxiety or uncertainty and a justification of behavior. Table 6.4 presents a overview of different functions of organizational culture.

---

6 ORGANIZATIONAL CLIMATE

Organizationational climate is a concept develop-ed by psychologists. In 1939, Lewin, Lippitt, and White examined the influence of experimentally created social climates on the behavior of boys in a group. Reiches and Schneider (1990) state that these authors neither define nor explicitly oper-ationalize the concept climate. There was some-thing in the environment influencing the behavior of individuals in a group. According to Reiches and Schneider, the concept of (organizational) climate was not fully explicated until the 1970s. These authors describe the development of organizational climate as an independent variable, as a moderator or as an intervening variable in an extended research model. Traditionally, organiza-tional climate has been studied from a func-tionalistic perspective (Schneider, 1975).

Ekvall (1987) describes two ontological interpretations of the organizational climate con-cept. One is realistic and objectivistic, the other is subjectivistic and phenomenological. According

TABLE 6.4

Functions of Organizational Culture.

Adjusting Internal Processes	Coordination and Cooperation
Adaptation to the external environment	How to handle customers, suppliers, government, and other outsiders
Result is:	Reduction of feelings of uncertainty Justification of behavior Identity Feelings of solidarity

to the objectivistic view, climate is an attribute of the organization. Climate refers to "a set of conditions that exist and have an impact on individual's behavior" (Denison, 1990, p.24). These conditions are "objective" characteristics of an organization and can be observed in several ways, for example, by organizational members as well as outsiders. Although organizational climate can only be assessed through perceptual data (Denison, 1990), in the objectivistic view climate does exist independently from these perceptions. In the subjectivistic approach, organizational climate is regarded as the organizational members common perception of the organizational situation. Organizational climate is the common perceptual and cognitive structuring of the situation. Organization members construct the organizational climate over time and events.

The distinction between the subjectivistic and the objectivistic view can also be described as: Is climate a stimulus or a response? In other words, is climate a characteristic of the organization, or is it an internal representation of an external stimulus? Some authors (James, James, & Ashe, 1990) pose that climate is "a product of personal values and remains a property of individuals irrespective of the empirical level of analysis, whereas culture is engendered by system values (and involves system norms) and is a property of the collective" (p.41). James et al. use the term "psychological climate" (PC), refering to organizational climate as aggregates of PC scores. The frame of reference for organizational climate is still the individual. The individual perceives and interprets his or her environment. Perceiving and interpreting situa-

tions are psychological processes and organizational climate indicates nothing more than an agreement on a PC variable or variables. That is, aggregated PC scores are shared phenomenological experiences and acquired meanings of the perceivers. In fact, organizational climate provides the opportunity "*to describe an environment in psychological terms*, that is, in terms of the shared acquired meanings of perceivers" (p.62). Note that these authors write "perceivers" and not organization members. The concept of organization members indicates a certain generality. Perceivers, however, are not necessarily representative of the organizations in question.

Other authors (DeCock, Bouwen, DeWitte, & DeVisch, 1986; Drexler, 1977; Rentsch, 1990) seen organizational climate as a property of an organization and consider consensus between organization members a criterion of organizational climate. Consensus implies shared perception. Respondents are considered to be representative of the organization.

This distinction between the subjectivistic and objetivistic view is theoretically clear. But, one has to ask the question: Does it matter empirically? Following Ekvall (1987), the distinction has not been kept empirically. "Most studies of organizational climate have made use of questionnaires in which the individual organization members have been asked to describe the climate by answering what is usually a large number of questions regarding conditions in the organization. The questions have been much the same, regardless of whether the researcher has adopted a realistic or phenomenological view of climate" (p.178). Also, perhaps more important, in both cases individual descriptions are aggregated to a certain level of analysis, for example, department or organization. Ekvall (1987) emphazises that "both approaches see perceptions and cognitions rather than attitudes, feelings, or abilities as the mediating link between situations and behavior" (p.178).

Rousseau (1988) clarifies the importance of the instruction level of a questionnaire in climate research. The instruction level of a questionnaire directs a respondent or informant to the appropriate frame of reference. It is necessary to specify the unit of analysis on which the individual is asked to focus (e.g. department, organization, or job) and to construct items on that level of analysis. If a researcher is interested in organizational climate, the items must be formulated on the organizational level and the instruction level must be the organization. An example of an instruction might be, "On the following pages short statements are presented which might be typical for your organization. Please, think about your organization as a whole when answering. The statement should capture your opinion about the whole organization, not only about the department in which you work daily." A corresponding item could be, "How often are work activities predictable?[1]" If the formulation of item were "How often are your work activities predictable?", the item would not be constructed on the organizational level, but on the, inappropriate, individual level.

In several organizational climate studies there is a lack of consensus between organization members on a high-aggregation level, like the organization. This could be the result of an inappropriate level of instruction or a lacking level of instruction (Rousseau, 1988; Schneider, 1990). Again, analogous to culture there can be several subclimates within an organization. A subclimate could refer to a certain department or a certain aspect, like a service climate. The research question determines the relevance of a specific frame of reference.

6.1   Organizational climate and organizational culture

Following Reiches and Schneider (1990), climate is widely defined as the common or shared perception of organizational policies, practices and procedures, both formal and informal. These organizational factors are easily observable for organization members. Climate descriptions are non-evaluative statements about conditions in the organization, based on individuals' perceptions as organization members. Rousseau (1990) argued that climate focuses on descriptive beliefs individuals hold regarding organizational conditions. These descriptive beliefs are influenced by individual characteristics and the position of the individuals in the organization. These descriptive beliefs are contrasted with normative beliefs, "which are more strictly a product of cultural processes" (Rousseau, 1990, p.159). As mentioned, culture refers more to deep-rooted assumptions, beliefs, and values that are taken for granted, that is, not directly observable and often preconscious.

Shared perceptions (climate) and shared assumptions (culture) are conceptually related. Both concepts refer to "the perceived logic of the internal social environment of a human organization" (Denison, 1990, p.31). New organization members will learn how to perceive and interpret organizational conditions correctly through socialization processes and symbolic interactions with other members. Through these learning processes important organizational assumptions and values will become internalized. That is, these values and assumptions are stored in cognitive schemata and, on basis of these schemata, meaning is attributed to perceived organizational conditions. In fact, new organizational members will undergo a cognitive, emotional, and perceptual training program, through which they learn how to perceive in a psychological relevant way and act accordingly.

Another similarity between climate and culture are that both concepts try to explain the impact of the organization or system on individuals. Also, both concepts are multi-dimensional. In an organization there could be a safety culture or climate and a service culture or climate.

Despite these similairities, there are important methodological and epistemological differences between climate and culture. Organizational climate has to do with individuals' perceptions of organizational behavior and of other observable conditions in an organization, whereas culture refers to invisible assumptions and values. If we include climate in the culture concept, we can consider climate as the manifestation of culture. The methodological differences are due to the different scientific backgrounds and traditions of climate and culture reseachers. The concept of organizational climate is rooted in psychology, with an emphasis on the perception of individuals. Traditionally, these perceptions are measured with questionnaires and related to other variables, such as performance or absenteeism (quantitative methods and statistics). The emphasis is on generalization of the results to the population. Culture, rooted in anthropology, is usually studied through hermeunitical research methods, like ethnography. Here, the results are interpreted from the research subject (clinical reference, see Geertz, 1973).

Moreover, in spite of the conceptual similarity between climate and culture Denison (1990) suggests maintaining the methodological differences. Perceptions are easily measured with questionnaires, but to describe basic assumptions and values, to decipher symbols and to unfold meaning into a richer, more complete and valid picture (or painting), one needs qualitative approaches. The advantage of both methods could be used in a hybrid design. For example, using questionnaires to scan the climate of an organization quickly, and using qualitative methods to validate results and get a more comprehensive view of meanings in the organization.

7 THE COMPETING-VALUES MODEL OF ORGANIZATIONAL CULTURE AND A CASE STUDY OF ORGANIZATIONAL CULTURE AND CLIMATE

The competing-values approach (CVA) (Quinn, 1988; Quinn & Rohrbaugh, 1983; Quinn & Kimberly, 1984); is an integrated framework on organizing. The CVA was originally developed to describe values underlying several organizational-effectiveness models. The CVA model is a powerful device, which can also be applied to organizations culture. An important assumption of the model is that "organizations can be characterized according to cultural traits or dimensions common

to all human organization" (Denison & Spreitzer, 1991, p.7).

The model consists of two dimensions (see Figure 6.1). The first dimension represents the organization's point of view. The focus can either be directed internally, which makes the organization itself, its processes or its people the central issue, or externally, which makes the relations of the organization with its environment the central issue. The second dimension is formed by flexibility and control. Control indicates that, to a certain extent, the behavior of organization members can be controlled. Flexibility signifies a certain degree of discretion for organization members. Combining these two dimensions gives four organizational culture orientations (Quinn, 1988). Organizations can score high on none, one, or any combination of these dimensions. The four cultural orientations are the support, the innovative, the rules, and the goal orientation (Van Muijen, 1994; Van Muijen, Koopman, Dondeyne, De Cock, & De Witte, 1992; Van Muijen & Koopman, 1994).

Central to the *support* orientation are concepts like participation, cooperation, people-based, social, mutual trust, group cohesion, and individual growth. Communication is often verbal and informal. Employees are encouraged to express ideas about their work and feelings about each other. Decision-making often runs through informal contacts. Commitment of the individual employee is emphasized. The *innovative* orientation is characterized by concepts like searching for new information in the environment, creativity, openness to change, anticipation, and experimentation. Communication is informal and usually flows in all directions. Control from above is neither possible nor required. Management assumes and expects commitment from and involvement of employees in their work and the organizational objectives. The focus of the *rules* orientation is on respect for authority, rationality in procedures, division of work, and normalization. The structure is hierarchical and communication is often written and top-down. Power is based on formal authority. The *goal* orientation emphasizes concepts like rationality, management-by-objectives, goal-setting, selected information, functionality accomplishment, and

FIGURE 6.1

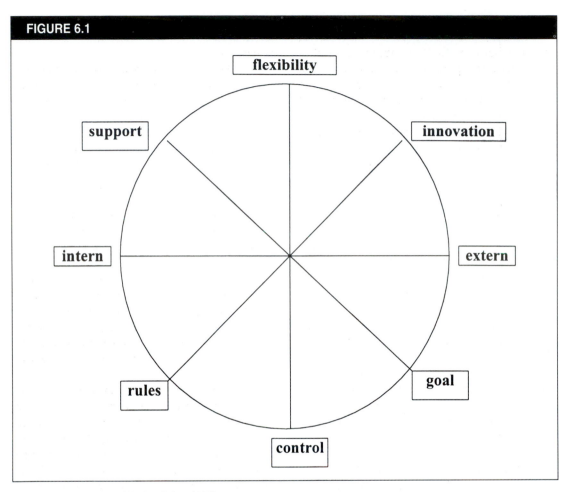

The competing values model (after Quinn, 1988).

contingency reward. The essence of this orientation is to realize the objectives in a rational way, taking the external environment into account.

The CVA model is *circumplex*. The circle (Figure 6.2) can be read from left to right and vice versa. This implies that the values of each orientation share some characteristics with values of the adjoining orientation. For example, the support orientation and the innovative orientation share an emphasis on flexibility, and the innovative and the goal orientation focus on the external environment. Among the values of the diametrical orientations there is tension. The values of the rules orientation emphasize stability and control, whereas the values of the innovative orientation stress flexibility and change. The values of the support orientation participation, cooperation, and mutual

trust are in stark contrast to the values competition (internal and external), accomplishment, and contingency reward. In other words, one would expect positive correlations among adjoining orientations, and negative of very low correlations among diametrical orientations.

As written before, the culture of an organization can be described in terms of these four orientations. There are several methods to study culture. The distinction between qualitative and quantitative methods was described earlier. A group of researchers from Europe and elsewhere has developed an questionnaire, the so-called "FOCUS-questionnaire", to measure the four cultural orientations. Over 100 organizations participated in their research (Van Muijen & Koopman, 1994). Part of the FOCUS-questionnaire measures the perceptions of behavior and of other observable conditions in an organization, that is, organizational climate. Remember that we consider climate as the manifestation of culture. The deeper layers of organizational culture, like values, could be studied by interviewing several important insiders and analyzing documents.

In the following case study the FOCUS-questionnaire was used to characterize the organization on the dimensions of support, innovation, rules, and goal orientation, and in addition several insiders were interviewed. The semi-structured interview-questionnaire was also based on the CVA-model.

The organization in this case study (Star) is one of the largest catering organizations in the Netherlands. Star employs over 5,500 people and operates in more than 900 locations, feeding over 375,000 people every day. The company has clients in business, industry, and the public-sector market, particularly government buildings and the prisons. The company has pioneered the tailoring of services to these markets, training its own experts and working closely with clients to understand the requirements of each sector. Besides its catering service, the organization also provides a party and event-catering service. The organization is divided in four regional areas. Each area has its own management, personnel, and other specialists. The CEO and the general Human Resource Manager from head office were interested in whether there was a corporate culture and whether there were regional differences in culture. The location of daily work activities is for most employees work in the client organization, not at the catering organization itself. After their socialization during the first weeks of employment at the catering organization, they spend most of their time at the client's organization and are thus socialized again.

FOCUS-questionnaires were sent at random to 50% of the employees. The instruction level was the catering organization, that is, respondents were asked to fill in the questionnaire focusing on the catering organization as a whole and not on the client organization where they worked daily. Figure 6.2 shows the results for the total organization. The catering organization is characterized by a relatively high score on the rules orientation, a

moderate score on the support orientation, and lower scores on the innovation and rules orientation.

In other words, respondents describe the organizational climate as internally oriented. Most work activities are organized according to procedures and rules. This explains why the score on the innovation orientation is low; the procedures inhibit new ways of working or product innovation. Organization members also perceive some characteristics of the support orientation. For example, the organization encourages and finances workers to follow courses relevant to their work. Although catering managers and workers are responsible for realizing their goals (goal orientation) the organization is not characterized by a goal orientation. One explanation was that on this orientation there is a significant difference between managers and workers. Managers indicate more pressure on achieving goals than workers resulting in a relatively low mean on the goal orientation. There were no significant regional differences.

These quantitative results are confirmed and explained in greater detail by the qualitaitive results. According to an informant, the organization is not innovative and not very client-oriented. He remarked: "If we are a client-oriented organization and a client needs pink elephants with green ties and blue socks, we ought to fulfil his wishes. However, what do we do? We deliver grey elephants with no ties and socks, and only on Thursday between 10 and 12 am."

The results from the interviews also present another explanation for the low score on the goal orientation and clarify the relatively high score on the rules orientation. Workers and managers are expected to realize their goals, but their reward does not depend on it. People are rewarded for following rules and procedures, even when these rules and procedures are, according to the opinion of most informants, contradictory to organizational goals. The fact that rules and procedures are so important also explains why there are no significant regional differences on the four cultural orientations. Rules and procedures tell people how to behave in general and in specific situations.

What can we learn from this case? Firstly, the

FIGURE 6.2

The results of Star on the four cultural orientations of the competing values model.

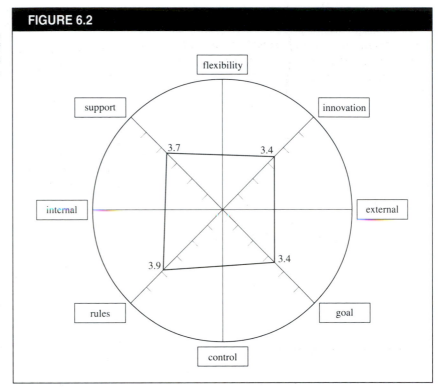

quantitative results were validated by the qualitative ones. There was no difference between behavioral patterens and organizational values. Therefore, organizational climate might be considered as the manifestation of organizational culture. Secondly, the results of the interviews clarified the quantitative results by providing some good explanations for unexpected outcomes. In this kind of studies, one could argue that in interpreting quantitative results one needs direct interaction with organizational members.

8   IN CONCLUSION

In the past, organizational culture has been described as another fad concept by critics. Research and practice, however, show that organizational culture has become an important scientific and practical concept. In particular, the relationship between leadership and organizational culture is now an important topic (Bass, 1988; Bryman, 1992; Den Hartog, Koopman, &

Van Muijen, 1996; Schein, 1992). Sashkin (1988), for instance, writing about visionary leadership, argues "the essential work of organizational leaders is defining, constructing, and gaining commitment to a set of shared values, beliefs, norms about change, goals, and people working together—that is, defining, building and involving people in an organization's culture" (p.136).

Another example of the growing interest in the relationship between leadership and organizational culture is found in the third edition of Yukl's book *Leadership in Organizations* (1994). A chapter on transformational and cultural leadership has been added in the third edition. Trice and Beyer (1991) examine the relationship between type of leadership and consequences for organizational cultures. They formulate a model comparing cultural change and maintenance leadership.

There is still a lot of interest in symposia about organizational culture during scientific congresses, for example, during the 23rd International Congress of Applied Psychology in Madrid, Spain, and the Academy of Management Meeting in Vancouver, Canada.

In practice, many organizations start a organizational development program by investigating the current organizational culture and formulating the desired one, comparable with the earlier mentioned operation Centurion of Philips. This can be very helpful, but it can also be dangerous to define organizational problems in terms of organizational culture. The danger is that organizational culture could then function as a scapegoat, especially for top management. Top management could claim that it is not their fault that the organization does not function as it should, but that the culture caused this situation. In other words, by overstressing the role of organizational culture, top management is able to conceal their own failure.

In conclusion, organizational culture is an important topic, because in an organization values, norms, and behavioral patterns influence daily practices and events.

NOTE

1. This is an example of the FOCUS-questionnaire (Van Muijen & Koopman, 1994).

REFERENCES

Argyris, C., & Schön, D.A. (1978). *Organizational learning: a theory of action perspective.* Reading, MA: Addison-Wesley.

Barley, S.R. (1983). Semiotics and the study of occupational and organizational cultures. *Administrative Science Quarterly, 28,* 393–413.

Bass, B.M. (1988). Evolving perspectives on charismatic leadership. In J.A. Conger & R.N. Kanungo (Ed.). *Charismatic leadership: The elusive factor in organizational effectiveness.* San Francisco: Jossey-Bass.

Bass, B.M., Burger, P.C., Doktor R., & Barett, G.V. (1979). *Assessment of managers: an international comparison.* New York: Free Press.

Bennis, W.G., & Nanus, B. (1985). *Leaders: The strategies for taking charge.* New York: Harper.

Bryman, A. (1992). *Charisma and leadership in organizations.* London: Sage.

Burawoy, M. (1981), Terrains of contest: Factory and state capitalism and socialism. *Socialist Review, 58,* 83–124.

Cock, R. de, Bouwen, R., Witte, J. de, & Visch, J. de (1986). *Organisatieklimaat en cultuur.* Leuven: Acco.

Cohen, A. (1974). *Two-dimensional man: An essay on the anthropology of power and symbolism in complex society.* Berkeley, CA: University of California Press.

Crozier, M. (1964). *The bureaucratic phenomenon.* Chicago: Chicago University Press.

Czarniawska-Joerges, B. (1992). *Exploring complex organizations.* Newbury Park, CA: Sage.

Danserau, F., & Alutto, J.A. (1990). Level-of-analysis issues in climate and culture research. In B. Schneider (Ed.), *Organizational climate and culture.* San Francisco: Jossey-Bass.

Deal, T.E., & Kennedy, A.A. (1982). *Corporate cultures.* Reading, MA: Addison-Wesley.

Denison, D.R. (1990). *Corporate culture and organizational effectiveness.* New York: Wiley.

Denison, D.R., & Spreitzer, G.M. (1991). Organizational culture and organizational development: A competing values approach. In R.W. Woodman & W.A. Passmore (Eds.), *Research in organizational change and development, 5,* 1–22.

Drexler, J. (1977). Organizational climate: Its homogenity within organizations. *Journal of Applied Psychology, 62,* 38–42.

Ekvall, G. (1987). The climate metaphor in organizational theory. In B. M. Bass & P. J. D. Drenth (Eds.), *Advances in organizational psychology.* Beverly Hills, CA: Sage.

Financial Times (1990). Philips to make sweeping cuts. 26 October.

Frost, P.J., Moore, L.F., Louis, M,R , Lundberg, C.C., & Martin, J. (1985) *Organizational culture.* Beverly Hills, CA: Sage.

Geertz, C. (1973). *The interpretation of cultures.* New York: Basic books.

Guest, D.E., Peccei, R., & Thomas, A. (1994). S*afety culture of safety performance: British Rail in the aftermath of the Clapham Junction disaster.* Paper presented at the 1994 Occupational Psychology Conference, Birmingham.

Handy, Ch.B. (1985). *Understanding organizations.* New York: Penguin.

Hartog, D.N. Den, Koopman, P.L., & Van Muijen, J.J. (1996). Linking transformational leadership and organizational culture. *The Journal of Leadership Studies, 3,* 68–84.

Heller, F.A, Drenth, P.J.D., Koopman, P.L., & Rus, V. (1988). *Decisions in organizations: A three-country comparative study.* London: Sage.

Hofstede, G. (1991). *Cultures and organizations.* London: McGraw-Hill.

Hofstede, G., Neuijen, J.A., Daval Ohayv, D., & Sanders, G. (1990). Measuring organizational cultures: A qualitative/quantitative study across twenty cases. *Administrative Science Quarterly, 35,* 286–316.

IDE-international research group (1981). *Industrial democracy in Europe*. Oxford: Clarendon Press.

IDE-international research group (1993). *Industrial democracy in Europe*. Oxford: Clarendon Press.

James, L.R, James, L.A., & Ashe, D.K. (1990). The meaning of organizations: The role of cognition and values. In B. Schneider, (Ed.), *Organizational climate and culture*. San Francisco: Jossey-Bass.

Jansen, N. (1994). *Safety culture: A study of permanent way staff at British Rail*. Amsterdam: Vrije Universiteit.

Kerr, J., & Slocum, J.W. (1987), Managing corporate culture through reward systems. *Academy of Management Executive*. New York: New Library.

Kilmann, R.H., Saxton, M.J., & R. Serpa (1985). Introduction: Five key issues in understanding and changing culture. In R.H. Kilmann, M.J. Saxton, & R. Serpa (Eds.), *Gaining control of the corporate culture*. San Francisco: Jossey-Bass.

Kroeber, A.L., & Kluckhorn, C. (1952). *Culture: A critical review of concepts and definitions*. Cambridge, MA: MIT Press.

Lammers, C.J. (1984). *Organisaties vergelijkenderwijs*. Utrecht: Het Spectrum.

Leach, E.R. (1976). *Culture and communication*. Cambridge: Cambridge University Press.

Lewin, K., Lippitt, R., & White, R.K. (1939). Patterns of aggressive behavior in experimentally created "social climates". *Journal of Social Psychology*, *10*, 271–299.

Louis, M.R. (1985). An investigator's guide to workplace culture. In: P.J. Frost, L.F. Moore, M.R. Louis, C.C. Lundberg, & J. Martin (Eds.). *Organizational culture*. Beverly Hills, CA: Sage.

Martin, J. (1992). *Cultures in organizations*. New York: Oxford University Press.

McGregor, D. (1960). *The human side of enterprise*. New York: McGraw-Hill.

Mead, M. (1949). *Male and Female*. Harmondsworth, UK: Penguin.

Mirvis, Ph.H., & Sales, A.L. (1990). Feeling the elephant: Culture consequences of a corporate acquisation and buy-back. In B. Schneider, *Organizational climate and culture*. San Francisco: Jossey-Bass.

Mitroff, I.I. (1982). *Stakeholders of the mind*. Paper presented at the Academy of Management meetings, New York.

Muijen, J.J. van (1994). *Organisatiecultuur en organisatieklimaat. De ontwikkeling van een meetinstrument op basis van het competing values model*. Amsterdam: Vrije Universiteit.

Muijen, J.J. van, Koopman, P.L., Dondeyne, P.D., De Cock, G., & De Witte, K. (1992). Organizational Culture: The development of an international instrument for comparing countries. In G. Hunyady, (Ed.), *Proceedings; Second European Congress of Psychology*, (pp.249–258) Budapest: Készült.

Muijen, J.J. van, & Koopman, P.L. (1994). The influence of national culture on organizational culture: A comparative study between 10 countries. *The European Work and Organizational Psychologist*, 4, 367–380.

Morgan, P. (1986). *Images of organizations*. London: Sage.

Neuijen, B. (1992). *Diagnozing organizational cultures*. Groningen: Wolters-Noordhoff.

Pennings, J.M. (1986). Organisatiecultuur als hefboom. *Bedrijfskunde*, *58*, 119–125.

Pennings, J.M., & Ch.G. Gresov (1986). Technoeconomic and structural correlates of organizational culture: An integrative framework. *Organization Studies*, *4*, 317–334.

Peters, Th.J., & R.H. Waterman (1982). *In search of excellence*. San Francisco: Harper & Row.

Pettigrew, A.M. (1979). On studying organizational cultures. *Administrative Science Quarterly*, *24*, 570–581.

Pondy, L.R., Frost, P.J., Morgan, G., & Dandridge, T.C. (1982). *Organizational symbolism*. Greenwich, CT: JAI Press.

Quinn, R.E. (1988). *Beyond rational management*. San Francisco: Jossey-Bass.

Quinn, R.E., & Cameron, K.S. (1988). Paradox and transformation. A framework for viewing organization and management. In R.E. Quinn, & K.S. Cameron (Eds.), *Paradox and transformation: Toward a theory of change in organization and management*. Cambridge: Ballinger.

Quinn, R.E., & Kimberly, J.R. (1984). Paradox, planning, and preseverance: Guidelines for managerial practice. In J.R. Kimberly & R.E. Quinn (Ed.), *Managing organizational transitions*. Homewood, IL: Richard D. Irwin.

Quinn, R.E., & Rohrbaugh, J. (1983). A spatial model of effectiveness criteria: Towards a competing values approach to organizational analysis. *Management Science*, *29*, 363–377.

Reiches, A.E., & Schneider, B. (1990). Climate and culture: an evolution of constructs. In B. Schneider, (Ed.), *Organizational climate and culture*. San Francisco: Jossey-Bass.

Rentsch, J.R. (1990). Climate and culture: Interaction and qualitative differences in organizational meanings. *Journal of Applied Psychology*, *75*, 668–681.

Rice, A.K. (1958). *Productivity and social organization: The Ahmedabad experiment*. London: Tavistock.

Roberts, N.C. (1986). Organizational power styles: Collective and competitive power under varying organizational conditions. *Journal of Applied Behavioral Science*, *22*, 443–458.

Rousseau, D.M. (1988). The construction of climate in organizational research. In C.L. Cooper & I.T. Robertson (Ed.), *International Review of Industrial and Organizational Psychology*, *3*, 139–158. New York: Wiley.

Rousseau, D.M. (1990). Assessing organizational culture: the case for multiple methods. In B. Schneider

(Ed.), *Organziational climate and culture*. San Francisco: Jossey-Bass.

Sackmann, S.A. (1991). *Cultural knowledge in organizations*. London: Sage.

Sashkin, M (1988). The visionary leader. In J.A. Conger, & R.N. Kanungo (Eds.), *Charismatic leadership: The elusive factor in organizational effectiveness*. San Francisco: Jossey-Bass.

Schermerhorn, J.R., Hunt, J.G., & Osborn, R.N. (1994). *Managing Organizational Behavior*. New York: John Wiley & Sons.

Schein, E.A. (1985). *Organizational culture and leadership*. San Francisco: Jossey-Bass.

Schein, E.A. (1992). *Organizational culture and leadership*. San Francisco: Jossey-Bass.

Schneider, B. (1975). Organizational climates: An essay. *Personnel Psychology*, *28*, 447–479.

Schneider, B. (1990). The climate for service. In B. Schneider (Ed.), *Organizational climate and culture*. San Francisco: Jossey-Bass.

Selznick, P.A. (1966) *TVA and the grass roots: A study in the sociology of formal organizations*. New York: Harper & Row (1st Edn 1949).

Smith, P.B., Peterson, M.F., Akanda, D., Callan, V. Cho, N.G., Jesuino, J., D'Amorim, M.A., Koopman, P.L., Leung, K., Mortazawi, S., Munene, J., Radford, M., Ropo, A., Savage, G., & Viedge, C. (1994). Organizational event management in fourteen countries: A comparison with Hofstede's dimensions. In A.M. Bouvy, F. van der Vijfer, P. Schmitz, & P. Boski, (Eds.), *Journeys into cross-cultural psychology*. Amsterdam: Swets & Zeitlinger.

Smircich, L. (1983). Concepts of culture and organiza-tional analysis. *Administrative Science Quarterly*, *28*, 339–358.

Steers, R.M., & Black, J.S. (1994). *Organizational Behavior*. New York: HarperCollins.

Storey, J. (1995). Human resource management: Still marching on, or marching out? In J. Storey (Ed.), *Human resource management: A critical text*. London: Routledge.

Tayeb, M. (1988). *Organizational and national culture: A comparative analysis*. London: Sage.

Tichy, N.M. (1982). Managing change strategically: The technical, political, and cultural keys. *Organizational Dynamics*, *4*, 59–80.

Trice, H.M., & Beyer, J.M. (1991). Cultural leadership in organizations. *Organization Science*, *2*, 149–169.

Trice, H.M., & Beyer, J.M. (1993). *The culture of work organizations*. Englewood Cliffs, NJ: Prentice-Hall.

Waldo, D. (1961). Organization theory: An elephantine problem. *Public Administration Review*, *21*, 210–225.

Weick, K.E. (1979). *The social psychology of organizing*. London: Addison-Wesley.

Weick, K.E. (1985). The significance of corporate culture. In P.J. Frost, L.F. Moore, M.R. Louis, C.C. Lundberg, & J. Martin (Eds.), *Organizational culture*. Beverly Hills, CA: Sage.

Wilpert, B. (1996). Management as risk factor in high hazard systems. In P.J.D. Drenth, P.L. Koopman, & B. Wilpert (Eds.), *Organizational decision-making under different economic and political conditions*. Amsterdam: Koninklijke Nederlandse Akademie van Wetenschappen.

Yukl, G. (1994). *Leadership in Organizations*. Englewood Cliffs, NJ: Prentice-Hall.

7

Organizational Psychology in a Cross-cultural Perspective

Pieter J.D. Drenth and Ben Groenendijk

1 INTRODUCTION

More and more frequently it is recognized that the activities of organizations are not restricted to any one country. There is an increasing number of contacts between organizations in various countries. National and cultural borders coincide less and less with the real demarcation lines for the sale of products and services, and for the recruitment, allocation, and training of personnel.

This applies to all sectors of the economy and is not restricted to the so-called "multinationals". Internationalization is the key word in market orientation, strategic policy, research, personnel management, competition, and cooperation. Recent socio-political developments, such as the growing unification of Europe, the opening of central and eastern Europe, and the increasing migration from countries with a lower standard of living or repressive regimes will only reinforce this international and intercultural orientation.

These developments raise a number of questions in the field of work and organizational psychology, for example:

- Does the culture of a country influence the manner in which an organization functions? If so, is it primarily the organizational structure that is influenced or rather the way in which various informal processes occur? Or is cultural influence perhaps restricted to the attitudes, values, and norms of organizations members, without affecting the manner in which organizations function?

- What should be paid attention to in the training of organization members who will be assigned abroad or who will maintain regular contacts with persons or organizations in other countries? In what way should certain cultural idiosyncrasies in organizational behaviour or in relationships between persons and groups of persons, different from those of the country of origin, be taken into account?

- Do organization principles that contribute to a more effective functioning in a given country have the same results in other countries. Is there, in that case, just one best recipe or are organizations in different countries effective in different ways?

Given these questions, the fact that so much research restricts itself to organizations in only country is surprising indeed. In any case, the implicit or explicit assumption of much of this research, that the research results are supposed to have general validity, should be received with reserve. Research that has the pretention of leading to statements about organizations in general cannot remain restricted to organizations in one given country.

One important reason for the reluctance to carry out cross-cultural research is perhaps the large number of methodological problems inherent in this type of study. Many of these problems, however, do not exclusively occur in cross-cultural research. They often play a role in non-cross-cultural research as well, though the researcher is often less aware of it. Thus, cross-cultural research can also lead to a clarification of previously often "automatic" applied concepts and nuances in traditional interpretations of work and organizational psychology in general.

A discussion of the general background of the subject of this chapter will be presented in section 2. In section 3 the methodological problems inherent in cross-cultural research will be examined. The following sections will discuss various aspects of the content of the chapter's topic, including:

- differences in attitudes, needs, expectations, and opinions of members of organizations (section 4);
- cross-national differences between organizations (section 5);
- the role of "culture" in these differences (section 6).

In section 7 the general frame of reference will be briefly handled again, while an attempt will be made to indicate how the most probable causal lines run. In the final section some conclusions and some expected developments in the cross-cultural research on organizations will be presented.

2   GENERAL FRAME OF REFERENCE

In the economic history of the past few centuries, one sees that with increasing industrialization more and more people are spending an important part of their lives in work organizations. Naturally, these employees have their own attitudes, needs, expectations, and opinions, which exercise influence on the organization. At the same time, does the organization influence the behaviour and attitudes of its members? It is obvious that the study of interactions between work organizations and the behaviour of employees is an interesting area of research, especially when placed against the background of intercultural differences.

In organizational psychology two main questions are dominant:

1. Direct relationships. What are the interactions between organizational characteristics and processes, on the one hand, and attitudes, work behaviour, and performance of people working in these organizations, on the other? We use the term "interactions", i.e. reference is made to the effects of organizational variables on the behaviour and attitudes of organization members as well as to the effects of behaviour and attitudes on (certain characteristics of) the organization.
2. Contingency factors. Under which conditions are certain organizational characteristics and processes related to certain attitudes (for example, commitment to the organization, satisfaction) or to certain work behaviour (for example, productivity, effort, absenteeism, personnel turnover)?

Many of the assumed conditions (also called contingent factors) in this second question are possibly embedded in the organization itself. Technology, nature of the work and product, size, centralization, formalization, specialization, etc. come to mind. Other contingent factors may be found in the individual of the group itself, such as age, sex, socio-economic level, rank in the organization, and education. Again, others are to be located in the broader physical and social environment, such as geographical conditions, political structures of the country, level of the country's development, unemployment level, and the dominant value system.

Within organizational psychology still other

questions occur, such as the question of the interrelationship between organizational characteristics, or the question of the relationship between work attitudes and work performance. However, the broad field of organizational psychology in principle deals with both "organizations" and "(behaviour of) individuals", and cannot restrict itself to one of these aspects.

Now, given the preceding definition of organizational psychology, the question of the subject-matter of cross-cultural research in organizational psychology still remains to be answered.

Brought into a *cross-cultural* perspective, the two general questions just designated could be transformed into the following (see figure 7.1, in which the numbers refer to the subquestions that follow):

1. Can cultural factors explain the differences in:
   1a. organizational characteristics, which might influence the work behaviour and performance of people in organizations?
   1b. attitudes and behaviour of people in organizations, which might influence various aspects of the organization?
2. Is culture a *contingent* factor in the relationship between organization and human behaviour?

The second question refers to the fact that the relationship between certain organizational characteristics (climate, size, formal characteristics, etc.), on the one hand, and work behaviour of the employees (job satisfaction, participative style, performance, etc.), on the other, may differ from one culture to another.

The second main question has been investigated only sporadically. By far the greatest amount of research has been devoted to differences in attitudes, needs, and expectations of organization members (section 4). In the light of subquestions 1a and 1b, however, this chapter will particularly focus on cross-national differences between organizations and the question of to what extent empirical evidence supports either of the hypothetical lines, or both. Section 6 examines the role of "culture" as a possible explanation of these differences.

In order to be able to answer those questions it is not enough to investigate whether organizations or individuals differ cross-*nationally*. The problem is that not all national differences can be considered cultural differences, in spite of the fact that in many publications the words "cross-cultural" and "cross-national" are used synonymously. Nations differ in language, legislation, religion, education, geographical and climate variables, economic and technological factors, and many other aspects. Many of these aspects are influenced by or have influence on cultural factors, but this still does not mean that they can be simply equated with culture. On the other hand, also within one nation, a large cultural variety can be found.

In a quite different approach "culture" is defined as everything that cannot be explained

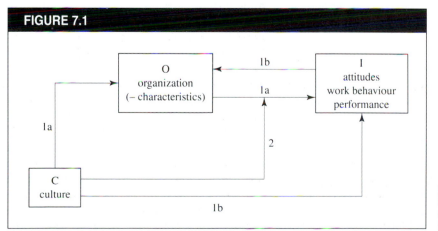

FIGURE 7.1

Hypothetical relationships between culture, organizations, and individuals.

through other identified factors; culture as a residue-factor, which remains in the "black box" after we have identified as many determinants as possible. This approach does not have much explanatory power either. We, therefore, completely agree with Jahoda (1980), who pleads for a specific choice and definition of what is meant by "culture".

A specific definition and reasoned choice of what is meant by "culture" as Jahoda (1980) demands is a prerequisite for a scientific discussion. In our view, "culture" should be conceptualized as the pattern of attitudes, values, and norms in a given society that exercise an influence on the behaviour of population groups. This patterns exhibits a certain stability over generations, although it does adapt itself to changing social and physical conditions. This description is in agreement with the much-quoted definition of Kluckhohn (1951), who defines the concept as "patterns of behaviour of human groups acquired and transmitted by symbols; the essential core of culture consists of traditional ideas, and especially their attached values". Lammers and Hickson (1979) define this concept, following Kroeber and Parsons (1958), a bit more sharply as "patterns of roles and norms embedded in certain paramount values".

It should be emphasized that this description of culture refers to roles and norms of larger (sub) populations and not of groups at a much lower level of aggregation, such as associations, institutes, companies, or even departments of a company. For this level of analysis the term "organizational culture" is used. For a discussion of this concept the reader is referred to Chapter 6 in this Handbook.

3   METHODOLOGICAL PROBLEMS

The difficulties in cross-cultural research caused by the large number of methodological problems have been described in more or less detail by many authors (Berry, 1980a; Berry et al., 1992; Brislin, Lonner, & Thorndike, 1973; Elder, 1976; Irvine & Carroll, 1986; Lonner & Berry, 1986a; Przeworski & Teune, 1970; Roberts, 1970).

In this section the following will be successively discussed: problems of translation, equivalence of concepts, differences in relationships, problems with response-sets, sampling difficulties, and finally the choice of the appropriate level of aggregation.

Translation

In many cross-cultural studies use is made of a questionnaire or interview form. These are often formulated in the mother tongue of the respondent. This is, however, not always the case; sometimes English questionnaires are used in other language areas. Apart from the problem that the questionnaire can be only used on that part of the population with an adequate command of English, the question still remains of whether the applied words and expressions have the same meaning for respondents outside of English-language countries as for people who use English as the daily vernacular. The simple utilization of English questionnaires outside of English-language areas should be discouraged as a rule. Naturally, this applies for other languages as well.

New problems naturally occur in translation. How is a comparable translation obtained? Can all concepts be well translated?

First, it is advisable to consider a number of guidelines for the choice of wordings in the original questionnaire, which make the translation easier. Brislin (1986) offers a list of these guidelines, such as: use of short sentences, use of the active form, avoidance of the subjunctive mood, avoidance of metaphors, choice of words that can easily be translated, etc.

Then there is the translation itself. A frequently applied technique is the so-called "back-translation" (see, for instance, Brislin, 1970). This technique involves the independent translation of the translated version back into the original language. The back translation and the original are compared and then, if necessary, the translation is adjusted. This method is also not without problems (see, for example, Bennett, 1977b). For many words, there are simply no good translation equivalents, especially when they have to be translated out of context (Osgood, 1967).

The so-called "decentring" method is an improvement of this technique (Brislin, 1976,

1986; Brislin et al., 1973). In this method, which is an extension of "back translation", the original version is not taken as the only criterion. After the back translation, the original version can be altered so that it is "translatable". In this way the translated version is a more equivalent alternative to the original version. The literal translatability is the criterion here just as with ordinary back translation.

It is assumed that well-translatable words refer to the same construct. But here also some question marks can be placed. Even well-translated quest-ionnaires cannot always be considered actually to measure the same things (to possess functional equivalence; see next section). Functional equiv-alence, as a rule, is considered to be the ultimate goal of the translation or adaptation (Elder, 1976; Osgood, 1967; Przeworski & Teune, 1970).

Faking and response sets

The problem of "faking" is a difficult obstacle in intra-cultural research. With this concept we are not exclusively thinking of the conscious distor-tion and embellishment of responses, but of a much more broadly conceived phenomenon, whereby a respondent presents himself other than he really is or expresses opinions other than those he really entertains, mostly on the basis of a subjective evaluation of the goal of the research situation (for an analysis of faking on question-naires see Van Esbroeck, 1982). In cross-cultural research this phenomenon can determine a still much larger part of the variance. In some cultures (e.g. Japan, China, Indonesia) the tendency "to please" the interrogator is perhaps a lot stronger than in other cultures. This "pleasing" will result in highly coloured information.

The same phenomenon will occur in tests and questionnaires to be used in cross-cultural research. We know that, in general, social desir-ability is often a significant determinant of res-ponses. But in some cultures the tendency to give socially desirable answers because of upbringing and tradition is stronger than in other cultures. Notably, in cross-cultural research, these differ-ences in social desirability could seriously damage the comparability of the scales. This reasoning also applies to the different kinds of response-sets. For example, the acquiescence-set can be fur-thered in East Asian countries by this "courtesy bias" (Elder, 1976) as well.

The response-set problem also can be encoun-tered in all kinds of other and more subtle variations. Response categories such as "often", "sometimes", etc. can vary widely in meaning, especially when the circumstances are rather diverse. This definitely plays a role in cross-cultural research. In a plant in a developing country an occasional consultation by the manager is perhaps experienced as "often", while in a Dutch or Scandinavian concern it will evaluated as "seldom". It is, therefore, important to formulate the response categories as concretely as possible.

Finally, one must not forget that large differ-ences between countries exist as to what one considers to be a proper and acceptable question. Deutscher (1973) points out that questions about income, family life, leisure, and the like are considered as a much greater breach of "privacy" in some countries than in others. That this will colour reactions does not require argument.

Conceptual, functional, and metric equivalence

If the measurement of a phenomenon in different cultures results in different scores, this can mean two things: either the phenomenon differs in nature or intensity, or the instrument used is not "equivalent". With respect to this equivalence, three different aspects may be distinguished:

First, *conceptual equivalence*. This requirement relates to the question of whether respondents in different cultures attach the same meaning or "definition" to the concepts used. For instance, in an international comparative study of the meaning of working (MOW, 1981, 1987) the same defi-nition of "working" should be used, in order to avoid that in one country only paid work and in another any useful activity in society, including voluntary work, is included. (Of course, we assume that these different "definitions" are not the very object of the research; Drenth, 1989.)

Secondly, *functional equivalence*. This require-ment means that the instruments (indices, scales, tests) measure the same thing in the different populations (Malpass & Poortinga, 1986; Poort-inga, 1975). A test for musical aptitude in culture A can have a strong intelligence-test character in culture B, as in this test use is made of concepts or words that are much less commonly known and therefore require more education or "intelligence" in culture B. Such a test is not functionally equivalent. A method to test this condition is based on a comparison of intercorrelations with other instruments or scales. If similar patterns of inter-relationships with other instruments in different cultures are found, functional equivalence can be assumed. Of course, this applies only when the concepts measured with the different instruments relate to each other similarly in those cultures.

Also different p-value (difficulty indices) of the items in two different populations is an indication of lack of functional equivalence. Van der Flier (1980) has based his so-called *deviance-index* on this phenomenon. If this index is large the test may not be used to generate conclusions on similarity or differences with respect to the attribute under study between the two populations.

Thirdly, *metric equivalence*. This even more rigorous requirement is to be applied if absolute or average scores in different populations are compared. Metric equivalence relates to the comparability—in quantitative terms and as far as the distribution is concerned—of data sets in different populations (cf. Berry, 1980b).

Various item-level analyses as well as the availability of external criteria or reference-scales are needed for the testing of metric equivalence (Malpass & Poortinga, 1986).

In individual psychology it seems that the aforementioned requirements are met only in the case of experimental psychological measures that are easy to operationalize (Drenth & Van der Flier, 1973; Poortinga, 1971). In cross-cultural research in organizations, the requirements already mentioned are often not met either in the measurement of individual attitudes and values or in the measurement of organizational characteristics. The more rigorous requirement of metric equivalence especially presents problems. We will return to this point in the following section.

Metric equivalence and differences in relationships

By far the largest part of cross-cultural research is concerned with score differences on one or more variables. This type of research will be handled in

detail also in this chapter. Nevertheless, from the discussion in the previous section it became clear that such comparisons between scores are not without problems. For Przeworski and Teune (1970) the fact that metric equivalence of the applied instruments is very seldom demonstrated is a reason to emphasize the differences in *relationships* among variables instead of simple differences in *level*. For such differences in relationship "only" the requirement of functional equivalence is to be met. Przeworski and Teune also propose an analysis strategy that should prevent a premature explanation of differences among organizations in terms of factors on a higher system level such as "culture". They advise first examining to what extent variables on a lower level, "individual variables", could explain the discovered differences.

Within organizational psychology this suggestion to focus attention primarily on differences in relationships is not taken very seriously. It will be understood that most researchers will find differences in level more interesting and more relevant.

The discussion of differences in level and differences in relationships seems to lead to an unsatisfactory conclusion. If the confirmation of differences in level must strictly meet the high requirements proposed, for example, by Poortinga (1975), and Przeworski and Teune (1970), such differences will be very seldom determined. Indirectly, one can still attempt to make such differences plausible. One possibility is to use several different methods to measure the same phenomenon (as in the study of Bennett, 1977a). Moreover, the use of techniques other than the usual questionnaire method can contribute to the plausibility of the conclusions (for example games or simulations, see Bass, 1977; Bass & Eldridge, 1973).

The problems that occur in research on differences in score level should, of course, be discerned in an overview of cross-cultural research. But in such a review there is an extra possibility to test certain conclusions regarding differences between cultures. In fact, the results of various studies in which comparable concepts were investigated can be compared with each other. If the conclusions of the various studies are in agreement, they become more convincing. We will make use of this possibility, especially in section 5.

Selection of countries, organizations, and respondents

The selection of the countries to be involved in the research and the compilation of the samples, organizations, and persons within the country should be based on theoretical and methodological considerations (see, for instance, Lonner & Berry, 1986). In fact, the solution is often highly influenced by practical conditions.

As for the choice of the *countries*, there are two approaches to choose from, depending on the question:

1. Maximum *similarity* between the countries; this model is justified when one wants to examine the influence of a certain independent variable on organizational characteristics. As an example one can think of the influence of the independent variable "capitalism versus socialism" on the extent of democratization in industrial organizations. In an ideal case one chooses countries that greatly differ on the designated dimension, but are as similar as possible on the remainder. The weakness of this approach is that the last requirement is hardly ever satisfied. Countries differ as a rule on a number of other features, on the basis of which plausible alternative explanations could be generated.

2. Maximum *differences* between the countries; this model is desirable when theoretical or causal relationships are examined. If, for example, one wants to demonstrate that the level of social security has an influence on absenteeism, or that the unemployment figures in a country affect the importance attached to having a paid job, the selection of countries that are clearly distinct with respect to these variables ("case independence"; Elder, 1976) is important.

As has already been said, pragmatic considerations and questions play an important part in the selection of the countries (can qualified co-workers for the project be found in the country involved, is there entry to the companies and cooperation on the part of the authorities, is there sufficient subsidy and the like?). Because of these reasons cross-cultural research is often restricted to a very small number of, often only two, countries.

The selection of *organizations* also is often not made according to the rules. Ideally, one chooses a sample in each country that is as comparable as possible with samples in other countries on aspects such as technology or size of the organization (see, for example, IDE, 1981a). In practice, this selection of organizations is often determined by practical considerations. Admission to companies is not always easy to obtain, especially when rather time-intensive research is involved. In addition, the concept of "organization" itself is not always uniform in different countries. The structure of organizations, their financial and organizational relationship to the mother company or the financial holding, can vary widely.

Once the selection of the company has been made, it is often less difficult to make a selection of respondents (IDE, 1981a), groups, work units (Koopman, Drenth, Bus, Kruijswijk, & Wierdsma, 1981), decisions (DIO, 1983; Koopman, Drenth, Heller, & Rus, 1991) or whatever the unit of analysis might be.

In the foregoing it was assumed that the choice of certain countries is made first, that subsequently organizations within the countries are chosen, and that finally the selection of respondents within the organizations takes place. Sometimes another route is actually followed. For instance, Hofstede (1979, 1980) compared the subsidiaries of the same multinational in 40 countries. One could say that the choice of the organization preceded the choice of countries and for a large part also determined the latter choice. This method has the important advantage that the organizations will not vary too much regarding salient characteristics. A disadvantage is that research is restricted to the one multinational concern and the generalizability is more limited.

Finally, we mentioned another, less well justified procedure, which is often encountered in cross-cultural research in organizational psychology, particularly in research on attitudes of organization members. We have in mind research that is based on samples of persons who "accidentally" participate in workshops or courses. This method may be convenient but the representativeness is almost always lost.

Level of aggregation

One last difficulty to be discussed concerns the level of observation and analysis. In cross-cultural organizational psychology this is naturally often the level of organizations. However, studying organizations data are collected at the level of individual members of the organizations. Here we encounter the difficulties related to the distinction between individual and aggregated data (Scheuch, 1966). When the level of analysis is the same as that of observation, we speak of *individual* data (this can be the level of persons, but also the level of decisions, departments, and organizations). Data are *aggregated* when the analysis level is higher than the observation level. This occurs, for example, when the analysis is done on the level of the department or organization, where the data consists of averaged scores of members of the department or organization.

Such changes in level are seen relatively often in cross-cultural research in organizational psychology. A few examples: the concepts of "division of power" and "total amount of power in the organization", as developed by Tannenbaum, are repeatedly used in cross-cultural comparative research between organizations (Tannenbaum, 1968; Tannenbaum, Kavcic, Rosher, Vianello, & Wieser, 1974; Tannenbaum & Cooke, 1979). In fact, this involves aggregated measurements based on average scores for the various hierarchical levels. Hofstede (1980) also makes use of aggregated data for each of the subsidiaries investigated by him.

A warning not to lose sight of this difference in level seems appropriate. Robinson (1959) long ago pointed out the danger of these, what he calls, "ecological" correlations. It is not admissible to drawn conclusions from correlations on a high level of aggregation about relationships on an individual level and vice versa. A relationship between the degree of unionization and the level of activity of the works council, established on the organization level, cannot simply lead to the conclusion that this relationship also exists on the

individual level. It could very well be that trade-union members are not active on the works council, but that with an increasing union membership precisely non-trade-union members become more active on the works council. Similarly, a correlation on the individual level can disappear on the organization level (the "Durkheimian Fallacy", Blalock, 1961).

Ecological correlations are often higher than individual ones; because of the process of averaging, part of the error variance drops out of the individual data. One does well to view these various kinds of correlations as separate realities and to be careful with interpretations at other levels of analysis.

Mutatis mutandis, what we have said so far is also valid for an aggregation at a still higher level, namely that of the country itself. One could establish average organization scores at the country level and relate these to socio-political norms, cultural factors, and the like. From the foregoing it will be clear that relationships on this level are not to be simply extrapolated to the level of the organization.

4   CULTURE AND ATTITUDES

By far the greatest part of cross-cultural research in organizational psychology pertains to attitudes, needs, expectations, and norms of organization members. From the organizational psychological perspective, as described in section 2, this research is only relevant if relationships can be established with organizational characteristics or operating modes of organizations. We will, therefore, refrain from reviewing extensively results of this type of research, and restrict ourselves to a discussion of a few often cited examples in order to indicate the possibilities and limitations of this type of research.

4.1   Clusters

A classic and often-cited study in this area is that of Haire, Ghiselli, and Porter (1966), which was carried out on a sample of over 3600 managers from 14 different countries. They found a large number of differences between the 14 countries, especially pertaining to attitudes and assumptions underlying management practices.

The most striking result of the research was the clustering of countries in the following five groups:

1. Northern Europe (Norway, Sweden, Denmark, and West Germany).
2. Latin Europe (Spain, Italy, France, and Belgium).
3. Anglo-American (England and United States).
4. Developing countries (India, Argentina, and Chile).
5. Japan.

The most salient differences between these clusters concern ideas about leadership and the satisfaction of a number of needs within the Maslow-hierarchy (somewhat modified by Haire et al., 1966).

In general, it seems that managers do not have a high opinion of the "capacity for leadership and initiative" of most people. Respondents from Europe (northern and Latin) have still less confidence in those capacities than do managers from other countries. This difference was not found on three other dimensions, which concerned attitudes with respect to participative leadership. Here the developing countries stood out from all the other countries owing to negative attitudes.

Secondly, there are differences in the extent of satisfaction of Maslow-needs. Especially the developing countries, but also the Latin European countries, were conspicuous for their low level of satisfaction. In northern Europe satisfaction is high. These needs were found to be the most important in the developing countries, the least in northern Europe.

Ronen and Shenkar (1985) have combined the results of a number of studies, which led to a clustering of countries, into a "cultural map" with the following eight clusters: Nordic, Germanic, Anglo, Latin, European, Latin American, Far Eastern, Arab, Near Eastern, and "independent" (i.e. rest category). This categorization concurs with "common-sense" ideas about country clusters. The reason for the exclusion of Africa and eastern Europe is simply the absence of sufficient data for these countries.

The cultural map, however, does not follow unambiguously from the empirical data. Griffeth and Hom (1987) conclude on the basis of an analysis of their own material and that of others that the result of clustering of countries is highly dependent on the chosen method (for instance, hierarchical cluster analysis or smallest-space analysis), the selected distance measure (correlation or Euclidic distance), and the interpretation of the researchers.

It is, therefore, too early to state that a "cultural map" of the world has been drawn. However, the clusters can function a useful expedient for the selection of countries for research, or for the formulation of hypotheses.

4.2 Restrictions

The discussed study of Haire et al. (1966) is illustrative for the enormous amount of research in relation to attitudes, values, norms, and opinions of organization members, as discussed by Barrett and Bass (1976), Tannenbaum (1980), and Bhagat and McQuaid (1982). More recently, Ronen (1986), Smith and Peterson (1988), Bhagat, Kedia, Crawford, and Kaplan (1990), and Poortinga (in Berry, Poortinga, Segall, & Dasen, 1992) have presented extensive reviews.

The research of Haire et al. (1966) has a number of limitations which are also applicable to most of the other studies in this area.

In the first place, many of these studies deal with attitudes of organization members, but do not include the organizations themselves in the research. It is obvious that such research can not say much about our earlier questions 1a and 1b.

Secondly, the question arises of whether the observed differences between countries are due to differences in the variables under study or to differences in the *meaning* of the concepts used. For example, differences in attitudes towards participation could also result from the different meanings attached to the concept of "participation". In this vein, one may question the applicability of the Western concept of participation for the more cooperative decision-making that occurs in Java (Martyn-Johns, 1977), or for the consensus-oriented approach through bottom-up procedures and lobby consultations in the Japanese ringi-system (Heller & Misumi, 1987).

In the third place, in each study in which differences between countries are found, one can ask to what extent these differences actually reflect cultural differences. In the case of the study of Haire et al. (1966), there are two arguments which plead for such a conclusion:

1. The clustering of countries into five groups shows a culturally meaningful picture. Culturally related countries often seem to go together in the same cluster and it seems that the clustering of the countries also follows an economic logic.
2. This picture is confirmed in a follow-up study by Ajiferuke and Boddewijn (1970), who related the data of Haire et al (1966), to a number of socio-economic indicators of attitudes and assumptions underlying management practices. The importance of the needs is predicted best from life-expectations, but the percentage of Roman Catholics and the average degree of urbanization are also important predictors. Need fulfilment and, especially, satisfaction could be predicted from the percentage of Roman Catholics and the percentage of illiterates. Ajiferuke and Boddewijn agree with the emphasis of Haire et al (1966). on economics as well as cultural explanations. They also point out that the variables themselves are more important than their labels, such as cultural, psychological, sociological, or economic.

In the fourth place, culture, as a rule, is defined in terms of values, norms, opinions, and attitudes. If, then, an attempt is made to explain the differences in values, attitudes towards work, and the like by means of "culture", the risk of circular reasoning is not imaginary. There are two ways to avoid this problem:

1. Culture can be defined at a macro-level (e.g. religious preferences, political tradition, educational level, etc.) and can thus be distinguished from attitudes, opinions, and values of individuals at the micro-level (Ajiferuke & Boddewijn, 1970).
2. Culture can be defined (and measured) at an individual, personal level, but at the same time a choice should be made of which values, attitudes, norms, and opinions are to be considered as "culture" and which are not. In this approach a number of personal characteristics, aggregated for certain cultural groups, are defined as "culture" and are distinguished from other personal variables that could be seen as "effects of culture". For the former the rule holds that they (a) are relatively stable over time, and (b) provide a more comprehensive explanation and description of behaviour and attitudes in different situations. Attitudes that exclusively concern the work situation will not be categorized as such.

It will have become clear, that the majority of the cross-cultural attitude research—especially if related to work attitudes—has not much to offer for cross-cultural organizational psychology and the main questions formulated in section 2.

4.3   Dimensions

Although the problems discussed in the previous section usually receive too little attention, there is an increasing interest in attempts to identify a restricted number of dimensions within the domain of attitudes in a cross-cultural context (see, for instance, Leung & Bond, 1989, Triandis et al., 1990). By far the best-known study in this field is that of Hofstede, who compared the reactions on a questionnaire with 32 questions on values and opinions within subsidiaries of the multinational IBM in 72 countries.[1]

His earlier analyses (Hofstede, 1980) were based on data from the 40 largest samples. Later data from another 10 countries (direct) and 14 countries (indirect) were used for additional analyses (Hofstede, 1983, 1991).

In this study the following four basic dimensions were identified:

- Power Distance (PDI): the extent to which the less powerful members of organizations and institutions (like the family) accept and expect that power is distributed unequally.
- Uncertainty Avoidance (UAI): the level of uncertainty and anxiety within members of a society caused by unstructured and ambiguous situations.

- Individualism–Collectivism (IND): the degree to which individuals are integrated into groups. In individualistic societies the ties between individuals are loose; everyone is expected to look after him or herself and their immediate family. In collectivistic societies people are integrated from birth onwards into strong cohesive ingroups; often the (extended) families continue protecting them, in exchange for unquestioning loyalty.
- Masculinity–Femininity (MAS): the extent to which social sex-roles are sharply defined. The male role is characterized by achievement orientation, assertiveness, competitiveness, and importance attached to material success. The feminine-pole indicates more overlap between the sex roles and a need with both men and women for good relations, modesty, care for the weak, and with importance attached to non-material aspects of life.

For these dimensions the restrictions discussed in the previous section are relevant. It is even conceivable that the dimensions themselves reflect a (Western) cultural bias. With this in mind the "Chinese Culture Connection" (1987) conducted a similar study in 22 countries, in which "Chinese values" formed the starting point for the construction of a questionnaire. In this investigation four dimensions were found, three of which concurred with the dimensions PDI, INV, and MAS of Hofstede. The fourth factor was different; it was called "Confucian Work Dynamism", as the ideas behind this factor are in agreement with Confucius' teachings (see also Hofstede & Bond, 1988). This dimension reflects the degree to which future-oriented values, such as perseverance and thrift, or values oriented toward the past and present, such as traditions and proper prescribed behaviour, are favoured.

5 DIFFERENCES BETWEEN ORGANIZATIONS

In section 4 it was pointed out that the majority of cross-cultural studies in organizational psychology are restricted to the study of attitudes,

needs, norms, and values of organization members. Our interest primarily concerns differences among organizations in different countries or cultures. Studies of these differences are discussed in various readers (e.g. Hickson & McMillan, 1981; Lammers & Hickson, 1979) and review articles (Lincoln & McBride, 1987; Roberts & Boyacigiller, 1984; Smith & Tayeb, 1988; Whiteley, 1990).

In view of the importance that we attach to cross-cultural research in which organizations are examined, two sections in this chapter (5 and 6) are devoted to this subject. In the present section the question of which cross-cultural differences among organizations in different countries are repeatedly being found will be handled. This discussion will focus on a restricted number of variables, which seem to reflect the mainstream of existing cross-cultural research of organizations. The question to what extent these differences may by considered as "cultural determined" will be discussed in section 6.

Social distance and power

In the 1950s the French sociologist Crozier studied the phenomenon of "bureaucracy" in government organizations in France (Crozier, 1964). Here, attention was especially paid to the dysfunctional aspects of bureaucracy. After a comparison with organizations in the United States and in the Soviet Union, Crozier (1964) concluded that these dysfunctional characteristics were in large part to be ascribed to French culture. Clark (1979) embroidered further on Crozier's study by examining to what extend the dysfunctional characteristics of bureaucracy mentioned by Crozier could also be found in three English factories that had a comparable market position (practically a monopoly), of approximately the same size, and used the same technology. Clark observed a large number of differences between the French and English factories. In the first place, French bureaucracy was typified by a large number of impersonal rules, drawn up by people not directly involved in the daily operations of the factory. In England the existing rules were made by both management and the trade-union representatives within the factory. In addition, the rules in England were often not aimed at covering all possible situations and their application was often open to interpretation by the managers and trade-union representatives. In the second place, there is a highly stratified social structure in France, while in England the social classes are less highly isolated. In the third place, local management in England was more autonomous with respect to the mother organization. Finally, in France the uncertainty that came about when everything could not be laid down in rules more often led to conflicts among the various groups within the organization. This is much less the case in England, which, for example, was evident from the more flexible manner in which machine stoppages were handled.

Lammers and Hickson (1979) distinguish at least two types of organization: a *classical* bureaucracy, which occurs especially in southern Europe, and a more *flexible* type of bureaucracy, which is supposed to be dominant in northern Europe and in North America. In developing countries the so-called "traditional organization" (which is in fact very similar to the Latin type) is supposed to be prevalent. This classification is supported by the results of the various studies in the book of Lammers and Hickson.

The study by Gallie (1978) of two French and two English oil refineries is comparable with that of Clark. In France, he found more social distance between workers and middle management. This result agrees with the more rigid stratification found in France by Clark. Further, Gallie observed a less unequal distribution of power in England. The large number of conflicts in the French oil refineries is ascribed to, among other things, these two differences between the organizations. In the study of Maurice (Lammers & Hickson, 1979, chapter 3; see also Maurice, Sorge, & Warner, 1980), organizations in France and West Germany were compared with each other. The results showed a less rigid stratification in West Germany than in France. In this respect, West Germany was more similar to England than to France.

It seems interesting to compare these results with the research, discussed in section 4, on the attitudes, needs, expectations, and opinions of employees.

The results of Hofstede with respect to the index for Power Distance are in line with the just given picture. The PD-index consists of three items, which can be briefly typified as follows (the descriptions are characteristic for a high PDI-score):

1. Non-managerial employees' perception that employees are afraid to disagree with their managers (this question is considered by Hofstede to be the core of his PDI).
2. Subordinates' perception that their boss tends to make decisions in an autocratic ("tells") or persuasive/paternalistic ("sells") way.
3. Subordinates' preference for anything but a consultative style in their boss.

The results point in the direction of a north–south distinction. English-language countries, Scandinavian countries, (former) West Germany, Austria, and Israel had a relatively low PDI-score. In contrast, Latin Europe, Latin America, and a number of Asian countries had a high PDI. Separate data (not from the same concern) for the former Yugoslavia prompt the surmise that this country belonged to the second group. Thus, West Germany and England were in the same group and even had the same PDI-scores. This result agrees with the findings of Clark, Gallie, and Maurice described earlier.

Here, it should be noted that in our opinion the power-distance of Hofstede, in contrast to what the words suggest, does not reflect real differences in power. The results of Hofstede are, for example, not in agreement with the results of Tannenbaum et al. (1974) in relation to the distribution of influence within organizations in five countries. Also in the IDE study (1979, 1981a) differences between twelve predominantly west European countries were found, using a measure for the distribution of influence derived from the study of Tannenbaum. For an overview the reader is referred to section 5.3 (Table 7.1).

It turns out that e.g. in Israel, which had the lowest PDI-score score among the 12 countries, the greatest differences in influence existed between top management and workers! The former Yugoslavia, the country with the highest PDI-score, had the smallest differences in influence. In any case, there seems to be no relationship between Hofstede's PDI and influence differences in the IDE study. The same is found in a replication study carried out 10 years later, in which surprisingly few changes in the patterns of influence distribution were found (Drenth & Wilpert, 1990; IDE, 1992).

Hofstede (1980, p.118) explains these differences between his own results and those of Tannenbaum et al. (1974) (we assume that this is also valid for the IDE results) concerning the distribution of power by suggesting that the PDI measures *informal* elements of hierarchy, whereas the influence question of Tannenbaum et al. is supposed to measure *formal* elements of hierarchy. But then, it is somewhat surprising that Hofstede views his PDI as conceptually related to the Aston dimension "centralization" (see Hickson & McMillan, 1981). Mintzberg (1979), among others, indicates that in this concept the formal side of the decision process is emphasized too much. It seems, therefore, that this concept has even less in common with the PDI than Tannenbaum's influence differences.

Child (1981) states that in different studies a stronger centralization in organizations was found in West Germany than in England, which was not supported by Hofstede's PDI-scores. Child concludes that the structural aspect of centralization is different from the participative/consultative style of the supervisor and the quality of the personal relations with his or her subordinates. The first aspect is measured in the Aston study, the latter by Hofstede's PDI. Differences in influence and power, as measured by Tannenbaum and in the IDE study seem to reflect "informal participation" rather than centralization according to the Aston-study.

Anyway, it seems that PDI can be interpreted as "leader–follower relations" or "social distance" rather than as differences in influence or power. This interpretation is also suggested by the context of the three items that constitute the PDI-index, as described in the foregoing.

The research results discussed in this section prompt the surmise that the north–south distinction of Lammers and Hickson in the first instance refers to a dimension that could be described as "rigid stratification", "social distance", or "informal participation". Probably this dimension reflects no differences in the division of power

within organizations. Regarding such differences in power, as studied by Tannenbaum et al. and in the IDE research, the distinction of north–south is less adequate.

Formalization and bureaucratic control

In the beginning of this section the study of Clark (1979) was discussed, who observed a number of differences between the French and English tobacco industry. One of these differences referred to the application of impersonal rules. In this section we will examine the extent to which other research results on the presence and use of impersonal rules also fit into the north–south distinction discussed in the previous section. The study of Aiken and Bacharach (1979) is interesting in this respect: a comparison was made between the local authorities in both the French- and Dutch-language areas of Belgium. A number of important differences were found:

- Social control in Flanders was more often based on interpersonal contact (such as direct supervision) and in Wallonia more often on impersonal rules (bureaucratic control).
- Still, respondents in Flemish organizations more often reported the presence of written documents such as job descriptions and documentations of the chains of command (formalization, see also Hickson, Hinings, McMillan, & Schwitter, 1974), but the Flemish often followed shorter routes in order to accomplish something than those indicated by the formal, prescribed procedures. This fact could explain why the greater formalization in Flanders did not lead to stronger bureaucratic control. Apparently, the rules were applied with more flexibility.
- The Flemish reported more often that they had varied work, while respondents in Wallonia more often called it routine work.

These observations are in agreement with the north–south distinction as sketched by Clark for Britain (north) and France (south).

It is surprising that countries like the former West Germany and Austria on this dimension seem to fit better into the "southern" than the "northern" cluster. The research results of Tannenbaum et al. (1974) concerning "opportunities provided by the job" seem to support this. According to Child and Kieser (1979; see also Child, 1981) organizations in West Germany had fewer rules, which, however, were more strictly followed and reinforced. Although there may have been more flexibility in West Germany than in France and England (Maurice et al., 1980), it can be concluded that in West Germany and Austria there was at the same time a relatively strong bureaucratic control.

A confirmation of this picture is found in the study of Hofstede (1980). His dimension "uncertainty avoidance" is measured by the UAI (Uncertainty Avoidance Index). This index consists of three items, among which is the question of whether respondents find that company rules should not be broken—even if the employee thinks it is in the company's best interest. The results show that respondents from Latin countries in Europe and America scored relatively high on this dimension and, therefore, have a strong tendency to avoid uncertainty. Scandinavian countries, The Netherlands, and especially English-speaking countries score low on the UAI. West Germany, Austria, and Switzerland (the latter being the least clear) showed a lower score than Latin countries, but a clearly higher score than other "Northern" countries. Hofstede's UAI seems to be a good indication of what is described as "bureaucratic control" in other studies. Also the extent of variation in the work seems to be connected to this.

Besides, Hofstede (1979, 1980) states that his UAI is conceptually related to the Aston dimension of "structuring of activities" (see also Hickson et al., 1974; Hickson & McMillan, 1981; Mintzberg, 1979). "Formalization" is a component of this dimension.

Within the Aston programme, data were collected in Britain, the US, Canada, West Germany, Poland, Sweden, Japan, Jordan, Egypt, India (Hickson & McMillan, 1981), and Iran (Conaty, Mahmondi, & Miller, 1983). Differences in formalization-scores are, however, not in agreement with Hofstede's findings with respect to UAI.

A more systematic comparison between the UAI and formalization can be made with the aid of formalization scores for 12 countries, as collected in the IDE research (1981a). In this research, the Aston measure for formalization was used. The UAI scores for these 12 countries are also available. The results are reported in Table 7.1 and show two things:

1. There is hardly any relationship between formalization (Aston), on the one hand, and uncertainty avoidance (UAI), on the other.
2. The results in relation to formalization do not seem to behave according to a "culturally sensible" pattern.

Generalizability

Table 7.1, besides giving the results for UAI (Hofstede) and the degree of formalization (IDE), also shows the results with regard to PDI (Hofstede) and the distribution of power (IDE). It seems that PDI and power distribution do not overlap, and neither do UAI and the degree of formalization. As has been mentioned, Hofstede's PDI seems related, rather, to the degree to which organizations are characterized by a participatory climate, rigid stratification, and social distance; his UAI might well be linked to the actual use of bureaucratic control in organizations.

The large majority of available research has confined itself to Western countries. Do the relations found in these countries also apply to countries outside the West? One non-Western country having a reasonable amount of comparable research material is Japan (for example: Cole, 1979; Dore, 1973; Lincoln & McBride, 1987; Misumi, 1985; Pascale & Athos, 1981; Takezawa & Whitehill, 1983). Most of this research compares Japan with the USA; Dore's study compares Japan with Britain.

According to Hofstede (1980), Japan is characterized by a relatively high PDI score, higher than in the USA and other Anglo-Saxon and northern European countries, but lower than France and other European and American Latin countries. This corresponds well to the "paternalistic" leadership system frequently attributed to the Japanese.

A number of direct comparisons, however, have shown little or no difference in the degree of participation between Japan and the United States (Pascale, 1978; Whitley, 1990); Japan, in fact, shows a less rigid stratification (Dore, 1973; Lincoln & Kalleberg, 1985; Whitley, 1990). This

TABLE 7.1

Ranking of 12 countries on four variables. (1 = little power inequality (IDE), low PDI (Hofstede), low UAI (Hofstede), little formalization (IDE).

	Inequality in power distribution	PDI	UAI	Formalization
Britain	6	6/7	3	10
Norway	2	3/4	4	5
Denmark	4/5	2	1	7
Finland	7/8	5	6	9
Sweden	3	3/4	2	1
Former West Germany	9	6/7	7	6
Israel	12	1	9	2
The Netherlands	4/5	8	5	4
Belgium	10/11	10	12	8
Italy	7/8	9	8	1
France	10/11	11	10	3
Former Yugoslavia	1	12	11	12

is clearly at odds with the PDI results. Lincoln, Hanada, and McBride (1986) encountered less formal decentralization in Japan than in the USA (Aston scale), but met with more informal decentralization in the actual workplace. This last result is at odds with Hofstede's assertion (1980) that the PDI is a measure of the informal aspects of power.

Furthermore, according to Hofstede (1980), Japan is characterized by one of the highest UAI scores. The strong affiliation that Japanese employees show with their companies (see Takezawa & Whitehill, 1983) can be seen as indicative of an avoidance of uncertainty. This also applies to the reported Japanese emphasis on the use of formal rules of work organization (Dore, 1973), and the apparently ready acceptance of rules and disciplinary measures laid down by management (Takezawa & Whitehill, 1983). Van Wolferen's description (1989) of Japan as a country in which conflict avoidance takes the form of an extensive system of rituals and intimidation is in line with this view:

In the Japanese sociopolitical order conflicts are avoided, shunned, disavowed, denied, ritually expelled, but seldom resolved ... In personal relations, psychological manipulation often takes the place of a frank discussion about the other's behaviour. p.541)

American employees see their work as being more varied than do Japanese employees (Kalleberg & Lincoln, 1988; Lincoln & Kalleberg, 1985). This might be taken to signify a Japanese tendency to regulate tasks and allow little flexibility or freedom; however, various authors have reported that Japanese organizations in fact employ less specific work roles (Dore, 1973), less division of tasks into subtasks (Cole, 1979), and a less far-reaching functional specialization of jobs (Lincoln et al., 1986). Evidently, fairly strong Japanese work formalization has not led to far-reaching specialization and differentiation in working roles.

These last findings do not square with an image of Japan as "risk-avoiding". They could mean that the Japanese do not avoid risk, but rather that they deal with uncertainty, ambiguity, and imperfection in an extremely subtle way (Pascale & Athos, 1981). It might also be possible that in the Japanese context, the differentiation of work roles is no indication of "uncertainty avoidance"; the relationship between a dimension such as "uncertainty avoidance" and actual behaviour need not, after all, be identical everywhere. Shouksmith (1987), for instance, has pointed out that the intention of staying with a given company (one of the UAI parameters) is influenced not just by cultural factors but also by other circumstances, such as the job-market situation.

In all, the results of research of stratification and participation do not accord with what one might expect on the basis of Japan's PDI score. With regard to the relationship between "uncertainty avoidance" (UAI) and "bureaucratic control" the picture is perhaps clearer. In a comparison between organizations in Japan, South Korea, and Taiwan, and organizations in the USA, Whitley (1990) arrives at a number of findings in various dimensions that are in broad agreement with these countries' UAI scores. These comparisons also demonstrate that it would be deeply mistaken to see Japan as "typical" of South East Asia. In several ways, many organizations in South Korea (and to a lesser extent in Taiwan) differ more from their Japanese than from their American counterparts. This, of course, puts Japan back in the "independent" category to which it was assigned in the research referred to in subsection 4.1.

This brings us to another relevant point: how large, or how important, are the observed differences between organizations in different countries anyway? Besides the differences between companies in different countries, after all, there are other differences between companies themselves that have to do with the branch of business, with technology, or with scale. Variations between countries are, in all probability, not the most significant source of variation in the characteristics and functioning of organizations.

Japan and the USA are generally perceived as being rather dissimilar. Nevertheless, Misumi concludes that, "Broadly speaking, the culture of Japan has much in common with that of the Western world even though its oriental heritage also produces noticeable differences" (1985, p.322), and Ouchi (1981) states that strong agreement exists between the policies and practices of large companies in Japan and the USA. The message is clear: there are similarities as well as differences between countries and cultures, and "culture" itself is just one of a number of factors

producing the actual differences between organizations.

6   CULTURE AND CONVERGENCE

This section will examine more closely the importance of "culture" in explaining the differences between organizations. Firstly, subsection 6.1 goes into the degree to which differences between countries (as noted in section 5) correspond to cultural factors. In subsection 6.2, attention is given to the observed dissimilarities in the distribution of power within organizations. Lastly, in subsection 6.3, we examine the hypothesis that cultural differences will disappear almost altogether as a consequence of economic and technological developments (the so-called "convergence hypothesis"). We also look at the plausibility of "psychological convergence", partly in relation to the "individual-collectivist" dimension.

6.1   Culture and organization processes

The fact that organizations in different countries (or groups of countries) themselves display differences does not entail that these differences are culturally determined. This can be demonstrated in several ways. Firstly, there is hypothesis-testing research of the kind carried out by Triandis (1972) and others. This method is particularly attractive where earlier research or theorizing has created the expectation of a role to be attributed to such cultural factors. However, hypothesis-testing cross-cultural research in organizational psychology is scarce. An example is provided by Triandis and Vassiliou (1972).

Another method of demonstrating that differences between countries are "culturally determined" parallels the method employed by Ajiferuke and Boddewijn (1970) with regard to attitudes (see section 4). Here, organizational differences are related to macro-level variables at the country level, such as dominant religion or degree of income differential. A disadvantage of this approach is that any genuinely unique characteristics of a given culture cannot be investigated (Agar, 1986). With regard to such unique characteristics, descriptive research of the kind often seen in cultural anthropology would probably be better placed.

Organization research almost never includes enough different countries to justify analyses like those of Ajiferuke and Boddewijn. For this reason, in this subsection we shall employ an intermediary step. It is likely that the PDI (which we interpret as "social distance") and Hofstede's UAI (the avoidance of uncertainty) correlate with within-organization processes (such as informal participation, the degree of stratification rigidity, and bureaucratic control). The relation between the latter indices and country-level variables (see Hofstede, 1980) therefore give (albeit indirectly) an indication of the culturally-determined character of differences between organizations.

In an analysis of geographic, economic and demographic factors, the PDI correlates most closely with the per capita Gross National Product (GNP), with latitude (distance from the equator), and with the population growth, three variables which are also mutually strongly correlated. Latitude, population size (not its growth), and GNP, in that order, explain almost 60% of the differences in PDI between countries. This accords with the north–south distinctions outlined in section 5.

Secondly, there appears to be a strong relationship between the PDI and the income differential in a given society. Countries with a low PDI frequently also show more balanced governmental power: there are regular elections, and coalition changes take place peacefully. Countries with a high PDI show more political violence. The PDI is therefore closely connected with processes taking place in society as a whole, and this points to cultural factors as well as to economic and geographical ones.

The UAI index has a conspicuously less close relationship with geographic, economic, and demographic indicators. A significant relationship does exist with GNP, but this is much weaker than that of the PDI with GNP. Hofstede has also drawn an interesting comparison with the data derived by Lynn & Hampson (1975) with regard to a number of medical and related indicators. In an ecological factor analysis of 18 richer countries, Lynn & Hampson found two factors, which they called "neuroticism" and "extraversion". Hofstede found that the first, for which the suicide and alcoholism

indices, for example, had high scores, was closely related to his UAI.

Thirdly, religious factors also appear to be important. In a random sample of 29 principally Christian countries, Hofstede found a strong relation between the percentage of Catholics (both Roman and Orthodox) and his UAI; in more Catholic countries, people were more inclined to avoid uncertainty. The UAI is therefore also related to aspects of wider society. Geographical, economic, and demographic factors play a lesser role here than in the PDI. For these reasons, it is very probable that between-country PDI and UAI differences and their related between-organization differences in areas such as "informal participation", "stratification rigidity", and "bureaucratic control" are at least partly determined by cultural factors.

6.2 Industrial relations and the distribution of power

The conclusion of the previous subsection does not, however, apply to "power differentials" as measured by Tannenbaum et al. in the IDE research project. In Yugoslavia and in Israeli *kibbutzim* Tannenbaum et al. (1974) found a smaller difference in influence between employees and top management than in Italy, Austria, and the United States, and associated these results to the ideologies and formal regulations existing in these countries. Naturally, this interpretation does not exclude a cultural explanation; a country's prevailing ideology and formal regulations might well reflect certain cultural norms and values, at any rate those unconnected with the north–south distinctions discussed earlier in this chapter.

In the IDE research (1979, 1981a), it seems that the found differences in power distribution between 12 countries are in great part to be explained by the existence of formal rules for participation. This is understood by the researchers as all formal, written regulations, and rules aiming at the support and promotion of employees' participation in organizations. These included not only legal regulations but also the results of collective bargaining and of the policy of management. Like Tannenbaum et al., the IDE researchers emphasize the possibility of human intervention in the power division. Power (in)equality is not, therefore, seen as a permanent and stable cultural fact or as the unavoidable result of technological developments.

This interpretation is supported by an analysis of the data from the IDE study, in which an attempt was made to find an explanation for the observed differences in *formal rules* on participation, as described already (IDE, 1981b). Three kinds of explanatory factors have been proposed: economic, cultural, and structural. The reasoning behind the *economic* explanation is that one can permit "participation" only under economically favourable conditions. It could be also defended that in technologically advanced (rich) countries more contributions from the personnel are necessary in decision-making. An index of economic growth and the national income per capita in 1975 were used as indices for the economic factor.

The *cultural* explanation aries from idea that employee-participation laws are rooted in attitudes and values in relation to cooperation, distribution of power, and the like. Three indices were used: political democracy, economic equality (ranking as far as income level is concerned), and cooperation orientation (ranking in terms of days lost due to strikes during the period 1967–1976).

Finally, the *structural* explanation is based on the idea that a system of employee participation will be developed only in cases where there is a strong position for both employees and employers. The strength of both positions was derived from a historical analysis of the system of industrial relationships in the country concerned.

In Table 7.2 the countries are ranked according to three criteria for employee-participation regulations (direct, indirect and by representation on the board of directors or council of commissioners). Further, the results are presented in relation to the various indices mentioned earlier for the three explanations. From this analysis it seems that the cultural explanation is the weakest.[2] The economic explanation also seems to be not very solid. There is a relationship with economic growth but not with prosperity.[3] The structural explanation finds most support. A strong position and organization of both employers and employees seem to form a favourable condition for the promotion of legislation in the area of employee participation in industrial organizations.

In this connection, some interesting research has been carried out into the negotiation arrangements employed by the labour relations found in various countries. On the basis of the OECD data for 17 countries, Bean (1985) concluded that a

TABLE 7.2

Formal rules in relation to participation and a number of possible determinants (1947–1975).

	Formal rules (1)	Position trade union (2)	Position management (2)	Economic growth (3)	Prosperity level (4)	Cooperation orientation (4)	Economic equality (4)	Political democracy (4)
Former Yugoslavia	A	?	?	1	3	1	1	?
Former West Germany	A	1	1	1	1	1	2	3
Sweden	A	1	1	1	1	1	1	1
Norway	B	1	1	1	1	2	3	1
The Netherlands	C	2	2	1	2	1	2	2
France	C	2	2	1	2	2	3	1
Belgium	D	2	2	1	2	2	2	2
Finland	D	2	1	1	2	3	2	1
Israel	D	1	3	1	3	2	1	3
Denmark	D	2	2	2	1	3	3	2
Italy	E	2	3	2	3	3	3	3
Britain	E	2	3	2	3	3	1	2

(1) A = many formal rules in relation to participation, E = few formal rules.
(2) 1 = strong, 2 = average, 3 = weak.
(3) 1 = quick, 2 = slow/stagnation.
(4) relative rank from 1 to and including 3.

relationship existed between the level of such negotiations (national, industrial, regional, company, or department) and the degree of centralization of employers' and employees' organizations. Austria, Norway, Sweden, and Denmark are, in both respects, centralist; the USA, Canada, and Britain are not. Poole (1986), concentrating more on the trade-union situation, examines other indicators indicative of "societal corporatism" and comes to similar conclusions. Both variables described by Bean, henceforth here referred to as "the centralization of industrial relations", are related to the level of trade union membership: the more centralized the industrial relations, the higher the percentage of union members in the workforce.

Comparison of the research results produced by Bean and by the IDE research project (1981a) reveals that the centralization of labour relations is associated with reduced power differentials within organizations. Evidently, growing influence at national or regional level means reduced influence differentials within individual organizations. Remarkably enough, Hofstede's research showed that centralized labour relations also correspond to a low PDI. As the degree of centralization of labour relations and the PDI both say more about the way power relations are constituted than about people's and organizations' influence on each other, it is possible that cultural factors are at work. In any event, the centralization of labour relations would appear to reflect a high level of consensus, which suggests a possible conceptual affinity with the PDI.

The regulatory framework sketched here (strong position for trade union and management—formal rules—more equal power distribution) can definitely not explain all the differences between countries. From a comparison between France and England it seems, for example, that a smaller number of rules and a weak position of management accompany a more equal power distribution in England. A possible explanation for this is perhaps the interpretation of Gallie (1978), who ascribes the greater social integration in English oil refineries to the strivings of the English trade unions for more control over the immediate work situation. At the organizational level, the unions were rather successful in

obtaining such influence. Relatively few formal rules are involved here. By contrast, the French unions have always been more oriented towards making the working class more conscious of its position and opportunities. They also have not been without success. The aspirations of French workers are higher than those of English workers, as far as the reformation of society as a whole is concerned. But they have less influence on the daily operations within the organization, partly because control over the immediate work situation is less strongly pursued and partly because of the unwillingness of French management to allow them such influence. The historical development of the system of industrial relations in both countries is considered of great importance by Gallie. This explanation emphasizes cultural elements which are specific in each of the two countries.

The conclusion could be that, as far as there is cultural influence on the (in)equality of power distribution, it should be perhaps sought in cultural characteristics that are *specific* for a given country. General cultural explanations such as those of Hofstede seem to have little applicability here.

6.3 Convergence hypotheses

This subsection will examine whether cultural factors are indeed negligible or of dwindling importance in the light of other developments (especially technological and economic) that to all intents and purposes now dominate the functioning of organizations. In this hypothesis, organizations in many different countries are increasingly coming to resemble one another as factors such as increasing industrialization, technological developments, communications and the media, general standards of living, and employee training all converge, with the remaining divergent factors (such as differences in natural resources, developmental level, demographic constitution, and specific aspects of culture) becoming less significant. Cultural factors are seen as having an important conservative influence. This standpoint is known as the "convergence hypothesis" and has been extensively described in the literature (Child & Kieser, 1979; Cole, 1973; Dore,

1973; Form, 1979; Kerr, 1983; Kerr, Dunlop, Harbison, & Myers, 1964; Lammers, 1983; Maurice, 1979; Neghandi, 1979; Pascale, 1978; Ronen, 1986).

It is not really possible to speak of "the" convergence hypothesis; there are several variants, with occasionally divergent outcomes (see Kerr, 1983). This chapter will confine its discussion to three observations on the main themes of this hypothesis (as agreed by most of the academic literature on the subject) and will go a little deeper into the principle of "psychological convergence".

1. Often it is not made sufficiently clear which personal or organizational characteristics are concerned in the hypothesized convergence process. In an analysis primarily directed at the distinctions between East (then communist) and West (capitalist), Kerr (1983) observed the following:

- broad convergence in six main categories of production and consumption, involving pragmatic, adaptive solutions (knowledge, the mobilization of production factors, production organization, work, lifestyle and pay);
- hybrids in economic and political structures, influenced by elites;
- abiding heterogeneity with regard to attitudes, feelings, and emotions, linked to "preindustrial beliefs and behaviours".

Seen from this "enlightened" convergence standpoint, differences in attitude and so on (as discussed in section 4) might remain, but differences between organizations (as discussed in section 5) need not ("pragmatic adaptiveness"). With regard to labour relations, too, as discussed in the previous subsection, a certain cultural diversity could remain.

2. Economic and technological factors are often presented as being in opposition to cultural factors. There is, however, little reason for assuming that these factors are mutually exclusive. Moreover, the premise that technological and economic factors exert an influence on organizational processes is itself hardly questioned at all. Research on the nature of the connections between these factors and the ways in which they influence each other might perhaps be more useful than research that presumes from the outset that these factors are diametrically opposed.

3. Empirical substantiation of the hypothesis is difficult if not impossible. The conception is based on a number of premises: that divergent cultural forces are weaker than convergent technological and economic forces, that the latter have more influence on organizations than the former, and that this gradually leads to organizations' internal structures and operational methods coming to resemble one another. The second premise, in particular, which can be compared with the concept of technological congruence (Perrow, 1970) or the ideas of a technological imperative and technological determinism, has been repeatedly criticized (Hickson, Pugh, & Pheysey, 1969; IDE, 1981a; Lammers, 1983; Mohr, 1971). Cross-sectional comparisons showing similarities or dissimilarities do not amount to empirical validation of convergence hypotheses. The systematic longitudinal research, which, strictly speaking, is necessary, has seldom been carried out; where it has (e.g. Fliegel, Sofranko, Williams, & Navin, 1979; IDE, 1992), it has not provided much support for convergence hypotheses.

One of the aspects of "convergence" is the so-called "cultural" (Fliegel et al., 1979) or "psychological" (Yang, 1988) convergence, an idea closely connected to the principle of "individual modernity" (Form, 1979; Segall, Dasen, Berry, & Poortinga, 1990). The best-known research in this area has been carried out by Inkeles and Smith (Inkeles, 1969; Smith & Inkeles, 1966, 1975). The central tenet is that certain human characteristics encourage participation in a modern technological society. Increasing industrialization, then, wherever in the world it occurs, will be associated with people showing openness to new ideas, independence from traditional authorities, belief in science and medicine, ambition, and so on. A "Modern Man" emerges whose values and behaviour are basically the same everywhere.

With reference to criticism of the principle of psychological convergence, Yang (1988) states that the concept of "individual modernity" has more than one dimension, and that psychological convergence may not pertain to all attitudes, values, and behaviours. According to this modified hypothesis, the specifically functional psychological characteristics that support individual adaptation to a certain kind of society (agrarian, hunting, industrial, etc.) would be particularly likely to converge. This would not necessarily be the case for other psychological characteristics.

The concept of "individual modernity" has been only broadly defined and can be seen as comprising various other psychological concepts (Segall et al., 1990; Yang, 1988):

- "*cognitive style*"; the analytical style (Gruenfeld & MacEachern, 1975; Witkin, Dyke, Faterson, Goodenough, & Karp, 1962) comprises social independence and can be characterized as modern;
- "*performance motivation*"; (McClelland, 1961) is primarily seen as a stimulus to economic development. Bhagat et al. (1990) note that cross-cultural research in this area, previously popular, had become rather scarce in the 1980s;
- "*individualism/collectivism*"; this dimension has enjoyed increasing attention (Kagitçibasi & Berry, 1989). Kagitçibasi (1989) has wondered whether this dimension actually replaces the concept of "performance motivation" as a possibly independent or contingent variable in the prediction of economic and other developments. Yang (1988) has shown that most (and certainly not the least important) components of modernism have a conceptual relationship with individualism.

The dimension of "*individualism/collectivism*" was discussed briefly in subsection 4.3, primarily in relation to Hofstede's work (1980). Kagitçibasi (1987; see also Kagitçibasi & Berry, 1989) also stresses that individualism and collectivism are probably not the opposite poles of a unidimensional concept. She also disputes the assumption that individualism is necessarily a question of progress, more or less imposed by industrialization and economic development, with collectivism held to be a sort of temporary state.

This brings us back to the theme of this subsection. Clearly, "individual modernity" is statistically linked to both individualism and economic development. This says nothing, however, about the nature (causal or otherwise) of the relationship. Economic, technological, and cultural factors seem to form an aggregate of components, which, given the sometimes extremely high correlations between them, are difficult to separate. Finally, the assumption is rather too readily made that the same developments are taking place all over the world and that in industrial societies the developments of the recent past will persist, practically unchanged, in the future.

7   SYNTHESIS

Let us look at a number of the matters discussed in this chapter in a slightly broader perspective. Does "culture" exert an influence on organizations and on the behaviour of people in organizations? If so, on what aspects of organizational and individual functioning is this influence seen? It has already been noted that much research has been confined to individual attitudes, needs, expectations, and opinions. The limited amount of research that has been done on the functioning of organizations in different countries has nevertheless produced a reasonably consistent picture.

With regard to formal organizational characteristics, such as the well-known Aston dimensions, there is little reason to assume that cultural factors exercise influence here. This does not mean that in this respect no differences between countries exist, but it is difficult to observe a culturally meaningful pattern in these differences. Organizations do not only have *formal* characteristics but they are also characterized according to the way in which they function. Such characteristics can be distinguished from the formal characteristics because they are more related to the daily operations of the organization, which do not always have to be in agreement with formally prescribed rules. In order to distinguish such organizational characteristics from formal organizational characteristics, they are called "*organizational processes*" (see, for example, Aiken & Bacharach, 1979).

Organizational processes cannot be sharply demarcated from the *behaviour* of organization members. If members of a given organization behave themselves systematically differently from members of other organizations (for example, in following the instituted rules), then there is a question of differences in organizational processes. A clear distinction can be made, however, between organizational processes and *attitudes* ("that which is going on in their heads").

Figure 7.2 contains a schematic representation of the research area, which in comparison with Figure 7.1 (section 1) contains a few new elements, In the first place, the concept of "organizational processes" discussed earlier is integrated in the scheme. The two part-classification "individual–organization" has been substituted by the given three-part classification individual-organizational processes–organizational characteristics. In addition, the possibility to distinguish "cultural individual variables" from other individual variables proposed in section 4 is taken into consideration. Such a description of culture in terms of attitudes, values, norms, and opinions is closely connected to the definition of Kluchkohn (1951) mentioned in section 2, in which ideas and, especially, the related values are considered to be the core of the culture concept. In order to make plausible that the individual variables under consideration are cultural in nature, an attempt could be made to relate them to system-level variables such as political and religious variables (see section 4 and 6).

The research discussed in sections 4 and 5 can be easily placed in this scheme. Cultural factors seem to have only little influence on formal organization characteristics. There is, however, a rather strong relationship between culture, on the one hand, and attitudes of organization members, on the other. Some organizational processes are predominantly determined by formal organizational characteristics. The discussion in section 6, for example, showed that the power distribution within an organization is largely determined by formal regulations regarding employees' participation. Other organization processes seem to be related to "culture". In this connection, two dimensions were mentioned in section 5: the first one can be described as "rigid stratification/social distance" and is related to the "power-distance" index of Hofstede. The second dimension can be called "bureaucratic control/routine work" and is related to Hofstede's index for "uncertainty avoidance". The relationships between these two dimensions, on the one hand, and the more (but not exclusively) attitude-oriented indices of Hofstede, on the other, strengthen the conviction that cultural influence on organizations predominantly occurs via the attitudes and values of organization members.

8   CONCLUSION

It will have become clear that better insight into the influence of "culture" on organizations will have to await further research. Unfortunately, this research area has been marred by a fragmentary approach, numerous methodological short-

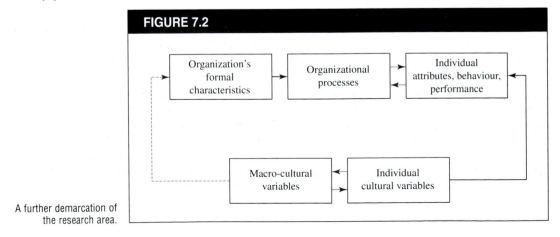

FIGURE 7.2

A further demarcation of the research area.

comings, and a limited congruity in research results. Cross-cultural and other comparative research has been subjected to strong criticism in these respects and not entirely without justification (Berry et al., 1992, ch. 13; Roberts, 1970; Roberts & Boyacigiller, 1984). We shall now try to indicate a number of ways in which this situation could be improved.

1. It must be acknowledged that much comparative research in this area displays a lack of clear conceptual definition and demarcation. This applies to the concept of "culture" itself as well as to the variables and dimensions by which cultural differences might be manifested. Earlier in this chapter we argued that "culture" should be seen as the pattern of attitudes, norms, and values showing a certain persistence over generations within a given society. In this vision expertise of psychologists can be utilized in the specification and operationalization of this pattern.

2. The majority of comparative research on organizations concerns differences in attitudes, needs, expectations, and concepts in employees. Given the limitations of the sample (limited to the members of certain organizations) and of the questioning (limited to the work situation), this research generally offers insufficient grounds for measuring differences between "cultures". The differences observed are, however, frequently presented as being "culturally determined". When culture itself is defined in terms of attitudes, norms, and values, the argument can become dangerously circular: "culture" determines "culture". This threat can be avoided by specifying which attitudes, norms, and values are to be seen as "cultural" and which are not.

3. In only a small number of instances have organizations in different countries or in different cultures actually been compared. Nevertheless, the observed differences in the attitudes, needs, expectations, and opinions of members of organizations have been used to support confident assertions on the comparability of the functioning of organizations. This is premature, even if a given study has found a relationship between certain attitudes, needs, expectations, and opinions, on the one hand, and organizational characteristics and processes, on the other. Furthermore, generalization from research results within countries to

the situation obtaining between countries is no more justified. Conclusions on the nature of "cultural" influence on the functioning of organizations will have to wait until organizations themselves have been subjected to cross-cultural comparison.

4. It was noted in section 3 that there were methodological advantages in comparing the patterns of relationships between variables in different countries and cultures. Such research is, however, scant. In most cases, different measurements are compared, on the assumption that these scores are directly comparable: a tall order.

The problem has been illustrated by a recent article by Singh (1990), who noted that for a given instrument and country, scores on Hofstede's four dimensions are not replicable. Hofstede reacted (1990) by qualifying the significance of the absolute values per country on the indices of the instrument he used; he rightly pointed out that the ideal instrument for cross-cultural comparison has simply not been available.

This is precisely the point. Ultimately, confident conclusions about the differences between cultures cannot justifiably be drawn on the basis of research, whose scores cannot be attributed absolute values because metric equivalency is absent or indeterminate. For this reason, the instruments employed in future cross-cultural research will have to meet higher standards—considerable increases in the required research effort, sample size, and sample variety notwithstanding.

5. Comparative research has been primarily limited to a small number of predominantly Western countries. The past 15 years, however, have seen a considerable expansion of activities in this area. Much of this is thanks to Hofstede (1980, 1983), who studied a large number of countries from widely different regions. Following the wave of interest in Japan, other South East Asiatic countries have enjoyed increasing notice (see, for example, Whitley, 1990).

During the 1970s, comparative research between countries in the West and countries in the then-communist Eastern Bloc was seldom if ever practicable, with Granick's study (1972, 1979) forming a noted exception. In 1987, Child and Bate published a book with the explicit intention of stimulating exchanges between East and West and facilitating comparative research. Given the speed of developments in today's eastern Europe, we may expect this exchange and comparative research to proceed apace.

Another notable development has been the increasing attention devoted in the 1980s to the People's Republic of China (Laaksonen, 1984; Shenkar & Ronen, 1987; Warner, 1987). A recent special issue of *International Studies of Management and Organization* (Shenkar, 1990) was entirely devoted to organizations and management in China.

Comparative studies of the poorer countries of Latin America, Asia, and especially Africa remain incidental. An undoubted contributory factor must be that these countries, in particular, are unlikely to show much interest in cross-cultural research, which promises them little practical benefit (Sinha, 1990). This argument is by no means limited to these countries; it is unclear, for example, whether eastern European countries are likely to show more interest in strictly theoretical exercises over the coming years.

It would be mistaken to sacrifice theoretical and methodological considerations to the "political relevance" of the research; ill-founded generalizations serve no-one's interests. On the other hand, a choice of research subject closely linked to existing problems (issues, perhaps, of personnel selection, training, the introduction and effects of new technology) can serve practical as well as scientific purposes.

Interest in cross-cultural and other comparative research on organizations may be expected to grow in the years to come. At the same time, more parts of the world are likely to become interested in the results of this research. The most can be made of these developments only where there is wider recognition of the theoretical significance as well as the practical usefulness of these studies. The recommendations made here are intended to contribute towards the ability of this research to meet such expectations.

NOTES

1. In section 3 some observations have already been made on

this sample. The companies are maximally comparable, but the generalizability can be questioned.

2. Again, this illustrates all the more difference between power inequality and formal rules in relation to participation on the one hand and Hofstede's PDI on the other. Two of the culture indices (political democracy and income level) agree with indices connected to the PDI.

3. For Hofstede's PDI this is precisely the opposite: a relationship with GNP but not with economic growth.

REFERENCES

Agar, M.H. (1986). *Speaking of ethnography*. Beverly Hills, CA: Sage.

Aiken, M., & Bacharach, S.B. (1979). Culture and organizational structure and process: A comparative study of local government administrative bureaucracies in the Walloon and Flemish regions of Belgium. In C.J. Lammers & J.D. Hickson (Eds.), *Organizations alike and unlike*. London, Boston and Henley: Routledge & Kegan Paul.

Ajiferuke, M., & Boddewijn, J. (1970). Socio-economic indicators in comparative management. *Administrative Science Quarterly, 15*, 453–458.

Barrett, G.V., & Bass, B.M. (1976). Cross-cultural issues in industrial and organizational psychology. In M.D. Dunnette (Ed.), *Handbook of industrial and organizational psychology*. Chicago: Rand McNally.

Bass, B. M. (1977). Utility of Managerial Self-Planning on a simulated production task with replications in twelve countries. *Journal of Applied Psychology, 62*, 506–509.

Bass, B.M., & Eldridge, L. (1973). Accelerated managers' objectives in twelve countries. *Industrial Relations, 12*, 158–171.

Bean, R. (1985). *Comparative industrial relations: An introduction to cross-national perspectives*. London: Croom Helm.

Bennett, M. (1977a). Testing management theories cross-culturally. *Journal of Applied Psychology, 62*, 578–581.

Bennett, M. (1977b). Response characteristics of bilingual managers to organizational questionnaires. *Personnel Psychology, 30*, 29–36.

Berry, J.W. (1980a). Introduction to methodology. In H.C. Triandis & J.W. Berry (Eds.), *Cross-cultural psychology* (Vol. 2). Boston: Allyn and Bacon.

Berry, J.W. (1980b). Ecological analyses for cross-cultural psychology, In N. Warren (Ed.), *Studies in cross-cultural psychology* (Vol. 2). London: Academic Press.

Berry, J.W., Poortinga, Y.H., Segall, M.H., & Dasen, P.R. (1992). *Cross-cultural psychology: research and applications*. Cambridge: Cambridge University Press.

Bhagat, R.S., & McQuaid, S.J. (1982). Role of subjective culture in organizations: A review and directions for future research. *Journal of Applied Psychology, 5*, 653–685.

Bhagat, R.S., Kedia, B.L., Crawford, S.E., & Kaplan, M.R. (1990). Cross-cultural issues in organizational psychology: Emergent trends and directions for research in the 1990s. In C.L. Cooper & I.F. Robertson (Eds.), *International review of industrial and organizational psychology* (Vol. 5). New York: Wiley.

Blalock, H.M. (1961). *Causal inferences in non-experimental research.* Chapel Hill: University of North Carolina Press.

Brislin, R.W. (1970). Back-translation for cross-cultural research. *Journal of Cross-Cultural Psychology, 5*, 139–161.

Brislin, R.W. (1976). Comparative research methodology: Cross-cultural studies. *International Journal of Psychology, 11*, 215–229.

Brislin, R.W. (1986). The wording and translation of research instruments. In W.J. Lonner & J.W. Berry (Eds.), *Field methods in cross-cultural psychology.* Beverly Hills, CA: Sage.

Brislin, R.W., Lonner, W.J., & Thorndike, R.M. (1973). *Cross-cultural research methods.* New York: Wiley.

Child, J. (1981). Culture, contingency and capitalism in the cross-national study of organization. In L.L. Cummings & B.M. Staw (Eds.), *Research in organizational behavior* (Vol. 3). Greenwich, CT: JAI Press Inc.

Child, J., & Bate, P. (Eds.), (1987). *Organization of innovation; East-West perspectives.* Berlin, New York: Walter de Gruyter.

Child, J., & Kieser, A. (1979). Organization and managerial roles in British and West German companies: an Examination of the culture-free thesis. In C.J. Lammers & D.J. Hickson (Eds.), *Organizations alike and unlike.* London, Boston and Henley: Routledge & Kegan Paul.

Chinese Culture Connection (1987). Chinese values and the search for culture-free dimensions of culture. *Journal of Cross-Cultural Psychology, 18*, 143–164.

Clark, P. (1979). Cultural context as a determinant of organizational rationality: A comparison of the tobacco industries in Britain and France. In C.J. Lammers & D.J. Hickson (Eds.), *Organizations alike and unlike.* London, Boston and Henley: Routledge & Kegan Paul.

Cole, R.E. (1973). Functional alternatives and economic development: An empirical example of permanent employment in Japan. *American Sociological Review, 38*, 424–438.

Cole, R.E. (1979). *Work, mobility and participation: a comparative study of American and Japanese industry.* Berkeley: University of California Press.

Conaty, J., Mahmondi, H., & Miller, G.A. (1983). Social structure and bureaucracy: A comparison of organizations in the United States and Pre-revolutionary Iran. *Organization Studies, 4*, 105–128.

Crozier, M. (1964). *The bureaucratic phenomenon.* London: Tavistock.

Deutscher, L. (1973). Asking questions cross-culturally. In D.P. Warwick & S. Osherson (Eds.), *Comparative research methods.* Englewood Cliffs, NJ: Prentice-Hall.

DIO, International Research Team (1983). A contingency model of participative decision-making: An analysis of 56 decisions in three Dutch organizations. *Journal of Occupational Psychology, 56*, 1–18.

Dore, R. (1973). *British factory–Japanese factory.* London: Allen & Unwin.

Drenth, P.J.D. (1989). Cross-cultural analysis of working: Definitions, centrality and normative views. In D.M. Keats, D. Monroe, & L. Mann (Eds.), *Heterogeneity in cross-cultural psychology.* Lisse: Swets & Zeitlinger.

Drenth, P.J.D., & Flier, H. van der (1973). Culturele verschillen en de vergelijkbaarheid van testprestaties. In P.J.D. Drenth, P.J. Willems, & Ch. J. de Wolff (Eds.) *Arbeids- en Organisatiepsychologie.* Deventer: Kluwer.

Drenth, P.J.D., & Wilpert, B. (1990). Industrial democracy in Europe: Cross national comparisons. In P.J.D. Drenth, J.A. Sargeant, & R.J. Takens (Eds.), *European perspectives in psychology* (Vol. 3). Chichester, UK: Wiley.

Elder, J.W. (1976). Comparative cross-national methodology. *Annual Review of Sociology, 2*, 209–230.

Esbroeck, R. van (1982). *Analyse van "faking"-gedrag bij adolescenten in beroepsinteressen-vragenlijsten.* Brussels: Vrije Universiteit.

Fliegel, F., Sofranko, A.J., Williams, J.D., & Navin, C.S. (1979). Technology and cultural convergence: A limited empirical test. *Journal of Cross-cultural Psychology, 10*, 3–22.

Flier, H. van der (1980). *Vergelijkbaarheid van individuele testprestaties.* Lisse: Swets & Zeitlinger.

Form, W. (1979). Comparative industrial sociology and the convergence hypothesis. *Annual Review of Sociology, 5*, 1–25.

Gallie, D. (1978). *In search of the new working class. Automation and social integration within the capitalist enterprise.* Cambridge: Cambridge University Press.

Granick, D. (1972). *Managerial comparisons of four deleveped countries: France, Britain, United States and Russia.* Cambridge, MA: MIT Press.

Granick, D. (1979). Managerial incentive systems and organizational theorie. In C.J. Lammers & D.J. Hickson (Eds.), *Organizations alike and unlike.* Boston and Henley: Routledge & Kegan Paul.

Griffeth, R.W., & Hom, P.W. (1987). Some multivariate comparisons of multinational managers. *Multivariate Behavior Research, 23*, 173–191.

Gruenfeld, L.W., & MacEachern, A.E. (1975). A cross-national study of cognitive style among managers and technicians. *International Journal of Psychology, 10*, 27–55.

Haire, M., Ghiselli, E.E., & Porter, L.W. (1966). *Managerial thinking: An international study.* New York: Wiley.

Heller, F.A., & Misumi, J. (1987). Decision making. In B.M. Bass & P.J.D. Drenth (Eds.) *Advances in organizational psychology.* Newbury Park, CA: Sage.

Heller, F.A., Drenth, P.J.D., Koopman, P.L., & Rus, V. (1988). *Decisions in organizations.* London: Sage.

Hickson, D.J., Pugh, D.D., & Pheysey, C. (1969). Operations technology and organizational structure; an empirical reappraisal. *Administrative Science Quarterly, 14,* 378–379.

Hickson, D.J., Hinings, C.R., McMillan, C.J., & Schwitter, J.P. (1974). The culture-free context of organization structure: A tri-national comparison. *Sociology, 8,* 59–80.

Hickson, D.J., & McMillan, C.J. (Eds.), (1981). *Organization and nation.* The Aston Programme IV. Westmead, UK: Gower.

Hofstede, G. (1979). Hierarchical power distance in fourty countries. In C.J. Lammers & D.J. Hickson (Eds.), *Organizations alike and unlike.* London, Boston and Henley: Routledge & Kegan Paul.

Hofstede, G. (1980). *Culture's consequences: International differences in work-related values.* Beverly Hills, CA: Sage.

Hofstede, G. (1983). The cultural relativity of organizational practices and theories. *Journal of International Business Studies, 14,* 75–90.

Hofstede, G. (1990). A reply and comment on Joginder P. Singh: "Managerial culture and work-related values in India". *Organization Studies, 11,* 103–106.

Hofstede, G. (1991). Empirical models of cultural differences. In N. Bleichrodt & P.J.D. Drenth (Eds.), *Contemporary issues in cross-cultural psychology.* Lisse: Swets & Zeitlinger.

Hofstede, G., & Bond, M.H. (1988). The Confucian connection: From cultural roots to economic growth. *Organizational Dynamics, 16,* 4–21.

IDE-International Research Group (1979). Participation: Formal rules, influence and involvement. *Industrial Relations, 18,* 273–294.

IDE-International Research Group (1981a). *Industrial democracy in Europe.* Oxford: Oxford University Press.

IDE-International Research Group (1981b). *Industrial relations in Europe.* Oxford: Oxford University Press.

IDE-International Research Group (1992). *Industrial democracy in Europe revisited.* Oxford: Oxford University Press.

Inkeles, A. (1969). Making men modern: On the causes and consequences of individual change in six developing countries. *American Journal of Sociology, 75,* 208–225.

Irvine, S.H., & Carroll, W.K. (1986). Testing and assessment across cultures. In H.C. Triandis & J.W. Berry (Eds.), *Handbook of cross cultural psychology* (Vol. 2), *Methodology.* Boston: Allyn & Bacon.

Jahoda, G. (1980). Cross-cultural comparisons. In M.H. Bornstein (Ed.), *Comparative Methods in psychology* (pp.105–148). Hillsdale, NJ: Lawrence Erlbaum Associates Inc.

Kagitçibasi, C. (1987). Individual and group loyalities, are they compatible? In C. Kagitçibasi (Ed.), *Growth and progress in cross-cultural psychology.* Lisse: Swets & Zeitlinger.

Kagitçibasi, C. (1989). Why Individualism/Collectivism? In D.M. Keats, D. Monroe, & L. Mann (Eds.), *Heterogeneity in cross-cultural psychology.* Lisse: Swets & Zeitlinger.

Kagitçibasi, C., & Berry, J.W. (1989). Cross-cultural psychology: Current research and trends. *Annual Review of Psychology, 40,* 493–531.

Kalleberg, A.L., & Lincoln, J.R. (1988). The structure of earnings inequality in the United States and Japan. *American Sociological Review, 94,* S121–S153.

Kerr, C. (1983). *The future of industrial societies: Convergence or continuing diversity.* Cambridge, MA: Harvard University Press.

Kerr, C., Dunlop, J.T., Harbison, F., & Myers, C.A. (1964). *Industrialism and industrial man.* New York: Oxford University Press.

Kluckhohn, C. (1951). The study of culture. In D. Lerner & H.D. Lasswel (Eds.), *The policy sciences.* Stanford, CA: Stanford University Press.

Koopman, P.L., Drenth, P.J.D., Bus, F.B.M., Kruijswijk, A.J., & Wierdsma, A.F.M. (1981). Content, process, and effect of participative decision-making on the shop floor: Three cases in the Netherlands. *Human Relations, 34,* 657–676.

Koopman, P.L., Drenth, P.J.D., Heller, F.A., & Rus, V. (1991). Strategic and practical decisions: A comparative analysis of 217 decisions in three countries. In N. Bleichrodt & P.J.D. Drenth (Eds.), *Contemporary issues in cross-cultural psychology.* Lisse: Swets & Zeitlinger.

Kroeber, A.L., & Parsons, T. (1958). The concepts of culture and of a social system. *American Sociological Review, 23,* 582–583.

Laaksonen, O. (1984). Participation down and up the line: Comparative industrial democracy trends in China and Europe. *International Social Science Revue,* 299–318.

Lammers, C.J. (1983). *Organisaties vergelijkenderwijs.* Utrecht: Spectrum.

Lammers, C.J., & Hickson, D.J. (Eds.), (1979). *Organizations alike and unlike.* London, Boston and Henley: Routledge & Kegan Paul.

Leung, K., & Bond, M.H. (1989). On the empirical identification of dimensions for cross-cultural comparisons. *Journal of Cross-Cultural Psychology, 2, 133–151.*

Lincoln, J.R., & Kalleberg, A.L. (1985). Work organization and workforce committment: A study of plans and employees in the US and Japan. *American Sociological Review*, *50*, 738–760.

Lincoln, J.R., Hanada, M., & McBride, K. (1986). Organizational structures in Japanese and US manufacturing. *Administrative Science Quarterly*, *31*, 338–364.

Lincoln, J.R., & McBride, K. (1987). Japanese industrial organization in comparative perspective. *Annual Review of Sociology*, *13*, 289–312.

Lonner, W.J., & Berry, J.W. (Eds.) (1986a). *Field methods in cross cultural psychology*. Beverly Hills, CA: Sage.

Lonner, W.J, & Berry, J.W. (1986b). Sampling and surveying. In W.J. Lonner & J.W. Berry (Eds.), *Field methods in cross-cultural psychology*. Beverly Hills, CA: Sage.

Lynn, B., & Hampson, G.L. (1975). National differences in extraversion and neuroticism. *British Journal of Social and Clinical Psychology*, *14*, 223–240.

Malpass, R.S., & Poortinga, Y.H. (1986). Strategies for design and analysis. In W.J. Lonner & J.W. Berry (Eds.), *Field methods in cross-cultural psychology*. Beverly Hills, CA: Sage.

Martyn-Johns, T.A. (1977). Cultural conditioning of views of authority and its effects on the business decision-making process with special reference to Java. In Y.H. Poortinga (Ed.), *Basic problems in cross-cultural psychology*. Amsterdam/Lisse: Swets & Zeitlinger.

Maurice, M. (1979). For a study of "the societal effect": Universality and specificity in organization research. In C.J. Lammers & D.J. Hickson (Eds.), *Organizations alike and unlike*. London, Boston and Henley: Routledge & Kegan Paul.

Maurice, M., Sorge, A. & Warner, M. (1980). Societal differences in organizing manufactering units: A comparison of France, West Germany and Great Britain. *Organization Studies*, *1*, 59–86.

McClelland, D.C. (1961). *The achieving society*. New York: van Nostrand.

Mintzberg, H. (1979). *The structuring of organizations*. Englewood Cliffs, NJ: Prentice-Hall.

Misumi, J. (1985). *The behavioral science of leadership*. Ann. Arbor, MI: University of Michigan Press.

Mohr, L.B. (1971). Organizational technology and organizational structure. *Administrative Science Quarterly*, *16*, 444–459.

M. O. W. International Research Team (1981). The meaning of working. In G. Duglos & K. Weierman (Eds.), *Management under different value systems*. Berlin: De Gruyter.

M. O. W. International Research Team (1987) *The meaning of Working*. London: Academic Press.

Negandhi, A.R. (1979). Convergence in organizational practices: An empirical study of industrial enterprise in developing countries. In C.J. Lammers & D.J. Hickson (Eds.), *Organizations alike and unlike*. London, Boston and Henley: Routledge & Kegan Paul.

Osgood, C.E. (1967). On the strategy of cross-national research into subjective culture. *Social Science Information*, *6*, 5–37.

Ouchi, W. (1981). *Theory Z*. Reading, MA: Addison-Wesley.

Pascale, R.T. (1978). Communication and decision-making across cultures: Japanese and American comparison. *Administrative Science Quarterly*, *23*, 91–110.

Pascale, R.T., & Athos, A.G. (1981). *The art of Japanese management*. New York: Warner Books.

Perrow, C. (1970). *Organizational analysis: A sociological view*. Belmont, CA: Needsworth.

Poole, M. (1986). *Industrial Relations: Origins and patterns of national diversity*. London, Boston and Henley: Routledge & Kegan Paul.

Poortinga, Y.H. (1971). *Cross-cultural comparison of maximum performance tests: Some methodological aspects and some experiments with auditory and visual stimuli*. Johannesburg: National Institute of Personnel Research.

Poortinga, Y.H. (1975). Limitations on intercultural comparison of psychological data. *Nederlands Tijdschrift voor de Psychologie*, *30*, 23–39.

Przeworski, A., & Teune, H. (1970). *The logic of comparative social inquiry*. New York: Wiley.

Roberts, K.H. (1970). On looking at an elephant. *Psychological Bulletin*, *74*, 327–350.

Roberts, K.H., & Boyacigiller, N.A. (1984). Cross-national organizational research: The grasp of the blind men. In B.M. Staw & L.L. Cummings (Eds.), *Research in Organizational Behaviour* (Vol. 6). Greenwich, CT: JAI Press Inc.

Robinson, W.S. (1959). Ecological correlations and the behavior of individuals. *American Sociological Review*, *15*.

Ronen, S. (1986). *Comparative and multinational management*. New York: Wiley.

Ronen, S., & Shenkar, O. (1985). Clustering countries on attitudinal dimensions: A review and synthesis. *Academy of Management Review*, *10*, 435–454.

Scheuch, E.K. (1966). Cross-national comparisons using aggregate data: Some substantive and methodological problems. In R. Merritt & S. Rokkan (Eds.), *The use of quantitative data in cross-national research*. New Haven, CT: Yale University Press.

Segall, M.H., Dasen, P.R., Berry, J.W., & Poortinga, Y.H. (1990). *Human behavior in global perspective. An introduction to cross-cultural psychology*. New York: Paramount Press.

Shenkar, O. (1990). Organization and management in China. *International Studies of Management and Organizations*, *20*.

Shenkar, O., & Ronen, S. (1987). Structure and importance of work goals among managers in the People's Republic of China. *Academy of Management Journal*, *30*, 564–576.

Shouksmith, G. (1987). Personnel Psychology. In B.M. Bass & P.J.D. Drenth (Eds.), *Advances in organizational psychology*. Newbury Park, CA: Sage.

Singh, J.P. (1990). Managerial culture and work-related values in India. *Organization Studies*, *11*, 75–101.

Sinha, D. (1990). Applied cross-cultural psychology and the developing world. *International Journal of Psychology*, *25*, 381–386.

Smith, D.H., & Inkeles, A. (1966). The OM-Scale: A comparative socio-psychological measure of individual modernity. *Sociometry*, *29*, 353–377.

Smith, D.H., & Inkeles, A. (1975). Individual modernizing experiences and psycho-social modernity: Validation of the OM scales in six developing countries. *International Journal of Comparative Sociology*, *3–4*, 154–173.

Smith, P.B., & Peterson, M.F. (1988). *Leadership, organizations and culture*. London, Beverly Hills, CA: Sage.

Smith, P.B., & Tayeb, M. (1988). Organizational structure and processes. In M.H. Bond (Ed.), *The cross-cultural challenge to social psychology*. Newbury Park, CA: Sage.

Takezawa, S., & Whitehill, A.M. (1983). *Work ways: Japan and America*. Tokyo: The Japan Institute of Labour.

Tannenbaum, A.S. (1968). *Control in organizations*. New York: McGraw-Hill.

Tannenbaum, A.S. (1980). Organizational Psychology. In H.C. Triandis & R.W. Brislin (Eds.), *Handbook of cross-cultural psychology* (Vol. 5). Boston: Allyn & Bacon.

Tannenbaum, A.S., & Cooke, R.A. (1979). Organizational control: A review of studies employing the control graph method. In C.J. Lammers & D.J. Hickson (Eds.), *Organizations alike and unlike*. London, Boston and Henley: Routledge & Kegan Paul.

Tannenbaum, A.S., Kavcic, B., Rosner, M., Vianello, M., & Wieser, G. (1974). *Hierarchy in organizations*. San Francisco: Jossey-Bass.

Triandis, H.C. (1972). *The analysis of subjective culture*. New York: Wiley.

Triandis, H.C., Bontempo, R., Leung, K., & Hui, C.H. (1990). A method for determining cultural, demographic, and personal constructs. *Journal of Cross-cultural Psychology*, *3*, 302–318.

Triandis, H.C., & Vassiliou, V. (1972). Interpersonal influence and employee perception in two cultures. *Journal of Applied Psychology*, *56*, 140–145.

Warner, M. (Ed.) (1987). *Management reforms in China*. London: Pinter.

Whitley, R.D. (1990). Eastern Asian Enterprise structures and the comparative analysis of forms of business organization. *Organization Studies*, *11*, 47–74.

Witkin, H.A., Dyke, R.B., Faterson, H.F., Goodenough, D.R., & Karp, S.A. (1962). *Psychological differentiation*. New York: John Wiley and Sons.

Wolferen, K.G. van (1989). *The enigma of Japanese power*. London: Macmillan. (Ned. vertaling: Japan, Rainbow Pockets.)

Yang, K. (1988). Will societal modernization eventually eliminate cross-cultural psychological differences? In M.H. Bond (Ed.), *The cross-cultural challenge to social psychology*. Newbury Park, CA: Sage.

8

Planned Change in Organizations and Organizational Development in the 1990s

René van der Vlist

1 INTRODUCTION

"Hoogovens [Dutch Steelworks] smouldering with ambition" Hans Buddingh reports with a sense of appropriate imagery in *NRC Handelsblad* of 10 April 1991. He continues: "The steel giant from IJmuiden hardly ten years ago a symbol of industrial depression experiences a cultural revolution: with Japanese management techniques top management tries to increase performance. Keywords are: efficiency, quality, and productivity."

The instrument for that purpose is a "Masterplan" to which the unions react sceptically, and to which the employees take a critical attitude. Buddingh puts forward that: "Many fear that everything is enforced from top level. It evokes resistance when a technologist from 'oxysteel 2' sometimes has to act as an operator within the framework of 'task integration', and playing a game of cards or eating together becomes impossible because of the tight work schedules."

Hoogovens imports its ideas from Japan, where its chief executive officer, Van Veen, paid a visit some three years ago. The goal of the Masterplan is, among others, to reduce the total costs by half a billion guilders within five years. For that matter, there will be no forced layoffs. According to Van Veen, companies need ambitious goals with which employees can identify. Also, his Japanese contacts have made it clear that many aspects should be dealt with simultaneously. Productivity is only one component of the costs. If the percentage of rejected products decreases, the costs decrease as well, and client relations improve simultaneously. In view of the Japanese experience, an approach is taken that makes use of the conventional line organization. Van Veen: "When you do not create a separate task group, or call in external experts, employees may view the plan as something of their own" (*NRC Handelsblad*, 10-4-91).

It is rather unusual for this *Handbook* to begin a contribution with a quotation this elaborate. However, here this is of extreme relevance. The quotation touches upon many points that should not be overlooked in the framework of a contribution to planned change and organizational development.

In that respect something has certainly changed compared with 10 years ago when the first edition of this *Handbook* was published. This change concerns the role of organizational development (i.e. planned change; see for the distinction between both concepts, section 3). Beer and Walton (1987) are most explicit. In their review article in *The Annual Review of Psychology* they postulate that organizational development (OD) traditionally consisted of a set of actions and interventions based on applied knowledge from psychology and "organizational behaviour" theory in order to improve the effective strength of organizations as well as the well-being of employees. Traditionally, interventions of this kind were the domain of consultants. Beer and Walton state, however, that OD knowledge and expertise gradually penetrate general management literature and from there the management practice itself. In their opinion, this means a broadening of the concept of organizational development as well, in the sense that not only should the OD adviser have disposal of knowledge on behavioural sciences, but also on "expertise in understanding and interpreting environmental changes" (p.340). Parallel to this, according to Beer and Walton, the role of the adviser changes as well. Whereas advisers initially occupied a leading, often initiating role, their role is now more modest: "consultants become actors in a process orchestrated by general managers" (p.340). Consequently, traditional boundaries of organizational development decline, and organizational development (i.e. planned change) should be viewed within the framework of an entity of organization theory, contingent thinking, management theory, etc. Before considering the relevance of, for example, a Japanese model, participant leadership, resistance to change, etc., in this contribution we will endeavour to clarify concepts like planned change, organization development, change skills (section 3). For that purpose, the "setting" will be discussed in section 2,

i.e. the background against which fundamental organizational change takes place. This background has to do with the fact that organizations have to function within an environment in strong motion. This requires organizations to adapt to these changes. For many organizations this adaptation means radical changes in which traditional organization principles should be reevaluated.

In section 4 the question is raised of whether such fundamental changes require either a new "design" for the organization or a "developmental" approach. Both conceptions are right now explicit subjects of argument. Section 5 raises the question of whether fundamental organizational change requires a revolutionary reversal, or whether it can be directed as an evolutionary process. In section 6 this results in a focus on resistance to change, and the role of executives in the framework of change processes. Primarily, this resistance has to do with what we call "cultural barriers" for organizational change. We will examine this more specifically. In section 8 recent developments will be discussed. Research now focuses more and more on the activities of OD consultants. In addition, theoretical progress may be observed in the context of new developments. This contribution ends with a summary.

2 THE NECESSITY OF FUNDAMENTAL CHANGES IN ORGANIZATIONS

Organizations are "open", input–throughput–output systems, where the output (partly) is used to reactivate the system. Input, throughput, and output, as well as the conversion of output in renewed input, each requests transactions between the organization and its environment. Emery and Trist (1965) use the term "transactional environment". Transactions do not take place in a vacuum. On the contrary, they are subject to conditions, boundary conditions, and environmental characteristics that may hinder transactions, simplify them, but in any case influence them. In short, transactions take place in a "contextual" environment. Boonstra (1991) outlines the aforementioned as a diagram in Figure 8.1.

2.1   The contextual environment

Katz and Kahn (1978, p.124) distinguish five sectors in the contextual environment that may influence organizational performance:

1. the value patterns of the cultural environment in which organizations are embedded;
2. the political structure and the accompanying issuing of laws and regulations that specify the formal legal status of organizations and set the boundaries of organizational authority and organizational practice;
3. the economic environment, especially competition on markets, raw materials, and employees;
4. the technological environment;
5. the physical environment, e.g. geographical factors, the climate, resources, etc.

Stated differently, organizations adapt to five "environments the cultural, the political, the technological, and the ecological" (p.125).

All these developments, adding "demographical developments" (the ageing of the population,

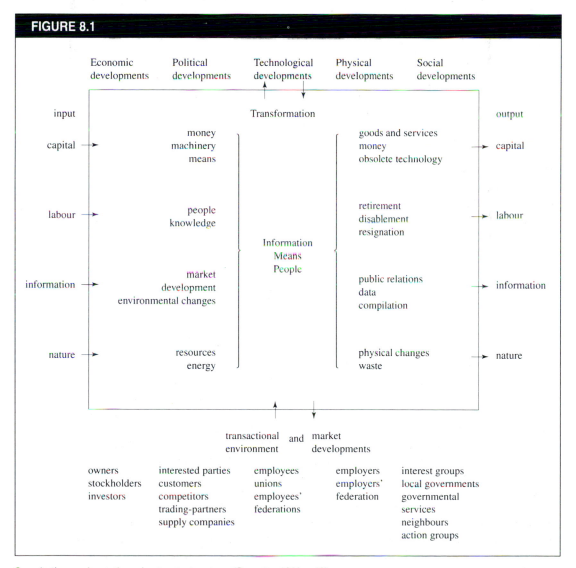

FIGURE 8.1

Organisations as input–throughput–output systems (Boonstra, 1991, p.12).

for instance), show increased interactions, the long-term effects being virtually unpredictable.

2.2   The transactional environment

"Right now there definitely is a demand in many companies to alter deeply engraved attitudes", said Peter Drucker in *NRC Handelsblad* of 30 April 1991. "Electricity and telephone companies in the past had the advantage of guaranteed profits by the government, whereas now they suddenly have to engage in a cutthroat competition. Customers demand just-in-time deliveries. Consumers become ever more particular as far as the quality and service are concerned. Employees quite readily march to court, with complaints about discrimination and sexual harassment."

And "there seems to exist a strong need for a radical change in most of the mechanical industries in the US (a fortiori those in Europe as well) in the way new products and models are conceived, designed, produced, and marketed a process that is eventually being contracted from years into a few months."

This may be a recent acknowledgement of what we actually already have known for some 20 years: The transactional environment to the world, consisting of capital-suppliers, customers, competitors, supply-companies, unions, employers' federations, and other interested parties, is on the move, and accelerating (see also Peters, 1987). The fact that this requires specific claims to organizations is illustrated by Bolwijn and Kumpe (1989). They argue that until the 1960s, the main market requirement (for industrial companies) was the price per product unit. Efficiency was practically the sole performance criterion, and the ideal company was the "efficient company". In the 1970s, another market requirement was added, "quality", so that besides efficiency, quality became a performance-criterion, with the ideal company becoming "the quality company". In the 1980s, the market-requirement prices, quality, and delivery-time, were important, as well as the performance-criteria efficiency, quality, and flexibility. The ideal-typical company thus became the "flexible company".

According to these authors, in the 1990s, the main issues will be the market-requirement prices, quality, delivery-time, and uniqueness (of the products to be delivered). Performance-criteria will be extended with "innovation", and the ideal-typical company becomes the "innovative company". The authors are convinced that the last added criterion or "market requirement", will be the most important one.

Bolwijn and Kumpe sketch recent and expected developments in industry, a field both authors are well versed in. Comparable developments, however, occur in other branches of industry as well as in the provision of services and government agencies (see for instance the memorandum "The Base of the Structure", by the Centrale Afdeling Organisatie van de Gemeente Den Haag (1981). In view of this memorandum, the local community decided for a radical reorganization of the internal organization. (See also Projectgroep Tangram, 1990.)

The conclusion of the aforementioned should be that organizations must be viewed as open systems that, if they want to survive, have to adapt themselves to changes in the environment. Conversely, organizations also influence their environment. Relevant changes in the environment of organizations concern persons, groups, authorities, and parties. The company, as it were, is doing business with the transactional environment directly, as well as the context within which these transactions must materialize. Even more important seems the observation that changes in the environment accelerate: The environment becomes much more dynamic, and it seems to be increasingly important to anticipate these changes (cf. Bolwijn & Kumpe, 1989).

2.3   Stability and turbulence

Changes in the environment of organizations relevant for those organizations happen continually. Theoretically, their intensity varies from nought to maximal. The question is what this implies. In a way organizations are comparable with biological organisms. In any case, the use of that metaphor (Morgan, 1986) may clarify matters. Organisations as open systems significantly depend on their environment. In contrast to organisms, where adaptation to changes in the environment are particularly genotypic, organizations are to a certain extent capable of fenotypical adaptation: Adaptation of the individual organization itself. That kind of adaptation requires minimal information about relevant characteristics of (changes in) the environment, and its translation into organizational goals, and the way these goals should be realized (strategy).

Although the dimension "Stability–Turbulence" (the terms are from Katz & Kahn, 1978, see p.125) should be interpreted as a continuum, it is nevertheless possible to formulate a characterisation of environments where, between certain types, the content of the strategy-formulation will differ fundamentally. Such an attempt was undertaken by Emery and Trist (1965), and further elaborated by Emery (1974). He distinguishes between:

a. placid, random environment;
b. placid, clustered environment;
c. disturbed, reactive environment;
d. turbulent environment.

(a) Placid, random environment

This is the most simple type of environment: goals and noxiants for the organization are randomly distributed. There is, in other words, no structure in the environment: No connection between the environmental parts (Ashby, 1960). Emery (1974) states that this resembles the classical market-idea of economists. An organization that must survive in such an environment, has no interest in an externally directed strategy, and is only able to enlarge its chances of survival by (compare Emery, 1974, p.21):

- increasing response capabilities: As will be shown, this is not unimportant;
- increasing the range of vision: increased range of vision in a random environment is equivalent to increasing the area of non-random environment immediately surrounding the system (Simon, 1956);
- increasing storage capacity (Simon, 1956), e.g. storage of natural resources and other commodities.

In other words, as far as strategy is concerned in this case, it is primarily directed internally: Increasing the range of vision, response capabilities, and storage capacity.

(b) Placid, clustered environment

Here the environment definitely has structure. That structure is in principle stable, barely susceptible to changes: Goals and noxiants are clustered, and the survival of the system also becomes dependent on knowledge of the environment and on an optimal location of the system in the environment (Emery, 1974, p.24).

When the organism/the organization has finally reached an optimal location, the system tends to bureaucratization or "mechanization".

(c) Disturbed, reactive environment

The most important characteristic of such an environment is that the structural aspect of the environment is susceptible to changes, and that knowledge of the environment is not eternal. This implies that knowledge that is adequate today might not suffice tomorrow. It is clear that organizations situated in this type of environment will have to investigate the environment continuously and act tactically. The relationship with the environment thus becomes a dominant factor.

A disturbed reactive environment is a common type of environment. Where disturbance is caused by competition with other systems, one possible strategy is to restrict competition by means of cooperation (i.e. mutual agreements) or even mergers. By implementing such a strategy, curtailing the number of competitors or even obtaining a monopoly position is possible. In the latter case the used strategy implies a return to the previous type of environment: placid clustered. Comparable strategies are aimed at obtaining a unique position by, for instance, development of a new brand. In all those cases where the organization succeeds in restoring this type of environment to the previous type, a process of routine action and mechanization will be started.

For that matter, organizations are usually only partly successful and even then only temporarily, in acquiring such a unique position. As a rule, the system should be aware of changes in the environment and should react instrumentally by making the relationship with the environment concrete: to pursue strategic policy.

(d) Turbulent environment

This is judged to be the most complex type of environment (Emery, 1974, p.28): "These are environments in which there are dynamic processes arising from the field itself" (p.28). Emery mentions a relatively simple example, i.e. overfishing. In his view this type of environment is so complex that it is difficult to imagine that individual systems may adapt to it on their own.

According to Emery, one of the most important causes for the emergence of this type of environment is the growth (via, among others, mergers and takeovers) of organizations and collaboration of organizations in order to accommodate the problems organizations experience when confronted with a disturbed reactive environment. The effect would in some cases not be the return to a placid clustered environment, however, but the creation of turbulence.

Although this effect is imaginable, the question remains of whether this is the sole cause of turbulence. The example of overfishing makes perfectly clear that turbulence may also be a consequence of too many independent units a typical characteristic of fishing on the North Sea given the possibilities offered by the environment. It seems to us that when similar forms of turbulence occur, joint policy, for instance through government interference, is the only solution. This interference should be directed at the development of such rules of play that promote a type of environment that we called "disturbed reactive". Examples are, among others, the German and American cartel law prohibiting all cartels, unless it can be established that the cartel is not in conflict with the general interest.

Adjustment to the environment

Disturbed reactive environments ("type c") lead to a strategic policy of the organization (response capabilities) at the input, throughput, and output side. The dynamics in the environment may, furthermore, be so extensive even without turbulence ("type d") that the policy necessitates continuous vigilance. The dynamics may even become so extreme that an external strategy (input; output) becomes virtually impossible. That would be the case if the predictability of the environment drops to a minimum. Such types of environment approach, in fact, "type a" environments. This would imply, in this case as well as with "type a" environments, that the strategy

should be directed internally this time in order to create "overcapacity", a readiness to meet diverse challenges.

This certainly is not an extravagant thought. Keuning and Eppink (1985) put forward that when an organization has explicitly formulated a strategy, a number of advantages is involved. It guides the activities of the organization, making the activities, as it were, perceptible as a pattern, thereby increasing cohesiveness between activities. On the one hand, an organization becomes clearly goal directed, whereas, on the other hand, coordination is improved. Some disadvantages mentioned, however, are that formulating a strategy costs time and money, and that, once a direction is chosen, it is difficult to change it, even when other possibilities occur. It is decidedly so that strategy-formulation takes place under conditions of incomplete information. This partial lack of knowledge apparently leaves the chance of "inaccuracies" with the selection process of the strategy to be followed (Keuning & Eppink, 1985, p.323).

That chance is obviously larger as "partial lack of knowledge" increases, and that seems to be the case (again, see Bolwijn & Kumpe, 1989; Peters, 1987, and many others). As for the policy directed at the environment, this implies that organizations will develop a preference for a relatively short-term policy. This expresses itself, among other thngs, in an investment policy directed at "times of recovering costs" of three years or less. For throughput policy (internally directed) this implies a relative preference for a strategic policy that increases the potential of the organization, enabling the organization to react effectively to environmental changes. This means flexibility of the organization, and the fostering of an innovative climate.

Adaptation to changes in the environment through which yet another appeal is done upon the throughput system of the organization requires either overcapacity of the system, or such a mode of operation that the need for a changed capacity can quickly be realized. In fact, this overcapacity can only be realized in two fundamentally different ways; overcapacity of parts or overcapacity of functions (Emery, 1967; Emery & Trist, 1973; see also Trist, 1981).

Overcapacity of parts

Overcapacity of parts implies task division in such a way that simple tasks result that can be carried out by low-skilled persons who can easily be exchanged if necessary, but who can also easily be attracted if need be (Trist, 1981).

Mechanistic organizations are of this kind. It is a common kind in Dutch society. Research by the Loon Technische Dienst (1986), for example, has shown that in Dutch organizations with more than 20 employees (in the private sector) at least 25% make use of, among others, work processes leading to short-cyclic work, with a time cycle of 90 seconds or less. This type of organization is Tayloristic in nature, and experienced its greatest boom in the first half of this century. Adapted models still seem to be dominant nowadays.

Yet, this type of organization is to some extent able to adapt to dynamic forms of "type c" environments. In many instances this does not lead to fundamental changes, however, but to adaptations that do not really disrupt the character of the organization. For instance, new technology may be put into action in such a way that it strengthens the "bureaucratic" tendencies of the mechanistic organization (see Frissen, 1989). Child, Ganter, and Kieser (1987) use the term "organizational conservatism" in this regard.

Also, the necessity for flexibility of the organization often does not lead to the acceptation of what, for instance, Trist (1981) called "a new paradigm of organising". We notice frequently that organizations of the mechanistic type adapt themselves in a way that matches the traditional paradigm: flexibility of the factor labour, manifesting itself, among other ways, in an increase of the number of part-time employees, call-up employees, temporary employees, as well as in outsourcing activities with irregular production processes. One way or another, this leads to a development where this type of organization will have a relatively small nucleus of permanent employees and a varying number of temporary employees. The pressure in the direction of this type of adaptation to environmental dynamics is so large that even obtained social rights, such as the laws governing dismissal, are a topic of discussion in the whole of western Europe. In other words, with some modifications in the socio-cultural and socio-economic environment traditional organizations of the mechanistic-bureaucratic type do not seem to encounter insurmountable difficulties adapting to turbulence. Whether this is also the case when innovation is added as a market requirement (see Bolwijn & Kumpe, 1989), however, remains to be seen (see also Van der Vlist, 1989).

Overcapacity of functions

Overcapacity of functions is the second alternative: Each component of the system (employees, task-groups) may perform multiple functions (see Trist, 1981, p.38).

This design principle is especially elaborated in the Socio-Technical Systems Design (STSD). In the Netherlands this is particularly the work of De Sitter (1986, 1989), and of Kuipers and Van Amelsfoort (1990; see also Chapter 4 of this *Handbook*). Application of the STSD design principle leads to an organization that is fundamentally different from the classical mechanistic-bureaucratic type. Instead of "maximum possible labour division", "minimal possible labour division" is the point of departure. Group tasks instead of individual tasks are the central issue. No external control but internal control and self-regulation is the leading coordination principle (see Kuipers, 1989). Participative management is essential.

The question is now whether extremely dynamic forms of "type c" environments necessitate fundamental changes, as have just been sketched. One answer to that question is given by Lawler (1989). Lawler puts forward that nowadays important changes take place in the way a range of big American companies are managed. In this regard the sense of commitment is stimulated by involvement of employees in the management of the organization: "Organization after organization in the United States is concluding that, unless they utilize their people more fully, they cannot compete in world markets" (p.91). Participative management might realize this, according to Lawler, because it could lead employees in non-management positions as well to think, assist in problem-solving, and control their own work activities (see also Walton, 1985): "This has the cost-effective impact of reducing the amount of management overhead needed to run an organization and tends to motivate individuals to do higher-quality work" (Lawler, 1989, p.91).

And that would implicate a development in the direction of socio-technical principles. Here, Lawler relates to the earlier work by Argyris, McGregor, and Likert (1957, 1960, and 1961, respectively). And so his contribution is titled "Participative Management in the United States: Three Classics Revisited". This implies that Lawler sees the ongoing development as a continuance of revisionism. Although he recognizes the emergence of a "new paradigm", he does not use the term socio-technical design. Yet, he applies the term "fundamental change". The article does not really create the impression that this change is revolutionary, which is not without importance, as we will see. Incidentally, I would like to remind the reader of the quotation from the interview with director Van Veen mentioned at the beginning of this contribution: obviously, the Dutch Steel Works are also considering a change process in the direction indicated by Lawler.

3.2 PLANNED CHANGE, ORGANIZATION DEVELOPMENT, AND THE STUDY OF CHANGE

Section 2 sketched the background for organizational change. Many organizations struggle with problems for which they need internal and external experts and consultants. Those problems may be simple in nature, like absenteeism and turnover problems, shortage of quality of delivered products and services, or sales problems. They can also be complex, like the introduction of integral quality control, flexibility of the organization, cultural change, and changes directed at improving the innovative capacity of the company or automatization. All of these can only be well understood against the aforementioned background. When consultants are used, a change problem is raised, and terms like "planned change" and "organizational development" become relevant. What do these terms actually mean?

The answer to this simple question is compli-cated. The first edition of this *Handbook* devoted two chapters to this point (Chapter 4.4 by Sopar [1984] and Chapter 4.9 by Bruining & Allegro [1984]). Sopar refers with the term organizational change to the purposeful and more or less accurate planned actions of which the final results are more or less accurately formulated. Those final results may contain a structural change, but this is not necessarily the case. Bruining and Allegro interpret organizational development as "determined, planned activities, directed at changing organizations or sub-systems" (p.4.9.1.). This is a description that, at first glance, hardly deviates from Sopar's. Bruining and Allegro subsequently distinguish between what they call the "process approach" and the "structural task approach". Both approaches fall, according to the authors, within the common denominator "organization development", although they have developed relatively autonomously during the 1950s (p.4.9.1.).

"The process approach is, on the one hand, directed at change in employees (opinions, attitudes, behaviour), and on the other hand, at organization processes (communications, policy-formulation and decision-making, problem-solving and conflict-resolution). Development of the members of the organization, and improvement of relational processes, respectively, might lead to a more adequately functioning organization" (p.4.9.1.). This approach makes use of process techniques and interventions from group dynamics "in order to realize open communication that offers opportunities for the development of alternative structures and processes within the organization". In other words: the process approach, although directed towards the development of members of the organization, could result in structural changes.

It concerns the realization of an organizational climate within which members of the organization can personally create conditions, structural ones as well, for effective functioning of self and the organization. The nature of the relationship between the consultant and the (members of the) organization will then foster a participative climate.

According to Bruining and Allegro (1984), this is an indirect approach emphasizing the *manner* of change and not the content. The role of the consultant is process oriented. In their evaluation of this approach (p.4.9.2/3) the authors conclude that one can hardly speak of "a well-considered, planned, and through scrutinised theoretical research sustained process": "This approach appears to be no more than an amorphous entity of techniques and models that is related, in some instances, to some theory" (p.4.9.3).

Structural task approaches are different in nature: "Publications with reference to the structural task approach are more of an organization-theoretical kind; focus more on diagnostic aspects; deal with the description of how organizational problems can be solved, and not so much with the developmental process, the strategy, or with implementation. This structural task approach is directed at changes of task and organization structures and at structural aspects like role relations. The changes of job-content and modes of operation influence attitudes, the organizational behaviour of the employee and his job relations" (p.4.9.3).

The authors partly see this movement as emanating from classical consultancy (scientific management and industrial engineering), directed by experts, but, on the other hand, also as a reaction to that classical approach, because use is made of the lessons, taught by the "human relations" movement (p.4.9.3). That means that this structural task approach makes use of substantial expert knowledge, on the one hand (with regard to the relations between structures and (dys)functioning of persons), but also, on the other hand, allows more and more for participation in the scope of change projects (p.4.9.4/3). The authors, though, conclude that both approaches, the process approach as well as the structural task approach, influence one another more and more (p.4.9.4).

Although Bruining and Allegro classify both approaches, the structural task approach as well as the process approach, by the common denominator "organization development", this may not be entirely correct. If one consults the views of "OD experts", the impression is created that organization development should rather be seen as a method of organizational change where the emphasis is put on the cultural line of approach (see Warrick, 1978, for a review).

Since then, the situation has not really changed.

French and Bell (1990) define in this regard organizational development as "a top-management-supported, long-range effort to improve an organization's problem-solving and renewal processes, particularly through a more effective and collaborative diagnosis and management of organization culture . . ." (p.17).

I would prefer to employ the term "planned change" for the structural task approach, or rather yet "systematic change". But, as organizational development may lead to structural change, planned or systematic change may utilize the techniques derived from group dynamics in order to procure those changes. Put differently: Organizational development is a process that starts group dynamically, and, with the aid of the client system, may result in changes that can also be structural. These results, however, are not presented from the very start: There is no concrete goal in organizational development. Planned change (i.e. the structural task approach) does have a concrete goal, but it is less clear about the process.

French and Bell (1991, p.180) are rather explicit on this point when they argue: "Although changes in structure are frequent outcomes of an OD-effort, most programs targeted from the outset at structural change are not OD as we have defined the field". According to these authors, OD demands "collaborative diagnosis" and "collaborative action planning". Structural interference, apparently deduced from theory-based expert knowledge, may come into conflict with the results of collaborative diagnosis and action planning, which after all do not imply structural interventions from the very start (see French & Bell, 1990, pp.180–181).

In a separate scheme (p.182) French and Bell summarize their views and sketch a continuum running from left to right, from "time and motion study" (a pre-eminently expert approach) via "unilateral forms of job enrichment", "work-restructuring" to ultimately "comprehensive OD". And, the more to the left in their scheme, the less OD.

For Marx (1978), the encompassing term is the "study of organisations in a broad sense" (p.19); the study of organizations (in a narrow sense), according to Marx, deals with "static" aspects of the enclosing domain: "It describes and analyses how organizations are constructed, and also regards organizations from a normative point of view. In the last case it tends not to take for granted what reality shows. It also indicates how organizations have to be designed, with a view to a large number of criteria, and under what conditions organizations ... can function more or less effectively" (p.19).

The study of change would then direct itself to the dynamic aspects of the enclosing domain: "It views in what way processes of change of and in organizations may be initiated, directed and ended systematically" (p.19).

The study of organizations in a more narrow sense and the study of change have been differentiated. The reasons for this are undoubtedly all kinds of less favourable experiences with reorganizations that were broached on account of the organizational point of view at the time. The classical approach often took the form of an expert report, which was concluded with recommendations on changes to be executed in the organization. The management of the organization often seemed convinced of the appropriateness of the recommendations, but noticed, after a shorter or a longer period of time, that it seemed unable to realize the proposed alterations: lacking knowledge and skills, and/or the cooperation of personnel and/or the means in order to lend force to its wishes. In short, the report disappeared.

Marx too notices that a certain differentiation occurred within the study of change. However, he does not see these as controversies, but rather as different strategies change-agents can use, and which may be applied in all sorts of degrees and dosages (p.31).

Here Marx probably does most justice to history: the oldest term is "planned change". Cozijnsen and Vrakking (1987, p.11) mention Lewin's introduction of this term as early as 1952. (That, in fact, is not very probable, as Lewin died in 1947. Posthumously, "Resolving Social Conflicts" (1948) and "Field Theory in Social Science" (1951) were published. Possibly, Cozijnsen and Vrakking refer to a reprint, but unfortunately they fail to mention what publication is meant. In any case, if it was Lewin who introduced the term it must have been before 1947.)

Benne, Bennis, and Chin (1962/1979) take it that the term was first used at the end of the 19th century. They state that the idea of representatives of the social sciences actively influencing the planning of social changes stems from that period. For that matter, that idea had led to severe controversies: In 1900 this controversy on planned change expressed itself in confidently ideological terms. Should mankind interfere by means of determined and collective effort in the present state of affairs in order to determine its collective future, or not? Or should one be more trusting to principles of automatic adaptation (p.14). Supporters of the social sciences as "science" thought that social sciences should refrain from interference in practical affairs, in accordance with the traditions of the physical sciences and the other social sciences, i.e. history, economy, and political theory.

Since then things have changed dramatically: Social work and other professions have shot up like mushrooms. Industrial and social management have become professions. They claim the right to initiate and guide changes in future behaviour and relationships of their client populations. This is most obvious in new professions like psychiatry, social work, nursing, counselling, management, and consultancy in all its forms (p.15). In the 1950s planning social change seemed completely accepted: "The question no longer was 'should we aim for planned change?', but: 'how should we design plans for specific changes in specific institutions and situations?'" (p.16).

The current model was "technocratic": In this model experts design plans that meet the needs of the people concerned. After the plan is made, those implicated in the plan will be treated by means of a monologue, and persuaded to give their consent.

In the "clinical model" the plan is made in cooperation with those concerned, and a dialogue takes place between the experts and the party concerned in order to inform them and to offer the opportunity for making, assessing, and changing of plans (p.17). The emergence of this "clinical model" (the expressions are from Gouldner, 1956) should be looked for around 1950, in any case shortly before the term "organizational development" came into practice, a term French and Bell attribute to various authors such as Blake, Shepard, Mouton, McGregor, and Beckhard, and surfacing for the first time in 1956 (see French & Bell, 1990, p.33).

Lewin has played an important role in this development, although he should not be regarded as an OD consultant "avant la lettre". He emphasized scientific research, the results of which could be useful to practitioners and social workers. His approach was more "technocratic" in nature than "clinical". Important to him was also "the function and position of research within social planning and action", and that particular function to him is "fact-finding" (see Lewin, 1948, pp.202–203). In his mind social research relates to two different questions: "the study of general laws of group life and the diagnosis of a specific situation". His relationship to practice was that of a professional researcher and he did not consider himself a "practitioner". I know I am taking a different stance from, for example, French and Bell, authors who describe Lewin to be a "prolific theorist, researcher and practitioner in interpersonal, group, intergroup and community relationships" (1990, p.25). Yet, reviewing Lewin's scientific work, I conclude that Lewin did undertake theoretical and applied research. He gladly shared his knowledge with social workers; however, he did not see himself in this role at all.

French and Bell (1990, p.24) argue that organizational development has three roots:

1. Lewin's work, especially in the field of "group dynamics" and the resulting T-group training. This is called the "Laboratory Training Stem" by French and Bell (p.24). After encountering problems with so-called "stranger" T-groups (T-groups for individual participants unknown to each other) this type of training in the form of "family labs" (teams, participants from the same group or organization) seemed reasonably successful in organizational development projects (see Blake & Mouton, 1979).
2. The Survey Research and Feedback Stem. According to French and Bell (1990), this is the second root of organizational development (p.32). Survey research and feedback

are particular types of action research. French and Bell describe this type as a certain intervention that gathers systematic data on the organization that are presented to individuals and groups at all levels of the organization. Subsequently, the data, as well as the following action stages, must be interpreted by the participants. This type of action research has two main components: an attitude survey and feedback workshops. Survey feedback methods were developed by and because of Likert's thesis ("A technique for the measurement of attitudes") in the Survey Research Center of the University of Michigan. In 1948 Likert became top manager of the Institute for Social Research, encompassing the Survey Research Center and the Research Center for Group Dynamics established by Lewin, when the latter institute moved from MIT (Massachusetts Institute of Technology) to Michigan after the death of Lewin. Because of this the first and second root of OD are very much entwined.

3. Action research would be the third root of organizational development. According to French and Bell action research includes: (1) a preliminary diagnosis, (2) data gathering from the client group, (3) data feedback to the client group, (4) data exploration by the client group, (5) action planning by the client group, and (6) action by members of the client group (p.20). It is a more encompassing concept than "survey feedback". Action research, according to French and Bell, is applied so much in organization development that "another definition of organization development could be organization improvement through participant action research" (p.21).

French and Bell point towards parallel developments in England, especially the Tavistock Institute in London and the work of Eric Trist. French and Bell conclude "Thus, there is a clear historical link between the group dynamics field and sociotechnical approaches to assisting organizations" (p.35). There certainly exists a historical relationship (as well as a relationship between the Tavistock Institute and the Netherlands Institute for

Preventive Medicine in Leiden, as well as between the latter institute and the Institute for Social Research in Michigan). However, this does imply that no differences in strategic insight exist within the world of planned change and OD, or on a conceptual level. Those differences are related to:

1. the role of knowledge, expertise, and especially organizational knowledge in the realm of planned change and OD;
2. the focus of change projects in organizations, and the role of ad hoc problems;
3. the question whether normative opinions/ notions on the design of organizations should guide the change process.

4   DESIGN OR DEVELOPMENT?

Many organizations function unsatisfactorily, and change is due. The emphasis is either on an understanding of what the organization should look like, should be structured, or on how social systems should be brought to change. Is the organizational change project oriented to concrete goals or is it directed towards improving what is now experienced as annoying?

Authors on organizational development are relatively clear: The goal is not concrete, but is formulated in abstract terms: "to improve an organization's problem solving and renewal processes" (French & Bell, 1990, p.17) and the pretext is here and now. The design approach, however (e.g. Boonstra, 1991; Dunphy & Stace, 1988), is planned in the sense that the goal is concrete (nowadays this is often a socio-technical design), leading to a change process that is focused and does contain less degrees of freedom. Meanwhile, to cover this controversy, the terms "design approach" versus "development approach" seem to have been established (compare Hopstaken & Kranendonk, 1989, especially Boonstra, 1991).

According to Boonstra, the design approach considers organizations as formal systems in which ad hoc problem-solving and related adaptations lead to increasing inadequacies. The problems of the organization can only be solved radically by redesigning the organization. This change is once only. "When the new organization is introduced and a stable situation is obtained, the change process is terminated" (p.67). These changes according to Boonstra are initiated, coordinated, and checked from the top of the organization. The consultant is predominantly an expert who is primarily oriented towards the design of the (new) work organization. He is inclined to use an empirical rational strategy of interventions (a strategy that presupposes that people are prepared to follow advice they know to be for their own good). "Participation during the design process or during implementation is problematic because distance is consciously taken from existing operations and procedures in the organization ..." (p.67).

Boonstra describes the design approach in powerful, almost ideal-typical terms. It will be clear that many variations exist. However, they have in common that a more or less final concrete goal is indisputable, making participation questionable. In contrast, Boonstra sketches the development approach: The development approach does not view organizations as a source of inadequacies, but as the result of knowledge, experience and insight that should be used as much as possible when change is due (p.67). The focus should not be design oriented, but problem-oriented. The change would be gradual "ideas from the basis of the organization playing an important role" (p.68). The existing organization is the point of departure, and members of the organization are involved in all stages of the change process: Participation is possible because of the point of departure's being the existing situation, and goals emerge during the process; goals can always be reconsidered and adjusted (p.68).

Boonstra strongly argues for a contingent application of both approaches, a design approach being preferable when it is necessary to act quickly (for instance, in a crisis), or when change is very radical. Also, when consensus on the nature of the intended change does not reach a reasonable level, or a substantial cutback of personnel seems necessary, or insufficient trust exists between top management and employees, a design approach is probably appropriate. The development approach would be more suitable in situations where:

- there is a reasonably functioning organization requiring some improvement;
- there is no crisis, so that improvements may be realized gradually;
- sufficient trust in the management exists, etc.

Both approaches have certain disadvantages. Boonstra rightly states that, because of the complexity, the abstract and often fundamental mode of thought of the design approach (think of socio-technical design), the management often hardly has any idea of the innovation process and the consequences for the organization, and the management fairly often pulls out, leaving the innovation to experts. This sometimes occurs with automation processes too, with all its consequences. For instance, a bad connection between the new technology and the work organization. Moreover, the organization usually strongly resists the enforced changes.

The development approach, however, has its own problems. The most important one seems to be that changes, when occurring at all, may be limited in nature and often are not fundamentally innovative. Moreover, a development approach takes much time, especially at the start. The obvious question is whether both approaches might be integrated, in order to combine the advantages of both and to avoid the disadvantages. This is what Koopman and Pool (1986) favour, as well as Hopstaken and Kranendonk (1989). Koopman and Pool argue that the approach to be chosen may fluctuate somewhat per phase, the management deciding on the outlines, but a more detailed filling in could be realized via the development approach (cf. Boonstra, 1991, p.72, for a more detailed discussion). Although such an integrated approach may be a feasible solution for manageable progress of a fundamental process of change, this solution is only partly satisfactory. The reason is that both approaches, the design approach and the development approach, employ different implicit conceptions of human nature and the meaning of participation, and these conceptions are hard to integrate.

The design approach is based on expertise: knowledge of the environment of the organization, and the resulting demands with regards to the organizational structure. Knowledge about people as well, i.e. what motivates people, and under what conditions people are willing to act for the benefit of the organization. The classical design approach is in that sense consistent; a model of human nature is employed that may well be combined with the fact that the organizational design is based on decisions made at the top. This human model is utilitarian, and is very suitable for a classical disciplinary scheme (cf. Foucault, 1975).

The design approach, which is based on (modern) Socio-Technical Systems Design, also called the new paradigm-thinking (Trist, 1981), however, has a completely different view on human nature. That design theory employs a view on human nature that is more pragmatic-humanistic, in the sense of Dewey (Dewey, 1939; cf., Sierksma, 1991, for a thorough discussion of the discrepancy between utilitarianism and pragmatism). Such a view on human nature is incompatible with the design of the organization being the domain of experts advising the top level of the organization. The developmental approach is quite consistent with this pragmatic-humanistic view on human nature, but its disadvantage (cf. Boonstra) is that changes that can be realized often are not fundamental in nature.

This problem can in fact be clarified in simple terms. If the head of a family (the top manager of a social system) has decided that "this summer a visit to Patagonia" would be the right way to spend the family holiday, then this implies a certain view on the positions and roles of the remaining members of the family. Given these plans, explanation (an appeal rational reflection) and coercion are the remaining strategies. Participation is not an issue here. Participation is quite possible with regard to minor decisions, such as the choice of clothing to be taken along, and if necessary the way the destination should be reached as well as the day of departure. An authoritarian decision, as in this example, corresponds very well with a classical view of human nature. It is much more difficult to combine with a pragmatic-humanistic model of man that has to allow for participation and democratic decision-making at all levels.

Modern STSD as a design theory can only deal with this dilemma in a paternalistic way. This means compromising, while manipulation is a constant hazard. Van Beinum (1990) comes to a radical conclusion. He states that the transition from the old to the new paradigm implies the introduction of more democratical structures, which has its consequences on how to execute change: "One can only develop democratic structures and processes by means of methods which embody the same principles, such as is the case in participative design, the search conference and democratic dialogue." In other words, goals and means should be compatible.

The question, of course, remains of what "participative design", "search conference", and "democratic dialogue" exactly yield. Is it indeed a "new paradigm" organization? This is not so plausible. In order to remain with the example: A democratic dialogue of family members will without doubt produce a nice holiday destination, but it probably will not be "Patagonia". This can be clarified with yet another example. Let us assume that a group of workers and supervisors come to the conclusion that Dutch is not very satisfactory as an official language. The group decides that an alternative has to be found by using participative methods. At the side is the expert who knows the alternative; let us say it is the French language. What are the chances of the group's reaching this conclusion? Very small indeed: The alternative deviates too much from existing practices. Modern sociotechnique as an organizational design theory deviates quite a long way from classical organization principles (which are not very suitable for democratic dialogue, anyway). Even when it would be possible to start a democratic dialogue in a classical environment of that nature, it is quite unlikely that this would be the key to a modern sociotechnical design. This means that supporters of participative redesign give more credit to participative and democratic dialogue than to the socio-technical design itself. And that is exactly the state of affairs. Particularly the Swedish beneficiaries of the (classical) socio-technical tradition give tremendous credit to participative redesign-methods, and especially to the democratic dialogue (Gustavsen & Engelstad, 1986, 1990). Here the design approach, in fact, is abandoned and preference is given to the developmental approach.

The Dutch version of sociotechnique, also called "modern sociotechnique" (De Sitter, 1989; Kuipers & Van Amelsfoort, 1990; Chapter 4 in this *Handbook*) is, on the other hand, more a design theory, and links up more with the so-called design approach. Boonstra (1991) calls his approach "integral organizational development", and takes an indicated middle position between design approach and developmental approach, already advocated by Koopman and Pool, where both approaches alternate in one and the same change project. I stated before that such a middle position is necessarily paternalistic, and the danger of manipulation is imminent. On the other hand, however, this approach is undeniably effective.

5   ORGANIZATIONAL CHANGE: EVOLUTION OR REVOLUTION?

It has already been mentioned that someone like Lawler (1989) comes to the conclusion that important changes in the functioning of organizations are necessary, and that those changes indeed are realized. Here, Lawler speaks of a "new paradigm". He does not underestimate the problems arising: "The adoption of a new paradigm takes much more than simply the statement of it" (p.94). Lawler notices a clear relationship between the developments of today and the early work of Likert, Argyris, and McGregor (see Lammers & Széll, 1989). However, he also notices discontinuity: "Indeed, the very point that organizations need to be restructured in almost every feature in order to adopt a new paradigm effectively is largely missing in the early writings on participative management" (p.95).

Although Lawler thus indicates that the introduction of this new paradigm necessitates total restructuring of the organization, he does not indicate that a sudden reversal is needed. Which leads to the question of whether such fundamental changes could also be implemented gradually. That is, via an approach in the direction of more participation, without a completely new design as a concrete prospect. This would have to be an approach that, other than the Swedish seemingly had in mind, should be directed from the top of the organization. This direction, then, would not anticipate a concrete goal, but only indicate the line of march. The main question then is: Is such a gradual change process possible or would it lead to failure as a rule?

Anyway, the question is of the utmost importance: some time ago the Committee on Organizational Research (COB) of the Dutch Social Economic Council published a report: "Cooperation in autonomous task-groups: practical experience in industry and the provision of services" (Joosse et al., 1990). In his preface to this report, Van Schaik, chairman of the COB/SER project team, states that companies have been occupied from way back with the question of how the efficiency and effectivity of the organization could be improved. "Little attention was given to the quality of work and organization. As a reaction an integral view was developed, so that work and organization could be organised according to the principles of the autonomous task-group. With this concept workers can organise the job in such a way that they as a team work together autonomously, in order to produce whole products or parts thereof. That way they take care of planning and preparation of their work, as well as the quality of their product . . ." (p.3). Joosse's survey concerns an evaluation of this practice found in 13 companies from industry and service provision in the Netherlands. It was not easy to find those companies. Very interesting is the following sentence from the report: "For participation in this research project almost one hundred companies were approached. In many instances these companies did not comply with an important criterion in order to participate in the research: actual experience with task-groups. This experience was not at all or only to a limited extent available." These, almost a hundred, companies were not approached overnight. They were approached on the basis of information justifying the sound assumption that the company possibly qualified for participation. Eventually, 13 companies were studied. Informally, the researchers admit that the companies could qualify after the researchers had reached a compromise: a very strict managing of the criterion would have yielded too few research cases. This means that only a few companies have realized this new "participative design based on socio-technical principles. However, it also means

that a much larger number of companies shows signs of development in this direction.

The 13 companies included in the research were without exception economically successful, as regards the implementation of the concept of autonomous task-groups: "economically, substantial improvements have been accomplished", the report mentions (p.15). The position of all the companies showing signs of development in the intended direction is not clear, unfortunately. Yet, one might interpret this as an indication of a transition from a classical mechanical structure to a feasible participative structure, knowing in-between stages suggesting the possibility of a more gradual development.

The idea that such in-between stages might be difficult to realize and in any case would be unstable, is based on the proposition of there being only two possible design principles for the design of organizations: maximum possible labour division (Kuipers calls this the classical engineering principle, characteristic scientific management), or minimum possible labour division, the leading construction principle of the socio-technical design theory (see Emery, 1979; Kuipers, 1989. Differently phrased, this proposition is also encountered in Hage, 1974, and Banbury, 1975). It would be difficult to combine both principles in one organization. A little less distinct, but certainly supporting this idea, is the insight of Leavitt (see Leavitt, 1965). Leavitt defines organizations as open, multivariate systems. Very well-known is the "diamond of Leavitt", depicted in Figure 8.2.

Actually, the four variables (tasks or goals of the organization, structure, technology, and people) are clusters of variables. These clusters of variables influence each other mutually, so that the whole tends towards a dynamic equilibrium. This means that changes introduced into one of these clusters have their effects in other clusters, so that a new dynamic equilibrium emerges. When the change that is realized is too superficial, not radical enough, the renewal will not be manifested elsewhere, and in time it can even be undone altogether. Leavitt certainly leaves some room for variation: The relations between these (clusters of) variables are not such that one determines the other completely. Yet, there is an "indicative

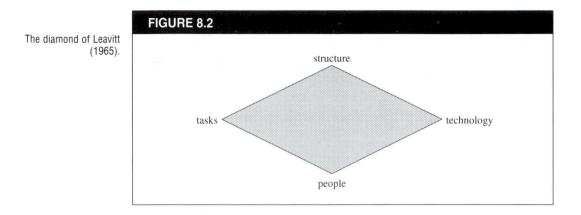

FIGURE 8.2

The diamond of Leavitt (1965).

dependency" (Van der Vlist, 1985, p.43), suggesting the possibility of a certain variation within a cluster. However, a fundamental change is only possible when the system is forced towards a completely new dynamic equilibrium. This insight corresponds with the assumption of Kuipers (Kuipers & Van Amelsfoort, 1990), that without a leading (new) construction principle the management "is only in a position for a 'piecemeal' approach. Possibly, this complies with the solution of problems where the existing concept of the organization is not under discussion, but it is unsuitable for solving more fundamental design problems" (p.200). Den Hertog (1980) calls such a limited approach a "billiard model": On the pretext of "there being a solution for every problem", the subdisciplines within the management sciences play billiards with symptoms without the causes disappearing. Finally, section 2 has already pointed at the concept "organizational conservatism" (Child et al., 1987) i.e. the inclination of organizations to incorporate innovations, for instance, new technology, in such a way that the organization as a socio-cultural construct maintains its identity (cf. Frissen, 1989).

The question here is: Is this an exaggerated gloomy note, or could it yet be possible to take some steps in the direction of a more fundamental change? (Lawler's "new paradigm", founded on a participative structure). Is evolution possible, or is revolution essential? If the latter is the case, a conversion will be painful and laborious, and perhaps on a societal basis fail to occur for the most part. This would mean that we would forever be stuck with a type of organization that is far from

optimal in view of the environmental developments. Perhaps there is more space, and intermediate forms are conceivable so that both extremes, an organization founded on classical design principles and an organization founded on "minimal labour division and participation, may be reconciled. The investigation by Joosse et al. (1990) holds indications in this direction, and suggests that reality is more complex and allows for variants that do not fit the somewhat schematical line of thinking many of us hold.

Literature pertaining to business administration and business economics also holds indications in this direction. Next to the same gloomy notes as those of the population-ecologists the strategic-choice literature exists. Population-ecologists take the stand that organizations react relatively slowly where threats and possibilities in their environment are concerned (Hannan & Freeman, 1989, p.70). The consequence is then that organizations are, as it were, carefully selected and innovation mainly takes place by new organizations' coming into being (see Schreuder, 1990). The strategic-choice literature, on the other hand, emphasizes the role of managers. This role is partly strategic in nature and directed at monitoring the developments in the environment as well as strategic decision-making, in order to tune the organizations to the environment.

Schreuder (1990) carried out research, directed at the question of "what are the factors determining whether a company successfully overcomes branch-problems" (p.307). Schreuder used as a criterion for branch-problems "that the added value at branch-level should have decreased with at least 20 per cent within the course of at least three years" (p.307). Thirty branches could be selected in that way. In the 30 selected branches pairs of companies were selected which: (a) found themselves at the same point of departure at the start of the branch problems, but (b) differed as much as possible concerning the success with which they tackled the problems (p.307). In 21 branches this scheme was successful, and the study was carried out in 42 companies, which could be compared in pairs.

Schreuder concluded that:

- Successful companies clearly take more measures directed at their potential market and commodities.
- Less successful companies take significantly more measures directed at diminishing costs (cutback in expenditure).
- In total, successful companies take considerably more measures (an average of 10.9) than less successful (7.7).
- In the categories organization and finances successful companies are more active.

Schreuder has also looked at the kind of measures within the category "organization." Here he used three subcategories management, internal organization, and diversification, and he states: "With regard to management measures it appears that the two groups of companies replace the top-management in the same number of cases (30%). The tendency exists in the successful companies, however, to reduce top-management; in less successful companies to extend top-management. In middle-management exactly the opposite is the case. Successful companies extend the second echelon sooner; less successful companies reduce sooner." Schreuder continues: "Apparently the more market-directed policy of successful companies is accompanied by decentralisation, while the cost-directed policy of less successful companies is connected with centralisation" (pp.309–310). What stands out is quite clear. Being successful in overcoming an enduring branch decline means in this time-span: more and decisive market sensitivity. This means decentralisation, i.e. divisionalization: putting responsibilities in the lower echelons of the organization, without transferring to a completely socio-technical design. Finally, Schreuder shows "that suc-

cessful companies take their management measures in average one year before the start of a branch decline, together with market-directed measures and adjustments of production volumes. Thus, they act in an anticipating way in this category. Less successful companies do not act anticipatorily anywhere. If they finally do react, the measures with respect to management and organization are the last ones taken.

Schreuder's study clearly shows that practice offers illustrations that can be seen as evidence by population-ecologists, but also examples appealing to strategic-choice theorists. It seems by the utmost importance that "success" depends upon early strategic decisions. Timely adaptation of the top of the organization is often deemed necessary. In other words: The pretext for fundamental changes, leading to a more decentralized, market-directed flexible structure, is the management of the organization. (This is hard to place in the "diamond" of Leavitt, unless the notion of "goals and tasks of the organization" is conceived of in a broad sense.) Sometimes, and maybe often, a timely change in top management is necessary. Though not always: The existing management should be able to start a fundamental change in course. Strategic insight as well as some sturdiness of the management will be needed. This (renewed) strategic insight may be a consequence of a trip to Japan (see the example at the beginning of section 1), but it could just as well be the consequence of a consciously employed technique like the "search conference" (Emery, 1987) or the "strategic-scouting-group" (Den Hertog & Dankbaar, 1989; see also Steensma, 1989).

The top management participates in such conferences in any case, but in addition often also representatives of the employees, in the Netherlands, for instance, the chair of the industrial council. Often the group is expanded with people from around the organization. Important is that the insight that restructuring of the organization is necessary, in the form of a more participative, flexible, client-and market-directed structure, cannot be realized without a "shock experience". At least not in the early stages of what may be seen as a societal conversion: Distancing oneself from classical organization principles, and working towards more organical, flexible, participative structures.

My impression is that this does not need to be a revolutionary process, in the sense that this restructuring of organizations has to take place within a relatively short period of time. What does seem to be necessary is a "revolution" in thinking by the top of the organization, leading to the first steps in the direction of restructuring, for example, in the form of divisionalization. Within these divisions, or relatively autonomous units, it certainly must be possible to work little by little towards participative structures. That in itself is rather difficult, because of "resistance to change" occurring in the entire organization, implying that changes in outlines have to be realized top-down.

6   RESISTANCE TO CHANGE: THE ROLE OF REPRESENTATIVES OF THE PROFESSIONAL STAFF AND (LOWER) SUPERVISORY STAFF

A development in the direction of a more participative structure implies another position for many members of the professional staff (the ones that take care of the brainwork in the classical structure), as well as a change in the position and role of executives and supervisors (who, in the role of line executives, obtain a greater responsibility in areas traditionally the responsibility of the professional staff, and who now must develop another style of leadership). To many this is not an obvious conclusion, and they show resistance to such changes. Resistance expressed as open protest, or in the form of passive resistance, inactivity, or ignorance and insecurity.

That resistance originates in different ways, and has a diverse background. Elsewhere I mentioned (see Van der Vlist, 1989):

- resistance as a reaction to the (alleged) attacks on the interest and power-position of supervisors and professional staff as a result of the introduced change;
- resistance as a reaction to the strategic and tactical tackling of the process of change;
- resistance as a result of cultural barriers, emanating from the fact that especially the

supervisors and professional staff experience their traditional position and matched conduct as appropriate. The implicit assumptions in the structure, the task-division and the procedures of the traditional organization (before the change) are, especially by the management, internalized as "fitting". These implicit assumptions show powerful features of McGregor's "theory X" (McGregor, 1960) (see also section 7).

Boonstra (1991) draws the conclusion that organizational changes are frustrated because of existing power-relations. "In organizational change different parties will more than is the case otherwise direct themselves towards safeguarding their own interests, objectives and power positions." He then states that organizational consultants should be aware that "political use of influence … is often essential in order to put organizational changes into motion" (p.38). Boonstra also explains that consultants have the power enabling them to fulfil that political role. As power sources he enumerates, among others, expertise (specific authority as a consultant), status (based on education, and as a representative of a possibly reputable agency), delegated informal power (as a result of the advice sought by the client system), delegated legitimate power (based upon acceptance and authorization of, mostly, the top management), the access to power centres, control of information and political abilities of the consultant (see Boonstra, 1991, pp.39–40).

This is not the only role played by the consultant in order to overcome the resistance of supervisors and professional staff. Other roles of consultants distinguished in the literature are:

- The procedural role (Marx, 1978). Here the structuring of one or more phases of the change process is concerned. The consultant formulates objectives for constituent processes, determines which activities should be carried out by whom, coordinates everything, and prevents stagnation.
- The expert role. The consultant uses his knowledge and cognitive skills in order to solve organizational problems (gathering data and formulating solutions based on theory and experience).

- The social-emotional role. The consultant guides members of the organization to analyze and improve interpersonal processes (see Beckhard, 1969; Boonstra, 1991; Van de Bunt, 1978). At the same time the consultant helps members of the organization to understand and accept the significance of the intended change.

Each and all of these consultant roles may be of service in overcoming resistance (of supervisors and professional staff) against change. In view of the power aspect that is greatest in the framework of the procedural role, and is unequivocal in the framework of the expert role, it may be advisable to work in teams of consultants where such a task division is achieved that the social-emotional role is used by the same member of the team continually, while the remaining roles are taken by (one or more) other members of the team of consultants.

Particularly in the framework of his social-emotional role the consultant employs "intervention techniques" at individual and group level. Blake and Mouton (1976) describe five of these techniques (or methods).

- The use of principles, theories, and models by the consultant in order to broaden the insight of the person(s) concerned, especially cognitive transfer of knowledge, among others, by means of education. Expert knowledge from the consultant is important here, but then as a power-neutral rational category.
- The catalytic intervention. This is an intervention where the consultant intervenes in a certain situation and adds something to change the character of that situation (for instance, making a suggestion, producing figures). Survey-feedback can be rated among this type of intervention.
- The confronting intervention. This is a more aggressive intervention technique in which the consultant confronts the relevant person(s) with their own behaviour or the consequences thereof.
- The prescriptive intervention, where the consultant prescribes what the person(s) should do, for instance, by way of exercise.
- The accepting intervention. This means that the consultant attempts to come into contact with feelings (tension, fear, ill-will) that may block someone. The consultant endeavours to help the person to express their feelings in order to solve the problems. This is mainly a non-directive technique, which may be compared with counselling.

Although the above-mentioned techniques may be seen as the most well known techniques, particularly because of publications by Blake and Mouton, this inventory is probably not exhausting, and a group-dynamics-trained consultant may invent additional techniques. The techniques intended can be applied at the individual as well as at group level.

A well-known technique mostly applied at group level, and catalytic in nature, is the "survey-feedback-method". This method includes systematic gathering of data through the help of questionnaires (for example, presented to employees or customers). The data gathered are subsequently presented to relevant individuals and groups, in order to analyze and interpret these data and to undertake actions on that basis (see section 3).

A variant of this method is Heller's "Group feedback analysis" (GFA), and is employed by him in leadership and decision-making studies (Heller, 1976; Heller, Drenth, Koopman, & Rus, 1988). The following example is taken from Heller (1976, pp.215–216). The example takes place in a bank, where it was decided to switch-over to a computerized accounting system. It was also decided to recruit new staff members in order properly to utilize the complex technology. The top level (level 1) did not think highly of the experience and abilities of their subordinates (level 2). Those subordinates were of another opinion, however. Application of the GFA technique clearly showed this discrepancy in opinions. Additional information, from other organizations as well as from other departments of the same bank, finally led the bank to deciding not to employ new staff members, but to utilize the knowledge and possibilities of already available staff members. A follow-up study six months later clearly showed the satisfactory functioning of the bank. One thing and another also led to less hierarchical leadership styles.

Another well-known group technique is the T-group, the "laboratory method of training" (see e.g. French & Bell, 1990). The method intends to make participants conscious about their until-then unconscious ideas, and about the effects of these unconscious ideas on their behaviour. These trainings, which may last from 3 to 14 days, and which may have a large impact, are usually attended by two trainers. Such trainings aim at increasing interpersonal competencies.

Finally, I mention group consultation as a technique, enabling all those involved to think about content and form of possible procedures and tasks to be performed per department or sector. In this latter case one recognizes aspects of a development approach (see section 4).

Resistance (of supervisors and professional staff), which should be seen as a reaction to (alleged) attacks on the interest and power-position, and which could be seen as a consequence of the proposed changes, requires, on the one hand, a power strategy at top-management level, but, on the other hand, negotiation and rational clarification. Eventually, supervisors and staff will have to be convinced of the necessity (and inevitability) of the proposed changes, in order to collaborate in a constructive way. This would not be possible without a certain attractiveness of that prospect. Negotiation and persuasion are due. That is no simple assignment, and in many situations the top management quickly abandons the initiative, enabling supervisors and staff members to safeguard their positions. Most of the time this is caused by the fact that participation is used too early and without a clear framework. The consultant, now in a procedural role, should guard against this.

Resistance caused by cultural barriers is probably the hardest to overcome. This is the result of the fact that this resistance, as an expression of the (until then existing) culture of the organization, is difficult to capture. Section 7 will deal with this more specifically. The aforementioned intervention techniques belong to the traditional equipment of the consultant. Its position, however, seems to be different now than compared with some 10 years ago. At that time it was the consultant, as OD consultant, who attempted to realize the desired changes that were formulated concretely or not. At this point the consultant is rather the assistant of the management that makes

the first move on the basis of vision. In that framework the consultant uses his expertise: helping and supporting. Beer and Walton (1987) state that managers start to recognise that they are the first to be responsible. Increasing competition, deregulation, changing values of personnel, and the increasing role of information technology dictate different requirements in organizations. Changes that require flexible organizations as well as educated managers who can realize those changes (p.345). And consultants become actors in a process orchestrated by general managers (p.340). This means that the emphasis now is on the general management of the organization itself.

7   CULTURAL BARRIERS FOR ORGANIZATIONAL CHANGE

After the elaboration in the preceding chapters that, because of changes in the environment, organizations are increasingly forced towards a more participative structure, the central question in section 5 was whether this is a revolutionary or an evolutionary process. It was made plausible that such structures may also be realized more gradually. Strategic insight at the top is essential here. Changes also start at that level and are, certainly in the initial phase, top-down and power-oriented. The latter is particularly necessary in order to avoid domination and obstruction of change by vested interests of supervisors and staff members. Yet, this is not enough to conquer all forms of resistance. An important source of resistance refers to the concept of organizational culture.

Without the need to present a formal definition of the concept of organizational culture, it may be clear that mainly implicit assumptions, beliefs, attitudes, shared by members of the group, are at stake. Essential is that these implicit assumptions are hardly ever discussed (see Chapter 4 of this *Handbook*). Schein (1985) argues that this entails basic assumptions developed by a group "as it learns to cope with its problems of external adaptation and internal integration" (p.9). Culture is significantly directional for behaviour.

The importance of the concept in this sense was

succinctly expressed by Allport (1948) in his preface to the reader *Resolving Social Conflicts* containing 13 articles written by Kurt Lewin (1948): In this preface Allport states: "The unifying theme is unmistakable: the group to which an individual belongs is the ground for his perceptions, his feelings, and his actions" (p.vii).

Interaction between group members, leading to a certain homogenization of notions on relevant domains probably is not the only factor influencing the development of a "group culture". Van Maanen and Barley (1985) mention four factors. The first one they call the ecological context. Organisations are involved with physical, social, and temporal aspects of the environment, related to the objectives of the organization (for example, a brickyard on the Rhine in a non-urban area in the 1990s). This same context exists for groups within this organization, although the specific task, the social coherence and the physical working space of the group, is added. This ecological context determines to a certain extent the nature of the problems experienced by the employees, and the kinds of solutions that are feasible.

A second factor mentioned by Van Maanen is differential interaction. The structuring of the organization has its effects on interaction patterns within the organization as well as within groups in the organization. It is this phenomenon to which Allport and Lewin were referring. Theories on the development of "social identity" (Tajfel, 1981) are akin to this. Interactions between group members in relation to matters relevant to the group, as well

as interactions with representatives from the environment, lead to the development of collective conceptions. These collective conceptions are then "guarded", preserved by processes with a reproductive and adaptive character. Collective "understandings" form the true implication of culture: Only when members of a group attribute similar meaning to what happens and facets of their situation, does a culture exist. Interaction is crucial: "through interaction, unique responses develop to problems that later take on trappings of rule, ritual and value" (Van Maanen & Barley, 1985, p.34). Van Maanen and Barley thus point to systems of meaning that develop as self-evidences that go without saying (see also Van der Vlist, 1991).

The cultural problems arising with the transition from a classical mechanical organization structure to a more participative structure (enabling the organization "to use its people more fully", as Lawler describes), I would now like to highlight by using a model based on the insight of Van Maanen and Barley, but supplemented with the findings of, among others, Schein (1985) and Smith and Peterson (1988). This is depicted in Figure 8.3.

Van Maanen and Barley (1985) pointed to the importance of the task structure and labour conditions (the ecological context). In this model the addition of "psychological characteristics of the situation" is new. Some clarification is called for: Katz and Kahn (1978) state that the greatest problem for every organization concerns behavi-

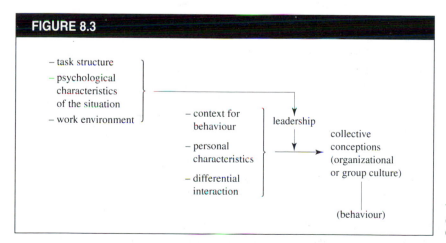

FIGURE 8.3

The development of an organizational-or group culture.

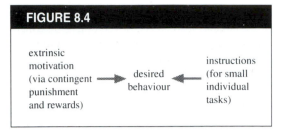

FIGURE 8.4

A model for behaviour control in classical mechanistical organizations. Authoritarian/utilitarian scheme.

our control of employees. Behaviour of people is flexible and capricious. In order to facilitate "concerted action", a certain behaviour control is necessary. Every organization knows, to quote Foucault (1975), a certain "disciplinary scheme". The ideal-typical classical mechanistical organization employs an "authoritarian/utilitarian" scheme, based on the assumption that people (employees) are mainly extrinsically motivated, and should be instructed in practically every activity (Figure 8.4).

As stated earlier, many organizations, also in the Netherlands, are of this type, although I have given a somewhat exaggerated sketch in Figure 8.4 for clarifying purposes. This scheme in its extreme form is found less often in reality. In Figure 8.3 this is indicated as "psychological characteristics of the situation" (in a classical organization). This is an essential factor in describing the context for behaviour. It is this context, together with personal characteristics of members of the group (organization), and differential interaction, which is crucial for collective understandings called "culture".

In a classical organization these conceptions, among others, refer to the meaning of work, conceptions of the management, the (minor) importance attached to the job, the outcome of one's own work, contacts with colleagues, etc. Generally the kind of conception meant is, that which Goldthorpe, Lockwood, Bechhofer, and Platt (1968) call an instrumental attitude with respect to the job, and which mainly refers to the importance attached to financial rewards. These collective conceptions are subsequently maintained, supplemented, and accentuated by actions by the supervisors, who as "cultural guards" attribute meaning to relevant events, like inter-

preting errors in the work process, i.e. caused by stupidity, non-motivation, negligence, etc. Group members also play an important role in maintaining the culture (cf. Schein, 1985; Smith & Peterson, 1988; Van der Vlist, 1991; Yukl, 1989).

A participative (possibly socio-technical) organization employs a more elaborate view of human nature, and utilizes what I would call a "self-regulating pragmatic" disciplinary scheme, in which the notion "pragmatic" should be interpreted in Dewey's (1915) use of the term. He does not view people as adjusting, reacting, or even passive, but as active, initiating, reinterpreting, and dynamic. This disciplinary scheme is depicted in Figure 8.5.

In a participative organization not only do a different task structure and different working conditions exist, but other "psychological characteristics of the situation" as well. Together with differential interaction (in groups and organizations), and influenced by personal characteristics of the members, this may lead to another culture, and other collective conceptions. That is possible when the supervisor behaves accordingly. Because of the (gradual) change of the organization from a mechanistic structure to a more participative structure, supervisors may maintain their position. It now becomes essential that these supervisors make explicit their understandings and suppositions, which have been implicit thus far (belonging to the old culture). They should also be willing to develop other understandings, in order to facilitate the cultural change process,

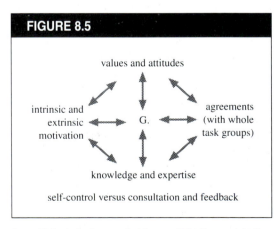

FIGURE 8.5

A model for behaviour control in a participative organization: Pragmatic-humanistic scheme.

including the changed task structure, the changed working condition, and the changed psychological characteristics of the situation, which facilitate change. This puts a strain on OD specialists, and time and effort of the management, the organization, and the consultant. In this sense the activities and interventions of OD consultants become supplementary and supportive for organizational change processes in which top management takes the lead. This supplementary role of OD consultants is particularly possible because the traditional values OD consultants adhere to (cf. French & Bell, 1990, pp.44–51) correspond with organizational changes in the direction of a participative structure (see also Faucheux, Amado, & Laurent, 1982; Jaeger, 1986).

Figure 8.3 depicts the genesis of an organizational or group culture. Due attention has been paid to the notion "context for behaviour", in order to clarify that the organizational and group culture has "fundaments", has "roots", which are not immediately visible, although they are decisive for development of culture, conceived of as "collective conceptions and attitudes". Culture is important for behaviour, it is "a kind of backdrop for action" (Smircich, 1985, p.58).

For many, behaviour itself is not considered to be part of this culture. Schein points to behaviour being another category. Behaviour is determined by varying combinations of cultural predispositions and situational contingencies originating from the momentary environment. That behaviour would then be an integration from the cultural predispositions and situational contingencies. The question could be posed of whether cultural change can also be reached in the opposite way, i.e. by procuring behavioural change. Certainly, clues exist in (social) psychology for this hypothesis. The social-psychologist Bem (1965, 1967) showed that experimental subjects, who could be persuaded to defend a point of view not matching their own attitude, would then change their attitude in such a way that the defended point of view was in agreement with their attitude. This was even more the case when the incentives to defend such a point of view were small.

Bem presented his research findings from a radical behaviouristic point of view: ideas, beliefs, attitudes we attribute to ourselves, they all are rationalizations we derive from our behaviour. Attitudes, etc. do not influence our behaviour, but just the other way around: situational contingencies summon behaviour, and conceptions, ideas, and attitudes are the by-products: "it is reasonable that we infer our own beliefs (when asked to reflect on them) from observations of our own non-manded behaviour" (Jones, 1985, p.90). That effect would be more substantial when the "incentives" to summon desired behaviour were smaller. Bem presented his ideas from a behaviouristic point of view. However, it will be clear that his data could just as well be comprehended from the cognitive dissonance theory. This issue will not be further examined here.

Behaviouristic principles are used in the framework of programmes indicated with the term "behaviour modification". The process leads to behavioural change by means of controlling the outcomes of behaviour (see also Chapter 2 in this *Handbook*; Davis & Luthans, 1980; Rietdijk, 1991).

In this approach it is essential not to try and change the culture of the organization or the group, but by means of positive and (in a minor way) negative reinforcers, the outcomes of behaviour should be managed for desired behaviour to take place. The process does not concern culture or anything preceding culture (see Figure 8.3). By now, behaviour modification has risen to a refined whole of techniques, which has been applied very successfully in a number of situations (for a review, see O'Hara, Johnson, & Beehr, 1985).

The success of organizational-behaviour modification ("OB-mod") programmes has led many an organization to the application of such programmes and to leave it at that. That is to say, without also changing the structure of the organization in such a way that the desired behaviour may be the result of a culture related to that structure (context, see Figure 8.3). In these cases the displayed behaviour is not "internalized". This also means that when creative and flexible behaviour is requested, behavioural modification is no solution, as OB-mod programmes need much more concrete behaviour definitions. "OB-mod" principles are not worthless; on the contrary, very valuable supplementary means can be distilled from its practice.

Strangely enough, a parallel can be seen in the

traditional actions of OD consultants with the mode of operation of OB-mod experts. Traditional OD consultants employed a whole of strategies and intervention techniques that were in fact meant to influence the culture of the organization or the group (Burke, 1987). French and Bell take a comparable, yet even more explicit view, and, moreover, they state that structural changes may be a consequence of OD activities, however, that programmes intending explicit structural changes, for the most part, are no OD programmes (cf. Chapter 3). In other words: OD consultants, too, worked "up-stream" from the right to the left in Figure 8.3, if they were occupied with structural changes at all. Just like behavioural change via behaviour modification may be successful, if only for a limited behaviour domain (very sensitive for inconsistencies in reinforcers), cultural change by way of OD programming may be possible. Here, too, cultural change does not represent a stable equilibrium, unless the basis of the culture the context for behaviour is also changed.

All the same, OD programmes may also be at the basis of the total process of organizational change. Conceptions on organizing are, as a rule, implicit, and culture-bound in a societal sense. When OD programmes are able to influence the conceptions top management holds, then there is no reason to replace the top management (Schreuder). Another aspect of such an OD programme could be a trip to Japan, as undertaken by the chief executive officer of the Dutch Steel Works. However, there are other possibilities, for instance, a search conference (Emery, 1987).

8   RECENT DEVELOPMENTS

Organisational development and planned change get a lot of attention in recent literature. Also, research on the activities of OD consultants is on the move. Fagenson and Burke (1991) investigated "individuals who attended a professional development program for organization development and human resource management practitioners" (p.7). This concerned OD specialists with at least three years' experience plus a thorough training, who were active as "internal"

consultants. A total of 71 professionals participated in the investigation. A questionnaire was presented in which 55 intervention techniques and OD activities were put forward. Participants were asked to indicate whether and how often they used each of these techniques. Fagenson and Burke factor-analyzed the item scores (principal components; varimax rotation), and found five factors with an eigen-value larger than 1, explaining 63.3% of the total item variance (p.10). The factors were named as follows: "employee development" (including career development, job-rotation, task redesign, job-evaluation, etc.); "strategy development" (strategic planning); "improvement of management style"; "cultural change", and "integration of (new) technology into the organization".

After some treatment of the data, they conclude that activities like improvement of the management style and strategy development occur most often (factors 2 and 3) (pp.11–12). In the discussion paragraph they state "it appears that much of what OD practitioners were involved in during the 1980's consisted of activities that facilitated organizational movement and change". Thus, with respect to the 1960s and 1970s things have certainly changed: "much of OD in the 1960's was process oriented. Involvement in human processural types of interventions appear to have been less prevalent in the eighties ..." (Fagenson & Burke, 1991, p.13). They also observe, as predicted by Sashkin and Burke (1987), and before that already observed by Bruining and Allegro (1984), a gradual integration of "human processural" and "technostructural approaches", although the latter's importance increases and is now used more often (Fagenson & Burke, 1991, p.13). So, OD practitioners no longer are "just process facilitators" (Fagenson & Burke, 1991, pp.13–14). This is a finding that fits the thesis of Beer and Walton (1987) I have already mentioned (see the introduction of this chapter).

That this is also necessary is pointed out by Porras and Silvers (1991). They commence their article with the observation that rapid changes in the environment of organizations necessitate quick reactions of organizations "in order to survive and prosper". They add: "planned change that makes organizations more responsive to environmental shifts should be guided by generally accepted and unified theories of organizations and organizational change ..." (p.51). Neither is available, according to the authors.

The great virtue of the article of Porras and Silvers is that the authors present a model of the change process itself. Actually, this model resembles Figure 8.3, the model depicting the genesis of an organizational culture. Essential in their model is the addition of OT, organizational transformation, leading to a (new) vision, a mission, tightly linked to the ideas of Lawler (1989). This (new) mission would, together with the effects of the process approach, i.e. the task-structural approach (Bruining & Allegro, 1984) which Porras and Silvers both consider OD, leads to "work-setting" changes concerning:

- organizing arrangements (i.e. changes in strategy, formal structure, policy, administrative systems, reward systems, and ownership relations);
- social factors (next to interaction processes, social patterns, management style, etc., they also mention culture);
- technology;
- physical setting (space configuration, physical ambience, interior design, architectural design).

This could then lead to cognitive change and behavioural change, to the advantage of the organization as well as of the employees.

It is a pity that they do not illustrate how changes, for example in "organizing arrangements", affect cognitive changes. Actually, part of the model seems to be a "black box". That is too bad, because it is certainly not impossible that certain cognitive changes can only be realized by means of fundamental changes in the "context of behaviour", as I sketched with reference to Figure 8.3. This could also explain why the results of Quality Circle programmes are mixed. The addition of QCs to an existing structure, implies that organizing arrangements are not so much altered, but rather expanded. In fact, this does not change the "context for behaviour" (cf. Lawler & Morhman, 1987).

The development of theories on the effects of interventions (of OD specialists, change agents or, even as a result of "accidental", not planned, events, like increasing turbulence of the environment), is, in the traditional critical-rationalistic notion of science, a detached process, in which the subject (the scientific researcher) gathers data on an object. Also the researcher has to abide to certain rules implying that "the researcher acts as 'objectively' as he is able to, without interference from personal opinions, preferences, observation modes, notions, interests and sentiments" (De Groot, 1961, p.172). The researcher endeavours to describe, to categorize, to register, to understand, and to explain phenomena. "furthermore, he is especially targeted towards predicting new phenomena, in order to finally control the sector in question by way of predictability, i.e. the ability to influence the phenomena" (De Groot, 1961, p.19).

Applied to OD and planned-change research, this view firstly implies a task-division between researcher and consultant. This is necessary because the subjective involvement of the consultant is in every possible respect inevitable where concrete interventions are concerned. Simultaneously, this means that the object of the researcher will not be limited to a concrete intervention. That object is, in accordance with this line of reasoning, the combination of a consultant, his or her applied intervention, and the concrete social system the intervention is aimed at. That does not simplify this type of research, also because the intervention and its effects do not take place instantly, but rather require (much) time as a rule. Research with regard to the effects of intervention methods is thus considered problematical. Beer and Walton (1987) mention four aspects:

1. The typical intervention research tries to isolate causal factors. Just as in "normal science", this research tries to identify the consequences of a single intervention, or a coherent whole of interventions, and by doing it ignores the systemic character of organizations. Furthermore, accidental factors like intervening incidents will preclude firm conclusions (Beer & Walton, 1987, p.343).
2. Much research is insufficiently longitudinal in nature.

3. The research is "flat". In general, research is rather precise as regards methodology and research instruments, but "it is often imprecise in depth and description of the intervention and situation" (p.343). Also, the nature and history of the group in question often are not included in the research, and the context is insufficiently recognized or even considered irrelevant.

4. The research often does not meet the needs of the users.

Attempts to achieve more precision and tighter scientific proof, with the aid of more complicated statistical techniques and more complex quasi-experimental test-cases, pass the fact that knowledge in the social sciences is also based on social constructions (p.344). The latter criticism is more fundamental. Here the main thing is not that this type of research is extremely difficult (and may e even impossible), but that knowledge in the social sciences is of a different nature than knowledge in, for instance, the natural sciences, and that what is "true" or "not true" may be partly (of even mainly) a time-limited social construction;it is relative, dependent on the observer and her social environment, and is partly based on conventions (cf. Carnap, 1966; Rorty, 1967; see also Van der Vlist, 1991, Ch. 8).

Other objections may be raised against forms of academic social-scientific research. Those ordinary forms are indicated by Liu as "observational research" (Liu, 1991). His objections to this kind of research are:

- The assumed total independency between the "observation" and the "phenomenon". It is a principle implying that research should not influence the object of study. Liu states that it is considered impossible in social science to comply with that principle. Referring to the Hawthorne effect, according to him a phenomenon neglected by researchers, he states that research practically always affects experimental subjects. Beer and Walton also point towards this effect. They mention research carried out by Blumberg and Pringle (1983) on socio-technical interventions "in which the 'control' group found out about the experimental group". As a consequence, further changes in the work situation were obstructed (Beer & Walton, 1987, p.343). The alternative prevention of the control group being informed could influence the significance of such an experiment. To put it briefly, there are always unintentional effects.

- Repeatability. This is an important basic principle in the natural sciences (classical physics), in order for a conclusion to be seen as valid. In the social sciences this is a problem "because many important human and social facts are unique, and not repeatable".

- Closure, independency, and additivity. This, third, principle of classical physics he calls the "laboratory principle". "Closure" means that one can remove an object from its context and study it without changing the object. Independency implies that characteristics of an object do not interact with one another. This is not the case where persons are concerned: characteristics are definitely closely connected, and changing one characteristic (i.e. cognitions) may lead to a change of other characteristics (like behaviour). Additivity, finally, is a characteristic of a set or group, just like independency: "The addition of a seventh apple to a set of six apples in a basket will not change the six apples". However, the addition of an extra member to a group will positively affect the other group members (see, for more criticism of positivistic research, Peters & Robinson, 1984).

Liu contrasts the principles of the positivistic academic research with "action research" as an alternative. Beer and Walton (1987) also choose this direction: "Rather than attempt to find the perfect quantitative methodology and 'scientifically' proof its value, OD should attempt to build a different model of knowledge" (p.344; see also Argyris et al., 1985). The kind of action research meant by Beer and Walton is not the detached type of research Lewin had in mind. To Lewin, action research meant interference in a social system (by a practitioner), and the study of its effect by a researcher (Lewin, 1947). The interpretation of the effects of the studied interference was either the task of the researcher only, or the task of the researcher and the practitioner. This interpretation might then lead to adjusted actions, etc. In other words: Lewin had his mind on a more traditional type of research. The action research Beer and Walton (1987), Liu (1991), Foote Whyte (1989), and many others have in mind, deviates fundamentally from this type of research. They use what Chein, Cook, and Harding (1948) already called "participant action research". It is a type of research where researcher and researched cooperate and together take the responsibility for the research, the interpretation of the results, the conclusions from that interpretation, and the following actions, for example, in the sense of alternative operating procedures of and within a social system (see also Greenwood & Gonzalez Santos, 1992).

Two out of three of the aforementioned roles (the role of the researcher, that of the consultant or social worker, and that of the "object') almost always disappear in this set-up, in the sense that both first roles integrate, and the researched also become researchers. Research and action integrate (Foote Whyte, Greenewood, & Lazes, 1989). Without dismissing this last type of research, on the contrary, the case histories described by Beer and Walton provide valuable material, which may be of great significance for the development of a theory of organization change, I still believe traditional research to be of great value. Although it is certainly true that "normal science . . . attempts to answer little questions precisely" (Beer & Walton, 1987, p.362), just this knowledge is of exceptional importance too.

In combining little bits of knowledge as well as logical thinking, the possibility of describing larger entities is opened up. This is certainly more detached than participative action research, although to a researcher this is no objectionable attitude. Such an attitude even enables research of a "meta" character as Fagenson undertakes: investigating the activities of consultants, the types of interventions, etc. That sort of research is also important.

9 SUMMARY

This contribution started with a quotation. This quotation made it clear that organizational change at the Dutch Steel Works is large scale, and that the organization itself tries to realize these changes. The point of departure is, without doubt, the management, and its altered views on organizations. The intended result is a participative structure, where broad and rich tasks of subordinates form a cornerstone, and where "participating leadership" prevails.

Section 2 tried to make plausible that changes in the environment of organizations pose problems for all or almost all organizations. Uncertainty about the environment, as well as the changeability of that environment makes it hard to predict developments. In order to anticipate unexpected developments quickly, organizations should become more and more flexible. The adaptability of organizations depends upon overcapacity of such systems. The system theory shows that this overcapacity can be realized through overcapacity either of parts or of functions. The first form implies an organization that drastically breaks down the tasks to be performed (maximum division of labour), so that, for example, the increased market requirements can be quickly intercepted by recruiting extra personnel. The flexibility of such systems, however, seems restricted; the necessary overhead is substantial, and the innovativity of the organization (an important new market requirement, see Bolwyn & Kumpe, 1989) is limited. "Overcapacity within functions" implies a structure of the organization that allows for broad and rich tasks of employees functioning in autonomous task groups. In other words, this is a matter of "minimum division of labour", and a structure and a mode of operation enabling the organization "to utilize people more fully" (Lawler, 1989). Here a "participative structure" is implied.

To realize this OD knowledge and expertise are used more and more. Different from 10 to 20 years ago, however, is that organizational development is no longer the leading force, though it plays a more supporting role in the developments now pressing everywhere. At the same time, this implies an expansion and fading of the traditional

OD domain: it is no longer a set of interventions with the aid of which especially the culture of the organization can be changed, organizational knowledge, too (in a more narrow sense), makes its appearance. This means, more than ever, a further integration of traditional OD (the process approach) and more task-structural approaches.

Fundamental organizational changes require a new design of the organization. In section 4 this led to the question: "design" or "development"? A design approach looks upon the existing organization as a whole of "grown inadequacies". This points to the piecemeal improvements and the necessary adjustments that organizations have tried to realize in the past, until the moment that these improvements are not adequate any more, and the organization, in fact, has to be redesigned. The "developmental approach" does not look at the organization as a source of inadequacies, but rather as a result of knowledge, insight, and experience (of employees) that should be put to use during the change process. Here the existing organization is the point of departure for change, and the organization members are involved in order to realize that change. Both approaches have their pros and cons. The design approach sometimes leads to accidents, and processes taking much more time than was foreseen. Developmental approaches often don't go a long way. Integration of both approaches is possible to a certain extent, while it is evident that both approaches, depending on the circumstances, have their advantages.

In section 5 the central question was whether the alluded-to organizational change (in the direction of a more participative structure) has to be the result of a "revolutionary" process, or may be realized more gradually. The latter should certainly be a possibility, given the fact that organizations exist with an in-between position between a classical machine bureaucracy and an organical (socio-technical) organization. A more gradual process in the direction of a more participative organization requires an action-inclined, differently oriented attitude of the top management. The importance of this was shown in the research by Schreuder (1990).

Without doubt, structural change (and mode of operation) of the organization meets with resistance. Especially resistance from supervisors and staff. This resistance may partly be understood from the fact that any restructuring may affect vested interests and power positions of those mentioned. Without a "power strategy", together with negotiation and clarification, this resistance may not be broken. On the other hand, resistance may also be based on the fact that the organization in its then existing form, can be seen as a socio-cultural phenomenon, with staff and especially supervisors being the "cultural guards": those who internalized the organization's implicit notions, attitudes, and theories. Breaking through such cultural barriers presupposes a different organizational structure, leading toward another "context for behaviour". However, this in itself is insufficient. Employees and especially leaders will have to behave differently, proceeding from another perspective (culture), so that the prospects of the new structure can be realized. In this context, traditional OD expertise may be used effectively, possibly supplemented with behaviour modification programmes.

Without these structural changes, which lead to a different context for behaviour, the traditional OD attempts and behaviour-modification programmes do not seem to render permanent effects. Certainly not when the intended effects entail greater flexibility, client-orientedness, and innovativity.

The development of knowledge in the areas of OD and planned change is dependent on theory development and research (both issues preferably going hand in hand). Research usually carried out is extremely difficult in the context of OD and planned change, and bristling with pitfalls. For some, this has been a reason to state the necessity of a completely different research methodology, sometimes even a different epistemology. Often action research is pleaded for where the responsibility for the research and its results is shared by both the researcher (interventionist) and the researched.

Case studies are the central issue in this type of research. Undoubtably this yields important material for theories on organizational change. This by no means implies that more common or traditional types of research should be avoided. In order to realize changes in organizations in the 1990s, it is a case of "all hands on deck".

REFERENCES

Allport, G.W. (1948). Foreword. In K. Lewin (Ed. G. Weiss Lewin), *Resolving social conflicts*. New York: Harper & Row.

Argyris, C. (1957). *Personality and organization*. New York: Harper.

Argyris, C., Putnam, R., & Switch, D.M. (1985). *Action science*. San Francisco/London: Jossey-Bass.

Ashby (1960). *Design for a brain* (2nd Edn). London: Chapman & Hall.

Banbury, J. (1975). Information system design, organizational control and optimality. *Omega, The Journal of Management Science*, 3, 4, 449–460.

Beckhard, R. (1969). *Organization development: Strategies and models*. Reading, MA: Addison-Wesley.

Beer, M., & Walton, A.E. (1987). Organization change and development. *Annual Review of Psychology*, 38, 339–367.

Beinum, H. van (1990). *Observations on the development of a new organizational paradigm*. Paper intended for the seminar on "Industrial Democracy in Western Europe". Keulen 26 February–2 March, 1990.

Bem, D. (1965). An experimental analysis of self-persuasion. *Journal of Experimental Social Psychology*, I, 199–218.

Bem, D. (1967). Self-perception: An alternative interpretation of cognitive dissonance phenomena. *Psychological Review*, 74, 183–200.

Benne, K.D., Bennis, W.G., & Chin, R. (1979). Geplande verandering in Amerika [Planned change in America]. In W.G. Bennis, K.D. Benne, R. Chin, & K.E. Corey (Eds.), *Strategieën voor verandering* [*Strategies for change*]. Deventer: Van Loghum Slaterus. (Translation of 3rd edition of *The planning of change* [1st edition in 1962]). New York: Holt Rinehart & Winston.

Blake, R.R., & Mouton, J.S. (1976). *Consultation*. Reading, MA: Addison-Wesley.

Blake, R.R., & Mouton, J.S. (1979). Why the OD movement is "stuck" and how to break it loose. *Training and Development Journal*, 33, 12–20.

Blumberg, M., & Pringle, C.D. (1983). How control groups can cause loss of control in action research: The case of Rushton Coal Mine. *Journal of Applied Behavioral Science*, 19, 409–425.

Bolwijn, P.T., & Kumpe, T. (1989). Wat komt na flexibiliteit? De industrie in de jaren negentig [What comes after flexibility? Industry in the nineties]. *M & O*, 2, 91–112.

Boonstra, J.J. (1991). *Integrale organisatieontwikkeling; vormgeven aan fundamentele veranderingspro-cessen in organizaties* [*Integral organization development; designing fundamental change processes in organizations*]. Utrecht: Lemma.

Bruining, G.R.P., & Allegro, J.T. (1984). Organisatieontwikkeling [Organisation development]. *Handboek A & O Psychologie*, 4.9.1.–4.9.36. Deventer: Van Loghum Slaterus.

Buddingh, H. (1991). Culturele revolutie moet hoogovens aan top brengen [Cultural revolution should take the Dutch Steel Works to the top]. *NRC Handelsblad*, 10-4-1991.

Bunt, P.A.E. van de (1978). *De organizatie-adviseur, begeleider of expert* [*The organization consultant, companion or expert*]. Alphen a/d Rijn: Samsom.

Burke, W.W. (1987). *Organization development: A normative view*. Reading, MA: Addison-Wesley.

Carnap, R. (1966). *Philosophical foundation of physics*. New York: Basic Books.

Centrale Afdeling Organisatie (1981). *De basis van de structuur* [*The basis of structure*]. Den Haag: Gemeentedrukkerij.

Chein, I., Cook, S., & Harding, J. (1948). The field of action research. *American Psychologist*, 3, 43–50.

Child, J., Ganter, H.D., & Kieser, A. (1987). Technological innovation and organizational conservatism. In J.M. Penning & A. Buitendam (Eds.), *New technology as organizational innovation*. Cambridge, MA: Ballinger Publications.

Cozijnsen, A.J., & Vrakking, W.J. (1987). Inleiding [Introduction]. In A.J. Cozijnsen & W.J. Vrakking (Eds.), *Inleiding in de organizatieveranderkunde* [*Introduction in organizational change*]. Alphen a/d Rijn: Samsom.

Davis, T.R.W., & Luthans, F. (1980). A social learning approach to organizational behavior. *Academy of Management Review*, 5, 281–290.

Dewey, J. (1915). Democracy and education. New York/London.

Dewey, J. (1939). Intelligence in the modern world. New York.

Drenth, P.J.D., Thierry, H., Willems, P.J., & Wolff, Ch.J.de (Eds.) (1984). *Handboek A & O psychologie* [*Handbook A & O psychology*]. Deventer: Van Loghum Slaterus.

Drucker, P.F. (1991). Verander de gewoonten, niet de bedrijfscultuur [Change the habits, not the organizational culture]. *NRC Handelsblad*, 30-4-1991.

Dunphy, D.C., & Stace, D.A. (1988). Transformational and coercive strategies for planned organizational change: Beyond the OD model. *Organization Studies*, 9, 317–334.

Emery, F.E. (1967). The next thirty years: Concepts, methods and anticipations. *Human Relations*, 20, 199–237.

Emery, F.E. (1974). *Futures we're in*. Centre for Continuing Education Australian National University, Canberra.

Emery, F.E. (1979). The assembly line; its logic and our future. In L.E. Davis & J.C. Taylor (Eds.), *Design of jobs*. Santa Monica, CA: Goodyear.

Emery, F.E., & Trist, E.L. (1965). The causal texture of organizational environments. *Human Relations, 18*, 21–32.

Emery, F.E., & Trist, E.L. (1973). *Towards a social ecology*. London: Plenum Press.

Emery, M. (1987). *The theory and practice of search conferences*. Paper presented at the Einar Thorsrud Memorial Symposium, Oslo, 1987.

Fagenson, E.A., & Burke, W.W. (1991). Organization development practitioner's activities and interventions in organizations during the 1980's. *Journal of Applied Behavioral Science*.

Faucheux, C., Amado, G., & Laurent, A. (1982). Organizational development and change. *Annual Review of Psychology, 33*, 343–370.

Foote Whyte, W. (Ed.) (1989). Action research for the 21st century: Participation, reflection and practice. Special issue of *American Behavioral Scientist, 32*, 5.

Foote Whyte, W., Greenewood, D., & Lazes, P. (1989). Participatory action research: Through practice to science in social research. In W. Foote Whyte (Ed.), Action research for the 21st century. Special issue of the *American Behavioral Scientist, 32, 5*, 513–551.

Foucault, M. (1975). *Surveiller et punir* [*Supervision and punishment*]. Paris: Gallimard.

French, W.L., & Bell Jr., C.H. (1990). *Organization development: Behavioral science interventions for organization improvement* (4th Edn). Englewood Cliffs, NJ: Prentice-Hall.

Frissen, P.H.A. (1989). *Bureaucratische cultuur en informatisering* [*Bureaucratic culture and computerisation*]. Den Haag: SDU-Uitgeverij.

Goldthorpe, J.H., Lockwood, D., Bechhofer, F., & Platt, J. (1968). *The affluent worker: Industrial attitudes and behaviour* (vol. I). Cambridge: Cambridge University Press.

Gouldner, A.W. (1956). Explorations in applied social science. *Social Problems, 3*, 173–181.

Greenwood, D.J., & Gonzalez Santos, J.L. (1992). *Industrial democracy as process: Participatory action research in Fagor Cooperative Group of Mondragon*. Assen/Maatricht: Van Gorcum.

Groot, A.D. de (1961). *Methodologie; grondslagen van onderzoek en denken in de gedragswetenschappen* [*Methodology: Foundations of research and thought in the behavioral sciences*]. Den Haag: Mouton & Co.

Gustavsen, B. (1985). Workplace reform and democratic dialogue. *Economic and Industrial Democracy, 6, 4*, 461–479.

Gustavsen, B. (1989). *Creating broad change in working life: the LOM programme*. Toronto: Ontario Quality of Working Life Centre.

Gustavsen, B. (1990). *A preliminary evaluation and summary of the LOM programme*. Stockholm: Arbetslivcentrum.

Gustavsen, B. (1991). *Dialogue and development; theory of communication, action research and the restructuring of work life*. Stockholm: Arbetslivcentrum.

Gustavsen, B., & Engelstad, P. (1986). The design of conferences and the evolving role of democratic dialogue in changing work life. *Human Relations, 39(2)*, 101–116.

Gustavsen, B., & Engelstad, P. (1990). Creating systems by dialogue: An emerging trend in organization development. In G. Bjerknes (Ed.), *Organizational competence in system development*. Lund: Student Literature.

Hage, J. (1974). *Communication and organizational control*. New York: John Wiley and Sons.

Hannan, M.T., & Freeman, J. (1989). *Organizational ecology*. Cambridge, MA: Harvard University Press.

Heller, F.A. (1976). Group feedback analysis as a method of action research. In A. Clark (Ed.), *Experimenting with organizational life: The action research approach*. New York: Plenum Press.

Heller, F.A., Drenth, P.J.D., Koopman, P., & Rus, V. (1988). *Decisions in organizations: A longitudinal study of routine, tactical and strategic decisions*. London/Beverly Hills, CA: Sage Publications.

Hertog, J.F. den (1980). The role of information and control systems in the process of organizational renewal. In M. Lockett & R. Spear (Eds.), *Organizations as systems*. London: The Open University Press.

Hertog, F. den, & Dankbaar, B. (1989). De sotiotechniek bijgesteld [Sociotechnique adjusted]. *Gedrag en Organisatie, 2, 4/5*, 269–289.

Hopstaken, B.A.A., & Kranendonk, A. (1989). *Informatieplanning in tweevoud* [*Information planning in duplicate*]. Leiden: H.A. Stenfert Kroese; dissertation.

Jaeger, A.M. (1986). Organization development and national culture; where's the fit? *Academy of Management Review 2*, 178–190.

Jones, E.E. (1985). Major developments in social psychology during the past five decades. In G. Lindzey & E. Aronson (Eds.), *The Handbook of Social Psychology* (Vol. 1, 3rd Edn, pp.47–108). New York: Random House.

Joosse, D.J.B. et al. (1990). *Zelfstandig samenwerken in autonome taakgroepen; praktijkervaringen in industrie en dienstverlening* [*Cooperation in autonomous task groups: practical experiences in industry and social services*]. Den Haag: COB/SER.

Katz, D., & Kahn, R.L. (1978). *The social psychology of organizations* (2nd Edn). New York: John Wiley and Sons.

Keuning, D., & Eppink, D. J. (1985). *Management en organizatie* [*Management and organization*] (3rd Edn). Leiden: H. E. Stenfert Kroeze.

Koopman, P.L., & Pool, J. (1986). De stuurbaarheid van besluitvormingsprocessen bij vernieuwing [The steering of decision-making processes in renewal]. In

A.J. Cozijnsen & W.J. Vrakking (Eds.), *Handboek voor strategisch innoveren; een internationale balans*. Deventer: Kluwer.

Kuipers, H. (1989). Zelforganizatie als ontwerpprincipe [Self-organization as design principle]. *Gedrag en Organisatie*, *2*, 199–222.

Kuipers, H., & Amelsfoort, P. van (1990). *Slagvaardig organizeren; inleiding in de sociotechniek als integrale ontwerpleer [Decisive organizing: introduction in sociotechnique as integral design]*. Deventer: Kluwer.

Lammers, C.J., & Széll (Eds.) (1989). *International handbook of participation in organizations*. Oxford: Oxford University Press.

Lawler, E.E. III (1989). Participative management in the United States: Three classics revisited. In C.J. Lammers & G. Széll (Eds.), *International handbook of participation in organizations, volume I: Organizational democracy: Taking stock*. Oxford: Oxford University Press.

Lawler, E.E. III, & Mohrman, S.A. (1987). Quality circles: After the honeymoon. *Organizational Dynamics*, *15*, 42–54.

Leavitt, H.J. (1965). Applied organizational change in industry: structural, technological and humanistic approaches. In J. G. March (Ed.), *Handbook of organizations* (pp.1114–1170). Chicago: Rand McNally.

Lewin, K. (1947). Frontiers in group dynamics. *Human Relations*, *1*, 150–151.

Lewin, K. (1948). Resolving social conflicts (Ed. G. W. Lewin). New York: Harper & Row.

Lewin, K. (1951). *Field theory in social science* (Ed. D. Cartwright). New York: Harper and Row.

Likert, R. (1961). *New patterns of management*. New York: McGraw-Hill.

Liu, M. (1991). Grondbeginselen van actieonderzoek [Foundations of action research]. *Gedrag en Organisatie*, *4*, 239–258.

Loon Technische Dienst (1986). *De omvang van het kort-cyclisch werk [The magnitude of short-cyclic work]*. Den Haag: Ministerie van Sociale Zaken en Werkgelegenheid.

Maanen, Van, J., & Barley, S.R. (1985). Cultural organization: Fragments of a theory. In P.J. Frost, L.F. Moore, M.R. Louis, C.C. Lundberg & J. Martin (Eds.), *Organizational culture*. Beverly Hills, CA: Sage Publications.

Marx, E.C.H. (1978). De organizatie-adviseur als procesbegeleider [The organization consultant as process companion]. *Maandblad voor Accountancy en Bedrijfshuishoudkunde. Themanummer Organisatieadviesprocessen*, *52*, 8/9, 387–396.

Marx, E.C.H. (1987). Organisatiekunde en organizatieveranderkunde [Knowledge of organizations and knowledge of change]. In A.J. Cozijnsen & W.J. Vrakking (Eds.), *Inleiding in de organizatieveranderkunde*. Alphen a/d Rijn: Samsom.

McGregor, D. (1960). *The human side of enterprise*. New York: McGraw-Hill.

Morgan, G. (1986). *Images of organization*. Beverly Hills, CA: Sage Publications.

O'Hara, K., Johnson, C.M., & Beehr, T.A. (1985). Organizational behavior management in the private sector: A review of empirical research and recommendations for further investigation. *Academy of Management Review*, *10*, 848–864.

Peters, M., & Robinson, V. (1984). The origins and status of action research. *Journal of Applied Behavioral Science*, *20*, 113–124.

Peters, T.J. (1987). *Thriving on chaos: handbook for a management revolution*. London: MacMillan.

Porras, J.L., & Silvers, R.C. (1991). Organization development and transformation. *Annual Review of Psychology*, *42*, 51–78.

Projectgroep Tangram (1990). *Verslag van het onderzoek naar de organizatiecultuur van de Gemeente Den Haag [Report of the investigation of organization culture in the city of The Hague]*. Den Haag: Gemeentedrukkerij.

Rietdijk, M. (1991). Gedragsmanagement [Behaviour management]. *Gedrag en Organisatie*, *4*, 320–331.

Rorty, R. (Ed.) (1967). *The linguistic turn*. Chicago: The University of Chicago Press.

Sashkin, M., & Burke, W.W. (1987). Organizational development in the 1980's. *Journal of Management*, *13*, 393–417.

Schein, E.H. (1985). *Organizational culture and leadership*. San Francisco: Jossey-Bass Publications.

Schreuder, H. (1990). Tijdige wijzigingen in management and leiderschap als element van organizatiestrategie [Timely changes in management and leadership as elements or organization strategy]. *Gedrag en Organisatie*, *3*, 5, 304–319.

Schutzenberger, M.P. (1954). A tentative classification of goal-seeking behaviors. *Journal Mental Science*, *100*, 97–102.

Sierksma, R. (1991). *Toezicht en taak, arbeidsbeheer tussen utilitarisme en pragmatisme [Supervision and task, labour policy between utilitarianism and pragmatism]*. Leiden/Amsterdam: SUA, dissertation.

Simon, H.A. (1956). Rational choice and the structure of the environment. *Psychological Review*, *63*, 129–138.

Sitter, L.U. de (1986). *Op weg naar nieuwe fabrieken en kantoren [On the way to new factories and offices]*. Deventer: Kluwer.

Sitter, L.U. de (1989). Moderne sociotechniek [Modern sociotechnique]. *Gedrag en Organisatie*, *2* (nr. 4/5), 222–253.

Smircich, L. (1985). Is the concept of culture a paradigm for understanding organizations and ourselves? In P.J. Frost, L.F. Moore, M.R. Louis, C.C. Lundberg, & J. Martin (Eds.), *Organizational culture*. Beverly Hills, CA: Sage Publications.

Smith, P.B., & Peterson, M.F. (1988). *Leadership, organization and culture*. London: Sage Publications.

Sopar, H. (1984). Organisatieverandering; een theoretische beschouwing [Organisational change; a theoretical consideration]. *Handbook A & O Psychologie*, 4.4. 1–3.3.30. Deventer: Van Loghum Slaterus.

Steensma, H. (1989). Sociaalpsychologische overwegingen en veranderkundige interventies bij sociotechnische zoekconferenties [Social-psychological considerations and change interventions in sociotechnical search conferences]. *Gedrag en Organisatie, 2, 4/5*, 347–361.

Tajfel, H. (1981). *Human groups and social categories*. London: Academic Press.

Trist, E.L. (1981). *The evolution of socio-technical systems; a conceptual framework and an action research program*. Toronto: Ontario Quality of Work Centre.

Vlist, R. van der (1985). On the inertness of organizations when it comes to improving the quality of work. In J. T. Allegro & H. Steensma (Eds.), *Trends in organization development*. Amsterdam: Stichting CCOZ.

Vlist, R. van der (1989). Weerstand van leidinggevenden tegen fundamentele veranderingen van de organizatie [Resistance of supervisors against fundamental organizational change]. *Gedrag en Organisatie, 2*, 305–315.

Vlist, R. van der (1991). *Leiderschap in organizaties, kernvraagstuk van de jaren '90 [Leadership in organizations, key question of the 90s]*. Utrecht: Lemma.

Walton, R.E. (1985). From control to commitment in the workplace. *Harvard Business Review, 63(2)*, 76–84.

Warrick, D. (1978). Definitions of OD by the experts. *The Academy of Management OD Newsletter*.

Yukl, G.A. (1989). *Leadership in organizations*, (2nd Edn). London: Prentice-Hall International.

9

Assessment of Organizational Change

Henk Thierry, Paul L. Koopman, and Dick de Gilder

1 INTRODUCTION

How are changes generally perceived in work organizations? Characteristic statements regularly encountered in the literature and in practice include examples like this:

> Companies and institutions are encountering radical changes more than ever, several of which usually emerge simultaneously. Moreover, changes are alternating at an ever-increasing rate and are becoming almost unpredictable. The globalization of the scale on which companies operate entails that no area of policy remains unaffected. In addition, flexible adaptation of the company is always a requirement.

This requires some qualification, of course: Future developments have always been hard to predict, also in those (few) cases in which systematic research lay at the root of making predictions. Who reviews the past, on the other hand, will observe patterns in changes occurred and assign meaning and sense to them. Consequently, the impression that the future is particularly difficult to predict in the present time may be reinforced. Another issue is whether all those changes are really so essential—that is, concern so-called "deep structures"—or merely mark more superficial problems of adaptation.

Yet the number of events that demand attention simultaneously in work organizations has increased considerably. Many administrators, managers and other employees devote a considerable part of their time to interpreting incomplete and ambiguous information (also see Chapter 14, Vol. 4, this *Handbook*). They attempt to gain insight into developments that can happen to them (Increase of energy prices? Closure of a department?). They are engaged in carrying out a drastic merger (What groups will remain? Who will be given what position?). In all such activities, they attempt to control, adjust, or resist change processes. Not only do many more administrators and employees seem to occupy themselves with change than several decades ago, but it is also recognized by many among them as being "much" and "overwhelming". In this sense, change can be seen as a burden involving much resistance. But it can also imply a challenge with all kinds of chances of improvement and innovation. Also, because many consequences can occur in an employee's life, change processes often evoke many emotions.

It is obvious that there is widespread attention to organizational change in the literature. In this Volume of the *Handbook*, change is discussed in each chapter in the context of a specific topic, strictly speaking. A more general profile—i.e., of planned change processes—forms the content of Chapter 8. Some general topics concerning organizational change also come up for discussion in this contribution. We shall go into the *diagnostics* and the *evaluation* of changes in and associated with an organization, under the heading of "assessment", as the multiple alterations confronting administrators, managers, and other members of the organization require structuring and interpreting. Sometimes it is easy to pinpoint which factors constitute the cause of events. Much more often, however, it seems that "everything" is connected with "everything", and the interest and the position of all sorts of groups within and outside the organization also exert influence on the interpretation of events (see, for example, Hickson, Butler, Cray, Mallory, & Wilson, 1986; Harrison, 1987). Some problems, moreover, are simply vague, and it also occurs that the problem forming the cause for a planned process of change, changes its nature in the meantime.

Structuring and interpreting changes are not sufficient, nonetheless. In order for a company to survive, it should also, in particular, be able to adapt itself. This entails that data from organization research are expected to produce unequivocal starting-points for the direction of a company or institution. In several cases, these starting-points exist: Specific goals can be set that can be achieved through focused interventions after a certain amount of time. Yet in various other cases the question of how to run business is much more complicated to answer: For instance, so many changes have occurred in areas excluded from the study that it has become unclear whether the actual research data still have any value whatsoever. Besides the issue of whether there are clear starting-points for policy, the *process* of change is also highly important: the way in which people, means and information are put to use to attain

certain goals. Diagnostics, evaluation, and policy-making: the research in the field of organizational change therefore often has to deal with some difficult problems.

In the second half of the 1970s interest in "assessment" of change processes in organizations (then called "organization assessment") developed in the United States. This interest was concentrated within the Institute for Social Research in Ann Arbor, Michigan, at first (see e.g. Lawler, Nadler, & Cammann, 1980; Seashore, Lawler, Mirvis, & Cammann, 1983). "Assessment" of organizational change (henceforth AO) aims at measuring the nature of organizational changes and the effect of change processes in a manner as "hard" as possible. In this sense, AO also implied an issue of criticism of research at that time concerning "organization development" (changes of attitudes and values) and "organizational change" (more structurally oriented organizational change; see also Chapter 8, Vol. 4, this *Handbook*). In that research, weak "designs" and hardly reliable and valid measuring instruments were used too often, because of which its results are multi-interpretable and hardly generalizable.

The use of the concept of "assessment" makes clear that the first consideration must be to make (aspects of) change measurable, actually to measure and to evaluate these. AO research does show some variety, however: For instance, research can be primarily *descriptive* and have a broad orientation. This occurs in the "broadband" research questions, for example (see, among others, Cronbach & Gleser, 1957, Chapter 11), that are hardly explicit, such as when it is the issue of whether the employees of a company are sufficiently focused on quality in their work. In this case, the emphasis is on the best possible diagnosis of what is understood by quality-oriented action and what is to be achieved with it, what attitudes and behaviour are connected with it, by what factors it is affected and what consequences arise from it. It cannot be told in advance whether there is indeed a problem (and, if so, whether this concerns the quality of the work), and therefore nor whether a change programme needs to be designed, implemented and evaluated. Another type of research pertains to the *effects* of specific, implemented changes, such as a new training and educational programme, the replacement of manual desk work by "on-line" computers, the homogeneity of departmental teams after a merger, and so on. Here diagnostic activities are also important, but the emphasis is generally on the extent to which objectives set beforehand (and other results) have been attained, and on the translation of the outcomes into new interventions (and policy to be pursued) in the near future. The two types of research do not differ in a principled way, however, but in emphasis.

In the next section we will go into the domain covered by AO more closely. After explaining various ways in which AO data can be used, several models will be discussed that can guide the choice of variables in AO research. Section 3 follows with a discussion of various methods and instruments that may be of use in AO research. In section 4, various phases of AO research are treated, such as entering into a contract and translating data into policy and action programmes. In the final section, a further positioning of AO is presented on the basis of three perspectives.

2 DOMAIN

2.1 "Assessment" of organization change: To what purpose?

It was stated in the closing section of the Introduction that "assessment" of organizational change can have a descriptive character, but can also be aimed at mapping the consequences of specific changes (for instance, certain interventions). The objective can, however, be even more ambitious and involve detecting cause–effect relations: in such research it is a matter of analyzing causal relationships between independent and dependent variables, and of the role of moderator variables. AO therefore covers a broad domain of problems.

In the remainder of this section we first give a further characterization of this domain by applying a distinction proposed by Lawler et al. (1980). Next we treat several models that may be essential to the design and the elaboration of AO research in practice, for instance, in connection with the pursuit of more effectiveness in work organiza-

tions. Nearly all examples of AO given so far pertain to decisions that are made by interested parties *within* a work organization. In addition, according to Lawler et al. (1980), decisions made by interested parties *outside* a company should also be distinguished, as well as those made by *researchers*. In some instances, AO data are assembled only once; to clarify the practical use of AO optimally, we shall assume in the following illustration of problems/decisions, nonetheless, that the same AO data are assembled repeatedly.

2.1.1 Organization—internal

AO data can be of use to interested parties within an organization when problems arise concerning, for example:

- *Management of Human Resources.* In many organizations quantified data on company results mainly or exclusively pertain to financial-economic variables (volume, sales, return on investments, etc.). Through systematic procedures, data can also be quantified concerning the quality of the employees, of their development, and the way they are managed. For instance, through "costing resources" (Cascio, 1991) the cost of actual turnover and absenteeism (due to illness, among other things) can be calculated; this also includes all cost of temporary replacement and of succession, of the time that line and staff managers spend on this, etc. Moreover, the proceeds of attempts to achieve improvement in these matters are considered. In turn, such data can again be related to periodical measurements of "commitment", job motivation, and satisfaction. Other examples concern the quantified consequences of change in training and educational methods, in leadership style, in compensation system, in reducing risks of accidents and illness, and so on. In a nutshell, a broadly varied and quantified representation of achieved departmental or company results can be obtained in this way. On such (and any other) data on the "added value" of Human Resources policy, decisions concerning the allocation of financial means in a new financial year can also be based.
- *The quality of policy.* This type of problem

links up with the preceding issue, but has a somewhat more limited range. Periodically obtainable AO data make it possible to assess pursued policy. This pertains to e.g. reorganization (the transition to decentralized "business units"), a different selection strategy (aptitude for a career within a company), a changed method of individual assessment (based more on critical performance factors), etc. Sometimes it is possible on the basis of AO data to redirect policy that is being enforced (so-called formative evaluation), if necessary. Frequently, however, only the final result can be assessed (summative evaluation).

- *(Systematic diagnosis and) change.* The aim is now evidently more modest than in the preceding problems. The development (improvement and deterioration) of a company can be evaluated periodically through a regularly repeated AO measurement—say, once every two years—of the strong and the weak aspects of the pursued corporate policy, and also of its consequences. Though the study now has a mainly exploratory nature, the outcomes of earlier AO measurements do produce all sorts of starting-points, for example in consideration of specifying the priority of change programmes.
- *Job selection.* Internal applicants can form a better notion of any other field of activity when provided with recent data (from a department and/or division) regarding, e.g., absenteeism and turnover, actual absenteeism and turnover, accidents in the past, job satisfaction, organizational climate, etc. Similar data on other organizations can be of use for whoever considers applying for a job elsewhere. Obviously, the AO data referred to here can also be important to external applicants.

2.1.2 Organization—external

This involves AO data (concerning one or several work organizations) that may be significant for the decisions to be made by individuals, groupings, or institutions that do not belong to that/those work organization(s), but do have an interest in it or can acquire one. Such decisions concern, among other things:

- *Investments.* Generally, individual or institutional investors who consider buying shares in a company go exclusively by the financial and economic results achieved in the past. Their decision-making might, however, benefit from the availability of periodically assembled AO data, for instance, on the organizational climate (such as dealing with insecurity), the degree of mutual collaboration, the focus towards innovation, etc.
- *Support operations.* AO data can provide important supplementary information on the effectiveness of support operations led by bank consortiums (and/or the government) of large companies or of a branch of industry. Such data refer to e.g. motivation, commitment, rate of supply of information and detection of problems, mutual relationships, innovative behaviour, etc.
- *Government policy.* Within the scope of the previous issue, AO data can be put to use for the evaluation of specific components of the government policy pursued, if they are available in a large scale and can be classified in terms of industrial sector and regional area, for instance. One might think of measures directed towards encouraging investment in companies, subsidizing a part of the cost of wages of either unemployed or disabled to be attracted, etc.
- *Regulation and control.* Here we have in mind control processes by the government, or an international organization, or the execution of legislation pertaining to individual companies and institutions. A clear example of this is recent legislation of the European Union, according to which each European company has to make a risk-inventory annually and has to develop plans, concerning safety, health, and the well-being of its own staff.

2.1.3 Researchers

AO data are indispensable in scientific research. As mentioned briefly in section 1, they enable researchers to make an inventory of a wide range of current problems or problems to be expected in the future in a work organization, or to rate the quality of a specific method (for instance, for training employees) in a comparative way, or to evaluate the effect of a particular change (say, privatization). Many such problems can be devised. It is this part of the AO domain in which high demands need to be placed on the quality of the study *par excellence*, because the method of research—in particular, the type of "design", the quality of the measuring instruments, and the data analysis—determine what type of answer a researcher can give (thus what decisions can be based on this). Precisely because research in a company in which changes are taking place is confronted with all sorts of "disturbing" difficulties, it is seldom, or is never, a matter of "true experimental design" (Cook & Campbell, 1976; Sackett & Larson, 1990; Cook, Campbell, & Peracchio, 1990; see also Chapter 2, Volume 1 this *Handbook*). Often some quasi-experimental design is involved, and also quite often data from a survey have to be sufficient, causing various threats to the validity of outcomes to become an issue; we shall return to these problems in section 3.

2.2 A framework

From the preceding outline, it becomes clear how varied the topics are about which all sorts of categories of interested parties—both within and outside a work organization—can make decisions in connection with AO data. If we limit our attention to internal organization affairs (the part of the domain to which AO has related most by far), it is remarkable, moreover, that problems of AO research exhibit a large variety. In some cases the problem is specific and well defined, embedded in a theoretical line of thought, whereas the study can be of a hypothesis-testing nature. One might think of the transition from a functional to a product-oriented work organization, for example, especially with regard to the consequences for motivation, commitment, skills, and performance of group members. But in various other situations the problem is rather vague or partly still unknown, whereas a coherent theoretical train of thought can hardly be drawn up (of course, all sorts of hybrids occur between the two extremes). For instance, during a reorganization process, researchers are presented with the question of how the resistance in employees opposing it is sup-

posed to be conceived of and how it can be reduced. How, then, does an AO researcher proceed and what considerations direct the choice of AO variables and instruments? The framework that is presented in Figure 9.1 contains several general theoretical concepts mentioned regularly in the literature when such a broadband design is required. It applies a global structuring in the AO domain based on the "open-system model" endorsed by many authors, either implicitly or explicitly. "Contingency-thinking" (no one best solution exists; what is effective also depends on certain situational characteristics) can easily be classified within it.

The main elements from Figure 9.1 are:

- *Input (resources)*: This consists of the raw materials, money, information, and knowledge that an organization extracts from the environment, and allocates in service of particular outcomes.
- *Output*: Products, services, and ideas that are mostly sold externally. Next to these "positive achievements" are negative indicators, such as absenteeism, turnover, waste.
- *Objectives*: These comprise both the strategic policy, aimed at the relation with the environment in the future, and its more concrete content in operational plans and performance goals at various levels in the organization.
- *Technology*: This concerns all processes and methods of transformation of input and output. It not only involves mechanical but also mental processes.
- *Culture*: The shared norms, values, convictions, and rituals regarding important aspects of the organization. It concerns identity, method of working and social intercourse, relations between managers and employees, etc.
- *Structure*: The formalized work relations among individuals, groups, and departments. These include job descriptions (in which authority and responsibilities are regulated), the grouping of functions within departments and divisions (horizontal and vertical differentiation), all sorts of rules and prescriptions about operations and coordination, rules for consultation and decision-making, but also

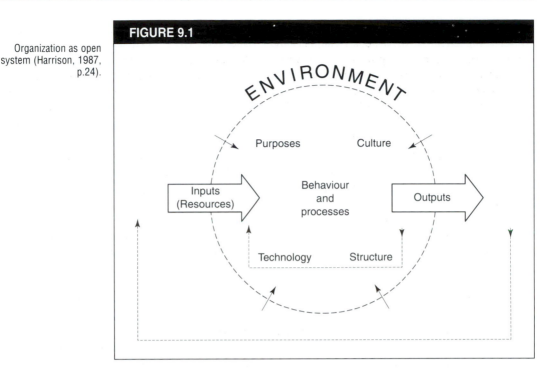

FIGURE 9.1

Organization as open system (Harrison, 1987, p.24).

instruments for personnel management (e.g. career lines, compensation systems, appraisal procedures).

- *Behaviour and processes*: Here one might think of the manner in which individuals and groups actually get on together: collaboration, conflicts, communication and consultation, behaviour focused on control and compensation, influence and power relations, leadership, the formulation of objectives and evaluation of performance, etc.
- *Environment*: A distinction can be made here between the "task environment" and the more general environment. The former pertains to those conditions and circumstances that directly affect the primary processes of the organization, such as the contacts with suppliers and customers, and the external industrial relations. The more general environment comprises economic, legal, social, technological, and market factors.

Other authors come up with, more or less, comparable classifications (e.g. Lawler, Nadler, & Mirvis, 1983; Gordon, 1987). For instance, Nadler (1981c) distinguishes the subdomains: tasks, indi-

viduals, groups, formal organizational regulations, the informal organization, the environment, and organization outcomes. Katz and Kahn (1981) mention motivation, leadership, organizational objectives and decision-making, conflict and conflict management, effectiveness and efficiency, organizational change, types and characteristics of organizations, and the interaction of organization and environment.

Authors place different emphases in choosing their variables and—by extension—their instrumentation. Some concentrate mainly on variables at the micro-level (e.g. perceptions, attitudes, performance), primarily using questionnaires. Others pay more attention to topics at the meso-level (e.g. organizational processes and issues of policy), in which interviews with key persons, observations, and document analysis may play important roles. Katz and Kahn (1981) argue that attention must be paid particularly to variables at what they term the "social-system level", because, according to them, this type of variable determines the largest part of the variance in organization-effectiveness, in contrast with variables at the individual level.

An example of the first design can be found in Porter et al. (1975, see Figure 9.2). Although factual variables at the organization (also called "objective") level have been incorporated into the model, attention is primarily focused on perceptions of task demands, task acceptance, individual performance, and such. These last topics can be found in Figure 9.2 in the blocks I to V. Other variables affect each of these variables and relations among them, respectively, for example the objective organizational expectations and demands regarding the individual (circle above box I). Hackman and Oldham (1976) also concentrate on the perceived aspects of task content. With regard to all sorts of other current topics in the field of work and organization, this approach has been and is used frequently.

An example of an approach at the meso-level is the so-called "field of forces" model introduced by Van der Torn (1986, see Figure 9.3). This model postulates three central processes in every organization. These stem from six forces active in and throughout the organization. The *policy-forming* processes develop from the tension between the force of vision and the force of reality; the *operational* processes take place in the tension

between the force of the objectives and the force of the means; the *organizational* processes pertain to the tension between the force of the existing form and the force of change (see also Hasper, 1989). To organize well means finding a balance between polar forces. When certain forces grow dominant, all sorts of negative effects develop. Vision that is not corrected by information from the environment becomes increasingly unrealistic: it means living in "dream castles". An excessive emphasis on objectives without attention to the means leads to matters being pushed to extremes. When form becomes dominant, bureaucracy develops along with a rigidified organization; if, on the other hand, change is overemphasized matters will not have enough time to develop and chaos will be imminent.

As early as 1967, Lawrence and Lorsch focused on the relation between differentiation and integration (see also Chapter 3, Vol. 4, this *Handbook*). Other authors also place emphasis on the characteristics of the organizational structure. One might think of the so-called "Aston studies" (for instance, Pugh & Pheysey, 1972). In recent years,

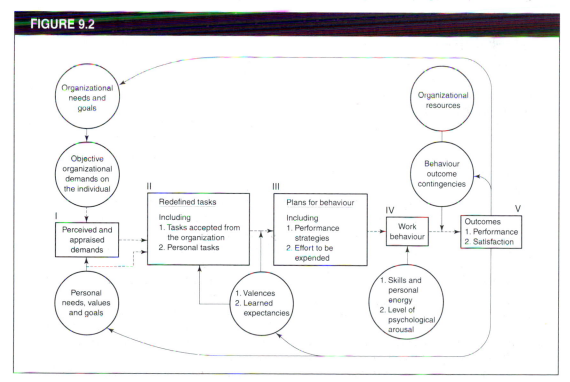

FIGURE 9.2

Model of individual performance in organizations (according to Porter, Lawler, & Hackman, 1975, p.121).

organizational culture has attracted more attention (Hofstede, 1984; 1991; Sanders & Neuijen, 1989; 1992; Schneider, 1990; Van Muijen & Koopman, 1992; see also Chapter 6, Vol. 4, this *Handbook*).

Obviously, there are also publications in which attempts are made to bring together all sorts of variables in an integrative model. Examples can be found in Ivancevich, Szilagi, and Wallace (1977) and in James and Jones (1974); see Hausser (1981) for a more extensive overview.

What demands, then, are to be made for a good AO model? Nadler (1981a) mentions the following: the model has to be (1) formulated explicitly; (2) based on research; (3) operationalized; (4) empirically motivated; (5) sufficiently credible ("face validity"); and (6) generalizable to various circumstances. These demands hold in general for any scientific theory, of course. In brief, AO therefore relates to a set of assumptions and methods for the research of changes in organizations. The choice of the specific variables is mainly determined by the objectives of a concrete research project in a given work organization. Nearly always the concept of effectiveness plays a role in these objectives.

2.3 Effectiveness

The answer to the question of what constitutes an effective organization is obviously connected with the policy choices of management. Although circumstances of market and competition, on the one hand, and government and corporate policy, on the other, can limit this freedom of choice considerably, in practice large differences in emphasis are found to exist in working out all the company objectives, and therefore concerning the primary effectiveness criteria.

At a theoretical level, survival, or continuity, may be viewed as the "ultimate" criterion for effectiveness (Hannan & Freeman, 1977; Sopers, 1992). The problem with this criterion, however, is that it is solely of use for retrospective research. More operational criteria in the relatively short term are required for other objectives, with a smaller "logical distance" with respect to independent variables (see e.g. Lawler, et al., 1983; Hufen & Leijten, 1989).

In a survey article, Campbell (1977) arrived at some 30 criteria for effectiveness. Quinn and Rohrbaugh (1983) elaborated them. On the basis of ratings by experts, the number of criteria has been reduced to the following:

1. Flexibility/adaptation/innovation.   The capacity to adapt the operational procedures to changing demands from the side of the environment.
2. Alert reaction (readiness). The chance that an organization will accomplish a new specified task successfully, when required.
3. Growth. In workforce, capacity, profit, and market share.
4. Interaction with the environment. The extent to which an organization interacts with its environment successfully and acquires scarce goods necessary for effective performance.
5. External evaluations. Rating by suppliers, customers, shareholders, and public.
6. Planning and the formulation of objectives. The extent to which an organization systematically develops plans and formulates objectives.
7. Level of performance. Volume of products or services that an organization makes.
8. Efficiency. Ratio in which a unit of products/services is weighed against the expenses that are made for it.

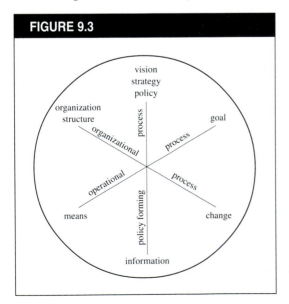

FIGURE 9.3

Van der Torn's "field of forces" model (1986).

9. Stability. The preservation of structure, function, and aids in time in spite of stress.
10. Check/control. The extent to which the management affects and controls the behaviour of the members of the organization.
11. Management of information and communication. The completeness, efficiency, and accuracy in analysis and distribution of information.
12. Conflict/cohesion. The involvement of members with the organization and the degree of openness versus conflict.
13. Development and training. The extent to which an organization provides means for the development of the members.
14. Morale. Both at the individual level (motivation, satisfaction), and at the group level (trust in the organization).

15. Quality. The quality of products/services.
16. Value of the members of the organization. The total value of individual members for the organization, based on various indexes.
17. Profitability. The assets minus the cost.

This collection of 17 aspects was further explored with regard to an underlying structure (Quinn & Rohrbaugh, 1983). The result of this—three dimensions—can be found in Figure 9.4. The first dimension (the horizontal axis) represents the "*focus*" of the organization. Effectiveness either has an internal, person-oriented emphasis (to the left) or an external, organization-oriented emphasis (to the right).

The second dimension (the vertical axis) is aimed at the *organizational structure*. Effectiveness now exhibits an emphasis on stability and

FIGURE 9.4

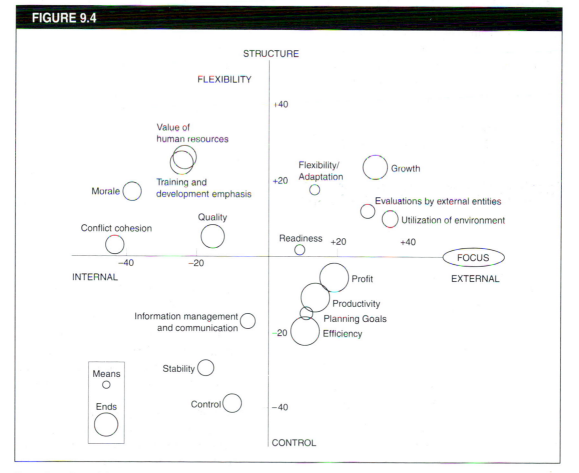

Three dimensions of the construct of effectiveness (Quinn & Rohrbaugh, 1983).

control (downwards) or rather an emphasis on flexibility and change (upwards).

The third (depth-)dimension concerning effectiveness reflects an *objectives–means continuum*. It involves an emphasis on efficient generation of products and services (foreground, large circles) versus an emphasis on planning and specialization of means (background, small circles).

From these three underlying dimensions the authors constructed a typology of four effectiveness models, that are related to various schools of thought within organization theory (Figure 9.5). The train of thought at issue is that views on effectiveness criteria are connected with the content of the organization theory adhered to.

The "human relations" model features a flexible structure and an internally directed organizational focus. The criteria in the top-left quadrant are: cohesion/conflict and morale as means, the value of members of the organization and further development of this as objectives. The "open-system" model combines a flexible structure with an external focus. Important criteria are: flexibility, alert reaction, and a positive image as means, and growth as the central objective. The "rational-

objective" model (bottom-right) has an external focus and a controlling structure. The effectiveness criteria planning and the formulation of objectives are important means, and the aim for efficiency, productivity, and profit are important as objectives. The "internal processes" model, finally, combines an internal focus with a controlling structure. Here the emphasis is on the management of information and communication as means, and stability and check/control as an objective (Quinn, 1988).

Often there are quite a lot of criteria for effectiveness and members of the organization disagree on the weight of the various criteria and/or the respective operational measures (Van de Ven, 1981; Cameron & Quinn, 1988). On this, Cameron (1986) states: "Organizational effectiveness is inherently paradoxical. To be effective, an organization must possess attributes that are simultaneously contradictory, even mutually exclusive." This is illustrated in the "competing-values model" developed by Quinn and Rohrbaugh (1983; Figure 9.5). Organizations sometimes have to aim for consolidation/continuity (internal-process model) and for expansion/adaptation (open-

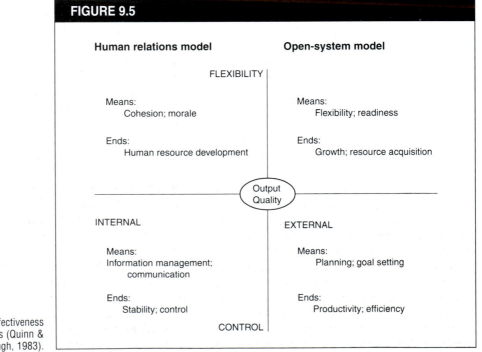

FIGURE 9.5

Human relations model   **Open-system model**

FLEXIBILITY

Means:
  Cohesion; morale

Means:
  Flexibility; readiness

Ends:
  Human resource development

Ends:
  Growth; resource acquisition

Output Quality

INTERNAL   EXTERNAL

Means:
  Information management;
    communication

Means:
  Planning; goal setting

Ends:
  Stability; control

Ends:
  Productivity; efficiency

CONTROL

Typology of effectiveness models (Quinn & Rohrbaugh, 1983).

system model), simultaneously, for maximization of output (rational objective model) and involvement of employees (human relations model).

3 ASSESSMENT OF ORGANIZATIONAL CHANGE: METHODS AND INSTRUMENTS

3.1 Introduction

Given the major importance that is attached to quantification of procedures within organizations in AO, it is understood that there is much attention for the quality of measuring instruments in the AO literature. In this section, first some remarks are made on methods of research. Next, a number of instruments are discussed that can be used in AO projects.

3.2 Methods of AO research

The research of change processes in organizations is a component of the research in industrial and organizational psychology in general (and of course of some other disciplines). It is this topic that Chapter 2, Vol. 1 in this *Handbook* is about. In reference to this, we will now take a closer look at some topics requiring specific attention in AO research.

Of course, the general rule applies that measuring instruments have to have high reliability and validity. This is no easy task, incidentally, as is evident from a description in the AO literature of the development of instruments (see, for instance, Nadler & Jenkins, 1983). When the objective of the AO project is limited to acquiring a better insight into the state of the organization at a given moment, and therefore it is merely a matter of diagnosing without organizational change being intended, good psychometric characteristics of measuring instruments are a necessary and sufficient condition to be able to do this diagnosis. Yet AO projects very often have more far-reaching pretentions. In reality, AO researchers mainly want to offer starting-points for the evaluation of organizational changes, to demonstrate causal and generally valid relations between the organizational change and its (positive) consequences. The developed measuring instruments mainly act as means to attain the objectives just mentioned. The internal and external validity of the organizational change programme are particularly important :

- *internal validity*: this is the extent to which it is justified to assume that the outcomes are really the consequence of, are caused by the organizational change carried through;
- *external validity*: here it concerns the extent to which it is justified to assume that the effects that have been found in a particular situation, can be generalized to other situations. In other words: whether the organizational change "works" equally well in other situations.

In promoting internal and external validity as much as possible, field researchers—and certainly those in the area of AO—are generally confronted with sore trials. There are many aspects that impede attaining high validity, aspects that usually cause *threats* of internal and external validity. Three types of such threats, which are not entirely independent, can be discriminated. We shall mention them briefly (see more detailed accounts in Cook & Campbell, 1976; Cook, Campbell, & Peracchio, 1990; Chapter 2, Vol. 1, this *Handbook*).

A first type is determined by using measuring instruments of insufficient quality; as stated earlier, good psychometric characteristics of measuring instruments are not a sufficient condition, but they are a necessary condition to obtain internal and external validity.

A second type of threat concerns the limitations that are located in the research situation. In order to demonstrate causal relations, a field experiment needs to be carried out in principle, involving an experimental and a control group, with at least a pre- and a post-measurement, and "random" allocation of individuals or groups of individuals to a single research condition. For various reasons, however, only few field experiments take place, and mainly survey and case studies are carried out. This practice entails that the objective of conducting an experiment, *the exclusion of alternate explanations* for the results found, is not achieved. As a consequence of the circumstances in which AO research is conducted, the number of alternate explanations is often countless.

The most important threat to internal validity in

AO research is without a doubt what is referred to by the term "history effect". This effect concerns all events (except the experimental "treatment") taking place between a pre-test and a post-test, which might affect the results of the study, and thus automatically make alternate explanations for the findings possible. This threat is so relevant for AO research because AO research projects always consume a great deal of *time*, mostly many months. It will be clear that many events (often irrelevant to the research project, in principle) can take place during this time that might affect the dependent variables, i.e. the results of the study. It hardly needs any argument that the external validity is also at stake in such events. An organizational change is often comprehensive. If such a "treatment" within an AO project cannot be considered as an important determinant of the outcomes unambiguously, however, the generalization of the findings to other situations and/or organizations will not be possible either.

A third type of threat to internal and external validity is tied up with the research process itself. Although this type of threat is often underexposed, much attention is paid to it in the AO literature. It mainly concerns the willingness of members of the organization, often taken for granted, to cooperate in the study. Argyris (1980) indicates in a somewhat anecdotal manner that assigned respondents are not always willing or able to provide the (right) information that the researcher wants to obtain from them. For instance, he discusses bank employees who approached an interviewer with distrust at first but who, having noticed that he had represented the supplied (yet deliberately incorrect) information neatly in a research report, invited him to do a new interview in which they would do their utmost to provide the desired, correct information after all. This example is intended to illustrate the justified concern that AO researchers have about this matter when carrying out their projects, a concern that began, of course, with the Hawthorne effect (Roethlisberger & Dickson, 1939). In order to avoid such response tendencies and those of a different kind (see Hoogstraten, 1988) that usually have to do with a certain distrust with respect to the researcher and their objectives, several AO researchers advocate informing the intended

respondents very well at any rate, but preferably involving them in the project from the outset, and allowing them to influence the content of the project (see Lawler, et. al., 1981, chapter 22; Argyris, 1980; Seashore & Mirvis, 1983). Such a procedure could also prevent forms of "bias" sometimes displayed by researchers. For instance, "elite bias" is involved when researchers cannot resist the temptation to approach those (groups of) respondents, in particular, who are favourable towards the study a priori, for instance, and/or can express themselves with more ease than other respondents. "Elite bias" can possibly be prevented once the acceptance of the researchers by *all* intended respondents has reached an acceptable level. This third type of threat to validity in itself has little to do with the quality of the measuring instruments itself, but more so with the manner in which these are applied, with monitoring of the research process by the researcher and by other interested parties. It shows once again that good measuring instruments alone are not a panacea.

The problems outlined here regarding internal and external validity have been acknowledged for a long time; yet this has not led to solutions that have resulted in a drastic increase of the number of field experiments. For this a number of reasons can be given; these mainly have to do with the last two types of threats to validity.

With regard to obtaining control groups, for instance, problems often arise in attempts to form a control group comparable with the experimental group. The reasons for this vary strongly: sometimes no comparable group exists, or it is necessary because of the drastic nature of the organizational change to look for other comparable departments instead or even for other organizations. In such a case, it would still be possible to construct a quasi-experimental research design, in which a non-equivalent research group (but probably an incomparable one) is used.

Frequently, however, the management of an organization decides that it is impossible or not desirable to exclude certain groups from participating in the change (actually, the latter is the consequence of setting up a control group). The sole possibility left then for the researcher, (besides a survey study) is the use of a "time-series design": a quasi-experiment in which no control group is present, but in which, because various measurements are carried out before and after the experimental manipulation, an important change in the pattern of results after the manipulation may be interpreted as a true effect of that manipulation (see also Chapter 11, Vol. 4, this *Handbook*).

Because of this, one might get the idea that the interests of a certain group or category within a work organization play a disproportionately major role. Whatever the definition of the relation between researcher and client a priori (see section 4), the client will always work out his/her own considerations regarding the access that is granted to certain groups within the organization, and the expenses involved in the project. Besides the management, however, there often are other interest groups that have to give their approval of the research project. In illustrating the problems tied up with the threat of the internal validity as a consequence of the research process itself, Seashore and Mirvis (1983) indicate that in several cases much time needs to be spent on creating a favourable research climate. The interested parties nevertheless sometimes refused to cooperate in certain subprojects in the study, for instance, because the researchers would violate privacy in the workplace, or because the researchers were still considered a kind of henchmen of management in the organization.

Another relevant issue relates directly to the outcomes of possible pretests. These can have a certain selective effect: The choice of organizational change in practice depends after all on the outcomes of the pretest. Members of the organization would look surprised, if, for instance, those aspects of their work or the structure of the organization were to change, which they consider to be all right.

The large number of possibilities that have occurred in the practice of AO research has caused organizations in which AO projects have been started ultimately to differ in all sorts of important respects. The type of organization, the type of change within those organizations, and the opportunities to carry out measurements, all vary a great deal. Furthermore, projects have various terms, and the periods of measurement also vary.

Besides the considerations mentioned here, it is highly important, of course, that the research method to be chosen fits the problem. The approach will have to be chosen, in accordance with the topic of research and the level of analysis. Questionnaires, for example, are particularly suitable for the measurement of attitudes and perceptions at the individual level, whereas observations and interviews qualify better for obtaining information on factors at the group and organization level. Often the researcher does the right thing to opt for a combination of various methods, in order to combine the advantages of different methods as much as possible in this way (Seashore, 1983). Table 9.1 gives an overview of the main advantages and drawbacks of questionnaires, interviews, observations, secondary analysis, and group discussions on the basis of "survey feedback" (see also Chapter 11, Vol. 4, this *Handbook*).

The interview is a flexible method. In nearly every AO procedure, interviews will occur at some times, especially during the first phases of the process. It enables the researcher to develop a tentative idea of the organization and of the workforce quickly. Yet the interview can also produce rich data in subsequent phases. There are, however, clear drawbacks. Interviews are time-consuming and vulnerable to various forms of "bias". Open-ended interviews, moreover, involve problems with the coding and interpretation of data.

Questionnaires offer many advantages. They are fairly easy to apply and score and, partly for this reason, less costly than interviews. Existing questionnaires have the further advantage of having reliability and validity coefficients that are already known. The main drawbacks are: little "empathy", low flexibility, and sensitivity for "bias". Questionnaires are especially suitable in obtaining specific data from large groups of individuals.

In principle, observation is a widely applicable research method. In many cases simply no alternative is available to watching things happen. Especially in the first phases of an AO observation it can be useful to get an idea of how the organization functions and where it fails. On the other hand, little-focused observation can soon

TABLE 9.1

A comparison of methods of data gathering on AO (according to Harrison, 1987, pp.19–21).

Method	Advantages	Disadvantages
Questionnaires Self-administered questions, forced-choice alternatives	Results that are easy to quantify and summarize; quick and cheap in the case of new data; suitable for large samples, repeated measurements, comparisons between departments/ organizations and norms; standardized instruments on the basis of previously tested items; very suitable for opinions/attitudes	Less suitable for data concerning processes and structures; unsuitable for intricate or sensitive cases; impersonal; risk of non-response, bias and erroneous information; danger of a too great a trust in standard instruments and procedures (not very open to new information)
Interviews Interviewer asks open questions previously structured in an interview scheme or list of subjects, or on the basis of on the spot evaluation	Flexible method to explore a wide range of subjects; can be applied as necessary before or during the interview; suitable for winning trust; abundant data, from which more insight can sometimes be gained into underlying factors	Cost: trained interviewers are expensive; danger of the interviewer and respondent being biased; comparison of un- or semi-structured interviews is limited; analysis and interpretation problematic
Observations Observation of people in their workplace	Especially suitable for registration of behaviour, so far as this is not analogous to opinions and feelings, perceptions, etc.; also directed at (effects of) situations; does not require the respondent to see things through the eyes of the interviewer (this can be important when dealing with complex concepts or delicate cases)	Limited access (in terms of time, distance, and confidentiality; sampling problems; expensive, requires trained observers; problems regarding bias and reliability; can interfere with observed behaviour
Secondary analysis Use of an organization's documents, reports, notices, unobtrusive measures (e.g. frequency of new ideas)	Unobtrusive data, through which less bias; often quantifiable; repeated measurements useful to register changes; data can be gathered in part by members of the organization; often cheaper and quicker than gathering new data; often suitable for data covering the whole organization and environment	Problems with regard to access, release, and analysis can increase costs; validity and reliability can decrease when data is used for purposes other than originally planned
Group discussions on the basis of survey feedback Discussions regarding group processes, perceptions of organization characteristics, etc. based on feedback from the researcher's aggregated data from individual members of the group	Further validation and supplementation of data gathered from questionnaires; interaction can stimulate thinking about and solving problems; strengthens involvement; stimulates self-diagnosis; can immediately be converted into action planning	Distortion possible owing to group processes (dominant members and views); presumes experience with group processes; dependent on a high level of confidence and cooperation in the group

become expensive, non-productive, and even misleading, because of the "bias" in one's own observation. In order to counteract this, trained observers are required and it needs to be registered precisely what to observe and how, how to score, etc.

Secondary analysis (also called document analysis or archive research) because the data are already available, offers countless possibilities. In the strength of this approach, however, lies also its weakness. Precisely because the data have been assembled for another purpose, validity problems arise quite easily. Access is often another problem. It is not always easy, for instance, to gain access to staff records or to obtain the desired data (performance, absenteeism) in the right format. It also requires further lengthy and boring donkeywork to organize the data and position them at the desired aggregation (Lawler, Seashore, & Mervis, 1983, pp.531–545).

Group discussion based on "survey feedback" (also called "group-feedback analysis") is a method in which the advantages of the questionnaire, notably the quantitative data, is combined with supplementary, more qualitative data. These can give a further explanation and validation of the tentative interpretations that are based upon the questionnaire. The argument can also lead to an onset for further action. Because of the direct involvement that can develop in the group discussion, survey feedback is not only known as a research method, but also as an important method of intervention (Heller, 1970; Bowers, 1973).

There are also other methods of research (than those mentioned in Table 9.1) that can produce useful AO data for different objectives. We will confine ourselves nonetheless to a reference to other literature (Runkel & McGrath, 1972; Weick, 1967; Roby, 1967; Bouchard, 1976; Fromkin & Streufert, 1976; McCall & Bobko, 1990; Chapter 2, Vol. 1, this *Handbook*). It is true in general that the aim for valid information must be central, whatever approach the researcher chooses. Insofar as information comes from members of the organization, an essential condition is that they have to be willing to provide this information authentically (Argyris, 1970). In this sense, an important requirement is approval of the objec-

tives and the method of AO. Suspicion or lack of interest is fatal for any AO.

3.3 Instruments

In this section several instruments are mentioned that can be used in connection with AO research. Given the multiplicity of instruments used, we do not, of course, aim at completeness (students of AO can orientate themselves further by means of the literature).

A separate question is what classification is chosen. For instance, the open-system model presented in Figure 9.1 might serve as a guide. Cozijnsen and Vrakking (1994) use a classification according to type of use: instruments of diagnosis, design, and change. Nonetheless, we favour a three-way classification according to approach, objective, and type of data (see also Andriessen, 1987; Hufen & Leijten, 1989).

1. *"Design"*.
   a. A quantitative-inductive approach, in which use is made mostly of standardized questionnaires, the representativeness of the respondents is carefully guarded, and attention is paid especially to the comparability and reliability of data. It is striking that in AO research, questionnaires are usually employed, despite the recognized disadvantages. The relative ease with which these instruments can be validated is likely to be responsible for this as well.
   b. A qualitative-deductive approach, in which experienced consultants, equipped with a sophisticated organization theory, collect problem-oriented information in a more qualitative (less standardized) manner. The solving of a specific problem is central. The utility of the research data for that concrete situation is of greater concern for consultants than the comparability with other situations.
   c. A pragmatic approach, in which the emphasis lies on the speed and low cost of the study.

2. *"Setting"*.
   In the following dichotomy, the distinction introduced in section 2.1 reappears, between AO research in aid of internal or external decision-

makers and AO research in consideration of an scientific problem.

a. An organizational diagnosis in one or more organizations that is aimed at signalling bottlenecks or at evaluating (government or corporate) policy or of specific interventions.

b. Organization-comparative research, in which data from several organizations are processed and compared, in aid of a scientific question.

3. *Type of data.*

a. Characteristics of codes derived from regis-

tration systems, also known as objective data (for instance, figures on average absenteeism).

b. Ratings, opinions, or attitudes derived from respondents, also known as subjective data. Though AO lacks a long history, there is still some differentiation anyhow. Category A in Table 9.2 is filled out most; mostly, instruments for the measurement of subjective data have been developed. Incidentally, we point out immediately that rather a lot of instruments in this subcategory might also have been classified under comparative research (and vice versa). Similarly, for example, the BASAM (Basic Questionnaire Amsterdam)

TABLE 9.2

Several AO instruments (adapted from Andriessen, 1987, in Kempen & Leijten, 1989).

			I	*II*
			Organization diagnosis: bottlenecks; evaluation of management/ interventions	*Comparative research*
A	Quantitative inductive	Objective data	• STTA[1] • EXCOM • RTA	• Aston scales • British Telecom Vol. II • RRPA
		Subjective data	• Various consultancy agencies • BASAM • Delftse meetdoos • WEBA • VAG • VOKIPO Focus • UV • OAI	• Comparative culture research (Hofstede) • IDE • MOAQ • JDI • JDS • British Telecom Vol. I
B	Qualitative deductive	Objective data	• Social indicators	• Comparative case studies (OTO)
		Subjective data	• Various consultancy agencies	• Comparative case studies (DIO)
C	Pragmatic ("quick-scan")		• Mintzberg (1979) • Beer (1980) • Shorter BASAM	• Shorter ASIA

[1] Abbreviations are explained in the text.

qualifies both for bottleneck and evaluative research, and for comparative research. The same also applies to, for example, the MOAQ (Michigan Organizational Assessment Questionnaire) and the JDI (Job Description Index). We will discuss both column classification methods from Table 9.2.

I. Organization diagnosis

As discussed earlier, AO instruments are supposed to meet a number of psychometric and other requirements. It is important, moreover, that there are clear norms. Various instruments qualify in this respect. But many other ones fail to do so: it is hard to comply with all these conditions in practice, for instance, in consultancies (Andriessen, 1987),

The SSTA questionnaire for socio-technical systems and task analysis was developed in the Netherlands (Van Eijnatten, 1985). Its core consists of four modules: task activities; aspects of work (rate, method, space, etc.); individual discretion; physical working conditions. The EXCOM (Experimental Computer-Aided Model Construction) is a computer-aided instrument of measurement that can play an important role during the designing process or the restructuring of a job.

The RTA—Requisite Task Attributes—is of American origin (Turner & Lawrence, 1965) and is of a somewhat earlier date. This instrument has inspired many researchers towards applying it or towards developing comparable lists. Consequently it has been included in Table 9.2. The scores on the six main attributes, i.e. variation, autonomy, required contacts, possible contacts, knowledge and skill, responsibility, are added and form the RTA index. In inventories developed by various consultancies, traces of the RTA can be found quite often.

The BASAM (Biessen, 1992; Biessen & Thierry, 1993) and the "Delftse Meetdoos" (Horn & Roe, 1986) again, were made in the Netherlands. They were both geared to obtaining subjective data. The BASAM consists of five modules: task characteristics, leadership, compensation (with separate versions for "profit" and "non-profit" companies), characteristics of the organization, and physical working conditions. The "Delftse Meetdoos" is primarily made up of characteristics of the organization, characteristics of the working situation (work content, work relations, working circumstances and conditions); characteristics of employees (e.g. abilities and needs); behaviour of employees (e.g. attention required, (mental) load); proceeds of organization and employees (consisting of eight indexes, such as satisfaction, health, absenteeism).

The WEBA (Projectgroep Welzijn bij de Arbeid, 1989)—welfare in work—is also an instrument from the Netherlands, by means of which an inventory is made of potential welfare risks, including: professional completeness of a function, organizing tasks, tasks with a longer cycle, job complexity, autonomy, contact possibilities, supply of information. Other questionnaires devised for the rating of function characteristics may be found in Algera (1981) and Van den Berg (1992).

The VAG (Questionnaire on Work and Health) was developed at TNO (Gründemann, Smulders, & Winter, 1994). This is intended to list not only risks in the field of welfare, but also those regarding health and safety, as well as regarding causes of sickness absenteeism. Apart from an overall rating of work, a distinction is made between: task content, task demands, work organization, working conditions and safety, leadership and colleagues, effect of work on private situation, compensation, physical and mental health, absenteeism due to sickness.

The VOKIPO (Short Organizational Climate Index for Profit Organizations) was developed in Belgium and is aimed at measuring a set of four culture orientations in organizations, based on the so-called "Quinn model" (see Figure 9.5). The distinction includes a supporting culture, an innovative culture, a regulative culture, and a culture characterized by clear objectives. A thorough revision of this list was finished recently, named FOCUS '93 (First Organizational Climate/Culture Unified Survey), with translations and data in a set of 13 countries in Europe (Van Muijen, Koopman, Dondeyne, De Cock, & De Witte, 1992; Van Muijen & Koopman, 1992; Van Muijen, 1994; Van Muijen, Koopman, & De Witte, 1996).

The UV (Extended Questionnaire) was constructed in The Netherlands for taking stock of opinions concerning the experiences with shiftwork (see Jansen, 1987, for example). These regard health, time-schedule characteristics, conveniences, inconveniences, and satisfaction. The OAI (Van de Ven & Ferry, 1980) (Organization Assessment Instrument) is an example of a series of scales in the USA specifically constructed for AO purposes. This includes all sorts of questions on the nature of the work (among other things, feedback, prescriptions, responsibility and the working unit, e.g. interdependence, method of consultation, treatment of differences of opinion).

There are a great many qualitative methods for setting an organizational diagnosis. Often, they are drawn up ad hoc by a company or a consultancy (see Thöne, 1988; Van Dalen & Hufen, 1989), but it also occurs that an instrument is realized by systematic analysis and research. Given this variety, we will refrain from mentioning specific instruments (see Cook, Hepworth, Wall, & Warr, 1981; Kastelein, 1985b; Budel, Donker, Valkenhoff, & Van der Vliet, 1985, for further details).

"Quick-scan" methods are intended to produce a description of various organization characteristics in a short time. Subsequently more focused, more thorough research can be set up on the basis of this. The shortened versions of more comprehensive instruments—such as for instance the BASAM (Biessen, 1992)—have often been made also for this purpose. Other initiatives for such a "quick scan" can be found in Mintzberg (1979, 1989) and Beer (1980), for example. Points for attention are: the content of functions, the arrangement of positions and departments, personnel management systems (such as recruitment, selection, training, promotion, compensation, working conditions), information systems, coordination mechanisms, performance-control procedures, and accounting and budget systems. Examples of a "quick scan" specifically specialized for social policy can be found in Groothuis (1987), Van der Leest and Van Duren (1989), and Kastelein (1985b).

II. Comparative research

The Aston scales (Pugh, Hickson, Hinings, & Turner, 1968, 1969) have been designed for the measurement of the structure of an organization, for the context thereof. Structural characteristics are specialization, standardization, formalization, centralization, and configuration (the structure in terms of roles and positions). Context characteristics regard origin and history, property, size, objective and function, technology, location, and dependence. British Telecom (1984, Vol. 2) contains several instruments aimed at approximately the same dimensions: organization context, organizational structure, and organizational processes (planning, organizing, managing, communicating, motivating, decision-making, controlling systems).

The RRPA (Jansen, 1987) (rota risk profile analysis) consists of a computer programme for rating 13 characteristics of regulations for working hours, notably regarding irregular and shiftwork, 6 of which relate to health, and the remaining 7 of which are in the social field.

The research program on culture conducted by Hofstede (1984) is an example of comparative organization and countries research in which data from respondents are used. Hofstede often uses four scales: power distance, uncertainty avoidance, individualism, masculinity. The project Industrial Democracy in Europe (IDE, 1981, 1993) is also a good example of comparative research. Within the same category we mention three American instruments. First, the MOAQ (Cammann, Fichman, Jenkins, & Klesh, 1983) (Michigan Organizational Assessment Questionnaire), which consists of six modules: general attitudes (motivation, satisfaction, and consequences), possible proceeds from the work, task characteristics, functioning of the workgroup, leadership, and compensation. The JDI (Smith, Kendall, & Hulin, 1985) (Job Description Index) measures the degree of satisfaction in five areas: work, compensation, promotion, leadership, and colleagues. The JDS (Hackman & Oldman, 1975) (Job Diagnostic Survey) is meant for the measurement of the components of the task characteristics model designed by the authors (see also Chapter 6, Vol. 3, this *Handbook*, for more detail).

The *Survey Item Bank Volume I* of British Telecom (1984) contains many questionnaires with regard to various aspects of job satisfaction. Numerous instruments regarding job perception have also been developed in The Netherlands. Examples are the VOS. D (Organizational Stress Questionnaire, see Bergen, Marcelissen, & Wolff, 1986), the Utrecht Coping List (UCL, see Schreurs, Van de Willige, Tellegen, & Brosschot, 1988), questionnaires regarding role ambiguity, role conflict, and tendency towards turnover (Zwaga, 1983), regarding conflict-management styles (Euwema, 1992) and regarding styles of leadership (Koopman, 1980; Den Hartog, Koopman, & Van Muijen, 1997), and use of power (Emans, 1988). An instrument for international comparative research into the meaning of working has been developed in the context of the Meaning of Working project (MOW, 1987).

In the category qualitative-deductive research, we point out various studies that are, at least in part, characterized by comparative case studies (Yin, 1989). First, the so-called OTO project (Research on Tasks and Organization, Andriessen, 1987), aimed at self-diagnosis of schools. Another project concerns the Decision-making In Organizations (DIO) project (Heller, Drenth, Koopman, & Rus, 1988), aimed at analysis of decisions at various levels in organizations. The decision-making study by Pool (1990) can also be characterized as such in part as well as the study by Van Veen (1993) into the use of Electronic Mail and the studies by Van Offenbeek (1993) and Van Duin (1997) into the introduction of information systems.

Finally, the "quick-scan" method: the abbreviated ASIA (1969) (Attitude Scale Industrial Labour) contains 15 questions. General job satisfaction can be measured by means of it (the entire ASIA pertains to seven different aspects of work).

This overview, in which by no means all existing instruments have been mentioned, shows how varied the AO instrumentation is. Various instruments are aimed at the diagnosis of a wide range of phenomena in organizations (characteristics, behaviour and/or attitudes), other ones have a much narrower orientation (e.g. organizational culture, working hours' regulations). A further issue is that particular topics are dealt with in rather a lot of questionnaires, although the substantive elaboration of it often shows many differences. This applies in particular to the topic of "task characteristics": understanding regarding

this topic is strongly determined by Hackman and Oldham's task characteristics model (see Chapter 6, Vol. 3, this *Handbook*). Yet it also applies to topics such as leadership, mutual relations, employment conditions, and working conditions; these are really standard topics in mapping job attitudes. Another remarkable aspect is that considerable differences in quality exist between instruments. Researchers—but also the users of results—would therefore be done a great favour, if, just as in the field of tests, (Evers, Van Vliet-Mulder, & Ter Laak, 1992) an "assessment" were to be carried out periodically for AO instruments (see e.g. Chun, Cobb, & French, 1975). The publication by British Telecom (1984, Vol. I and II) goes quite a way in that direction, but the rating of the various instruments could definitely be made tighter.

4   PHASES IN "ASSESSMENT" OF ORGANIZATIONAL CHANGE

4.1   Influence and expertise

So far, we have not paid any attention in this chapter to the roles of clients in AO projects and to the relations between clients on the one hand, and AO researchers on the other. First of all, several aspects regarding influence and expertise of these "parties" will be discussed. Next, a phase model will be treated extensively.

What kind of relation exists between a researcher and a client in making AO data-based decisions? Heller (1986, p.4ff) distinguishes five models:

1.   Traditional: purely scientific. By this Heller means more basic or more applied research in which "science" provides the rules of the game. The researcher specifies the problem, formulates the hypotheses, selects the instruments, and measures in a longitudinal design under circumstances controlled as much as possible. Application of results is not of immediate interest to the researcher.

2.   Building bridges between researcher and user. The conduct of the study rests with the researcher, but the client collaborates in its execution, receives feedback and gives the

outcomes an interpretation of his own, if necessary. The researcher assists the client in applying the results.

3. Equality between researcher and client. Topics for research may be chosen by one "party" or the other. The method of research is also specified by mutual arrangement.

4. Client requests professional assistance. If the client has a problem, a researcher is consulted, who usually does not assemble any new data; the assistance depends on expertise and the researcher's prior experience.

5. Client dominates the search process. If the client requests assistance, a consultant is brought in, who does not necessarily have to be an expert in the respective topic involved. Solutions are based on what is known from the literature, experience elsewhere and the use of common sense.

These models differ in the influence that the researcher and the client have on the nature and the course of the study (or consultation project), on the changes to be introduced and hence also in the quality of the expertise brought in. The same topics play a role in the centre–periphery–model developed by Staw (1980). Staw's central question is how policy-makers in organizations can be assisted in making better decisions based on AO data than before. Staw states that those decisions often pertain to causal inference: What causes are responsible for what consequences? Policy-makers from practice usually go by some sort of "lay psychology" (statements about behaviour in which one's own experience plays a major role). Interpretations based on them may well be of high quality, but the problem is that mostly, in methodological respect, they are not motivated. A researcher–client relation would be linked to this, in which the researcher is in the (knowledge) centre and supplies his or her client (s) with theoretical and practical knowledge and insights and gives all sorts of recommendations for changes. But, Staw states, are the theories of expert researchers really so much better founded than those of their clients? Whoever takes notice of the vulnerability of the research carried out and asks the question, for instance, of how generalizable outcomes are, has no alternative but to be

modest. For this very reason, another type of client–researcher relation is preferred. The decision-making client occupies its centre and the researchers (in the periphery) teach managers in whatever way they are able to, and allowed to treat data and how questions from practice can be made suitable for research. In this way, generally speaking, managers get a better idea of the contributions that researchers can make towards solving their problems.

In Chapter 2, Vol. 1, this *Handbook*, three kinds of relations between research and action (or policy) were distinguished. Research that preceded (any) action is called "descriptive". Research that takes place during action (or change) is called "action research": action-supportive research, feedback research, or self-examination can be distinguished here. Finally, "evaluative" research: This is conducted *after* the action (or intervention). As described earlier, a concrete AO project can pertain to the three kinds meant here combined, but also to each of them separately.

The place of AO within a process of "organizational learning" can also be explained by means of Kolb's "experiential learning model" (Wolfe & Kolb, 1984, p.128). Certain concrete experiences or events lead to reflection and more focused observations. In turn, these give cause for the formulation of more general ideas and hypotheses, which are subsequently tested more seriously in new situations. In many cases, AO is a cyclical process comprising the steps of global problem detection, data assembly, interpretation, more precise identification of problem areas, initiation of action programmes, and evaluation of them (see Figure 9.6). Other stages consisting of fewer steps occur as well, though, for instance when there is a case of repeated use of an instrumentation. The steps can also have another order.

In the literature on AO and organizational change (and organization development) various phase classifications can be found (see e.g. Kolb & Frohmann, 1970; Seashore, Lawler, Mirvis, & Cammann, 1983; Harrison, 1987, p.5; Harvey & Brown, 1988, pp.43,124; Twijnstra & Keuning, 1986, p.77; French & Bell, 1990, p.101). The most important steps and points for attention in AO are summarized in nine phases in Table 9.3.

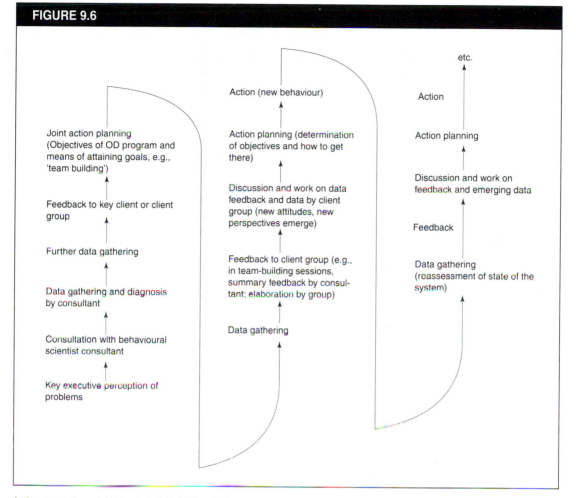

FIGURE 9.6

Action-research model (French & Bell, 1990, p.101).

4.2 Intake and contract

During the first two phases the contact is realized between the principal and the researcher/consultant (who is quite often called a project manager). They discuss mutual expectations and opportunities with respect to both content and procedure (Jonker, 1993). The researcher attempts to get a good impression of changes that have occurred, of problems involved in them, and of their inducement and cause. The difficulty tends to arise quite often that the issue that the researcher has been contacted about is not the main problem (though only further research can give a decisive answer on this matter). There can also be a hidden agenda. Moreover, what plays a part in this is with whom the researcher has contact in these phases and who

has to act as informants. Usually a third party (that is, organization members concerned) will already be involved in the discussion in this phase. These are the members to whose functioning the research pertains primarily, on whose information and cooperation the success of the AO depends and/or who will have to benefit from the results of the research.

Agreements will have to be made between these parties. In north-western Europe, there is usually also consultation in this phase with, or information is passed on to administrators of, the unions. Moreover, the works council often existing in this part of Europe should give its approval as well. In these phases, however, it is eventually a matter of the contract between the project manager and the

TABLE 9.3

Phases of AO.

Phase	Principal activities	Points for attention
Intake	– exploration – assess willingness to participate in project	– first impression of problem – occasion/cause – who is the interested party?
Contract	– formulate assignment – time schedule	– who is the principal? – nature of problem
Design	– choice of approach and methods	– approach, setting, data (§ 3.4) – role client – role researcher
Research	– gather information – handling and analysis – interpretation	– feedback: nature, form, speed
Reporting	– to principal – interested parties	– role of interested parties in interpretation – norms
Intervention	– plan changes – introduce changes (perhaps on a trial basis) – repeated measurement	– translation of results in concrete actions/policy – role advisers – adjustment of policy?
Evaluation	– final measurement – interpretation	– effect of changes – other actions/policy?
Diffusion	– prepare changes for other business units – implement changes – assessment/measurements	– institutionalization of decisions
Finalization	– follow-up	– repeat?

principal. It is the principal who formulates the objectives and makes the means available. Agreements with this party (psychological contract) are also important, depending on the type of problem, i.e. the extent to which a good solution depends on collaboration between the partners.

But who is the principal? Sometimes the researcher/consultant is brought in at too low a level. The principal is supposed to be the one who can be held responsible for tackling the problem that is the cause for AO. If the problem goes beyond the boundaries of a department it is usually the management team or the board of administrators. Sometimes there is not so much a concrete cause, as an AO instrumentation is used at set times to evaluate the effect of applied interventions and to map the current changes. In this case, the manager/director responsible for social policy often acts as a principal.

The researcher will need to ask herself whether she finds herself sufficiently competent in the domain of the research problem and whether her instrumentation matches well enough. A further question that the researcher needs to ask herself in this phase is whether, both substantively and procedurally, there is sufficient preparedness and scope to make the project a success, to be able to consider the problem initially defined as a tentative one, and to test its correctness and completeness within the organization in a kind of pilot phase. In addition, scope to be able to find out in conversations with those immediately involved whether there is a sufficient basis of trust, with prospects of valid information and involvement in any action (Argyris, 1970, 1992). The researcher has to consider the fact that groups of involved employees may have rather different opinions on the nature of a problem, on the content and the design of a study, on the interpretation and the results, and on the measures required afterwards. Each of these stake-holders (see Chapters 2 and 14, Vol. 4, this *Handbook*) will attempt to influence the AO project.

In particular, the following questions need to be answered in this phase (Van De Ven, 1981; Kastelein, 1987):

- What are the reasons for executing an AO project?
- What part of the organization is covered?
- What topics are dealt with?
- What point of view is used and what is its theoretical and empirical support?
- What methods and techniques are the members of the organization confronted with?
- What sources of information are available?
- What kind of (mental) load do they mean, for whom, and for how long?
- What rules of the game apply?
- How much time is there between introduction of the study and reporting?
- What does reporting entail?
- Who are the users of/deciders on this information?
- What can the organization do with it? What actions or interventions are considered?
- What is it going to cost?

After this kind of brief "attainability study" (for instance, several conversations, insight into certain documents, global observation of certain workplaces), several agreements are made. What is highly important in this is that the, potentially adjusted, problem and/or purpose is subscribed to by both principal and partners, and that agreement is reached regarding the question how, in what form and order, reporting will be carried out to whom. Other agreements pertain to questions such as who determines what is going to be done with the results, what measures are taken to guarantee the confidentiality of the data, what other rules of conduct the researchers employ, and who acts as a contact for the researchers (see also McCall & Simmons, 1969; Lawler, 1981). It is wise for a researcher/consultant to establish a small steering committee or supervising committee, when consensus of opinion has been reached on the previous issues. This can fulfil an important role in observing the objectives of the AO project and in passing on information regarding data from and opinions about the study held among members of the organization. Once the agreements have been made, the first two phases have come to an end.

4.3 Design

The design of the study, the selection of the instruments, and the further shaping of the procedures are central throughout the design phase. The selection of the instruments obviously correlates very closely with the purpose and problem of the AO project. If the purpose is broad and global, "modules" will generally be used: standard instruments that represent certain components of the policy, complemented in places by company-specific questions. An advantage of working with such modules is that researchers have gained experience with them elsewhere and have "norm scores" at their disposal, by means of which the organization is provided with some kind of frame of reference in interpreting its own data (see section 3.3). If a specific problem is at issue, however, the design will contain more tailoring. Depending on the extent to which the research problem exhibits open ends, and the level of the organization where the main variables are assumed to be, the research design will be characterized by either a more open, flexible or a more closed, standardized approach.

An important question that the researcher needs to ask himself (again) in this phase is: what measures are necessary and possible in order to stimulate the involvement of the parties in the study and thus to boost the probability of valid responses? Two aspects play a role in this: optimum supply of information and the degree of participation or self-examination respectively. First, as regards the supply of information, especially when the partners have the opportunity to provide ideas and to make suggestions concerning any specific variables that might be included in the AO study (as a complement), AO may be seen as an approach that is accessible to members of the organization and "open".

It is highly important nonetheless that every party individually is adequately informed about the why, what, when, and how of AO, about the rules of the game and the ethical code, and about the question on what may further be expected from the study in terms of reporting and any follow-up activities. And even then it is quite possible that certain (groups of) employees develop a resistance to the study, to the method employed, to the (interpretation of) results, or to suggestions for change. But if careful supply of information is left undone, it is very probable that more distrust will develop. In turn, this usually leads to less valid information: socially desirable responses increase, information that might constitute a threat to one's own position is suppressed, and so on.

The second issue concerns the division of labour between the researcher and the organization (members), which was touched on earlier. In some cases it is possible that the organization carries out (a part of) the AO project independently. This is only practicable if (Andriessen, 1987):

- the instrumentation has been standardized to a high degree;
- the execution can take place fast and with ease;
- the data can be analyzed fast and with ease;
- the results can be presented in an orderly fashion.

It also occurs that members of a work organization are schooled during an AO project and trained in order to carry out AO themselves in the future.

Yet self-examination is considered less suitable in acute problems and in conflicts in which management or particular groups of employees are in some way involved as a party. In such situations, it is highly probable that the results,

in so far as they even come to light, vanish into a drawer or that the execution of changes is obstructed. In the following section we assume that the study involves some form of cooperation between the researcher and the members of the organization.

4.4 Research and reporting

After the data have been assembled, they need to be processed and analyzed. Subsequently, there is often quite a long period of "calm" for the partners: the researchers occupy themselves with analysis of the data and tentative interpretation of the outcomes. Usually, not much can be reported about them in the meantime, because tentative findings can often be placed within another perspective due to later processing operations. Consequently, those involved might get the impression that "nothing is happening", that "unfavourable figures" are being kept away, etc. For this reason, this is a vulnerable phase. But we argue that the researcher should not attempt to solve the problem outlined by merely carrying out some simple data operations and, for instance, by merely calculating means, variances, and summations. The question about what analyses qualify better cannot be answered in general terms; moreover, this topic goes beyond the scope of this chapter. We do note, nonetheless, that the original "intention" of AO—to measure changes and their effects in a way as "hard" as possible—entails that as much is taken from the data as is possible in terms of methodological criteria. We hold the view that the expertise meant here should be part of the researcher's "tool-kit". Such expertise is hardly ever at the client's disposal. It is this very aptitude that enables the researcher to construct justified interpretations, show caution if necessary, and to draw conclusions where possible. At the same time, it is this aptitude that enables the principal and/or employees at stake to make a contribution of their own towards the interpretation of the results. Reporting style is also important in this connection. It is remarkable, really, that little attention is paid to this topic within AO research. For instance, it is recommendable to present results of (advanced) statistical operations in graphical form. Practical experience (for example, with the BASAM, Biessen, 1992) points out that it is perfectly possible to present the outcomes of complicated analyses in a form comprehensible for many employees. Some examples are given in Figure 9.7.

Example I pertains to three measurements: a first and a second measurement among employees of an organization, and a measurement among members of the management team. The results are given as standardized cluster scores. Example II refers to the outcomes of a multiple-regression analysis in which it is examined which variables make their own contributions to the explanation of performance differences. Of the three variables the first (task complexity) is of highest importance; motivation comes next, and so on. The outcome of a variance analysis is mentioned. In example III results of analyses of variance are

shown: The various groups differ strongly or hardly at all in satisfaction. In this way, of course more data can be included in the graphs (for instance, concerning the level of significance). Quite frequently in qualitative research (for instance, a case study), a protocol is made or an overview of strengths and weaknesses.

This brings us to feedback. This sometimes takes place in phases: First, specific feedback at group or departmental level, and then aggregated information at organization level. This procedure is also known as either "survey feedback" (Bowers, 1973) or "group-feedback analysis" (Heller, 1969, 1970). Feedback at group level is used for further validation and as a complement to the questionnaire data. In addition, a discussion on this topic can lead to concrete suggestions for change.

The probability of acceptance of the procedure and willingness to start doing something with the material is higher when the feedback complies with the following characteristics (Lawler, Nadler, & Mirvis, 1983; Huse & Cummings, 1985; Harrison, 1987):

- relevant and comprehensible for the members of the organization;
- descriptive rather than evaluative;
- clear and specific, referring to concrete behaviour and recognizable situations;
- short time between data assembly and feedback;
- credible, with indications for the validity of the information;
- respecting emotions and motivation instead of invoking helplessness or a defensive attitude;
- limited in size;
- practical and practicable, briefly mentioning matters that the members themselves can do something about;
- with open-ends, leaving space for the members to give their own interpretation and present proposals for action.

The exact form of the feedback varies according to the type of data assembled and the intended objective of the core report. Nadler (1981b) distinguishes seven different ways of feedback that vary according to the composition of the

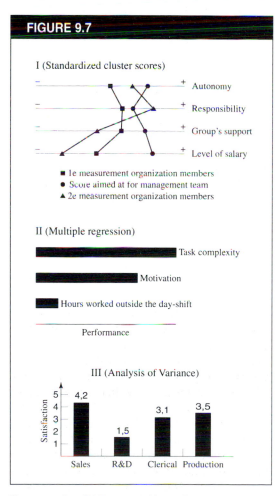

FIGURE 9.7

I (Standardized cluster scores)

- 1e measurement organization members
- Score aimed at for management team
- 2e measurement organization members

II (Multiple regression)

III (Analysis of Variance)

Three examples of data presented in graphs.

group to which feedback takes place, the order in which groups of individuals are dealt with, and the issue of whether an external or internal consultant/ researcher is involved in the feedback (see also Van de Vall, 1980).

4.5   Intervention and evaluation

On the basis of the interpretation of the data reported, the important phase of planning interventions and implementing them now follows, along with the phase of evaluating the achieved results. Incidentally, these phases do not only have to come *after* the research phase: in particular forms of action research, these phases alternate constantly. Such a cyclical method of working is described by Shepard (in French & Bell (1990, p.102).

We will first go into the role of the researcher/ consultant and her relation with the members of the organization: it is complex. There are various possibilities (see also Chapter 2, Vol. 1, this *Handbook*), varying from the pure researcher role through a combined role in which aspects of organizational advice and supervision of certain activities have also been included to forms of research by the organization itself (Seashore & Mirvis, 1983). In most cases, the company will want some form of advice from the researcher. In whatever way this is formalized, it is important that clarity is provided for the parties. When the role of the researcher is not clear, the members of the organization will resolve this ambiguity by making assumptions themselves, for instance, by viewing the researcher as a spy for management (Lawler, Nadler, & Mirvis, 1983).

Furthermore, it is important for optimum co-operation by the parties that they can look forward to "reasonable proceeds" for their preparedness and energy to provide honest and possibly threatening information as regards the way the organization or department functions. If proceeds are fair, one might think of the probability that the information will be taken seriously by management, on the one hand—such a declaration of intent can be formalized, given the agreements about further procedures—and, on the other, the confidentiality with which the individual data are treated. Clear agreements should also be made about the latter, possibly registered in a code (see, for instance,

Mirvis & Seashore, 1981; Seashore & Mirvis, 1983) and the ethical code for (industrial and organizational) psychologists in various countries.

Researchers often feel that there is a certain onesidedness in the relation with the organization, that they are the demanding party. Yet this is not often the case. Members of the organization sometimes need to put forward their own view in the company, test certain ideas before an outsider, to take a new look at existing problems, or simply to give vent to their feelings (especially at the top, where it sometimes gets lonely, especially in periods of reorganizations). This does presuppose that the researcher is seen as a serious interlocutor; not every type of problem is adequate for handling by a junior researcher (Table 9.4).

As the researcher becomes more involved in action planning it is inevitable that he/she becomes (more still) a part of all sorts of power processes in the organization (Breuer, 1985). AO seldom takes place in a political vacuum: A principal usually wants to achieve something with it. Members of the organization guess this and will allow their participation also to be dependent on a satisfying answer to this question. The researcher's credibility is tested on, for instance, the consistency of his behaviour with the official account of the principal. AO itself is not a neutral event either: It releases a lot of energy, creates expectations, often opens old wounds, and so on. It is advisable therefore to have lucid role expectations for this phase.

Expectations regarding the role of the researcher, her own ideas about it, and current options in this connection are influenced by whether she is either externally employed (for instance, in a research agency/consultancy) or internally employed (and thus in the relevant organization). This theme has been the topic of scientific research only rarely (though see Van de Vall, 1980). From what is available it appears that an external researcher can often set a stranded situation in motion and that her contribution quite often gives cause for high expectations. Sometimes, however, these expectations are pitched so high that the results can only be disappointing. The internal researcher has the advantage in a field of which the external one is usually hardly aware: He or she knows the game of formal and informal balance of power within the organization. When it comes to decision-making in a company—for instance, concerning interventions—it is essential that the right players are treated in the right order. Cooperation between an external and an internal researcher/consultant can therefore produce advantages.

So far we have acted as though the planning of an intervention (an individual intervention, a series of measures, a coherent policy programme) produces no particular difficulties. But this is often not the case. First, a methodological or content-specific problem is involved. Whenever data have been assembled in consideration of certain expectations or specific hypotheses, a first question is to what extent the quality of the research design permits making valid inferences. A second question is to what extent the results support the expectations or hypotheses. It often occurs that there is "some distance" between them: the support is mediocre, or the support is available in certain respects and not in others. Statements (for example, recommendations on changes) are surrounded by a degree of uncertainty in such cases.

A second problem concerns the mapping of research results to one or more interventions (irrespective of the form of an intervention). First, the question is raised as to what level(s) of analysis the intervention must refer to. Suppose that a study shows that many members of the organization (individual level) are dissatisfied with their work, but also with their compensation and their supervision. It is not a very logical step to consider interventions that are at that individual level only. But at what level then: of the group (leadership?), of a division (task restructuring?), and/or of the entire company (compensation?)? A second important question is for which criteria improvement is pursued. Is the observed dissatisfaction in itself a disadvantage? Or does it lead to negative consequences regarding job motivation, involvement, or performance? Or is higher turnover feared, in the long run? Here, one recognizes the theme of short- versus long-term criteria as well. There is a third question in close connection with this: What insight exists regarding the time required to achieve a particular result by means of a particular intervention? Very little research on this topic—the choice of interventions—has been conducted in connection with AO yet (but see, in the context of research into social indicators, Bauer, 1966; Sheldon & Moore, 1968; Campbell & Converse, 1972; Stöber & Schumacher, 1973).

Finally, we will make some remarks on typical pitfalls in which the researcher can end up, in evaluative research of change processes or developmental processes in organizations (henceforth OO). In most of the OO programmes, there is not so much a single independent, manipulable vari-

TABLE 9.4	
Elements of exchange in AO relations (cf. Lawler et al., 1981 p.503).	
Perceptions of how the organization functions	Guarantees anonymity/confidentiality
Feelings regarding people, processes, tasks	Reflecting on what the organization looks like
Time and energy for data gathering	A chance to put a certain view forward
Risk of giving less sociably acceptable answers	A listening ear
Admittance to meetings and archives	A new look at problems
Assist with interpretation	Advice/recommendations with regard to changes
Involvement in interpretation of diagnosis in action	Assist with changes

able and a single dependent variable. Rather, one has to deal with a package of interventions, and some operations cannot be predicted as such, but just correlate with other measures that were intended. In the same way, it is a matter of a multitude of outcomes, some of which are non-intended. Ultimately, various ways are imaginable in which certain actions lead to results.

To measure the effects of such a programme, both the preparation and the introduction have to be registered with great care, the behaviour of the partners has to be observed, repeated measurements carried out, and so on. And even then, numerous questions still arise, such as (Mirvis, 1983): Which objectives have been realized to a higher degree, which ones to a lesser degree? Was the programme equally effective in the entire organization? To whom (project management, employees) or to what (characteristics of the programme, circumstances) can particular results or failures be ascribed? Have certain preconditions been modified in the course of time and what

effect has this had on the results of the programme?

OO programmes often follow a certain phasing of activities (see e.g. McLennan, 1989). An AO project has to link up with this as well as possible and record the main activities, processes and—intended and non-intended—effects by means of a variety of methods. Continuous measurements (observation), repeated measurements (question-naires), and periodical measurements (behaviour, effects) can be integrated in a complex AO design (Heller et al., 1988; Lawler et al., 1983, p.38; see Figure 9.8).

Some examples may clarify this. Assume that a research team is involved in an OO programme that is directed towards enhancing the quality of the work and organization (Van Duren & Van Manen, 1992), the quality of the service (Sadler, 1988; Vinkenburg, 1988), a more client-oriented organizational structure, for instance, local police (Cozijnsen, 1989) or patient-oriented healthcare (Van Zonneveld, 1993), with the particular

FIGURE 9.8

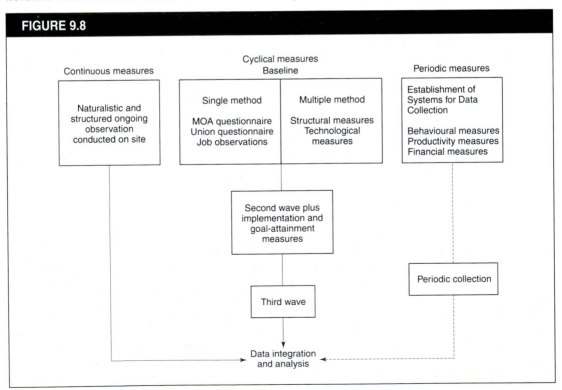

Illustration of a complex measuring programme. Reprinted with the kind permission of John Wiley & Sons Inc, from Lawler et al., 1983, Organizational change and the conduct of assessment research. In S.E. Seashore, E.E. Lawler, P.H. Mirvis, & C. Cammann (Eds.). Copyright (1983) John Wiley & Sons Inc.

question to follow the process critically by means of measurements during the process of change, suggestions for readjustment, and an evaluation afterwards. A shared feature of such programmes is that the concrete activities are primarily aimed at several specific interventions (for instance reformulation of tasks, rearrangement of various organizational units, influencing attitudes with respect to the client), but that the organization intends to realize more remote objectives in due time in doing so (higher effectiveness of the organization). Such a programme and the activities of the research team may be globally described in phases (see on this matter e.g. Mirvis, 1983; Vinke & Thierry, 1984; Thierry, Koopman-Iwema, & Vinke, 1988).

4.6 Diffusion and finalization

If the results of the preceding phase are positive, an important question is in what way the changes introduced can assume a durable nature. This institutionalization not only pertains to the (altered) action of members of the organization—for instance, much more attention to quality—but also to support it within the organization (say, a small department for quality control). Now it occurs quite often that interventions have not been initiated for an entire company, but only—"experimentally"—in a particular department. In this connection, "experimentally" can refer to a research design in which the consequences of one or several specific changes have been analyzed. But it can also mean "first gain experience" with an intervention: As described earlier, employees have many doubts about the supposed consequences of an intervention. By gaining experience, the decision concerning the definitive introduction (or cancellation) of an intervention is postponed. In both cases, attention is due to the diffusion of it in the other departments of the company.

Most of the AO phases are usually skipped in those other departments: a simple assessment of opinions or a shortened measuring procedure is often sufficient, after which the introduction of the interventions takes place by means of instruction. In a more general respect, Diffusion can also pertain to *learning to tackle* a problem and a change programme. After a company has com-

pleted an AO project with the assistance of a researcher, during its finalization, the researcher observes to what extent the company can handle current and future problems by itself.

5. "ASSESSMENT" OF ORGANIZATIONAL CHANGE IN PERSPECTIVE

5.1 A tool-kit?

"Assessment" of organizational change takes place by means of a multicoloured set of methods and instruments for diagnosing and evaluating behaviour of (people in) organizations and of changes in them. These methods and instruments are not viewed in isolation, but are embedded in various assumptions or models, both regarding the rules for conducting research and with regard to the approach of clients and principals. AO data can therefore provide an important contribution to the solution of problems or, generally speaking, to decision-making. Now does this mean, as a question regularly posed in the literature goes, that AO mainly revolves around a series of instruments, a tool-kit, so to speak? Or does AO form part of a particular theory that, indeed not always equally explicit, affects the procedure in research on organizations?

In order to answer this question, and in conclusion of this chapter, we shall outline three perspectives (the transition among which can be gradational).

5.2 Organization and behaviour

If AO research pertains primarily to gaining insight into the *state* of an organization, the researcher is committed to a theory on organizations and on the behaviour of people within it. An apt illustration of this is the open-system theory that was briefly mentioned in section 2.2 (according to Harrison, 1987). It provides the researcher with a framework that enables him or her to make a broad structuring and to make a choice from all sorts of possibilities (because the problem is broad and hardly specified as yet). This structuring involves the selection of variables about which data are to be assembled, making decisions concerning dimensions that are to be held constant as much as possible, the selection of criterion variables (for instance, norms) and the type of "theoretical" explanation. In the open-system theory, this explanation pertains to the relations between concepts such as input, troughput, output, and environment.

The example clarifies that, strictly speaking, no theory is involved, but a theoretical conception. For this reason, we prefer the term "model". A model regarding organization and behaviour enables the researcher to chart the relatively unknown field tentatively. This field-marking nature is also characteristic of all sorts of other organization models: The description of them in terms of a metaphor illustrates each of their points of view or characteristic methods of explaining (Morgan, 1986, 1993; Lammers, 1993; see also Chapters 2 and 3, Vol. 4, this *Handbook*). For instance, one speaks of a mechanistic (the organization as a wheel) and an organic model ("natural" adaptation to changing internal and external relations). In other cases, the organization is viewed as a brain system (data flow and methods of problem-solving), as a set of paradoxes (co-existing, mutually exclusive phenomena), as bankrupt property (surviving despite continuing negative results), and so on. (See also Quinn & Cameron, 1988; Meijer & Zucker, 1989.) Each point of view contains a very general pattern of explanation—that also has some influence on the selection of variables and on the processing of the data—but not a series of hypotheses and predictions, derived from a theory. Hence, a theoretical conception, usually of use in order to get acquainted with the state of an organization.

5.3   Change of behaviour and organization

Yet the "state" of an organization—which was discussed just now—refers to a cross-section at a certain point in time. The state can be viewed as a kind of photo: originating from all sorts of change processes and in its turn giving cause for new alterations. Because all sorts of specific questions often arise regarding these changes, AO research can secondly pertain to the *evaluation of changes*. This involves the consequences of planned interventions and the effects of external or internal unpredicted alterations with which an organiza-

tion is confronted (for example, shifts in consumer behaviour) that can be rather drastic. Now the researcher cannot limit herself to using a theoretical notion (and thus a general model) concerning organization and behaviour. What is needed is a specific theory concerning one of the many aspects that may be involved in the evaluation of changes. A first important question is at what level(s) change has found its origin. Many levels qualify for this, as is evident from nearly every chapter in this Volume of the *Handbook*. One might think of the individual employee (for instance, ageing), the task content (restructuring), the group (modified composition), leadership (more emphasis on quality), the organizational structure (in terms of decentralized business units), the culture (more emphasis on security), the market (more competitors), etc.

A second important question in theoretical respect is what should be understood by change. Here we only point out the difference in view between change as "factual" change of a social system, and change as a shift in the "meaning assignment" by a person to whatever happens to her or him (see also Chapters 8 and 6, Vol. 4, this *Handbook*).

A third question of theoretical importance concerns the nature of interventions to be considered: these take place at the micro-level, for instance (say, sensitivity learning in a group), or at the macro-level (for example, merger of companies). Interventions further occur in either a so-called "soft" area (attitudes) or a "hard" area (new equipment); they are central (administrative centre) or peripheral (warehouse management), and so on. What considerations and expectations guide this choice? Heller (see Chapter 10, Vol. 4, this *Handbook*) believes that behavioural science (including industrial and organizational psychology) has a blind spot for the (predominant) meaning of structural interventions (such as in the field of technology and legislation). A fourth theoretically relevant question is how the researcher interprets the often multiple causes for resistance to change and subsequently deals with them in practice. A fifth important question is what consequences changes have. Consequences pertain to dependent variables, for instance (e.g. job behaviour, attitudes), to an altered problem, to shifts in the positions of power held by groups of individuals, and to the issue of who can claim a success.

We do not claim, of course, that one specific theory regarding changes can shed light on all these questions. We do think, on the other hand, that AO research in which changes are evaluated, is hardly conceivable without an adequate theory focused on either content or process. In this way, we also make a claim about the relation between AO and a theory in general: without a theory, this type of research on change is out of control. AO pertains to the tool-kit of the work and organizational psychologist in diagnostics and evaluation on the one hand, but on the other hand "instruments" thus made available make it possible to give a first judgment of the extent to which specific theories are suited the problem in question, i.e. on the basis of the variables that are involved in research each time and the type of explanation sought.

5.4 Determinants and consequences

Third, AO research may involve causal problems: gaining a better insight into cause–effect relations, and into the role of moderator variables. One might think of the question of whether increased attention given by employees to the quality of service is realized more effectively by means of a programme aimed at influencing their motivation or instead by purchasing other equipment and receiving skill training. This type of research problem should be supported by a sound theory. Furthermore, hypotheses and expectations derived from it need to be tested in (field) experimental research. As indicated earlier in this chapter, practical circumstances in a company or institution often make it necessary to select a more vulnerable form of research than researchers would prefer. Research results can also contribute to decision-making in a useful way in that case, nonetheless. This chapter started from the observation that organizational changes are increasing in number, magnitude, and rate. Periodical "assessment" of organizational change is, however, not taking place at a large scale yet. We have the optimistic expectation, nonetheless, that systematically designed AO research will lead to a better understanding of changes and, possibly, to improved control.

REFERENCES

Algera, J. (1981). *Kenmerken van werk.* Lisse: Swets & Zeitlinger.

Andriessen, J.H.T.H. (1987). Zelfonderzoek op scholen: Organisatiediagnose op nieuw terrein. *OTO-Conferentie "Leraar tot (w)elke prijs".*

Argyris, C. (1970). *Intervention theory and method: A behavioral science view.* New York: Wiley.

Argyris, C. (1980). Some unintended consequences of rigourous research. In E.E. Lawler, D.A. Nadler, C. Cammann (Eds.), *Organizational assessment.* New York: John Wiley & Sons.

Argyris, C. (1992). *Organizational learning.* Cambridge, MA: Blackwell.

Asia (1969). *Attitudeschaal voor industriële arbeid.* Den Haag: Commissie Opvoering Produktiviteit/SER.

Bauer, R.A. (Ed.)(1966). *Social indicators.* Cambridge: MIT Press.

Beer, M. (1980). *Organizational change and development: A systems view.* Santa Monica, CA: Goodyear.

Berg, P.T. van den (1992). *Persoonlijkheid en werkbeleving.* Amsterdam: Vrije Universiteit.

Bergen, G.P.A., Marcelissen, F.H.G. & Wolff, C.J. de (1986). *Handleiding Vragenlijst Organisatiestress.* Nijmegen: Katholieke Universiteit. Intern Rapport.

Biessen, P.G.A. (1992). *Oog voor de menselijke factor. Achtergrond, constructie en validering van de Basisvragenlijst Amsterdam.* Lisse: Swets & Zeitlinger.

Biessen, P.G.A., & Thierry, H. (1993). Basisvragenlijst Amsterdam: ontwikkeling en gebruik. In M.J. Schabracq, & J. Winnubst (Eds.), *Handboek Arbeid en Gezondheidspsychologie.* Utrecht: Lemma.

Bouchard, T.J. (1976). Field research methods. In M. D. Dunnette (Ed.), *Handbook of industrial and organizational psychology.* Chicago: Rand McNally.

Bouwen, R. (1990). Innovatie en conflict: Het paradigma van gedeelde betekenis. In J. von Grumbkow (Ed.), *Perspectieven op organisaties.* Heerlen: Open Universiteit.

Bowers, D.G. (1973). OD techniques and their results in 23 organizations: The Michigan ICL study. *Journal of Applied Behavioral Science, 9,* 21–43.

Breuer, F. (1985). Organisatiediagnose in de praktijk. *M&O, Tijdschrift voor Organisatiekunde en Sociaal Beleid, 39,* 401–415.

British Telecom (1984). *Survey item bank.* Bradford: MCB University Press.

Budel, H.J., Donker, A.A., Valkenhoff, R.E.G., & Vliet, L.P. van der (1985). Organisatiediagnose in een ministerie. *M&O, Tijdschrift voor Organisatiekunde en Sociaal Beleid, 39,* 416–425.

Cameron, K.S. (1986). Effectiveness as paradox. *Management Science, 32,* 539–553.

Cameron, K.S., & Quinn, R.E. (1988). Organizational

paradox and transformation. In R. E. Quinn & K. S. Cameron (Eds.), *Paradox and transformation: Toward a theory of change in organization and management*. Cambridge, MA: Ballinger.

Cammann, C., Fichman, M., Jenkins, D., & Klesh, J.R. (1983). Assessing the attitudes and perceptions of organizational members. In S. E. Seashore, E. E. Lawler, P. H. Mirvis, & C. Cammann (Eds.), *Assessing organizational change*. New York: Wiley.

Campbell, A., & Converse, P. E. (Eds.) (1972). *The human meaning of social change*. New York: Russell Sage Foundation.

Campbell, J.P. (1977). On the nature of organizational effectiveness. In P. S. Goodman & J. M. Pennings (Eds.), *New perspectives on organizational effectiveness*. San Francisco: Jossey-Bass.

Cascio, W.F. (1991). *Costing human resources*. Boston: PWS-Kent Publishing Co.

Chun, K.T., Cobb, S., & French, J.R.P. (1975). *Measures for psychological assessment*. Ann Arbor, MI: Institute for Social Research.

Cock, G. de, Bouwen, R., Witte, K. de, & Visch, J. de (1986). *Organisatieklimaat en –cultuur*. Leuven: ACCO.

Cook, J.D., Hepworth, S.J., Wall, T.D., & Warr, P.B. (1981). *The experience of work: A compendium and review of 249 measures and their use*. London: Academic Press.

Cook T.D., & Campbell, D.T. (1976). The design and conduct of quasi-experiments and true experiments in field settings. In M.D. Dunnette (Ed.), *Handbook of industrial and organizational psychology*. Chicago: Rand McNally.

Cook, T.D., Campbell, D.T., & Peracchio, L. (1990). *Quasi-experimentation*. In M. D. Dunnette & L. M. Hough (Eds.), *Handbook of industrial and organizational psychology* (2nd Edn., Vol. 1). Palo Alto, CA: Consulting Psychologists Press.

Cozijnsen, A.J. (1989). *Het innovatievermogen van politie-organisaties*. Deventer: Kluwer.

Cozijnsen, A.J., Vrakking, W.J. (Eds.) (1994). *Handboek Organisatie-Instrumenten*. Alphen a/d Rijn: Samsom.

Cronbach, L.J., & Gleser, G.C. (1957). *Psychological tests and personnel decisions*. Urbana: University of Illinois Press.

Dalen, J.C. van, & Hufen, P.G.M. (1989). *Organisatiediagnose: Theorie en praktijk*. Leiden: Spruyt, Van Mantgem & de Does.

Duin, S. van (1997). *Management van automatiseringsprojecten*. Amsterdam: Vrije Universiteit.

Duren, A.J. van, & Manen, M. van (1992). *Integraal veranderingsmanagement*. Assen: Van Gorcum.

Eijnatten, F.M. van (1985). *STTA: Naar een nieuw werkstruktureringsparadigma*. Eindhoven: Nederlandse PHILIPS Bedrijven.

Emans, B.J.M. (1988). *Machtsgebruik*. Dissertatie Rijksuniversiteit Groningen.

Euwema, M.C. (1992). *Conflicthantering in organisaties*. Amsterdam: VU-press.

Evers, A., Vliet-Mulder, J.C. van, & Laak, J. ter (1992). *Documentatie van tests en testresearch in Nederland*. Assen: Van Gorcum. Amsterdam: NIP.

French, W.L., & Bell, C.H. (1990). *Organizational development: Behavioral science interventions for organizations improvement* (4th Edn). Englewood Cliffs, NJ: Prentice-Hall.

Fromkin, H.L., & Streufert, S. (1976). Laboratory experimentation. In M. D. Dunnette (Ed.), *Handbook of industrial and organizational psychology*. Chicago: Rand McNally.

Gordon, J.R. (1987). *A diagnostic approach to organizational behavior* (2nd Edn.). Boston: Allan and Bacon.

Groothuis, G.J. (1987). Sociaal profiel. In *Methoden, technieken en analyes voor personeelsmanagement* (I.6.1.1–4). Deventer: Kluwer/NVP.

Gründemann, R.W.M., Smulders, P.G.W., & Winter, C.R. de (1994). *VAG: Vragenlijst Arbeid en Gezondheid*. Lisse: Swets & Zeitlinger.

Hackman, J. R., & Oldman, G. R. (1975). Development of the Job Diagnostic Survey. *Journal of Applied Psychology, 60*, 159–170.

Hackman, J.R., & Oldham, G.R. (1976). Motivation through the design of work: Test of a theory. *Organizational Behavior and Human Performance, 16*, 250–279.

Hannan, M.T., & Freeman, J. (1977). Obstacles to comparative studies. In P. S. Goodman & J. M. Pennings (Eds.), *New perspectives on organizational effectiveness*. San Francisco: Jossey-Bass.

Harrison, M.I. (1987). *Diagnosing organizations: Methods, models, and processes*. London: Sage.

Hartog, D.N. Den, Koopman, P.L., & Muijen, J.J. Van (1997). *Inspirirend leiderschap in organisaties*. Schoonhoven: Academic Service.

Harvey, D.F., & Brown, D.R. (1988). *A experiential approach to organization development*. Englewood Cliffs, NJ: Prentice-Hall.

Hasper, W.J.J. (1989). *De onderneming als individualiteit*. Alphen a/d Rijn: Samsom/NIVE.

Hausser, D.L. (1981). Comparison of different models for organizational analysis. In E. E. Lawler, D. A. Nadler, & C. Cammann (Eds.), *Organizational assessment*. New York: Wiley.

Heller, F.A. (1969). Group feed-back analysis: A method for field research. *Psychological Bulletin, 72*, 108–117.

Heller, F.A. (1970). Group feedback analysis as a change agent. *Human Relations, 23*, 319–333.

Heller, F.A. (1986). *The use and abuse of social science*. London: Sage.

Heller, F.A., Drenth, P.J.D., Koopman, P.L., & Rus, V. (1988). *Decisions in organisations: A three country comparative study*. London: Sage.

Hickson, D.J., Butler, R.J., Cray, D., Mallory, G.R., & Wilson, D.C. (1986). *Top decisions.* London: Jossey-Bass.

Hofstede, G. (1984). *Culture's consequences: International differences in work related values.* London: Sage.

Hofstede, G. (1991). *Cultures and organizations: Software of the mind.* London: McGraw-Hill.

Hoogstraten, J. (1988). *De machteloze onderzoeker.* Meppel: Boom.

Horn, L.A., & Roe, R.A. (1986). *De Delftse meetdoos voor kwaliteit van arbeid: Oriëntatie voor gebruikers.* Delft: TU Delft.

Hufen, P.G.M., & Leijten, A.T. (1989). Organisatiediagnose doorgelicht: Een verkennend onderzoek. In J.C. van Dalen & P.G.M. Hufen (Eds.), *Organisatiediagnose: Theorie en praktijk.* Leiden: Spruyt, Van Mantgem & de Does.

Huse, E., & Cummings, T. (1985). *Organizational development* (3rd Edn.). St Paul, MN: West.

IDE—International Research Group (1981). *Industrial Democracy in Europe.* Oxford: Clarendon Press.

IDE—International Research Group (1993). *Industrial democracy in Europe revisited.* Oxford: Oxford University Press.

Ivancevich, J.M., Szilagi, A.D., & Wallace, M.J. (1977). *Organizational behavior and performance.* Santa Monica: Goodyear.

Jansen, B. (1987). *Dagdienst en ploegendienst in vergelijkend perspectief.* Lisse: Swets & Zeitlinger.

James, L.R., & Jones, A.P. (1974). *Organizational structure: A review of structural dimensions and their conceptual relationships with individual attitudes and behavior* (Technical report No. 74–19). Fort Worth, TX: Christian University.

Jonker, J. (1993). *In termen van beelden: Een kwalitatief onderzoek naar het ontstaan van adviesrelaties.* Assen: Van Gorcum.

Kastelein, J. (1985a). *Modulair organiseren doorgelicht.* Groningen: Wolters-Noordhof.

Kastelein, J. (1985b). Doorlichten van kleinere eenheden. *M&O, Tijdschrift voor Organisatiekunde en Sociaal Beleid, 39,* 426–435.

Kastelein, J. (1987). Doorlichtingsperspectief. *Interface,* May, 6–15.

Katz, D., & Kahn, R.L. (1981). Organizations as social systems. In E.E. Lawler, D.A. Nadler, & C. Cammann (Eds.), *Organizational assessment.* New York: Wiley.

Kolb, D., & Frohmann, A. (1970). An organization development approach to consulting. *Sloan Management Review, 12,* 51–65.

Koopman, P.L. (1980). *Besluitvorming in organisaties.* Assen: Van Gorcum.

Lammers, C.J. (1993). *Organiseren van bovenaf en van onderop.* Utrecht: Het Spectrum.

Lawler, E.E. (1981). Adaptive experiments. In E.E. Lawler, D.A. Nadler, & C. Cammann (Eds.), *Organizational assessment.* New York: Wiley.

Lawler, E.E., Nadler, D.A., & Cammann, C. (1980). *Organizational assessment.* New York: John Wiley & Sons.

Lawler, E.E., Nadler, D.A., & Mirvis, P.H. (1983). Organizational change and the conduct of assessment research. In S.E. Seashore, E.E. Lawler, P.H. Mirvis, & C. Cammann (Eds.), *Assessing organizational change.* New York: Wiley.

Lawrence, P.R., & Lorsch, J.W. (1967). *Organization and environment.* Boston: Harvard University.

Leest, D.J.B. van der, & Duren, J.A.A. van (1989). Human resource management. In J.C. van Dalen & P.G.M. Hufen (Red.), *Organisatiediagnose: Theorie en praktijk.* Leiden: Spruyt, Van Mantgem & de Does.

McCall, G.F., & Simmons, J.L. (1969). *Issues in participant observation: A text and reader.* Reading, MA: Addison-Wesley.

McCall, M.W., & Bobko, P. (1990). Research methods in the service of discovery. In M.D. Dunnette & L.M. Hough (Eds.), *Handbook of industrial and organizational psychology* (2nd Edn., Vol. 1). Palo Alto, CA: Consulting Psychologists Press.

McLennan, R. (1969). *Managing organizational change.* Englewood Cliffs, NJ: Prentice-Hall.

Meijer, M.W., & Zucker, L.G. (1989). *Permanently failing organizations.* London: Sage.

Mintzberg, H. (1979). *The structuring of organizations. A synthesis of the research.* Englewood Cliffs, NJ: Prentice-Hall.

Mintzberg, H. (1989). *Mintzberg on management: Inside our strange world of organizations.* New York: The Free Press.

Mirvis, P.H. (1983). Assessing the process and progress of change in organizational change programs. In S.E. Seashore, E.E. Lawler, P.H. Mirvis, & C. Cammann (Eds.), *Assessing organizational change.* New York: Wiley.

Mirvis, P.H., & Seashore, S.E. (1981). Being ethical in organizational research. In E.E. Lawler, D.A. Nadler, & C. Cammann (Eds.), *Organizational assessment.* New York: Wiley.

Morgan, G. (1986). *Images of organization.* London: Sage.

Morgan, G. (1993). *Imaginization: The art of creative management.* London: Sage.

MOW-International Research Team (1987). *The meaning of working.* London: Academic Press.

Muijen, J.J. (1994). *Organisatiecultuur en organisatieklimaat.* Amsterdam: Vrije Universiteit. [Dissertatie.]

Muijen, J.J. van, & Koopman, P.L. (1992). Organisatiecultuur en organisatieklimaat: De ontwikkeling van een internationaal bruikbaar instrument. In G. B. van Hees (Ed.), *Arbeids-en Organisatieonderzoek in Nederland* (pp.63–76). Amsterdam: SISWO.

Muijen, J.J., Koopman, P.L., & Witte, K. de (1996). *FOCUS op organisatiecultuur.* Schoonhoven: Academic Service.

Muijen, J. van, Koopman, P.L., Dondeyne, P., De Cock, G., & De Witte, K. (1992). Organizational culture: The development of an international instrument for comparing countries. In G. Hunyady (Ed.), *Proceedings of Second European Congress of Psychology.* Budapest. Amsterdam: Vrije Universiteit.

Nadler, D. A. (1981a). Role of models in organizational assessment. In E. E. Lawler, D. A. Nadler, & C. Cammann (Eds.), *Organizational assessment.* New York: Wiley.

Nadler, D.A. (1981b). Using organizational assessment data for planned organizational change. In E.E. Lawler, D.A. Nadler, & C. Cammann (Eds.), *Organizational assessment.* New York: Wiley.

Nadler, D.A. (1981c). Managing organisational change: An integrative approach. *Journal of Applied Behavioural Science, 13,* 191–211.

Nadler, D.A., & Jenkins, G.D. (1983). Observation ratings of job characteristics. In S.E. Seashore, E.E. Lawler, P.H. Mirvis, & C. Cammann (Eds.), *Assessing organizational change.* New York: Wiley.

NIP (1989). *Beroepsethiek voor psychologen.* Amsterdam: Nederlands Instituut voor Psychologen.

Offenbeek, M.A.G. van (1993). *Van methode naar scenario's: Het afstemmen van situatie en aanpak bij de ontwikkelijng van informatiesystemen.* Amsterdam: Vrije Universiteit.

Pool, J. (1990). *Sturing van strategische besluitvorming: Mogelijkheden en grenzen.* Amsterdam: Vrije Universiteit.

Porter, L.W., Lawler, E.E., & Hackman, J.R. (1975). *Behavior in organizations.* New York: McGraw-Hill.

Projectgroep EXCOM (1990). *EXCOM: Een computerondersteunend meetinstrument voor de kwaliteit van de arbeid.* Voorburg: Ministerie voor Sociale Zaken en Werkgelegenheid.

Projectgroep Welzijn bij de Arbeid (1989). *Functieverbetering en organisatie van de arbeid: Welzijn bij de arbeid (WEBA).* Vooorburg: Ministerie van Sociale Zaken en Werkgelegenheid.

Pugh, D.S., Hickson, D.J., Hinings, C.R., & Turner, C. (1968). Dimensions of organization structure. *Administrative Science Quarterly, 13,* 65–105.

Pugh, D.S., Hickson, D.J., Hinings, C.R., & Turner, C. (1969). The context of organization structures. *Administrative Science Quarterly, 14,* 91–115.

Pugh, D.S., & Pheysey, D.C. (1972). A comparative administration model. In A.R. Negandhi (Ed.), *Modern organization theory: Contextual environmental, and socio-cultural variables.* Kent, OH: Kent State University Press.

Quinn, R.E. (1988). *Beyond rational management: Mastering the paradoxes and competing demands of high performance.* San Francisco: Jossey-Bass.

Quinn, R.E., & Cameron, K.S. (Eds.) (1988). *Paradox and transformation: Towards a theory of change in organizations and management.* Cambridge, MA: Ballinger.

Quinn, R.E., & Rohrbaugh, J. (1983). A spatial model of effectiveness criteria: Towards a competing value approach to organizational analysis. *Management Science, 29,* 363–377.

Roby, T.B. (1967). Computer simulation models for organization theory. In V. H. Vroom (Ed.), *Methods of organizational research.* Pittsburgh: University of Pittsburgh Press.

Roethlisberger, F.J., & Dickson, W.J. (1939). *Management and the worker.* Cambridge, MA: Harvard University Press.

Rosenthal, R. (1991). *Meta-analytic procedures for social research.* London: Sage.

Rosenthal, R., & Rosnow, R.L. (1991). *Essentials of behavioral research: Methods and data analysis.* New York: McGraw-Hill.

Runkel, P.J., & McGrath, J.E. (1972). *Research on human behavior.* New York: Holt, Rinehart & Winston.

Sackett, P.R., & Larson, J.R. (1990). Research strategies and tactics in industrial and organizational psychology. In M.D. Dunnette & L.M. Hough (Eds), *Handbook of industrial and organizational psychology* (2nd Edn., Vol. 1). Palo Alto, CA: Consulting Psychologists Press.

Sadler, P. (1988). *Managerial leadership in the post-industrial society.* Aldershot: Gower.

Sanders, G.J.E.M., & Neuijen, J.A. (1989). Bedrijfsculturen in kaart gebracht. In J.C. van Dalen & P.G.M. Hufen (Eds.), *Organisatiediagnose: Theorie en praktijk.* Leiden: Spruyt, Van Mantgem & de Does.

Sanders, G.J.E.M., & Neuijen, J.A. (1992). *Bedrijfscultuur: Diagnose en beïnvloeding.* Assen: Van Gorcum.

Schneider, B. (Ed.) (1990). *Organizational climate and culture.* San Francisco: Jossey-Bass.

Schreurs, P.J.G., Willige, G. van de, Tellegen, B. & Brosschot, J.F. (1988). *De Utrechtse Coping Lijst: Handleiding.* Lisse: Swets & Zeitlinger.

Seashore, S.E. (1983). Issues in assessing organizational change. In S.E. Seashore, E.E. Lawler, P.H. Mirvis, & C. Cammann (Eds.), *Assessing organizational change.* New York: Wiley.

Seashore, S.E., & Mirvis, P.H. (1983). Doing independent assessment research. In S.E. Seashore, E.E. Lawler, P.H. Mirvis, & C. Cammann (Eds.), *Assessing organizational change.* New York: Wiley.

Seashore, S.E., Lawler, E.E., Mirvis, P.H., & Cammann, C. (1983). *Assessing organizational change.* New York: Wiley.

Sheldon, E.B., & Moore, W.E. (Eds.) (1968). *Indicators of social change. Concepts and measurement.* New York: Russell Sage Foundation.

Smith, P.C., Kendall, L.M., & Hulin, C.L. (1985). *The revised Job Description Index.* Bowling Green: Dept of Psychology at Bowling Green State University.

Sopers, J.M.M. (1992). *Turnaround management: Het saneren van ondernemingen in moeilijkheden.* Leiden: Stenfert Kroese.

Staw, B.M. (1980). The experimenting organization: Strategy and issues in improving causal inference within administrative settings. In E.E. Lawler, D.A. Nadler, & C. Cammann (Eds.), *Organizational assessment*. New York: John Wiley & Sons.

Stöber, G.J., & Schumacher, D. (Eds.) (1973). *Technology assessment and quality of life*. Amsterdam: Elsevier.

Thierry, H., Koopman-Iwema, A.M., & Vinke, R.H.W. (1988). *Toekomst voor prestatiebeloning?* Scheveningen: Stichting Maatschappij en Onderneming.

Thöne, T.J.F. (1988). Managementcultuur: Meetbaar en bestuurbaar. In J.J. Swanink (Ed.), *Werken met organisatiecultuuur: De harde gevolgen van de zachte sector*. Vlaardingen: Nederlands Studie Centrum.

Torn, J.D. van der (1986). Management in het krachtenveld van de organisatie. *M&O, Tijdschrift voor Organisatiekunde en Sociaal Beleid, 40*.

Turner, A.N., & Lawrence, P.R. (1965). *Industrial jobs and the worker. An investigation of response to task attributes*. Boston: Harvard Graduate School of Business Administration.

Twijnstra, A., & Keuning, D. (1986). *Organisatieadvieswerk*. Leiden: Stenfert Kroese.

Vall, M. van de (1980). *Sociaal beleidsonderzoek*. Alphen a/d Rijn: Samsom.

Veen, J.M. van (1993). *Toy or tool? Electronic mail as an organizational medium*. Amsterdam: Vrije Universiteit.

Ven, A.H. van de (1981). A process for organization assessment. In E.E. Lawler, D.A. Nadler, & C. Cammann (Eds.), *Organizational assessment*. New York: Wiley.

Ven, A.H. van de, & Ferry, D.L. (1980). *Measuring and assessing organizations*. New York: Wiley.

Vinke, R.H.W., & Thierry, H. (1984). *Flexibel belonen: Van cafetariaplan naar praktijk*. Deventer: Kluwer.

Vinke, R.H.W., & Thöne, T.J.F. (1989). Management, cultuur en innovatie. In J.C. van Dalen & P.G.M. Hufen (Eds.), *Organisatiediagnose: Theorie en praktijk*. Leiden: Spruyt, Van Mantgem & de Does.

Vinkenburg, H. (1988). *Dienen en verdienen*. Deventer: Kluwer.

Weick, K.E., (1967). Organizations in the laboratory. In V.H. Vroom (Eds.), *Methods of organizational research*. Pittsburgh: University of Pittsburgh Press.

Wolfe, D.M., & Kolb, D.A. (1984). Career development, personal growth, and experiential learning. In D.A. Kolb, I.M. Rubin, & J.M. McIntyre (Eds.), *Organizational psychology: Readings in human behavior in organizations*. Englewood Cliffs, NJ: Prentice-Hall.

Yin, R.K. (1984). *Case study research: Design and methods*. London: Sage.

Yin, R.K. (1989). *Case study research*. (2nd Edn.) Newbury Park, CA: Sage.

Zonneveld, A.M. van (1993). *Zorg voor verandering*. Utrecht: Rijksuniversiteit Utrecht (dissertatie).

Zwaga, P.G.J. (1983). *Rolproblemen in algemene ziekenhuizen*. Assen: Van Gorcum.

10

The Levers of Organizational Change: Facilitators and Inhibitors

Frank Heller

INTRODUCTION

Nobody can doubt that organizations are undergoing substantial changes. The past decade and a half in particular seems to have witnessed an acceleration of this process and there is now an extensive discussion about the alleged need for continuous change (Brown & Eisenhardt, 1997).

Some organizations grow rapidly; others decline as quickly. Agreed or hostile takeover bids, voluntary or involuntary mergers, and employee or management buy-outs, have taken place at an unprecedented rate. Computer and other technological changes are everyday events.

This is not, however, the scenario that by tradition psychologists have in mind when they talk of organizational change. Organizational psychologists and behavioural-science consultants have tended to concentrate their interest on achieving changes in organizations through individuals or groups, occasionally also by manipulat-

ing structures like committees. One of the questions that can be asked is whether the phenomenon of organizational change does in fact owe a significant part of its dynamic to the work of the behavioural social sciences. Alternatively, or in addition, one can ask questions about the extent to which social-science interventions tend to be successful (Heller, Pusic, Strauss, & Wilpert, 1998).

Since there is an understandable reluctance on the part of researchers and consultants, as well as editors of journals, to publish articles on failure to achieve change, the impression may have been gained that organizational change is more easily accomplished than is in fact the case (Clark, 1976). Given this inevitable bias in the published literature (but see Mirvis & Berg, 1977), a meta-analysis is unlikely to produce reliable results for the universe of change efforts. Nevertheless, we will review one recent large-scale meta-study to relate its results to other evidence.

For the purpose of this chapter, we will for the most part content ourselves with a selective review of the literature and an emphasis on theoretical contributions that might help us to understand the reason behind successful or unsuccessful efforts at organizational change.

THE NATURE OF NATURAL RESISTANCE

In November 1970, Donald Schön started the series of Reith Lectures for the British Broadcasting Corporation, which were later published as a book (Schön, 1971). He made out a strong theoretical case, backed by examples, for a basic socio-psychological need for security and constancy in our lives which he called "the stable state". This need is so strong that it becomes institutionalized in every social domain. The stable state is important to us because it acts as a bulwark against the discomfort of uncertainty and helps us deal with the threats inherent in change. The concept of a built-in need for a stable state should be seen as part of a *homeostatic system*, which relates our inner life to external circumstances.

To help accomplish and then preserve the stable state, people build up a series of social institutions: government, religious faith, family, and a host of similar groupings around one's immediate locality. The institutions create predictability and make us feel secure until some unexpected or unwelcome change penetrates the homeostatic defences and creates tensions and anxiety. The discomfort created by tension and anxiety ushers in a search for a new equilibrium. Such a search can take two forms. It can look for a novel solution in an attempt to reach a higher level of integration to re-establish the stable state; or it can more simply try to re-enact the original circumstances and aim for an equilibrium at the former level.

As novel solutions require imagination and ingenuity, it follows that, in the majority of cases, the tendency is to adopt the second and easier solution. What we call "resistance to change" is usually the result of trying to escape from anxiety due to the loss of a stable state by fighting to return to the familiar pre-crisis set of circumstances without searching out new, and possibly better, options created by the challenge of change.

The need for predictability and stability receives support from our biological inheritance. There is, of course, a need for organisms to adapt to changes in external circumstances, but these changes at lower levels of the evolutionary scale came about primarily through the slow process of developing viable mutations rather than by any rapid behavioural or social process of adaptation. Although people are probably unique in being capable of responding to psychological and socially conditioned changes, we know from the analysis of Chinese brainwashing and other attempts to carry out changes in thought patterns (during the Korean War and elsewhere), that permanent changes in value orientation could not be achieved (Brown, 1963, Chapter 11). Certain techniques, particularly long periods of isolation and enforced sleeplessness, linked with repetitive exhortations, and alternating extreme brutality with less harsh treatment, soon lead to complete disorientation, breakdown of self-esteem, and pliability. In one well-documented case of a Dr Vincent, this type of treatment by his captors went on for over three years and his case was then intensively studied after his release by Dr Robert Lifton. Brown, who reviews this and other cases of similar treatment, concludes that "most of the subjects had succeeded in neutralizing the ideological effects of their experiences, but—as might be expected—nobody who has once been through the process of thought reform ever wholly throws off the new light in which he has seen himself". (Brown, 1963, p.283).

Having reviewed a wide range of evidence of the effects of different forms of persuasion from propaganda, advertising, psychological warfare, religious conversions, and indoctrination to psychotherapy and brainwashing, Brown (1963, pp.297–301) concludes that "attitudes are difficult to change (a) when they are part of the individual's basic personality structure, and (b) when they are a function of the group situation or environment within which he is virtually trapped ... The significant point is that neither political indoctrination, nor brainwashing, showed any permanent results of the type intended, except in those cases who might have been expected to accept the beliefs engendered, even if they had been offered them under normal circumstances."

If we accept the evidence of a built-in human

need for homeostatic stability and extreme resilience to influence from outside, we will no longer be surprised to hear that socio-psychological methods alone will frequently fail to produce lasting organizational change.

Several other theorists have worked along analogous lines to explain organizational resistance. Staw (1982) put forward two motivational counter-forces to change. One is called "escalation", which drives people to a relentless and ineffective perseverance of behaviour so that they invest more and more resources, even when the outcomes are clearly negative. He gives the example of Vietnam and George Ball's correct prediction that the war would escalate as losses increased, drawing the US ever deeper into a losing situation (Staw, 1982, p.90). The second counter-force to change is commitment, which is like a glue that fixes individuals to a rigid line of behaviour. Commitment can be treated as an attitudinal force or as a structural condition of behaviour and he specifically mentions loyalty as a structural mechanism that presumably is reinforced by rituals. It is an interesting comment, because a fair amount of work by organizational psychologists seems to be designed to create organizational loyalty and attachment in the expectation that it will be helpful to management (Steers, 1977; Morrow, 1983).

At the end of the article, Staw concludes that these two counter-forces to change are so formidable that he wonders how organizations can ever manage to carry out any successful adaptation to changing circumstances.

An excessive attachment to a given line of thinking or action has been shown to have quite baleful consequences. Irving Janis calls the phenomenon *Groupthink* and has used it to analyze a large number of major political disasters, like Pearl Harbor, the Bay of Pigs, and Neville Chamberlain's sell-out to Hitler (Janis, 1982). In his more recent writing, he elaborates on these encapsulated decision practices and gives many more examples (Janis, 1989, 1992).

Using a structural rather than psychological analysis of change, Kanter (1983) finds various organizational conditions that resist adaptation to new situations. She mentions specifically the process of segmentation with emphasis on bound-

aries between functions, between management and labour, and between central staffs and field operations. The examples of Ford UK and British Leyland in the section below on "Crises, the environment, and change" fit this conceptual schema.

DEPENDENCY

Another way of describing and conceptualizing resistance to change is to draw attention to the dependency culture, which can operate at the national as well as the organizational level (Miller, 1993). At the organizational level, hierarchy inevitably creates a measure of dependency among subordinates, particularly where structures are designed to be near-permanent rather than flexible, rotational or matrix-like (Kingdon, 1973). Though it is now widely recognised that some form of hierarchy is inevitable in large-scale modern organizations (Abell, 1979), dependency needs can be substantially reduced through a variety of organizational democracy measures from consultation to delegation and semi-autonomous working groups. However, these measures are more talked about than practised (Heller, in press).

At the national level, the methods of instruction used in the educational system can play a major role in strengthening a child's dependency feeling and it is often only at university that students are encouraged to be self-reliant in their exploration of knowledge. Miller (1993) believes that a dependency culture is often reinforced by state welfare policies. In some countries, at the end of the Second World War "warriors could return to be suckled by the bountiful national breast …" (p.286).

It is plausible that a combination of these various dependency pressures, going back to the relationship between mother and child, play an important part in reducing the proclivity for spontaneous or self-generating change dynamics in organizations. Dependency and equilibrium theory reinforce each other. Equilibrium theory draws on the long time-span of evolution and morphogenesis where defences against change have penetrated deeply into the genetic code. Dependency theory adds synergy by showing how social and structural determinants within our own lifetime reinforce the evolutionary trend. Further reinforcement of dependency theory comes from evolutionary psychology (Nicholson, 1997).

DISPOSITIONAL OR GENETIC STABILITY

From quite a different direction there is another source of evidence to support the stable state. It comes from longitudinal research on attitudes by psychologists backed by genetic studies of twins

A frequently used measure of change is satisfaction and in organizational psychology the dependent measure is often called *job satisfaction.* Staw and Ross (1985) were able to use a US national random sample of over 5000 men traced through longitudinally between 1969 and 1972. The individuals in this sample experienced changes in employers and in the nature of their work, but the data from a one-item measure of job satisfaction showed a correlation of .33. From this, the authors argue that what they call *dispositional influences* affect job attitudes to an important extent and there may have been a tendency to put too much weight on the effect of other factors as determinant of job attitudes. Though they accept possible limitations of the data, for instance the one-item measure, they find other supportive evidence. The study by Schneider and Dachler (1978) used the extensively validated Job Description Index and found that during an interval of 16 months, there was substantial consistency, giving average correlations of .56 for managers and .58 for non-managers, as well as stability of factor structure over time.

Staw, Bell, and Clausen (1986) were able to test their previous work on a different longitudinal sample, using Intergenerational Studies conducted by the Institute of Human Development at the University of California at Berkeley. They used a combination of data from three studies covering almost 50 years, and show that scores as well as factor structures showed consistent stability over

time: effective measures, from as far back as adolescence, are useful predictors of subsequent work attitudes (Staw et al., 1986). Combining their evidence from both studies, Staw et al. put forward several policy implications:

1. part of the psychological literature seems to have exaggerated the importance of situational determinism;
2. it may be necessary to re-examine arguments from the OD (Organizational Development) literature in the light of evidence of attitudinal stability over time;
3. similarly, it now seems that improvements in job design may more frequently fail than we have tended to believe.

An alternative interpretation accepted by Staw et al. is that, to demonstrate substantial attitudinal change, organizational interventions need to be stronger and more pervasive (Staw et al., 1986).

Other psychologists and geneticists have referred to the Staw et al. analysis in their own work. Arvey, Bouchard, Segal, and Abraham (1988), using a sample of 34 monozygotic twins reared apart from an early age, found correlations of .31 for general job satisfaction and .32 for intrinsic satisfaction. In spite of the small sample, they argue that though the hereditary factor is not overwhelming, there is nevertheless evidence of heritability, which suggests that organizations find it more difficult to affect or control job satisfaction than is commonly believed. Much more extensive studies of twins, particularly from the Minnesota research, also conclude that attitude and personality factors may be rooted in genetic individuality (Bouchard, 1984; Bouchard, Lykken, Segal, & Wilcox, 1986). Reviewing the evidence, Holden (1987) suggests that a variety of social attitudes are affected by deeper personality traits, which are to some extent influenced by genetic factors.

Notwithstanding genetic and acquired preferences for homeostasis, we have to recognize that there are social, psychological, and structural factors that influence organizational life and that appear to have exerted increasing authority over the rate of change in the past few decades.

TECHNOLOGY AS AN AGENT OF CHANGE

Throughout history, technology has been the major lever of change in the organization of human work activity. This goes back to pre-history but is probably most clearly documented in the social history of the industrial revolution, which, in Britain, started in the 18th century with a series of inventions in textile machinery and the use of water and steam power. As a consequence, the process of moving the main locus of work from the extended family home to separate places of work began and has only very recently started to reverse itself with the advent of networking and distance working based on computer technology (Holti & Stern, 1984; Haddon & Lewis, 1994).

Though the dominance of technology in deciding the nature of work cannot be denied, its pre-eminent position has often been challenged at the theoretical level and the undesirable consequences of the technological imperative are frequently criticized by social scientists.

Historic amnesia has allowed modern analysts to concentrate on two major developments in the 20th century: Taylorism and Fordism. The former was based on a preoccupation with scientific principles applied to the design of work and the selection and motivation of people at work. Fordism, by contrast, was the ruthless application of a pragmatic idea about task sequences in relation to space. Both developments conquered the world and are still with us, albeit in increasingly ameliorated forms.

A theoretical breakthrough came with the research leading to the elaboration of the socio-technical model in the 1950s. The early work of Eric Trist and his colleagues is well known and has been extensively diffused throughout the social sciences (Trist & Bamforth, 1951; Trist, Higgin, Murray, & Pollock, 1963; Cummings & Srivastva, 1977; Bamber & Lansbury, 1989, Trist & Murray, 1990; Van Eijnatten, 1993).

At the broad policy level, the sociotechnical model draws attention to unavoidable duality of two aspects of the work system. In the absence of the unmanned factory or automatic transportation system, technology always has to operate with and

through people. Hence it is argued, and has been demonstrated, technology alone cannot be maximized without reducing the effectiveness of the total system. By the same token, if technology is designed entirely in line with the maximum demands of people, overall system effectiveness will also be reduced. Consequently, there is a need to analyze both the social and technical components together to achieve optimum overall effectiveness. In practice this usually leads to a suboptimization of both components, but the exact arrangement will be contingent on the different circumstances in each case (Herbst, 1972; Mumford, 1983; Heller, 1997a).

Woodward's (1958, 1965) pioneering work claimed that technology had to be a major variable in organizational analysis and that aspects of organizational structure were determined by the shape of technology. Since then, there has been a proliferation of research on the relative impact of variables like technology or size on other dimensions of organizations and their decision processes. The well-known Aston studies (Pugh, Hickson, Hinings, Macdonald, Turner, & Lupton, 1963; Pugh & Hickson, 1976) set the pace and led to a considerable literature in support or critical of the role of technology as a source of influence or an agent of change (for instance, Aldrich, 1972; Khandwalla, 1974; Zuboff, 1988).

Aldrich re-examines the extensive Aston data using path analysis. The Aston studies accumulated cross-sectional data and therefore felt diffident about making very clear-cut causal claims for their variables. Aldrich believes that his path-analysis methodology overcomes this problem to some extent and from this position claims that causality goes from technology to structure and then to size (Aldrich, 1972, p.28).

On a more general level, researchers have often taken positions on whether technological change has been beneficial or hostile to the life of people in organizations, whether it has led to deskilling or an emphasis on higher levels of training (Collingridge, 1982).

Ellul (1980) has no doubt that the industrial system has become completely determined by technology and that the effect is almost entirely negative. Our modern apparatus of communication, including advertising, public relations, and even entertainment have, he claims, the single function "to adapt man to technology, to furnish him with psychological satisfactions . . . that allow him to live and work effectively in this universe" (Ellul, 1980, p.313). Two other important social analysts have taken a critical stance towards technology. Habermas (1971) is concerned about the force science and technology exert in destabilizing power relationships in modern society, and Vickers (1972) sees certain aspects of modern technology as undermining the tranquillity of social life, which needs stability and continuity rather than change or growth.

Similarly, Mumford (1966) argues that technology, which leads to standardization, eliminates the uniquely personal and creative elements of human organization. But not everybody comes to such dismal conclusions (Taylor, 1971; Macdonald, Lamberton, & Mandeville, 1983). Cotgrove, Dunham, and Vamplew (1971) use a detailed study of work design and technology at Britain's Imperial Chemical Industries (ICI) to argue that technology sets limits to what can be achieved by organizational change. A study of a nylon-spinning factory describes how ICI sought to bring about major improvements in work attitudes and satisfactions, and in morale and productivity, by changes that included devolving responsibilities from supervisors to operatives, and the introduction of flexible working arrangements through job-enlargement. Despite the marked successes achieved by the experiment, the researchers emphasize its limits.

"What is remarkable about this experiment is how much could be achieved through small organizational changes. But the limits are there. It is the constraints of the technology that underline the limits to job-enlargement and job enrichment . . . the pervading influence of the technology emerged particularly dramatically in the marked differences between the three main areas in the plant" (Cotgrove et al., 1971, p.136).

"Within the limits set by the technology, the exercise can be judged to have done much that it set out to do. But these limits are real. The relations between men and machines are substantially determined by the machines themselves, and therefore, in the last analysis, by those who design and make the machines. It is here, on the evolution of a more human technology, that we must focus if we are to make real progress towards work which is meaningful and satisfying." (Cotgrove et al., 1971, p.143).

In any case, the reviews of the literature can leave one in no doubt that technology was, is, and will continue to be, a major factor in bringing about organizational change (Mesthene, 1972; Schmeikal, Hogewey-de Haart, & Richter, 1983; Daukbaar, 1997).

THE ROLE OF FORMAL AND INFORMAL STRUCTURES

Among structural factors, apart from technology, changes in the law as well as less formal policy changes can be seen to have had consequences for organizational behaviour. I will mention only two examples.

The European system of industrial relations that developed after 1945 made provision for various forms of organizational democracy. In Germany, the structural arrangements go back to 1905, when a Prussian Mining Act made working committees obligatory for all Prussian mines employing at least a hundred people. In 1951, a codetermination law for the coal, iron, and steel industries gave worker representatives one-half of the seats on the Supervisory Board in the Federal Republic of Germany. In the following year the Works Constitution Act gave worker representatives in other industries one-third representation on the Supervisory Board. Since then various acts have extended the participative arrangements further, so that elected worker representatives operate at several levels of large as well as small organizations. The early 1950s saw similar but even more radical legal developments in Yugoslavia, where worker representatives dominated the top decision-making *fora* and were legally entitled to hire and fire management. Many other European countries have developed organizational democracy legislation, notably the Netherlands and the Scandinavian countries (IDE, 1981a). A few, like Britain and Italy and, of course, many countries outside Europe—notably in the United States—have preferred to leave participation to voluntary actions by management.

Part of the debate about whether to support such legal developments revolved around doubts that formal structural impositions could change behaviour (Emery & Thorsrud, 1969). Organizational psychologists as well as managers believed that democratic behaviour on the shop-floor could only be influenced by voluntary leadership practices and organizational designs geared to the level of the organization at which behaviour was to be influenced (Tannenbaum, 1968; Thorsrud, 1977). Legal provision for formal representation was often thought to be a hindrance rather than a help in bringing about lower-level employee participation.

To resolve this and similar inconclusive debates, a group of European researchers set up a comparative study, including countries that had a wide variety of legal structures in support of industrial democracy and some that relied entirely on voluntary measures. The results of this 12-country comparison found significant statistical support for the view that legal structures exert a measurable influence on behaviour (IDE, 1981b):

"Given the framework of the hierarchy, introducing more rules for employee participation is the most efficient way of increasing employee involvement, particularly that of employee representatives, and of equalising the distribution of power" (IDE, 1981b, p.328). Ten years later a further IDE study came to similar conclusions (IDE, 1993).

Although the findings from the IDE (Industrial Democracy in Europe) research have clear policy implications for governments, it was recognized that decisions of this importance are more likely to be influenced by political arguments than by statistical results. Partly for this reason, but also as a means of checking the conclusions from the larger study, a team from The Netherlands, Yugoslavia, and Britain undertook a longitudinal in-depth study lasting five years, but using similar measures of participation (DIO, 1979, 1983). Instead of using formal legal structures applicable to a whole country as the independent variable, the research introduced a new measure called *Status Power*. Status Power was a quantitative assessment at the level of an organization of the amount of formal, often written authority given to a hierarchical level or a committee. At a non-legal

level, this new structural measure was thought to have similarities with the assessment of external formal statutory support, which the IDE research had found to be a predictor of behaviour. Status Power was decided voluntarily by each organization, but it was incorporated in policy and often written down by describing the authority given to groups of individuals or committees.

In line with the hypothesis, Status Power was found to be a strong predictor of the amount of *de facto* influence of all levels of the organization (Heller, Drenth, Koopman, & Rus, 1988, p.209). This demonstrates the important role that organizational structures can play in influencing behaviour. In the case of Status Power, the structure can be introduced as part of a company's organization development programme, independently of prevailing national laws. This finding is of some importance in many current debates about the most appropriate way of achieving organizational change.

The evidence from these two research programmes should not be interpreted as a structural equivalent of the *technological imperative*. In both studies, other factors, like leadership style and training, also played an important part in organizational change, but the evidence strongly suggests that, without the help of structure, change would not have taken place or would not have lasted any length of time.

CRISIS, THE ENVIRONMENT, AND CHANGE

The kind of organizational changes described in the financial pages of our newspapers are very frequently seen as responses to economic crises, or at least external competitive pressures. Organizational psychologists have been slow to take environmental changes into account, despite evidence from an impressive range of popular analysts, like Peter Drucker (1968) and Alvin Toffler (1970, 1980). There is also no shortage of evidence from careful scholarly analysis, of which Chandler's *Strategy and structure* (1962) was an early example.

Looking at organizations through the eyes of an

historian, Chandler studies the rise and development of large businesses from the late 19th century until the post-Second World War period (Chandler, 1977). From this perspective he attributes the major initiating role for change to business strategy and therefore to the visible hand of management in developing policies to fit changing circumstances. These changing circumstances precipitated crises, which were nearly always environmental; they include new or accelerating market forces and technological developments. In successful companies, and he has made a close study of DuPont, General Motors, Standard Oil of New Jersey, and Sears Roebuck, these pressures are accommodated in changes of strategy, which, in turn, require an adaptation of structures, for instance to a multi-divisional decentralized arrangement. He argues that the broad market forces acting on these four companies were very similar and therefore the structural changes followed more or less the same line. However, details of strategy and the way administrative changes were introduced show that managers have a reasonable measure of choice over timing and detail. He distinguishes between structural innovation based on creative responses and defensive adaptations, which allow change to remain within the current philosophy supported by custom and practice.

At about the same time, Burns and Stalker (1961) published their very influential study of 20 Scottish and English organizations in which they analyze "how management systems changed in accordance with changes in the technical and commercial tasks of the firms, especially the substantial changes in the rate of technical advance ..." (Burns & Stalker, 1961, p.4). Organizations develop either mechanistic or organic forms. In the mechanistic system, control was exercised hierarchically through the use of formal authority. Interaction between people was largely confined to the chain of command, irrespective of the problems dealt with or the competence of the people involved in the decision process. By contrast, under the organic system, power and authority was exercised flexibly in relation to the needs of each specific organization and took account of the experience and competence of the people. As situations or problems changed, so did the methods of exercising authority and control.

The English study took place at a time of major change in market conditions characterized by a rapid decline in government purchases and a correspondingly increased emphasis on making an impact on the competitive open market. The Scottish study saw similar environmental changes, but these were more the result of the introduction of new technologies. The researchers came to the conclusion that organic methods of organization were better adapted than mechanistic methods to conditions of change. While environmental and market conditions are probably the most important factors in determining whether the work organization develops organic or mechanistic trends, Burns and Stalker found that managerial leadership factors were also important, in particular the strength of personal commitment and the extent to which the managing director could correctly interpret the technical and commercial organization.

A few years later (1967) Lawrence and Lorsch at Harvard published research that further emphasized the determining influence of an organization's external environment on the structure and behaviour of employees. Studying ten American companies in the plastics, containerization, and food industries, they came to conclusions that support the work of Chandler and Burns and Stalker in opposing a one best solution for organizations. The older philosophies based on the idea of a one best solution ignored different market and technological conditions, and pretended that the environment could be ignored when designing appropriate structures or behaviour patterns. Lawrence and Lorsch were able to make some comparisons between companies that were more or less successful by traditional economic criteria and between companies in relatively stable, compared with more uncertain and turbulent, environments. The adjustment of successful companies to different degrees of uncertainty and unpredictability is superior to that of unsuccessful companies. The plastics industry was an example of a dynamic environment characterized by uncertainty and a high rate of change. To be effective in these conditions required a differentiated and flexible way of thinking and behaviour, while in the more stable container industry, much less differentiation and flexibility was sufficient to cope with the situation.

Where differentiation was a necessary condition for effective adaptation to the environment, it was found that a complementary mechanism, which they called integration, was also necessary. Integration was defined as the state of collaboration among departments that are required to achieve unity of effort by the demands of the environment (Lawrence & Lorsch, 1967, p.11). These two concepts, differentiation and integration, were found to be useful for understanding how the successful companies adapted their organizational structure and management behaviour to different degrees of environmental pressures.

In their conclusions, Lawrence and Lorsch used these ideas to illustrate the value of contingency theory to management educational programmes. In companies that need high flexibility and therefore low formalization of structure and procedure, a form of sensitivity training in which people learn to cope with unstructured and ambiguous situations would be appropriate. However, where organizations can be successful with a low degree of differentiation and integration, they feel that much more structured educational methods would be indicated.

In their analysis of organizational change, McKinlay and Starkey (1988) say that the prime mover of contemporary organizational innovation has been the changed conditions of international competition, specifically the decline and fragmentation of previously stable mass markets (p.556). They give four case examples, including Ford UK, which tried unsuccessfully to introduce Japanese-type Quality Circles in response to extremely competitive and turbulent conditions. Failure was due to an excessively mechanistic management style, which insisted on a quick top-down decision implementation. It happened after a top Ford manager had visited Japan and seen how effective their Quality Circles were. Unfortunately he did not stay in Japan long enough to understand their decision culture, which insists on slow consultative processes. After this failure, Ford UK was under pressure to use an American employee-involvement scheme, which had been very carefully introduced in the US with full trade-union cooperation. To use these methods, Ford UK had to change its own structure and culture away from the traditional line–staff, top-down style, based on a short-term profit mentality.

A further example of the effect of the environment on structure and behaviour comes from a study of British Leyland (BL), the predecessor of Rover, which was later absorbed by BMW. The British motor industry had been very successful after the Second World War, when competition was severely limited, but later the industry lagged behind European and Japanese producers, particularly after import tariffs were removed in 1970. BL was the only major completely British-owned car manufacturer and, by 1974, it had become quite uncompetitive. The decline had been exacerbated by the oil crisis, which nobody had foreseen. Bankruptcy of the privately owned company was avoided by the government's underwriting its debts and agreeing to invest very considerable sums of public money on condition that the previously anarchic multi-union industrial-relations system, which was held responsible for very low productivity, was changed (Dunnett, 1980).

As a consequence of the new government policy, BL management and unions agreed to devise an employee-participation scheme at three levels of BL, which at that time still employed about 130,000 workers. A small team from the Tavistock Institute negotiated an action research project, which was warmly accepted by unions and management and which was financed independently of the company. The project monitored the new industrial-relations structure over a period of five years from 1976 to 1980 (Heller & Varelidis, 1977; Varelidis & Heller, 1980). Management and unions had always coexisted precariously under a very aggressively handled collective-bargaining scheme frequently interrupted by both official and unofficial stoppages. Under the pressure of imminent bankruptcy, they managed to work out an entirely new method of regular discussions, which worked quite effectively, particularly at the top level, where senior management, including the Managing Director, would meet the top level of elected shop stewards. They evolved a reasonable understanding of the functional difference between consultation and collective bargaining, although the same people would carry out both activities. Restrictive practices were relaxed, strikes became less frequent and unions supported management plans for the development of new cars and even helped to find the name for a successful new model. Something like a Quality Circle scheme was discussed and supported by unions but in the end it was not adopted by BL middle management, who had difficulty adjusting to the new collaborative ideas.

However, the market for cars had become even more competitive and BL's financial position had deteriorated. In October 1978, Michael Edwardes was appointed as the new Managing Director, with a clear brief to improve the balance sheet. He closed one big factory and changed the production plan, with consequent reduction of 25,000 jobs and further closure of 13 plants. Michael Edwardes had no sympathy with consultation and never attended a meeting of the top-level Consultative Council. The scheme, which had grown reasonably firm roots over the first two years, limped on for another two years, but collapsed in September 1979.

Though the personality of Michael Edwardes was incongruent with the nature of participation, the researchers concluded that such an organizational scheme could, in any case, not survive the extreme environmental pressures of extensive plant closures and mass redundancies. There was a reversion to the old familiar structure of collective bargaining, but even this did not survive intact when several major strikes were lost.

It seems that innovative new and quite flexible structures, like the employee-participation scheme, could develop fairly well under competitive economic pressures when survival was the objective. The participation scheme was built up as an organic entity, to use the Burns and Stalker terminology, in parallel with the mechanistic collective-bargaining arrangements. However, when turbulence of the environment exceeds a certain threshold, the adaptive structures can no longer be sustained (Heller & Varelidis (1977). Emery and Trist (1965) describe such situations as turbulent fields, where variations and changes inside the organization are compounded by being enveloped and attacked by external conditions.

The normal interdependence between company and environment no longer operates because of a "gross increase in their area of relevant uncertainty. The consequences which flow from their actions lead off in ways that become increasingly unpredictable . . ." (Emery & Trist, 1965, p.249).

The question raised by Emery and Trist's theoretical analysis of this extreme condition is whether there is some possibility of counteracting the degenerative consequences of what they call *Type 4* turbulence by the emergence of cohesive social values that could constitute a significant binding force for all members involved in the turbulence. No such cohesive values existed in British Leyland at that time

CHANGE OR STAGNATION?

Most of the evidence we have reviewed so far shows that neither people nor organizations find it easy to change (Brunsson & Olsen, 1993). There seem to be various built-in predispositions favouring stability, which can only be altered with great effort. A certain measure of predictability is a necessary condition for social interaction in work as well as in leisure activities, and this brings with it resistance to untried ideas or new forms of behaviour. The existence of the steady state, whether culturally or genetically supported, is with us everywhere. Uncertainty creates insecurity, and as it escalates this becomes turbulence and, eventually, chaos.

The other side of this equation is stability, which prevents progress and this, too, can lead to turbulence and chaos. Opposition to technological innovation in agriculture and irrigation engineering can lead not only to lower standards of life and to illness, but also mass starvation (Max Neef, 1982).

We have seen that there are examples of what can be called noxious stability, where an unwillingness to reassess the *status quo* and adjust current thinking and behaviour, can lead to disaster. Janis's examples of Groupthink are one source of evidence at the level of individuals and groups, and there are case studies of failures at national level from Gibbon's 18th-century classic *Decline and fall of the Roman Empire* to Corelli Barnett's *Collapse of British power* (1972) and Wiener's (1981) *English culture and the decline of the industrial spirit*. Organizational failures as a result of mal-adaptation are more frequently written up in newspapers than in books, but much insight can be obtained by reading Chandler (1962, 1977) and reports of failure of business strategies in the motor-car industry by Williams, Williams, and Haslam (1987) and Dunnett (1980).

PHASES AND CONTINGENCIES

A meta-analysis of business failures divides the process of decline into five stages (Weitzel & Jonsson, 1989):

1. blindness to incipient problems;
2. change is recognized but no action is taken;
3. inappropriate action is taken;
4. crisis;
5. irreversible failure.

This extensive review of the literature supports the view that the danger signals come from outside the organization and that a preoccupation with internal dynamics may reinforce blindness to the real problems. In their stage 1, a measure of commitment by employees may be helpful, but by the time the decline reaches stage 3, loyalty may be a severe hindrance. At this point resistance to taking appropriate action is due to excessive centralization of analysis and action at the top rather than the lower levels, where the problems are more accurately felt. Warnings from subordinates are swallowed up in Groupthink.

Crisis-stage 4 is seen by Weitzel and Jonsson (1989) as the time when revolutionary changes in structure, strategy, personnel, and ideology are necessary (p.105). Outside observers and experts are mentioned as having great potential for helping the organization at this stage, but this points up the difficulty facing social scientists, who would surely want to be involved earlier. If, during the crisis stage, revolutionary changes in personnel are necessary, this would almost certainly include the top executive. Large consultant companies are sometimes called in by the board of directors and may propose such root-and-branch changes, but social scientists normally operate at lower levels. It would seem to follow that they would have to work during stages 1 to 3. Is this an advantage or a hindrance?

Action researchers would certainly like to be involved at the earliest possible moment to enable them to contribute to the correct diagnosis and to steer the organization away from severe crises. However, if our analysis so far is correct and the five-stage road to disaster described by Weitzel and Jonsson is accepted, then change agents face a dilemma. One self-imposed problem, on which I elaborate below, is the current trend among many action researchers to minimize the fact-finding research stage and to delve almost immediately into client collaboration and change (Elden & Chisholm, 1993). In relation to Weitzel and Jonsson's analysis, this could prevent the action researcher from being aware of the critical antecedents facing the organization at a given phase of the crisis.

Resistance to change is inversely related to the progression of the stages. It is obviously difficult to get a foothold in what Weitzel and Jonsson call stage 1, where blindness to early indicators is the chief characteristic. Resistance is also strong during the following stage, which they characterize by inaction, where leaders are said to become more authoritarian and adopt an increasingly narrow vision. Stage 3 offers the greatest opportunity, because the organization is now said to be susceptible to some kind of action. But this is also the time when, according to Weitzel and Jonsson, the dominant coalition begins to break up, when decisions tend to concentrate at the top, and when lower levels, who often have the correct diagnosis, are asked to show silent loyalty to the boss and deference to the previous—and by now possibly outdated—goals and mission statements.

Nevertheless, this seems to be the stage when action researchers could use the moderately high levels of stress in their favour and encourage serious examination of alternatives, because this is the time when a climate amenable to change can be attained and conflict can be managed and subordinated to the need for survival (Weitzel & Jonsson, 1989, p.103).

It seems possible that one of the reasons why action research is so often fraught with difficulties is this restriction of opportunity for effective action to a single phase in an extended process of organizational life; if the researcher or consultant is brought in too early or too late, the chances of success are seriously diminished.

Two possibilities suggest themselves. Large companies sometimes have a resident social-science adviser who may be able to judge the appropriate timing for external intervention (Klein, 1976; Klein & Eason, 1991). The other possibility, which can be used by both small and large companies, is to have one or more trusted social scientists attached to an organization on a long-term basis, who come in at more or less regular intervals to discuss current events or emerging problems.

Schön, whom we have used earlier to describe the basic human need for a stable state, approaches the problem from a different perspective. He, too, is interested in finding ways of encouraging change in modern organizations as well as in society as a whole, and he describes some of the classical methods that have been used to achieve, or at least to attempt, change (Schön, 1971). The prime method is based on the centre–periphery model.

The centre is where knowledge and experience reside and where innovation is thought to take place. The task is therefore one of diffusion from the centre to the periphery. When this is not successful, the remedy is to strengthen the links that tie the periphery to the centre, and when this fails, reward and punishment are used as a form of social Pavlovian conditioning to make the periphery more responsive.

In business organizations, the centre is the apex of the pyramid and the centre–periphery model easily translates into centralized decision-making. Given this diagnosis, it would be tempting to suggest decentralization as a way of increasing the rate of change, but, in his last Reith Lecture, Schön (1971) has more unusual, though tentative, suggestions to offer.

First, one must distinguish between organiza-tions embedded in a relatively calm environment in which the centre–periphery model of enforcing change may work well, at least for a time. He uses the Coca Cola company as an example of success-fully imposing a single innovative product on a vast periphery. But even here, problems may surface in some phases. The dark brown liquid was not very popular in Africa, where consumers preferred an orange colour. In any case, the centre–periphery model operates well only when the message is simple, when the environment is stable, and when the periphery is fairly homo-geneous. In practice, this combination of circum-stances is rare. A similar clearly formulated contingency approach has been developed by Dunphy and Stace (1988; Stace, 1996) and will be described later.

When the environment is unpredictable or even turbulent, and when centralized decisions are attempting to deal with complexity and diversity of needs at the periphery, the normal change model fails. Instead it creates confusion, apathy, resistance, or even outright rebellion. So what is the remedy? Schön suggests a system of flexible networking with the objective of creating a self-learning system in the periphery as well as in the centre, and he is able to give a few examples. Sometimes a single person can run a successful network; he mentions the *tolkach* in the early years of Soviet Russia, who, although officially classi-fied as a criminal, was able to soften the inadequa-cies of the Soviet centre–periphery planning model. When one factory produces too many nuts but lacks bolts, while another factory has a surfeit of bolts, the *tolkach*'s network allows for this imbalance to be ameliorated.

Although Schön does not mention it, I suppose that within organizations there is room for people who are variously called progress chasers or troubleshooters, but more importantly, matrix organizations or decentralized semi-autonomous working groups, which come close to his idea of networks and self-generated learning systems. Under these conditions, new ideas arise in res-ponse to what he calls "existential knowing" in response to local needs and are locally implemented in what Mary Parker Follet (1950) used to call the "law of the situation".

ORGANIZATIONAL INTERVENTION

This brings us, naturally, to the main field of activity for organizational psychologists. The literature on intervention methods is enormously large and varied and any selection is bound to be seen as unfair by numerous protagonists. An early account of the field is covered by Argyris's (1970) well-known *Intervention theory and method*, and a much more superficial but more recent attempt to bring the available diversity together in one volume was published by Huczynski (1987).

It may be useful to start by drawing a distinction between Organizational Development (OD) and other approaches. OD is a relatively new subject. It was reviewed for the first time in the *Annual Review of Psychology* by Friedlander and Brown in 1974. In its origin and until quite recently, it was primarily concerned with changing people rather than organizations. To that extent the term Organization Development was misleading, because the emphasis was on individual attitudes, values, and leadership behaviour, and on sensitivity to interpersonal relations. Of course, it could be claimed that changing people was a necessary first step to changing organizations, but this claim is not easily sustained in the light of current knowledge.

In his 1977 review of the same field, Alderfer describes OD as at once a professional field of social action and an area of academic study (p.197) but then, as now, it is much more highly developed as a tool of professional consultancy than as an academic discipline. There seem to be at least two reasons for this. In the first place OD has grown out of efforts to improve managerial skills and was seen as part of investment in practical aspects of training within the personnel function. The available resources were therefore spent on the development of programmes rather than on research. The second reason is the inherent difficulty of applying traditional psychological assessment methods to this quite complex multi-faceted field. To begin with, it took OD some time before it was prepared to look at factors like organizational power, the existence of coalitions, the role

of conflict, the role of unions, pressures from competitive markets, and other environmental forces (Wilpert, 1995).

In the absence of a systems approach, which would include these facets, the aim of improving the effectiveness of organizations was illusory, though most traditional research methods would find it difficult to do justice to such an array of variables.

One of the most widely used change theories and derivative methods stems from Kurt Lewin (1954), later adapted by Schein and Bennis (1965) and Schein (1980), and has three phases: unfreezing, changing, and refreezing. Though widely disseminated through the professional literature, consultancy and change-agent training, the difficulties are frequently sidestepped, though fully acknowledged by the originators. Schein (1980), for instance, draws attention to the following problems: (1) the change process cannot start before the previous attitudes or behaviour are first unlearned; this is difficult because they are deeply embedded in the personality and entrenched relationships; (2) unlearning attitudes, values, and self-images is "inherently painful and threatening" (p.209); (3) to unfreeze established patterns, they must be disconfirmed by the discovery that the assumptions, values, etc. are not validated; and (4) the disconfirmation "must set up sufficient guilt or anxiety to motivate a change" (p.210). This creates ethical problems for the change agent, who has to decide when it is right to induce discomfort, guilt, and anxiety without inflicting lasting psychological problems.

These four problems apply only to the unfreezing stage and further difficulties are acknowledged for the other two stages.

Trist and his colleagues at the Tavistock Institute have also borrowed from Lewin's field experimental work and added important refinements. Trist (1989) describes how the development of change theory derived from the crisis situations produced by the Second World War and its aftermath. Attempts to unfreeze attitudes and values led to the discovery of T-groups and the laboratory method of training, where individuals were taken out of their ordinary lives and organizational settings to help them unlearn old values and learn new ones in a group-dynamic setting. However, Trist acknowledges that this kind of situation-specific learning does not carry over into real-life settings: "the stranger's human relations training laboratory was not in itself a method of effecting organizational change" (p.43). This conclusion about the ineffectiveness of learning in artificially created learning situations is strongly confirmed by other research, for instance Fleishman et al.'s (1955) carefully controlled before and after study of foremen with the International Harvester Company in the United States.

Heller (1970) has developed a method of facilitating organizational change also derived from Lewin's pioneering theory. Group Feedback Analysis (GFA) has been used in a variety of different settings (Heller, 1976; Brown & Heller, 1981; Heller & Brown, 1995) to analyze, challenge, and—when appropriate—disconfirm current attitudes, values, and behaviour preferences. The disconfirming is achieved when groups are required to analyze and explain differences in attitudes, values, and behaviour. These differences cannot always be justified either in personal or organizational terms, or in relation to existing values or theory. The disconfirming process owes much to evidence derived from dissonance experiments (Festinger, 1958).

Unlike T-groups, Group Feedback Analysis attempts to facilitate organizational learning through existing work situations and therefore does not suffer from the unlearning due to transition from the cultural island of special-purpose groups back to the real-life situation. Furthermore, the feedback data used in GFA groups are anonymous and therefore do not create the stress and anxiety often characteristic of T-group type work. By the same token, if we accept Schein's requirement that unfreezing should be inherently painful and threatening (Schein, 1980, p.209), GFA may not always achieve the desired results (Heller, 1997b).

Argyris has used several approaches to intervention but is best known for his single- and double-loop learning model. Single-loop learning does not question or try to understand the underlying values people hold. People espouse, that is to say, pretend to have, certain values, but in practice they do not use them. Single-loop learning occurs,

for instance, when managers are asked to be more democratic in their decision-making and to consult their subordinates. They may be told that subordinates like participation and that this will improve morale and efficiency. But people who try to follow these injunctions often hold deeply felt competitive and autocratic values, which would lead them to fear a loss of prerogatives if they allowed subordinates to exercise real influence. The consequence of this is likely to be a form of pseudo-participation by gestures but avoiding the reality of decentralization. Single-loop learning may work for simple, routine tasks such as using certain accounting procedures, but is unlikely to change a manager's leadership style for more than a short period.

To accomplish long-lasting changes on emotional and cognitively complex tasks, it is necessary to achieve deep insight into the governing value positions a person holds and to challenge them effectively, if necessary. This allows people to obtain congruence between espoused values and values in use; they then achieve double-loop learning (Argyris, 1985).

Argyris is the first to admit that double-loop learning is not easily brought about. For most people the gap between espoused values and action is very large; attempts to create double-loop learning often fail, even under favourable learning conditions (Argyris, 1982, pp.73–77).

In his more recent writings, Argyris (1985) has refined his concepts, now called Model I, II, OI, and OII, being descriptions of different theories-in-use. These theories are related to a description of a number of defensive routines that make the transition from superficial to insightful action difficult, so that it requires much practice and therefore a long time (Argyris, 1993, p.254).

It seems that we learn our espoused values quite early in life and they are then reinforced when we join organizations. To change in adulthood, when we have progressed to our present position with these espoused values, requires substantial deprogramming. The obstacles seem to be similar to those identified by Schein and Bennis (1965) which we described earlier.

Kurt Lewin, whose genius started so many organizational change developments, is also credited with having initiated a way of relating scientific research to organizational change by involving the client organization or at least a selection of key actors in the formulation and development of the research and change process (Lewin, 1946). The method was called *Action Research* (AR) and several variants have been used (Elden & Chisholm, 1993; Rapaport, 1970; Susman & Evered, 1978). Earlier we gave some examples.

One important ingredient of the theory sustaining AR is the assumption that resistance to change can be reduced by allowing those involved in the change to participate in the process, for instance by some form of joint decision-making (Coch & French, 1948). Researchers at the Tavistock Institute developed a number of approaches to Action Research, including the important discovery of the socio-technical relationship (Clark, 1976; Trist, 1989), which was adapted and used in a number of important change experiments in different parts of the world (Heller, 1997c).

LARGE-SCALE CHANGE PROJECTS

Probably the two largest systematic project-based attempts to introduce organizational change anywhere started in Norway and Sweden in the late 1980s. These two Scandinavian countries have a long history of research to democratize organizational life going back to collaborative work between the Tavistock Institute in London and the Oslo Work Research Unit in the late 1960s (Emery & Thorsrud, 1969, 1976). The early studies were with individual enterprises but later, particularly in Sweden, several fairly large-scale projects operated simultaneously with firms in different parts of the country. The Swedish URAF programme during 1969–1973 worked with 10 relatively large firms, a 1982–1986 Development Programme operated with 40 companies, whereas the extremely ambitious five-year LOM Programme finished in 1992 and covered 148 organizations in the private and public sectors.

In Norway, a five-year study called SBA based on the Norwegian Work Life Centre came to an end in 1993. It covered 98 projects involving 516 enterprises and is seen as a fifth-generation democratization programme. Both LOM and SBA were given assured finance, they exchanged information and experiences, and both were formally evaluated by independent groups of assessors (Naschold, 1993; Snow & Hanssen-Bauer, 1993).

Though to some extent the objectives and approaches of the LOM and SBA programmes differed, they shared a common action-research philosophy, sometimes called participative action research or PAR (Whyte, 1991). Action research has a long and fairly controversial history, but all variants of this approach have a common preoccupation with facilitating change by translating knowledge and experience into action. The PAR used in the LOM and SBA programmes has a very heavy *action* and a light *research* orientation, and this has been critically evaluated from the point of view of scientific knowledge creation (Heller, 1993).

As the objective of this chapter is to assess the feasibility and propensity of stimulating organizational change, the two Scandinavian longitudinal programmes using action research are of considerable interest. Both programmes draw on extensive past self-critical experience. The earlier work had led to disappointingly little diffusion and imitation. The researchers felt that the encapsulation may have been due to the prominent part played by the researcher in planning and executing the programme. Later action projects put much more emphasis and responsibility on the client system to organize its own analysis and development with the researcher in attendance. This, too, failed to galvanize change or diffusion. Consequently, the SBA and LOM programmes were designed to produce a critical mass of coordinated experience to demonstrate the viability and utility of democratization at work within a socio-technical framework and to move from the individual to a systems-level approach (Chisholm & Elden, 1993).

The two extensive evaluation reports conducted at the end of the five-year programmes provide a valuable and unusual opportunity to assess the change potential of theories and methods developed and honed over nearly three decades. Positive conclusions and useful lessons can undoubtedly be derived from these large-scale longitudinal experiments, but there are also important caveats.

Perhaps one should wait another five years and re-asses the cumulative experience then (Quale, 1996).

In the meantime the following tentative conclusions are extracted from the Norwegian evaluation report.

The programme has been "more successful at an individual project level than at a branch or regional and national levels. At the national level the outcome was far below the original goals" (Davies, Naschold, Pritchard, & Reve, 1993, p.iii). At the enterprise level, 64% of the organizations want to continue with the work although only 30% are prepared to pay for it themselves. Over 50% of the firms who participated in the programme have incorporated or will incorporate some expertise into their own organizations.

It is on the level of the overall mission, which was seen to be assisting Norwegian organizations and industries to become internationally competitive, that the report becomes pessimistic. To begin with, in spite of Norway's long history and international reputation for introducing direct-participation measures, there was a shortage of enterprises that wanted to join the SBA approach. There was very little diffusion between enterprises or to regional or national levels, and there was little publicity and a noticeable lack of genuine support from key firms and top Norwegian management; unions and the government paid only lip service.

The LOM programme in Sweden was larger and more substantially financed. The primary objective of introducing organizational change to help Swedish industry improve its productivity and competitiveness in an increasingly complex and turbulent economy is the same as SBA's. Whereas SBA worked with individual companies and a range of measures, including network diffusion, based on previous research evidence, LOM put more emphasis on establishing clusters and networks between organizations and used extensive communication methods and participative action research to accumulate local knowledge and produce improved organizational practices.

The results, as described in the Evaluation Report (Naschold, 1993), are mixed. By its own high expectations a success rate of 33% in innovative communicative development and 15% for innovation in the technology, organization, and personnel areas seems meagre (p.10). The programme is also criticized for its "exclusive process orientation (which) ... precludes any effort towards a design orientation. The programme ... appears to be seriously under-instrumentalized" (p.14) and showed serious limitations in the adequate control of processes of communication, which were relied on as the main instrument for introducing change. These limitations "are reflected in the limited effectiveness of operational process control and level of innovation development achieved by the LOM Programme" (p.14). Although the intention was to concentrate on bringing organizations together as clusters and networks, 75% of projects were run on an individual basis and in the minority of cases where clusters were formed, "only one or two meetings were held" (p.130).

However, these apparently disappointing results have to be put into a comparative framework, for instance by setting them against the successes and failure of the very large-scale German government-supported Humanization of Work, or its successor Work and Technology programmes. The German research investment started in 1974 and so far has had little success in establishing intra-sectorial networks and even less success with encouraging cross-sectorial collaboration (p.130). By comparison with the heavily financed German programmes, the LOM "achievement is something to be proud of, particularly in view of the short duration of the Programme" (pp.135–136).

META-ANALYSIS OF CHANGE

So far, we have reviewed theories and research studies in the area of organizational change without pretending that our analysis is representative of the available literature. We felt justified in this approach for two reasons. In the first place, a very significant area of social science is—in one way or another—concerned with change, and this makes the subject unmanageable. Second, though a few meta-studies of organizational change have been attempted, they have their own limitations. However, one meta-study overcomes a number of the methodological problems and reaches interesting policy-relevant conclusions. Macy and Izumi (1993) selected 131 North American field studies on organizational change and subjected the results to detailed meta-analysis, using individual, group, and organizational-level data from single and multiple sites. They aggregated the results at the organizational level to draw conclusions about the strength and weakness of various change-design features. Although the authors consider the sample to be large in comparison with previous studies, they are aware that their selection discarded 92% of the available literature because it did not fit in with their methodological requirements. The main objective of Macy and Izumi's meta-study was to discover which organizational change levers resulted in measurable output effects. They divided the change levers into three categories: (1) structural, (2) human resources, and (3) technological. Their output measures were: (a) financial, (b) behavioural indicators of business success like turnover and absenteeism, and (c) employee attitudes, beliefs and perceptions. Their extensive data pool also enabled them to separate out (i) structural changes (amelioration to hierarchy, physical layout, multi-skill training, etc.) from (ii) team-development practices (team-building, group-process training, open information, etc.), (iii) semi-autonomous work arrangements (including job enrichment and task enlargement), (iv) goal setting, management development (performance appraisal and recruitment assessment), (v) financial reward and employee recognition.

The results are reported in a fairly uncompromising way. Companies that use individual change levers do not, in general, achieve significant improvements although structural changes on their own yield better results than human resources and technology change levers used in isolation. Macy and Izumi are particularly critical of the claims by a substantial number of firms as well as consultants and change agents that very significant output improvements can be achieved by concentrating on human-resource redesign alone.

The improvements in performance recorded in this study are much larger than those reported in previous meta-research on organizational change. By far the most significant financial results came from change strategies that simultaneously combined structural, technological, and human-resource action levers. Consistent with this integral and holistic approach is the finding that within an overall change strategy, the role of semi-autonomous work teams and goal-setting procedures are particularly powerful. On the other hand, they report that none of the 18 commonly implemented action levers was significantly associated with changing employee attitudes (p.289). They quote other studies that have come to similar conclusions demonstrating the resistance and scepticism people show *vis-à-vis* the originators of the change process.

One important limitation of the Macy and Izumi study is its concentration on intra-organizational processes. Given the other evidence we have reviewed, it seems likely that most of the companies that instituted a multi-faceted change programme were subjected to strong external economic and competitive pressure in which changing technology could have played a significant part. Given strong exogenous pressures with the attendant time constraints, it seems likely that companies would choose to introduce, more or less simultaneously, structural, technical, and human-resource changes. When external pressures are moderate or low, there might be a temptation to be cautious and introduce changes piecemeal. This interpretation would suggest that the real change levers are environmental.

CHANGE UNDER TURBULENCE

Ever since the 1930s, stimulated by the important work of Elton Mayo, and later Rensis Likert and Chris Argyris, the dominant behavioural-science philosophy on organizational improvement and change has been based on individual or group learning, creating new values, delegation to lower levels, democratizing decision-making and developing consensus and loyalty through appropriate leadership methods. Situational factors and environmental influences were often ignored or played a minor role. It may be that these fairly gentle and incremental approaches to organizational development were appropriate in a certain epoch and in some circumstances, but with the advent of discontinuity (Drucker, 1968) and extreme shifts in environmental turbulence (Emery & Trist, 1965), their appropriateness had to be questioned.

Dunphy and Stace (1988) reviewed the evidence and came to the conclusion that abrupt transformational changes induced by external circumstances required different approaches. The transformational changes could have different origins; they could be based on economic or technological factors, deliberate policies of diversification, mergers, acquisitions, or takeovers. Dunphy and Stace suggest a two-by-two typology yielding four change strategies appropriate for different contingencies: (1) participative evolution; (2) charismatic transformation; (3) forced evolution; and (4) dictatorial transformation. They believe that the traditional organization development literature favours type (1) but under pressure leans towards type (2). Consultants who organize change through designing control systems will favour type (3), whereas corporate strategy consultants may opt for type (4).

Incremental change may be appropriate when the environment is benevolent or slow moving, but transformational change is needed when the environment is hostile or turbulent.

The typology is based on a model of environmental–organizational fit and has been criticized on the grounds that this tends to ignore personal power-based motives for instituting or resisting organizational change (Dunford, 1990). However, the contingency model allows a wider range of transformation choices and has since been expanded. The authors subjected their models to a preliminary test in a number of case studies of Australian firms, which included high, medium, and low performers. The results confirmed and extended the contingency model (Stace & Dunphy, 1991). Medium- and high-performing companies used a variety of change approaches, whereas lower performers were timid and preferred fine-tuning. The case studies cover interviews with 450 executives in 13 organizations. Eleven of the 13 companies used a directive change style and none of the 450 interviewees

rated the organizational change style as collaborative. The authors conclude that though there are differentiated change strategies, the dominant approach in their sample of firms is not that of participative evolution or charismatic transformation, and therefore not in line with the methods widely advocated in the organizational-development literature (see also Kochan & Dyer, 1993).

Furthermore, if organizations change their strategies to achieve a high degree of fit with the environment, then one would expect organizations to change their strategies over time, as environmental requirements are unlikely to remain fixed. Using Miles and Snow's (1978) four different generic business strategies and a longitudinal analysis, they find that human-resource and change strategies tend to adjust over time to changes in environmental conditions (Dunphy & Stace, 1990).

The tough and rapid transformational approach to change has been taken one step further and given a new name. It is called *re-engineering* and is alleged by its protagonist to be an essential response to the constantly changing requirements of the world economic situation (Hammer, 1993). Re-engineering advocates a completely new start, by literally scrapping existing structures and policies and redesigning business to follow the basic process of service or product horizontally from the receipt of an order or customer request to the final delivery. During the process of transformation several ingredients have familiar names: the use of information technology, quality control, multi-skilling, product redesign, and team working. The emphasis, however, is on radicalism and shock treatment, and Hammer is aware of a high failure rate (Buchanan, 1997; Kets de Vries & Balasz, 1997).

There can be little doubt that during the next decade we will hear of several more transformational strategies, even if the names given to them are newer than the context they describe.

CONJECTURES AND CONCLUSIONS

As we look over the evidence reviewed in this chapter we notice that several theories and quite a number of strands of evidence converge and support each other. Several authors are prepared to take issue with the OD literature and with prescriptions based on the assumption that lasting organizational change can be achieved:

- by concentrating entirely on intra-organizational manipulations, and in particular
- by concentrating on personnel or human-resource considerations or on any other single pressure for change;
- by attempting to change people's attitudes, values, or interpersonal sensitivity.

We have seen that biogenetic factors operate as a constraining influence and are reinforced by various dependency experiences from infancy through adulthood and further supported by the almost universal experience of hierarchy in politics and organizations.

Of course, biological and psychological development takes place throughout a person's life, but even then there are periods —as in adolescence or after bereavement—when adjustments, though incremental, are painful until an equilibrium is re-established.

These considerations have to be reconciled with everyday experience of changes in organizations, including our schools, churches, political parties, and the places where we work. Most social analysts tell us that our century has seen a higher rate of change than any other period in history (Tinbergen, Dolman, & Van Ettinger, 1977) and this rate seems to be increasing with every decade (Toffler, 1970, 1980; Walton, 1987).

The most obvious and most visible example comes through our experience of technology and particularly computers. From the 1960s to 1980s, computers established themselves in nearly all offices, in most schools, and in many private homes. The versatility of these machines, particularly through a frenetic evolution of software capability, proceeds by rapid incremental changes almost every few months. Hundreds of millions of people in industrialized countries have had their work redesigned quite drastically by an ever increasing variety of technological changes (Andriessen & Koopman, 1996).

As Mumford (1994) has observed, in spite of the well-documented and extensively tested validity of the socio-technical model, most technological design pays little or no regard to it. However, the technical-fix approach often fails and then socio-technology may get a chance.

So technology is a powerful lever of change and a second, even more powerful, lever is economic pressure based on the vagaries of the trade cycle, competition, and the unpredictable but visible hand of the market (North, 1990). In some cases new laws initiate change, for instance in regulating company structures (two-tier boards), safety provisions (the Swedish system), ethical requirements (insider trading), and industrial relations (organizational-democracy laws). Finally, there are political-system changes exemplified since the late 1980s in central and east European countries. These four levers of change: technology, economic crises, laws, and political systems are external to organizations but may help trigger intra-organizational adjustments as described by Macy and Izumi (1993).

We started this chapter by asking two questions. First, whether the phenomenon of organizational change owes a significant part of its dynamic to the work of the behavioural sciences, for instance psychology. Second, one can ask questions about the extent to which social-science interventions tend to be successful.

In answer to the first question, the evidence we have reviewed suggests that social-science change agents, business consultants, and managers could usefully re-examine their beliefs about organizational change. It seems that far from being progenitors of dynamic processes, they are—for the most part—innocent bystanders or at best midwives to a process over which they have little control. If they are professionals or scientifically trained, they may be able to hitch their expertise to work with the external change levers and to facilitate, improve, and speed up the process or anaesthetize the birth pangs of transitions or protect organizations from taking the wrong medicaments.

One way of illustrating this limited but important role is to look again at the well-documented and controlled experiment of Kurt Lewin, who persuaded American housewives to change their food purchasing from butter to margarine and from meat to offals. It was a considerable achievement when we remember how fond Americans are of eating meat and how malodorous and tasteless margarine was in the 1940s. Lewin's group-consensus decision method shifted purchasing behaviour by about 30%! Lewin's innovation demonstrated the superiority of the group decision methods over alternatives like lectures and leaflets which put forward the same arguments (Lewin, 1947, 1954).

We must not forget, however, that the motivation behind the change experiment was the need for America to help the Allies, who were then engaged in a struggle for survival against Hitler's ruthless war machine. America had not yet joined the Allies but its conscience was aroused.

The second question is about the success of social-science-designed interventions. There is clearly a connection here with the answer to the first question, but concern now is not with the external change levers, but with the way environmental pressures are translated into organizational processes. To go back to the birth metaphor, the question is about the success of social-science midwifery. The results are very mixed. There have probably been as many failures as successes, but failures are reported more reluctantly (Brunsson & Olsen, 1993).

The evidence we have reviewed suggests that designs that encourage participation and a degree of influence-sharing before and during the change, reduce resistance and facilitate transition. Autocratic, imposed change may be successful over a short time-span; the effect of democratic or charismatic benevolent leadership seems to last longer. But how long? The evidence is unclear (Heller, Pusic, Strauss, & Wilpert, 1998).

It seems likely that the power of the environment not only initiates the original changes, but can also bring intra-organizational processes to an end, even though in themselves they have been successful. Recent developments in the Volvo company illustrate the dilemma. Kalmar and Uddevalla were two highly innovative manufacturing designs based on humanistic socio-technical principles. The Kalmar plant attracted world-wide attention. The slightly greater cost of its innovative design was compensated by the reduced labour turnover and higher-quality output attributed to the flexible, group-based working methods (Aguren, Hansson, & Karlsson, 1976; Gyllenhammar, 1977; Auer & Riegler, 1990). Uddevalla was even more innovative and challenged the alleged superiority of the Japanese car-production system (Berggren, 1993).

However, by April 1993, both factories were closed. The European, and in particular the Scandinavian, social-science community was incredulous and stunned. It seems that, to a large extent, the prolonged down-turn in the European economy and the particularly severe crisis in the European car industry, decided Volvo on closing its two smaller production plants. A few years later, the Uddevalla factory was reopened but not in its original innovative design (Sandberg, 1995).

Is it simply the case that nothing lasts forever and organizational change is no exception?

REFERENCES

Abell, P. (1979). Hierarchy and democratic authority. In L.E. Karlsson & V. Rus (Eds.), *Work and power*. Beverly Hills, CA: Sage.

Aguren, S., Hansson, R., & Karlsson, K.G. (1976). *The Volvo Kalmar plant*. Stockholm: The Rationalization Council.

Alderfer, C. (1977). Organization development. *Annual Review of Psychology, 1977*, 197–223.

Aldrich, H. (1972). Technology and organisation structure: A re-examination of the findings of the Aston Group. *Administrative Science Quarterly, 1972, 17*, 26–43.

Andriessen, E., & Koopman, P. (Eds.) (1996). The introduction of information and communication technology (ICT) in organizations [Special issue]. *European Journal of Work and Organizational Psychology, 5* (3).

Argyris, C. (1970). *Intervention theory and method: A behavioral science view*. Reading, MA: Addison-Wesley.

Argyris, C. (1982). How learning and reasoning processes affect organizational change. In P.S. Goodman and Associates (Eds), *Change in organizations*. San Francisco: Jossey-Bass.

Argyris, C. (1985). *Strategy, change and defensive routines*. Boston: Pitman.

Argyris, C. (1993). *Knowledge for action: A guide to overcoming barriers to organizational change*. San Francisco: Jossey-Bass.

Argyris, C. and Schön, D. (1974). *Theory in practice: Increasing professional effectiveness*. San Francisco: Jossey-Bass.

Arvey, R.D., Bouchard, T.J. Jr., Segal, N.L., & Abraham, L.M. (1988). Job satisfaction: Environmental and genetic components. *Journal of Applied Psychology, 1989, 74*, 187–192.

Auer, P., & Riegler, C. (1990). Post-Taylorism: The enterprise as a place of learning organizational change. A comprehensive study on work organization changes and its context at Volvo. *Swedish Work Environment Fund & WZB.*

Bamber, G., & Lansbury, R. (1989). *New technology: International perspectives on human resources and industrial relations.* London: Unwin Hyman.

Barnet, C. (1972). *The collapse of British power.* London: Eyre Methuen.

Berggren, C. (1993). *The Volvo experience: Alternatives to lean production.* Basingstoke: Macmillan (previously published by ILR Press, Cornell, 1992).

Bouchard, T.J. Jr. (1984). Twins reared together and apart: What they tell us about human diversity. In S.W. Fox (Ed.), *Individuality and determinism: Chemical and biological bases.* New York: Plenum.

Bouchard, T.J. Jr., Lykken, D.T.; Segal, N.L., & Wilcox, K. (1986). In A. Demirsian (Ed.), *Human growth: A multidisciplinary review.* London: Taylor and Francis.

Brown, A. & Heller, F. (1981). Usefulness of Group Feed-back Analysis as a research method: Its application to a questionnaire study. *Human Relations, 34, 2*, 141–156.

Brown, J.A.C. (1963). *Techniques of persuasion: From propaganda to brainwashing.* Middlesex: Penguin.

Brown, S.L., & Eisenhardt, K. (1997). The art of continuous change: Linking complexity theory and time-paced evolution in relentlessly shifting organizations. *Administrative Science Quarterly, 42*, 1–34.

Brunsson, N., & Olsen, J. (1993). *The reforming organization.* New York: Routledge.

Buchanan, D.A. (1997). The limitations and opportunities of business process re-engineering in a political organizational climate. *Human Relations, 50*, 51–72.

Burns, T. & Stalker, G.M. (1961). *The management of innovation.* London: Tavistock Publications.

Chandler, A.D. (1962). *Strategy and structure.* Cambridge, MA: MIT Press. (2nd Edn. 1969.)

Chandler, A.D. (1977). *The invisible hand.* Boston: Harvard University Press.

Chisholm, R., & Elden, M. (1993). Features of emerging action research. *Human Relations, 46, 2*, 275–298.

Clark, A.W. (Ed.) (1976). *Experimenting with organisational life: The action research approach.* New York: Plenum.

Coch, L., & French, J.R.P. (1948). Overcoming resistance to change. *Human Relations, 1*, 512–533.

Collingridge, D. (1982). *Critical decision-making: A new theory of social choice.* London: Frances Pinter.

Cotgrove, S., Dunham, J., & Vamplew, C. (1971). *The nylon spinners: A case study in productivity bargaining and job enlargement.* London: Allen & Unwin.

Cummings, T.G. and Srivastva, S. (1977). *Management of work: A socio-technical approach.* Kent: Kent University Press.

Daukbaar, B. (1997). Lean production: Denial, confirmation or extension of sociotechnical system design. *Human Relations, 50*, 567–583.

Davies, A., Naschold, F., Pritchard, W., & Reve, T. with the assistance of B. Olsen, T. Sørum, R. Saeveraas and B. Willadssen (1993). *Evaluation report.* Commissioned by the Board of the SBA Programme, June 1993.

DIO (Decisions in Organizations) (1979). A comparative study in Britain, the Netherlands and Yugoslavia. *Industrial Relations, 18*, 295–309.

DIO (Decision in Organizations) (1983). A contingency model of participative decision making: An analysis of 56 decisions in three Dutch organizations. *Journal of Occupational Psychology, 56*, 1–18.

Drucker, P. (1968). *The age of discontinuity: Guidelines to our changing society.* London: Pan Piper Book.

Dunford, R. (1990). A reply to Dunphy and Stace. *Organization Studies, 2*, 131–135.

Dunnett, P.J.S. (1980). *The decline of the British motor industry.* London: Croom Helm.

Dunphy, D., & Stace, D.A. (1988). Transformational and coercive strategies for planned organizational change: Beyond the OD model. *Organizational Studies, 9*, 317–334.

Dunphy, D., & Stace, D.A. (1990). *Under new management: Australian organizations in transition.* Sydney: McGraw-Hill.

Eijnatten, F.M. van (1993). *The paradigm that changed the work place.* Stockholm: The Swedish Centre for Working Life; Assen: Van Gorcum.

Elden, M., & Chisholm, R. (Eds.) (1993). Emerging varieties of action research: Introduction to the Special Issue. *Human Relations, 46*, 121–142.

Ellul, J. (1980). *The technological system.* New York: Continuum.

Emery, F.E., & Thorsrud, E. (1969). *Form and content in industrial democracy.* London: Tavistock Publications.

Emery, F., & Thorsrud, E. (1976). Democracy at work. *A report of the Norwegian Industrial Democracy Program.* Leiden: Martinus Nijhoff.

Emery, F.E., & Trist, E.L. (1965). The causal texture of organisational environments. *Human Relations, 18*, 21–33.

Etzioni, A. (1988). *The moral dimension: Toward a new economics.* New York: The Free Press.

Festinger, L. (1958). The motivating effect of cognitive dissonance. In G. Lindzer (Ed.), *Assessment of human motives.* New York: Rinehart & Company.

Fleishman, E.A., Harris, E., & Burtt, H. (1955). Leadership and supervision in industry. *Ohio State University Educational Research Monographs No.33.* Ohio University Press.

Follett, M.P. (1950). *Dynamic administration*. London: Pitman.

Friedlander, F., & Brown, L.D. (1974). Organization Development. *Annual Review of Psychology, 25,* 313–341.

Gibbon, E. (1854–55). *The history of the decline and fall of the Roman empire* (Ed. W. Smith, London).

Gyllenhammar, P. (1977). *People at work.* London: Addison-Wesley.

Habermas, J. (1971). *Toward a rational society.* London: Heinemann.

Haddon, L., & Lewis, A. (1994). The experience of teleworking: An annotated review. *The International Journal of Human Resource Management, 5,* 193–223.

Hammer, M. (1993). Re-engineering work: Don't automate, obliterate. *Harvard Business Review, 90,* 4, 104–112.

Heller, F.A. (1970). Group Feedback analysis as a change agent. *Human Relations, 23,* 319–333.

Heller, F.A. (1976). Group feed-back analysis as a method of action research. In A. Clark (Ed.), *Experimenting with organizational life: The action research approach.* New York: Plenum Press.

Heller, F.A. (Ed.) (1986). *The use and abuse of social science.* London and Beverly Hills, CA: Sage Publications.

Heller, F.A. (1993). Another look at action research. *Human Relations, 46,* 10, 1235–1242.

Heller, F.A. (1997a). Sociotechnology and the environment. *Human Relations, 50,* 605–624.

Heller, F.A. (1997b). *Influence at work.* The Tavistock Institute Paper TTI No. 2T–717.

Heller, F.A. (1997c). *Is action research real research: Yes and no.* Tavistock Institute Paper.

Heller, F.A., (in press). Influence at work. *Human Relations.*

Heller, F.A., & Brown, A. (1978). Group Feed-back analysis applied to longitudinal monitoring of the decision process. *Mimeograph*: Tavistock Institute of Human Relations.

Heller, F.A., & Brown, A. (1995). Group feedback analysis applied to longitudinal monitoring of the decision making process. *Human Relations, 48,* (7).

Heller, F.A., Drenth, P., Koopman, P., & Rus, V. (1988). *Decisions in organizations: A longitudinal study of routine, tactical and strategic decisions.* London and Beverly Hills, CA: Sage Publications.

Heller, F.A., Pusic, E., Strauss, G., & Wilpert, B. (1998). *Organizational participation: Myth and reality.* Oxford: Oxford University Press.

Heller, F.A., & Varelidis, N. (1977). A current British development in industrial democracy. *Paper to Second International Conference on Participation, Workers' Control and Self-Management*, Paris, September 1977.

Herbst, P.G. (1972). *Sociotechnical design.* London: Tavistock Publications.

Holden, C. (1987). The genetics of personality. *Science 237,* 598–601.

Holti, R., & Stern, E. (1984). *Social aspects of new information technology in the UK: A review of initiatives in local communication; distance working; and education and training.* London: Tavistock Institute.

Huczynski, A. (1987). *Encyclopedia of organizational change methods.* London: Gower Press.

IDE (Industrial Democracy in Europe research group) (1981a). *European industrial relations.* Oxford: Oxford University Press.

IDE (Industrial Democracy in Europe research group) (1981b). *Industrial democracy in Europe.* Oxford: Oxford University Press.

IDE (Industrial Democracy in Europe research group) (1993). *Industrial democracy in Europe revisited.* Oxford: Oxford University Press.

Janis, I. (1982). *Groupthink.* Boston, MA: Harcourt Brace.

Janis, I. (1989). *Crucial Decisions.* New York: Free Press.

Janis, I. (1992). Causes and consequences of defective policy making: A new theoretical analysis. In F.A. Heller (Ed.), *Decision making and leadership.* Cambridge: Cambridge University Press.

Kanter, R.M. (1983). *The change masters.* New York: Simon & Schuster.

Kets de Vries, M., & Balazs, K. (1997). The downside of downsizing. *Human Relations, 50,* 11–50.

Khandwalla, P. (1974). Mass output orientation of operations technology and organizational structure. *Administrative Science Quarterly, 1967, 12,* 1–47.

Kingdon, R.R. (1973). *Matrix organization: Managing information technologies.* London: Tavistock Publications.

Klein, L. (1976). *New forms of work organization.* Cambridge: Cambridge University Press.

Klein, L., & Eason, K. (1991). *Putting social science to work.* Cambridge: Cambridge University Press.

Kochan, T., & Dyer, L. (1993). Managing transformational change: The role of human resource professionals. *The International Journal of Human Resource Management, 4,* 569–590.

Lawrence, P. & Lorsch, J. (1967). *Organization and environment: Managing differentiation and integration.* Boston: Graduate School of Business Administration, Harvard University.

Lewin, K. (1946). Action research and minority problems. *Journal of Social Issues, 2,* 34–36.

Lewin, K. (1947). Group decision and social change. In T. Newcomb & E. Hartley (Eds.), *Readings in social psychology.* New York: Henry Holt & Co.

Lewin, K. (1954). Studies in group decision. In D. Cartwright & A. Zander (Eds.), *Group dynamics: Research and theory.* London: Tavistock Publications.

Macdonald, S., Lamberton, McL., & Mandeville, T. (Eds.) (1983). *The trouble with technology: Explorations in the process of technical change.* London: Frances Pinter.

Macy, B., & Izumi, H. (1993). Organizational change, design and work innovation: A meta analysis of 131 North American field studies 1961–1991. *Research in Organizational Change & Development, 7,* 235–313 (Eds. W.A. Pasmore and R.W. Woodman).

Max-Neef, M.A. (1982). *From the outside looking in: Experiences in barefoot economics.* Uppsala: Dag Hammarskjöld Foundation.

McCalman, J. & Paton, R. (1992). *Change Management: A guide to effective implementation.* London: Paul Chapman.

McGregor, D. (1960). *The human side of enterprise.* New York: McGraw-Hill.

McKinlay, A., & Starkey, K. (1988). Competitive strategies and organizational change. *Organization Studies, 9,* 555–571.

Mesthene, E. (1972). Harvard University Program on Technology and Society: A final review 1964–1972. Cambridge, MA: Harvard University Press.

Miles, R.E., & Snow, C.C. (1978*). Organization, strategy, structure and process.* New York: McGraw-Hill.

Miller, E. (1993). *From dependency to autonomy: Studies in organization and change.* London: Free Association Books.

Mirvis, P., & Berg, D. (Eds.) (1977). *Failures in organization development and change: Cases and essays for learning.* New York: John Wiley & Sons.

Morrow, P. (1983). Concept redundancy in organizational research: The case of work commitment. *Academy of Management Journal, 8,* 486–500.

Mumford, E. (1983). Participative systems design: Practice and theory. *Journal of Occupational Behaviour, 4,* 47–57.

Mumford, E. (1994). *Tools for change: Modern miracles or dangerous disasters?* Manchester: Manchester Business School.

Mumford, L. (1966). *The myth of the machine. I: Technics and human development.* New York: Harcourt Brace.

Naschold, F. (1993). *Evaluation report commissioned by the Board of the LOM Programme.* Berlin: Science Center.

Nicholson, N. (1997). Evolutionary psychology: Toward a new view of human nature and organizational society. *Human Relations, 50,* 1053–1078.

North, D.C. (1990). *Institutions, institutional change and economic performance.* Cambridge: Cambridge University Press.

Pugh, D.S., Hickson, D.J., Hinings, C.R., Macdonald, K.M., Turner, C., & Lupton, T. (1963). A conceptual scheme for organizational analysis. *Administrative Science Quarterly, 8,* 289–315.

Pugh, D.S., & Hickson, D.J. (1976). *Organizational structure in its context: The Aston programme* (Vol. 1). Saxon House-Lexington Books.

Quale, T. (1996). Local development and institutional change: Experience from a "fifth generational" national programme for the democratization of working life. In P.J.D. Drenth, P. Koopman, & B. Wilpert (Eds.), *Organizational decision-making under different economic and political conditions.* New York: North Holland.

Rapaport, R.N. (1970). *Mid-career development: Research perspectives on a developmental community for senior administrators.* London: Tavistock Publications.

Sandberg, A. (Ed.) (1995) *Enriching production: Perspectives on Volvo's Uddevalla plant as an alternative to lean production.* Aldershot, UK: Avebury.

Schein, E.H. (1980). Planned change theory. *Organizational Psychology* (3rd Edn, pp.243–247).

Schein, E.J., & Bennis, W.G. (1965). *Personal and organizational change through group methods: The laboratory approach.* New York: John Wiley & Sons.

Schmeikal, H., Hogeweg-de Haart, H., & Richter, W. (Eds.) (1983). *Impact of technology on society: A documentation of current research.* Oxford: Pergamon Press (A publication of the Vienna Center).

Schneider, B., & Dachler, P.H. (1978). A note on the stability of the job description index. *Journal of Applied Psychology, 63,* 650–653.

Schön, D.A. (1971). *Beyond the stable state. The 1970 Reith Lectures.* London: Maurice Temple-Smith.

Snow, C.C., & Hanssen-Bauer (1993). *Nordvest Forum Evaluation Study Report.* Oslo: The Norwegian Worklife Centre.

Stace, D. (1996). Dominant ideologies, strategic change and sustained performance. *Human Relations, 49,* 553–570.

Stace, D.A., & Dunphy, D. (1991). Beyond traditional paternalistic and developmental approaches to organizational change and human resources strategies. *International Journal of Human Resources Management, 2,* 263–283.

Staw, B.M. (1982). Counterforces to change. In P.S. Goodman & Associates (Eds.) *Change in organizations.* San Francisco: Jossey-Bass.

Staw, B.M., & Ross, J. (1985). Stability in the midst of change: A dispositional approach to job attitudes. *Journal of Applied Psychology, 70,* 469–480.

Staw, B.M., Bell, N.E., & Clausen, J.A. (1986). A dispositional approach to job attitudes: A lifetime longitudinal test. *American Science Quarterly, 31,* 56–77.

Steers, R.M. (1977). Antecedents and outcome of organizational commitment. *American Science Quarterly, 22,* 46–56.

Susman, G., & Evered, R. (1978). An assessment of the scientific merit of action research. *Administrative Science Quarterly, 23, 4,* 582–603.

Taylor, J.C. (1971). High technology leads to more democracy: Some effects of technology in organizational change. *Human Relations, 24,* 105–123.

Tannenbaum, A.S. (Ed.) (1968). *Control in organizations.* New York: McGraw-Hill.

Thorsrud, E. (1977). Democracy at work: Norwegian experiences with non-bureaucratic forms of organization. *Journal of Applied Behavioural Science, 13,* 410–421.

Tinbergen, J., Dolman, A., & Ettinger, J. van (1977). *Reshaping the international order: A report to the Club of Rome.* London: Hutchinson.

Toffler, A. (1970). *Future shock.* New York: Bantam Books.

Toffler, A. (1980). *The third wave.* London: Pan Books.

Trist, E.L. (1989). Aspects of the professional facilitation of planned change. In R. McLennan (Ed.), *Managing organizational change.* Englewood Cliffs, NJ: Prentice-Hall.

Trist, E.L., & Bamforth, K.W. (1951). Some social and psychological consequences of the longwall method of coal getting. *Human Relations, 4,* 3–38.

Trist, E.L., Higgin, G.W., Murray, H., & Pollock, A.B. (1963). *Organizational choice.* London: Tavistock Publications.

Trist, E.L. & Murray, H. (Eds.) (1990). *The social engagement of social science, Vol I.* London: Free Association Books.

Varelidis, N., & Heller, F. (1980). The British Leyland Employee Participation Experiment. *Final Report of Research Project to the Department of Employment.* Tavistock Institute Paper.

Vickers, G. (1972). *Freedom in a rocking boat: Changing values in an unstable society.* Harmondsworth: Penguin Books.

Walton, R.E. (1987). *Innovating to compete: Lessons for diffusing and managing change in the workplace.* San Francisco: Jossey-Bass.

Weitzel, W., & Jonsson, E. (1989). Decline in organizations: A literature integration and extension. *Administrative Science Quarterly, 34,* 91–109.

Whyte, W.F. (Ed.) (1991). *Participatory Action Research.* London: Sage Publications.

Wiener, M. (1981). *English culture and the decline of the industrial spirit.* Cambridge: Cambridge University Press.

Williams, K., Williams, J., & Haslam, C. (1987). *The breakdown of Austin Rover: A case study of the failure of business strategy and industrial policy.* Leamington Spa: Berg.

Wilpert, B. (1995). Organizational behavior. *Annual Review of Psychology, 46,* 59–90.

Woodward, J. (1958). *Management and technology.* Pamphlet of the Department of Scientific and Industrial Research. London: HMSO.

Woodward, J. (1965). *Industrial organization theory and practice.* London: Oxford University Press.

Zuboff, S. (1988). *The age of the smart machines: Tradition and innovation.* Cambridge, MA: MIT Press.

11

Motivation and Satisfaction

Henk Thierry

1 INTRODUCTION

The why and whither of human behavior is one of psychology's concerns of old: What is it that gets us moving and keeps us going? Is that cause located "within" the person, or is it to be found in the "external" environment, or are both person and situation always involved? Why do we sometimes feel ourselves "driven" to do something, while at other times our attention is, as it were, "drawn" to an event, possibly one that has not yet taken place? What is the explanation for the fact that part of our behavior—and we often only realize this after-wards—occurs almost without particular thought, as if it were automated? Why is it that a backlog in work challenges some people to work harder to catch up, whereas it makes others feel blocked? How come one individual is always looking for risks, whereas another person prefers life to be ordered and predictable at work and at home? Is it that people are primarily motivated by long-term views and plans, much as a chief executive officer presents the company's objectives for the next year relative to the results achieved in the preced-ing fiscal year? Or is the audience more sensitive to the commitment and trust he or she radiates in outlining the mission? Is motivation perhaps

affected more by the frequency with which the results of individual performance behavior are monitored in relation to goals set?

A second issue is closely linked with this: Where does satisfaction fit into all this? Is a person highly motivated when (s)he is somewhat dissatis-fied with her/his situation and, as a consequence, wants to effect change? How do we account for the person who is dissatisfied but also "demotivated"? Is there something like a "spillover" effect? In other words: Is dissatisfaction with, say, job content a causal agent of dissatisfaction in other work-related domains? And may satisfaction with e.g. one's career development lead to all-round job satisfaction? Are satisfied workers also productive workers, or are they merely less inclined to apply for another job? And again: Is satisfaction pri-marily affected by somebody's situation or are dispositional factors also involved?

With respect to both major issues there is a large body of literature, which grows by the year. Yet their roles within psychology are different. Moti-vation concerns one of the fundamental determi-nants of (human) behavior: It addresses the cause, the intensity, the duration, and the direction of the individual's behavior. Motivation has always been a major theoretical subject in psychology. But the issue of "what gets us moving and keeps us going" relates, and not only in a linguistic sense, to concepts like motive and attitude towards life. On the one hand, this clarifies why in other disciplines—such as economics, sociology, theology, and philosophy—attention is devoted to human motivation. On the other hand, it explains why motivation tends to be a popular subject: Everybody wonders from time to time about the motives for his/her own and others' behavior, often from the perspective of how to influence other people. This chapter, however, deals almost exclusively with psychological concepts and approaches, tailored primarily to the domain of work and organization.

Despite motivation being a core subject area in psychology—or possibly because of it—there is no comprehensive, widely accepted general motivation theory. Quite a large number of approaches are in fact theories about particular aspects, addressing e.g. particular elements of behavior. Other theories claim to cover more ground, but these are usually selective with respect to the conditions to which they apply. Thus it is not surprising that empirical research tends to be somewhat fragmented. As is so often the case in psychology, this is partly due to a lack of consensus and consistency regarding the definition of core concepts, operationalizations, research designs, samples, and data-analysis techniques. Many studies, however, address only a few aspects of the motivation of behavior and are not embedded in a broader research program.

Nevertheless, the impression of great variety, if not fragmentation, is supported in part by the tendency of some authors to stress the particular, perhaps even exclusive, nature of a theory, a hypothesis, or a research outcome. This fails to place sufficient emphasis on the relationship, or even the correspondence, with the earlier ideas and data of others. Moreover, each epoch has its particular "schools": According to Staw (1984), motivation research in the 1970s subscribed either to reinforcement concepts, or to need theories, or to expectancy theory (we return to these theories later in this chapter). Luthans and Martinko (1987) emphasize slightly different major concepts but, however that may be, such "schools" promote some convergence in research. Students of one school tend not to stress any correspondence between their work and that of major concepts developed in a competing school, yet it is our impression that the late 1980s and early 1990s have shown an increasing convergence of and relationships between major research themes (see also Kanfer, 1990). This is certainly partly the result of a number of large, comprehensive research programs. In addition, quite a number of theories share some common elements—as we hope to show later—even though these are expressed in different ways.

In section 2, the main framework will first be introduced, according to which some 10 theories of motivation, relevant to the domain of work, will subsequently be discussed. Then we turn to some connecting themes between motivation theories.

There are probably even more publications relating to *satisfaction* than to motivation, but satisfaction has a much shorter history. During the epoch of "scientific management", Taylor (1911) used words like "attitude" and "belief" in describing supervisors and workers. Similar terms were used by Mayo (Roethlisberger & Dickson, 1950) at the onset of the "human relations" movement in the second part of the 1920s. Yet the first large-scale research into satisfaction did not take place until the early 1930s (Hoppock, 1935).

The subject of satisfaction was neglected for a long time within psychology probably because from the behavioristic perspective—or rather, from a mechanistic perspective on conditioning and reinforcement—satisfaction was conceived of as a purely "introspective" phenomenon. After all, introspective events are not open to scientific analysis and enquiry.

Yet despite the fact that behaviorism has gradually lost its hold, theoretical progress regarding satisfaction has nonetheless been very modest. A number of theories are at best merely descriptions of the way in which the concept of satisfaction is measured, as we shall see in section 3. For some time now, points of critique have maintained that many researchers apply satisfaction atheoretically (e.g. Locke, 1976; Staw, 1984; Schneider, 1985; Griffin & Bateman, 1986). Another remarkable feature is that psychology's interest in satisfaction is not widespread, but restricted to a few of its domains (such as work and organizational psychology).

Nevertheless, empirical satisfaction research, in

which satisfaction is considered not only as a dependent, but also as an independent variable, has garnered some highly useful results. Moreover, effective instruments have been designed in various countries. Consequently, in recent years, the discussion regarding the nature of the concept of satisfaction has been revived. One feature of this discussion is its questioning of the widely held view that satisfaction merely consists of a set of attitudes structurally determined by situational variables. Satisfaction may also be conceived of in terms of a person's needs or motives, or as a component of a person's mood state, or as a fairly stable personality variable.

Section 3 begins with some definitions; these are followed by a framework in the light of which several models and theories relevant to the domain of work and organization are discussed. In this context the theoretical nature and the determinants of satisfaction are addressed. Various methods and instruments for measuring satisfaction are then outlined, including some rather more technical features often encountered in the course of conducting satisfaction research. The final part of that section reviews the question of whether a relationship between satisfaction and performance exists and, if so, how it is to be seen in terms of cause and effect. We conclude this chapter by voicing some concerns about the future of motivation and satisfaction research.

2 MOTIVATION

2.1 Definition and classification

Any theory that addresses the explanation for and the influencing of the motivation to perform a task should meet three criteria, according to Cummings and Schwab (1973). The key questions are:

1. What it is that draws a person's attention? How is that person activated?
2. How is motivation channeled into the performance of a task?
3. How does behavior remain motivated: is it, for instance, when a need is satisfied or a goal is attained?

Lawler (1973) adds to these a fourth point that a satisfactory motivation theory should also examine which general categories of outcomes are preferred by individuals.

These four criteria help in assessing the formal quality of motivation theories. They do not contribute towards defining the concepts of "motive" and "motivation". Widely varying definitions have been put forward that have at times resulted in confusion. A well-known distinction differentiates between "need" theories and "goal" theories. *Need* theories, in their classical form, assumed the existence of some basic, primary physiological needs oriented towards the individual's survival. When these needs are activated—e.g. when a person becomes hungry or thirsty—drives develop that *push* the person, as it were, to search for opportunities to satisfy the needs. Once the need is satisfied, the internal balance returns. Later theories broadened the concept to include "psychological needs"; these included that of Lewin (1938), e.g., who emphasized that all needs are cognitive in nature (see also Locke, 1976; Locke & Henne, 1986). Following Maslow (1954), who termed his five categories "needs", the concept of need is used in many theories in a very general sense (desire, want, wish, and so forth). As a consequence, the distinctive contrast between "need" and "goal" has been lost.

Goal theories assume that when a person considers particular goals (or outcomes) to be attractive or worthwhile, behavior will be produced to achieve them. Unattractive outcomes will cause efforts to be initiated to prevent these from occurring. Goals or outcomes *draw* a person in a certain direction, as it were, and challenge him or her to greater efforts. According to Tolman (1932), this also occurs with primary motives: In the case of a physiological deficiency it is of vital importance to achieve very specific goals. Motives are cognitively represented through goals: the individual designs a "mental map" and develops, through learning processes, expectations about the relationship between behavior and outcomes (see also Lewin, 1938, 1951).

Our definitions of the concepts of motive and motivation are related to the "goal" theories. Yet, in our opinion, it is not only cognitive but also reinforcement processes that affect the motivation of behavior (we return to this at the end of section 2). Moreover, we prefer a definition in which process characteristics are given more emphasis than content features. *Motive,* then, is the systematic preference for or against a category of outcomes (see also Vroom, 1964). Suppose a person finds the motive of "getting recognition from others" important; incidentally, the fact that different motives are often of simultaneous importance to a person is not relevant here. Then she or he strives to obtain a whole range of "marks" of recognition, both verbal and non-verbal, both in material and in immaterial form. We call these marks or signs of recognition from others "outcomes" (also "rewards"); the level of recognition the person is striving for represents the goal the person is pursuing. The preference is of a systematic nature: The relevant motive is of frequently recurring importance to the individual.

Motivation bears upon an important behavioral dynamic. On the one hand it reflects what someone considers to be attractive (or unattractive), and on the other it denotes the way in which this is to be achieved (or avoided; see also Lawler, 1973). Thus motivation is defined as the process relating to the category of outcomes an individual wants to achieve or to avoid as well as to the specific actions necessary to attain this.

Our definition emphasizes process characteristics. Moreover, in defining motives we did not specify the nature of preferences and dislikes people at work might have in general. This distinction between process and content is used to categorize motivation theories (e.g. Campbell, Dunnette, Lawler, & Weick, 1970). *Content* theories address *what* it is in the person and/or his or her environment that attracts attention, causes behavior to occur, and keeps doing so. These theories specify the kind of needs a person has, the nature of the outcomes pursued by him/her, and so forth. *Process* theories, on the other hand, deal with the issue of *how* behavior is energized, how it is channeled, how it is maintained or changed. The latter theories stress the dynamic nature of motivation, its course and development, and the manner in which the most important variables relate to one another.

In practice this distinction should be used

carefully. Exclusively content-oriented theories do not explain how an individual goes about trying to get what (s)he considers important; in other words, how behavior develops over time. Process theories do precisely that but they fail to account for the causes of behavior. Moreover, there are hardly any "pure" content or process theories: It is almost always a matter of the focus shifting more towards one than the other.

We hold that motivation theories can be understood even better if yet another dimension is used. This dimension bears upon the distinction between reinforcement and cognitive theories. *Reinforcement* theories conceive of motivation in terms of drives and non-cognitive forms of learning (Staw, 1984; Petri, 1986). Positive outcomes ("rewards") reinforce the bond with the immediately preceding behavior of an individual (this is called positive reinforcement): A person who gets attention (and values this) when (s)he gets to the workplace on time, will repeatedly arrive on time. Negative outcomes ("punishment") will cause, sooner or later, the extinction of that particular behavior–outcome relationship. A third form, negative reinforcement, occurs when manifesting a particular behavior (e.g. performing adequately) causes the withdrawal of a negative reward (e.g. continued criticism). Essentially, the individual is considered to be a passive organism, subject to reinforcement processes.

Cognitive theories share the common notion of a person as actively processing information. The person perceives signals, interprets them, stores them in the memory system, and retrieves them when necessary. (S)he designs representations of the environment, develops intentions and expectations, learns purposefully, behaves effectively, and compares him/herself with others. Compared with reinforcement theories (S-R), cognitive theories have at least *S*timulus-*O*rganism-*R*esponse connections, but, according to Ilgen and Klein (1989), a particular school of thought is better described in terms of O-S-O-R links. Such theories are usually derived from attribution theory: The environment is not conceived of as an "objective" reality that exists independently of the observer, but rather as a "subjectively colored" construction of the "cognizing organism". Between these opposite poles of the dimension lie a whole range of positions. If we combine both dimensions, the following classification of theories may be constructed, which will be further discussed in the rest of this section (see Figure 11.1).

For the sake of readability the above classification is somewhat general. Hull's drive-reduction theory, for example, is characterized on the one hand as a reinforcement theory, and on the other as tending more towards being a content theory than a process theory. The classification is not meant to provide absolute scores, but rather relative ones: for instance, equity theory is clearly more cognitive and more process-oriented, whereas Maslow's theory is more cognitive and more content-oriented than Hull's, and so forth. Remarkably, there is a good balance between content theories and process theories, while reinforcement theories are underrepresented (for theories not discussed in this chapter, see Vroom, 1964; Campbell & Pritchard, 1976; Petri, 1986; Ilgen & Klein, 1989; Kanfer, 1990; Ford, 1992; Thierry, Koopman, & van der Flier, 1992).

2.2 Hull: Drive reduction

Hull's theory may be seen as a highly systematic attempt to explain human (and animal) behavior in terms of physically defined variables (e.g. Orlebeke, 1981) without using any cognitive constructs or processes. Behavior, according to Hull (1943, 1951), is a function of the interaction between the number of times this behavior has successfully satisfied a need (the "habit") and the strength of the drive caused by that need (see also Petri, 1986). Consequently, there are two components: the *learning* component and the *drive* (or motivation) component. When one component is absent (equal to 0), no behavior is manifested.

The learning component in Hull's theory is based on Thorndike's "law of effect": Learning occurs when a connection is established between a stimulus and a response as an effect of reinforcement. Given the variety of responses to the same stimulus (or situation), the response which is satisfactory (is "effectual") will be more strongly connected to that stimulus. When an organism experiences a particular need that it can satisfy

FIGURE 11.1

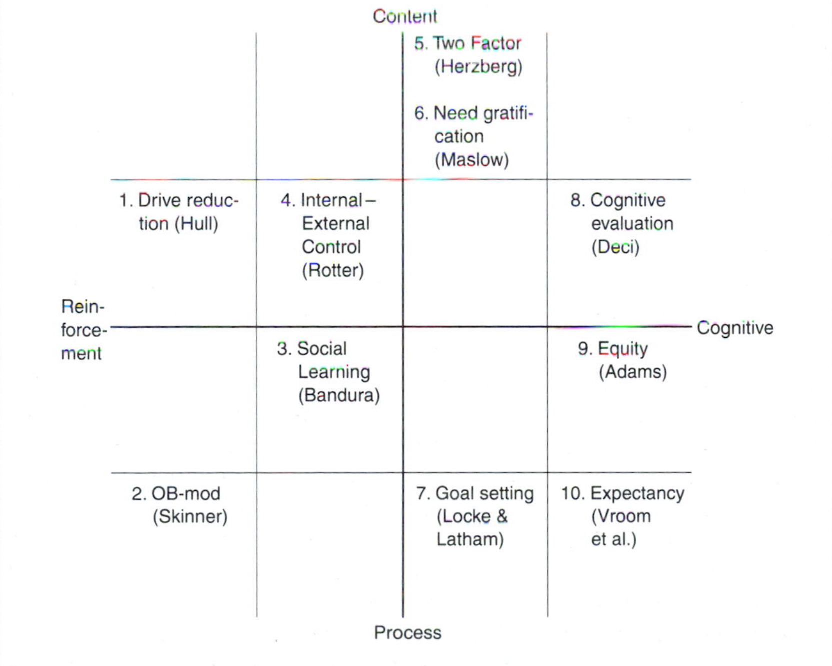

Motivation theories represented along two dimensions.

through specific behaviors, then these behaviors are more likely to occur should that need arise again. The probability of this behavior's occurring is thus determined by the frequency with which this stimulus–response connection (the habit) has arisen as well as by the degree of need satisfaction that resulted. The habit thus specifies the *direction* of behavior relating to a particular stimulus. A satisfactory explanation of behavior, however, must also specify its *strength*.

This latter issue is addressed through the drive component, according to Hull. Each organism has what are termed primary drives, which are biological in nature and are geared to the individual's survival. They bear upon nutrition, activity, care of offspring, and so forth. In the case of hormonal or organic deprivation, the organism is motivated to restore the imbalance. Drives arise that provide the energy source to signal to the organism that something is amiss (e.g. hunger pangs in the stomach). Thus the organism is alerted to (primary or secondary, that is learned) opportunities in the environment—the habit, mentioned earlier—for making up the deficiency. The more successful this is, the more the basic need is satisfied; consequently, the drive becomes increasingly weaker. Petri (1986) states, however, that a drive is not always caused by a need. Sexual drives, for example, are not rooted in an individual's need for survival. Similarly, an unmet basic need does not always lead to behavior: A person experiencing a shortage of oxygen will feel a sense of euphoria and will not be motivated to effect change. It was precisely this that gave rise to the drive concept as the direct "igniter" of behavior. Drives, however, can also be learned (secondary). Secondary drives develop through occurring simultaneously with primary drives: drives based on the need for social contact or status develop, e.g. during the process of satisfying the primary need for activity. Thus, drive and habit interactively determine eventual behaviors, according to Hull. The drive constitutes the "pushing force" or motivator for satisfying the need; the habit determines the way (the stimulus–response connection) in which the need will be satisfied.

Changes in the strength of the reinforcements can thus only gradually affect behavior because the "habit" component changes only gradually.

What then is the explanation for drastic behavioral changes? This led Hull to later introduce a separate motivational variable, namely the *incentive* or Stimulus K. This incentive represents characteristics of a particular goal object. The changing value of that goal may thus affect motivation directly. Spence (1958) has elaborated the incentive concept; according to him it is based on the so-called "anticipatory goal response". Whereas a drive "pushes" the organism, as it were, towards behavior, the value of an unmet goal "pulls" the organism towards behavior.

It is not surprising that this theory has stimulated laboratory experiments, primarily with animals. These provide some empirical support for Hull's theory, also with regard to human behavior. Yet critical comments predominate in the literature, relating for example to the way drive and incentive are combined in the one theory, its poor predictive power regarding the learning of simple or complex tasks, and the assumption of a direct relationship between the degree of deprivation and the activity level of an organism. In relation to this last, Sheffield et al. (cited in Petri, 1986) have shown that learning through reinforcement may occur without any reduction in drive and may even increase motivation.

The mechanistic nature of Hull's approach, its limited applicability in explaining *human* behavior and, principally, its "deliberate" neglect of cognitive and other mental variables have also received extensive criticism. We would like to stress, however, that the addition of the incentive concept does appear to bridge the gap towards these latter variables. Nonetheless, Hull's theory scarcely plays any role in problems of work and organization (Koopman-Iwema, 1980; Orlebeke, 1981).

2.3   Skinner and behavior modification

In the previous section it was found that, according to Hull, specific primary needs underlie the creation of drives. For this reason we categorized his theory in Figure 11.1 as being more one of content than of process. Comparable content issues are absent from Skinner's operant conditioning theory (Skinner, 1948). Yet here, too, Thorndike's law of effect is discernible. In classical conditioning (Pavlov, Watson) reinforcement bears upon making connections between different *stimuli:* An unconditioned stimulus (say food) is repeatedly paired to a neutral stimulus (say noise), which gradually assumes the properties of a "conditioned" stimulus. Over time the conditioned stimulus may evoke the "natural" response (say chewing). According to Skinner, however, reinforcement is essentially the strengthening of a response through the *effect*, which is linked with it (see also Petri, 1986). Someone who reacts aggressively and experiences as a consequence that he gets others where he wants them, will tend to be aggressive in the future, not only under comparable conditions but also in other situations (generalization). Behavior, according to Skinner, is determined by what *follows* it. In order to explain this it is not necessary to use ambiguous concepts such as motivation, autonomy, intention, and so forth (Skinner, 1990). Any society may be designed in such a way that desirable behaviors are reinforced and undesirable behaviors are unlearned through the effects linked with behaviors (Skinner, 1948). These effects may vary in amount, quality, and frequency, and in terms of the contrast between them and effects that have occurred previously.

Although Skinner's thinking has found some support it has been severely criticized by others. Operant conditioning has been called mechanistic (no recognition of cognitive variables and processes), characterized as positivistic (only observable and measurable concepts are acceptable), and deemed atheoretical in nature (since a closed system of reinforcement is used: Mitchell, 1976). Moreover, operant conditioning would more or less imply a negation of the dignity and the individuality of the human being; consequently, everyone's behavior could be determined by manipulating effects.

Some of the criticisms are certainly valid. The majority of current motivation theories consider cognitive processes to be very important, if not dominant (see Figure 11.1). Yet the critics of operant conditioning theory should also be aware that a whole range of individual behavior is partly determined by effects that have occurred previously. All sorts of habits, experiences, opinions developed over the years, acquired knowledge, scripts, schemas and so forth—in March and

Simon's terminology (1958): routine programs—often affect, directly and immediately, a part of our behavior, and color, as a matter of course, a part of our perceptions (see also Motivational Systems Theory, Ford, 1992). Normally, this is not something we think about: we are not "aware" of it. Partly as a result of this a variety of dysfunctional, undesirable behaviors may be exhibited, possibly because their reinforcement in the past occurred by chance or inadvertently. Then again, other behaviors might be required, e.g. as a result of the introduction of new technology, while it proves to be difficult to design reinforcers that are sufficiently strong. Why, then, do we not change the conditions of behavior in a more systematic manner?

This perspective is fundamental to the "behavior modification" movement, applications of which are well known in e.g. psychotherapy. In the domain of organizational behavior (abbreviated to "OB-mod") the following approach is implemented (see Luthans & Kreitner, 1975):

1. *Identify* that part of performance behavior which is problematic.
2. *Measure* the frequency with which the behaviors in question are exhibited in order to have a comparison standard.
3. *Analyze* which factors determine these behaviors and which outcomes are caused under current conditions.
4. *Intervene* by changing the situational conditions to such an extent that desirable functional behavior is more likely to occur (reinforcement), while the probability of undesirable, dysfunctional behavior's occurring is reduced (extinction).
5. *Evaluate* through systematic observation and measurement of the results.

OB-mod has been applied for quite some time over a wide range of subject areas. Most interventions focus on feedback on work behavior (e.g. Komaki, Heinzmann & Lawson, 1980); research evidence shows that these are generally very effective. A considerable amount of data is also available concerning other OB-mod interventions, such as performance appraisal (Komaki, Collins, & Temlock 1987), work behavior of commercial assistants and clients, leadership behavior, financial incentives, safety at work and absenteeism (an overview of research is, e.g., given in: Luthans & Martinko, 1987; Davey & Cullen, 1988). It is our view that there is still too little attention paid to the relative usefulness of OB-mod techniques (see also Staw, 1984).

2.4   Bandura: Social Learning Theory

This theory lies between reinforcement and cognitive approaches, as Figure 11.1 shows. In fact, it forms an interesting and important attempt to integrate cognitive and operant conditioning concepts. Yet, reinforcement is its major theme. If we understand this concept in mechanistic terms, according to Bandura (1977, 1986), and assume that learning merely consists of giving responses and experiencing their effects, then reinforcement would constitute not only a passive, but primarily a very cumbersome strategy, which is determined to a great extent by trial and error. A whole range of potential reinforcers would compete with one another incessantly to attract the person's attention. Yet each human being also exists in a *social* environment in which learning occurs through observing the behaviors of others.

Someone who perceives another person as a role model—this is termed "modeling"—observes a great many characteristics. These bear in part upon the model-person him/herself (e.g. his/her skill level), upon the model's behavior, upon the interactions between the model and other human beings, and upon the consequences of the model's behavior. The observer stores these in his/her memory (visually or symbolically) and retrieves them when necessary. These representations are subsequently transformed into movements and actions: however, the act of observing a mechanic, e.g. assembling a carburetor, does not lead to the acquisition of that skill. The observer's own expertise in this regard is thus important, in addition to which training and coaching are needed. The observer is motivated to exhibit this behavior if the model's behavior produced outcomes that the observer deems to be attractive. This last point illustrates what is meant by *vicarious reinforcement.* By observing whether the model's behavior is punished or rewarded the observer is likely to adjust his or her behavior

accordingly. In other words, the observer does not need to experience all behavior–outcome relationships at first hand in order to learn which behavioral preferences (s)he has. (S)he develops ideas and interpretations based upon the experience gained vicariously through the model. In this way the observer gains a more rapid understanding of the design of stimulus–response links. This is also the setting for the development of norms in order to make social comparisons.

We now turn to the meanings of reinforcement, according to Bandura. He prefers the concept of *regulation* to that of "reinforcement". The primary meanings of regulation are not mechanical, but—as indicated before—informational and motivational in nature. Information allows the person to construct hypotheses concerning effective behaviors; motivation stems from expectations caused by the effects experienced by the model. Outcomes may first regulate the person's behavior through external reinforcement: biofeedback and relaxation techniques are among the more well-known examples. In addition to the second form, vicarious reinforcement, mentioned earlier, there is a third form: self-regulation. Here, the person sets his/her own behavioral norms, and punishes or rewards him/herself for the behavior exhibited. The concept of *self-regulation* has triggered various contemporary approaches to better understand the role of cognitive processes for attaining goals (e.g. Kanfer, 1990; Ford, 1992; Farr, Hofman, & Ringenbach, 1993).

One of the famous concepts in Social Learning Theory is also *"self-efficacy"*. This concept concerns the person's expectation regarding the extent to which (s)he is able successfully to engage in a particular activity or to achieve a specific desired outcome. In conceptual terms self-efficacy is closely related to expectancy (Bandura, 1977; Locke & Henne, 1986)—which is discussed later in this chapter—but it comprises more aspects. Expectancy concerns the relation between a person's effort and his/her performance; self-efficacy includes the person's evaluation of his/her aptitude and knowledge, and also the person's adaptability (see also Gist & Mitchell, 1989). The stronger the self-efficacy, the greater the expectation that behavior will be successful and the higher the level of performance will be.

The person who expects to achieve a desired result will make a greater effort and will cope more effectively with difficult conditions.

These years a considerable body of research relevant to Social Learning Theory has been conducted (e.g. Bandura, 1986; Locke & Henne, 1986; Luthans & Martinko, 1987). Research on self-efficacy has displayed an increasing divergence from Social Learning Theory (e.g. Bandura, 1982; Gist & Mitchell, 1989; Vrugt, 1992). There are no studies in which all aspects of Social Learning Theory have been verified. Bandura makes repeated claims that this theory can explain almost every type of behavior, although various parts of it are scarcely testable; such claims are detrimental to the theoretical status of Social Learning Theory (see also Thierry, 1989). The significance of modeling, however, presents a more positive picture. Models, in person or on video or TV, appear to affect observers' learning and motivation processes under a great variety of conditions. Such results have important consequences for the visibility of trainers, teachers, and leaders, and more generally, for all those wishing to influence others. However, the psychological determinants of this process have not always been unequivocally established.

Furthermore, self-efficacy scores appear to be good predictors of performance behavior. In other words, this is a consistent "construct", although issues concerning the relations between cognitive and affective aspects still remain (see also Schwarzer, 1992).

2.5   Rotter: Internal–external control

The concept of the "locus of control of reinforcement" forms the central focus of Rotter's "Social Learning Theory". In order to avoid confusion with Bandura's theory of the same name, the title of this paragraph uses a term taken from that concept. Rotter takes as his point of departure (1954, 1966, 1975) that "The potential for a specific behavior directed toward a reinforcement to occur in a particular situation is a function of the expectancy of the occurrence of that reinforcement following the behavior in that situation and the value of the reinforcement in that situation." This means that the behavior in a specific situation depends, on the one hand, on the expectation that

this behavior will lead to a specified result ("reinforcement") and, on the other, on the value of that result.

We have already come across the main points of this argument in Bandura's theory, namely in the context of the informational and motivational meanings of reinforcement (regulation). More specifically, the concepts of "expectancy" and "value" are apparent in most of the more cognitively tinted theories (although different terms may be used) and most explicitly in expectancy theory (see section 2.11).

According to Rotter, on the basis of experiences and learning processes in specific situations people develop broad, so-called generalized, expectations, and norms regarding the relationships between behavior and its effects. An example of such an expectation is the "internal–external control" of effects dimension (the so-called "I–E dimension"). Rotter defines this as a personality variable and he has developed a scale to measure it, which has become widely known. One pole of this dimension is formed by the "internal locus": the person considers him/herself to be cause of his/her behavior and feels in control of circumstances. The other pole is formed by the "external locus": the person considers him/herself to be the plaything of external forces which lie outside his/her power (e.g. fate or powerful others) and over which (s)he has no control. The assumption here is that in the same situation, people who are more internally oriented will exhibit different behavior from those who are more externally oriented.

There has been extensive research (see also Rotter, 1975) showing that this assumption is correct. For example, high internal control appears to go hand in hand with a more participatory and social-emotional style of leadership and to be accompanied by more satisfaction (for a more detailed account see: Spector, 1982; Petri, 1986; Luthans & Martinko, 1987).

This theory has not escaped criticism either, however, and we will concentrate on three main points of contention. First, a good deal of research has been conducted in which attention has focused exclusively on I–E as a personality variable and failed to examine its interaction with situational variables. The latter would imply, e.g., that not only the I–E expectations but at the very least also the value of reinforcements would be measured. Second, there is some doubt whether, based on general personality variables, specific behaviors can be predicted. In that context, the use of scales with I–E items which relate specifically to the behavior in question have been advocated.

The third point of criticism has been leveled by supporters of attribution theory. For example, Weiner (1974) is of the view that people can attribute the cause of the results (success–failure) of their performance to one or more of the following four sources:

1. their capacities;
2. their efforts;
3. the difficulty of the task; and
4. luck.

On the basis of this, according to Weiner, their expectations regarding future results can be predicted. These four sources can be categorized along two dimensions: 1 and 2 are I-oriented, whereas 3 and 4 are E-oriented; 1 and 3 are relatively stable characteristics, whereas 2 and 4 are more variable. Research—relating almost exclusively to performance behavior—has now shown that the stability dimension exerts a greater influence on changes in the expectations regarding future results than the I–E dimension. This means that previous experiences (particularly achievements) determine the expectations regarding the outcomes of future behavior only when the causes of those previous experiences are attributed to stable variables (see also Vinke, 1996). As Rotter has not identified the stability dimension it is assumed that his scale does not clearly distinguish between measuring aspects of I–E and of stability. Weiner (1985) later developed a three-dimensional model (see also Carver & Scheier, 1981; Ilgen & Klein, 1989).

2.6   Herzberg: Two-factor theory

This theory is both of a more content-oriented and cognitive nature than the theories discussed thus far (see Figure 11.1). It holds for both this theory and that of Maslow in section 2.7 that although research has lost interest in them, many managers in work organizations attach a good deal of importance to them (see also Schneider, 1985). Locke's (1976; Locke & Henne, 1986) criticism is particularly trenchant: both theories enjoy popularity chiefly in "organizational behavior textbooks" without there being any justification for this at all. We will return to this point later in the chapter.

Herzberg, Mausner, and Snyderman (1959) asked their respondents (mid-level administrative and commercial staff in Pittsburgh, USA) to examine the points in their career at which they had experienced very positive feelings. They were then asked to indicate the causes of this, which attitudes occurred and what effects arose. Subsequently, they were asked about the times they had experienced very negative feelings; the same follow-up questions were then asked. The researchers were employing the Critical Incidents Technique (see Chapter 4, Vol. 3 in this *Handbook*). The criteria for the selection of these incidents was "internal": they were chosen by the respondents themselves.

It appears from Herzberg et al.'s (1959) report that the "causal" events could be classified into four categories. As regards positive feelings, the most commonly mentioned features were as follows:

1. *Achievement and recognition*. The successful completion of a task was reported relatively often. Getting recognition, often on the basis of performance, was also indicated.
2. *The work itself, responsibility, promotion.* The first theme concerns among other things the challenge involved in the work, its varied nature, and the opportunity to carry out a task from beginning to end. Responsibility concerns such things as working without supervision, being in charge of others, etc. When promotion was mentioned, it had been unexpected in 50% of the cases. This category occurred less frequently than the first.
3. *Salary*. Generally this related to a rise. This category was mentioned even less frequently than the previous one.
4. *Other*. This category includes 10 factors with a low frequency, including status and

the policy, and the management of a company.

Thus, according to the research, the most important factors relate to the *work itself:* They are *intrinsic.* The feelings that arise in that context primarily bear upon recognition and performance, opportunities for growth, responsibility, and the work itself. The authors now draw the conclusion that the feelings of *self-actualization* and *growth* are the key to the creation of satisfaction.

The occurrence of negative feelings clearly involves a different sequence of "causes". The four categories mentioned become rather jumbled up. Therefore we will mention only the separate factors: policy and management of the company; technical-procedural side of leadership behavior; recognition; salary; interpersonal relations with superiors; the work itself.

These aspects relate primarily, according to Herzberg et al., to the *work context:* They are *extrinsic.* That is why they evoke such feelings as *being thwarted as regards opportunities for promotion* but also of *being unfairly treated.* According to Herzberg, factors such as the work itself, recognition, and salary—which we also encountered in the context of satisfaction—now have another meaning: they often go hand in hand with dissatisfaction with the policy and the management of the company.

Two-factor theory bears upon two interconnected themes. The first theme relates to the distinction between work content and work context factors. Work-content factors, according to Herzberg et al. (1959), are responsible for the creation of satisfaction (the so-called "satisfiers"). If an element is missing in one or more or these factors—e.g. if a person has no responsibility—this does not result in dissatisfaction but in a neutral feeling: It doesn't matter. They call these intrinsic factors *motivators.* Incidentally, we would like to point out that this terminology ("satisfiers are motivators", "motivators can only create satisfaction", etc.) has not exactly contributed to a clarification of the concept of satisfaction compared to that of motivation.

Conversely, work-context factors can only cause dissatisfaction ("dissatisfiers"), namely if something is lacking—e.g. in the domain of

leadership. If, however, there is nothing wrong, then satisfaction does not occur, but again a neutral feeling: You don't notice them. These aspects must be taken care of—hence the term *hygiene factors*—if dissatisfaction is to be avoided.

The second theme of the two-factor theory focuses on the more general relationship between situational factors and attitudes. As a rule, researchers assume that these factors are located on a *continuum:* a positive influence from a factor is supposed to lead to increased satisfaction and a negative influence from the same factor to increased dissatisfaction. It seems preferable, according to Herzberg et al. (1959), to assume that satisfaction and dissatisfaction are not opposite poles, but instead form independent variables.

In 1959, the authors categorized their theory as a hypothetical interpretation, thus recognizing that it contains a certain amount of speculation. A few years later, this reticence on the part of Herzberg (1966)—the other authors were no longer involved—has disappeared. Furthermore, in his view a general theory of human nature exists: The Old Testament figure of Adam represents the hygiene-seeker (shelter; hiding away), whereas Abraham is the manifestation of the "motivated" being (on the way to unknown horizons).

Were there in fact any research outcomes that justified the making of such leaps? It is certainly the case that this theory has made a profound impression. The emphasis that it placed on content features had strong appeal for the business community. Furthermore, during the 1960s there was increasing interest in the opportunities for the job enlargement and job enrichment. Herzberg's plea for "job enrichment" (e.g. 1968, 1976) now formed a logical corollary to his theory. People will derive more satisfaction from tasks to which extra "vertical" task elements have been added; these increase the opportunities for individual responsibility, scope for decision-making, and growth. In satisfaction research, too, Herzberg's work offered a considerable challenge, principally because it represented a break with the more classical definition according to which satisfaction and dissatisfaction are part of one continuum and do not have any fundamentally different causal factors. This led to an abundance of empirical research into the validity of the theory.

The results of this research have led to what is known as the "Herzberg controversy". If Herzberg's research method is followed, his theory can generally be supported; if, however, any other method is used, then the theory is almost never supported. This means that Herzberg's results are method linked and that his "theory" is probably based on an artifact of this method. If a person is satisfied, then he puts the reasons for this down to himself (intrinsic); if he is dissatisfied, then he attributes the reason to his environment (extrinsic).

We would like to stress, however, that Herzberg was one of the first to stress the importance of the distinction between intrinsic and extrinsic variables. The meaning of that distinction, however, is different from what Herzberg stated: Work-content variables often appear to be of great importance as regards the occurrence of *both* satisfaction and dissatisfaction. Work-context variables are often less important in both respects.

Once the theory proved to be untenable, researchers lost interest in it. According to Schneider (1985), this loss of interest was also caused by the theory's failing to take sufficient account of individual differences. Perhaps this point does apply in particular to the approach that comes up in the following section (for further reading on Herzberg see Thierry, 1968, 1969; Thierry & Drenth, 1970; Locke, 1976; Locke & Henne, 1986).

2.7 Maslow: Need gratification and satisfaction

In common with Herzberg's theory, this theory has become widely known among the business community, through the publications of McGregor (e.g. 1960) among others. Maslow (1954) assumes a hierarchy of human needs, which he divides into five categories. Although each category is given a simple "label" it should not be forgotten that each type of need comprises quite a large number of different behavioral phenomena; a small selection of these are given. The five categories are:

1. Physiological needs (e.g. hunger, thirst, fresh air, sex).

2. Need for security (for example, for method and order in life, for safety).
3. Need to belong (the "social" needs, such as affection, friendship, contact with others, love)
4. Need for recognition and esteem. A distinction is made between:
   a. needs for self-respect, self-confidence, desire to achieve, competence;
   b. needs for respect from others, reputation, status, power.
5. Needs for self-actualization (i.e. personal growth, development, "becoming what you can be").

If a number of basic conditions are met—such as living in freedom and having an understanding environment—then, according to Maslow, each person will strive to satisfy these needs in the order in which they are listed. A person will only seek to satisfy a need from a "higher" category if the need from the "lower" category that directly precedes it has largely been satisfied ("gratification"). The motivation towards behavior is thus determined by the lowest need that exists at any particular time. As soon as this need is satisfied, it loses its motivating power ("satisfaction"). Just prior to this, a "higher" need can begin to act as a motivator. In Maslow's view, it is only the need for self-actualization that will never reach a final state of satisfaction. The more this need is met—i.e. the more it is "satisfied"—the stronger the need for self-actualization will become. Maslow argues that if there is healthy development, people will pass through all the need categories to finally get around to the need for personal growth and development. In Maslow's view, a person's development can be described according to the need level that (s)he is endeavoring to satisfy.

The fact that this theory has gained widespread popularity is perhaps primarily due to its clarity (at least at first sight) and with its intuitively appealing structure. Yet objections have been raised from various sources, particularly regarding content and ethics, whereas there is very little empirical support for the theory as a whole. A first point is that each need category has a rather complex composition, that—partly due to this—many problems have occurred in operationalizing (aspects of) needs, and that difficulties have thus also arisen in unambiguously classifying a behavioral aspect under one category. Alderfer's research is interesting in this context (e.g. 1972). He identifies three needs: "existence" (material existence), "relatedness" (interpersonal social), and "growth" (personal growth). In his view, this framework is conceptually more correct; furthermore, there is no rigid hierarchic relationship between these three needs. This last aspect refers to a second point of criticism. The assumed hierarchical structure implies that the "following" need can only function as a motivator once the "previous" need has been satisfied. Yet it regularly appears that behavior is aimed at simultaneously satisfying various categories of needs. It also occurs that behavior is oriented towards "higher" needs while "lower" needs are not satisfied or may even be neglected. Latham (1988) mentions a third problem: how exactly should Maslow's theory be applied? Is the idea that a company or organization should direct policy principally towards satisfying the three "lower" needs so that each employee will almost automatically focus on the two "higher" needs? Which behavior indicates that this is actually happening and that it is effective? We would like to add that a commonly occurring "application" has been the establishing of a link between Maslow's lower needs and Herzberg's hygiene variables. Consequently, extraordinarily *little* emphasis was laid on aspects such as work situation, security, pay, etc.; after all, these aspects were not really important anyway, were they? Particularly as a result of these points of criticism, the tenability of the concept of "need" has been increasingly called into question (see also Wahba & Bridwell, 1976; Staw, 1984; Petri, 1986; Locke & Henne, 1986; see also section 2.1).

Duijker (1975, 1976) has pointed out that Maslow's hypothesis that it is possible to determine whether a person's development is "healthy" is scientifically untenable and ethically "intolerable". Then Maslow argues that people can be characterized by the need level that they have satisfied, his implication being that there is a hierarchy of people. In addition, as was mentioned earlier, this theory provides no recognition of the role of a whole range of individual-linked variables, such as personality traits, biographical data,

skill levels, etc. (see also Huizinga, 1970; Koopman-Iwema, 1980; Ten Horn, 1983; Pinder, 1984).

2.8 Locke and Latham: Goal setting

In order to clearly understand the concept of "goal" it is necessary first to examine Locke's fairly specific description of the concepts of "need" and "value" (Locke, 1969, 1976, 1986). *Needs* are innate: They are fundamental in nature and their objectives are the survival and well-being of the organism. In addition to physical needs—such as food, regulating temperature, etc.—there are psychological needs: self-esteem, growth, etc. Deprivation of a need does not automatically create the motivation to exhibit goal-oriented behavior, because the individual must discover by means of cognitions which need is at issue, what his/her options for acting might be, etc. Locke's belief that a need theory such as this cannot take account of individual differences is an important one. Such differences are addressed, however, in the concept of *values*: these relate to what an individual wants to preserve or attain. They reflect what the individual considers to be good or bad and include both moral beliefs and short-term preferences. For example, a person wishing to have a career (need) might be able to become a sports instructor or a programmer (both are values).

The meaning of *goal* corresponds to a value but is far more specific. It conveys the way in which the individual wishes to put his/her values into practice and which actions need to be performed in order to achieve this. In terms of the previous example, the goals bear upon the training, performance, and actions, etc. that will be necessary to achieve them. According to Locke, cognitions play an important role in these three concepts: people learn for instance how values can be reached via goal setting and actions. They develop expectations, e.g. about themselves (self-efficacy; see section 2.4), etc.

The actual goal-setting theory is based on a number of simple hypotheses (see also Locke & Latham, 1984). There is strong motivation to increase performance when:

● the goal set is *high* (i.e. is rather difficult);

- the goal is *precisely* formulated (i.e. it specifies what must be done when);
- there is regular *feedback* (i.e. in terms of the goal to be achieved);
- the goal is *accepted* by those concerned.

What actually happens if goals are set that meet these four conditions? A goal specifies the direction of action as well as that (amount, quality) which must be achieved. Assuming that the person has a certain degree of freedom of action in his work, it subsequently leads to sustaining the required behavior. Compared with OB-mod, (or operant conditioning; see section 2.3), the view underlying the goal-setting theory is that the cognitions involved in setting a goal function as *mediator* and *moderator* variables respectively, with respect to the relation between reinforcers on the one hand (e.g. participation, pay, recognition, etc.) and behavior on the other (performance). Locke and Latham (1990b) integrated these notions in the so-called High Performance Cycle.

A considerable body of literature has become available, derived partly from laboratory experiments and partly from practical situations (see also Locke & Latham, 1990a). From this it appears that if the four conditions are met, goal setting leads to the accepting of challenges, clearer expectations from others regarding the person's work, and spontaneous competition. In particular, setting goals raises or improves the level of performance and increases job satisfaction and satisfaction with performance. This theory has, furthermore, provided the stimulus for the development of a number of important personnel and organization management methods, while the theory is also used to explain why existing methods function effectively. These include the situational interview in selection situations, performance appraisal (Behavior Observation Scale), and training for problem-solving. Such applications have been greatly benefited by the existence of a handbook providing practical guidance (Locke & Latham, 1984, 1990a). Various authors argue that this theory is one of the most valid contemporary motivation theories (see also Pinder, 1984; Staw, 1984; Schneider, 1985).

"Goal-setting" theory remains for many a fascinating research theme. Nevertheless, the question is whether the reported results can be interpreted content-wise. In Figure 11.1 we characterized this theory as processual because it provides a psychological explanation of the way in which behavior develops, although not the "why and whither". The empirical fact that goals that are consciously set can radically influence performance does not in itself provide an explanation. Perhaps "goal setting" is primarily (as the title of a 1984 publication describes it) a *method*—albeit a successful one. The fact that this method often appears to deliver the desired results could be explained in terms of OB-modification (section 2.3), self-efficacy (2.4), and probably also expectancy (2.11) (further reading: Kanfer, 1990; Kleinbeck, Quast, Thierry, & Häcker, 1990; Tubbs & Ekeberg, 1991; Ford, 1992; Erez, Kleinbeck, & Thierry, forthcoming).

2.9   Deci: Cognitive evaluation

In the motivation theories that have so far been reviewed in this chapter an important, if not dominant, role is assigned to situational variables. Reinforcement occurs because a worthwhile outcome is linked with previous behavior. Cognitions concerning internal or external "loci" (Rotter, see section 2.5) are based on generalizations regarding what the person has experienced and learned. Goals—often set by third parties—that meet specific conditions (Locke & Latham, see section 2.8) can determine motivation and performance. By shaping features of the (work) situation—at least, so many theories assume—the nature, intensity, and direction of (working) people's motivation can be influenced.

Yet is this hypothesis correct when the individual considers his/her own feelings and experiences? Is it not often the case that the cause of specific behavior is located "within the person"? In other words, can behavior not also be *intrinsically* motivated without there being any extrinsic cause? Deci's cognitive evaluation theory has a bearing on this theme (Deci, 1975; Deci & Porac, 1978; Deci & Ryan, 1985). His theory provides a remarkable elaboration on the theme central to attribution theories: To what do people attribute the causes of their own and others' behavior?

Deci holds that each person has two basal, survival-oriented needs: the need to be *competent* and the need to *be personally the cause* of one's own behavior ("personal causation", see DeCharms, 1968). That is why each person seeks out situations which challenge him/her up to a certain point after which (s)he endeavors to face up to the challenges. Intrinsically motivated behavior is that behavior which a person chooses to make him/herself feel competent and self-determining. This behavior will, however, be interrupted from time to time as a result of primary drives aroused by hunger, thirst, etc. (for other descriptions of intrinsic motivation, see Thierry, 1990).

The core subject area of Deci's theory concerns the effect of extrinsic inducements on intrinsic motivation. A person works on a particular task on the basis of intrinsic motives. Now, suppose that each time something is achieved or a particular result is attained (s)he immediately receives a financial reward for it (the so-called "contingent" payment). The person's experience will then be that (s)he is no longer the cause of his/her own behavior. The "locus of causality" shifts: the person's re-evaluation implies that (s)he will attribute the "locus" to the external "source" that hands out the reward, and thus his/her intrinsic motivation will plummet. Why is this? According to Deci, each outcome has two components: a *behavior-controlling* and an *informative* component. In the example, the former is at issue: someone else or something else determines, through the giving of a reward, what is preferable. A cause located outside the person governs his/her behavior.

If the person receives a contingent verbal reward—e.g. an appreciative word is given for each achievement—then it is the informative component is involved, probably as far as men are concerned. The person receives "feedback" about his competence and self-determination, on the basis of which intrinsic motivation remains high. A word of praise to a woman, on the other hand, creates dependence on the "speaker": such behavior control decreases intrinsic motivation. Deci does not explain how this difference can be accounted for, however. If (financial or verbal) inducements are *not* given on a contingent basis—such as when a person is paid for a particular period—then intrinsic motivation remains unchanged. If the contingent financial reward is

dispensed with, then intrinsic motivation increases once again.

Deci designed his theory on the basis of a series of laboratory experiments. The following is a typical example. In the first round each subject is given a number of puzzles to solve. A break is then announced: the researcher leaves the room but the subject is observed, e.g. via a monitor. The subject can do whatever (s)he wants: read the paper, have a cigarette, etc. but (s)he may also solve puzzles. Deci's main interest is this *break behavior:* if the person chooses voluntarily to continue solving the puzzles, then this, according to Deci, denotes intrinsic motivation. If the subject does something else, then the intrinsic motivation is clearly lower and the extrinsic motivation is higher. After the break, the second round, the instruction is given corresponding to the experimental condition concerned (contingent-financial, contingent-verbal, etc.). After once more solving a number of puzzles there is another break. According to Deci, test subjects in the contingent-financial condition less frequently do puzzles in the second break.

There are two reasons why cognitive evaluation theory has attracted considerable interest. This is due in the first place to the hypothesis concerning the relationship between extrinsic outcomes and intrinsic motivation (and outcomes); according to Deci, this relationship is a negative one. A contingent financial reward leads to lower intrinsic motivation. Adherents of operant conditioning theory (section 2.3), however, think that positive interactions occur between both kinds of outcomes: They reinforce each other. Furthermore, according to expectancy theory (section 2.11) the effects are additive: They occur alongside each other. Second, the potential practical implications are significant: Working with deadlines set by a third party and the regular assessment of learning achievements are supposed to have a negative effect on intrinsic motivation. The same is considered to be the case with those forms of performance-related pay in which performance is immediately and frequently remunerated. And if a person's intrinsic motivation is high—it is expected that this will occur when the quality of work is high—would it suffice to have a minimum of leadership and coordination from his/her supervisor? And could the pay then perhaps be slightly reduced (after all, (s)he is working on the basis of "intrinsic" motives)?

Over the past 15–20 years, aspects of cognitive evaluation theory have been put to the test in a fairly large number of experiments (for an overview, see Koopman-Iwema, 1982; Thierry, 1990; Vinke, 1996). In the first place, it was apparent from these that there is little empirical support for the theory and thus also for its supposed practical implications. There was most support for the point that dispensing with extrinsic inducements can lead to higher intrinsic motivation. However, this result can also be accounted for in terms of dissonance reduction (see section 2.10). Unfortunately, in response to this controversy Deci and Ryan (1985) have reformulated their theory in such a way that it has become untestable. They argue, for example, that the quality of an outcome (behavior controlling or informative) is no longer determined by its "source" but solely by the nature of the attribution which the person makes. Second, the theory has been severely criticized for its lack of logical consistency (Bandura, 1977; Locke & Henne, 1986). Elsewhere we have commented that the distinction between intrinsic and extrinsic motivation, which has been made not only by Deci, cannot be upheld either logically or content wise (and in fact is based on a fallacy; Thierry, 1990). That distinction reflects the well-known person-situation dilemma: Is behavior primarily or exclusively determined by personality traits or, on the contrary, by situation variables? Motivation towards behavior does not arise either through aspects "outside of" or "inside" the person, but occurs through frequently complicated *interactions* between personality traits and situation variables.

2.10 Adams: Equity theory

In his theory of social comparison, Festinger (1950, 1954) argues that each human being has a tendency to evaluate his/her opinions and skills. If objective norms for this are lacking, then the person will seek others who differ as little as possible from him/her in order to compare him/herself with them. If the comparison proves to be positive, the person is pleased. A negative result produces dissonance and the person will endeavor to modify his/her behavior accordingly. If (s)he

compares a particular *opinion* with someone else, then (s)he will attempt to make this as similar as possible to that of the other person (the tendency to uniformity). If, on the other hand, it is *a skill* that is being compared, then the person will endeavor to distinguish him/herself from the other person and try to be just that bit better (the tendency to discriminate).

In his theory on distributive justice, Homans (1961) has developed this process of comparison in terms of investments, costs, and outcomes. Suppose a female employee wonders whether she receives an equitable immaterial and material reward for her performance compared with a male colleague. Investments refers to inputs of a fairly general nature: e.g. her age, training, experience, etc. In addition she has had costs: efforts made, risks taken, working pace, etc. Against this there are outcomes, such as status, recognition, payment, and attention from others. If the profit (i.e. the difference between inducements and costs) both for her and her colleague is proportional to the investments, then there is distributive justice. If the relationship is disproportionate, then dissatisfaction will result: that triggers the introduction of changes.

Adams—whose theory we will examine in rather more detail—holds that Homans is not nearly specific enough about the events that can lead to injustice and also about the effects of this (Adams, 1963, 1965). In an exchange relationship each person strives, according to Adams, to achieve a *balance* between his inputs and his outcomes compared to that of the referent other(s) as the person perceives it. Inputs includes both investments and costs (Homans), such as training, effort, intelligence, etc. Outcomes includes e.g. the performance, pay, recognition, and criticism received (these examples show that some costs—in Homans' terms—can be considered as outcomes). The question of whether a particular attribute is defined by the person as an input or as an outcome depends primarily on whether the person *recognizes* that attribute. Subsequently, it depends on his/her assessment of whether the attribute is *relevant* to the comparison. The deciding factor in the choice of the referent other(s) is their relevance to the person (who is comparing him/herself) in the comparison process.

The degree of "equity" is now, according to Adams, determined by the ratio between one's own inputs and outcomes relative to that of the referent other. Equity occurs when this relation is seen as *equal* ("consonance"). If the relationship is unequal—feeling of inequity—"dissonance" occurs: The dissatisfaction resulting from this motivates the person towards behavior to restore the balance. In Figure 11.2 we illustrate various forms of (in)equity. The assumption is that a person is comparing the relation between her efforts and payment with that of someone else.

We can see that three forms of consonance occur (a, d, and e): A distinctive feature is that the *relationship* is seen as equal. The unequal relationship is characteristic of the three forms of dissonance (b, c, and f).

The behavior of the person to reduce the dissonance depends among other things on the type of dissonance that occurs. Furthermore, the person can make use of the fact that some attributes are additive—e.g. make more effort, get less criticism—whereas others are exchangeable (what was "formerly" an input will "from now on" be seen as an outcome, etc.). Options for the person include:

1. *Changing the inputs:* in b (Figure 11.2) the person could for example reduce his effort whereby he strives for a low/low : high/high ratio (this form of consonance corresponds to type e). Suppose it is a case of overpayment (type c): It is likely that the person will try to increase his inputs. Adams assumes that input-reduction will occur more frequently in the case of underpayment than the increase of inputs will occur in the case of overpayment, because people tend to minimize their "costs" and maximize their "profit".

2. *Changing the outcomes:* in case b the person can also attempt to get more pay (striving for consonance form a). In the case of c, reduction of pay could also be considered. However, in view of Adams' assumption about human behavior referred to above, it is likely that outcome-increase will occur more frequently where there is underpayment than outcome-reduction where there is overpayment.

3. *Cognitive "reinterpretation":* let us assume that the person considers that the changes mentioned in 1 and 2 above are not possible or are not effective enough. The person can resort to reinterpretation, "distortion" of components of the relationship. In type f, e.g., the person comes to the conclusion that (s)he has after all come up with a pretty

FIGURE 11.2

		Person	Other	Result
a.	Effort	high	high	Consonance
	Payment	high	high	
b.	Effort	high	high	Dissonance ('underpayment')
	Payment	low	high	
c.	Effort	low	low	Dissonance ('overpayment')
	Payment	high	low	
d.	Effort	high	high	Consonance
	Payment	low	low	
e.	Effort	high	low	Consonance
	Payment	high	low	
f.	Effort	high	low	Dissonance (maximum)
	Payment	low	high	

Examples of consonance and dissonance in Adams' theory.

smart approach (for which, of course, (s)he cannot be rewarded "in this setting"; the person adds an outcome); furthermore, (s)he thinks that "you could tell" that the other person was really having trouble carrying out his/her tasks (the person adds an input to the other person). Adams also points out that it is rather difficult fundamentally to reinterpret one's own inputs or outcomes.

4. *Retreat:* a more radical option is that the person tries to leave the situation and e.g. resigns. This may be preceded by a period of increasing absenteeism, a decreasing feeling of involvement, increasing apathy, etc.

On the basis of this theory a large number of laboratory experiments have been carried out. One of the findings is that the theory receives more support if the person and the referent other are in a direct exchange relationship with each other than if they are indirectly connected via a third party, e.g. an employer. Furthermore, it emerges that the motivation to strive for consonance is stronger in the case of undervaluing (i.e. underpayment) than in that of overvaluing.

This implies, according to Syroit (1984), that there are situations in which the person does not strive for complete balance but is apparently satisfied with a *partial* elimination of the dissonance that is occurring. Yet the theory is unclear regarding the circumstances under which the person is apparently able to tolerate some inequity.

Another criticism is that the definition of inputs or outcomes is unsatisfactory. Depending on how it suits the person, various features can sometimes fall into one category and sometimes into the other. A similar criticism bears upon the factors that determine the choice of a referent other: The theory does not make it clear which these are. Thus, for example, research by Patchen (1961) and Goodman (1974) reveals that these choices can take place on "instrumental" grounds; with a view to a specific form of consonance another factor may be selected. This raises the fundamental question of the extent to which (this form of) social comparison is "generically" original.

Another handicap is that practical applications of the theory in field situations have met with little success. Although on more than one occasion the theory was able to offer a workable explanation,

there is still a great deal lacking in its predictive power in situations outside the laboratory (for a more detailed account, see Campbell & Pritchard, 1976; Rijsman & Wilke, 1980; Syroit, 1984). In various other social-comparison theories the importance of procedural justice (in addition to distributive justice) is stressed. Such procedures may contribute to the establishment of more stable reference norms for assessing fairness or justice (see e.g. Hermkens, 1995; Thierry, 1998).

2.11 Expectancy theory

This motivation theory—of a cognitive and processual nature—has enjoyed a dominant position for more than 25 years. The theory has formed the point of departure for a considerable body of empirical research, while its core subject areas have been developed in approaches in various other domains, e.g. pay and leadership (see Chapters 12 and 13, Vol. 4, of this *Handbook*). Various components of the theory or operationalizations of them have been subjected to criticism over the years, however; it is partly due to this that there are quite a number of "versions" in circulation. We will begin our discussion with an account of Vroom's (1964) formulation of the theory; then important changes and points of criticism will be addressed.

Vroom's conceptualization displays a strong affinity with the views of Lewin (1938, 1951), while ideas from Edwards' "Subjective Utility Theory" (1954) can also be discerned. Furthermore, it was possible to build on earlier work by Georgopoulos, Mahoney, and Jones (1957). Vroom identifies three models: the motivation model, the valence (or job satisfaction) model, and the performance model. According to the *motivation model*, motivation towards specific behavior is considered to be dependent on:

- the expectation that this behavior will lead to particular outcomes;
- the valence or attractiveness of these outcomes for the person.

The symbolic notation for this is:

$$F_i \stackrel{n}{\underset{j=1}{=}} f\Sigma (E_{ij} V_j), \text{ where:}$$

F_i : the force which is exerted on an individual to act.

E_{ij} : the expectation that behavior $_i$ will lead to outcome $_j$.

V_j : the valence of outcome $_j$.

n : the number of outcomes.

To take an example: the motivation to make a great effort (F_i) is dependent both on the extent to which there is an expectancy that great effort will lead to a qualitatively higher level of performance (E_{ij}) and on the extent to which the person finds a higher level of performance attractive (V_j).

To describe valence, Vroom uses the term "value" of an outcome: this relates to the actual degree of satisfaction which arises as a result of procuring that outcome. The valence of the outcome stands for the anticipated ("expected") degree of satisfaction.

But how does an outcome attain valence for a person? The *valence model* bears upon this. Vroom expresses this as follows:

$$V_j \overset{n}{\underset{k=1}{=}} f\Sigma\,(V_k\,I_{jk}), \text{ where:}$$

V_j : the valence of outcome $_j$.

I_{jk} : the observed instrumentality of outcome $_j$ in order to achieve outcome $_k$.

V_k : the valence of outcome $_k$.

n : the number of outcomes.

A person's preference, neutral attitude or aversion, with regard to a particular outcome is, according to Vroom, a function of the instrumentality of that outcome to reach other outcomes and the valence of those other outcomes. Another example: The valence of a qualitatively higher level of performance for a person is determined by the instrumentality of that performance for earning money, acquiring status, and increasing the chances of promotion *as well as* the valence of money, status, and promotion opportunities for the person in question (the valence of the last three outcomes is again determined by the extent to which it expected that these will be instrumental to obtaining other attractive outcomes, etc.). The instrumentality of an outcome thus bears upon the extent to which a person thinks that it will lead to attaining other outcomes. It is a so-called outcome–outcome relationship. This deviates from

the concept of expectancy (which we came across in the motivation model), which concerns the relationship between behavior and its effects or outcomes.

In the *performance model* it is argued that a person's performance is determined not only by his/her motivation but also by that person's competence. This third model will not be further discussed here.

The valence model is often used in research into job satisfaction and into the preference for and the choice of a profession. Over the years it has undergone few changes (see also Mitchell, 1982). On the other hand, many changes have been made in the motivation model, which of the three is the one that has been used most frequently in research. The following are the most important modifications as far as both models are concerned:

1. Making a distinction between *first- and second-level outcomes*. First-level outcomes bear upon the work behavior of the person in question. These outcomes acquire valence if they are expected to lead to obtaining second-level outcomes (e.g. money, status). Differentiating first-level from second-level outcomes serves to condense, as it were, Vroom's valence and motivation models. The first-level outcomes (e.g. a particular performance level) are explained by the Motivation Model, as a function of the expectation that specific efforts will lead to this performance level and of the valence of that performance level. The valence of the performance level is explained by the Valence Model, i.e. it is dependent on the extent to which this performance level is seen as instrumental to attaining second level outcomes (money, status) and on the valence of those outcomes.

This integration means that we can confine ourselves to one formula; we have chosen Lawler's (1973):

$$F_i \overset{n}{\underset{o=1}{=}} f\Sigma\,[(e\text{--}{>}p)(p\text{--}{>}o)V_o], \text{ where:}$$

F_i : the strength to act.

$e\,\text{--}{>}p$: the expectation that a specific effort will lead to a particular performance.

$p\text{--}{>}o$: the expectation that a particular

performance will result in a specified outcome.

V_o : the valence of the outcome.

n : the number of outcomes.

2. A second modification, which was in fact already assumed in 1., concerns the distinguishing of *different kinds of expectation*. Expectancy-1 (which corresponds to the e−>p relationship referred to in 1.) is the same as Vroom's concept of expectancy. Expectancy-2 (see the (p−>o) relationship in 1.) corresponds to the concept of instrumentality. Vroom's expectancy involves a probability estimate with values ranging from 0.00 (totally uncertain) to 1.00 (totally certain). Instrumentality bears upon a correlation between two outcomes and can thus vary between −1.00 (negative relation) and +1.00 (positive relation). As both kinds of expectancy can be formulated as a probability relationship, diverse researchers have switched over to working exclusively with correlational links.

3. A number of variables from the work situation is added to the model, and various "feedback loops" are also introduced. This has been the principal reason for the sharp increase in the model's complexity, although the changes were made on the assumption that a more contingent approach would benefit the predictive power of the model. Figure 11.3 shows an example of this; it has been derived in part from Lawler (1971, 1973).

The backbone of this model is formed by the relationship between (1) a person's motives and expectations, (3) his/her efforts, (8) his/her performance, (10) the outcomes obtained, and (12) the degree of satisfaction. This relationship is influenced by a number of variables (the unbroken lines), whereas the degree to which the behavior has led to satisfactory outcomes has a feedback effect on various components of the motivation cycle (the dotted lines). There now follow some brief comments on this:

- The motives of a person and his/her expectations (1) regarding the effects of his/her efforts (e−>p) and of his/her performance (p−>o) are influenced by such things as that person's habits, experience in similar situations, observations of others, etc. (2). The resulting action is called the effort (3).
- The extent to which the person's effort results in performance (8) is influenced by individual features (4), e.g. the person's

FIGURE 11.3

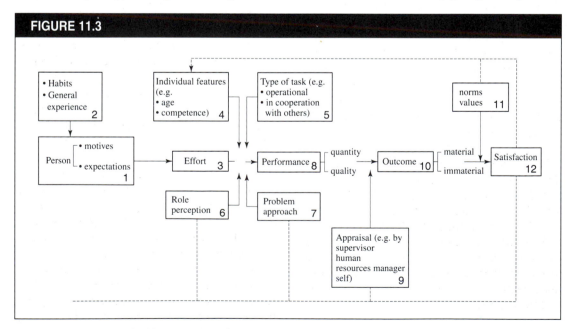

Work-motivation model, derived from expectancy theory.

competence, the type of work (5), the person's perception of what is expected of him/her (6), and by the way in which (s)he tackles a problem (7), e.g. as a whole or one aspect at a time.

- The extent to which the person's performance produces outcomes (10) for him/her is influenced by the way in which that performance is perceived and appraised by others (9).
- The relation between outcomes acquired and the person's satisfaction with these (12) is influenced in turn by norms and values (11) regarding what the correlation between effort and performance on the one hand and the outcomes on the other ought to be. For ease of comparison, a number of lines have not been drawn in; for example, the extent to which acquired outcomes give rise to satisfaction is obviously also determined by the motives which the person has.
- The more unsatisfying the result, the more the person will try to effect changes in his/her own behavior and possibly in that of others (9).

Incidentally, scarcely any examples of studies exist, in which the meaning of all the types of variables mentioned in Figure 11.4 have been simultaneously examined. This kind of model sets stringent standards for the quantity and quality of data, which often cannot (e.g. for practical reasons) be fully met. This may partly be the reason why the proposed refinements and additions to expectancy theory have not led to a better explanation and prediction of behavior (see Van Eerde & Thierry, 1996, for various meta-analyses). The average correlation between predictions based on the expectancy model and criterion behavior (often, performance) still appears to lie between .25 and .30. If we confine ourselves to the valence (satisfaction) model discussed earlier, however, then the results are considerably better (for an overview, see e.g. Mitchell, 1982).

As mentioned earlier, a number of points of criticism have been raised over the years, bearing partly upon "technical" problems, and partly upon fundamental issues. Those relating to technical problems include:

- The outcomes that a researcher includes in a

study are not automatically relevant for all respondents. How many levels (first, second, etc.) should they be relevant for? Should both positive and negative valence outcomes be included?

- If instrumentality (and fairly often expectancy) is defined as a correlation between two variables, then in principle this should be able to assume any value between -1.00 and $+1.00$. Suppose that a researcher is interested in expectations that exist among employees regarding the relationship between their performance and the social-emotional behavior of their supervisor. If the researcher restricts him/herself to one or two questions (as generally happens)—e.g. the extent to which a high level of performance leads to highly social-emotional behavior on the part of the leader—then (s)he is in fact assuming that the answer given applies "across the board". It is quite possible, however, that non-linear links exist, such as when it is anticipated that both a high level of performance and a poor performance will lead to increased attention from the supervisor (though for different reasons), whereas an average performance is accompanied by little attention, etc. This means that quite a large number of (interval) positions need to be distinguished per variable (Thierry, 1991).

- From a theoretical point of view, the concept of effort is distinctly useful. Problems arise, however, when it has to be identified and operationalized in respondents' behavioral cycle, because effort cannot always clearly be differentiated from the concept of performance. The person who wishes to achieve a high level of performance carries out a whole range of actions, sets intermediate goals, produces partial achievements, etc. Which of these behaviors can unequivocally be termed "effort"?

- The terms in the model—e.g. performance (as criterion), instrumentality, outcome—should not just be multiplied together (e.g. Koopman-Iwema, 1980; Mellenbergh, Molendijk, De Haan, & Ter Horst, 1990; Evans, 1991). Yet even if that does happen, adding the "predictors" sometimes leads to a higher correlation with the criterion than multiplying them (see also Ilgen & Klein, 1989). A more fundamental question is whether choice situations—the person must actively make a choice—come up as often in practice as many researchers tend to assume. For example, there must be a "discrete" setting, in which the problem with which the person is confronted deviates from the type of events that he had experienced up to now. The person must, according to Carver and Scheier (1981), experience at least some uncertainty regarding the course to be taken. Yet, how often does such uncertainty arise? March and Simon (1958) have pointed out that for a whole range of decision-making problems a network of alternatives is called on (so-called "evoked alternatives"). This network consists of a set of well-known ways, tested solutions, and generally established assessments. If there is a structured problem, usually of an operative nature, then the person resorts in general to a standard program (see Chapter 14 of this *Handbook* for a more detailed treatment of this theme).

Up to now we have addressed the question of how often choice situations arise to which expectancy theory relates. A more fundamental question is whether the assumption is actually correct that an individual first sets goals (pursues certain outcomes), then develops expectations about the ways in which these can be achieved, and subsequently behaves accordingly. Adherents of attribution theory assume a different sequence: for example, Weick (1979) argues that the person interprets in retrospect, *after* his/her behavior, which goals were pursued, and which causes underlay that behavior. Furthermore, much everyday behavior, according to the "information-processing" approach (e.g. Langer, 1978; Taylor & Fiske, 1978), is of a *non*-cognitive nature. People often analyze their situation on the basis of rough "scripts" and let their decisions be guided by prototypes, general outlines, and bias. According to Salancik and Pfeffer (1977), however, *social* factors play an essential role in processing and interpreting information. The views, opinions, and attitudes of others in the person's environment determine to an important extent what the person perceives. This "social information processing" theory, however, is almost exclusively applied in analysing task variables (see also Ilgen & Klein, 1989; and Chapter 6, Vol. 3 of this *Handbook*) and until now has not led to an essentially modified approach (see also Stone, 1992).

Though some important basic assumptions of expectancy theory are disputed, this does not prove that those assumptions are often incorrect. On the contrary, over the past couple of years researchers have once more shown increasing interest (e.g. Van Eerde & Thierry, 1996). A contributing factor has certainly been the fact that, other than had been assumed for some time, "goal setting" and expectancy reach the same predictions (see also Ilgen & Klein, 1989; Locke & Latham, 1990a). Nevertheless, further research is needed into the conditions under which path–goal choice situations occur. In addition to the themes briefly indicated earlier, attention should furthermore be devoted to such questions as:

- can the person determine his/her own behavior to a fair extent?
- with regard to "expectancy" and instrumentality, does the person take account of obstacles and chance factors can influence his/her own performance? Does the person change his/her cognitions about this during a behavioral cycle?
- are the outcomes really dependent on the person's behavior, and if so, how much time elapses between the two? (see also Mitchell, 1974; Feather, 1982; Ilgen & Klein, 1989).

2.12   Determinants of motivation

In this chapter we have discussed motivation theories classified along two dimensions: content versus process and reinforcement versus cognitive. In the commentary on the first dimension we pointed out that a satisfactory theory should examine both the "what" and the "how" of motivation. It is apparent from the previous sections that most theories comply with this requirement, albeit in different ways.

The second dimension, in our view, contains *differences in emphasis* but not contradictions. Reinforcement, on the one hand, can of course be interpreted as mechanistic without any role at all being assigned to cognitions. And cognitions may obviously be seen as operations and constructions of the autonomous person who is constantly creating his world anew. It is our view, however, that regulating mechanisms (habits, learned behavior–outcome relationships, scripts, programs) play a prominent role in a whole range of the person's "cognitive" representations, opinions, intentions, etc. They occur immediately in each representation of possible future behavior. One of the criticisms of expectancy theory (section 2.11) bears upon this theme: The person makes use of routine programs for a number of decisions. On the other hand, it is our view that conscious cognitive operations cannot be excluded from reinforcement processes. The person is not a passive creature with no will of its own who is subject to reinforcement processes; (s)he can change behavior–outcome relationships and add to them selectively. Bandura's theory (section 2.4) provides an example of this. But it is also true of "OB-modification" (section 2.3). Reinforcement can also be one of the explanatory concepts in "goal setting", etc.

To sum up, we argue that the theme of *"behavior–outcome relationships"* forms the core subject area in almost every motivation theory. A few theories place more emphasis on the way in which outcomes are related to the person's "preceding" behavior; others are more concerned with the way in which behavior is influenced by ensuing outcomes. Yet each time it is the *same* type of relationships that are at issue: In part, these are learned and have become a component of the basic behavioral repertoire; in part, they can moreover be intentionally constructed or changed. Reinforcement and cognitive operations are not antitheses but are simultaneously occurring, *interactive* processes in the motivation of behavior. Motivated behavior can be defined as the result of interactions between "habits" and "intentions".

The various theories could also have been described along a third dimension: *dispositional variables versus situational characteristics* (Thierry, Koopman, & Van der Flier, 1992). The theme sketched here addresses, on the one hand, the question of whether certain innate needs (not purely physiologically determined), motives or qualities are attributed to the person, which are therefore of a fairly stable nature (with regard to time and situation). On the other hand, there is the basic assumption that the differences in motivation between people can be accounted for almost exclusively by the variation in work (situation) variables. In the past couple of years the discussion on this has flared up, in particular as regards satisfaction; for this reason we will return

to this briefly in the next section. What is remarkable is that in the (more) content-oriented motivation theories either this aspect is not pursued at all or it is assumed that needs have arisen through learning processes. This means that the dominance of situational variables tends to be taken for granted. In the domain of work and organization, then (in addition, of course, to bio- and demographical variables), attention focuses particularly on five determinants: work content (primarily task features); leadership and management; social relationships among people; work conditions; labour conditions (e.g. pay). These will not be discussed here: In this *Handbook* they come up in other chapters (Vol. 3, Chapters 6, 13, and 15; Vol. 2, Chapter 6; and Chapter 12, respectively). It is our view, however, that an "internal" (dispositional)—"external" (situational) antithesis is rather unproductive, and that an "interactional" approach based on both orientations might be expected to be more fruitful.

3   SATISFACTION

3.1   Definition and categorization

We have already come across this concept a number of times in our review of motivation. Generally speaking, satisfaction plays a role in every motivation theory, namely, whenever the question arises of the extent to which a particular need is satisfied or an important motive is achieved. In a number of the motivation theories that we have discussed, however, satisfaction has an even more specific, pronounced meaning: In Maslow's theory, it determines whether a need at a higher level in the hierarchy will produce behavior. Herzberg's two factors—motivators and hygiene variables—are even quite often called after the exclusive effects that they are supposed to evoke: "satisfiers" and "dissatisfiers". This has persuaded some authors to categorize Maslow's and Herzberg's approaches under the heading of satisfaction theory. The latter also applies fairly often to Adams' "equity" theory, which chiefly focuses on the behavior that will occur as a result of dissatisfaction (dissonance) (see also Schneider, 1985). In the same way, the "information-processing" and the "social-information-processing" theories (Staw, 1984; Griffin & Bateman, 1986), which were touched on in section 2.11, are treated as satisfaction theories. Furthermore, Vroom's satisfaction (valence) model has already been examined in the discussion on expectancy theory. In other words, it appears at least that there is a close conceptual relationship between motivation and satisfaction.

Nevertheless, definitions of (work) satisfaction are often fairly meaningless. Locke (1976, p.1328) argues that it is the result of a person's *perception* that her job enables her to actualize the motives—in Locke's terminology, values—which are important to her. Ten years later the emphasis has changed slightly (Locke & Henne, 1986): Satisfaction with the work is the *pleasant emotional state* which flows from someone realizing his/her motives (values) in the work. According to Schneider (1985), the key issue is *attitudes*—evaluations, feelings—*towards outcomes* or circumstances, whereas Griffith and Bateman (1986) emphasize that the central idea is a *global concept*, which is constructed out of *specific facets* (satisfaction with the job, pay, etc.). Our general description runs as follows: Job satisfaction concerns the degree to which the person is satisfied with (aspects of) his/her job and job situation. It implies that a need is satisfied, a motive is achieved, and a goal is met. Incidentally, we also use the term satisfaction to indicate the *degree* of (dis)satisfaction.

In the foregoing, fairly widely accepted definitions, a direct or indirect link is thus established with motivation, although aspects relating to content will not be discussed here. It is equally remarkable that although a great many results from satisfaction research appear each year, the criticism that its theoretical background is very weak continues to grow (see also Staw, 1984; Schneider, 1985; Locke & Henne, 1986; Biessen, 1992). Griffin and Bateman (1986) describe satisfaction as one of the most "a-theoretical" subjects within work and organization psychology.

In our view it is not so much that a separate, "independent" theory needs to be developed about satisfaction, but rather that the concept should be embedded in a model or theory on the motivation of work behavior. It is not only the various definitions of satisfaction that give occasion for

this, but particularly the conclusion that satisfaction—whether in a general or in a more specific sense—plays an integral role in motivation theories. On the basis of the motivation model shown in Figure 11.3—the main outline described in section 2.11 can be used to represent, if necessary with some additions or omissions, a number of motivation theories—we will mention three different lines of approach regarding the concept of satisfaction. Within the context of each line of approach, theories about particular aspects can, of course be designed regarding the specific role of satisfaction within it. Our three categories consist of:

1. Satisfaction as the *result* of a behavioral cycle. It reflects the person's evaluation of the outcomes (s)he has produced in relation to needs, motives, values, or goals that are important to the person. Theoretically, it is the (often causal) relationship between motives, behavior, and outcomes that is of particular importance.

2. Satisfaction as a component of the *controlling and regulating system*. The emphasis is now placed on the extent to which the evaluation of the result causes the introduction of changes. Anyone who is not satisfied with what (s)he received is motivated to go in search of possible improvements. These might concern others (e.g. the way in which the person is appraised), or the approach to a task, but might also relate to the goals set or motives, etc. If, on the other hand, the person is satisfied, then (s)he will strive to repeat the behavioral cycle unless other motives start to become more dominant. Theoretically, the causal relationship between outcomes, behavior, and motives is the central issue. The role which satisfaction plays in social comparison theories—e.g. "equity" theory—provides an illustration of this line of approach.

3. Satisfaction as a *cause* of behavior. Here, the emphasis is on the behavior that arises partly as a result of (dis)satisfaction, such as making complaints, absenteeism, employee turnover, hazardous lifestyle, etc. A person who is dissatisfied with the outcomes produced (see 1.) and does not consider him/herself capable of altering them (see 2.) will be more likely to strive for outcomes outside work or possibly in another organization.

If a person is happy about the extent to which (s)he can learn from his/her work, then the feeling of involvement will probably increase, just as the number of hours that (s)he spends on that work will increase, etc. From a theoretical viewpoint, it involves the causal relationship between (dis) satisfaction and behavior, whereby the considering of alternative modes of behavior is of particular importance.

These lines of approach have a certain hierarchic relation to each other. More importantly, all three can be categorized as motivation issues without designating any one particular motivation theory. Satisfaction can certainly be defined in conceptual terms as an evaluation or a feeling of satisfaction. But the circumstances under which it is being examined ("point of view") make a big difference.

The third approach will not be further discussed in this chapter (for an overview, see Locke & Henne, 1986; Griffin & Bateman, 1986; see also Chapter 6, Vol. 2 of this *Handbook*). First of all we will discuss four satisfaction theories. Two of these do not actually reflect much more than the way in which the concept is measured. Nevertheless, a basic order can be established (see Figure 11.4).

Satisfaction theories differ from each other in the extent to which they either assume the existence of "*needs*" or that solely *situational variables* are reviewed. We already came across this dimension in section 2.12; the question of whether "needs" are innate, however, does not play a special role here. In the three theories concerned in Figure 11.4 (discrepancy; need fulfillment; facet satisfaction) only the presence of certain needs or motives is assumed; the content of these is left

aside (we would like to point out that Figure 11.4 only indicates a sequence and does not show absolute positions).

After these theories have been discussed, various types of measuring instrument will be sketched, after which we turn to the question of whether it is preferable to define satisfaction as a global concept or as a concept composed of specific facets. This section concludes with a discussion of the relation between satisfaction and performance. (Readers wishing to familiarize themselves further with satisfaction or with the theories we have not discussed are referred to Vroom, 1964; Campbell, Dunnette, Lawler, & Weick, 1970; Lawler, 1973; Locke & Henne, 1986; Griffin & Bateman, 1986; Cranny, Smith, & Stone, 1992.)

3.2   Satisfaction theories

3.2.1   Discrepancy

A considerable number of satisfaction studies are based on the following assumption: Satisfaction is dependent on the extent to which the outcomes which the person perceives him/herself to have received correspond to those which (s)he needs and thus strives for at work. This idea has been developed in the so-called discrepancy model, which has achieved recognition chiefly through the work of Morse (1953), Porter (1961), and Locke (1969). In the model, satisfaction is defined as "degree of discrepancy": The more the outcomes aimed for and the perceived outcomes of the work correspond with each other, the greater the level of satisfaction.

The way in which the concept of discrepancy has been operationalized in the research also

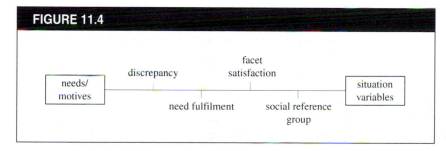

FIGURE 11.4

Order of satisfaction theories.

shows a large number of variations. A first feature concerns to which components the discrepancy relates. One component nearly always concerns the actual outcomes perceived by the person (the so-called "is now" score; see section 3.3). But the other component can relate to a whole range of features; thus it can cover what the person "wants", what (s)he finds "attractive", what (s)he "prefers", what (s)he considers of "importance", what (s)he feels "should" be, what (s)he "expects", or what (s)he has become "adjusted to". Research has shown that the choice of formulation is highly important. Furthermore, it happens fairly often that in addition to asking the question of e.g. what (s)he wants, the person is also asked what is of importance to him/her. A second point concerns the question of *how* the components relate to each other: Fairly often the difference between "wish" and outcome is determined (hence the name discrepancy model), but it also occurs that the product is calculated or that the difference is corrected using a weighting factor, etc. Research has shown, however, that such variations regularly lead to divergent results (see also Wall & Payne, 1973; Ferratt, 1981). In section 3.3 we return to a number of these problems.

3.2.2   *"Need fulfillment"*

According to this theory, satisfaction is determined by the extent to which the work and the work situation produce outcomes worthwhile to the person (Vroom, 1964; Lawler, 1973). In terms of expectancy theory (section 2.11) both "value" and "valence" are involved: Satisfaction thus relates not only to outcomes that have already been acquired but also to those that it is anticipated will be acquired or will be able to be avoided. The sort of questions used to measure satisfaction are of the so-called "is now" type: Questions or descriptions that are as factual as possible are given to the respondent for appraisal. For example: How often does your supervisor consult with you? This regularly adopted approach thus assumes that the degree of satisfaction will be reflected in the appraisal of actual statements or questions: The person's description also indicates what (s)he considers worthwhile and attractive, or alternatively what (s)he finds unimportant.

3.2.3   *Facet satisfaction model*

This model, developed by Lawler (1973), combines equity theory (section 2.10) with discrepancy (section 3.2.1) (see Figure 11.5).

Reading from right to left, we see first that satisfaction is determined by the discrepancy between what the person feels (s)he should receive and what from his/her own observation (s)he actually receives. The conception regarding what should be received—and this is the second point— depends not only on the inputs (the qualifications) which (s)he thinks (s)he has and the requirements of the job, but also on the relationship observed by him/her between the inputs and outcomes of the referent other(s). The perception of the outcomes actually obtained is, on the one hand, determined by his/her actual outcomes and, on the other hand, by the outcomes that the other(s) produced. Various aspects, moreover, affect the perception of inputs and of job features.

A number of studies, e.g. in the domain of pay, make use of aspects of this model. Some of these suggest the inclusion of additional variables, such as actual salary (Berkowitz, Fraser, Treasure, & Cockhran, 1987), and perceived adequacy of the salary system (Dyer & Theriault, 1976; Weiner, 1980). Heneman & Schwab (1985) have argued that salary satisfaction should be conceived in terms of four components (see also Miedema, 1994).

3.2.4   *"Social reference group"*

Both in discrepancy theory and in need-fulfillment theory it is assumed that the person evaluates his/her outcomes in relation to what (s)he is striving for, irrespective of the motive or goal. According to social reference group theory, however, this evaluation occurs in relation to viewpoints and features of the group or (socio-economic) category to which the person belongs. It is on this last aspect that particular stress is laid. Thus, themes that already played a role in the research into *social indicators* (see Chapter 12, Vol. 2, this *Handbook*)—particularly in the area of "quality of working life"—are gaining increasing importance in satisfaction research. For example, the following distinctions are made: size of the town of residence; number of employees; number of union members; amount

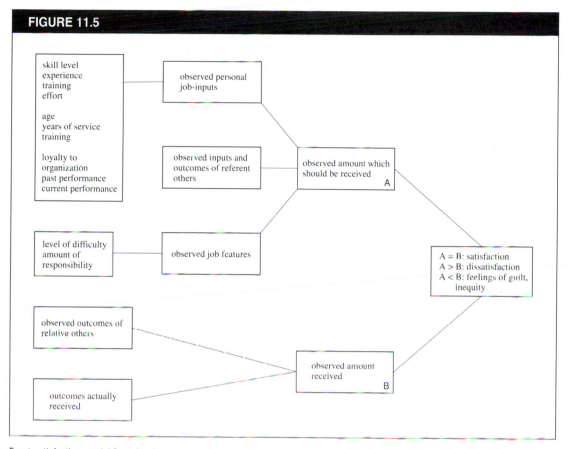

FIGURE 11.5

Facet satisfaction model from Lawler.

and allocation of wages and salaries; level and distribution of purchasing power; quality of housing and amenities; etc. The line of thought now is that a person evaluates features of her work (situation) in terms of her frame of reference. An illustration: Two people earn exactly the same income; the income of the one falls into the top income category in the organization in which she works, whereas the other's income belongs in the middle category in her company; the two people will differ in their levels of satisfaction.

It goes without saying that the researcher should not just collect data at random on a whole range of themes but should at the very least have a notion (in fact, a theory about a particular aspect) of the relation between satisfaction and those themes. Furthermore, *norms* will need to be developed based on previous research. On the basis of this it is then determined which degree of satisfaction is indicated by the answers—mostly of the descrip-

tive type—to a questionnaire (section 3.2.2 and 3.4).

The frame of reference in the examples given was primarily of a socio-economic nature. It can also bear upon someone's personal past and future: a combination of both—for which the term adaption level is used—is aimed at in the construction of the well-known "Job Descriptive Index" (see also section 3.4, and, more generally, Katzell, Barrett, & Parker, 1961; Hulin, 1966; Ronan, 1970; Locke, 1976; James & Tetrick, 1986; Ironson, Smith, Brannick, Gibson, & Paul, 1989; Biessen, 1992).

3.3 Determinants

The theories that have just been reviewed do not really deserve the name. In all four an indication is given of how satisfaction should be measured but concepts such as needs, motives, or goals are only referred to in very general terms. This also goes for the situational variables; which they are and how satisfaction can then be influenced are not discussed. Incidentally, as in the case of motivation, there is a reasonable amount of agreement in the literature regarding which aspects often influence satisfaction. In the following summation (see Griffin & Bateman, 1986; Biessen, 1992; Miedema, 1994), the reader will recognize, on the one hand, core subject areas from motivation theories and, on the other hand, features that are arranged in a more descriptive way. These are: demographic aspects; goal setting (see section 2); job design (see Chapter 6, Vol. 3 of this *Handbook*); organization characteristics (see Chapter 2, this volume of the *Handbook*); leadership (Chapter 13, this volume of the *Handbook*); participation in decision making (Chapter 13, Vol. 3); labour conditions (Chapter 12); individual differences.

The appending of that last category is interesting: In addition to biographical variables, Griffin and Bateman also mention "self-esteem" and expectations. This implies that the influence of job and/or organizational characteristics on satisfaction can be moderated in any way whatever by these types of variables; the same applies in reverse to the effects of such personality aspects. However obvious this conclusion may be, a dominant effect is usually ascribed in many models and theories to situational variables on their own.

What are the reasons underlying this? In the past decade there has been an ongoing discussion on this theme, which has chiefly been promoted by Staw (see Staw, 1984; Staw & Ross, 1985; Staw, Bell, & Clausen, 1986). It concerns whether a person's satisfaction level is not also influenced by dispositional variables and thus displays a certain stability over time and situations. For example, Staw et al. (1986) found that over a period of 50 years part of the variation in satisfaction among respondents could be explained in this way. Arvey, Bouchard, Segal, and Abraham (1989) even mention genetic components: They were able to account for about 30% of the variation in job satisfaction in identical twins who were raised separately. Such an interpretation has been challenged by Gerhart (1987) and more particularly by Davis-Blake and Pfeffer (1989).

This breathes new life into an old but, from both

a theoretical and practical point of view, highly important theme: The interrelationship between personality traits and situational variables. Davis-Blake and Pfeffer raise the point that demonstrating stability in scores (temporal and situational) is not sufficient reason for inferring the existence of dispositions, but that the phenomenon of stability needs to be embedded in a theory. In our view, he is right; such theories are still few and far between.

Yet it is also necessary—and Pfeffer does not draw this obvious conclusion—that similar theories should be designed regarding the role of a whole range of situational variables. We anticipate that research in this area will also shed more light on the nature of the interactions between both categories of variables. The first point is whether, theoretically speaking, interactions are accepted. A second point concerns decision-making rules regarding the role of so-called "strong" versus "weak or ambiguous" situations (Mischel, 1977). In strong situations, certain "situational" features have a dominant role and personality variables a subordinate one, for example, in the event of an "external" threat occurring. Weak situations are far less structured and leave a lot of room for the differences between people. Is a person able—and this is the third point—to "adapt" to particular job variables? Can the differences between people in this regard be attributed to a personality variable or is it in fact an indication of interaction?

3.4   The measuring of satisfaction

Satisfaction can be measured in various ways, i.e., by means of questionnaires, interviews, behavioral observations, clerical data (e.g. on absenteeism), and critical incidents. The choice of method for measuring satisfaction is determined by a number of considerations; we will focus on some of these. It is well known that no method is perfect (see Chapter 2, Vol. 1 of this *Handbook*): Each has its weaknesses, hence the recommendation to use more than one method in a study wherever possible. A second question concerns the insight that the researcher has gained beforehand into the problem which (s)he is going to study, into the idiosyncrasies of the population or sample, etc. The more limited the insight, the more an "open" method—e.g. an interview—might be appropriate, perhaps by way of a preliminary enquiry. A third aspect is linked to some extent with the second: To what extent does the researcher have access to instruments whose reliability and validity have been established in previous studies (see also Chapter 9, Vol. 4, this *Handbook*)? Considerations of time available and funds are also important in this context. A fourth question is whether the nature of a problem to be looked at might render the use of certain kinds of methods undesirable or impossible: Sometimes a study is pointless, e.g. if, in completing a questionnaire, the participants might prematurely be able to ascertain what the intention of the study is, etc.

In practice, however, questionnaires constitute the most frequently used method of measuring satisfaction; we hold that there are often well-founded reasons for this. In the rest of this section we will restrict ourselves to this method, focusing in particular on three types of scale (see Koopman & Werkman, 1973):

1. simple evaluation;
2. description;
3. weighted evaluation.

Simple evaluation: Statements or questions are put to the respondent, who then gives his/her "assessment" by choosing one of the response alternatives each time. An example of a statement might be: "my supervisor gets on well with his staff". The possible responses might range from "agree completely" to "disagree completely". This type of scale has formed the basis for the development of a considerable body of instruments, which in the Netherlands include: "How do you feel about your job?" (NIPG, 1958), "Attitude Scale for Industrial Labour" (ASIA, 1969), and the "Questionnaire for staff and management in industry" (Van der Graaf & Huizinga, 1969). Instruments developed later in this country have regularly been based on these "examples". Current questionnaires include The Delft Box (TU Delft) and the Basic Questionnaire Amsterdam (BASAM; Biessen, 1992). Examples from the United States include the "Minnesota Satisfaction Questionnaire" (Weiss, Dawis, England, & Lofquist, 1967) and the "Survey of Organizations" (Taylor & Bowers, 1972). This method ties in

perfectly with the definition of satisfaction in terms of "need fulfillment" (see section 3.2.3).

Description: Here, the respondent has to appraise the accuracy of descriptions of his/her work (situation) in the form of statements or adjectives. The contribution that the various answers will make to the degree of satisfaction is stipulated in advance. One of the most well-known examples of this is the "Job Descriptive Index" (Smith, Kendall, & Hulin, 1969, 1985), which is generally considered to be one of the best validated questionnaires. It differentiates five categories, i.e. "work, supervision, coworkers, pay, promotions". Items include: "my work is useful"; "my pay is bad". The way in which the authors have designed this scale provides a good illustration of the "social reference group" theory (section 3.2.4). They define satisfaction as a function of the difference between what the person expects and experiences in relation to the person's *perceived real or potential alternatives* in a given situation. Norms are developed, which differentiate according to gender, income, training, years of service, and "community prosperity" (this last is composed of five indices).

Weighted evaluation: A respondent's opinion about an aspect of his/her work (situation) is linked up with what (s)he wants, and/or finds attractive, and/or considers important about it, etc. As we have already seen in the discrepancy model (section 3.2.1), this can be done by calculating the difference between the two scores, or the product, or by weighting the discrepancy score, etc.

Although the *discrepancy model* is used very frequently, various objections have been raised, while, in addition, various preconditions need to be met, which in practice are regularly not complied with. The following example serves to illustrate this:

	5	4	3	2	1	
Desire: frequently		___ x ___				rarely
Observed factuality: frequently				___ x __		rarely

Here we see two 5-point scales: the degree of satisfaction can range between +4 and –4; in our example the score is +2. The first remarkable thing is that the values that satisfaction can theoretically take can vary per item: if the perceived outcome is

3, satisfaction varies between +2 and −2. If the outcome is 2, then there is a variation from +3 to −1, etc. Thus, standardized scores are required. A second point is that it is the size of the discrepancy that is at issue and not the composite scores. In other words: a discrepancy of 5–3 is considered identical to a 3–1 discrepancy; total satisfaction (discrepancy score is 0) in the case of 5–5 is the same as 1–1. A number of objections to this have arisen. In terms of our example: Frequently desiring and receiving information is equated with rarely desiring and receiving information. Third, a dissatisfaction score of e.g. +2 (wanting more than you have) is equated with a score of −2 (having more than you want). Based on research using "equity" theory, this assumption must be called into question.

Application of the discrepancy model assumes that the two scores are *independent* of each other. It now appears that this is not usually the case: The desire score often increases in proportion to the perceived outcome. This might be due to the tendency always to award a "desire" a higher score, or it might be due to an intrinsic relation: The person becomes used to a particular outcome level—e.g. having influence—and wants gradually to increase it. It can also point to the role of a third factor that influences both scores (for instance, changing job). Furthermore, satisfaction is often linked with a criterion variable, such as performance. Then the condition applies that both scores must also be independent of this variable; this condition is also frequently unable to be met.

In the product or *interaction model*, both scores are multiplied. In the example we just gave, the satisfaction would come to 4 x 2 = 8. This is an attempt to remove one of the objections to the discrepancy model—the lack of interaction between desire and outcome. Other difficulties now arise, however. Suppose that the desire score equals 1. The greater the perceived outcome (e.g. 3, 4, or 5) the greater the satisfaction (i.e. 3, 4, or 5). It is difficult to see why someone with a satisfaction score of 1 (desire and outcome are scored equal) should be less satisfied that someone with a score between 2 and 5 (whereby the outcome increasingly exceeds the desire). Furthermore, the product scores must be standardized, because a number of values between 1 and 25

cannot occur. Subsequently, the chance factor increases sharply if the product is correlated with a criterion measure; the latter is often the intention of the study (for a more detailed discussion, see Koopman-Iwema, 1980; Mellenbergh et al., 1990; Evans, 1991). We have come to the conclusion that it is often preferable in practice to adopt the descriptive method (or simple evaluation).

In the second part of this section we have chiefly discussed verbal methods of measuring satisfaction. It is also recommended, however, to consider the use of *non-verbal* measures. These do not usually relate to separate items but to the facets differentiated in a study (e.g. the work, the physical working conditions, etc.), or to the general or "overall" satisfaction. A well-known method is Kunin's (1955) "Faces Scale": These faces—11 in the original version—range in expression from perfectly blissful to deeply distressed. The respondent chooses the face which best represents his/her attitude or feeling. Research has shown that this scale has a high validity. The degree of satisfaction can also be shown along a straight line where only the poles are named, or using a diagram, etc.

3.5   Weighting facets

Up to now in this section, satisfaction has dealt principally with the degree of satisfaction with *facets* of the work (such as work content, leadership, etc.); within each facet, a whole range of elements (the items on a scale) can be further differentiated. An important question, however, is how the researcher can gain insight into a person's general ("overall") satisfaction with his/her work (situation). As we mentioned earlier, this question can be approached from three different angles (see section 3.1).

First of all, the researcher can use the *global* method. This usually means that employees are given one question in which they are asked to evaluate their work or work situation. A format frequently used for this is: "How do you feel about your work on the whole?" It was probably Hoppock (1935) who first made use of this type of question. Sometimes a number of general questions are asked and the answers from these are then averaged. A second method uses "composite" scores. A number of items are selected from all the scales that represent satisfaction facets. This selection may take place on the basis of the factor loading (see the abridged ASIA, 1969; BASAM, Biessen, 1992). The averaged sum score then indicates the degree of overall satisfaction; in other words, the total consists of the sum of the parts. This characterization is also applicable to a third method: *summed* facets. Overall satisfaction is determined by adding the relevant facet satisfaction scores. Comparative research has shown, however, that the correlations between global scores, on the one hand, and composite and/or summed scores, on the other, are not particularly high. Furthermore, differences occur in the correlations with independent criterion variables.

What might account for such differences? Two trends of interpretation can be identified. The first highlights the fact that by making use of the global method the researcher in a sense is transferring his own research problem—how can overall satisfaction be measured?—to his respondents. Such a broad question is too complicated, however; as a result, the researcher *cannot effectively interpret* the responses to it. Thus it appears that there is always a high percentage of respondents who indicate that they are satisfied and that this percentage—with the exception of the period during the Second World War—has gradually increased. In recent years, 80–85% have tended to indicate that they are satisfied. The dilemma is now that an outcome like this often displays a sharp deviation from the satisfaction scores, which relate to the various facets separately. Furthermore, such a "high" degree of satisfaction—not in line with expectations—can go hand in hand with a high level of absenteeism and a high turnover. In fact, the answer to this type of question is simply too open to interpretation.

According to the second trend, a global question in part *measures* different components of a person's overall job satisfaction than the composite or the summed methods. A global question is more "inclusive": In answering it, the person not only includes the work facets relevant to him/her but also events outside work (see also Arvey & Dewhirst, 1979). Overall satisfaction consists of more than just the sum of the parts (facets). A number of studies (e.g. Scarpello & Campbell,

1983; Ironson et al., 1989) have in fact shown that global scores display a higher correlation with criterion scores than the other two types of score but that summed facet scores are workable and useful for organization questions where broad diagnoses are required (see also Smith, 1992).

It is our view that for the time being restraint is called for in the use of the global method. The researcher will first have to ascertain whether the question (or questions) concerned are sufficiently reliable and valid, e.g. by examining the global question's predictive value.

If the scores for various facets are used, then the question arises of whether weighting should occur: Are all the facets of equal importance? It would appear to go without saying that both from an intuitive as well as a content viewpoint, facet satisfaction scores should be weighted by the respondent. If we compare a facet such as "independence at work" with that of "physical working conditions", for example, then the widely held view is that by and large the former will carry most weight as far as the degree of overall satisfaction is concerned. For this reason, respondents are regularly asked to allot a weighting factor to each of the separate facets identified in a study by prioritizing them or awarding them an interval score (in the previous section we saw that this can also be done per item). Subsequently, the researcher multiplies, divides or adds up this factor with the facet satisfaction score.

The results of extensive empirical research, however, have shown that weighting either furnishes no improvement or leads to metrically misleading findings. Unweighted summing of facet-satisfaction scores, on the other hand, results in more reliable and valid data. How should these results be explained? In the discussion of the "weighted evaluation" method, a number of conditions relating to weighting were mentioned, which in a study are often not able to be met. Hoekman (1970) has stressed, furthermore, that in the simple summing of facets (or items) effective score discrepancies (weights) occur and that an extra weighting—especially when, as is usually the case, a good few facets have been included in a study—chiefly serves to increase the joint variance.

3.6 Satisfaction and performance

In particular around the time of the "human relations" movement (see Chapter 2 of this *Handbook*) it was widely held that satisfied employees would achieve a high and effective level of performance. Empirical research has since shown that this statement, put in such general terms, has no support: Positive correlations were sometimes found, then at times negative ones would crop up and then it frequently occurred that no correlation could be observed at all. Based on a survey of a large number of studies, Vroom (1964) arrives at an average correlation of .13; subsequent studies have not revealed any essential differences, although emphasis is repeatedly placed on the role of moderating variables (see also Schwab & Cummings, 1970; Lawler, 1973; Wanous, 1974; Locke, 1976; Griffin & Bateman, 1986; Katzell, Thompson, & Guzzo, 1992).

Various authors have stressed that there is little point in relating overall job satisfaction to a general index of performance because the important things are which facets affect a person's satisfaction and which components are used in the measuring of performance (see also Fisher, 1980). Others suggested the possibility that a third variable might influence both satisfaction and performance, but in opposite directions: Triandis (cited by Schwab & Cummings, 1970) argued that the pressure to increase production, for example, would decrease satisfaction but would increase performance (at least in the short term). The influence exerted by a number of characteristics relating to the person, the work, the organization, etc. on this relationship has also been pointed out, and furthermore attention has been drawn to the incorrect assumption, which is frequently made, that a linear relationship exists between satisfaction and performance.

The sequence of the two themes can also be reversed, depending on the line of approach that is taken (see section 3.1) and the theory (e.g. "goal setting" or "expectancy") that is adhered to. Performance then results in a certain degree of satisfaction. Performance bears upon the means by which the person is able to acquire outcomes, whereas satisfaction reflects the extent to which outcomes have been obtained. A number of variables can in turn influence this relationship. It is our view that it is both theoretically and empirically advisable to introduce a dichotomy.

1. *Performance leads to satisfaction.* This assumes that the more the performance corresponds to what was aimed at, the higher the satisfaction will be (*positive* correlation). The person is thus prompted to repeat the behavioral cycle concerned as often as possible. This relationship can be moderated by a number of variables, which may relate to the person, the work group, the task, the organization, etc. Satisfaction thus reflects the result.

2. *Dissatisfaction leads to performance.* A distinctive feature of motivated behavior is that the person strives to actualize needs or motives that have not yet been satisfied. The person is thus always dissatisfied in some respects. If (s)he anticipates that achieving a high level of performance will ensure that the motives in question will be actualized, then in that situation there is a *negative* correlation between satisfaction and performance. Of course, a number of variables can moderate this relationship. Here, satisfaction is a component of a steering and regulating system.

The foregoing implies that future research into the correlation between satisfaction and performance needs to make a clearer distinction between the various components of satisfaction (and of performance) and this in turn affects the type of causal relationship that is assumed. It means, however, that it is not right to sum up studies of this relationship in one average correlation coefficient.

4 CONCLUSION

It is our view that in recent years more cohesion has arisen in research and theory building in the domain of motivation. On the one hand, the product of this has been a greater consistency in a number of core research programs. On the other hand, a limited number of themes—particularly concerning the relationships between performance behavior and its outcomes—turn up in every theory.

This convergence does not occur in the field of satisfaction research. We are of the opinion, however, that both subjects, in a theoretical as well as an empirical respect, correspond far more closely than is usually assumed. Given all the differences in emphasis that can be placed on it, the theme of satisfaction forms a series of subsidiary domains within the broader subject of motivation. Among other things, this means that satisfaction research can take advantage of the relatively more solid foundation of motivation approaches. Motivation research in its turn can profit in particular from the extensive armoury of empirical instruments that has been developed in the domain of measuring satisfaction. Both concepts give rise to a discussion regarding the degree to which stable personality variables play a significant role. We anticipate important contributions from the research that needs to be carried out into this regarding the interactional relationships between personality and situational variables and the correlation between motivation and satisfaction.

REFERENCES

Adams, J.S. (1963). Toward an understanding of equity. *Journal of Abnormal and Social Psychology, 67*, 422–436.

Adams, J.S. (1965). Inequity in social exchange. In L. Berkowitz, (Ed.), *Advances in experimental social psychology* (Vol. 2). New York: Academic Press.

Alderfer, C.P. (1972). *Existence, relatedness and growth: human needs in organizational settings.* New York: Free Press.

Arvey, R.D., & Dewhirst, H.D. (1979). Relationships between diversity of interests, age, job satisfaction and job performance. *Journal of Occupational Psychology, 52*, 17–23.

Arvey, R.D., Bouchard, T.J., Segal, N.C., & Abraham, L.M. (1989). Job satisfaction: Environmental and genetic components. *Journal of Applied Psychology, 74*, 187–192.

ASIA (1969). *Attitudenschaal voor industriële arbeid.* Den Haag: Commissie Opvoering Productiviteit/SER.

Bandura, A. (1977). *Social learning theory.* Englewood Cliffs, NJ: Prentice-Hall.

Bandura, A. (1982). Self-efficacy mechanism in human agency. *American Psychologist, 37*, 122–147.

Bandura, A. (1986). *Social foundations of thought and action: a social-cognitive view.* Englewood Cliffs, NJ: Prentice Hall.

Berkowitz, L. Fraser, C., Treasure, F.P., & Cockhran, S. (1987). Pay equity, job gratification, and comparisons in pay satisfaction. *Journal of Applied Psychology, 72*, 544–551.

Biessen, P.G.A. (1992). *Oog voor de menselijke factor: achtergrond, constructie en validering van de basisvragenlijst Amsterdam.* Lisse: Swets & Zeitlinger.

Campbell, J.P., Dunnette, M.D., Lawler, E.E., & Weick, K.E. (1970). *Managerial behavior, performance, and effectiveness.* New York: McGraw-Hill.

Campbell, J.P., & Pritchard, R.D. (1976). Motivation theory in industrial and organizational psychology. In M.D. Dunnette (Ed.), *Handbook of industrial and organizational psychology.* Chicago: Rand McNally.

Carver, C.S., & Scheier, M.F. (1981). *Attention and self-regulation: A control-theory approach to human behavior.* New York: Springer.

Cranny, C.J., Smith, P.C., & Stone, E.F. (1992). *Job satisfaction.* New York: Lexington.

Cummings, L.L., & Schwab, D.P. (1973). *Performance in organizations: Determinants and appraisal.* Glenview: Scott, Foresman & Co.

Davey, G., & Cullen, C. (1988). *Human operant conditioning and behavior modification.* Chichester: Wiley.

Davis-Blake, A., & Pfeffer, J. (1989). *Just a mirage: The search for dispositional effects in organizational research.* Manuscript. Graduate School of Business, Stanford University.

DeCharms, R. (1968). *Personal causation: The internal affective determinants of behavior.* New York: Academic Press.

Deci, E.L. (1975). *Intrinsic motivation.* New York: Plenum Press.

Deci, E.L., & Porac, J. (1978). Cognitive evaluation theory and the study of human motivation. In M.R. Lepper & D. Greene (Eds.), *The hidden costs of rewards.* New York: Wiley.

Deci, E.L., & Ryan, R.M. (1985). *Intrinsic motivation and self-determination in human behavior.* New York: Plenum Press.

Duijker, H.C.J. (1975). *Norm en descriptie in de psychologie.* Amsterdam: Noord-Hollandse Uitgevers Mij.

Duijker, H.C.J. (1976). De ideologie der zelfontplooiing. *Pedagogische Studiën, 10*, 358–373.

Dyer, L., & Theriault, R. (1976). The determinants of pay satisfaction. *Journal of Applied Psychology, 61*, 596–604.

Edwards, W. (1954). The theory of decision making. *Psychological Bulletin, 51*, 380–417.

Eerde, W. van, & Thierry, H. (1996). Vroom's expectancy models and work related criteria. *Journal of Applied Psychology, 81*, 575–586.

Erez, M., Kleinbeck, U., Thierry, H. (Eds.) (forthcoming). *Work motivation in the context of a globalizing economy.* Lawrence Erlbaum.

Evans, M.G. (1991). The problem of analyzing multiplicative composites: Interactions revisited. *American Psychologists, 46*, 6–15.

Farr, J.L., Hofman, D.A., & Ringenbach, K.L. (1993). Goal orientation and action control theory: implications for industrial and organizational psychology. In C.L. Cooper & I.T. Robertson (Eds.), *International review of industrial and organizational psychology 1993*. Chichester: Wiley

Feather, N.T. (1982). Expectancy-value approaches: Present status and future directions. In N.T. Feather (Ed.), *Expectations and actions: Expectancy-value models in psychology*. Hillsdale, NJ: Lawrence Erlbaum.

Ferratt, T.W. (1981). Overall job satisfaction: Is it a linear function of facet satisfaction? *Human Relations, 34*, 463–473.

Festinger, L. (1950). Informal social communication. *Psychological Review, 57*, 194–200.

Festinger, L. (1954). A theory of social comparison. *Human Relations, 7*, 117–140.

Fisher, C.D. (1980). On the dubious wisdom of expecting job satisfaction to correlate with performance. *Academy of Management Review, 5*, 607–612.

Ford, M.E. (1992). *Motivating humans: Goals, emotions and Personal Agency Beliefs*. London: Sage.

Georgopoulos, B.S. Mahoney, G.M., & Jones, N.W. (1957). A path-goal approach to productivity. *Journal of Applied Psychology, 41*, 345–353.

Gerhart, B. (1987). How important are dispositional factors as determinants of job satisfaction? Implications for job-design and other personnel programs. *Journal of Applied Psychology, 72*, 366–373.

Gist, M.E., & Mitchell, T.R. (1989). *Self-efficacy: A theoretical analysis of its determinants and the process of change*. Seattle: University of Washington, WP88-21.

Goodman, P.S. (1974). An examination of referents used in the evaluation of pay. *Organizational Behavior and Human Performance, 12*, 170–195.

Graaf, M.H.K. van der, & Huizinga, G. (1969). *Bedrijfsenquête staf-en kaderpersoneel*. Den Haag: Commissie Opvoering Productiviteit.

Griffin, R.W., & Bateman, T.S. (1986). Job satisfaction and organizational commitment. In C.L. Cooper & I. Robertson (Eds.), *International review of industrial and organizational psychology 1986*. Chichester: Wiley.

Heneman, H.G., & Schwab, D.P. (1985). Pay satisfaction: Its multidimensional nature and measurement. *International Journal of Psychology, 20*, 129–141.

Hermkens, P. (1995). Sociale vergelijking en rechtvaardigheid van beloning. *Gedrag en Organisatie, 8*, 359–371.

Herzberg, F. (1966). *Work and the nature of man*. Cleveland: World Publishing Co.

Herzberg, F. (1968). One more time: How do you motivate employees? *Harvard Business Review, 46*, 1, 53–62.

Herzberg, F. (1976). *The managerial choice: To be efficient and to be human*. New York: Dow Jones-Irwin.

Herzberg, F., Mausner, B., & Snyderman, B.B. (1959). *The motivation to work*. New York: Wiley.

Hoekman, K. (1970). Satisfactie-meting: Over-weging en modellen. In P.J.D. Drenth, P.J. Willems, & Ch.J. De Wolff (Eds.), *Bedrijfspsychologie: Onderzoek en evaluatie*. Deventer: Kluwer.

Homans, G.C. (1961). *Social behavior: Its elementary forms*. New York: Harcourt Brace & World.

Hoppock, R. (1935). *Job satisfaction*. New York: Harper & Brothers.

Horn, L.A. ten (1983). *Behoeften, werksituatie en arbeidsbeleving*. Dissertatie, TH Delft.

Huizinga, G. (1970). *Maslow's need hierarchy in the work situation*. Groningen: Wolters-Noordhoff.

Hulin, C.L. (1966). Effects of community characteristics on measures of job satisfaction. *Journal of Applied Psychology, 50*, 185–192.

Hull, C.L. (1943). *Principles of behavior*. New York: Appleton-Century-Crofts.

Hull, C.L. (1951). *Essentials of behavior*. New Haven, CT: Yale University Press.

Ilgen, D., & Klein, H.J. (1989). Organizational behavior. *Annual Review of Psychology, 40*, 327–351.

Ironson, G.H., Smith, P.C., Brannick, M.T., Gibson, W.M., & Paul, K.B. (1989). Construction of a job in general scale: A comparison of global, composite and specific measures. *Journal of Applied Psychology, 74*, 193–200.

James, L.R., & Tetrick, L.E. (1986). Confirmatory analytic tests of three causal models relating job perceptions to job satisfaction. *Journal of Applied Psychology, 71*, 77–82.

Kanfer, R. (1990). Motivation theory and work and organizational psychology. In M.D. Dunnette & L.M. Hough (Eds.), *Handbook of industrial and organizational psychology* (revised Edn., Vol. 1). Palo Alto, CA: Consulting Psychologists Press.

Katzell, R.A., Barrett, R.S., & Parker, T.C. (1961). Job satisfaction, job performance, and situational characteristics. *Journal of Applied Psychology, 45*, 65–72.

Katzell, R.A., Thompson, D.E., & Guzzo, R.A. (1992). How job satisfaction and job performance are and are not linked. In C.J. Cranny, P.C. Smith, & E.F. Stone (Eds.), *Job satisfaction*. New York: Lexington.

Kleinbeck, U., Quast, H.H., Thierry, H., & Häcker, H. (1990). *Work motivation*. Hillsdale, NJ: Lawrence Erlbaum.

Komaki, J., Heinzmann, A.T., & Lawson, L. (1980). Effects of training and feedback: Component analyses of behavioral safety program. *Journal of Applied Psychology, 65*, 261–270.

Komaki, J., Collins, R.L., & Temlock, S. (1987). An alternative performance measurement approach: Applied operant measurement in the service sector. *Applied Psychology: An International Review, 36*, 71–89.

Koopman, P.L., & Werkman, B. (1973). Het verhoudingsmodel bij de meting van satisfactie. In P.J.D. Drenth, P.J. Willems, & Hh.J. De Wolff (Eds.), *Psychologie van arbeid en organizatie*. Deventer: Kluwer.

Koopman-Iwema, A.M. (1980). *Macht, motivatie, medezeggenschap*. Assen: Van Gorcum.

Koopman-Iwema, A.M. (1982). De puzzel van het prestatieloon—arbeidsgedrag en motivatie. *Psychologie*, 15–21.

Kunin, T. (1955). The construction of a new type of attitude measure. *Personnel Psychology*, *8*, 65–78.

Langer, E.J. (1978). Rethinking the role of thought in social interaction. In J. Harvey, W. Ickes, & R. Kidd (Eds.), *New directions in attribution research*. Hillsdale, NJ: Lawrence Erlbaum.

Latham, G.P. (1988). Employee motivation: Yesterday, today and tomorrow. In J. Hage (Ed.), *Futures of organizations: Innovating to adapt strategy and human resources to rapid technological change*. Lexington, MA: DC Health.

Lawler, E.E. (1971). *Pay and organizational effectiveness*. New York: McGraw-Hill.

Lawler, E.E. (1973). *Motivation in work organizations*. Monterey: Brooks/Cole.

Lewin, K. (1938). *The conceptual representation and the measurement of psychological forces*. Durham, NC: Duke University Press.

Lewin, K. (1951). *Field theory in social science*. New York: Harper & Row.

Locke, E.A. (1969). What is job satisfaction? *Organizational Behavior & Human Performance*, *4*, 309–336.

Locke, E.A. (1976). The nature and causes of job satisfaction. In M.D. Dunnette (Ed.), *Handbook of industrial and organizational psychology*. Chicago: Rand McNally.

Locke, E.A., & Henne, D. (1986). Work motivation theories. In C.L. Cooper & I. Robertson (Eds.), *International review of industrial and organizational psychology 1986*. Chichester: Wiley.

Locke, E.A., & Latham, G.P. (1984). *Goal setting: A motivational technique that works*. Englewood Cliffs, NJ: Prentice-Hall.

Locke, E.A., & Latham, G.P. (1990a). *A theory of goal setting and task performance*. Englewood Cliffs, NJ: Prentice-Hall.

Locke, E.A., & Latham, G.P. (1990b). Work motivation: The high performance cycle. In U. Kleinbeck, H.H. Quast, H. Thierry, & H. Häcker (Eds.), *Work motivation*. Hillsdale, NJ: Lawrence Erlbaum.

Luthans, F., & Kreitner, R. (1975). *Organizational behavior modification*. Glenview, IL: Scott, Foresman & Co.

Luthans, F., & Martinko, M. (1987). Behavioral approaches to organizations. In C.L. Cooper & I. Robertson (Eds.), *International review of industrial and organizational psychology 1987*. Chichester: Wiley.

March, J.G., & Simon, H.B. (1958). *Organizations*. New York: Wiley.

Maslow, A.H. (1954). *Motivation and personality*. New York: Harper & Row.

McGregor, D.C. (1960). *The human side of enterprise*. New York: McGraw-Hill.

Mellenbergh, G.J., Molendijk, L., Haan, W. de, & Horst, G. ter (1990). The sum-of-products variable reconsidered. *Methodika*, *4*, 37–46.

Miedema, H. (1994). *De achterkant van het salaris*. Assen: Van Gorcum.

Mischel, W. (1977). The interaction of person and situation. In D. Magnuson & N. Endler (Eds.), *Personality at the crossroads*. Hillsdale, NJ: Lawrence Erlbaum.

Mitchell, T.R. (1974). Expectancy models of job satisfaction, occupational preferences and effort: A theoretical, methodological and empirical appraisal. *Psychological Bulletin*, *81*, 1053–1077.

Mitchell, T.R. (1976). Cognitions and Skinner: Some questions about behavioral determinism. *Organization and Administrative Science*, April, 63–69.

Mitchell, T.R. (1982). Expectancy-Value models in organizational psychology. In N.T. Feather (Ed.), *Expectations and actions: Expectancy-value models in psychology*. Hillsdale, NJ: Lawrence Erlbaum.

Morse, N.C. (1953). *Satisfaction in the white-collar job*. Ann Arbor: The University of Michigan.

NIPG (1958). *Hoe denkt u over uw werk?* Leiden: Nederlands Instituut voor Praeventieve Geneeskunde.

Orlebeke, J.F. (1981). Motivatie. In J.F. Orlebeke, P.J.D. Drenth, R.H.C. Janssen, & C. Sanders (Eds.), *Compendium van de psychology* (Vol. 4). Muiderberg: Coutinho.

Patchen, M. (1961). *The choice of wage comparisons*. Englewood Cliffs, NJ: Prentice-Hall.

Petri, H.L. (1986). *Motivation: theory and research*. Belmont: Wadsworth (2nd Edn.).

Pinder, C.C. (1984). *Work motivation*: Glenview, IL: Scott Foresman.

Porter, L.W. (1961). A study of perceived need satisfaction in bottom and middle management jobs. *Journal of Applied Psychology*, *45*, 1–10.

Rijsman, J.B., & Wilke, H.A.M. (Eds.) (1980). *Sociale vergelijkingsprocessen*. Deventer: Van Loghum Slaterus.

Roethlisberger, F.J., & Dickson W.J. (1950). *Management and the worker*. Cambridge, MA: Harvard University Press.

Ronan, W.W. (1970). Individual and situational variables relating to job satisfaction. *Journal of Applied Psychology*, *54* (monograph).

Rotter, J.B. (1954). *Social learning and clinical psychology*. Englewood Cliffs: Prentice-Hall.

Rotter, J.B. (1966). Generalized expectancies for internal versus external control of reinforcement. *Psychological Monographs*, *80*, 1–28.

Rotter, J.B. (1975). Some problems and misconceptions

related to the construct of internal versus external control of reinforcement. *Journal of Consulting and Clinical Psychology, 43*, 36–67.

Salancik, G.R., & Pfeffer, J. (1977). An examination of need-satisfaction models of job attitudes. *Administrative Science Quarterly, 22*, 427–456.

Scarpello, V., & Campbell, J.P. (1983). Job satisfaction: Are all the parts there? *Personnel Psychology, 36*, 577–600.

Schneider, B. (1985). Organizational behavior. *Annual Review of Psychology, 36*, 573–611.

Schwab, D.P., & Cummings, L.L. (1970). Theories of performance and satisfaction: A review. *Industrial Relations, 9*, 408–430.

Schwarzer, R. (Ed.) (1992). *Self-efficacy: Thought control of action*. London: Hemisphere Publishing.

Skinner, B.F. (1948). *Waldon Two*. New York: Macmillan.

Skinner, B.F. (1971). *Beyond freedom and dignity*. London: Bantam Books.

Skinner, B.F. (1990). Can psychology be a science of mind? *American Psychologist, 45*, 1206–1210.

Smith, P.C. (1992). In pursuit of happiness: Why study general job satisfaction? In C.J. Cranny, & P.C. Smith, & E.F. Stone (Eds.), *Job satisfaction*. New York: Lexington.

Smith, P.C., Kendall, L.M., & Hulin, C.L. (1969). *The measurement of satisfaction in work and retirement*. Chicago: Rand McNally.

Smith, P.C., Kendall, L.M., & Hulin, C.L. (1985). *The job description index* (rev. Edn.). Bowling Green: Dept. of Psychology, Bowling Green State University

Spector, P.E. (1982). Behavior in organizations as a function of employee's locus of control. *Psychological Bulletin, 91*, 482–497.

Spence, K.W. (1950). Behavior therapy and selective learning. In M.R. Jones (Ed.), *Nebraska Symposium on motivation, Vol. 6*. Lincoln, NE: University of Nebraska Press.

Staw, B.M. (1984). Organizational behavior: A review and reformulation of the field's outcome variables. *Annual Review of Psychology, 35*, 627–666.

Staw, B.M., & Ross, J. (1985). Stability in the midst of change: A dispositional approach to job attitudes. *Journal of Applied Psychology, 70*, 469–480.

Staw, B.M., Bell, N.E., & Clausen, J.A. (1986). The dispositional approach to job attitudes: A lifetime longitudinal test. *Administrative Science Quarterly, 31*, 56–77.

Stone, E.F. (1992). A critical analysis of social information processing models of job perceptions and job attitudes. In C.J. Cranny, P.C. Smith, & E.F. Stone (Eds.), *Job satisfaction*. New York: Lexington.

Syroit, J.E.M.M. (1984). *Interpersonal justice: A psychological analysis illustrated with empirical results*. Dissertation: Katholieke Universiteit Brabant.

Taylor, F.W. (1911). *Principles of scientific management*. New York: Harper & Row.

Taylor, J.C., & Bowers, D.G. (1972). *Survey of organizations*. Ann Arbor, MI: Institute for Social Research.

Taylor, S.E., & Fiske, S.T. (1978). Salience, attention, and attribution: top of the head phenomena. *Advances in Experiential Social Psychology*, 249–288.

Thierry, H. (1968). *Loont de prestatiebeloning?* Assen: Van Gorcum.

Thierry, H. (1969). *Arbeidsinstelling en prestatiebeloning*. Utrecht: Het Spectrum.

Thierry, H. (1989). Imperialisme of contingentie. In H. Thierry & A. Evers (Eds.), *Psychologie en Hoger Onderwijs: toekomstverkenningen*. Lisse: Swets & Zeitlinger.

Thierry, H. (1990). Intrinsic motivation reconsidered. In U. Kleinbeck, H.H. Quast, H. Thierry, & H. Häcker (Eds.), *Work motivation*. Hillsdale, NJ: Lawrence Erlbaum

Thierry, H. (1991). De merits van de expectancy theorie. *Gedrag en Organisatie, 4*, 305–319.

Thierry, H. (forthcoming). Theories on compensation: the perspective of the reflection theory. In M. Erez, U. Kleinbeck, & H. Thierry (Eds.), *Work motivation in the context of a globalizing economy*. Lawrence Erlbaum.

Thierry, H., & Drenth, P.J.D. (1970). De toetsing van Herzbergs two factor theorie. In P.J.D. Drenth, P.J. Willems, & Ch.J. De Wolff (Eds.), *Bedrijfspsychologie, onderzoek en evaluatie*. Deventer: Kluwer.

Thierry, H., Koopman, P.L., & Flier, H. van der (Eds.) (1992). *Wat houdt mensen bezig?* Utrecht: Lemma.

Tolman, E.C. (1932). *Purpose behavior in animals and men*. New York: Appleton-Century-Crofts.

Tubbs, M.E., & Ekeberg, S.E. (1991). The role of interventions in work motivation: Implications for goal-setting theory and research. *Academy of Management Review, 16*, 180–189.

Vinke, R.H.W. (1996). *Motivatie en belonen: de mythe van intrinsieke motivatie*. Deventer: Kluwer.

Vroom, V.H. (1964). *Work and motivation*. New York: Wiley.

Vrugt, A. (1992). Waargenomen eigen competentie en arbeidsmotivatie. In H. Thierry, P.L. Koopman, & H. van der Flier (Eds.) *Wat houdt mensen bezig?* Utrecht: Lemma.

Wahba, M.A., & Bridwell, L.G. (1976). Maslow reconsidered: A review of research on the need hierarchy theory. *Organizational behavior and human performance, 15*, 212–240.

Wall, T.D., & Payne, R. (1973). Are deficiency scales deficient? *Journal of Applied Psychology, 58*, 322–326.

Wanous, J.P. (1974). A causal-correlation analysis of the job satisfaction and performance relationship. *Journal of Applied Psychology, 59*, 139–144.

Weick, K. E. (1979). *The social psychology of organizing* (2nd Edn.). Reading: Addison-Wesley.

Weiner, B. (1974). An attributional interpretation of expectancy-value theory. In B. Weiner (Ed.). *Cognitive views of human motivation*. New York: Academic Press.

Weiner, B. (1985). An attributional theory of achievement motivation and emotion. *Psychological Review, 92*, 548–573.

Weiner, N. (1980). Determinants and consequences of pay satisfaction: A comparison of two models. *Personnel Psychology, 33*, 741–757.

Weiss, D.J., Dawis, R.V., England, G.W., & Lofquist, L.H. (1967). Manual for the Minnesota Satisfaction Questionnaire. *Minnesota Studies in Vocational Rehabilitations*. Bulletin 22.

12

Compensating Work

Henk Thierry

1 INTRODUCTION

In recent years, organizations in most industrialized countries have been faced with events and problems relating to pay and, more broadly, to working conditions that could often be summed up in three words: *flexibility, differentiation*, and *market orientation.*

Strictly speaking, flexibility denotes the capacity of an object to be bent or twisted without it breaking (see *American Heritage Dictionary of the English Language*, 1969). In other words: the object or system is tailored to and developed for specific circumstances without its core being altered. In practice, we hardly ever come across this definition any more. In most cases, what flexibility really implies is: organizational change. Flexibility occurs in at least six domains: working hours (e.g. flexitime); employment contracts (including via employment agencies); job content (rotation, enrichment, etc.); workplace (at the client's office; teleworking); work relations (including self-regulating teams), and working conditions. These six areas are linked in a number of respects. More flexibility in the area of working conditions often means that employees' or managers' pay can more easily be adjusted, for example, to changes in a business unit or in the market. It also means that the pay should reflect to a greater extent the organization's degree of success. And sometimes what is meant is that the pay should be based more on effort or performance.

These last two meanings really have more to do with the second concept that we mentioned at the beginning: differentiation. This is understood to mean that differences between objects or systems need (more) emphasis. Differentiation in working conditions is nearly always taken to mean that differences in (individual or group) performance or contribution should likewise be reflected in the pay (and possibly in other working conditions).

Market orientation was briefly mentioned earlier: This, it is generally assumed, indicates that the working conditions in a company or institution need to have a certain "sensitivity" to market changes. This draws attention particularly to the fact that the pay should be less dependent on regulations (at national, sectoral, and company level). In this view, the pay of personnel is partly dependent on the results achieved at the level of the individual, the group, the business unit, or the organization as a whole. An example of this, which at least in north-west European labour relations is seen as a rather fundamental change, is the system of gain sharing[1]: This means that the basic pay of each staff member is reduced. If things are going well in the company, then more can be earned than previously through bonuses; if, on the contrary, things are going badly, then the pay reverts to the lower level. And via so-called "deferred" forms of pay—such as, for instance, options and shares, dividends from a pension fund—a results-oriented approach is combined with an attempt to bind managers (and others) long term to an organization.

The developments briefly sketched so far occur in many countries, although each country has its own emphasis. This raises various important questions. One point that particularly comes to the fore from the trade-union angle is the extent to which employees can be protected from the (too) direct effects of market fluctuations on their income. A second important point is of a more instrumental nature: To which features of the "result" (such as performance, productivity, profit, or payout) can pay be linked? Is it advisable to include the results of individual (performance) evaluation in this? A third point is whether more flexible, differentiated, and market-dependent pay is effective. This raises the question of how to determine whether the pay package is of a "strategic" nature, in other words, whether it is consistent with and contributes to the achieving of the policy of an organization. This covers not only the mission statement and the corporate plan (where these are present) of a company, but also the culture of the whole organization and of parts of it. It is important in that context, moreover, whether pay plays a role in the planning or the implementation of changes within the organization. And the last but not least important point is whether there is good cohesion between pay and other parts of the personnel and organization policy.

Psychologically speaking, there is an interesting problem formulation in this introduction. Apparently, it is taken for granted that pay affects or can affect individual, group or organization-wide behaviour in the workplace. But what is this assumption actually based on? The consideration of that question forms the core of this chapter. First, we examine a number of theories which shed light regarding the conditions under which pay has meaning for individual working behaviour. This leads—in section 3—to an account of the different meanings of pay. In that context various strategic objectives are assessed, which, from a policy viewpoint, can be pursued by means of pay. Linking up with this, in section 4, is a discussion of various pay systems, focusing in each case on the results of empirical research. In a short concluding section we sketch a number of important questions for future research.

2 PSYCHOLOGICAL THEORIES ABOUT PAY

2.1 Perspective

A psychological theory about pay should answer the question of how the income that a person earns on the basis of his work can influence his work behaviour. The theory needs to make clear which meanings that person's pay can have for him and how as a result of this his motivation, performance and/or satisfaction might undergo a change. Clarification is also needed as to which variables, as determinants, can cause changes in those meanings. The following is an example of one of these variables.

A member of staff earns $50,000. The reader is asked how s/he plans to allow that staff member to benefit from an extra $5,000 that is made available. The reader could choose to allow 12 monthly portions of just over $400 and pay these together with the monthly salary. Another option is to sound out that staff member's preferences regarding both the form in which and the time when an extra payment will be made. The reader could pay out a bonus from time to time (until the $5,000 is reached) for excellent performance by the staff member; the amount of the periodic bonus as well as the frequency with which it is given can both be varied.

There are, of course, other options for allocating the $5,000. These three examples are intended to show that from the same amount, depending on the system adopted, very different meanings can be "read into" it by the recipient. In the reader's first system, the staff member probably considers the monthly portion as a part of his salary for the job (based on the value of his job). After a few months he might think he has a right to the additional amount, while there is a possibility that after a time he does not even notice the amount. In the second system there is an attempt to make pay instrumental to certain wishes or needs: The main thing is now its "expected usefulness" to the recipient. And in the third system it is obvious, owing to the link that is established with performance, that the pay will be seen by the recipient in relation to the job targets set, and is likely to be compared with what his colleagues are getting. Apart from the pay system there are of course other aspects that affect the meanings of pay; we will return to this later.

Owing to the—almost self-evident—correlation established earlier between pay on the one hand and motivation, performance and satisfaction on the other, it is also understandable that in developing theories on pay this relationship particularly is elaborated on. For there are hardly any (work and organizational) psychological theories that have been developed predominantly with a view to pay. There are, however, other more general motivation theories that appear to have implications for the meaning of pay or demonstrate a specific elaboration of this theme.

In a number of these theories the concept of *reinforcement* is a central one: Motivation is then interpreted in terms of motives or as a non-cognitive form of learning (Staw, 1984; Petri, 1986). Positive inducements reinforce the relationship with previous behaviour; negative inducements lead to its disappearance. Strictly speaking, these "reinforcers" "happen to" the person as she is seen as a passive organism. Other theories are "cognitive" in nature (see, for example, Vroom, 1964; Lawler, 1973). In these the person is depicted as an active processor of information who conceptualizes representations of his or her environment. Motivation is determined by the expectations and the intentions that the person has regarding how events will turn out, by objectives that she pursues and by the values she has. Both reinforcement and cognitive theories accentuate the relationships between behaviour and inducements, although there is a difference in interpretation regarding the nature of the causality between them.

We have examined this theme more fully in Chapter 11, Vol. 4, of this *Handbook*. Furthermore, various theories examining the meaning of pay have already been considered in the context of motivation. This is why we will confine ourselves to a short summary wherever this seems appropriate (see also Gerhart & Milkovich, 1992, and, for theories from other disciplines, Thierry, 1997).

2.2 Drive reduction

Hull (1943) takes as his point of departure that behaviour is based on the interaction between the number of times that this behaviour has successfully fulfilled a need (the habit) and the strength of the drive which is aroused by this need. His theory thus contains, at least in its original form, a learning and a drive (motivation) component.

The role of pay becomes clear if we examine further the way in which drives operate. Each individual has, according to Hull, a number of primary needs, such as for food, activity, etc. If one of these needs is unsatisfied—i.e. an organic or hormonal lack arises—then the organism is motivated to do something about it. Drives arise to relieve the need. In addition to primary responses, habits—"learned" stimulus–response bonds—will point the way to satisfy the need. Money often forms a good means to supply a need and thus to reduce the force of a drive. Thus money (pay) can be important: The individual associates the occurrence of basic needs and drives *and* the gradual reduction of these with the presence of financial resources. Pay can then take on the meaning of a drive (which is acquired, "learnt'): This can manifest itself without there being any lack of a basic need.

Pay can also be important because it can serve to reduce anxiety (Brown, 1961). The line of reasoning, however, remains the same. An example: Young children associate their painful experiences—falling; touching a sharp object—with worried, anxious behaviour from their parents. Suppose now that their parents also react in this way if they have financial problems: The children will then transfer their own anxiety to money. They are motivated to earn money (later) in order to reduce their anxiety. This drive gradually becomes self-supporting in nature.

2.3 (Partial) reinforcement

According to the operant conditioning theory

(Skinner, 1969)—and the "organizational behavior modification" school related to it (see Luthans & Kreitner, 1985)—it is not necessary to use the concept of drives, as Hull does, to explain how reinforcement comes about. A particular behavioural reaction is reinforced, according to Skinner, through the effect that is linked to it. If money regularly occurs together—in time and space—with the primary satisfying of a need, then it gradually takes on the meaning of a secondary ("learned") reinforcer. Incidentally, contrary to Hull's findings, such a reinforcer can only be effective if a person has been deprived of a need. But that does not have to be the "original" need because the role of money can be *generalized* with respect to all kinds of other needs. Pay is often of such importance because it is a pluriform reinforcer.

What happens, though, if the reward for particular behaviour is withheld every now and then? Animal research has shown that pigeons coo more and rats run to the centre of a maze faster if from time to time no food is provided (see, e.g., Amsel, 1972; Ferster & Skinner, 1957; Petri, 1986; Mawhinney, 1986). This is also termed the "stretching effect": A particular reinforcer requires increasingly improved performance. Do such effects occur with people as well? We will look at this question more closely.

One of the oldest experiments we know was carried out by Yukl and Latham (1975). Planters of very young trees (seedlings) could process about two boxes—each containing about 1000 seedlings—per day. While the normal hourly rate for each planter was guaranteed, three experimental groups were started. In the first group, for each 1000 seedlings there was a bonus of $2: This formed the so-called Continuous Reinforcement (CR) condition. Each member of the second group, after planting 1000 seedlings, had to guess whether a particular coin tossed up would come down heads or tails. If they guessed right, they received $4; if they were wrong, they got no bonus. Because this form of Variable Ratio (VR)—or partial reinforcement—gives a 50% chance of a correct answer, this second condition was termed VR(2).

In the third condition there was VR(4): The outcome of two tossed coins had to be guessed. A correct guess yielded a bonus of $8. Reckoned over a longer period of time these conditions—based on the calculation of probability—would yield the same bonus to the members of the groups involved. It is therefore interesting to examine whether certain reinforcers result in higher performance than others. Contrary to the expectations of the researchers (that VR would produce the best results), the CR group showed a performance increase of 33%. The VR(4) group achieved an 18% increase, whereas the VR(2) group achieved 8% *less*; the performance of a control group remained more or less the same. Shortly afterwards a similar experiment was run (Yukl, Latham, & Pursell, 1976): in this, each planter was faced in succession with the CR and with both VR conditions. Once again, the CR condition resulted in the highest performance; moreover, VR(4) was found unattractive.

Since the end of the 1970s, comparable experiments have been carried out during the summer months among trappers of small beavers. These beavers are active at night, they strip young trees and thus form a threat to forestry in the north-west of the United States and Canada (see e.g. Latham & Dossett, 1978; Saari & Latham, 1982). Here once again the effects of the CR, VR(2), and VR(4) conditions were studied. With CR there was a consistent rise in performance. However, this occurred particularly among the inexperienced trappers. Experienced trappers performed best under the VR(4) condition. Furthermore, the latter system in particular was seen as a form of job enrichment: The trappers reported, among other things, on challenge, variety, and a pleasant excitement in their work.[2]

Yet no univocal conclusions can be drawn from these experiments as regards the effectiveness of partial reinforcement. The same goes for the results of other experiments dealing with, for example, reducing absenteeism, improving sales performance and travelling on public transport. It was apparent that continuous reinforcement led to better performance in nearly all cases in which a comparison could be made with a prior situation and/or that of a control group (in which no link existed between work behaviour and pay).

In the field study of the relative effectiveness of

partial reinforcement, a number of special problems occur. An initial problem is the lack of transparency regarding the criteria used to define the concept of performance. Can the 1000 seedlings from the first experiment be considered an adequate measure of this, or would it have been better to choose the planting of one young tree after another? Or would another component of the action process—digging a hole, taking one seedling out of the box, etc.—have been more appropriate? Closely linked to this is a second problem: when is there a continuous reinforcer-related performance and when a partial one? Shouldn't the CR condition with the beaver trappers have involved the bonus being received immediately after a beaver was trapped? And wasn't the period between the performance of a task and receiving the payment for it too long in various VR experiments? Mawhinney (1986) points out another difficulty: Supposing, as a result of increased performance, more bonus is earned in a particular VR condition—which in fact happened fairly often—then a basic precondition of "stretching" (that the pay remains level) has not been fulfilled. In fact, according to Mawhinney again, the effectiveness of VR can only be studied in a controlled laboratory situation.

Nevertheless, it may be stated that pay for performance generally—almost always with CR; fairly often with VR—led to increased performance. Does the amount of the performance-related pay (which is often called incentive or bonus pay) play the most important role in this? Dickinson and Gillette (1993) argue that this question needs to be analyzed, starting from the kinds of reinforcement that a work environment offers. Reinforcers can be formal or informal in nature, given by colleagues or managers, be work-related or involve profits from outside work, etc. (see also Mawhinney & Gowen, 1990). In practice, reinforcers frequently tend to counteract each other.

The effect of an incentive can be to improve someone's performance. But it is just as likely that the incentive will persuade a staff member to spend more time on his work. If the *work* that someone does is strongly reinforced through financial and non-financial inducements, then it is to be expected that a small incentive will have a

considerable influence on his performance. If there are strong reinforcers of someone's activities *outside* work (for example, making contact with a particular man or woman), then an incentive will produce no effect. If an incentive is large, it is to be expected that the person will become uncertain as a result of the variation in pay that can occur, particularly if he or she does not have much influence on the result (performance or productivity). That is why Dickinson and Gillette anticipate that performance-related pay will lead to better performance than fixed pay (according to job value), but that the amount of the incentive pay is irrelevant. In the simulation experiments which they discuss, an incentive can, for example, add up to 0, 3, 11, 20, or 35% (above the basic pay). The relevant research (Frisch & Dickinson, 1990; Leary et al., 1990; Riedel, Nebeker, & Cooper, 1988; two experiments in Dickinson & Gillette, 1993) has repeatedly shown that the stated expectation is correct. The *fact* of performance-related pay, *not the amount*, determines the performance level. The authors make the interesting suggestion that if payment for results is introduced, staff members should be allowed to choose how much the incentive that applies to them will be.

To conclude this section we return briefly to the difference between continuous and partial reinforcement that was introduced in the experiments with seedling planters and beaver trappers. An interesting question is whether CR in these experiments should not be seen as some kind of partial reinforcement. It was never the case that a direct payment was made immediately following the performance. The reinforcers came some time later. This is probably typical of the reinforcement of a number of forms of work behaviour. Why does an author who cannot get his thoughts down on paper take up his pen again? Because experience has taught him that after a time he will succeed. Similarly, the salesman who, despite fruitless calls on clients, perseveres in trying to obtain orders: Because he *expects* to succeed after a time. This concept is central to the following theory.

2.4 Expectancy

As described in Chapter 11 (this *Handbook*), a person's choice of a behavioural alternative according to this theory is determined by the interaction of three components (see also Van Eerde & Thierry, 1996):

1. the expectation ("expectancy") that a particular effort will lead to a particular performance;
2. the expectation (instrumentality) that producing that performance will lead to particular inducements being obtained;
3. the attractiveness of these inducements.

Lawler (1971) has targeted the second and third component upon the theme of reward. The *importance* of reward is thus determined by the interaction of:

a the extent to which reward is seen as a good means of satisfying certain motives;
b the importance of these motives.

Suppose that a person is striving for a high measure of security in his life. Suppose too that he expects that (more) pay will offer the means for achieving this. The product of both values now represents the importance of pay for him as far as this motive is concerned. If (more) security is not interesting for him, then pay plays no role for him in this respect, even though he might be of the opinion that it would provide him with security.

In order to understand the "total" importance of pay to a person, it is necessary to examine both components regarding each relevant motive. Lawler illustrates this using the motives identified by Maslow (see Figure 12.1).

The total importance of pay for a person is thus made up of the sum of the diverse products (of instrumentality of pay and valence of a motive). If a person indicates, for example, via a questionnaire, that pay is of great importance to him, then—without any more data—the researcher will still not know very much. The latter is well aware that the instrumentality of the pay is highly valued. In addition it may be that the person feels he has few other means at his disposal for achieving his goals. This would explain the result that regularly emerges from research that the more junior staff consider pay more important than those further up the hierarchy. If, on the other hand, a person can see a variety of options for achieving his objectives then—as long as the other variables remain constant—pay will be of lesser importance.

Lawler does not subscribe to all aspects of Maslow's theory (see Chapter 11, Vol. 4, of this *Handbook*). His principal emphasis is on the instrumental nature of pay in relation to salient motives. The concept of classifying the six motives into a hierarchy does not pay any special part in this. He distances himself in particular from the view that Pay should "belong" with the two "lower" motives: pay is in principle, according to Lawler, more or less instrumental with regard to *every* motive.

In the "theory of reasoned action" by Ajzen and Fishbein (e.g. 1980), we encounter various ideas from "expectancy theory". Actual behaviour, according to Ajzen and Fishbein, is determined by a person's intentions. These intentions are the result of two interacting variables. The first is the attitude towards behaviour. This attitude is built up from "beliefs" about the link between behaviour and outcomes in relation to the estimated value of those outcomes. The second variable that

FIGURE 12.1

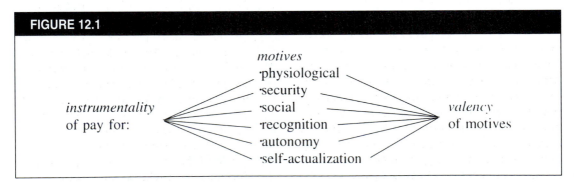

Importance of pay (Lawler, 1971).

affects intentions is the subjective norm: This norm has to do with the views of relevant others regarding the person's behaviour; the motivation of the person to conform to those others also plays a part. Langedijk (1995, 1997) has used this theory to predict the choices for working conditions that employees and managers might make where flexible compensation is adopted (such as, e.g., the Cafeteria Plan).

2.5 A hygiene variable?

In this section a view emerges that is clearly at variance with the basic idea outlined so far. As is well known, the two-factor theory (Herzberg, Mausner, & Snyderman, 1959; Herzberg, 1966) states that the *work-content characteristics*—also called intrinsic factors, motivators, "satisfiers'— can give rise to satisfaction, but never to dissatisfaction. If something is lacking with regard to a characteristic of the work content, it causes a feeling of indifference: It doesn't matter. Conversely, *work context characteristics* (extrinsic aspects; hygiene; "dissatisfiers') can cause dissatisfaction but not satisfaction. If such aspects are "okay", then a feeling of indifference also arises. In short: Work context aspects must be adequate, but they do not motivate; by emphasizing intrinsic aspects of work people are really challenged in their job.

Intrinsic aspects relate primarily to performance and gaining recognition for performance. Additional features are the challenges and responsibilities of the work and getting promotion. Context aspects consist, among other things, of the policy and management of the company, leadership styles, and interpersonal relations.

The position of pay is interesting here. In their original publication (1959, pp.82–83) Herzberg et al. devoted a separate passage to this. Pay proved to be mentioned just as often in relation to satisfaction as in relation to dissatisfaction. As a "producer" of satisfaction the respondents apparently interpreted pay as a sign of recognition, as a sign that they were performing well and that progress at work was being made. In relation to dissatisfaction the pay denoted an unfair pay system: increases were given too late or grudgingly; the differentials of pay compared with the more experienced personnel or those who had just joined the company were too small. Incidentally, it is worth pointing out how much these results conform to the "expectancy" theory approach discussed in the previous section.

Yet Herzberg et al.— in our opinion, not supported by their research data—have categorized pay as a "dissatisfier", a work-context variable. Pay is thus not "really" important: With a view to motivation and performance all the emphasis, according to Herzberg, should be on the quality and the content of the work and on fostering personal growth in the workplace. This plea has been warmly received by the "job enrichment" movement, as is demonstrated elsewhere (see Chapter 11, Vol. 4, of this *Handbook*). But it also went down well with many managers and personnel officers. They found a connection between the idea derived from Maslow's theory that pay indicates one or more needs at a "lower" level. From this grew the conviction that pay has little or no significance for the motivation of individual working behaviour.

This "conviction" appears to be particularly persistent. It is remarkable that since the late 1960s researchers have not shown any more interest in the two theories so that no (recent) research exists to support this conviction. It is probably also as a consequence of this conviction that the number of experiments with pay in practice has remained so modest for so long.

2.6 Cognitive evaluation

According to Deci (1975; Deci & Ryan, 1985) a clear distinction must be made between intrinsic and extrinsic motivation. Each person has two basic needs: The desire to be *competent* and striving to *be the cause* of one's own behaviour. Based on this, each person is in search of challenging situations. Intrinsic motivation occurs when a person chooses behaviour that gives her the feeling of being self-determined and competent. The outcomes of that behaviour *inform* her of the extent to which it has succeeded each time and lead to a continuance of intrinsically motivated behaviour. But when an inducement for that intrinsically motivated behaviour is given by someone else, the person will no longer locate the cause of her behaviour in herself. A process of re-evaluation occurs: The person experiences the inducement as *controlling her behaviour* from a source outside herself (extrinsic). As a consequence the intrinsic motivation decreases: The motivation is being determined by extrinsic causes.

Analogous to this, pay, according to Deci, can have two meanings. If someone is paid on the basis of the time he has worked—i.e. a *fixed* wage per hour, day or month, for example—then the intrinsic motivation does not undergo any change. A fixed wage apparently has a meaning that is informative about capacity and "self-causation'. But if he receives payment for his *performance—* per piece, for the quality or speed—then the inducement for his behaviour is determined by a third party. Owing to this dependence he will attribute the inducement for his behaviour externally. Consequently, the intrinsic motivation will be lower (and the extrinsic motivation higher).

Despite the fact that there has been severe criticism of this theory and of the distinction between intrinsic-extrinsic motivation as such (see, e.g., Thierry, 1990; Vinke, 1996; Chapter 11, Vol. 4, of this *Handbook*), the concept of intrinsic motivation has exerted a good deal of attraction in practice. To a lot of managers it suggests that if a person finds his job stimulating, then "the rest" is hardly of any importance to his motivation and performance. "The rest" includes such things as the working conditions, and thus the pay. Earlier we came across the—in itself incorrect—notion derived from Maslow and Herzberg that payment has little meaning anyway for relevant working behaviour. To this is now added that on no account should use be made of performance-related pay because negative consequences can be expected. We will elaborate on the validity of this last conclusion in section 4.

2.7   Contributions–inducements

In the theories that have been reviewed so far, payment in general has been linked with particular (performance) results of working behaviour, namely as one of the inducements for this. There are considerable differences of opinion in these theories, incidentally, regarding the nature of those links. In the approaches touched on in this section, payment is also seen as an inducement: Now, however, this concerns the relationship with the contribution made by the person to the work, and then in the framework of an exchange model.

The first school of thought is social psychological in origin. Against the background of Festinger's theory of social comparison (1954), Homans (1961), in his theory of *distributive justice*, argues that a person's investments, costs, and inducements must be in proportion to the comparative ratios of a referent other. Investments are contributions of a general, longer-term nature, such as age and experience. Costs are much more specific contributions such as effort made, risks taken. They can also be seen as negative inducements. Positive inducements include status, pay, recognition. If the profit (the difference between yields and costs) both for the person and for the other is disproportionate to the investments, then the resulting dissatisfaction forms the trigger for introducing change.

As mentioned in Chapter 11 (Vol. 4, of this *Handbook*), Adams' *"equity" theory* (1963) is an attempt to specify more clearly how injustice arises and what the consequences of this are. On the basis of his input(contributions)–outcome (inducements) model—which is often illustrated using the combination effort–reward—he not only outlines diverse forms of dissonance but also various ways in which dissonance can be reduced (see Syroit, 1984).

The meaning of pay in this type of approach thus not only depends on the outcome of the comparison with one (or more) *other(s),* but also on the *characteristics* (attributes) that the person includes in her comparison. These characteristics refer not only to contributions but also to other inducements. Research using, among other things, the Input–Outcome Questionnaire (Tornow, 1975; Von Grumbkov, 1980) shows that this distinction is not so straightforward. Furthermore, it appears that the person is able to "adapt" the choice of the referent other(s). This referent might be, as was assumed earlier, another person with whom social interaction does or does not exist. The referent can also be constituted by the person herself in the past or in the future. In Folger's "Referent Cognition Theory" (1986) the person compares herself with so-called "referential rewards": These are inducements that the person considers both available *and* attractive. The group as a referent is found in Runciman's "Relative Deprivation Theory" (1966), whereas Berger, Zelditch, Anderson, and

Cohen (1972) emphasize that the person uses stable reference structures, such as, for example, opinions about an equitable distribution of income according to age. Hermkens (1995) points out, incidentally, that it is not only the *outcome* of comparisons with referents that is involved, but also the *procedures* that are followed for this. This "procedural justice" is seen as determining some-one's general attitude to a company; the "distribu-tive justice" mentioned earlier is seen as primarily affecting a person's satisfaction with her pay (Miceli & Lane, 1991).

In the second school of thought the *contract* between the individual member of staff and the organization is used as an exchange model. Bar-nard (1938) was probably the first who system-atically tailored the "contributions–inducements" model to target the working behaviour of employees and essential leadership tasks. Simon (1947; see also March & Simon, 1958) made productive use of this for clarifying individual decisions regarding whether or not to join an enterprise and regarding the quality of individual working behaviour. It is within this framework that the concept of "limited rationality" was developed: This concerns on the one hand individ-ual decision-making and on the other hand the resources that the organization can deploy for this. Although this "administrative science" approach concerns the individual who must make choices between contributions and inducements, consider-ation is also given to the (organizational) influenc-ing of that process.

Belcher and Atchison (Belcher, 1974; Belcher & Atchison, 1976) have used the contract model to draw attention to uncertain and unbalanced aspects in the employment contract between employee and employer. They argue that the usual employment contracts hardly specify any exchange relations other than those between labour and income, whereas both parties have many more expectations about each other's non-material contributions and inducements. Those expectations, however, are generally incomplete and only specified in part. They argue in favour of specifying considerably more exchange relations in employment contracts, for example, regarding the flexibility and sense of responsibility expected from a staff member on the one hand and the

satisfying social relations and a certain status expected from an employer on the other. Current research addresses e.g. the concept of the *psycho-logical contract,* according to which perceptions of rights and duties of both employee and employer, as well as their mutual expectations, constitute core themes. Perceived contract viol-ations may affect motivation, satisfaction, per-formance, and other "behaviour" at work (like absenteeism), and may also impact upon the formal contract between parties (e.g. Rousseau, 1990; Robinson & Rousseau, 1994; Robinson, 1997; Makin, Cooper, & Cox, 1997).

The "agency" theory is economic in origin (see, e.g., Holmstrom, 1979; Nalbantian, 1987; Eisen-hardt, 1988; Beatty & Zajac, 1994) and relates to the exchange process within an organization between a "principal" (for example, an employer) and an "agent" (an employee) who is taken on to the staff. Each party will endeavour to protect their own interests and achieve maximum utility. If the employee in taking care of her own interests also promotes the interests of the employer, there is no problem. But suppose now that the "agent" were to rest on his or her laurels, is oriented towards short-term gains or perhaps steals organization property, whereas the interests of the "principal" lie in a high level of yields, which will ensure the survival of his company in the long term: How are such risks dealt with? A first important point is the extent to which parties are prepared to accept risks or tend to shift these as much as possible. A second point is whether the "principal" is in a position to record the behaviour of the "agent" (monitoring) and if so, whether the costs of this are not extremely high. Take, for example, employees who carry out service and maintenance for clients or staff members who have specialist knowledge. In such situations it is almost impossible to regularly monitor the behaviour of an "agent" or to evaluate him or her. In such cases, the "principal" will try to shift the risks which he or she runs as much as possible on to the shoulders of the "agent" by making a part of the pay dependent on performance (via a performance bonus, options on shares, etc.). The more averse the "agent" is to taking risks, the more he or she will try to get "compensation", for example, in the form of a higher level of pay. The "agency" theory thus attempts to offer an explanation for the pay "structure" (the systems and forms) and the level of pay in an organization.

3 MEANINGS OF PAY

3.1 Four categories

The theories discussed in the previous section each in their own way provide an answer to the question of *how* pay can acquire meaning for an individual. This always involves the relationship between the pay (as a reward) and the contribution to or the results of working behaviour. However, *what* the meanings of pay are have not yet been indicated; only Lawler has drawn attention to the instrumental nature of pay.

We now examine four kinds of meaning which pay can have in principle for its "recipient". These four meanings are identified in our "reflection theory" of pay, which will be dealt with after that. Subsequently, the perspective is shifted and we address the strategic and "managerial" functions of pay.

The reflection theory is based on the idea that the developing and retaining of one's self-identity are essential for the person's "internal" organization (for a more detailed discussion, see Thierry, 1992a, 1992b, forthcoming; Miedema-Van den Heuvel, 1994; Van den Heuvel & Thierry, 1995). The internal organization should be continually coordinated with internal and external changes. This is why the person scans incoming information for signals that might concern himself. Working people thus pay attention to such things as (the appraisal of) their performance, power differences, social relations, etc.; one of the reasons for comparing oneself with others is to affirm one's self-identity (Austin, 1977). An important component of work and working conditions consists of the payment made for it.

Pay has no "intrinsic" meaning. It acquires meaning because it contains information about "other" areas which are generally of great importance to the person. Pay *reflects* opportunities and events in four domains:

1. *Motivational properties*. Pay has meaning in proportion to how much the person sees pay as a good means of achieving important motives and worthwhile goals. For instance, many employees expect to get more security in their lives, for example, by buying an insurance policy. They can also expect to receive recognition via their pay for the level of their job or for the quality of their performance, etc. This first category of meaning is directly derived from the "expectancy" theory discussed in section 2.4.

2. *Relative position*. This has two dimensions. Pay can, in the first place, contain information about the amount of progress made in the work *vis-à-vis* set *task goals* (i.e. the position of the person with respect to the goal). This "feedback" makes clear to a staff member the extent to which her results are on course or have already answered their purpose. In the second place, pay can inform the staff member about her position vis-à-vis *others*. It describes her effectiveness in relation to other members of the group or department, comparable staff posts in other companies, managers and their subordinates, members of the same occupational group, etc.

Various theories relate to both components of relative position. These concern the various contributions–inducements theories which were discussed in section 2.7 (social comparison theory, agency theory, contract model), but there is also the "goal-setting" theory (Locke & Latham, 1990), which addresses the role of feedback in increased performance. This second meaning, relative position, essentially relates to the regulation of working behaviour.

3. *Control*. This meaning is also of a regulatory nature and refers to the "dependence" of a staff member. Pay reflects the extent to which a staff member has been able to influence others, such as for example his/her manager, colleagues, clients, and suppliers. But pay can also reflect that those others exert influence on him or her, and equally that the quality of tools and equipment has an influence. The level of "dependence" is determined by a person's position in the organizational hierarchy, his or her "role set", and the amount of autonomy in the work. Thus, a person can read (just as with the other meanings) his or her degree of "control" from the amount of pay, the (reasons for) variation in it, the composition of the pay package, whether or not s/he receives a bonus, etc.

The social comparison theory and agency theory mentioned in section 2.7 are also relevant to this third meaning. The reader is referred to the Resource Dependence theory (Pfeffer & Salancik, 1978) as well, which relates to features that can provide individuals and groups in an organization with more relative power.

4. *Spending.* In the fourth place, pay denotes the goods and services purchased. It is not the purchase itself that is the key issue, but the extent to which important motives and goals (see "motivational properties") are realized. Of particular importance are the *utility* of the spending and also the *ease* or the difficulty with which it is done. Indirect references to this are found in the expectancy theory (section 2.4) and in contribution–inducement theories (section 2.7).

For measuring these four meanings, scales have been constructed and validated based on data from a large number of Dutch organizations (Biessen, 1992; Miedema-van den Heuvel, 1994; Van den Heuvel & Thierry, 1995; Thierry, forthcoming). From the research it appeared that in practice correlations fairly often occur between relative position and control, as well as between motivational properties and spending. Yet a solution based on (the intended) four factors appears to provide the best fit.[3]

The extent to which pay reflects these four meanings each time is influenced by a number of aspects. In the first place, the "structure" of the pay in an organization plays a role: This involves such elements as the pay system in question (salary for the job with or without performance bonus, etc.), the form of payment (individual, per group, or per business unit), and the practical implementation (degree of secrecy, participation of staff members, etc.). A second important aspect is the extent to which the pay policy is integrated into the strategic company policy and, also in this context, the extent to which other instruments of Human Resource policy (such as selection, evaluation, and management development) are tailored to the goals to be achieved via payment (we will come back to this in the following section).

3.2 Meanings and working behaviour

The key points of the reflection theory of the influence of pay on individual work behaviour are shown in Figure 12.2.

If a staff member has some knowledge and insight regarding the systems according to which he or she is paid, the pay will have more effect on his or her motivation, performance, and satisfaction, the more meaning that pay has for him or her (i.e. score higher on the four categories of meaning). We assume that payment that is not considered very instrumental, which says little about the progress in someone's work (also in relation to others), which reveals little about his/her influence, and which hardly affects his/her spending

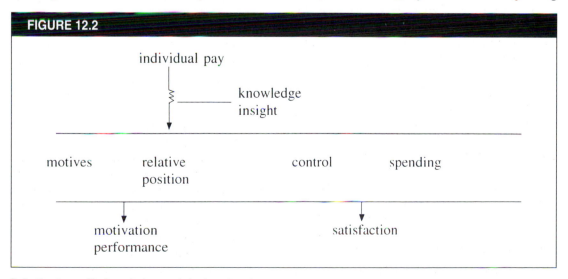

FIGURE 12.2

Reflection theory: The impact of pay on behaviour at work.

(for example, because the pay is very low), also has hardly any effect on work behaviour. If we wish to extend one or more meanings, then it is required that the condition in a certain area to which pay refers—e.g. via the relative position—and changes in it, are to be expressed in the pay via the pay system implemented.

In section 4 we will come back to the way in which the concept of *performance* can be operationalized, for example, in the context of systems of performance-related pay. As regards the operationalising of the *satisfaction* with pay, Lawler's model (1971) has had a good deal of influence. In it, Lawler combines "equity" theory (section 2.7) with the discrepancy model (according to this latter model, the degree of satisfaction with an object is determined by the difference between what the person desires regarding the object and the person's own perception of what he has received from it). A person is, according to Lawler, entirely satisfied with his pay if the amount that he *ought to* receive matches his own perception of what *has been* received. The opinion regarding the desired pay is influenced by features of the person (such as, e.g., skill, experience and previous performance), by perceived features of the job (e.g. level, degree of difficulty, etc.) and by the perceived contributions and inducements of referent others. The perception of the amount "actually" received is influenced by, among other things, the amounts that the referent others receive. Lawler's model has been adapted and expanded by Dyer and Theriault (1976): For instance, the extent to which the person considers the pay system appropriate has been added as a component seen as directly influencing pay satisfaction. Furthermore, the amount that people wish to receive is considered dependent on the cost of living, on financial needs, and on the financial scope. Crosby (1976) argues, on the basis of her relative deprivation model, that someone experiences more dissatisfaction with his/her pay, if he/she:

- finds more discrepancy between the desired and received pay;
- finds that a referent other has received more;
- had expected more based on the pay in the past;

- has no high expectation of better pay in the future;
- feels entitled to more pay;
- does not consider him/herself responsible for not receiving more pay.

It is interesting that the aspects identified by Crosby show fairly low intercorrelations (see also Sweeney, McFarlin, & Inderrieden, 1990). Heneman and Schwab (1985) are of the opinion that pay or salary satisfaction has been incorrectly defined as a one-dimensional concept. In their Pay Satisfaction Questionnaire they identify the following four dimensions (see also Scarpello, Huber, & Vandenberg, 1988).

- pay level: satisfaction with the amount of the salary;
- pay raises: satisfaction with the amount and the equity of increases;
- pay benefits: satisfaction with fringe benefits;
- pay administration: satisfaction with the salary policy in practice.

Miceli and Lane (1991) argue against including all possible determinants of pay satisfaction in one model, but advocate differentiating relevant determinants according to satisfaction with pay level, benefit level, pay system within job, pay system between jobs, and benefit system respectively. Furthermore, these determinants should be adopted for both the current and the expected situation.

In the Dutch research on the reflection theory of pay, Miedema-Van den Heuvel (1994) has adapted the PSQ scales for the Dutch industrial relations climate and subsequently validated them. Her data shows that a solution based on four factors—in accordance with the assumed four dimensions—offers the best fit. Furthermore, it appears that only the "relative position" meaning accounts for the fact that there is some variation in the four satisfaction dimensions. Research since then (Thierry, forthcoming) shows that "relative position" is one of the more important meanings for interpreting dimensions of pay satisfaction, but also that other meanings of pay can account for pay satisfaction (see also Shaw, 1996).

The role of the moderating variables *knowledge and insight* shown in Figure 12.2 is less clear than might first have been thought. Of course it is true that pay systems of which staff members have no knowledge or which they do not know enough about generally do not produce the effect for which they were introduced (see, e.g., Thierry, 1987). But the minimum amount of knowledge necessary for pay to be effective is not known (see Miedema-Van den Heuvel, 1994). Furthermore, another question is whether knowledge and insight always fully *precede* the influencing of working behaviour. In theories in which the concept of "reinforcement" is central, it is the successful inducement–behaviour relations from which the person gains the experience of how connections in relations are shaped. The person might deduce, initially based on inducement–behaviour relations that occur and that he had not expected, how her knowledge and insight are lacking. There is a possibility that cognitive processes are especially important—in this case, concerning the functioning of a pay system—when some experience is gained with links between inducements and behaviour. We consider research into this of great importance.

In Figure 12.3 an overview is given of the principal determinants of the meanings. We assume that six groups of determinants affect the meaning that a person's pay has for him or her. We briefly comment on these, starting at the bottom. First, we point out the characteristics of the person. Apart from the knowledge and insight referred to in Figure 12.2, the meaning attached to pay can be influenced by e.g. a person's age, education, previous income, etc., but also by certain personality characteristics. One such is "negative affect": A dispositional variable that indicates the extent to which facets of the person, of others, and of the world in general are interpreted by him/her as negative, unsuccessful, failing. For instance, George, Brief, Webster, and Burke (1989) found that workers with a high score on negative affect consider a system of performance-related pay as potentially damaging to their welfare.

Meanings of pay can, in the second place, be influenced by the requirements of the job. Features of this—such as the number of different abilities and skills that are required, or the extent to which independent decisions can be taken—are con-

sidered in the periodic individual performance appraisal. The result of this often affects the decision of whether or not to award a pay increase (see section 4). Features of the job can also form a part of a system of performance-related payment. At the same time they determine to an important degree how dependent staff members are on each other.

This brings a third category of determinants into view: Features of the group(s) within the company to which the staff member relates. Thus a staff member compares, for example, his contributions and inducements (e.g. pay) with those of one or more colleagues. Furthermore, group members can through their actions often exert direct influence on his work, e.g. on the quality of it (and thus indirectly on his pay). The group also influences the behaviour of individual members via the norms (for example, regarding differentials in pay), values, and goals subscribed to by the members (see Hermkens, 1995; Thierry, 1997).

Work unit (the fourth category) is understood to mean the department or unit in which a staff member works. Features of this include the opinions and behaviour of the leader: The extent to which s/he supports a staff member and gives feedback on the progress and results of the work can have a considerable influence on the meanings which the pay has. The quality of the pay systems adopted also falls into this category.

The determinants reviewed so far in most cases probably affect directly the meanings of pay. Expectations are that the two categories that will now be addressed play a more indirect role. Organisational characteristics such as technology and the degree of (de)centralization, primarily affect the work unit and the job, and via these the meanings attached to pay. Thus, a more decentralized structure often offers more opportunities for tuning pay characteristics with what is of great importance for the working process of a department or division. A characteristic such as culture probably has both a direct and an indirect effect. Furthermore, it is a matter of two-way traffic: On the one hand, the culture in an organization emerges in the policy and practice relating to pay, through which it is predicted that culture can also affect the meanings. On the other hand, the pay

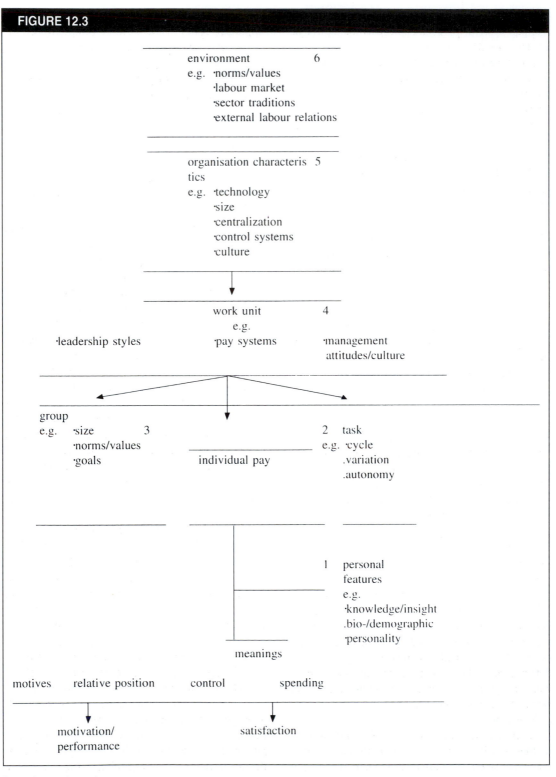

FIGURE 12.3

Determinants of meanings.

structure can influence the culture in an organization (Lawler, 1990; Gomez-Mejia & Balkin, 1992; Thierry, 1993).

Environmental characteristics—the sixth and final category—relate among other things to the job market and the industrial relations between employers" organizations and unions. The relative scarcity of employees affects among other things the level of pay. That, of course, also applies to the agreements made regarding working conditions.

The reflection theory is of a temporary nature, on the one hand because data regarding individual work performance is difficult to compile in practice, on the other hand because research into its possible validity in other countries (with their different cultures and traditions as regards industrial relations and working conditions) has only recently started.

3.3 Strategic pay

In recent years there has been increasing interest in strategic pay (see Lawler, 1990; Gomez-Mejia & Balkin, 1992). "Strategic pay" means that when determining the way in which its staff members are paid, an organization takes account of its general strategic policy objectives. These objectives are quite often summarized in a "mission statement": This contains the organization's principal challenges, problems, and opportunities, the main features of the business plan, the deployment of people and resources, the meaning of (changes in) the organization culture, the consistency between organizational and personal instruments, etc. Such policy objectives actually need to be regularly adjusted or completely revised from time to time, particularly when the organization is operating in uncertain markets and (societal, political, and economic) developments are difficult to predict. Strategic pay means that where decisions about important components of the pay are concerned—such as salary level, salary differentials, the extent of performance pay, direct or deferred pay, choice of benefits, etc.—account is continually taken of the extent to which the main features of the strategic company policy are reflected in it.

Gomez-Mejia and Balkin (1992) mention 17 themes (which are partly interconnected) with regard to which a choice must be made. These themes can be divided into three categories:

1. *Basis for pay*, including pay for the job or pay for skills; individual or aggregate pay; corporate or business unit performance as basis.
2. *Design*: fixed or incentive pay; frequency of (bonus) pay, etc.
3. *Administration*: for example, centralized or decentralized decision-making; secrecy or openness.

Gomez-Mejia and Balkin, also on the basis of empirical data, have identified two pay strategies that can be defined more or less as the two poles of one continuum. One strategy is termed *algorithmic*: It is a standardized method of pay in which according to previously determined criteria it is primarily the job that is rewarded, the maturity (e.g. experience) of the individual staff member carries more weight than her performance, while decisions about pay are usually taken at the top of the organization. The algorithmic strategy is suited to organizations with a rather bureaucratic structure and whose strategic policy is characterized among other things by the attempt to maintain existing market positions ("defenders", as Miles & Snow put it, 1978). The other strategy is called *experiential*: This is a flexible method, sensitive to market changes, oriented towards rewarding performance in the longer term, whereby skills and risk-taking among other things can also be rewarded. The experiential strategy is suited to companies with a more organic structure, in which decisions about pay are taken by the lower echelons in the organization and whose strategic policy is characterized by growth and change ("dynamic growth", as Miles & Snow express it, 1978). We are of the opinion that further research into strategic pay is of great importance, particularly into the question of what determines the degree of "fit" between the strategic company policy and the pay structure.

But what should be understood by "strategic" pay if there are no strategic company objectives and no mission statement in an organization? In that case, it could be based on strategic or *managerial functions* of pay, which, in view of the pay systems adopted in practice, are apparently put first and foremost. To that end, we link up with the meanings of pay identified earlier, but now from the angle of the manager, who, also via pay, wishes to achieve certain objectives. If the manager wishes to influence the working behaviour of his staff through their pay, then the systems concerned will have to "score" highly on a number of the meanings. We identify six managerial functions of pay (Thierry, Koopman-Iwema, & Vinke, 1988; Lawler, 1990). We mention a number of relevant systems to illustrate each function and we will return to these in section 4.

Based on the salary system that an organization has adopted, it can be discovered which managerial or strategic objectives are apparently being pursued. Other objectives can also be set for the pay, such as, for example, influencing the organization culture, changing the organization structure, and cutting labour costs. We are of the opinion, however, that such functions are of a more indirect nature and can be pursued via one or more of the six functions mentioned.

---

4   PAY SYSTEMS

4.1   Introduction

In most countries a staff member's pay is the result of applying three or four principles. These vary greatly, however, in the way they are worked out, not only between countries, but also between industrial sectors (e.g. government as opposed to industry) and within a company between categories of personnel (for example, the shop floor as opposed to executive level). In general, the job value is very important for determining the level of pay: The point of this first principle is which qualifications are necessary for a job—compared with other jobs—and how much is paid for them on the job market generally speaking. In determining the *job salary*, regarding which in north-west European countries guidelines are incorporated as a rule in a collective agreement, the company can also take account of internal considerations. A company, however, can also make use of "wage surveys": Each year, various firms of consultants publish the results of national and international surveys of salary levels (and fringe benefits) for a whole range of jobs. In order to determine the job value, job evaluation (see Chapter 8, Vol. 3, this *Handbook*) is fairly often used. Generally, the

major part of the pay is accounted for by the job salary. In the Netherlands that is more than 90%. This only refers to the level of the job; a staff member's actual performance is not taken into consideration.

This last is central to the second principle: *pay for performance*. As a rule, a performance above a certain norm or standard is rewarded with a premium or bonus. A "structural" pay increase is sometimes awarded: The fixed salary then rises one or more steps up the relevant salary scale. In the Netherlands, just over 20% of personnel subject to a collective agreement (in companies and establishments with 20 or more employees) fall under a such a system. In other countries, performance-related pay is applied on a larger scale, although over the years considerable variations occur. These are caused among other things by changes in the regulations laid down by national governments, the changing views of entrepreneurs, managers and unions, far-reaching technological changes, and other elements concerning the organization of the work process (for example, more autonomous units).

A third principle concerns the *fringe benefits*. We are not thinking of social security here, but of additional provisions ('benefits') that have been agreed per company and/or per sector. These involve, for example, (supplementary) pension coverage, health insurance (or reimbursement of certain expenses due to illness), or life insurance. Within a company, these can vary greatly.

Fourth, there are the so-called *'perquisites'* (or "perks", emoluments): These are quite often exclusively applicable to categories of senior personnel. These are a mixed bag of allowances, for example, for mileage (or a company car), for telephone calls and for membership of clubs. But they also include canteen subsidies, allowance towards mortgage-interest repayments, favourable savings schemes, etc., which in some sectors of industry apply to all employees.

For the remainder of this section a slightly different format will be used. Job value related pay is left aside (see Chapter 8, Vol. 3). First of all, systems of performance-related pay are highlighted. After that the Cafeteria or flexible compensation systems will be considered (whereby choices can be made from among fringe benefits

TABLE 12.1.	
Managerial functions of pay.	
Function	*System/Method*
1. *Attracting* personnel on the job market	* Job salary (via job evaluation or via wage survey) * Performance-related pay (if high performers are sought) * System that suits the organization culture (e.g. Flexiplan at Dow Chemical Europe)
2. *Keeping* competent staff members	* Keep bonus: stock options; shares; market allowance * Profit-sharing * Gain-sharing (Scanlon or Rucker Plan) * Cafeteria Plan
3. *Stimulating* good or high performance	* Performance-related pay (various alternatives)
4. *Learning* new working behaviour (new technology; reorganization)	* Performance-related pay (rewarding risk-taking behaviour) * Skill pay
5. *Compensating* for inconveniences of the job (e.g. dirty work, unsocial hours)	* Via job evaluation in job salary * Separate bonus
6. *Preventing* or *solving* conflicts	* Via job evaluation in job salary * Profit-sharing

and perks), and finally incidental pay will be examined.

4.2 Performance-related pay

4.2.1 Two characteristics

The principle of performance-related pay involves on the one hand defining what constitutes a *normal performance*, i.e. a performance that in average circumstances can be achieved by the appropriate staff members (selected, trained, with the necessary experience) using normal effort (see also Van Silfhout, 1995). In quite a lot of cases it is obvious what is meant by "performance", for example, for a salesman who sells or leases photocopiers. But often it is harder, such as when as a result of new technologies the intervention of a worker in the process is sporadic (process operators), or his/her contribution takes place in project groups whose configuration constantly changes (consultants of hard- and software systems). And thus work study

is required, which is necessary anyway in order to determine what a "normal" performance is (see also section 4.2.6). If the work study is carried out properly, then each of the phases that the products or services to be provided go through will be examined to see how, using as few resources as possible (efficiency), the objectives set can be achieved as well as possible (effectiveness). This also includes the analysis of working methods that experienced staff members apply.

On the other hand, performance-related pay involves *linking* the performance to a bonus. Sometimes we see that a bonus is awarded just for achieving the performance norm; in other cases the bonus only applies to performances better than the norm. Figure 12.4 illustrates this principle.

In Figure 12.4 a performance norm is given along the horizontal axis and along the vertical axis some bonus percentages are shown, in addition to the rate for the job. In many countries it

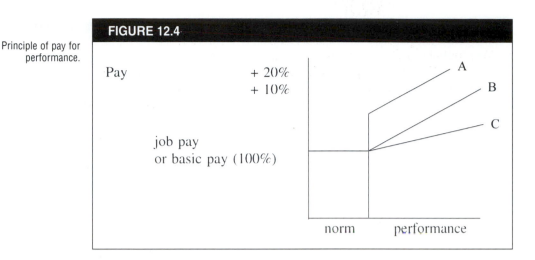

Principle of pay for performance.

FIGURE 12.4

is the case that the rate for the job—set at 100%—is always paid (thus also for performances where the norm has not been achieved). Line A represents the example where a bonus is given for achieving the norm. In this case that is 10% (i.e. 10% of the rate for the job, so that the pay amounts to 110%). If the performance is better, then the bonus rises proportionally. On Line B only performances above the norm are given a bonus. Line C forms one of the numerous other options: to start with, 50% of the increased performance is rewarded (termed "half-over'), but the better this becomes, the lower the bonus ('degressive, curvilinear" relation).

4.2.2 Piece-rate pay

One of the oldest forms of performance related pay is pay per piece: The job pay is not guaranteed. For each piece of work—say mowing $1m^2$ of grass—a certain amount is given. If a rate for the job or basic pay is guaranteed, then we talk of *piece rates*. As a result of the technological developments in trade and industry, there are no longer many examples of "piece" production for which simply the number produced forms an adequate criterion of performance. But if people are set on that, a bonus can of course be paid per parcel delivered, per sausage made, per bicycle, car, or aeroplane built.

Elsewhere we have published the results of some thousands of studies from the past 40 years into the functioning of systems of performance-

related pay and of fixed pay (Thierry, 1987). Nearly 40 of these involved piece rates. In 34 studies, a higher performance was reported and in 5 a better organization of the work. That last is remarkable, because piece-rate work rarely involves any previous work study. There are hardly any negative results against this. Piece rate is, in many respects, a simple system that is easily understood.

4.2.3 Performance-bonus ("tariff") system

If the number of pieces cannot be determined (as in process production) or do not form a relevant criterion, a *performance-bonus* (also called: *tariff or measured-rate*) *system* can be applied. Generally, some prior research *is* carried out into this, because norms are relevant to e.g. the pace at which the work is carried out, or the quality of the product, or the use of expensive materials, etc. Mostly, requirements also have to be specified for the working methods and tools and/or additional materials to be used. The calculation of the bonus is in accordance with the principle described in Figure 12.4. If various features of the expected performance are simultaneously of importance, then we talk of *multifactor pay*. The performance-bonus scheme is followed, but norms are set for more performance aspects, such as for quality (which, for example, may vary within set tolerance limits), for being economical with energy or with raw materials, for hygiene in the workplace (e.g. if light-sensitive materials are being used), etc. (readers interested in further details of the technical aspects of these and other wage systems are referred to: Thierry, 1969; Marriott, 1971; Lawler, 1971; Koopman-Iwema & Thierry, 1981; Milkovich & Newman, 1984; Wallace & Fay, 1988; Thierry, Koopman-Iwema, & Vinke, 1988; Rock & Berger, 1991; Bruns, 1992; Wilson, 1995).

A mixed picture emerges from the survey of research mentioned here. On the plus side are a better cooperation and, especially, a higher performance, which is at times impressive. It is not possible to check the extent to which the higher performance is caused by the linking of performance and pay or by the results of the preceding work studies. But the downside includes such things as lower performance, complaints about the norms, a lack of insight into the relation between performance and pay, and mistrust, including fear of "cutting'. Cutting the norms (or rates) means that when performances are regularly better than the norm, the norm is tightened without the bonus being adjusted (although it is probable that cutting only very seldom occurs, the fear of it has a clearly negative effect on working behaviour).

Performance-bonus schemes can have favourable results for staff members and for the company. But great demands are made: The performance features for which norms are set must be relevant (and thus may not exclude important aspects) *and* they must be able to be influenced by the staff members. New work studies are needed on a regular basis in order to incorporate modifications in the work (owing to changes in technology and organization) into the norms. Furthermore, the system needs to be easily understood by members of staff (see also Miceli & Lane, 1991).

4.2.4 Merit rating

It is common practice with merit rating that staff members are evaluated once a year by their manager—usually in November or December. The results of this are given "financial shape'. Figure 12.5 shows a typical example.

We have borrowed the foregoing characteristics from an arbitrarily selected appraisal instrument, which is used for the appraisal of each staff member. For each characteristic, one (poor) to four (excellent) points can be awarded. On the right is shown the conversion of the total result into the bonus percentage. In addition, it quite often happens that there is a departmental budget, which the manager has to observe when determining each person's bonus. The appraisal result can also be expressed in positions (steps) on the salary scale that applies to the relevant job. In some cases the percentage bonus to be awarded may be greater, the higher the job level. In companies that apply profit-sharing, the appraisal result can determine what percentage of the maximum amount of profit to be allocated is to be awarded.

In order to appraise personnel in an effective way, quite a lot of skill is needed. There are

---

FIGURE 12.5

characteristics	appraisal				result		
	1	2	3	4			
	poor	adeq.	good	excell.		score	bonus
· quantity							
· quality					total		
· dedication						6 - 10	0
· initiative						10 - 15	3%
· human relations						15 - 21	6%
skills						21 - 24	9%
· general impression							

Merit rating.

various traps into which appraisers (and also appraisees) regularly seem to fall; these are focused on in detail in Chapter 4, Vol. 3 of this *Handbook*. We will briefly examine a few of these, precisely because this system, relatively speaking, is widely used. The objective of the personal appraisal is often to identify and discuss the good as well as the less satisfactory aspects of the *performance over the previous period*. A second objective is quite often to reach agreements about the *objectives for the coming period*, often in the context of special emphases to be laid (such as follow-up courses or training, being given a number of new tasks, etc.; we will leave aside the effects on pay for the time being). In many cases features such as those shown in Figure 12.5 are used: Apart from the quantity and quality of the work, dedication, initiative, and human-relations skills are considered. Comparable features are, for example, responsibility, accuracy, creativity, ability to express oneself, etc. Such characteristics are fairly often called behavioural features, but actually involve skills, sometimes a combination of personality characteristics and skills. It is considered an advantage of the somewhat abstract nature of such features that they are applicable to all the jobs in an organization. But if they are applied in order to appraise staff members in a specific job, then a number of tricky problems emerge. For example, it is not clear exactly what each feature means; this often leads to a whole range of misunderstandings or differences of opinion during a round of appraisals. Furthermore, there are hardly any features relevant to every job in an organization. Moreover, the features that are lacking are often precisely those specific to one job. The impression is also often given that someone's performance is entirely determined by his personality characteristics and skills; mistakenly, no account is taken of all kinds of situational aspects that also determine performance. This is why it is usually less problematic if, in view of the two objectives mentioned, the appraisal is based on concrete and practical results, or on specific, perceptible, "critical" behaviours, which determine success in a job.

The annual nature of the appraisal subsequently renders its "feedback" effect debatable; the time span is far too long (see among others Bannister &

Balkin, 1990). Events that occurred earlier in the year have gradually faded. But those, too, who wish to perform better after an evaluation are not encouraged because their potential behavioural change will not be appraised for a long time (or possibly not even noticed).

Now what happens when a payment is linked to the appraisal result? In most cases, when awarding bonuses the manager has to keep to a budget. In addition, a "forced distribution model" may be used: A number of classes is identified (e.g. four), which differ from each other as regards bonus percentage, while it is determined in advance for each class which percentage of personnel may be assigned to it. Sometimes all staff members are arranged in order of their performance results. Far more often the "normal distribution model" is used. An interesting question is why a normal distribution should be fair. More important in this context is the issue of how the manager acts when certain staff members are given a very positive appraisal (and thus should get a relatively high bonus), while the performance of other staff members has certainly not decreased. How can the manager then justify the bonus of the latter being reduced?

Although merit rating has been adopted on a fairly large scale in a number of countries, research into its effectiveness has remained very limited. But from what is available (among others, Thierry, 1987; Milkovich & Wigdor, 1991; Heneman, 1991; Marsden & Richardson, 1994) it appears that the problems referred to earlier regularly crop up in practice. As a consequence of these factors, staff members do not understand the connection between their performance (appraisal) and the pay received, which contributes to the dissatisfaction with this system. Marsden and Richardson (1994) observe that the majority of respondents in one of the larger British government services is in favour of the principle of payment for results: A large majority of them, however, thinks that merit rating has no effect on their motivation and their performance behaviour, and that it leads to dissatisfaction and a lower morale.

Kipnis and Schmidt (1988) point out, furthermore, that there is a relation between the way in which a staff member tries to influence his or her manager (being friendly? logical arguments?) and both the performance appraisal and the pay.

4.2.5 Gain sharing: The Scanlon Plan

A division- or organization-wide system such as the Scanlon Plan can be appropriate if the structure of the group or the department is such that identifying the performance levels achieved is not meaningful. The Plan certainly deserves serious consideration if an emphasis is to be laid on the involvement of staff members in the division or company as a whole.

A distinctive feature of the Scanlon Plan is the conviction that all staff members can contribute considerably to the success of the company through their proposals and ideas, and that they should share in its financial gains. This collective decision-making process about the work can be given shape via a structure of committees. In each department a small committee is set up, in which a few staff members and their manager participate. It has the task of stimulating the other staff members to come up with ideas and proposals, both about existing problems and about issues that it is felt could be solved in a more effective way. The committee evaluates the proposals and has a modest budget to implement the ideas that it has approved—insofar as they exclusively concern its own department. More large-scale and expensive proposals go through the central committee (which includes members of the departmental committees). Depending on the programmes already underway and whether there is a well-developed collective decision-making culture, a different form of participation may be chosen other than via committees (see Lawler, 1986).

Subsequently, an index must be found in which the results of this collective decision-making process can be made visible. Scanlon chose for this purpose the relation between the labour costs (wages + salaries) and the value of the production. Such an index must display a certain stability, at any rate if we want to be able to attribute the variations that occur in the index principally to variations in the quality of the collective decision-making process (scope of ideas applied, nature of (un)detected problems, etc.). For this reason it is advisable to analyze, in the light of available company data, how the proposed index would

have behaved in previous years—i.e. before the introduction of the Scanlon Plan. Say that the relation between the labour costs and the product value in previous years was around 0.26. This is then used as the norm for the coming years, provided that no fundamental changes occur in the products to be made, in the production process and in the organization of the work. Figure 12.6 shows the results in a particular month after the introduction of the Plan (taken from De Jong & Thierry, 1979).

We can see that the labour costs in a particular month have amounted to 23% of the acquired product value. Clearly, as a result of the ideas put forward and the proposals introduced, more or better results have been achieved and/or the costs have been lower. Applying the norm (26%) yields the sum to be distributed. In various enterprises a part of this goes to the company itself (e.g. 20%). In the example shown in Figure 12.6, a sum is only reserved for months showing an unexpectedly poor result (so that a modest bonus can still be paid out). The remaining part is distributed among all the staff; this is usually done pro rata according to monthly salary.

In many contemporary companies, the relation between labour costs and production value would not form an accurate index, principally because as a result of changes constantly taking place—i.e. before the introduction of the Scanlon Plan—a great deal of variation in both components occurs. There are, however, a number of better alternatives (see e.g. Frost, Wakeley, & Ruh, 1974; Thierry & De Jong, 1979; Schuster 1983; Belcher, 1991).

Between the two main themes of the Scanlon Plan—participation on the one hand and sharing in the financial profits on the other—information forms an essential link. The analysis of the periodic results must also take place against the background of ideas that have been introduced and proposals that have been rejected. Conversely, via this analysis, attention is drawn to a number of problems that need proposals to be developed for solving them. From our research overview (Thierry, 1987) it appears that in many cases good results have been achieved, chiefly positive attitudes and increased productivity. On the downside are negative attitudes, including from executive staff, and an irregular bonus.

4.2.6   Payment for performance or results?

In section 3.3 we examined the theme of strategic pay: This is understood to mean that for decisions regarding (systems of) payment, the main points of the company policy are kept in mind. The question of whether payment for results can or should be adopted is therefore also a strategic one. In this section attention is focused on a number of systems aspects. The question is, what conditions does a system of performance-related pay actually have to satisfy?

First, the concept of *performance*: In practice,

as a rule the first question that gets asked is how is it possible to measure or appraise an, often individual, performance. Because staff members often have to rely on others in carrying out their work, it is better to begin with an analysis of the extent to which staff members are *dependent* on each other in their work (see also Lawler, 1981; Pritchard, 1995; Pritchard et al., 1988). If a group is substantially dependent on what happens elsewhere in a company, then even a higher level of analysis must be chosen, for example, a department or a division, until a considerable degree of technological (and organizational) independence is reached. This can result in only an organization-wide performance-related payment being suitable

---

FIGURE 12.6

month: February

- *actual results:*

  labour costs   fl   254,114.-

  value of production fl   1,101,372.-

  ratio   : $\dfrac{253,114}{1,101,372} = 0.23$

- norm   :   0.26

                       :   0.26 x 1,101,372 = fl 286,357.-

- difference   :   fl 286,357 - fl 254,114 = fl 32,243.-

- distribution   :   set aside against worse months: 25%

                            0.25 x fl 32,243.- = fl 8,061.-

                            to be divided among all personnel:

                            0.75 x fl 32,243.- = fl 24,182.-

An example of gain sharing.

(see section 4.2.5). Group or individual payments might also be possible, but only if the result of such an analysis shows this. For the essential thing in every system of performance-related pay is that—at whatever level of analysis—the performance to be identified should be *relevant* to the core activities of the department and/or the company and should be sufficiently open to influence by the staff members in question. If the analysis of interdependencies is missed out—and as a result the chosen level (often individual) at which performances are determined is too low—then the performance of the task cannot be sufficiently influenced by *those* staff members who will be rewarded for its results. If the requirement is made that staff members must be able *fully* to influence the performance factors concerned, this is running the risk that these factors are not very relevant.

In our view, as far as performance-related payment is concerned, the foregoing means that performance should not relate to more or less peripheral (or vague) aspects, but only to so-called *critical* performance factors. These are features that in essence reflect the purpose for which a job, a group, a department, or a division has been created. For instance, a performance factor for an auxiliary power station is the provision of electricity at times when consumption is far greater than usual. And a maintenance store needs to have certain parts in stock and be able to supply others within a certain time, etc. The PROMES (Productivity Measurement and Enhancement System) method developed by Pritchard et al. (1988; Pritchard, 1995) can provide one way of identifying such factors.

A second point emerges from this: Both in new technologies and in contemporary organizational forms, increasing emphasis is being laid on *groups* (or even larger units) (see e.g. Markham, 1988). Thus it would seem more obvious to adopt group performance-related payments than individual performance related payments. From the research overview referred to earlier, it appears that it is chiefly individual implementation that has led to increased performance. But as regards group performance-related payments, too, there are more studies that show an increase in performance than a decrease. It is clear that group pay is vulnerable on a number of points: The number of members cannot be very large, the members must understand the system, and it appears to be advantageous if they can redistribute the group bonus received if need be.

This concludes our discussion of performance-related pay. There are, incidentally, a number of forms of payment and savings—which we cannot deal with here—which some authors include under pay for performance. These include skill pay, whereby a pay increase is awarded for each relevant diploma; profit-sharing (Weitzman & Kruse, 1990); staff shares; share options, etc. In principle, performance-related pay is consistent with the central theme that runs through pay theories: establishing a link between performance results and inducements. Furthermore, performance-related pay can score highly on the four meanings considered essential for influencing individual working behaviour (see section 3.2). But it will be clear from the foregoing that in practice a system of performance-related pay does not "automatically" satisfy the conditions laid down. It must meet fairly stringent requirements if it is to produce any effect.

4.3 Cafeteria Plan

The Cafeteria Plan—also called Flexiplan—derives its name from the, albeit limited, opportunities for self-service in the compilation of a package of working conditions. Underlying this is the idea that most staff members have little or no influence on the fringe benefits and perks that apply to them. This means that nearly everyone is receiving a number of conditions that are not appreciated or of which they are not even aware (e.g. because the employer pays the premium). On the other hand, other conditions are often attractive but are not part of the package. The Plan aims at giving personnel choices, so that everyone can get the set of conditions that suits their own circumstances and preferences. Figure 12.7 gives an example of this.

The staff member in this example can spend the sum of £4000 annually. In many cases the amount becomes available through periodic pay increases (or through compensation for rises in the cost of living), and through selling (extra) free days, but there are also examples whereby other components can be contributed. In our example we can

FIGURE 12.7

available: £ 4,000

alternatives		costs
· extra holiday (£ 300 per day)	2	£ 600
· saving up days: (educ.) leave	7	£ 2,100
· additional collec- tive insurance		£ 500
· increase in pension level		--------
· savings scheme		£ 500
· cash payments		£ 300
		£ 4,000

Cafeteria plan: Some options.

see that seven free days have been set aside for later. If this is done in subsequent years, then a very long trip could be taken, for instance, a sabbatical leave could be arranged, etc. The staff member can also participate in an insurance and savings scheme.

This type of plan was first introduced in the late 1960s in a number of American companies. Given that the level of social security in the USA is considerably lower than that in western Europe, the plans adopted there tend to be more concerned with basic facilities (medical expenses; disablement; pension). After a slow start in the 1970s (see e.g. Vinke & Thierry, 1984), these days the Plan is being implemented in the USA on a fairly large scale. In western Europe various examples exist, among them in Germany, in the United Kingdom, and in the Netherlands. Choices to be made bear primarily on free time, saving schemes, insurance

plans, and, increasingly, to pension plan options. Incidentally, the definition of the Plan is also relevant. In many companies certain categories of staff have choices in a limited area, such as e.g. the method of compensation for overtime. We are of the opinion that it is only a real Cafeteria Plan if all the personnel concerned can compile a "menu" from a number of alternatives.

The research until now has been on a modest scale. From the start, however, it has focused on the degree of predictability of the choices to be made by the staff (see Nealey & Goodale, 1964; 1967), because insurance companies wanted to guard against "adverse selection'. This last means that only high-risk personnel opt for a particular form of insurance. The results of previous and recent research (e.g. Thierry & Croonen, 1980; Vinke & Thierry, 1983; Langedijk, 1995, 1997) point out among other things that the choices made by personnel are hardly influenced by their satisfaction with the work but more by their satisfaction with one or more dimensions of pay, by a number of biographical features (age, education), by expected effects of choices, and to some extent by the opinions of referent others regarding the choices made. Unfortunately, there has not yet been any research into the extent to which the use of a Cafeteria system in practice affects the motivation and performance of staff. What has been apparent from sounding out companies that have adopted the Plan is that staff who participate—on a voluntarily basis—are satisfied with the Plan.

We anticipate that the Cafeteria Plan will score highly, particularly on the "motives" and "influence" meanings and, to some extent, on the "spending" meaning (as distinguished in the reflection theory, section 3).

4.4 Incidental pay

In the Introduction, the need of many organizations for (more) flexibility came up. Thus, managers would like to have the opportunity regularly to show their appreciation to staff promptly—individually or in groups—and also in financial terms when exceptional efforts or results have been produced.

In various companies forms of incidental pay have been introduced for this purpose. These include:

- being given a lunch;
- being given a dinner for two;
- attending an expensive conference;
- going on a business trip;
- participating in a conference with a short paid holiday attached;
- having a holiday that includes a seminar, etc.

The first two are obviously the most frequently adopted. To this end, for example, a manager is given a number of tickets per month to hand out. If the performance or effort has been such that a conference or a holiday is appropriate in the manager's opinion, then he should at least consult with his superior. The decision-making procedures for this are kept short: If a lot of time is involved, the intended effect—a prompt sign of appreciation—would be negated.

Unfortunately, we are not aware of any research into the effects of incidental pay. We tentatively anticipate that it will show a fairly high score on the "relative position" meaning (section 3).

5 CONCLUSION

From the first three sections of this chapter it may be concluded among other things that pay can have a considerable effect on behaviour in the workplace. From the fourth section it is clear that in practice something is frequently lacking, at least from the perspective of the influence intended. This means that the pay not only has less significance for personnel than it might, but also produces less benefit for the company than is desired. In addition, it must be remembered that the total labour costs always form an important item of expenditure and even, in labour-intensive companies, the most important item. With a view to reducing both discrepancies indicated, we make a number of recommendations for future research.

First, a more general point. Research into the role of pay in staff motivation, performance, and job satisfaction occupies only a minor position. We advocate allowing more scope for research into the effects and results of pay, including on themes such as (re)designing tasks and jobs, learning, and actually using new capabilities and skills as a result of introducing new technology, working in groups whose composition regularly changes, etc. But we are also thinking of the role of pay in more conventional, equally contemporary subjects, such as producing high-quality work, promoting involvement, supervising individuals and groups, career planning, the functioning of various forms of consultation, the development of a cohesive organization culture, etc.

Second, we mention an area that we have just dealt with by implication. Virtually every company is regularly faced with more or less far-reaching changes, which, whether planned or not, occur in increasingly rapid succession. As we pointed out in the Introduction, many companies do not actually know the role that can or should be played by pay in that context. This is why it is necessary that attention should be paid in research to diagnosing strategic policy objectives for an organization from the perspective of which forms and systems of payment best reflect those objectives. Based on theories about behaviour–inducement relations it may be expected that the "strategic" pay referred to here fairly often implies that new, perhaps even temporary, forms of payment are introduced at an *early* stage of a change process, partly so that other behaviour and other forms of cooperation will be quickly learnt. Running parallel to this is the interesting theme of the consistency of Human Resource instruments during change and reorganization processes.

In addition, there is a considerable need for further research into the effectiveness of systems and forms of payment. Thus it in fact remains an open question whether results-oriented pay *generally speaking* leads to other (better?) performance, productivity, or return on investment results than fixed pay. The same question applies to profit-sharing. We also find this theme in merit rating. Furthermore, effectiveness not only concerns performance, but of course also motivation, involvement, satisfaction, organizational citizenship, etc. We need to bear in mind that the answer to this question can only be given in a contingency model, i.e. it is dependent on the degree to which an organization gives the pay strategic shape.

NOTES

1. Unfortunately, the term "gain sharing" also refers to systems such as those of Scanlon, Rucker, et al., whereby all members of staff share in the results of improvements (for example, in productivity) that have been reached through greater commitment and involvement.
2. From a conversation in the summer of 1989 with the ex-foreman of these beaver trappers, we found that each worker indicated at the *end* of each week which of the conditions (CR, VR) he wanted his performance of the previous week to fall under. The operationalizing of the VR conditions was thus completely in the air.
3. Implementation of the English-language version of these scales in a sample survey by American MBA students (Shaw, 1996) shows that a solution based on three factors ("control" has been dropped) seems more satisfactory. Data from other countries will be available later.

REFERENCES

Adams, J.S. (1963). Toward an understanding of inequity. *Journal of Abnormal and Social Psychology, 67*, 422–436.

Ajzen, I., & Fishbein, M. (1980). *Understanding attitudes and predicting social behavior.* Englewood Cliffs, NJ: Prentice-Hall.

American Heritage Dictionary of the English Language (1969). New York: Houghton Mifflin.

Amsel, A. (1972). Behavioral habituation, counter conditioning, and a general theory of persistence. In A.H. Black, & W.F. Prokasy (Eds.), *Classical conditioning II. Current research and theory,* New York: Appleton-Century-Crofts.

Austin, W. (1977). Equity theory and social comparison processes. In J.M. Suls, & R.L. Miller (Eds.), *Social comparison processes.* Washington.

Bannister, B.D., & Balkin, D.B. (1990). Performance evaluation and compensation feedback messages: An integrated model. *Journal of Occupational Psychology, 63*, 97–111.

Barnard, C. I. (1938). *The functions of the executive.* Cambridge, MA: Harvard University Press.

Beatty, R.P., & Zajac, E.J. (1994). Managerial incentives, monitoring and risk bearing: A study of executive compensation, ownership and board structure in initial public offerings. *Administrative Science Quarterly, 39*, 313–335.

Belcher, D.W. (1974). *Compensation administration.* Englewood Cliffs, NJ: Prentice-Hall.

Belcher, D.W., & Atchison, T.A. (1976). Compensation for work. In R. Dubin (Ed.), *Handbook of work, organization and society.* Chicago: Rand McNally.

Belcher, J.G. (1991). *Gain sharing.* London: Gulf Publishing Company.

Berger, J., Zelditch, M.B., Anderson, B., & Cohen, B.P. (1972). Structural aspects of distributive justice: A status value formulation. In J. Berger, M. Zelditch, & B. Anderson (Eds.), *Sociological Theories in Progress.* (Vol. 2). Boston: Houghton Mifflin.

Biessen, P. (1992). *Oog voor de menselijke factor. Achtergrond, constructie en validering van de Basisvragenlijst Amsterdam.* (*The human factor: background, construction and validation of the Basic Questionnaire Amsterdam.*) Amsterdam: Swets & Zeitlinger.

Bruns, W.J. (1992) (Ed.) *Performance measurement, evaluation, and incentives.* Boston: Harvard Business School Press.

Brown, J.S. (1961). *The motivation of behavior.* New York: McGraw-Hill.

Bulcke, F. van den (1989). *Beloon inzet met kapitaal.* (*Reward effort with capital.*) Antwerpen: De Financieel-Economische Tijd.

Crosby, F. (1976). A model of egoistical relative deprivation. *Psychological Review, 83*, 95–113.

Deci, E.L. (1975). *Intrinsic motivation*. New York: Plenum Press.

Deci, E.L., & Ryan, R.M. (1985). *Intrinsic motivation and self-determination in human behavior*. New York: Plenum Press.

Dickinson, A.M., & Gillette, K.L. (1993). A comparison of the effects of two individual monetary incentive systems on productivity: Piece rate pay versus base rate pay. *Journal of Organizational Behavior Management, 14*, 3–83.

Donaldson, L. (1990). The ethereal hand: Organizational economics and management theory. *Academy of Management Review, 15*, 369–381.

Dyer, L., & Theriault, R.D. (1976). The determinants of pay satisfaction. *Journal of Applied Psychology, 69*, 69–78.

Eisenhardt, K.M. (1988). Agency and institutional theory explanations: The case of retail sales compensation. *Academy of Management Journal, 31*, 488–511.

Eerde, W. van, & Thierry, H. (1996). Vroom's expectancy models and work-related criteria: A meta-analysis. *Journal of Applied Psychology, 81*, 575–586.

Ferster, C.B., & Skinner, B.F. (1957). *Schedules of reinforcement*. New York: Appleton-Century-Crofts.

Festinger, L. (1954). A theory of social comparison. *Human Relations, 7*, 117–140.

Folger, R. (1986). A referent cognitions theory of relative deprivation. In J.M. Olson, C.P. Herman, & M.P. Zauna (Eds.), *Relative deprivation and social comparison: The Ontario Symposium*: (Vol. 4). Hillsdale, NJ: Lawrence Erlbaum.

Frisch, C.J., & Dickinson, A.M. (1990). Work productivity as a function of the percentage of monetary incentives to base pay. *Journal of Organizational Behavior Management, 11*, 13–33.

Frost, C.F., Wakeley, J.H., & Ruh, R.A. (1984). *The Scanlon Plan for organization development*. East Lansing: Michigan State University Press.

George, J.M., Brief, A.P., Webster, J., & Burke, M.J. (1989). Incentive compensation as an injurious condition of work: A study of labelling. *Journal of Organizational Behavior, 10*, 155–167.

Gerhart, B., & Milkovich, G.T. (1992). Employee compensation: Research and practice. In M.D. Dunnette & L.M. Hough (Eds.), *Handbook of industrial and organizational psychology*. (2nd Edn, Vol. 3). Palo Alto, CA: Consulting Psychologists Press.

Gomez-Mejia, L.R., & Balkin, D.B. (1992). *Compensation, organizational strategy and firm performance*. Cincinnati: South-Western Publishing Company.

Grumbkov, J. von (1980). *Sociale vergelijking van salarissen*. Tilburg: Van Spaendonck.

Guzzo, R.A. (1988). Financial incentives and their varying effects on productivity. In P.A. Whitney, & P. Ochsman (Eds.), *Psychology and productivity*. New York: Plenum Press.

Heneman, H.G. (1985). Pay satisfaction. In K.M. Rowland & G.R. Ferris (Eds.), *Research in personnel and human resources management*. (Vol. 3). Greenwich, CT: JAI Press.

Heneman, R.L. (1991). *Merit pay: Linking pay increases to performance ratings*. Reading, MA: Addison-Wesley.

Heneman, H.G., & Schwab, D.P. (1985). Pay satisfaction: Its multidimensional nature and measurement. *International Journal of Psychology, 20*, 129–141.

Hermkens, P. (1995). Sociale vergelijking en rechtvaardigheid van beloning. (Social comparison and pay justice.) *Gedrag & Organisatie, 8*, 359–371.

Herzberg, F. (1966). *Work and the nature of men*. Cleveland, OH: World Publishing Co.

Herzberg, F., Mausner, B., & Snyderman, B.B. (1959). *The motivation to work*. New York: Wiley.

Heuvel, H. van den, & Thierry, H. (1995). Over de reflectietheorie: betekenissen van beloning. (On reflection theory: meanings of pay.) *Gedrag & Organisatie, 8*, 372–386.

Holmstrom, B. (1979). Moral hazard and observability. *Bell Journal of Economics, 10*, 74–91.

Homans, G.C. (1961). *Social behavior: Its elementary forms*. New York: Harper, Brace & World.

Hull, C.L. (1943). *Principles of behavior*. New York: Appleton-Century-Crofts.

Jong, J.R. de, & Thierry, H. (1979). *Zeggenschap en beloning. (Participation and pay.)* Assen: Van Gorcum.

Kipnis, D., & Schmidt, S.M. (1988). Upward-influence styles: Relationship with performance evaluations, salary and stress. *Administrative Science Quarterly, 33*, 528–542.

Koopman-Iwema, A.M., & Thierry, H. (1981). *Payment for results in the Netherlands: An analysis*. Dublin: European Foundation for the Improvement of Living and Working Conditions.

Langedijk, M.C. (1995). Maatwerk binnen het arbeidsvoorwaardenpakket. (Tailor-made working conditions.) *Gedrag & Organisatie, 8*, 439–458.

Langedijk, M.C. (1997). *Flexibel belonen: De keuze voor arbeidsvoorwaarden op maat (Flexible pay: Choosing tailored working conditions.)* Assen: Van Gorcum.

Latham, G.P., & Dossett, D.L. (1978). Designing incentive plans for unionized employees: A comparison of continuous and variable ratio reinforcement schedules. *Personnel Psychology, 31*, 47–61.

Lawler, E.E. (1971). *Pay and organizational effectiveness*. New York: McGraw-Hill.

Lawler, E.E. (1973). *Motivation in work organizations*. Monterey: Brooks/Cole.

Lawler, E.E. (1981). *Pay and organization development*. London: Addison-Wesley.

Lawler, E.E. (1986). *High involvement management*. London: Jossey-Bass.

Lawler, E.E. (1987). The design of effective reward systems. In J.W. Lorsch (Ed.), *Handbook of organizational behavior*. Englewood Cliffs, NJ: Prentice-Hall.

Lawler, E.E. (1990). *Strategic pay*. London: Jossey-Bass.

Leary, K., Roberts, S., Trefsgar, D., Kaufman, J., Cassel, C., Jones, C., McKnight, J., & Duncan, P. (1990). *Pay for performance*. Paper presented at the Annual Conference of the Association for Behavioral Analysis, Nashville.

Locke, E.A., & Latham, G.P. (1990). *A theory of goal setting and task performance*. Englewood Cliffs, NJ: Prentice-Hall.

Luthans, F., & Kreitner, R. (1985). *Organizational behavior modification and beyond*. Glenview, IL: Scott, Foresman & Co.

Makin, P., Cooper, C., & Cox, C. (1997). *The psychological contract in organizations*. Schoonhoven: Academic Press.

March, J.G., & Simon, H.A. (1958). *Organizations*. New York: Wiley.

Markham, S.E. (1988). Pay-for-performance dilemma revisited: Empirical example of the importance of group effects. *Journal of Applied Psychology, 73*, 172–180.

Marriott, R. (1971). *Incentive payment systems*. (4th Edn). London: Staples Press.

Marsden, D., & Richardson, R. (1994). Performing for pay? The effects of "merit pay" on motivation in a public service. *British Journal of Industrial Relations, 32*, 243–261.

Mawhinney, T.C. (1986). Reinforcement schedule stretching effects. In E.A. Locke (Ed.), *Generalizing from laboratory to field settings*. Lexington, MA: Heath and Co.

Mawhinney, T.C., & Gowen, C.R. (1990). Gainsharing and the law of effects as the matching law: A theoretical framework. *Journal of Organizational Behavior Management, 11*, 61–75.

Miceli, M.P., & Lane, M.C. (1991). Antecedents of pay satisfaction: A review and extension. *Research in Personnel and Human Resources Management, 9*, 235–309.

Miedema-Van den Heuvel, H. (1994). *De achterkant van het salaris*. (*The backside of salary*.) Assen: Van Gorcum.

Miles, R.E., & Snow, C.C. (1978). *Organizational strategy, structure, and process*. New York: McGraw-Hill.

Milkovich, G.T., & Newman, J.M. (1984). *Compensation*. Plano: Business Publications.

Milkovich, G.T., & Wigdor, A.K. (1991) (Eds.) *Pay for performance: Evaluating performance appraisal and merit pay*. Washington: National Academy Press.

Nalbantian, H.R. (1987). Incentive compensation in perspective. In H. R. Nalbantian (Ed.), *Incentives, cooperation, and risk sharing. Economic and psychological perspectives in employment contracts*. Totowa: Rowan & Littlefield.

Nealey, S.M. (1964). Determining worker preferences among employee benefit programs. *Journal of Applied Psychology, 48*, 7–12.

Nealey, S.M., & Goodale, J.G. (1967). Worker preferences among time-off benefits and pay. *Journal of Applied Psychology, 51*, 357–361.

Perrow, C. (1986). *Complex organizations: A critical essay*. (3rd Edn). New York: Random House.

Petri, H.L. (1986). *Motivation: Theory and research*. (2nd Edn). Belmont, CA: Wadsworth.

Pfeffer, J., & Salancik, G.R. (1978). *The external control of organizations: A resource dependence perspective*. New York: Harper & Row.

Pritchard, R.D. (Ed.) (1995) *Productivity measurement and improvement: Organizational case studies*. London: Praeger.

Pritchard, R.D., Jones, S.D., Roth, P.L., Stuebing, K.K., & Ekeberg, S.E. (1988). Effects of group feedback, goal setting, and incentives on organizational productivity. *Journal of Applied Psychology, 73*, 337–358.

Riedel, J.A., Nebeker, D.M., & Cooper, B.L. (1988). The influence of monetary incentives on goal choice, goal commitment, and task performance. *Organizational Behavior and Human Decision Processes, 42*, 155–180.

Robinson, S.L. (1997). Trust and breach of the psychological contract. *Administrative Science Quarterly, 41*, 574–599.

Robinson, S.L., & Rousseau, D.M. (1994). Violating the psychological contract: Not the exception but the norm. *Journal of Organizational Behavior, 15*, 245–259.

Rock, M.L., & Berger, L.A. (1991). *The compensation handbook*. (3rd Edn). London: McGraw-Hill.

Rousseau, D.M. (1990). New hire perceptions of their own and their employer's obligations: A study of psychological contracts. *Journal of Organizational Behavior, 11*, 389–400.

Runciman, W. (1966). *Relative deprivation and social justice*. London: Routledge & Kegan Paul.

Saari, L.M., & Latham, G.P. (1982). Employee reactions to continuous and variable ratio reinforcement schedules involving a monetary incentive. *Journal of Applied Psychology, 67*, 506–508.

Scarpello, V., Huber, V., & Vandenberg, R.J. (1988). Compensation satisfaction: Its measurement and dimensionality. *Journal of Applied Psychology, 73*, 163–171.

Schuster, M. (1983). Five years of Scanlon Plan research: A review of the descriptive and empirical literature. In C. Crouch & F. Heller (Eds.), *Organizational democracy and political processes*. Chichester: John Wiley.

Shaw, J.D. (1996). *A confirmatory factor analysis of pay meaning dimensions on an English speaking sample*. Paper presented at the Southwest Academy of Management Conference.

Silfhout, R.K. (1995). De effectiviteit van prestatiebe-loning (The effectiveness of pay for performance). *Gedrag en Organisatie, 8,* 399–418.

Simon, H.A. (1947). *Administrative behavior.* New York: The Free Press.

Skinner, B.F. (1969). *Contingencies of reinforcement.* Englewood Cliffs, NJ: Prentice-Hall.

Staw, B.M. (1984). Organizational behavior: A review and reformulation of the field's outcome variables. *Annual Review of Psychology, 35,* 627–666.

Sweeney, P.D., McFarlin, D.B., & Inderrieden, E.J. (1990). Using relative deprivation theory to explain satisfaction with income and pay level: A multi-study examination. *Academy of Management Journal, 33,* 423–436.

Syroit, J.E.M.M. (1984). *Interpersonal justice: A psychological analysis illustrated with empirical results.* Dissertation. Tilburg: Tilburg University.

Thierry, H. (1969). Arbeidsinstelling en prestatiebelon-ing. (*Work Attitudes and Performance Related Pay.*) Utrecht: Het Spectrum.

Thierry, H. (1987). Payment by results systems: A review of research 1945–1985. *Applied Psychology: An International Review, 36,* 91–108.

Thierry, H. (1990). Intrinsic motivation reconsidered. In U. Kleinbeck, H.H. Quast, H. Thierry, & H. Häcker (Eds.), *Work Motivation.* Hillsdale, NJ: Lawrence Erlbaum.

Thierry, H. (1992a). Pay and payment systems. In J.F. Hartley & G.M. Stephenson (Eds.), *Employment relations: The psychology of influence and control at work.* Oxford: Blackwell.

Thierry, H. (1992b). Payment: Which meanings are rewarding? *American Behavioral Scientist, 35,* 694–707.

Thierry, H. (1993). Vital conditions for effective per-formance-related payment. In P. Dempsey (Ed.), *Manufacturing Europe 1993.* London: Sterling Publications.

Thierry, H. (forthcoming). Theories of compensation: The perspective of the reflection theory. In M. Erez, U. Kleinbeck, & H. Thierry (Eds.), *Work motivation in the context of a globalizing economy.* Mahwah, NJ: Lawrence Erlbaum.

Thierry, H., & Croonen, J.J.F. (1980). Does the Cafe-teria Plan pay off? An empirical research study. *Management Decisions, 18,* 303–312.

Thierry, H., & Jong, J.R. de (1979). *Naar participatie en toerekening: theorie en praktijk.* (*Towards Partici-pation and gain sharing: Theory and practice.*) Assen: Van Gorcum.

Thierry, H., Koopman-Iwema, A.M., & Vinke, R.H.W. (1988). *Toekomst voor prestatiebeloning?* (*Has per-formance-related pay any future?*) Scheveningen: Stichting Maatschappij en Onderneming.

Tornow, W.W. (1975). The development and appli-cation of an input–outcome moderator test in the perception and reduction of inequity. *Organizational Behavior and Human Performance, 6,* 614–638.

Vinke, R.H.W. (1996). *Motivatie en belonen: de mythe van intrinsieke motivatie.* (*Motivation and reward: The myth of intrinsic motivation.*) Deventer: Kluwer.

Vinke, R.H.W., & Thierry, H. (1983). Het Cafetaria Plan: een nieuwe weg in belonen? (The Cafeteria Plan: a new way of compensation?) *M & O, 37,* 152–169.

Vinke, R.H.W., & Thierry, H. (1984). *Flexibel belonen: van Cafetaria Plan naar praktijk.* (*Flexible compen-sation: From Cafeteria Plan towards practice.*) Deventer: Kluwer.

Vroom, V.H. (1964). *Work and motivation.* New York: McGraw-Hill.

Wallace, M.J., & Fay, C.H. (1988). *Compensation theory and practice.* Boston: PWS-Kent Publishing Company.

Weitzman, M.L., & Kruse, D.L. (1990). Profit sharing and productivity. In A. S. Binder (Ed.), *Paying for productivity.* Washington, DC: The Brookings Institute.

Wilson, T.B. (1995). *Innovative reward systems for the changing workplace.* New York: McGraw-Hill.

Yukl, G.A., & Latham, G.P. (1975). Consequences of reinforcement schedules and incentive magnitudes for employee performance: Problems encountered in an industrial setting. *Journal of Applied Psychology, 60,* 294–298.

Yukl, G.A., Latham, G.P., & Pursell, E.D. (1976). The effectiveness of performance incentives under con-tinuous and variable ratio schedules of reinforce-ment. *Personnel Psychology, 29,* 221–231.

13

Leadership: Theories and Models

Erik J.H. Andriessen and Pieter J.D. Drenth

1 INTRODUCTION

The Chinese book of wisdom *Tao Te King* (600 BC) contains the following dictum: Most leaders are despised, some leaders are feared, few leaders are praised, and the rare good leader is never noticed. This tells us that even in the very distant past leadership was controversial, but in recent times the position of leaders has become especially complicated. Leadership has come under pressure in politics, in social institutions of all kinds (church, school, family, clubs), and in labour organizations. Matters like authority, responsibility, centralized decision-making power etc., which in the past were never questioned, have now been replaced by new ideas like the primacy of the group, the deposability of the leader, one man one vote, and a dutiful role for the leader. Even where such far-reaching ideas have not been adopted there are, nevertheless, changes. For instance, with respect to the bases of power distinguished by French and Raven (1959), it is clear that in many institutions the rewards and punishments controlled by the leader have, from

1980, been replaced by power based on expertise and at best reference power. Not everyone is finding it easy to adapt to the new expectations—this is especially true of those in business; not infrequently this is a source of serious conflicts.

To a large extent research and development of theories about leadership seem to reflect the confusion already manifest in reality. The theory that leaders have charismatic authority over their followers through their personal qualities has been abandoned. The scientific approach, which attempts to identify special leadership properties that could, once they had been made measurable, serve as basis for selection, is no longer in vogue. The search for the "one best way of management", which could be taught in training courses, has ended (however, see Blake & Mouton, 1982).

The area is swamped with competing models: the contingency model, the multiple linkage model, transformation leadership, transactional leadership, symbolic leadership, socially interactive leadership—and it is becoming difficult to retain a global view.

However, confusion is partly due to the research methodology applied. We will list a number of possible objections to classical leadership research.

• This research is conducted almost exclusively through questionnaires. In many cases the psychometrical properties of these questionnaires are, to say the least, dubious. Furthermore, it is well known that many irrelevant factors influence the answers to questionnaires. This problem is compounded when the aspects of leadership thus measured are compared with dependent variables like satisfaction, attitude towards leadership, or estimated performance, which have also been measured on the basis of questionnaires. It may well be that the common variance, that is due to the methods used, explains the relations found. It is, furthermore, not unlikely that the frequent application of self-descriptions, aggravates rather than diminishes the problems.

• A leader's style or manner of working is often estimated through the computation of an average based on the various judgments of subordinates or superiors. The idea is that differences between group members are due to chance fluctuations, which are neutralized by this averaging. But different judgments can actually represent "true variance", as the leader's behaviour (particularly towards his subordinates) is not as unchangeable as is assumed, and this all too easily overlooked.

• The bulk of leadership research is still correlational. This means that it is often impossible to get at what is really interesting: causal relations. Even if leadership style and satisfaction were measured by different instruments it remains to be seen whether it would be permissible to deduce from the correlation that the style was the cause of the satisfaction. Various other explanations offer themselves, such as:

a. Satisfaction is the cause of the style of management.
b. Satisfied group members attribute certain behaviour to the leader.
c. Style and satisfaction reinforce each other.
d. There is a third variable that influences both (performance, reward).

• It is anything but clear what the relevant dependent variables are in leadership research. Campbell (1977) emphatically argues that the following factors—though frequently used—should be avoided: overall judgements of performance, general labour-satisfaction indices, objective production measures, and group measures for absenteeism or turnover. The logical distance between these variables and leader behaviour is too great. Besides, they are to a large extent determined by various other technological and/or economic factors.

On the other hand, this confusion is partly due to the use of simplistic theoretical models. Those involved in this research do not sufficiently realize that interaction between leader and group (members) is a complex socio-psychological phenomenon that in turn forms part of an even more complex organizational system.

In this chapter we hope to go some way towards untangling this complex situation. After starting with a definition of the concept of leadership and a brief analysis of the various viewpoints from which organizations and their modes of leadership can be regarded, we move on to discuss and criticize a number of the classic approaches employed to define leadership in terms of individual characteristics or behavioural styles. Section 5 argues that a more differentiated view of leadership is required. This view holds that leadership plays only a limited role in motivating people, that leader and individual group members influence each other in a process of continuous mutual interaction, and that leadership itself is just one element in a complex set of organizational processes. The subsequent section discusses a number of modern leadership models, and the last section presents the first attempt at a model representing a synthesis of these various new ideas.

2 PREMISES

In this chapter we shall focus on the behaviour of leaders in large organizations. That is, we shall mainly focus on the leadership of officially appointed authorities in organizations characterized by hierarchical relations, complex structures, and a highly differentiated technology. We shall largely ignore phenomena such as the emergence and functioning of leaders in small informal groups. However, the one cannot always be clearly separated from the other. Even in formal organizations informal groups with informal leaders are formed.

In his *Handbook of leadership* Stogdill (1974) gives various descriptions of the concept of "leadership". For instance, it can be seen as a personal property, as the art of inducing obedience, as a way of convincing people or of exercising influence, as an instrument for reaching goals, as the result of interaction, as a role differentiated in group processes, or as a form of structuring. We feel that the last five elements in particular are most important, among other things because they occupy a central place in modern leadership theories.

We will therefore employ the following definition of the concept of leadership: *Leadership is that part of the role of a (appointed or elected) leader that is directly linked to influencing the behaviour of the group, or of one or more members of the group, and that is expressed through the direction and coordination of activities that are important in connection with the tasks of the group (within the organization).*

Leadership behaviour, then, is only part of the activity of a leader. It is particularly true of managers in large organizations above the direct supervisoral level that they usually spend their time dealing with affairs that are only indirectly related to supervising group members. Writing reports, administration, calling, maintaining relations with suppliers or customers, and meetings with colleagues all appear to take up much of the manager's time (Campbell, Dunnette, Lawler, & Weick, 1970; Mintzberg, 1973, Prahalad & Doz, 1984).

Hemphill (1960) and Stewart (1970) analyzed the activities and time allocation of a large number of managers. Stewart identified five groups of functions:

Group 1 (for example, sales manager, general director) was characterized by much traveling, attending conferences, negotiating, and contacts outside the organizatlon.

Group 2 (for example, acting manager, head of accountancy) was characterized by much reading, writing and making reports, and analysis and interpretation of technical affairs.

Group 3 comprised a heterogeneous group of functions that involved divergent managerial activities (simulation, directing, decision-making) carried out in cooperation with colleagues.

Group 4 (for example, chief of maintenance) was characterized by short, quick contacts, inspection of the production processes, and solving crises.

Group 5 (for example, director of planning, head of training) spent much time in committees, and was mainly preoccupied with coordinating different aspects of personnel management.

This analysis shows that various managerial functions require divergent forms of knowledge and skills, as well as divergent forms of behaviour. Directing subordinates is one aspect of their function; sometimes it is of minor importance.

The fact that we focus on leadership behaviour as it takes shape in large complex organization has a few other implications. Direct personal management is an element of the complex of processes taking place in such an organization. The leader's behaviour is not something abstract but is often largely determined by properties of the organization, such as the production process or current ideas about management. Moreover, the behaviour and performance of group members are— quite apart from what their boss says—also directed and limited by all sorts of rules and formal procedures or by the nature of the production process. This means that in certain cases leadership may well be rather less important than is often assumed. At least it implies that the study of leadership behaviour cannot be separated from that of the characteristics of the organization as a whole.

3   PERSPECTIVES ON ORGANIZATIONS

Organizations and processes in organizations are complex. One can study them through different approaches and these different approaches produce divergent analyses. Moreover, they can lead to very different recommendations as to what are the most desirable or most effective forms of organization and management. In the course of time a number of such approaches have crystallized. In the following paragraphs we shall briefly describe each of them. For a more detailed discussion the reader is referred to Chapter 2 of this *Handbook*.

Taylorism

The rapid industrialization that took place in the previous century and the increasing size and complexity of organizations and production processes gave rise to attempts to find more and more refined methods of controlling the behaviour of large numbers of workers, in order to achieve high productivity and an efficiently conducted business. This development was closely intertwined with the ideal of management characterized by McGregor (1960) as "Theory X": Most workers want to earn as much as possible, and want to work as little as possible; they are unwilling and unable to carry responsibility and must be kept in line by "stick and carrot" methods, i.e. enticement and coercion. Therefore tasks were carefully analyzed and split up, so that workers only had to perform a limited number of simple activities. It was "scientifically" established (hence scientific management) how these activities (e.g. hand-and-arm movements) could be carried out as fast and efficiently as possible. In this context, supervision meant keeping a strict watch and using the available means of reward and punishment to induce individuals to reach a high level of production.

Human Relations

The first to cast doubt on the idea that the individual pursuit of gain was the primary motive of workers in organizations were social scientists, who analyzed the actual processes taking place within groups of workers. The well-known Hawthorne studies and investigations on cohesive working groups who limited their own production caused attention to shift to social relations, groups norms, and cooperation as important motives of human behaviour (Homans, 1950). At the same time they felt they had traced important determinants of (job) satisfaction.

Leadership was thought to be effective if it satisfied the need for social contacts. A leader had to be sensitive to the feelings and problems of subordinates, and mutual trust was to be the basis of group relations. It was assumed that this form of supervision would enhance the satisfaction of group members and would in turn result in stronger work motivation. It soon became clear that this model was simplistic. A large number of empirical studies (summarized by Brayfield & Crockett, 1955, and Vroom, 1964, among others) showed that in many cases there was a very weak link between worker satisfaction and motivation.

Later versions of this model (the neo-human relations school) stated that in order to promote both satisfaction and motivation, the leader should not only focus on people but also be task-oriented (Fleishman & Harris, 1962; Blake & Mouton, 1964). Likert (1967) propagated this approach—still more or less exclusively focused on the single group—and turned it into an organization network; as a "linking pin" the group leader was himself a member of another group on a higher level of the organization. Organizations should consist of a pyramid of such groups, supplemented by work groups particularly created for specific tasks, to be made up of members from various levels and departments. If all these groups had supporting leaders and if high performance was aimed for, the organization would be maximally effective.

Human resources and participation

One of the results of post-Second World War changes in technology and market relationships, and the quick ageing of products, was that organizations had to adapt more and more rapidly to new circumstances. This required increasing flexibility on the part of the organizations themselves, and increasing creativity and adaptability on the part of the members of these organizations. People became aware of the fact that hitherto too little use had been made of the talents of members of the organization (Miles, 1974). For this reason it was argued that decisions should be made at those levels of the organization where the required knowledge was available (Likert, 1967), that consultation should involve both leader and group members, and that leadership should be participatory.

Moreover, it was assumed that participation would not only lead to better decision-making, but would also lead to a lessening in the resistance to change and would motivate people to a higher level of performance. The assumption was that every human being wants to have a say and a certain amount of responsibility; under a participative leader people would be prepared to realize this need. Lammers (1975) calls this approach to participation one of the forms of functional democracy. The assumption is that a certain degree of participation is functional to the aims of the organization, because it makes more effective use of the available information capacities and expertise and because it motivates people. This functional democracy is to be distinguished from structural democracy in which participation in decision-making is a purpose in itself (see also this *Handbook*, Chapter 4).

Systems model

The starting point of many approaches is a perspective—often never made explicit—on organizations referred to by terms such as (structural) functionalism or the Systems Model. Organizations are viewed in the light of their goals and their function in society. One talks about the goals of the organization as if one could take for granted that all members of the organization equally work to attain those goals. Organizations are made up of subsystems whose functions can be explained in the light of the goals of the organization as a whole. Conflicts arise when the subsystems are not well adjusted to each other; alongside other mechanisms, leadership will see both to the attuning of subsystems to one another and to the attuning of the goals and activities of group members to those of the organization (Katz & Kahn, 1978). This attuning process can be enhanced by appealing to the fact that the formally appointed leader is after all the boss, or by appealing to the members' social obligations to one another, their responsibility with regard to the organization's goal, or to the efficiency and productivity principle.

Organizations as political arena: The multiple parties model

The multiple parties model of organizations is based on the idea that social systems are the outcome of the process of interaction between various groups or "parties". This view implies that organization structures and coordination mechanisms are not so much functional requirements for achieving the organization's goals, which everybody subscribes to, as control mechanisms of the dominant group, or at best as compromises resulting from "negotiations" or exchange relations between various parties. The original Marxist approach only recognizes two parties or classes, i.e. the workers and the representatives of capital. Modern theories acknowledge the existence of more groups, which have their own values, goals, and interests, their own definition of the situation, and their own strategies for reaching these goals. Two examples of an analysis based on this perspective are Beyne's (1973) study of relations in the British Ford Motor Company, and Baldridge's (1971) study of the organizational structure of New York State University.

This perspective particularly centres on the notion of power. People may derive power from various sources, for instance, from their official position, from the fact that they control rewards and punishments, from expertise, or from personal charm. One reason for the attractiveness of power is that it gives access to privileges. Through various strategies, which are not always consciously pursued, powerholders (particularly managers) try to maintain or increase their power (see, for example, Mulder, 1977). According to this perspective, people engage in many, sometimes temporary, coalitions in this power game in order to reinforce their own position.

Conclusion

As is often the case with conflicting approaches, each of the perspectives discussed here contains elements that are valuable. This is especially true of the last two approaches, the systems model and the multiple parties model: It is impossible to say that the one is more correct or more adequate than the other. The value of either way of thinking depends on its usefulness for specific scientific or social goals. Very often an integration or combination of aspects of the theories will yield useful insights (Lammers, 1980).

4 LEADERSHIP TRAITS AND LEADERSHIP STYLES

The insight that the exercise of leadership is a part of organizational processes, and that the nature and the effects of leadership are therefore strongly dependent on that context, is relatively new. Until quite recently, theories confined themselves to the leader's personality and characteristics.

4.1 Leadership traits

The theory of leadership traits is founded on the assumption that leaders posses certain personal qualities, such as courage, intelligence, strength of character, vision, or charisma, which their followers do not possess. Despite its persistence in the public mind, this approach has enjoyed waning scientific interest since the 1950s, particularly because it has proved impossible to find a single set of characteristics that enables a clear and reliable distinction to be drawn between good and bad leaders or, for that matter, between leaders and followers. This was found to be the case both in large organizations (Stogdill, 1948, 1974) and in smaller groups (Mann, 1959).

Nevertheless, time and again this type of research has been given a new lease of life. Bass (1981) has discussed hundreds of leadership-trait studies. He, too, concludes that leadership as such is not a property of an individual's personality, but there are nonetheless certain fixed personal characteristics that seem to play a part in the exercise of leadership. Recent studies which made use of so-called "meta-analyses" have also had positive findings on the contribution made by personal characteristics to observable variation in leadership performance (Kenny & Zaccaro, 1983; Lord, De Vader, & Alliger, 1986). House (1977), who developed the Path–Goal theory, which makes particular use of the roles played by situational and behavioural variables (see section 6), also calls for renewed attention to leadership traits. A related approach is one that stresses not so much individual skills and personality traits, as managers' *motives* (especially motives related to power and performance) (McClelland, 1975; McClelland & Boyatzis, 1982) or patterns of motives (Stahl, 1983; Cornelius & Lane, 1984).

House and Baetz (1979, p.352) argue for a more differentiated approach than the traditional one, aimed at finding universal relations, i.e. traits that are important in all situations. They argue that certain characteristics are only important in certain circumstances. This can be demonstrated with the help of Stogdill's correlations of .38, .40, and .60 between athletic capacities and leadership in youth groups, whereas in other situations the same capacity hardly plays a role at all.

Personal characteristics can also moderate the effect of leadership behaviour on production and satisfaction (cf. Johnson, Luthans, & Hennessy, 1984). This warrants giving careful attention to House and Baetz suggestion to concentrate on analyzing the *interactions* between certain traits, and to discover the possible relations between leaders' characteristics and leadership behaviour rather than those between leaders' characteristics and group performance.

This less universal, strongly differentiated approach may help to dispel the bad reputation that the study of leadership traits has acquired, and thus confirm the common-sense view that some "have a natural aptitude" for leadership and others do not.

4.2 Leadership styles

Although insight into the personal characteristics of leaders may be useful for selecting leaders, in everyday life it is far more important to know how certain kinds of behaviour affect attitudes and behaviour of the group. It is usually not so very important to know which properties cause a leader to behave as he or she does. Moreover, the causes for a given behaviour may differ considerably.

For instance, regulating behaviour may be due to a variety of reasons or motives. A person may like to put things in order because he fears unforeseen events, but he may also do it for aesthetic reasons. Leaders may want to share power because they are afraid of burning their fingers, or because they adhere to theory Y, or because they appreciate their colleagues, or because they feel that by letting them share they can improve the relationship (Vollebergh, 1973, p.235).

Empirical research on leadership as it takes shape both in small informal groups and in formal organizations resulted in the identification of a limited number of dimensions or so-called "leadership styles". In the following section, special attention will be devoted to *consideration, initiating structure*, and *participation*, the three basic dimensions according to—among others—Campbell et al., 1970). The first two have primarily been measured by means of the "Ohio State Leadership Scales" (see Fleishman, Harris, & Burt, 1955). In addition, a few other classifications will be briefly discussed.

Consideration and initiating structure

Research on small groups has repeatedly demonstrated the existence of two central functions, i.e. fulfilment of the group task and stimulating and taking care of good mutual relations. On the basis of factor analyses of behaviour descriptions of numerous formal organizations, researchers from the Ohio State University came to similar conclusions. They named the two dimensions "initiating structure" and "consideration". In the Dutch literature these are usually described as instrumental and social leadership (Philipsen, 1965) or task-oriented and socio-emotional leadership (Mulder, Ritsema Van Eck, & Van Gils, 1967).

Consideration

This reflects the degree to which the leader's behaviour towards the group members is characterized by mutual trust, development of good relations, sensitivity to the feelings of group members, and openness to their suggestions.

Initiating structure

This reflects the degree to which a leader is bent on defining and structuring the various tasks and roles of group members in order to attain group results.

Various scales were devised with which these dimensions could be measured: the Leadership Opinion Questionnaire—a Likert-type scale which measures how the *leader* thinks she should behave—and three versions of the Leader Behavior Description Questionnaire (the 1957 SBDQ, the 1957 LBDQ, and the revised version of the latter the 1963 LBDQ-XII). The last three measure how group members perceive the actual behaviour of their leader. With the help of these scales numerous studies have been carried out. Surveys

of these studies can be found in Korman (1966), Kerr and Schriesheim (1974), and elsewhere. Stogdill's handbook (1974) also supplies much information on this subject.

Summarizing the results of the many studies we can conclude that socio-emotional leadership is positively related to satisfaction of the group members, whereas task-oriented leadership is positively related to group performance. It should be noted that task-oriented leadership without personal attention to group members may have negative effects on satisfaction and even on performance (Fleishman & Harris, 1962; Schriesheim & Murphy, 1976). This could imply that socio-emotional leadership has a moderating effect on the relation between task-oriented leadership and performance. If socio-emotional leadership scores high, there is a positive relationship between task-oriented leadership and performance; if socio-emotional leadership scores low, the relationship is low or negative. These and similar results lead to the conclusion that the ideal leader should combine both aspects of leadership. Consequently, training courses like those of Blake and Mouton (1964) take this "one best way" as the gospel truth.

Reddin (1970) and Kerr, Schriesheim, Murphy, and Stogdill (1974) adopt a more subtle perspective, asserting that the best approach depends on the situation and on the task in hand; in so doing they move a step closer to the contingency approach (see the following section).

Although the scales mentioned in the foregoing were carefully constructed, and much energy was spent in validating and improving them, they have met with rather severe criticism. Schriesheim and Stogdill (1975) and Schriesheim, House, and Kerr (1976) in particular studied the comparability of the various scales. They discovered that the scales only partly measure the same thing, and on the basis of this discovery they were able to explain the divergent results of various studies. Notably the early versions of the initiating structure scales appeared to measure two dimensions. On the one hand, high production is highlighted with items such as "he emphasizes the meeting of deadlines", and "he encourages overtime work". On the other hand, there are items that deal with the structuring, i.e. clarifying, of situations; for example, "she lets group members know what is expected of them", and "she schedules the work to be done". The original SBDQ scale contained both kinds of items and therefore produced ambiguous results. Thus giving greater weight to performance may have a negative effect on professional workers, whereas structuring the problem may have a postive effect. The subsequent versions of this scale were clearly oriented towards the structuring of activities.

Moreover, the "Consideration" scale too does not contain a completely homogeneous set of items. A distinction can be made between warmth and trust on the one hand, "he is friendly and approachable", and participation and decision-making on the other, "he acts without consulting the group". Unfortunately, in the last version of the consideration scale (LBDQ-XIII) the second dimension is over-represented. Participative leadership will be discussed in greater detail later. In their analysis of the Ohio State Leadership Scales. Schriesheim and Kerr (1974, 1977) conclude that the psychometric properties leave much to be desired. But this does not alter the fact that this type of research, carried out with the help of the existing versions of the scales, has yielded valuable results.

Participative leadership

We can be rather brief about this leadership style. First, this subject is discussed in various other chapters of this *Handbook* (see Chapters 4, Vol. 2, and 16, Vol. 4). Second, an extensive survey of the numerous studies in this field has been published by Locke and Schweiger (1979). Third, the conclusions drawn in this overview hardly differ from conclusions made by others long ago (see, for instance, Drenth & Thierry, 1970). A number of these conclusions can be summarized as follows:

1. Participative decision-making usually leads to satisfaction with this decision-making. According to Locke's survey, this obtains for both laboratory studies and for correlational and longitudinal field studies: in 60% of the studies there was a positive correlation, in 30% no correlation, and in 10% a negative correlation. Similar figures can be deduced from Stogdill's (1974) data (67%, 20%, and 8%). It is not always clear which processes are responsible for this relation.

A plausible explanation would be that, on the one hand, participation meets the need for participation as such—in that it implies the acknowledgement of someone's contribution or makes use of someone's knowledge or skills (Wall & Lischeron, 1977)—whereas, on the other hand, it offers the possibility of attaining other important goals (better decision-making, better relations, more information).

2. Participative decision-making rarely leads to increased motivation, performance, or productivity. According to Locke, in 22% of the cases there was a positive relationship, in 56% there was no relationship, and in 22% there was a negative relationship. Stogdill's results are 30%, 57%, and 13%, respectively. Presumably, the reason for this is that the relations between the participation concept, which varies considerably according to the situation, and the performance concept, which is determined by numerous factors, are very complex and largely depend on situational variables (see section 5).

3. Many factors have been tested for their moderating effect on the relationship between participation and performance (Drenth & Thierry, 1970; Koopman, 1980). Without going into the details of this research, the most important of these results are as follows.

The principal factors are frequently held to be the levels of knowledge, intelligence and expertise amongst the group members (Locke & Schweiger, 1979; House & Baetz, 1979): the more these conditions are fulfilled, the more effective participative leadership becomes. The same applies to motivation and the perceived need for participation amongst the group members (Vroom, 1964; House & Baetz, 1979). The nature of the task in hand (routine/complex, structured/unstructured, problem-free/crisis situation, see Thomson & Tuden, 1959; Duncan, 1973; Vroom, 1967; Vroom & Yetton, 1973; Mulder et al., 1967; Mulder, De Jong, Koppelaar, & Verhage, 1986) and the importance of the decision to be taken (Heller & Wilpert, 1981; Heller, Drenth, Koopman, & Rus, 1988) also play a significant role. The more complex and important the task, the more effective the participative leadership. The nature of the environment must also be mentioned: The less controllable and the more turbulent the situation, the more effective participation becomes (Vroom & Yetton, 1973). The acceptance of the leader figure and the trust placed in that person (Fiedler, 1967) and that person's influence in higher echelons (Pelz, 1951, 1952) also appear to be important moderators. Heller et al. (1988; see also Koopman & Drenth, 1980a; Drenth & Koopman, 1984) showed that, besides the importance of the decision, the particular phase of the decision-making process also mattered. In implementation or development phases, for instance, authoritarian behaviour by top management has more negative effects than it does in the finalization of the decision-forming process. The same study also showed that in more serious conflicts, reduced mutual trust and vaguer objectives actually raised the effectiveness of participative leadership. Finally, an influencing factor that deserves mention is the regulation and formalization of such discussions, which means that these discussions are taken more seriously (Koopman, 1980).

It is indeed remarkable that most overviews pay practically no attention to instruments for measuring the degree of participative leadership. From the short descriptions of the various studies we gather that researchers often use their own instruments. Contradictory or at least obscure results are probably partly due to the use of non-comparable or psychometrically weak instruments. The scale of Koopman and Werkman (1973), developed in The Netherlands, has been used often in a shortened version in a variety of studies (Zanders, Van Büchem, & Van Berkel, 1978; Andriessen et al., 1984). The psychometric properties of this scale are satisfactory. The scale contains a series of Likert-type items that inquire into the degree to which the leader usually informs or consults group members. Yet, at the same time the nature of this scale is evaluative. A completely different instrument investigates the degree to which group members are involved in decision-making on specific issues. The positions on the response scale usually include the following range: not involved; being consulted; joint decision-making; and the possibility of taking decisions independently (Vroom & Yetton, 1973; Heller 1971; Heller, Drenth, Koopman, & Rus, 1988; IDE, 1981). This

scale also has reasonably good psychometric-properties.

Other leadership styles

Besides the social-emotional, task-oriented, and participatory styles of leadership that have been mentioned, a great many other leadership styles have been put forward and operationalized.

The classic *Survey of organizations* (Taylor & Bowers, 1972), for instance, describes four more scales by which to measure leadership dimensions. These measure support (letting group members know that they are valuable and important), goal emphasis (stimulating enthusiasm for work), work facilitation (removing barriers that hamper work) and interaction facilitation (turning a group into a solid team). The significance and the value of these scales is less than entirely clear. Schriesheim and Kerr (1977) are rather negative about the psychometric qualities of these scales; neither is it clear to what extent they are independent of the Ohio State Leadership Scales.

Also the scales published by Bass, Farrow, Valenzie, and Solomon (1975) for measuring direction, negotiation, consultation, participation, and delegation are not entirely different from other well-known scales. The last three of these dimensions, which show a relatively high mutual correlation, are clearly related to the concept of participative leadership. Their direction dimension approaches the concept of task-oriented leadership.

Drehmer and Grossman (1984) directed their attention to the measurement of a climate of trust and mutual respect. Starting from a large number of critical incidents, they developed a checklist that determined in which phase (of the progression towards complete trust) the leadership behaviour was situated. These nine phases were characterized as follows: attention, support, collective feedback, stimulation, development of autonomy, setting limits, personal competence, independent personal and professional growth, and loyalty and commitment. The authors call their model hierarchical, which would imply that each phase has to be passed through, before the next phase can be implemented. An attractive aspect of this model is that not only the behaviour of the leader, but also that of the follower is included in the analysis; it is, in fact, more of an interaction model. Its implications for organizational development are clear (see Banner & Balsingname, 1988).

Another model that deserves looking at in this respect is the PM (Performance and Maintenance) leadership model developed by Misumi (1985; Misumi & Peterson, 1985, 1987). For decades, Misumi has researched leadership in the Michigan tradition, especially in the Japanese context. His two main dimensions, performance and maintenance, bear an unmistakable resemblance to the task-oriented and group-oriented leadership styles, respectively. Together, these two dimensions form what he calls the morphological aspect of leadership; he also distinguishes a dynamic dimension. If they are to be effective, the P and M functions have to be realized in specific ways for each specific situation. This context is not summed up by a couple of generalizable aspects, an approach frequently employed in the contingency approach (see section 6), but should be analyzed specifically and idiosyncratically for each particular case. Misumi employs extensive interview schemas and measuring instruments to this end. In this way he simultaneously gauges the leadership style and the organizational culture in which it is found, and he incorporates both these measurements into his insights into effective leadership. The culture-relatedness of the behaviour corresponding to a particular style was demonstrated empirically by Smith, Misumi, Taylor, Peterson, and Bond (1989).

The last development to be examined here is the renewed interest for the old Weberian concept of charisma in leadership (see, for instance, Conger & Kanungo, 1988). House (1977) had already noted that there were leaders who seemed to be able to inspire their followers, to bind them to him emotionally and to excite their commitment, a phenomenon for which it was impossible to account satisfactorily using the classic terminology of behavioural styles. Along the same lines, Burns (1978) distinguished between two forms of leadership: transactional and transformational. In transactional leadership, leader and follower take part in a transaction, a deal, so to speak; here, agreements and the exchange of certain behaviours and rewards do not necessarily lead to a

lasting, deep attachment between the two. Transformational leadership, on the other hand, does lead to this strong bond, and leads to a situation where both leader and follower are encouraged to attain ever greater levels of motivation, energy, and achievement. The initiative for this inspiring and transformative relationship is a matter for the charismatic leader.

This idea has been further elaborated and operationalized by Bass (1985a, 1985b), who developed a scale and a Multifactor Leadership Questionnaire, with five subscales, to be completed by the subordinates. The questionnaire asks respondents to indicate, on a five-point scale (0–4), the degree to which a given statement applies to the leader. Each scale comprises 10 items, and the complete list generates a five-dimensional profile.

There are two transactional scales: contingent reward (for instance, the leader tells me what I have to do in order to ensure that my efforts are rewarded) and management by exception (for instance, the leader is happy that I go on working as I have always done). There are three transformational scales: charisma (for instance, I have faith in the leader's ability to deal with any kind of setback), individualized consideration (for instance, the leader gives personal attention to neglected group members), and intellectual stimulation (for instance; the leader stimulates me to think about old problems in new ways).

The research carried out by Bass, Waldman, Avolio, and Bebb (1987) since the development of the model appears to support the assumptions underlying the model. First, it appears that transformational leadership can be found in a wide variety of organizational settings and is by no means limited to top management echelons. Second, transformational leadership generally appears to be positively correlated to subordinates assessments of their leader s effectiveness, the esteem in which they hold their leader, their preparedness to make extra efforts on the leader s behalf, and so on. While the same applies to transactional leadership, the correlations are clearly weaker (Bass, 1985b; Bass et al., 1987; Avolio & Bass, 1987; Hater & Bass, 1988). It is to be hoped that future research and data in this area will be based on the use of hard criteria rather than the subjective judgments of subordinates, which run too great a risk of generating spurious correlations through common method variance.

4.3 Summary

The theories and empirical inquiries discussed so far all belong to a rather simplistic tradition, which could be called the trait or style approach. "Trait" is an underlying individual property. "Style" refers to the leader's more or less stable way of behaviour. Characteristics of the style approach are: universalism (the "one best way" of leadership), defining leadership in terms of a number of broad dimensions, a simple casual model (leadership causes satisfaction and improves performance), and correlational questionnaire research in which perceptions are treated as descriptions and individual variation as error. Campbell (1977, p.228) sums up the following points of criticism:

> Consideration and initiating structure have been recognized as both too simple and too complex. They are too simple in that two factors simply cannot reflect the complexity of what leaders do . . . They are too complex in that scores on these two variables are several steps removed from behavioral bedrock and represent a considerable amount of inference on the part of the respondent.

To a greater or lesser degree these points of criticism apply to all leadership-style dimensions. The dimensions can be seen as factors of a higher order. However, both for research and for leadership practice it is necessary to focus on more specific forms of behaviour. The notion of "leadership style" suggests that leaders always behave in the same way towards all group members. So long as leaders are described in terms of only a few dimensions, we will not gain a deeper insight into the complexity of the behaviour of divergent types of leaders. Besides, in practice and particularly in connection with the training of leaders a much more specific approach of leadership behaviour is called for. It is hardly useful to tell a boss that she should give more support or be more sensitive to certain needs if she is not told how she should react to the behaviour of group members. Theories and approaches that to some degree remedy these problems will be discussed below.

5 CHARACTERISTICS OF MODERN LEADERSHIP APPROACHES

Typical of the traditional leadership approaches was the simplicity of their conceptual schema as illustrated in Figure 13.1.

Behaviour (and attitudes) of group members were believed to be wholly or largely determined by the behaviour of the leader, which in turn was largely determined by his (personal) characteristics. Moreover, leadership behaviour could be described in terms of a permanent "style" of management. This style of management was to be adjusted to the motives of group members. True, there were different opinions as to the most effective style: Directive, open and supporting, or democratic, depending on which human motives one saw as most important, i.e. the need for guidance and stimulation, sociability or participation.

Nevertheless it was generally accepted that in everyday practice leaders could be characterized by a particular style, and the gospel of a particular leadership style (for instance, Likert's supportive leadership, Blake and Mouton's 9.9. style) was spread with missionary zeal. That this zeal brought grist to the missionaries' mill (witness book sales

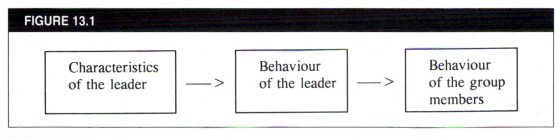

FIGURE 13.1

| Characteristics of the leader | ——> | Behaviour of the leader | ——> | Behaviour of the group members |

Traditional leadership model.

and the popularity of this kind of leadership training) might well have something to do with the simplicity of these approaches. However, reality appeared to be more complicated than these approaches and theories assumed. Modern insights led to new theories about leadership based on the following psychological and organizational assumptions:

1. Human behaviour is determined by many factors. The traditional motives—money, sociability, participation—are motivating factors only under certain conditions. Moreover, there are other needs that also determine motivation, and other factors besides motivation that determine behaviour.

2. Leadership is one aspect of the total set of activities that take place in an organization. Interaction between leader and group members takes place within the context of various situational factors. Therefore, contextual (e.g. technology, power relations, general climate) and situational factors (e.g. nature of the decision, personality of subordinates) also determine leader behaviour and type of management.

3. Leader and group members influence each other continually, i.e. leadership behaviour is liable to change, partly due to the way a leader reacts to the behaviour of group members.

4. Modern organizations require other forms of leadership than more traditional organizations.

In the following sections these characteristics of modern leadership theories will be developed and combined into a new leadership model.

5.1   A differentiated model of man

At the start of this chapter various views on people and organizations were discussed. It appeared that most of these views were based on rather one-sided ideas about human motivation. The workers were either motivated only by money or only by social needs, or only by the need for autonomy. Meanwhile it has become rather clear that people have many needs, and that a number of these needs can be realized in work situations.

The literature provides various classification schemes of human needs. Maslow's (1954) division, despite the criticism on his theory, offers a good starting-point: Human needs can be classed into physiological needs, the safety need, belongingness or social needs, recognition need, and the need for self-actualization. Alderfer (1972) simplified this classification and refers to three types of needs: existence needs, relatedness needs, and growth needs. Central to modern leadership theories is the idea that if a leader wants to influence the behaviour of his group members she must adapt to their needs by making rewards (incentives) available that meet these needs. A good leader is sensitive to what group members need in given situations. People's motivation is determined not only by the availability of certain rewards, but also by whether or not they expect to attain these rewards through their efforts. If good relations with colleagues exist independently of whether or not one works hard, this incentive will not motivate people to higher performance.

There are also other factors that determine the behaviour of group members, and if leaders want to direct this behaviour they must take them into account. Campbell and Pritchard (1976) summarized these factors in a model (the sequence of the boxes does not imply that we are dealing with a causal chain).

In principle the boxed elements in Figure 13.2 can be influenced (at least partly) by a leader. People take their capacities with them to work but the boss can help to develop experience and skills. A boss can also play in important role in making clear what is expected of group members. In modern leadership theories, like that elaborated in "Management by objectives", which focuses on management through formulating joint goals (Drucker, 1954), this is seen as one of leadership's most important functions. Obviously, there are not only official goals (= expectations of the management), but also types of more or less explicit expectations of others (colleagues, higher personnel, subordinates, trade unions, family members etc.), which also partly determine behaviour. The following three elements of this model are concerned with motivation, which was discussed in an earlier section.

The last box contains elements related to the *conditions* under which group members carry out their work. The nature of the task and the working

FIGURE 13.2

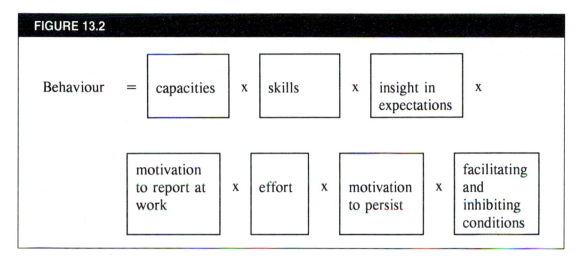

Determinants of human performance.

conditions strongly influence employees' attitudes, behaviour, and perceived experience. Job design does indeed warrant careful attention. This is usually arranged outside the working group itself; however, the head of a department can frequently make an important contribution to this design. Lawler (1985) has given clear indications of a leader's possible role with regard to job design and the working situation.

The concept of boundary function (Katz & Kahn, 1978, p.532) is relevant here. It is precisely a leader's task to arrange relations between the subsystems within an organization (obtaining materials, disposing of the product, and so on) in such a way that the group members work together as effectively as possible. The same idea is elaborated in Yukl's multiple-linkage model (1981), in which it is put forward that a leader's most important responsibilities have to do with marshalling the skills and energies of employees and the other resources available to the organization.

Wofford and Srinivasan (1983) have developed a similar train of thought into a comprehensive theory, which found support in a number of laboratory experiments. According to this theory, the behaviour of group members is determined by four elements: their competence, their motivation, their role perception, and the limitations determined by the setting. These four behavioural determinants correspond to four necessary leadership activities, namely those activities carried out to:

1. promote the choice and development of skill and competence (recruitment, training, etc.);
2. promote employee motivation (goal-setting, encouragement, rewards, etc.);
3. clarify the organization s aims and expectations (structuring the situation);
4. reduce the limitations offered by the environment (technology, working conditions, organizational structures).

In these terms, an effective leader is one who (1) keeps a sharp eye on shortcomings in these four areas and analyzes the problems accordingly, and (2) takes the necessary steps to provide the missing ingredients.

Ashour (1982) has shown that for each of these types of activity, a leader can work in an operant-conditioning (using rewards and punishments, see section 6.4) or in an cognition-clarifying manner.

5.2 Mutual influence of leader and group members

Most studies dealing with the relation between leadership and group satisfaction, group performance or other criteria are correlational. Positive correlations often lead to the conclusion that the behaviour of the leader is the reason behind, and a determining factor in, the attitudes and performance of the group. Of course, there are many situations in everyday life in which a new leader "sets a new course", and is consequently the reason for changes in the attitudes and behaviour of the group. Systematic studies (laboratory experiments or longitudinal field studies) have demonstrated that a change of leader can cause a change of group behaviour. House and Baetz (1979, p.347) give a survey of studies that show that leadership has influenced the dedication and motivation of group members, their adjustment to change, their turnover and absenteeism, the quality of their decisions, their acceptance of decisions taken, their group productivity, and the profits of the enterprise. It seems appropriate in this context to note the importance of the time factor. Leadership behaviour comes into being and grows in permanent interplay with the group and the environment. However, other studies have shown that there is often no relationship between the leader and group performance (Stogdill, 1974; Locke & Schweiger, 1979), or that the cause–effect relation can be the other way around (Lowin & Craig, 1968; Farris & Lim, 1969). For example, higher performance by the group can lead to less close supervision by the leader.

Studies by Graen and Cashman (1975) show that the process of interaction can be even more complex. When new members join the group, a long process may follow whereby leader and group members (and group members among themselves) will feel each other out as it were and test each other's reactions. During this process an exchange relation develops, which determines whether or not the leader will assign a group member certain tasks, give information or support the group member in his or her relations with other members of the organization. The group member in turn shows a degree of dedication, conformity, cooperation etcetera (Jacobs, 1970).

This exchange model has been tested and elaborated in a number of studies (Graen & Novak, 1982). In their wake, Green, Fairhurst, and Snavely (1986) have elaborated on the related concept of the control chain and have applied it in particular to the long-term reactions of managers to repeatedly bad performance by group members. Such control chains apparently display certain constant patterns.

5.3 Leadership as part of organizational processes

The fact that the interaction between leader and group members is embedded in an organization that has a formal structure, employs a certain technology, employs certain control processes, and has an external environment in its turn, is not adequately reflected in most theories of leadership (Neuberger, 1984, 1985).

The attention for contingency theories that arose in the 1960s admittedly included an acknowledgement of the importance of certain micro-structural variables, such as task structure, group relations (Fiedler, 1967; Heller, 1971) and group norms (Hollander, 1964, 1979). Nevertheless, as organization theories have shown, human behaviour is also determined by the nature of the production process, by rules and regulations, and by communication patterns.

In this connection some useful light is thrown onto the situation by the work carried out by Kerr and his colleagues (Kerr, 1974; Kerr & Jermier, 1978), in particular their concept of substituting for leadership. This concept arises from the idea that situational factors can exist that provide so much structure or support that group members can derive all their motivation and job satisfaction from these factors alone, and that, as far as this support or structure is concerned, the intervention of a leader is superfluous. This does not mean, however, that the leader becomes altogether superfluous as such—as has been argued, for instance, in a classic study by Lieberson and O'Connor (1972). The leader has other responsibilities too, and leadership does influence the results attained by an organization (Thomas, 1988).

Examples of such substitution of supportive leadership are intrinsically satisfying tasks, professional orientation, or a cohesive working group. Examples of such substitution of structuring leadership are routine tasks, formalized plans, or rules and procedures.

Others have also attempted to categorize leadership within the framework of different forms of behaviour manipulation (see for example Miner, 1982). A particularly well-argued synthesis from the organizational point of view is provided by Mintzberg (1979, 1983a). Mintzberg shows that direct leadership can be regarded as one of the coordination mechanisms used to attune the behaviour of individuals and groups to the aims of the organization. The activity differentiation that follows specialization and task division creates the need for integrative mechanisms by which the members of organizations can be directed and controlled (Lawrence & Lorsch, 1967).

Mintzberg distinguishes between five such coordinating mechanisms:

- direct supervision;
- rules, regulations and procedures;
- goal-setting;
- professional training;
- mutual consultation.

In a later publication (Mintzberg, 1983b) he identifies five types of organization, including machine-bureaucracy and professional organizations . In certain types of organizations, claims Mintzberg, certain types of coordination mechanisms dominate. For instance, the larger and the more bureaucratic an organization becomes, the more direct supervision is replaced by rules and regulations. In professional organizations (e.g. hospitals, architect's bureaux, universities), however, coordination by means of training and mutual consultation are of great importance. Naturally, the role of the manager is different in each of these situations.

It has become clear that management is only one of many coordination mechanisms, and is itself determined by other mechanisms. There are three ways in which external variables and aspects of the situation, like organization structure, technology, or group relations, can play a part; these are indicated by arrows a, b, and c in Figure 13.3.

We will devote some attention to these three ways of exercising influence.

a. Influence of situational characteristics on leader behaviour

Although, traditionally, leadership was taken to be an independent variable, many studies have shown that the behaviour of the leader is also dependent on situational factors. The degree to which the leader is forced to behave in a certain way is highly variable. In bureaucratic organizations, first-level supervisors usually have little freedom of movement. On the other hand, the manager and owner of a small enterprise can largely determine his own policy and leadership style (although it should be borne in mind that this type of leader is also constrained by government regulations, collective labour agreements, type of personnel, etc.). This phenomenon is confirmed by various empirical studies. Thus an elected (as opposed to an assigned or appointed) leader appears to take more initiative (Carter, Kaythorn, Schriver, & Lanzetta, 1951) and to have more power and influence (Raven & French, 1958).

Furthermore, many studies have demonstrated the importance of management expectations and of management philosophy, on the one hand, and the nature of decisions, on the other (Heller, 1976; Wilpert, 1977). The level of the organization itself is an important differentiating factor with regard to leadership. Katz and Kahn (1978, p.536) distinguish three basic types of leadership behaviour.

- "Origination", i.e. policy-making, creating and changing structures (particularly at top level). In order to be able to do this one needs complete

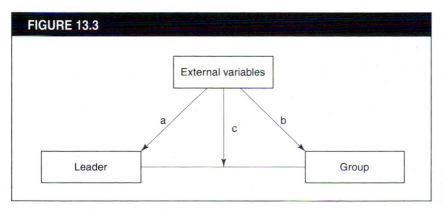

FIGURE 13.3

External variables

a   c   b

Leader   Group

The impact of aspects of the situation on leader–group relations.

insight into both the system as a whole, including its subsystems, and the demands, developments, and possibilities of the environment. According to Katz and Kahn, this "systemic perspective" is more important to top managers than interpersonal skills.

• "Interpolation", i.e. development of ways of effecting policies (particularly at the middle level). This presupposes a two-way orientation whereby ideas can be handed from top to bottom, and vice versa. This requires interpersonal skills and a keen insight into organization processes.

• "Administration", i.e. making use of the existing structure and effecting procedures and regulations (particularly at the lower level). This mainly requires technical and procedural knowledge.

Although every level requires its particular dominant type of leadership, a sufficient degree of each of the three types of leadership will have to be represented at each level. Insufficient attention at top level to policy, change, and adjustment can result in a rigid, bureaucratic organization. Insufficient attention at top level to routine control functions can lead to inefficiency and irritations, and to rivalry or lack of integration at lower levels (Katz & Kahn, 1978, p.570).

b. Aspects of the situation and the behaviour of group members

As mentioned already, the behaviour of individuals depends on more factors than leadership behaviour alone. Naturally this also holds for group attitudes and behaviour: These depend partly on all sorts of factors outside the leader's sphere of influence. In the first place we are alluding to task characteristics and group processes. Yet, organizational characteristics also appear—usually in a very complex way—to have considerable impact on the behaviour and attitudes of group members (James & Jones, 1976, Mintzberg, 1979).

All this means that it is doubtful whether a leader is always equally important to group behaviour. Hall (1972) therefore wonders whether there is convincing evidence that leadership has significant effects. Practical experience and common sense suggest that it does; but Pfeffer (1978) warns against such reasoning. Human beings constantly search for the causes of what happens to them, partly because that enables them effectively to control events. They particularly look for factors that are controllable, and dislike attributing causality to an obscure complex of human interaction, rules, structures, and objects. Where there is success there must be a hero; where there is a failure there must be a scapegoat.

We would like to argue that the need for leadership is in evidence not only in practice but also in theory and empirical research. Katz and Kahn (1978, p.530) mention a number of reasons:

• No organization scheme or scenario can be so exhaustive as to cover all activities.

• Organizations are open systems and are embedded in a constantly changing environment. Every change in the environment brings on changes in the organization.

• An organization consists of subsystems that are often not completely adjusted to each other, as they have different goals. The leader typically has a boundary function; that is to say, it is her task to regulate relations with other groups, so as to create optimal working conditions for her own group.

• Members of an organization are at the same time members of other systems (family, trade union, club). These systems may also cause changes in the leader's behaviour. It is the leader's task to react to these changes in order to keep the organization running.

c. Situational aspects and the part they play in the relationship between leadership (behaviour), group attitudes, and group behaviour

Theories that contend that the effect of a certain type of leadership on the performance and satisfaction of group members is partly determined by aspects of the situation, are called contingency theories. A well-known (if strongly criticized) example is Fiedler's theory (1967), which states that the success of task-oriented or relation-oriented leadership is dependent on the leader's formal power, task structure, and group relations (see the following section).

A contingency theory that has recently become

popular is the situational leadership theory put forward by Hersey and Blanchard (1982). According to this theory, there are four basic types of leadership, based on the combination of more or less task-oriented leadership activities. The effectiveness of these types of leadership depends particularly on what the authors call the maturity of the group members.

Kerr et al. (1974) present a long list of moderator variables based on an elaborate analysis of studies carried out with the help of the Ohio State Leadership Scales "consideration" and "initiating structure". Their most important findings are the following:

- Structuring leadership will be most desired and appreciated in crisis or at least stress situations, e.g. as a result of pressure of time, conflicts, physical danger, or other factors (see also Mulder et al. 1967). Recently, this was confirmed by Katz (1977) with respect to group conflicts.
- If tasks are very routine or if the person in question is very experienced or competent there is no insecurity and therefore little need for structuring leadership. In such cases, satisfaction of group members is primarily linked to "considerate" leadership.
- Contrary to expectation, the effects of hierarchical position, expectations of group members with respect to the most adequate leadership style, concurrence between leadership style of the direct supervisors and the manager on the next rung of the ladder, and communication with the top level appear to be rather unclear. In some studies they had a positive moderating effect; in others the effect was negatively moderating, or completely absent.

These conclusions confirm House's Path–Goals theory (House, 1971; House & Dessler, 1974), in which many of the variables mentioned earlier are integrated into a consistent model (see the following section).

However, these studies pay little attention to the moderating effect of the characteristics of the organization structure, technology, and other "macro" variables. Vollebergh (1973) deals with the subject in a rather impressionistic way; he defines certain types of leadership with the help of

two dimensions, namely, the degree of planning (improvisation vs. bureaucracy) and the degree of participation (hierarchical vs. participative). The four types that can be defined on the basis of these dimensions are each taken to be effective in certain organizations. Classical entrepreneurship (hierarchical but not very bureaucratic) is suitable for small organizations that require quick decisions. The inspiring leader (non-bureaucratic, oriented towards participation) suits the smaller organizations or departments in which various types of competent people should form a solid team, e.g. a project organization. The controller (hierarchical as well as bureaucratic) suits those organizations that need to be rigidly structured in order to avoid mistakes (for instance, administrative organizations). Finally, the role of manager (both structuring and oriented towards participation) is primarily effective in large organizations with complex links between divergent departments.

The parallels with Mintzberg's model described above are clear. Hunt and Osborne (1980) too have attempted to include macro-organizational factors into an explanatory model, their so-called multiple-influence model.

Moreover, we should not lose sight of more general social and environmental factors, important examples of which are given by certain groups of employees' rising levels of professional qualification and their increasing articulacy at work. We may expect such employees to appreciate a different kind of leadership (Lawler, 1985), one which relies less on direct supervision and guidance, and more on creating favourable conditions.

Finally, we would draw attention to a development in which the traditional approach is relinquished still further by supposing that differences between group members descriptions of their leader are in fact anything but random fluctuations, and that the leader's behaviour and that of the group members is far from homogeneous.

This is concerned with two forms of inconsistency in the leader's behaviour, namely:

1. a leader behaves in one way with one employee and in a different way with another;

2. a leader behaves with an employee in one way at one moment and in a different way at another moment.

Together, this is referred to as cross-situational specificity, and it represents the opposite of cross-situational consistency, that is, a style of leadership that remains the same in all circumstances. Research is then directed towards the analysis of vertical dyad linkages, that is, the interactions between the leader and a specific group member (see section 6.4). In an analysis of this kind which covered a series of groups within a large organization, Graen and others (Graen, Alvares, Orris, & Martella, 1970; Graen & Cashman, 1975; Dansereau & Dumas, 1977) came to the conclusion that in many groups these dyadic interactions took several different forms.

To be sure, in his reaction to this article Cummings (1975) states that to presuppose heterogeneity of behaviour is as generalizing as to presuppose homogeneity. Dansereau and Dumas (1977) present a method by which one can decide in a concrete research situation which of the two suppositions corresponds to reality. It can safely be assumed that in some situations—for instance, where group members work close to each other and on the same tasks—the leader shows rather consistent behaviour, if only because unequal treatment is likely to be seen as unfair. Besides, in very cohesive groups it is probably more effective if the leader approaches the group as a whole instead of approaching each member individually (Schriesheim & Kerr, 1977, p.38). Nevertheless, the authors' call for a more differentiated approach is very important, as it appears to take account of the notion that leader behaviour is not always as consistent and unchangeable as traditional theories suppose.

Although the argument has long been decided in favour of the contingency approach (situational leadership), the one-best-way claim is still occasionally made. Blake and Mouton published an interesting article, which argued for the consistent use of their 9-9 style, that is, leadership directed towards both the task required and towards the human relations involved (Blake & Mouton, 1982). However, their leadership styles actually refer more to the principles and intentions underlying leadership activities than to concrete behaviour—behaviour that their model also sees as changing according to the circumstances.

6 A FEW RECENT THEORIES

The previous section described a number of factors that ought to be incorporated into a leadership theory. Six modern approaches to the subject which do this to some degree at least, will now be discussed.

These six approaches can be subsumed into three categories:

1. *Static contingency theories*, that is, theories in which a number of more or less objectively ascertainable situation characteristics are held to determine which of a limited number of leadership styles is the most effective. We will discuss Fiedler's contingency theory (section 6.1), the Path–Goal theory put forward by House (section 6.2) and Vroom and Yetton's decision-making approach (section 6.3).

2. *Interaction models*, that is, models of the changing interactions between a leader and individual group members. We will discuss the rewards and punishments approach (section 6.4) and the leader–follower interaction approach (section 6.5).

3. *Leadership in organization*. Concepts of leadership as one of a range of coordination and control mechanisms within organizations are described at various points in this chapter. An in-depth analysis of organization-theory concepts and approaches is, however, beyond the scope of this article; we shall confine ourselves to one example, a theory put forward by Smith and Peterson (1988).

6.1 Fiedler's contingency theory

Fiedler's theory (1967) is certainly worth mentioning since it is one of the first of the contingency models. The central idea is that the effect of a certain type of leader behaviour on group performance depends on the situation (see Figure 13.4).

Rather than measure leadership behaviour, Fiedler measures (with the help of a semantic differential questionnaire) a personal property, *an*

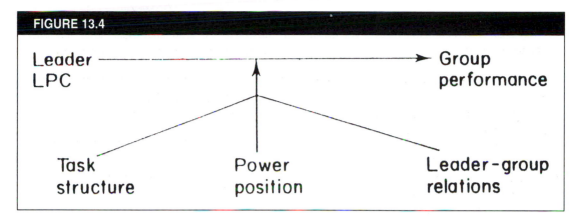

FIGURE 13.4

Fiedler's contingency theory.

attitude, of the leader, i.e. his attitude towards the "least preferred coworker" (LPC). A high LPC score is interpreted as strongly relation oriented, a low LPC score as strongly task oriented.

At the same time three aspects of the situation are measured with the help of questionnaires, i.e. the degree to which the task is routine and/or clearly structured, the degree to which the power position of the leader is guaranteed by the organization and the degree to which the group climate is favourable.

On the basis of numerous empirical studies, Fiedler concludes the following:

● Highly task-oriented leadership is most effective in groups in which conditions are relatively favourable (i.e. good relations and the presence of one or both of the other factors), or in those cases where all these factors are unfavourable.

● Highly relation-oriented leadership is most effective when the other conditions prevail, i.e. when the task is sufficiently structured yet the leader–group relations and/or the leader's formal power position are rather poor.

● The leader's attitude (as represented in the LPC score) is hard to change. Consequently, it is suggested that the selection and appointment of the leader should happen in such a way that he ends up in the right groups, or that the leader's attitudes are being diagnosed, whereupon the aspects of the situation might be changed so as to create the most favourable combination of leader and situation (Fiedler, Chemers, & Maker, 1976).

Fiedler's theory has met with severe criticism (for

example, Graen et al., 1970; Schriesheim & Kerr, 1977). The most important critical observations are:

● The LPC scale shows insufficient conceptual, substantial, and predictive validity. One important issue is the fact that the LPC variable is unidimensional, whereas the Ohio State Studies have demonstrated that task and relation-oriented behaviour can occur simultaneously. "Thus we must conclude that after twenty-five years the LPC remains a measure in search of a meaning" (Stinson, 1977). Furthermore, homogeneity often scores high, but it appears that in many studies stability (test-retest) is very low. The latter is important, as the LPC variable is supposed to measure a stable personality trait.

● The selection, measuring, and differential weighting of the three aspects of the situation are conceptually obscure, and in various studies they have been changed in an *ad hoc* manner. Moreover, the model in Figure 13.4 shows that the choice of these three aspects is rather arbitrary and incomplete.

● The theory is static. There is no room for change: The LPC variable is taken to be unchangeable, and if a leader wants to be effective she must see to it that the situation does not change either. According to the theory, the leader can afford to be strongly task oriented when leader–group relations are favourable. It remains to be seen whether these relations continue to be favourable if the leader is exclusively task oriented.

These and other criticisms show that the theory is rather vulnerable. Nevertheless, during the 1960s and the early 1970s this model stimulated much theorizing and research; in this respect, it certainly has exerted important influence.

In a later series of publications culminating in the book *New approaches to effective leadership* (Fiedler & Garcia, 1987), three new parameters were introduced: Whether or not the task requires cognitive capacities, intelligence (of leader and group members), and whether or not the leader is working under stress. The theory holds that if a task-oriented leader is stress-free, then the leader's intelligence will correlate with group-performance levels to the degree to which the leader enjoys support from the group. If this is not the case, then the leader's intelligence will have less influence on group performance, including tasks requiring fewer cognitive skills. If the leader is less directive and more relationship oriented, then it is the intelligence of the group that is linked to group-performance levels, especially in tasks requiring more cognitive skills, but only if the leader supports the group. If he does not, then it is the external factors in particular (e.g. the difficulty of the task) that determine group performance.

The book puts forward a considerable amount of experimental and empirical support for (parts of) this newer cognitive variant, and it would seem to represent an enrichment of classical theory in the field. Whether the book answers every point of criticism and weakness that has been made against it however, is open to question. The issue will doubtless remain a subject of debate for the time being.

6.2   The Path–Goal theory

Following Evans (1970), House (1971) based his theory about leadership behaviour on the expectation theory of work motivation. According to this theory, people's motivation to work depends both on the importance (the valence) they attach to certain results that are to be attained (the outcomes) and on the expectation that their behaviour will actually cause them to obtain these results (see also Vroom, 1964). The behaviour of the leader should supply rewards (valent outcomes), e.g. by reacting with open and social leadership to desired behaviour (= consideration). Besides the leader's instructions and structuring (= initiating structure) should be such that they help the group members to attain their goal. The latter, also called role clarification, means that the group members' expectations about their chances of attaining their goals (path–goal relation) are reinforced. This leads to two conclusions:

1. The leader is effective (i.e. he motivates his people) if he makes satisfaction of group member needs (i.e. receiving valent outcomes) dependent on their behaviour.
2. The leader is effective insofar as his behaviour (rewarding or structuring) is complementary to what the situation is already producing.

House distinguishes two groups of situational factors, namely, characteristics of group members (notably, perception of their own skills. "locus of control" orientation and authoritarianism), and characteristics of the environment (notably, task structuring and structuring of the organization). In discussions and empirical studies the degree of task structuring received most attention. The second proposition implies that if the task itself is very structured, i.e. routine, the leader should not give instructions or do much supervising, as this is superfluous and causes frustration. She should instead adopt a considerate and supportive form of leadership, i.e. be friendly, open, and helpful, in order to compensate for the monotonous task or the formalistic organization. Tests of the Path–Goal theory have been limited to an analysis of the moderating effect of task structure on the relationship between leadership behaviour and performance, satisfaction, or expectations of group members.

In their survey article Schriesheim and Kerr (1977) conclude that hitherto the empirical support for the theory, notably the aforementioned effect on task structure, is rather weak. Possible explanations are twofold. First, the rather unfortunate operationalization of leadership behaviour: for lack of any better alternative, the Ohio State Leadership Scales for "consideration" and "initiating structure" were used in many cases. Schriesheim himself developed specific Path–Goal scales for measuring consideration and initiating structure (Kerr & Jermier, 1978, p.392).

A number of other aspects of leadership behaviour aspects have also been examined within the framework of the Path–Goal theory (Fulk & Wendler, 1982), namely upward-influencing, performance-oriented, and arbitrary punishment behaviour. Such behaviour did indeed contribute towards the (dis)satisfaction of the group members, and also towards the clarification of roles, but did not contribute towards their motivation or performance.

Secondly, all kinds of other factors that could influence relations were not taken into account. The study by Downey, Sheridan and Slocum (1976) demonstrates that hierarchical differences (with the attending differences in task preferences) interact with task structure. Managers appear to prefer a great deal of independence. As a result, structuring leadership did enhance their performance but it also caused dissatisfaction. In the long run this could lead to lower performance. Hammer and Dachler (1975) argue for a more explicit use of the expectation theory, which they believe will improve the conceptualization of notions like "path" and "goals".

Partly on the basis of our model (Figure 13.4) we can make the following criticisms of the Path Goal theory:

1. House and Dessler's (1974) formulation in particular pays little attention to the actual behaviour of the members, to group performance as a whole, or to the feedback effect on the perception and behavior of the leader. The longitudinal research carried out by Downey et al. (1976) illustrates the importance of these factors.
2. Apart from task structure there are various other aspects of the environment that, either by themselves or in a process of interaction, might influence the relationship between leader behaviour and the group.
3. Although the theory explicitly postulates that leadership behaviour should be adjusted, i.e. to the performance of group members, most empirical studies only use operationalizations of general leadership styles.

Despite these criticisms, the Path–Goal theory offers a model that in principle can encompass many variables and phenomena relevant to the effects and determinants of leadership behaviour. For further verification of the theory, many of these variables and their effects should be defined and operationalized more explicitly.

6.3 Leadership as decision-making

Vroom and Yetton (1973) have developed a detailed theory about the conditions under which different ways of decision-making are most effective. The five ways of decision-making vary with respect to the degree to which group members are involved in the decision-making of the leader. These various decision-making strategies can he compared with the levels in the Influence–Power continuum (IPc), mentioned by Heller (1971), and the participation levels used in recent research on industrial democracy in Europe (IDE, 1981), and complex decision-making (Heller et al., 1988).

The five ways of decision-making are the following:

1. *autocratic-l (AI)*: the leader makes the decision without making enquiries of the group;
2. *autocratic 2 (AII)*: the leader makes the decision after selective enquiries;
3. *consultative-l* (CI): the leader makes the decision after asking individual group members for solutions;
4. *consultative 2 (CII)*: the leader makes the decision after consulting and discussing with the whole group;
5. *group method (GII)*: the group (which includes the leader) makes the decision.

Certain aspects of the situation are important in determining which strategy is chosen. Unlike other contingency theories, Vroom and Yetton's model focuses not so much on general organization, group, or task characteristics as on the characteristics of specific decisions. According to the theory, seven characteristics are important (see the questions in Figure 12.6). The effectiveness of decisions is defined in terms of the quality of the solution and the motivation of group members to cooperate in its implementation. In fact, the model consists of a number of rules for decsion-making that determine which methods of decision-making are more and which less effective, given a certain combination of decision-making characteristics.

The "acceptance-rule" can serve as an example: If effective implementation of a decision requires that group members accept it, and if it is not certain that an autocratic decision will be accepted, then strategies AI and AII (autocratic decision-making) are unsuitable.

The theory is in the first place meant to be normative. That is to say, on the basis of an extensive study of the literature, Vroom and Yetton have drawn up rules that specify how a leader should behave in order to reach a given goal. This normative model is represented in Figure 13.5.

Vroom and Yetton (1973) and Jago and Vroom (1975) have investigated whether the normative model has also an empirical character, i.e. to what degree leaders actually behave according to this model. They conclude that leaders do indeed adjust their behaviour to the situation, i.e. the nature of the problems confronting them. However, they only do this within limits. Apparently, many leaders showed less variation in their behaviour than the model postulates.

Some are less, others more participative than the model prescribes. From this the authors deduce that to some extent leaders adopt a certain personal style, which manifests itself in various situations. Nevertheless, the theory needs further testing. Vroom and Yetton have actually used two research strategies, both of which are reputational in character. First, managers were asked to mention decisions they had had to make in the past and to describe the decision-making process followed. Second, managers were confronted with a series of standardized problems and subsequently asked how they would go about making a decision.

Jago and Vroom's (1975) research seems a step in the right direction. They asked group members to describe (predict) how their leader would make certain decisions. This study also led to the conclusion that the leader adjusts his decision-making style to the problem. However, there was practically no agreement in the descriptions that the group members and the leaders themselves gave of the latter's strategy.

The model is therefore not yet empirically tested, and it remains uncertain whether managers who do make decisions in the "prescribed" manner are really more effective than those who do not. No matter how self-evident the links, empirical research can lead to completely different results. Thus Koopman and Drenth (1980a) found that in a situation of conflict rather than of consensus, decision-making is indeed linked to effectiveness.

Finally, when we compare Vroom and Yetton's theory with the model in Figure 13.4 it becomes clear that the theory's scope is limited. First, it is only concerned with a specific part of leadership, namely, ways of decision-making. Other forms of interaction between leader and group members, such as daily contact, supervision of work, or discussion of a group member's personal problems, are not taken into account. Furthermore, no attention is devoted to conditioning characteristics of the organization or the group. However, it is likely that the same decision-making style applied to the same problems in (departments of) organizations with varying power relations or managerial climate would yield wholly different results. This may explain the limited variance of the decision-making style of Vroom and Yetton's managers. It is possible that some of them behaved more autocratically or participatively than prescribed by the model, because they bore in mind the general climate of the organization, and their own bosses' wishes. Nevertheless, this theory is clearly an improvement on the traditional universal theories. One does not often come across such an accurate specification of leader behaviour and aspects of the situation.

6.4   Rewards and punishments

Fourthly, we would like to discuss approaches that devote particular attention to the leader's use of punishment and reward. These approaches are sometimes explicitly based on operant-conditioning theory (Scott, 1977; Sims, 1977). Sims (1977) defines leadership as "a process of supervisory structuring of reinforcement contingencies in the environment". His operant-conditioning theory is based on the idea that group member behaviour is particularly determined by stimulus–response–reward chains in the work environment.

In an organization there are various sources of reward: colleagues supply friendship; the organization supplies wages, promotion, secondary labour conditions; the task supplies intrinsic

FIGURE 13.5

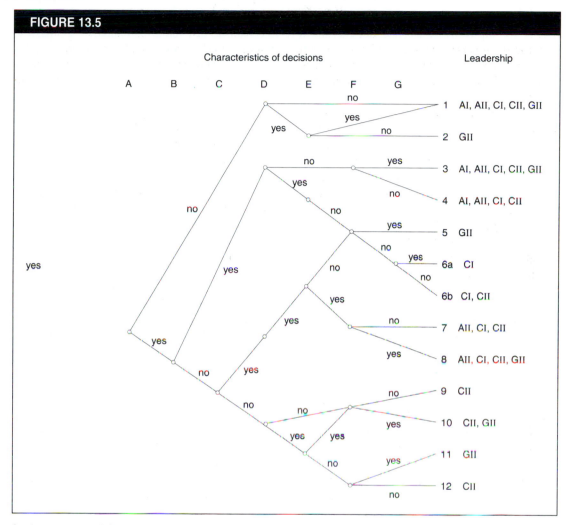

Contingency model of decision-making by Vroom and Yetton (1973).

Definition of decision characteristics:
A. Is there a quality requirement such that one solution is likely to be more rational than another?
B. Do I have sufficient information to make high quality decisions?
C. Is the problem structured?
D. Is acceptance of decision by subordinates critical to effective implementation?
E. If I were to make the decision myself, is it reasonably certain that I would be accepted by my subordinates?
F. Do subordinates share the organizational goals to be attained in solving this problem?
G. Is conflict among subordinates likely in a preferred solution?

satisfaction; and the leader gives compliments, acknowledgement, and pleasant tasks. The leader therefore plays an often crucial role in devising "contingencies of reinforcements". She does this in two ways. If tasks are not completely routine she is the one who determines the "discriminative stimuli" (i.e. indicates how group members should act), among other things by assigning tasks.

Sims (1977, p.134) believes that what is called "initiating structure" or "goal specification" in leadership style traditions in fact comes down to defining the stimuli and indicating the correct response. Besides indicating the correct stimulus and response, the leader's task consists of giving a reward for the correct response.

It is well known from conditioning theory that

giving rewards should be directly dependent on the nature of the response and should follow closely on the response. Furthermore, conditioning experiments have yielded all sorts of reward schemes. According to Sims, some of these can be used in a work situation.

He devised a questionnaire—the Leader Reward Behaviour Questionnaire—with which this reward behaviour of the leader can be evaluated by group members. With the help of factor analysis three dimensions could be identified:

1. *Positive Reward Behaviour* (example: Your boss would be very interested if you would suggest new and better ways of working);
2. *Advancement Reward Behaviour* (example: If you asked him for a transfer your boss would help you get it);
3. *Punitive Reward Behaviour* (example: Your boss would be angry with you if your work wasn't as good as that of the others in your department).

Whereas "Initiating Structure" and "Goal Specification" specify that which precedes group-member behaviour, "Leader Reward Behaviour" specifies what comes after it. The theory was tested in a study of 61 workers at various levels in different types of organization. Positive Reward Behaviour and, to a lesser degree, Advancement Reward Behaviour appear to be positively correlated with performance. Punitive Reward Behaviour was not related to performance level.

It is also interesting to ask why and when punishments or rewards are employed. In an examination of the literature, Podsakoff (1982) has identified large number of the situational characteristics (group size, organization policy, task structure, and the like), group-member characteristics (performance level, gender, interpersonal attraction, and so on), and leader characteristics (personality, gender, and so on) one might suppose to have an influence on the matter. However, only a very few of these determinants turn out to have an unambiguous influence: Rewards turn out to be more important than punishments, particularly in smaller groups, given that the group members work hard and that their leaders are confident and experienced.

The danger that this line of thought harbours a mechanistic or even a manipulative approach to leadership is not entirely illusory, but certain of its ideas are valuable none the less. Among them is the distinction between response-specifying (initiating structure) and reward-assigning behaviour (reward behaviour), and the attention to the fact that a leader's effectiveness depends on the way in which she reacts directly to the behaviour of group members.

6.5   Leader–follower interaction and attribution

Earlier in this chapter we drew attention to the possibility of inconsistency in a leader's behaviour, as this behaviour is primarily determined by interaction with (necessarily diverse) subordinates. The vertical dyad linkage concept based on this idea has been accorded empirical support from a number of different studies (Zahn & Wolf, 1981; Graen & Novak, 1982; Vecchio & Gobdel, 1984; Crouch & Yetton, 1988).

Leaders and employees do indeed appear to influence each other's perceptions, attitudes, and behaviour, and leaders employ different behavioural styles with different employees. These studies, and others (e.g. Podsakoff, 1982) also had a third, and rather sobering, conclusion: The variable that appears to invoke the most predictable behaviour in the leader is the performance level of the group members. Leaders reward those who do well and do not reward, or punish, those who do not do so well.

Green and Mitchell (1979) have used notions from the attribution theory to understand an aspect of leadership that is often neglected, namely, the impact of behaviour of group members on leader behaviour. According to this theory, the reactions of a leader to the behaviour of his group members is dependent on how he interprets and explains this behaviour. The leader will attribute that which a group member does to her specific characteristics and/or the nature of the task and/or the nature of the context within which the group member performs her task (group and organization characteristics). For instance, he will compare the behaviour of one group member with that of another, or performance on one task with performance on another or behaviour at one moment with behaviour at another. The more complex the situation (for instance, as a result of the size of the workgroup, heterogeneous tasks, geographical space, etc.), the less the leader will be inclined to seek or use all available information; instead, he will confine himself to very simple causal interpretation schemes in order to "explain" a given level of performance of a group member (see, for instance, Figure 13.6).

The leader's reactions (e.g. rewards, punishments, nature of supervision, expectations of the group members) will depend on what he considers to be the cause of that behaviour. If he thinks that a group member's failure is due to external factors he will give support and consideration; if he feels that it is due to group member's remissness, he will be inclined to motivate her through either negative or positive sanctions. If he feels that high performance of group members is a result of his close supervision, he will be inclined to continue this type of leadership. And if he attributes a group member's behaviour to lack of understanding of the task, he will probably react with structuring behaviour.

The central idea behind the attribution theory is that the leader's reaction is not directly linked to the observable behaviour of a group member, but to causes that determine that behaviour *according to the leader*. The group member herself goes through a similar process of attributing causes to her own behaviour. In cases where these two attribution processes lead to different conclusions, the odds are that conflicts will arise. In fact, this is extremely likely, according to Green and Mitchell.

A variety of socio-psychological processes lie at the root of this.

Observers are rather inclined to attribute an actor's behaviour to *internal* factors, whereas the actors themselves are strongly inclined to emphasize the importance of *external* causes.

These general processes also appear to be at work in leader–group member interactions. Moreover, there are a number of variables that influence the way in which leaders assess the behaviour of those around them: attributes of the group members and of the leader (gender, race, and more personal characteristics such as perceived locus of control, etc.), congruities and incongruities in these attributes, the psychological distance between the leader and the group, the complexity of the situation and the seriousness of the consequences of certain behaviours, can all influence the way in which a leader accounts for the group's behaviour (see Johnson et al., 1984; Dobbins, Pence, Orban, & Sgro, 1983). The whole process is shown diagrammatically in Figure 13.7.

However, leaders in formal organizations cannot determine their behaviour and reactions solely on the basis of their own causal explanations. They are tied to rules and procedures and to the conduct of higher managers. Thus a boss may attribute the tardiness of a group member to external factors (e.g. his car tyres were slashed), but the rules of the organization prescribe that the missed hours shall not be paid. In such cases it is important to know what leaders do when their own attributions are in conflict with the policy of the organization. One

---

FIGURE 13.6

		attributed cause	
		personal	situational
assumed stability of behaviour	high	capacities	task complexity organization
	low	exertion	luck/bad luck

Causal interpretaton schema.

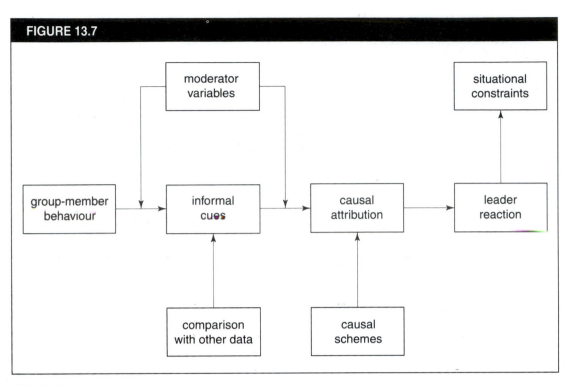

FIGURE 13.7

Attribution theoretical model of leadership reactions.

can assume that factors such as the leader's power position (partly) determine the extent to which either her own attributions or those or organizational policy will prevail.

6.6 The management of meaning

Smith & Peterson (1988) have built on the idea that leaders and group members within organizations react to each other. This interaction takes place within a framework of the organization's structure and culture, and it is this framework that partly determines one party's interpretation and attribution of the other party's behaviour.

This theory comprises, firstly, a cognitive choice model, as shown in Figure 13.8.

In a sense this is actually a kind of contingency approach; the situation plays an important role. However, in this model the situation is not an objective fact, but is construed in a certain way by the leader and by the group members, a way which depends on the nature of their attention, their attributes, and their own motives

Secondly, the theory concerns the way in which the social context imbues actual events and leader-

ship behaviour with meaning, and therefore determines their effects. A leader moves in a network of relationships and roles, which determine, to a greater or lesser extent, his interpretation of a given event and therefore his reaction to it. The group members and the others (colleagues and superiors) with whom a leader has a relationship react, in turn, to the meaning they attach to the leader's behaviour. The same people define what they regard as effective leadership on the basis of their own value systems. For these reasons the art of good leadership consists not so much in accurately assessing the objective situation, but rather in influencing the interpretations that others give to that situation. Smith and Peterson speak of leadership as the management of meaning (see also Smircich & Morgan, 1982).

For all this, over the course of time, behaviour patterns and interpretations take on a certain degree of routine. The habits and practices which then arise contribute towards the organizational culture, which in turn affects the interpretations made by the various players in this organizational game. Neither can Smith and Peterson avoid

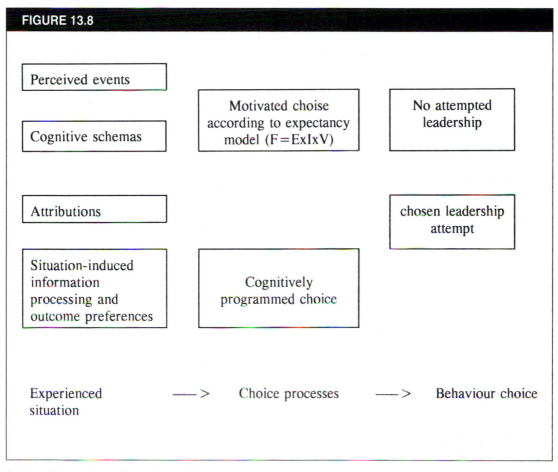

FIGURE 13.8

Smith and Peterson's cognitive choice model.

having to categorize leadership aspects into task-oriented and relationship-oriented aspects, although in their view this amounts to no more than distinguishing *what* a leader should do, without providing useful answers to the question of *how* it can best be done in a given context. The most important departure from previous leadership-style theories and contingency theories is that it holds task and relationship orientation not to be the objectively ascertainable characteristics of a certain leader or a certain type of leader behaviour, but rather as ways that leaders, followers, and often observers make sense out of their experience of more specific actions. Every leader must struggle with the need to adapt her behaviour to forms that will be experienced by others in the role set in the manner intended (p.158).

7 FINALLY: A COMPREHENSIVE MODEL

Some surveys about leadership, which appeared in the 1970s (for example Hunt & Larsson, 1977; McCall & Lombardo, 1978), present a rather pessimistic picture of the field. There is certainly little optimism in the discussion of research results and theories. This negative assessment primarily concerns research and theories within the realm of what we called the "style" paradigm. This approach is characterized by:

- exclusive attention to a number of general leadership styles;
- the assumption that leadership and group

behaviour are homogeneous—confinement to shopfloor-level work groups in large organizations;

- confinement to only a few dependent variables (satisfaction, motivation, and performance);
- scant attention to aspects of the situation other than qualities of the leader and the group;
- a simplistic cause-and-effect model (leadership→result);
- an exclusive reliance on correlational questionnaires in gathering data.

Moreover, as a consequence of this approach, training courses focused on teaching leaders "the one best way", i.e. a leadership that was both task-oriented and human-oriented, and, more recently, preferably also participative.

During the 1960s in particular, the contingency approach led to more attention to the environment in which leaders and group members function. In leadership training courses leaders were now taught that there were environments in which other combinations of the two leadership styles could be effective (Reddin, 1970, 1971). In the 1970s, however, the "style" paradigm came under more vigorous attack. This is not to say that then the route to new approaches, theories, and research became clearly mapped. In his concluding remarks at the third Southern Illinois University Leadership Symposium, Miner (1975) decribed the situation as follows:

> This state of high uncertainty and its concordant frustrated desire for real understanding presently characterizes the leadership field more than any other single thing; we simply do not know what we want to know.

None the less, some new and promising developments have emerged, although so far they have been little tested; some have been discussed in this chapter. Future approaches to the problem of leadership should focus on a number of elements brought to light in this review. We will finish by enumerating those elements and thus—in a sense summarize and present our conclusions on the arguments we have developed in this chapter.

From the discussions of the previous sections we can conclude that theories on leadership have to be complex—that is to say, they have to be able to take account of large numbers of variables and the interactions between them. This is not to say, however, that the process entails drawing up long lists of factors, all of which might be relevant in some way or other. There has to be further specification of the effects of different *kinds* of factors.

In a model of our own construction (Figure 13.9) we have endeavoured to integrate the most relevant and frequently considered of these variables and links. Those interacting processes (within and between groups and leaders) that directly determine or moderate the central group process have been placed at the centre of the model. Naturally, the model does not have an ontological, empirically tested status, but a heuristic one.

The model clearly shows that, in our opinion, leadership can hardly be isolated from the whole complex of dynamic processes. It can be assumed however, that the determining effect of leadership on the attitudes and behaviour of group members will be stronger when aspects of the situation are less clearly structured and less pressing.

With the help of this model we will now discuss a number of the better known and more recent theories in the field of leadership.

- Leadership is part of an organization process. Leader behaviour, like the behaviour of group members, is strongly determined and restricted by structure, technology, role expectations, control mechanisms, and other characteristics of the environment.
- Leaders at various levels of the organization have widely differing functions and tasks that appeal to divergent capacities, cognitive processes, and social skills.
- The effect of leader behaviour is dependent on the expectations and goals of the group members and on the conditions in the environment.
- Leader and group members constantly interact. In the course of this interaction they create complex exchange relations, which, through changes in the composition of the group or in the

environment, are themselves constantly subject to change.

- Developing one specific style and sticking to it may be dysfunctional. It is more important that a leader understands the expectations and goals of group members, the complexity and dynamics of the situation, and the possible changes that may occur.

- Leaders only devote a limited amount of their time to direct supervision. Often their work is extremely fragmentary and their function is largely a boundary one, i.e. they maintain contacts with colleagues, superiors, suppliers, clients, trade unions, etc. In these contacts they serve their own interests and the interests of the group in order that it may function optimally. They enter into coalitions or into conflicts. In short, they play their role in the organization's power game.

- Leadership serves two group aspects: group-task work and the maintenance of mutual relations. However, the behaviour that actually contributes to this, and the degree to which certain behaviour is perceived as being effective, depends on the specific context and the role-set interpretations.

- In an organizational context that is not subject to too much change, the significance of leadership behaviour can become stable over time.

FIGURE 13.9

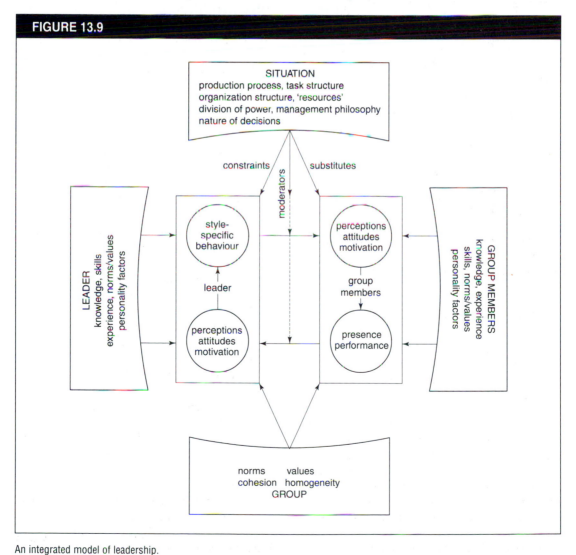

An integrated model of leadership.

To a certain extent, therefore, traditional contingency theories, which prescribe certain specific behaviour in specific circumstances, are of some real value. However, modern organizations in particular are subject to rapid processes of internal and external change. For this reason, leaders also derive benefit from a theory that can throw light on the ways in which their behaviour is affected by others as well as how it is interpreted and thereby exerts influence.

Indeed, it is quite understandable that today, with more stable organizations than ever turning into turbulent working environments, traditional static contingency theories are making way for dynamic interaction theories and interpretation theories.

Leadership research within this context of change will have to make much more use of techniques other than questionnaires. Longitudinal research will be needed to reveal process dynamics, and attention will also have to be given to those dependent variables that are directly linked to leadership, that is, the expectations and perceptions of individual group members and their direct reactions to leader behaviour.

Finally, one last word on a problem in the leadership of groups and organizations that receives next to no attention in the leadership research literature: the issue of succession. An analysis of the most critical factors involved in leadership succession (Gordon & Rosen, 1981) has shown just how important this subject is. The process of succession and replacement can itself strongly influence group culture and behaviour. New leaders sometimes feel compelled to conform, or, indeed, to rebel against their predecessor's behaviour. Gordon and Rosen have developed a model for the study of succession processes and have called for more intensive research in this area. In their view, the effectiveness of many leaders—especially in the beginning—is strongly determined by the characteristics of the previous history and the way in which succession took place.

We would add that the succession issue looks set to become increasingly important in the future. In many bureaucratic organizations large numbers of directors, managers, and departmental heads have spent years doing the same job. Modern, flexible organizations will be characterized, however, by project groups, temporary joint ventures, job-changing, and mobility. Frequently, leaders will guide groups for a much shorter time period. The way a person *becomes* a leader, and the *first* interactions between leader and group, will therefore become increasingly important in determining group performance and relations.

REFERENCES

Alderfer, C.P. (1972) *Existence, relatedness and growth: Human needs in organizational settings.* New York: Free Press.

Andriessen, J.H.T.H., Drenth, P.J.D., & Lammers, C.J. (1984). *Medezeggenschap in Nederlandse bedrijven.* Amsterdam: Noord-Hollandse Uitgevers Maatschappij.

Ashour, A.S. (1982). A framework of cognitive-behavioral theory of leader influence and effectiveness. *Organizational behavior and human performance, 30*, 407–430.

Avolio, B.J., & Bass, B.M. (1987). Charisma and beyond. In J.G. Hunt (Eds.), *Emerging leadership vistas.* Boston: Lexington.

Baldridge, J.V. (1971). *Power and conflict in the university.* New York: Wiley.

Banner, D.K., & Balsingame, J.W. (1988). Towards a developmental paradigm of leadership. *Leadership and Organization Development Journal, 9, 4*, 7–16.

Bass, B.M. (1981). *Stogdill's handbook of leadership.* New York: Free Press.

Bass, B.M. (1985a). Leadership: good, better, best. *Organizational Dynamics, Winter*, 26–40.

Bass, B.M. (1985b). *Leadership and performance beyond expectations.* New York: Free Press.

Bass, B.M., Farrow, D.L., Valenzie, E.R., & Solomon, R.J. (1975). Management styles associated with organizational task, personal and interpersonal contingencies. *Journal of Applied Psychology, 60*, 720–729.

Bass, B.M., Waldman, D.A., Avolio, B.J., & Bebb, M. (1987). Transformational leadership and the falling dominos effect. *Group and Organization Studies, 12*, 73–87.

Beyne, H.H. (1973). *Working for Ford.* London: Penguin.

Blake, R.R., & Mouton, J.S. (1964). *The managerial grid.* Houston: Golf Publishing.

Blake, R.R., & Mouton, J.S. (1982). Theory and research for developing a science of leadership. *Journal of Applied Behavior Science, 18, 3*, 275–291.

Brayfield, A., & Crockett, W. (1955). Employee attitudes and employee performance. *Psychological Bulletin, 52*, 396–424.

Burns, J.M. (1978). *Leadership*. New York: Harper & Row.

Campbell, J.P. (1977). The cutting edge of leadership: An overview. In J.G. Hunt & L.L. Larson (Eds.), *Leadership, the cutting edge*. Carbondale: Southern Illinois University Press.

Campbell, J.P., Dunnette, M.D., Lawler, E.E., & Weick, K.E. (1970). *Managerial behavior, performance and effectiveness*. New York: McGraw-Hill.

Campbell, J.P., & Pritchard, R.D. (1976). Motivation in industrial organizational psychology. In M.D. Dunnette (Ed.), *Handbook of industrial and organizational psychology*. Chicago: Rand McNally.

Carter, L.F., Kaythorn, W., Schriver, E., & Lanzetta, J. (1951). The behavior of leaders and other group members. *Journal of Abnormal and Social Psychology, 22*, 396–424.

Conger, J.A., & Kanungo, R.N. (1988). *Charismatic leadership: The elusive factor in organizational effectiveness*. San Francisco: Jossey-Bass.

Cornelius, E.T., & Lane, F.B. (1984). The power motive and managerial succes in a professionally oriented service industry organization. *Journal of Applied Psychology, 69*, 320–339.

Crouch, A., & Yetton, P. (1987). Manager behavior, leadership style, and subordinate performance: An empirical extension of the Vroom–Yetton conflict rule. *Organizational Behavior and Human Decision Processes, 39*, 384–396.

Crouch, A., & Yetton, P. (1988). Manager–subordinate dyads: Relationships among task and social contacts, manager friendliness and subordinate performance in management groups. *Organizational Behavior and Human Decision Processes, 41*, 65–82.

Cummings, L.L. (1975). Assessing the Craen/Cashman model and comparing it with other approaches. In J.G. Hunt & L.L. Larsson (Eds.), *Leadership frontiers*. Kent, OH: Kent State University.

Dansereau, F., Dumas, M. (1977). Pratfalls and pitfalls in drawing inferences about leader behavior in organizations. In L.G. Hunt & L.L. Larsson (Eds.), *Leadership, the cutting edge*. Carbondale: Southern Illinois University Press.

Davis, T.R.V., & Luthans, F. (1979). Leadership reexamined: A behavioral approach. *Academy of Management Review, 4*, 237–248.

Dobbins, G.H., Pence, E.C., Orban, J.A., & Sgro, J.A. (1983). The effects of sex of the leader and sex of the subordinate on the use of organizational control policy. *Organizational Behavior and Human Performance, 32*, 325–343.

Downey, H.K., Sheridan, J.E., & Slocum, J.W. (1976). The path–goal theory of leadership: A longitudinal analysis. *Organizational Behavior and Human Performance, 16*, 156–176.

Drehmer, D.E., & Grossman, J.H. (1984). Scaling managerial respect: A developmental perspective. *Educational and Psychological Measurement, 44*, 763–767.

Drenth, P.J.D., & Koopman, P.L. (1984). A contingency approach to participative leadership: How good? In J.G. Hunt, D.M. Hosking, C.A. Schriesheim, & R. Stewart (Eds.), *Leaders and managers: International perspectives on managerial behavior and leadership*. New York: Pergamon.

Drenth, P.J.D., & Thierry, H. (1970). Onderzoek naar effectief leiderschap. In P.J.D. Drenth, P.J. Willems, & C.J. de Wolff (Eds.), *Bedrijfspsychologie. Onderzoek en evaluatie*. Deventer: Kluwer.

Drucker, P. (1954). *The practice of management*. New York: Harper.

Duncan, R.B. (1973). *Modifications in decision making structures in adapting to the environment*. Evanston, IL: Northwestern University.

Duncan, R.B. (1973). Multiple decision-making structures in adapting to environmental uncertainty: The impact on organizational effectiveness. *Human Relations, 26*, 273–292.

Evans, M. . (1970). The effects of supervisory bahavior on the path–goal relationship. *Organizational Behavior and Human Performance, 5*, 277–298.

Farris, F., & Lim, F. (1969). Effect of performance on leadership cohesiveness, influence, satisfaction and subsequent performance. *Journal of Applied Psychology, 53*, 490–497.

Fiedler, F.E. (1967). *A theory of leadership effectiveness*. New York: McGraw-Hill.

Fiedler, F.E., Chemers, M.M., & Maker, L. (1976). *Improving leadership effectiveness: The leader match concept*. New York: Wiley.

Fiedler, F.E., & Garcia, J.E. (1987). *New approaches to effective leadership: Cognitive resources and organizational performance*. New York: Wiley.

Fleishman, E.A., & Harris, E.F. (1962). Patterns of leadership behavior related to employee grievances and turnover. *Personnel Psychology, 15*, 43–56.

Fleishman, E.A., Harris, E.F., & Burt, H.E. (1955). *Leadership and supervision in industry*. Columbus: Ohio State University.

French, J.P.R., & Raven, B.H. (1959). The bases of social power. In D. Cartwright (Ed.), *Studies in social power*. Ann Arbor: University of Michigan.

Fulk, J., & Wendler, E.R. (1982). Dimensionality of leader–subordinate interactions: A path–goal investigation. *Organizational Behavior and Human Resources, 30*, 241–264.

Gilmore, T.N. (1982). Leadership and boundary management. *Journal of Applied Behavioral Science, 18, 3*, 343–356.

Gordon, G.E., & Rosen, N. (1981). Critical factors in leadership succession. *Organizational Behavior and Human Performance, 27*, 227–254.

Graen, G., Alvares, K., Orris, J.B., & Martella, J.A. (1970). Contingency model of leadership effectiveness: Antecedent and evidential results. *Psychological Bulletin, 74*, 286–296.

Graen, G., & Cashman, J.F. (1975). A role making model of leadership in formal organizations: A developmental approach. In J.G. Hunt & L.L. Larson (Eds.), *Leadership frontiers*. Kent, OH: Kent State University Press.

Graen, G., Dansereau, F., & Minami, T. (1972). Dysfunctional leadership styles. *Organizational Behavior and Human Performance*, 7, 216–236.

Graen, G., & Novak, M.A. (1982). The effects of leader–member exchange and job design on productivity and satisfaction: Testing a dual attachment model. *Organizational Behavior and Human Performance*, 30, 109–131.

Green, S.G., Fairhurst, G.T., & Snavely, B.K. (1986). Chains of poor performance and supervisory control. *Organizational Behavior and Human Decision Processes*, 38, 7–27.

Green, S.G., & Mitchell, T.R. (1979). Attributional processes of leaders in leader member interactions. *Organizational Behavior and Human Performance*, 23, 429–458.

Hall, R.M. (1972). *Organizations: Structure and process*. Englewood Cliffs, NJ: Prentice-Hall.

Hammer, T.H., & Dachler, H.P. (1975). A test of some assumptions underlying the path goal model of supervision: Some suggested conceptual modifications. *Organizational Behavior and Human Performance*, 14, 69–75.

Hater, J.J., & Bass, B.A. (1988). Superior's evaluations and subordinate's perception of transformational and transactional leadership. *Journal of Applied Psychology*, 73, 695–702.

Heller, F.A. (1971). Managerial decision making, *A study of leadership styles and power sharing among senior managers*. London: Tavistock.

Heller, F.A. (1976). Decision processes: An analysis of power sharing at senior organizational levels. In R. Dubin (Ed.), *Handbook of work, organizations and society*. Chicago: Rand McNally.

Heller, F.A. (1973). Leadership, decision making and contingency theory. *Industrial Relations*, 12, 183–199.

Heller, F.A., & Wilpert, B. (1981). *Competence and power in managerial decision making*. Chichester: Wiley.

Heller, F.A., Drenth, P.J.D., Koopman, P.L., & Rus, V. (1988). *Decisions in organizations: A three-country comparative study*. London: Sage.

Hemphill, J.K. (1960). *Dimensions of executive positions*. Ohio State University: Bureau of Business Research, no. 98.

Hersey, P., & Blanchard, K.H. (1982). *Management of organizational behavior: Utilising human resources*. Englewood Cliffs, NJ: Prentice-Hall.

Hollander, E.P. (1964). *Leaders, groups and influence*. New York: Oxford University Press.

Hollander, E.P. (1979). Leadership and social exchange processes. In K.J. Gergcen, M.S. Greenberg, & R.H. Willis (Eds.), *Social exchange: Advances in theory and research* (pp.103–118). New York: Winston-Wiley.

Homans, G.C. (1950). *The human group*. New York: Harcourt.

House, R.J. (1971). A path–goal theory of leader effectiveness. *Administrative Science Quarterly*, 16, 321–328.

House, R.J. (1977). A theory of charismatic leadership. In J. G. Hunt & L. L. Larson (Eds.), *Leadership: The cutting edge*. Carbondale: Southern Illinois University Press.

House, R.J., & Baetz, M.L. (1979). Leadership: Some empirical generalizations and new research directions. In B. Staw (Ed.), *Research in organizational behavior I*. Greeenwich, CT: JAI Press.

House, R.J., & Dessler, G. (1974). The path–goal theory of leadership: Some post hoc and a priori tests. In J. G. Hunt & L. L Larsson (Eds.), *Contingency approaches to leadership*. Carbondale: Southern Illinois University Press.

Hunt, J.G., & Larsson, L.L. (Eds.) (1977). *Leadership: The cutting edge*. Carbondale: Southern Illinois University Press.

Hunt, J.G., & Osborne, R.N. (1980). *Beyond contingency approach to leadership*. Birmingham: Management Center, University of Aston.

IDE, International Research Group (1981). *Industrial democracy in Europe*. Oxford: Oxford University Press.

Jacobs (1970). *Leadership and exchange in formal organizations*. Alexandria: Human Resources Research Organization.

Jago, A.G., & Vroom, V.H. (1975). Perceptions of leadership style: Superior and subordinate descriptions of decision-making behavior. In J.G. Hunt & L.L. Larson (Eds.), *Leadership frontiers*. Kent, OH: Kent State University Press.

Jago, A.G., & Ragan, J.W. (1986a). The trouble with leader match is that it doesn't match Fiedler's contingencies model. *Journal of Applied Psychology*, 71, 555–559.

Jago, A.G., & Ragan, J.W. (1986b). Some assumptions are more troubling than others: Rejoinder to Cheiners and Fiedler. *Journal of Applied Psychology*, 71, 564–565.

James, L.R., & Jones, A.P. (1976). Organizational structure: A review of structural dimensions and their relationships with individual attitudes and behavior. *Organizational Behavior and Human Performance*, 16, 74–113.

Johnson, A.L., Luthans, F., & Hennessy, H.W. (1984). The role of locus of control in leader influence behavior. *Personnel Psychology*, 37.

Katz, R. (1977). The influence of group conflict in leadership effectiveness. *Organizational behavior and Human Performance*, 20, 265–286.

Katz, D., & Kahn, R.L. (1978). *The social psychology of organizations* (2nd Edn.). New York: Wiley.

Kenny, D.A., & Zaccaro, S.J. (1983). An estimate of variance due to traits in leadership. *Journal of Applied Psychology*, 68, 678–685.

Kerr, S. (1974). Substitutes for leadership. In J.G. Hunt & L.L. Larsson (Eds.), *Contingency approaches to leadership*. Carbondale: Southern Illinois University Press.

Kerr, S., & Jermier, J.M. (1978). Substitutes for leadership: Their meaning and measurement. *Organizational Behavior and Human Performance, 22*, 375–403.

Kerr, S., & Schriesheim, C.A. (1974). Consideration, initiating structure and organizational criteria: An update of Korman's 1966 review. *Personnel Psychology, 27*, 555–568.

Kerr, S., Schriesheim, C.A., Murphy, C.J., & Stogdill, R.M. (1974). Towards a contingency theory of leadership based upon the consideration and initiating structure literature. *Organizational Behavior and Human Performance, 12*, 62–82.

Koopman, P.L. (1980). *Besluitvorming in organisaties*. Assen: Van Gorcum.

Koopman, P.L., & Drenth, P.J.D. (1980a). Komplexe besluitvorming in organisaties. *Gedrag, 8*, 361–379.

Koopman, P.L., & Drenth, P.J.D. (1980b). Een contingentie-model voor participatie in complexe besluitvorming. *Mens en Onderneming, 6*, 464–478.

Koopman, P.L., & Werkman, B. (1973). Het verhoudingsmodel bij meting van satisfactie. In P.J.D. Drenth, P.J. Willems, & C.J. de Wolff, *Arbeids-en Organisatiepsychologie*. Deventer: Kluwer.

Korman, A.K. (1966). "Consideration", "initiating structure" and organizational criteria: A review. *Personnel Psychology, 25*, 349–361.

Lammers, C.J. (1975). Self-management and participation: Two concepts of democratization in organizations. *Organization and Administrative Sciences, 5*, 17–33.

Lammers, C.J. (1980). *Ontwikkeling en relevantie van de organisatiesociologie*. Leiden: Universiteit van Leiden.

Larson Jr., J.R. (1982). Cognitive mechanisms mediating the impact of implicit theories of leader behavior on leader behavior ratings. *Organizational Behavior Performance, 29*, 129–140.

Lawler, E.E. (1985). Education, management style, and organizational effectiveness, *Personnel Psychology, 38*.

Lawrence, P.R., & Lorsch, J.W. (1967). Differentiation and integration in complex organizations. *Administrative Science Quarterly, 12*, 1–47.

Lieberson, S., & O'Connor, J.F. (1972). Leadership and organizational performance: A study of large corporations. *American Sociological Review, 37*, 117–130.

Likert, R. (1967). *New patterns of management*. New York: McGraw-Hill.

Likert, R. (1971). *The human organization*. New York: McGraw-Hill.

Locke, E.A. (1978). The ubiquity of technique of goal setting in theories and approaches to employee motivation. *Academy of Management Review, 3*, 594–601.

Locke, E.A., & Schweiger, D.M. (1979). Participation in decision making: One more look: In B. Staw (Ed.), *Research in organizational Behavior I*. Greenwich, CT: JAI Press.

Lord, R.G., Vader, C.L. de, & Alliger, G.M. (1986). A meta-analysis of the relation between personality traits and leadership perception of validity generalization procedures. *Journal of Applied Psychology, 71*, 402–410.

Lowin, A., & Craig, J. (1968). The influence of level of performance on managerial style. *Organizational Behavior and Human Performance, 3*, 440–458.

Lowin, A., Hrapchak, W.J., & Kavanagh, M.J. (1969). Consideration and initiating structure: An experimental investigation of leadership traits. *Administrative Science Quarterly, 14*, 238–253.

Mann, R.D. (1959). A review of the relationship between personality and performance in small groups. *Psychological Bulletin, 56*, 241–270.

Maslow, A. (1954). *Motivation and personality*. New York: Harper & Row.

McCall, M.W., & Lombard, M.M. (1978). *Leadership: Where else can we go*. Durham, NC: Duke University Press.

McClelland, D. (1975). *Power: The inner experience*. New York: Irvington.

McClelland, D., & Boyatzis, R.E. (1982). Leadership motive pattern and longterm success in management. *Journal of Applied Psychology, 67*, 737–743.

McGregor, D. (1960). *The human side of enterprise*. New York: McGraw-Hill.

Miles, R.E. (1974). Leadership: Human relations or human resources. In D.A. Kolb, I.M. Rubin, & J.M. McIntyre (Eds.), *Organizational Psychology*. Englewood Cliffs, NJ: Prentice-Hall.

Miner, J.B. (1975). The uncertain future of the leadership concept: An overview. In J.G. Hunt, & L.L. Larsson (Eds.), *Leadership frontiers*. Kent, OH: Kent State University Press.

Miner, J.B. (1982). The uncertain future of the leadership concept: Revisions and clarifications. *Journal of Applied Behavioral Science, 18, 3*, 293–307.

Mintzberg, H. (1973). *The nature of managerial work*. New York: Harper & Row.

Mintzberg, H. (1979). *The structuring of organizations*. Englewood Cliffs, NJ: Prentice-Hall.

Mintzberg (1983a). *Power in and around organizations*. Englewood Cliffs, NJ: Prentice-Hall.

Mintzberg (1983b). *Structure in fives: Designing effective organizations*. Englewood Cliffs, NJ: Prentice-Hall.

Misumi, J. (1985). *The behavioral science of leadership* (Ed. M.F. Peterson). Ann Arbor: University of Michigan Press.

Misumi, J., & Peterson, M.F. (1985). The performance–maintenance (PM) theory of leadership: Review of a Japanese research program. *Administrative Science Quarterly, 30*, 198–233.

Misumi, J., & M.F. Peterson (1987). Developing a

performance–maintenance (PM) theory of leadership. *Bulletin of the Faculty of Human Sciences*, Osaka University, *13*, 135–170.

Mitchell, T.R., & Wood, R.E. (1980). Supervisors responses to subordinate poor performance: A test of an attributional model. *Organizational Behavioral and Human Performance*, *25*, 123–138.

Morgan, G. (1986). *Images of orgnization*. Beverly Hills, CA: Sage.

Mulder, M. (1977). *Omgaan met macht*. Amsterdam: Elsevier.

Mulder, M., Jong, R.D. de, Koppelaar, L., & Verhage, J. (1986). Power, situation and leader's effectiveness: An organizational field study. *Journal of Applied Psychology*, *71*, 566–570.

Mulder, M., Ritsema van Eck, J.R. & Gils, M.R. van (1967). *Structuur en dynamiek van een grote organisatie; een veldstudie op zee*. Leiden: NIPG.

Neuberger, O. (1984). *Führung*. Stuttgart: Enke.

Neuberger, O. (1985). *Unternehmenskultur und Führung*. Augsburg: Universität Augsburg.

Pelz, D. (1951). Leadership within a hierarchical organization. *Journal of Social Issues*, *7*, 49–55.

Pelz, D. (1952). Influence: A key to effective leadership in the first line supervisor. *Personnel*, *29*, 209–217.

Pfeffer, J. (1978). The ambiguity of leadership. In M.W. McCall & M.M. Lombardo, *Leadership: Where else can we go*. Durham, NC: Duke University Press.

Philipsen, H. (1965). Het meten van leiderschap. *Mens en Onderneming*, *3*, 153–171.

Podsakoff, P.M. (1982). Determinants of a supervisor's use of rewards and punishments: A literature review and suggestions for further research. *Organizational Behavior and Human Performance*, *29*, 58–83.

Prahalad, C.K., & Doz, Y.L. (1984). Managing managers: The work of top management. In J.G. Hunt, D.M. Hosking, C.A. Schriesheim, & R. Stewart, *Leaders and managers: International perspectives on managerial behavior and leadership* (pp.366–374). New York: Pergamon Press.

Raven, B.H., & French, J.R.P. (1958). Group support, legitimate power, and social influence. *Journal of Personality*, *26*, 400–409.

Reddin, W.J. (1970). *Managerial effectiveness*. New York: McGraw-Hill.

Reddin, W.M. (1971). *Effective management by objectives: The 3-D method of MBO*. New York: McGraw-Hill.

Schriesheim, C.A., House, R.J., & Kerr, S. (1976). Leader initiating structure: A reconciliation of discrepant research results and some empirical tests. *Organization Behavior and Human Performance*, *15*, 297–321.

Schriesheim, C.A., & Kerr, S. (1974). Psychometric properties of the Ohio State Leadership scales. *Psychological Bulletin*, *81*, 756–765.

Schriesheim, C.A., & Kerr, S. (1977). Theories and measures of leadership: A critical appraisal of current and future directions. In J.G. Hunt & L.L. Larsson (Eds.), *Leadership, the cutting edge*. Carbondale: Southern Illinois University Press.

Schriesheim, C.A., & Murphy, C.J. (1976). Relationships between leader behavior and subordinates satisfaction and performance: A test of some situational moderators. *Journal of Applied Psychology*, *61*, 634–641.

Schriesheim, C.A., & Stogdill, R.M. (1975). Differences in factor structure across three versions of the Ohio State Leadership scales. *Personnel Psychology*, *28*, 189–206.

Scott, W.E. (1977). Leadership: A functional analysis. In J.G. Hunt & L.L. Larson (Eds.), *Leadership: The cutting edge*. Carbondale: Southern Illinois University Press.

Shull, F.A., Delbecq, & Cummings, L.L. (1970). *Organizational decision making*. New York: McGraw-Hill.

Sims, H.P. (1977). The leader as manager of reinforcement contingencies: An emperical example and a model. In J.G. Hunt & L.L. Larson (Eds.), *Leadership: The cutting edge*. Carbondale: Southern Illinois University Press.

Smircich, L., & Morgan, G. (1982). Leadership: The management of meaning. *Journal of Applied Behavioral Science*, *18*, *3*, 257–273.

Smith, P.B., Misumi, J., Taylor, M., Peterson, M., & Bond, M. (1989). On the generality of leadership style measures across cultures. *Journal of Occupational Psychology*, *62*, 97–109.

Smith, P.B., & Peterson, M. (1988). *Leadership, Organizations and Culture*. London: Sage.

Stahl, M.J., (1983). Achievement, power and managerial motivation: Selecting managerial talent with job choise exercise. *Personnel Psychology*, *36*, 775–789.

Stewart, R. (1970). *Managers and their jobs*. London: Pan.

Stinson, J.E. (1977). The measurement of leadership. In J.G. Hunt & L.L. Larsson (Eds.), *Leadership: The cutting edge*. Carbondale: Southern Illinois University Press.

Stogdill, R.M. (1948). Personal factors associated with leadership: A survey of the literature. *Journal of Psychology*, *25*, 35–71.

Stogdill, R.M. (1974). *Handbook of leadership: A survey of theory and research*. New York: Free University Press.

Stogdill, R.M., & Coons, A.E. (Eds.) (1957). *Leader behavior: Its description and measurement*. Columbus: Ohio State University, Bureau of Business Research.

Taylor, J.C., & Bowers, D.G. (1972). *Survey of organizations: Toward a machine scored standardized questionnaire instrument*. Ann Arbor, MI: Institute of Social Research.

Thierry, H., Jong, J. de (1979). *Naar participatie en toerekening*. Assen: Van Gorcum.

Thomas, A.B. (1988). Does leadership make a difference to organizational performance. *Administrative Science Quarterly*, 388–400.

Thomson, J.D., & Tuden, A. (1959). Strategies, structures and processes of organizational decisions. In J.D. Thompson, P.B. Hammmond, R.W. Hawkes, B.H. Jonker, & A. Tuden (Eds.), *Comparative studies in administration*. Pittsburgh, PA: Pittsburgh University Press.

Vecchio, R.P., & Gobdel, B.C. (1984). The vertical dyad linkage model of leadership: Problems and prospects. *Organizational Behavior and Human Performance*, *34*, 5–20.

Vollebergh, J.J.A. (1973). Leiderschap en organisatie. In P.J.D. Drenth, P.J. Willems, & C.J. de Wolff (Eds.), *Arbeids-en Organisatiepsychology*. Deventer: Kluwer.

Vroom, V.H. (1964). *Work and motivation*. New York: Wiley.

Vroom, V.H. (1967). Leadership. In M.D. Dunnette (Ed.), *Handbook of industrial and organizational psychology*. Chicago: Rand McNally.

Vroom, V.H. (1988). *The new leadership: managerial participation in organizations*. Englewood Cliffs, NJ: Prentice-Hall.

Vroom, V.H., & Yetton, Ph.W. (1973). *Leadership and decision making*. Pittsburgh, PA: University of Pittsburgh Press.

Wilpert, B. (1977). *Führung in deutschen Unternehmen*. Berlin: De Gruyter.

Wall, T.D., & Lischeron, J.A. (1977). *Worker participation*. London: McGraw-Hill.

Wofford, J.C., & Srinivasan T.N. (1983). Experimental tests of leader–environment–follower interaction theory of leadership. *Organizational behavior and human performance*, *32*, 35–54.

Yukl, G. (1981). *Leadership in organizations*. Englewood Cliffs, NJ: Prentice-Hall.

Zahn, G.L., & Wolf, G. (1981). Leadership and the art of cycle maintenance: A simulation model of superior–subordinate interaction. *Organizational Behavior and Human Performance*, *28*, 26–29.

Zanders, H.J.G., Büchem, A.L.J. van, & Berkel, J.J.C. van (1978). *Kwaliteit van arbeid 1977*. Den Haag: Ministerie van Sociale Zaken.

14

Complex Decision-making in Organizations

Paul L. Koopman, Jan Willem Broekhuijsen, and André F. M. Wierdsma

---

1 INTRODUCTION

Complex decisions in organizations usually involve broad lines of strategy. What products or services ought to be developed? In what markets should the company operate? Will the aim be to achieve the lowest costs in the branch, or to provide the best quality and optimal service? What degree of diversification is best? Some authors speak of strategic decisions, being top management decisions, involving considerable company resources, committing the firm with implications for its profitability far into the future, requiring coordination of many businesses or many functional areas of the firm, and requiring the involvement of factors external to the firm (Pearce & Robinson, 1988; Taylor, 1992). Such issues imply other decisions on the most appropriate organizational structure, technology, management style, and organizational culture, sometimes called tactical decisions (Koopman, Drenth, Heller, & Rus, 1993).

Because the quality and the acceptance of such decisions is vital to a company's functioning—indeed, often to the mere survival of an organization—complex decision-making has traditionally been a focus of attention in the management literature (Ansoff, 1965; Andrews, 1980; Porter, 1980; Hill & Jones, 1989; Arnold, 1992). Alongside these sources, with their often normative and typically rational approach to decision-making, are more recent studies, which tend to take a more descriptive, empiristic viewpoint (Hickson, Butler, Cray, Mallory, & Wilson, 1986; Pettigrew, 1986; Donaldson & Lorsch, 1983; Quinn, Mintzberg, & James, 1988; Heller, Drenth, Koopman, & Rus, 1988; Beach, 1990; March, 1994). These studies clearly show that complex decisions generally take an entirely different course from the one recommended by the classical literature.

The development in literature has made rationality a central issue. Some of the questions raised are: To what extent does thinking precede action? (Lawrence, 1985; Starbuck, 1985). What is the relationship between facts and intuition? What is the role of information? When are rational planning systems wise? How are political contrasts reconciled?

In this chapter we want to start by investigating what *perspectives* on decision-making the literature has to offer. Four models will be discussed, which make widely divergent assumptions about the *behaviour* of the actors. Thus they primarily focus on behavioural rationality. Sometimes actors try to maximize their yield; sometimes they are satisfied with "acceptable" solutions (Gladstein & Quinn, 1985). In certain situations, actors have solutions (e.g. budgets) at hand and are on the look-out for problems (March, 1988); in other situations they primarily seem to be after power.

After examining decision-making from the point of view of the actors, we want to consider the time perspective. Complex decisions often run a lengthy course, in which several phases can be distinguished. The literature offers a variety of phase models. They deal with the *process* rationality, or the order in which certain aspects are completed during the decision-making process (e.g. diagnosis, search, choice, implementation). They also pay attention to how logical aspects and political aspects are interwoven in a single project. The number of interruptions, such as delays and feedback cycles to earlier phases, are another important factor.

Next, the *context* in which decision-making takes place is discussed. The context largely determines the degrees of freedom management has in organizing and steering the decision-making process. Determining factors, in addition to the topic itself, are the nature of the organization and of the environment. What limitations do existing rules impose? If the environment becomes more threatening, what implications does it have for decision-making? Under what circumstances is "no-nonsense management" possible?

After this analysis at the organizational level we turn to the *individual manager* and his role as decision-maker. Here we go into questions such as: What characterises the work of a manager? What makes a topic become a problem? What factors give a problem so much priority that it is tackled? When is it important, when is it possible to decide quickly; when is it better or necessary to

take more time? What repercussions do decisions have for a manager's "track record" and thus for his career chances? How can the manager limit his risks and strengthen his image as a successful manager? There are widely divergent opinions on the meaning of complex processes. The same may be said of the role played by individuals in such processes. Active "management of meaning" therefore often brings up the rear in a decision-making process.

In conclusion, the more concrete tools of management are discussed. What instruments are available for complex decision-making? What experience has been acquired with them? What instruments are useful under what circumstances? What limitations must be reckoned with?

2 VIEWS OF DECISION-MAKING

2.1 The classical or rational model

The classical or rational model is normative in nature; it prescribes the ideal way of acting in decision-making situations. It offers a basis for quantitative disciplines such as econometrics and statistics. It assumes that the decision-maker strives for a decision with a maximum yield. It also makes the rather simplistic assumption that the decision-maker is aware of all alternatives and their possible consequences, at least the short-term ones (see Figure 14.1).

The model's usefulness is thus largely limited to situations with the following characteristics (Harrison, 1995):

1. There is only one decision-maker.
2. The decision-maker has only one goal.
3. The goal can be described in quantitative terms.
4. There is a limited number of solutions and they are known to the decision-maker.
5. The best alternative can be "calculated".

Other variants of the rational model allow for several decision-makers and more than one goal. But the basic assumptions are always known goals, unlimited availability of information, the lack of cognitive limitations as well as limitations in time and costs, quantifiable alternatives. Decision-making is regarded as a logical process in which decision-makers try to maximize their objectives in an orderly series of steps. In doing so, they continually assess what actions or alternatives, with what chances of success, will contribute to which fairly short-term goals. The rational model is prescriptive in that it sets down steps for decision-makers in a logical order, and recommends that opportunities and results are quantified whenever possible (Yates, 1990; Goodwin & Wright, 1991).

Several models were developed as alternatives to the normative rational model (MacCrimmon, 1985; Shrivastava & Grant, 1985; Koopman & Pool, 1990; Taylor, 1992). They are based more on the actual behaviour of decision-makers in organizations. Research has shown that, in actual practice, decision-makers behave entirely differently than recommended by the rational model. In addition, the assumptions made by the rational model with respect to the situation have seldom turned out to be realistic. Or, in the words of Taylor (1992, p.971): "If behaviors that appear to deviate from calculated rationality are seen to be intelligent, then models of calculated rationality may be considered deficient, both as descriptions of how decisions are made and as prescriptions about how decisions should be made."

On the other hand, rational-analytic models make valuable contributions to strategic decision-making by providing relatively precise and quanti-tative input through forecasting models and decision-analysis solutions to more limited subproblems (Lawrence, 1985; Winter, 1985; Taylor, 1992). Further advances in decision analysis are foreseen for the near future, for instance, greater use of expert systems to describe decision-making and computerized intelligent decision systems to provide normative aids for improving decision-making on an even broader scale (Howard, 1988; see also section 6.2).

We will now review several alternative models.

2.2   The behavioural or organizational model

An initial adaptation of the rational model to the practice of decision-making concerns the *information-processing capacity of decision-makers*. Simon (1947, 1957) and March and Simon (1958) focused attention on several frequent restrictions with which decision-makers are faced. For instance, because of their limited cognitive capacities, decision-makers use only part of the relevant information. Time and money considerations also play a role in determining whether there will be a search for more information and how long it will last. The search process generally stops when a "satisficing solution" has been found: Alternatives are not studied exhaustively.

Other researchers, mostly involved in laboratory research on decision-making behaviour,

FIGURE 14.1

Model	Primary criterion	Key ingredients
Rational (classical)	Maximized outcome	Clear objective; quantified utilities; exhaustive alternatives; computational decision-making strategy
Organizational (behavioural)	Satisficing outcome	Limited subjective probabilities; non-exhaustive alternatives; moderately structured process
Garbage can	Unspecified chance	Unclear or inconsistent goals; a technology that is obscure and little understood by members; a highly variable member participation
Political (arena)	Acceptable outcome	Multiple objectives; coalition formulation; compromise or bargaining decision-making strategy

Four decision-making models (adapted from Harrison, 1987, p.78).

have pointed out more specific limitations of human decision-making (Tversky and Kahneman, 1974; Kahneman & Tversky, 1984). Oversimplification processes primarily occur in more complex, ambiguous decision-making situations (Rowe & Boulgarides, 1992). Hogarth (1987) described two major conclusions from the research on intuitive thinking. First, a great many studies have confirmed that even simple laboratory tasks require more information-processing capacity than humans have. Second, cognitive research has revealed that people misperceive information content, process information sequentially to accommodate their poor integrative capacity, and have very limited memory. Schwenk (1988) investigated several of these mechanisms, most of which are seen in strategic decision-making. Basically, decision-makers become fixated on one solution at an early stage and give insufficient consideration to alternatives. The catastrophic results this can have is well explained by Janis (1982, 1992). His "group-think" concept, or the phenomenon that a great many highly unrealistic assessments of reality can exist in a small group of relatively isolated decision-makers, serves as an explanation of catastrophes such as the Watergate affair and the Bay of Pigs crisis.

If we look, with Simon (1957), at information-seeking in decision-making situations, we see the following picture. The search for solutions mostly starts close to home. First solutions are explored with which the organization successfully tackled its problems in the past. By following existing procedures and current policy, people try to avoid uncertainty. Only when old recipes and rules of thumb fail to work do they start to look for new possibilities.

Other characteristics of Simon's model are that the goals are fairly broad, that there are limited and subjective chance estimates, that not all alternatives are known and that the process is often poorly structured and short-sighted. The "administrative man" makes do with the alternative that offers him just enough satisfaction with respect to his aspirational level, while avoiding as far as possible unnecessary investments in time.

The limitations inherent in individual decision-making as described can be minimized by creating the proper sort of organization. Limited personal information-processing and analysis of the environment are compensated by establishing various organizational units and a division of labour (March & Simon, 1958).

But there are also a number of *limitations within the organization*. For instance, organizational goals are seldom entirely clear. There are often several changing goals that must be achieved to a certain level of acceptance. Decision-makers often have insufficient control of relevant situational factors here. This makes feasibility an important criterion.

The result is that decision-making often takes place step by step. This is called "incrementalism" and "muddling through" (Lindblom, 1959, 1980; Mintzberg, 1994). Rational-analytic and incremental strategic decisions differ in the following ways: How decision-making is initiated, how goals are used, how means are linked to ends, how choices are made, how comprehensive or analytically complete the decision-making is, how comprehensively decisions are integrated into strategy (Fredrickson & Mitchell, 1984). Gradually, decision-makers develop a definition of the situation that is workable for them. It is a simplified model of reality, embracing both goals and solutions. Often the goals are not clear from the start, but are defined or elaborated along the way.

A good example of this is how a government office works. The precise goals of the minister for whom they must prepare policy are often not explicitly known. Civil servants at various levels use a great many different tacks to anticipate possibly desired policy. Often they must rely on isolated remarks by the minister or replies to questions from the Dutch House of Parliament. From such signals they try to infer what proposals might be acceptable to the higher echelon. In this way, policy gradually takes shape by means of interaction between the top and the staff. Van der Krogt and Vroom (1991) therefore called it the dialogue model.

Lindblom's attempt to adjust the rational (or as he called it, the "root" or "synoptic") model so that it more clearly described what actually took place in organizational practice has evoked many reactions. An often-mentioned point of criticism was the inherent conservatism that appeared from it

(Etzioni, 1967). The step-by-step manner of working makes the introduction of fundamental changes a laborious process. Quinn (1980), however, showed that a step-by-step manner is the only "logical" possibility in complex and ambiguous situations from the point of view of attainability.

Another point that requires attention when decision-making is seen as an organizational activity is that an organization is not a unity. Organizations are composed of departments, divisions or other units, and are not "unitary" structures (Allison, 1971). The task division in organizations leads to a limited view of problems and solutions. Production workers readily see problems as caused by inefficient production methods, sales people by improper marketing techniques, and so on. At the same time, they try to seek the solution in the area of production or sales and thus to safeguard the involvement and influence of the department.

Cyert and March (1963) also discussed decision-making in the light of the organizational context, and presented four characteristics. The first is that conflicts that arise from the diversity of interests and preferences of the coalition partners are usually not really resolved. Conflicts are brought back to acceptable proportions by means of a variety of procedures ("quasi-resolution of conflict"). To ensure a certain coherence among the various subsolutions, the organization strives for satisficing rather than maximal results, and devotes its attention to the successive achievement of contrasting goals, where time acts as a buffer (Cyert & March, 1963). A second characteristic of organizational decision-making is the avoidance of uncertainty, for example, by bringing the environment under control as much as possible through agreements and contracts (Pfeffer & Salancik, 1978; Thompson, 1967). Third, organizations only seek solutions to specific problems. Once a problem is solved, the search stops. The search process takes place according to three rules: First look in the neighbourhood of the problem, then in the neighbourhood of known alternatives, and try to pass off as many problems as possible to weak sectors of the organization. The fourth and final characteristic is that organizations learn from their experiences. This implies

that search procedures (the rules according to which attention is divided) and the goals of the organization adapt themselves in the course of time to the changed circumstances.

2.3 The garbage-can model

In the "garbage-can model" organizations are seen as "organised anarchies" characterized by unclear or inconsistent goals, a technology that is obscure and little understood by members, and a highly variable member participation. Cohen, March, and Olsen (1972) based their description of this model primarily on experiences with decision-making processes at universities. The university is considered the prototype of the garbage-can model. According to these authors, organizations can be viewed as collections of (1) problems, (2) solutions, (3) participants, and (4) choice opportunities (these are situations in which participants are expected to link a problem to a solution, and thus make a decision).

These four elements are more or less randomly mixed together in the "garbage can". Combinations arise almost unpredictably. There is no a priori chronology. Solutions can precede problems, or problems and solutions can wait for a suitable opportunity for a decision. Clearly, the traditionally assumed order "identification and definition of the problem, search for solutions, consideration of alternatives and selection" is reversed. "Although it may be convenient to imagine that choice opportunities lead first to the generation of decision alternatives, then to an examination of their consequences, then to an evaluation of those consequences in terms of objectives, and finally to a decision, this type of model is often a poor description of what actually happens" (Cohen et al., 1972, p.2).

Concepts such as "garbage-can model" and "anarchy" can be misleading. The authors certainly do not imply that no systematic decision-making can be discovered in such organizations. On the contrary, the central message of these authors is that the seeming anarchy has a structure and an organization, which form a reasonable, although not optimal, answer to the great environmental uncertainty in which the participants find themselves.

In order for decision-making to progress, it is

essential that the organization manages to attract sufficient attention from the participants to solve the problems in question. However, participants generally have more on their minds. Thus it is not unusual that decision-making takes place without explicit attention to the problem, or even by simply postponing the problem. The authors, however, see it as the task of management to coordinate and steer the required attention in a direction desired by the organization (March, 1988).

2.4 The political or arena model

Where the garbage-can model emphasizes the variable participation of the members and the lack of clarity of the system, the arena model assumes that the various players have divergent and some-times contrasting goals. Conflict and the way in which it is handled are thus the focal points of the arena model. The organization is seen as a band of changing coalitions, and decision-making is pri-marily a political process in which negotiations play a central role (Bacharach & Lawler, 1986; Pettigrew, 1973). The primary criterion is not the "right" decision, but a decision acceptable to all (George, 1980; Koopman & Pool, 1990; Hosking & Morley, 1991; Koopman, 1992).

The division of tasks among organization mem-bers mentioned under the organization model has one inevitable side effect: Differences in the division of power. In their "strategic contingency theory of intra-organizational power", Hickson, Hinings, Lee, Schneck, and Pennings (1971) described how the division of power in organiza-tions lies in the control of critical dependencies. The power of departments is dependent on the extent to which they can reduce environmental uncertainty for the organization, the extent to which they can be replaced, and the extent to which the activities are central (that is, how large a part of the organization will come to a standstill if a department discontinues its work). The strategic contingency theory is an extension of the earlier work of Emerson (1962).

Pfeffer and Salancik (1978) also elaborated on this. Owing to differentiation processes in society and the organization and to the different segments of the environment with which the various parties must deal, differences of opinion arise on goals

and on technology. Differentiation within the organization also leads to increasing interdepen-dence among the various organizational members, which may result in differences of opinion on all manner of scarce resources such as budgets, staffing, etc. Pfeffer (1981) stated that conflict does not automatically lead to attempts to gain control. Because the investments and risks involved in the exertion of power are by no means small, the problem must be sufficiently important: Chances of success must be good. This is not the case, for example, when power is strongly concen-trated with one party.

Another view of power is that there are demon-strable power sources. In their classical article, French and Raven (1959) distinguished five sources of power: reward, force, legitimacy (accepted or legitimate power differences, as in stratified organizations), reference (the power that comes from identification with popular persons, charisma), and expertise. Another important power source is control of the available infor-mation (Pettigrew, 1973; O'Reilly, 1983). The person who determines how, on the basis of what information or which alternatives, a decision will be made often has more influence on the final result than those who actually decide.

In order to play the game successfully, a person must not only have access to sufficient power sources, but also the will and the capacity to use them (Mintzberg, 1983). Use of language and legitimation of the exercise of power are essential elements of the power game (Pfeffer, 1981; Clegg, 1987). A great many studies have shown that the "logical rationality" (factual argumentation) of decision-making processes is often made subordi-nate to the "political rationality" (internal power relations).

An important question that has been studied is: "What requirements must the political constel-lation—that is, the system of power relations within the organization—meet in order to be able to implement strategic changes?" A study by Pettigrew (1986) indicated that this is only poss-ible in large organizations under extreme pressure from the environment. Excellent managers gener-ally turn out to be very skilful at utilizing the (unexpected) opportunities of the context.

3 PHASING AND PROCESS RATIONALITY

What the above-mentioned models have in common is that they all make some statement about *behavioural* rationality, be it assumed or advocated, in the classical model. As we have seen, limited cognitive capacities, insufficient time and resources, lack of insight in the functioning of the organization, and conflicting interests among participants are all threats to rational behaviour.

In the models to follow, emphasis lies on the *process* rationality. Naturally, these two categories are not mutually exclusive. But the angle of approach is different. Assuming that, in strategic decisions, logical and political problems must together be brought to a solution, the central question is how this actually happens. In what order do certain activities take place? Is there a logical order, or should we speak of chaos? What actors or parties are active during which phases of the decision-making? Does information play an important role in the preparation of the decision, or primarily in the legitimation of a decision that was reached more on political grounds?

3.1 Chaos or structure?

There are several phase models of decision-making in the literature. A typical example is the model of Brim, Glass, Larvin, and Goodman (1962), in which the following steps take place: (1) identification of the problem, (2) seeking information, (3) generation of possible solutions, (4) evaluation of alternatives, (5) selection, and (6) implementation of the decision. A similar, but more elaborated phase model can be find with Janis (1989, p.91). Other authors use a somewhat rougher classification, because a sharp distinction between steps 2 and 3 and between 4 and 5 is seldom found in practice (see e.g. Witte, 1972). Based on a study of 25 strategic decisions, Mintzberg, Raisinghani, and Théorêt (1976) observed that three central phases were always found: "identification", "development", and "selection" (see Figure 14.2).

Several supporting processes run parallel to these three central decision-making phases: decision-making control processes, communication processes, and political processes. In addition, the picture is further complicated by the effect of several "dynamic factors". Interruptions, delays, and feedback loops are important in complex decision-making processes. Strategic management is not a matter of steady progress from one activity to the next, but a dynamic process with acceleration and delays, "comprehension cycles", in which those involved gradually get more of a grasp on a complicated question, and "failure cycles", in which they must return to previous phases, when, for example, no acceptable solution can be found because of conflicts. Also, many processes are prematurely stopped or blocked because of political or technical reasons. Mintzberg et al. thus arrived at the following typology of decision-making processes:

1. Simple impasse: As a result of contrasting interests, decision-making is blocked in the diagnosis phase.
2. Political design: The decision-making meets impasses and interruptions in the design phase.

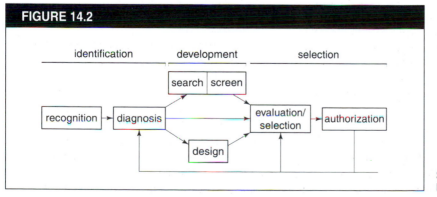

FIGURE 14.2

Simplified phase model of Mintzberg et al. (1976).

3. Basic search: Decision-making emphasizes a search for existing solutions, and involves uncontested technical decisions.
4. Modified search: A technical modification of an existing solution is taking place.
5. Basic design: Demands much creativity, few interruptions, and little political activity.
6. Blocked design: Like "basic design", but with additional resistance that is recognized too late.
7. Dynamic design: A complicated process with many interruptions, a long duration and repeated feedback loops to earlier phases.

Nutt (1984) studied the manner in which solutions to complex problem situations were generated. In his analysis of 73 decision-making processes he distinguished 5 different phases (formulation, concept development, detailing, evaluation, and implementation) and three main activities (search, synthesizing, and analyzing). The combination of phases and activities led to a typology of five different ways in which "solutions" were found (Table 14.1). They were termed as follows:

- Historical process (41%): In this case solutions or ideas of others (e.g. other organizations) are imitated, even if there is no immediate problem. The problem follows the solution. A subcategory is the "pet idea", hobby-horses of decision-makers, for which an occasion is sought to put them into practice.
- Off-the-shelf (30%): This approach uses the tender method. Competition arises among various solutions offered from outside, and these offers are then evaluated.
- Appraisal (7%): This is an attempt to find "objective data" to back up a chosen solution. However, Nutt's remark that this resembles the scientific method is not entirely correct.
- Search (7%): Possible solutions are sought to a newly discovered problem. There are no firm ideas about this. The search is passive and takes place through familiar contacts. If a solution is found, it is immediately adopted.
- Nova process (15%): Solutions are designed either by outsiders (advisers) or by the decision-makers themselves.

If we compare this classification with the work of other researchers, then its correspondence to the work of Mintzberg et al. (1976) is immediately apparent. Their division of the development phase into search-and-screen and design activities is clearly recognizable in Nutt's classification.

In Nutt's typology, solutions do not always follow problems, but sometimes precede them. In some cases it is not so much the solution that must be sought, but the problem. O'Reilly (1983) discussed the role of information in decision-making and also recognized these possibilities. Preferences or desired solutions are often present

TABLE 14.1

Nutt's typology (1984).

Type of process	Characteristics	Problem definition	Search for alternatives	Detailing	Evaluation	Implementation
Historical process	Imitate the ideas of others	X		X		X
Off the shelf	Evaluation criteria are based upon characteristics of the alternatives	X		X	X	X
Appraisal	Seek a rationale	X			X	X
Search	Passive, delegated	X				X
Nova process	New ideas are designed with the help of experts	X	X	X	X	X

before the search for information starts. Information is then used to support, sell, or defend these preferences. Naturally, we can no longer speak of an objective or rational choice in such a case.

3.2   The rules of the game

The organization can be seen as the context within which decision-making processes take place. This means that such processes are subject to the structural division of authority and tasks that prevails in the organization. "For decision-making, an organization is the rules of the game", as Hickson et al. (1986) stated. There are large differences in the number of decision-making procedures among different types of organizations. Governmental organizations are frequently characterized by detailed rules and delineation of authority, whereas business and industry often have fewer such rules. The delegation of authority—traditionally more or less hierarchical—is not fixed, but can itself be the subject of decision-making (Child, 1972; Bobbitt & Ford, 1980).

Most decisions take place within the network of accepted rules and agreements. This is primarily true of operational and tactical decisions, which are often made at middle and lower levels (Nutt, 1976). Sometimes, however, a decision is so new and exceptional that the existing structure is not adequate. Wilson, Butler, Cray, Hickson, and Mallory (1986) named four factors that make routine decisions impossible: unusual facts, conflicts between players, new topics, and an unusual source from which the problem arises. These factors mean that the usual rules and procedures are no longer applicable. The bounds are broken, so new negotiations must be held about the rules of the game. The more powerful players, those who control important resources or skills, are naturally in the strongest position.

Rather than use the existing organizational structure, agreements can be made about the procedure to be followed for each individual decision-making process. Mintzberg et al. (1976) called the use of such "decision controls" meta-decision-making. Under this heading come agreements about who does what when, what criteria will be applied, and what the planning will be. This is actually the determination of the structure of the decision-making process (Kickert, 1979) or—as Van der Krogt and Vroom (1991) put it—decisions about the way in which decisions will be made. The latter authors viewed these as the most important or strategic decisions, because they establish the limits of the rest of the decision-making process. In this way, the top of an organization can exert significant influence on the final result without necessarily making direct decisions. However, firm agreements about the procedure to be followed can also work out unfavourably. For instance, the formalized procedures of governmental bodies often elicit counteractions: Lower echelons learn to apply the rules to their advantage (Morgan, 1986). This decreases flexibility and increases administrative immobilization (Allison, 1971; Koopman & Algera, 1989; Koopman, 1991).

In addition to organizational structure and meta-decision-making, legislation is a third constraint. For example, the Dutch Works Council Act states that the Works Council has the right to advise management or to endorse decisions in a number of areas. The Large Companies (Structure) Act (1971) and the Civil Code also set down certain competencies and obligations for the Board of Supervisory Directors and Board of Directors (or management) (De Jongh, 1987). Finally, trade-union organizations can insist on being involved in a number of decisions (such as reorganizations, mass dismissals, mergers) on the basis of collective labour agreements or the Socio-Economic Advisory Council's merger code. International research has shown that such formal regulations largely determine the distribution of influence in decisions (Heller et al., 1988; IDE, 1993).

3.3   Information or politics dominant?

In another study of 217 complex decision-making processes in organizations in England, (former) Yugoslavia, and The Netherlands, empirical support was found for such phases as "start, development, finalization, implementation" (Heller et al., 1988; Koopman et al., 1993). But this study also showed that the steps were not always found neatly ordered in this fashion. Many processes were divided into a number of subdecisions in which the main activities of search, evaluation, and selection occurred. The nature of these decision-making processes was therefore more circular than sequential. Nevertheless, profiles could be sketched for the various groups in the organization (top management, lower and middle management, workers, professional staff, and works council) on the basis of their participation in the various decision-making phases. The following profiles were found to be typical (see Table 14.2):

1. Dominance without responsibility: A certain group sets a decision-making process in motion, but does not play an active role in the further process. This profile was typical of the management of a (former) Yugoslavian paper mill.
2. Dominance with responsibility: In this situation a group has a high involvement score in the first and the third phases, but a low score in the second and fourth phases. This pattern was applicable to the management of a municipal transport company in the Netherlands and to the workers in a (former) Yugoslavian metal-working plant.
3. Overcommitment: One group is dominant during all phases of the decision-making process. This was found for the management of a Dutch steelworks, the local management and the concern staff of a regional office of the Netherlands Railways,

and the professional staff of a paper mill in (former) Yugoslavia.

4. Controlled participation: A group is very active in both the development and the implementation phases. Their efforts, however, are "controlled" by other groups whose activity is concentrated in the start-up and finalization phases. Controlled participation was primarily found for the middle management of two English companies and the workers of a municipal transport company in the Netherlands.
5. Dependent participation: A group only becomes involved at the time of implementation. This was most strongly the case for workers in a Dutch steelworks.
6. No participation: A group shows little or no involvement in any of the four phases. This was primarily found for the workers in an English paint factory.

Based on these four phases (start, development, finalization, implementation), the question of how to interpret the various phases remains. For this we want to compare two points of view. The first is that of Sfez (1978). This author approaches decision-making as an integration process of knowledge and power. According to Sfez, the first and the third phases are primarily characterized by power processes. During the second and fourth

---

TABLE 14.2

Typology of participation profiles (Heller et al., 1988).

Type of participation profile	Participation per phase			
	Start-up	Development	Finalization	Implementation
1. Dominance without responsibility	H	L	L	L
2. Dominance with responsibility	H	L	H	L
3. Overcommitment	H	H	H	H
4. Controlled participation	L	H	L	H
5. Dependent participation	L	L	L	H
6. No participation	L	L	L	L

H = High, L = Low

phases knowledge aspects are central. The second point of view is that of Enderud (1980). He assumes, as does Sfez, that the power game makes up an essential part of strategic decisions. But they differ in opinion about the question of in which stage the power struggle is concentrated. According to Enderud, this happens as early as the second phase, generally inside a small group that operates behind closed doors. The primary function of the third phase is the official legitimation of decisions. This implies approval by the authorized bodies and the creation of some acceptance among those directly involved (see Table 14.3).

It is no simple matter to say which view is more correct. The applicability of the two approaches might well depend on certain circumstances, particularly the degree to which the decision-making process is formalized, and the problem towards which the decision-making is directed. In the democratized decision-making structure at Dutch universities during the 1970s, departmental and university councils, in which all groups of personnel and students were represented, had fairly effective control of all important decisions. This control came about primarily through participation in the first and the third phases: Problem identification and the choice of the ultimate solution. However, after the universities had moved from a period of growth into one of cut-backs, the importance of the second phase was found to have increased: More and more solutions were fairly definitively prepared in an informal and/or confidential circuit in which a small group of professional managers and a few experts played important roles. Research of the course of retrenchment processes in business and industry points in the same direction: In crisis situations, management assumes power. The official discussion of the plans with the works council serves as legitimation, but seldom leads to adaptation of the contents (Koopman, 1992). In this sort of situation the model of Enderud would seem to be more realistic than that of Sfez. In another study Fahey and Naroyanan (1983) found that political activities tend to emerge at every stage of stategic decision-making, from problem-finding to implementation and control.

The previously mentioned study of complex decisions in seven English, (former) Yugoslavian, and Dutch companies (Heller et al., 1988) found widely divergent participation profiles. For instance, in the Dutch and the English companies the lowest amount of participation (summed over the various groups within the organization) was found in the first and the third phases, the highest in the second and the fourth. In the terms of Sfez: The participation level was lower in the power phases than in the knowledge phases. In (former) Yugoslavia the reverse was the case: There, the greatest amount of participation was found in the first and the third phases. This suggests that when decision-making is more formalized and public (universities in the 1970s, (former) Yugoslavia), it should more largely follow the classical phase model, because the legitimation of the process is then more strongly guaranteed. Theoretically, the works council thus has a grasp of the diagnosis of the problem via the first phase and of the choice of the ultimate solution via the third phase. Whether this legal power base is effectively converted into actual power is highly dependent on what happens in phase two, in which middle management and staff groups play an important role.

TABLE 14.3		
Interpretation of Sfez	Four main phases	Interpretation of Enderud
Power	1. Start-up	Exploring
Knowledge	2. Development	Negotiating
Power	3. Finalization	Legitimation
Knowledge	4. Implementation	Adjustment

Phase models of Sfez (1978) and Enderud (1980).

4 THE CONTEXT

In the previous section we reviewed several decision-making models. The strength, but also the weakness, of a model is that it highlights a certain aspect of the object of study. This shifts other characteristics somewhat to the background. Depending on the concrete case with which we are dealing, one model or another offers a more true-to-life or useful description of reality. This depends on the nature of the problem in question as well as the context (organization, environment) in which it occurs (Koopman & Pool, 1992; Pool & Koopman, 1993). A few of these contingencies and their influence on the manner of structuring decision-making processes will now be explored.

4.1 Novelty and complexity of the problem

Depending on the novelty and complexity of the problem, higher and more creative investments will have to be made in a variety of search behaviour. When problems are more familiar and surveyable, the organization can rely more strongly on "schedules" that were effective in the past. Mathematical models, computer simulation and such can offer support here. In less familiar, little-structured problems, the decision-maker must rely more on intuition, rules of thumb, and heuristic techniques (Simon, 1977).

As research has repeatedly borne out, the logical rule "the more complex the problem, the more analysis is necessary" is put into practice

ever so seldom (Beach & Mitchell, 1978). This can partly be explained by the fact that analysis activities are viewed as cost items. People are not always willing to pay these costs. In part, it also depends on the presence of other strategic factors, particularly the amount of conflict. O'Reilly (1983) studied the conditions under which available information is actually utilized. These are summarized in Table 14.4.

The way in which the search process takes place is often entirely different from the assumptions made by the classical model. In 233 decision-making processes relating to the purchase of a computer, Witte (1972) registered the frequency with which the activities "seeking information, developing alternatives, evaluation of alternatives" occurred in 10 different time intervals. The frequencies found differed greatly from the assumed frequencies. The most striking conclusion was that "seeking information" was the most frequent activity during all time intervals.

According to other studies (Nutt, 1984), however, "solutions" are often imitated or borrowed from the neighbours or the competition, without a thorough analysis. Many computers that were bought on a whim have been put in cold storage: They turned out not to be the solution to the company problem.

4.2 Amount of agreement on goals and means

As early as 1959, Thompson and Tuden developed a typology based on the amount of agreement about goals and means (ways in which the goals are to be achieved). According to these authors,

---

TABLE 14.4

Information is more readily utilized when:
- it comes from a powerful source
- it is impossible to verify
  (no other source available)
- the information is important to a person's position
- the information is easily accessible
- it comes from a credible source
- it supports desired outcomes
- using the information does not lead to conflict
- the information is offered directly
  (not via third parties)

When is available information utilized in the decision-making? (O'Reilly, 1983).

there is a best-fitting "strategy" for each of the four types of problems. If there is agreement about both goals and means, the decision can be calculated. In practice, this usually means delegating it to experts (Vroom & Yetton, 1973). If the means to the desired end are unclear, experts will have to reach a solution through consultation ("majority judgment"). If there is conflict about the goals, consultation between the parties involved is necessary, for example, via a representative body. If agreement is lacking on both goals and means, say Thompson and Tuden, the organization is endangered. In this situation, only charismatic leadership ("decision by inspiration") is said to be able to prevent the organization from disintegrating. Axelsson and Rosenberg (1979) and McMillan (1980) gave similar typologies.

At the Bradford University in England Hickson et al. (1986) studied 150 "top decisions" in 30 different organizations. The researchers classified each decision-making process using 12 process categories such as: duration, formal and informal interaction, negotiating scope, interruptions, and delays in the process. Two fundamental process dimensions were distilled from these process variables: discontinuity and dispersion. The discontinuity dimension indicates whether a process has many delays and interruptions, resulting in a longer duration. The second dimension, dispersion, indicates how many groups are involved in the process. If the cases studied are classified according to their scores on these two dimensions, a typology of three process types results: sporadic, fluid, and constricted processes.

Sporadic processes are characterised by bursts of activity alternated by still periods, a lengthy duration and much informal contact. They have delays and obstacles, for example, because a

report must be awaited or because of resistance. Information of varying quality and from various corners of the organization is used. Sporadic decisions are authorized at the highest level. Fluid processes are more regular and linear. They take place mostly in committees, project groups, and meetings. The duration is shorter, in terms of months rather than years. The information used comes from fewer sources and is less ambiguous. Constricted processes are characterized by more delays, more information sources, and less formal communication than fluid processes. On the other hand, the decision has undergone more preparation (less negotiating scope) and less activity is unleashed in the organization.

The characteristics of the process proved to be highly related to the nature of the topic, in particular, the complexity and the political import (see Figure 14.3). These results are thus entirely in agreement with those of Thompson and Tuden (1959), Axelsson and Rosenberg (1979), and Pool (1990).

According to some authors, the number of cells can even be reduced to two: Goals and means sometimes overlap. Means often form intermediate steps or subgoals. So the amount of "conflict" can be reduced to one dimension. Pinfield (1986), limiting himself to strategic decisions, distinguished "structured, orderly but iterative" processes and more unpredictable "anarchical" processes. The explanatory value of these process types, he stated, depends on whether or not there is consensus on the goals to be achieved.

Fahey (1981), based on a study of six strategic decisions, also reduced reality to two contrasting types: "rational-analytical" and "behavioural-political". However, he saw the amount of complexity (uncertainty, novelty) as the primary factor

FIGURE 14.3			
		Socio-political import	
		Low	High
Technical complexity	Low	(no cases)	constricted
	High	fluid	sporadic

Typology of decision-making processes of Hickson et al. (1986).

in determining the decision-making process. Grandori (1984) combined the factors of uncertainty and conflict on one continuum, and distinguished five process types on this basis (see Table 14.5).

"Optimizing" (cf. the rational model) is only possible when the alternatives and consequences are known and there is no conflict on goals. "Satisficing" can be seen as a form of optimizing in which the costs of the search for alternatives is also a factor. The different aspiration levels of the various actors set limitations to the search process. When both the alternatives and their consequences are unclear, an "incremental" approach necessarily results. The process takes place step by step. If uncertainty and conflict increase even more, one must resort to more heuristic techniques. Grandori mentioned "cybernetic" and "random" strategies. An example of the former is a situation in which a person must repair a broken machine with which he is not familiar. The decision-maker can only proceed by trial and error and see whether it works. An extra complication arises when the decision-maker has no information about workable past solutions. Then he must rely entirely on a "random" or chance strategy).

4.3   Type of organization

Several authors assume a relationship between organizational characteristics and the course of decision-making processes. Fredrickson (1986) reversed the traditional statement of Chandler that "structure follows strategy". In his view, strategic decision-making process are largely determined by structural characteristics of the organization in which they take place. As structure variables Fredrickson cited centralization, formalization,

and complexity. In his view, these characteristics were best represented by three of Mintzberg's (1979) structural configurations, the simple structure, the machine bureaucracy, and the professional bureaucracy. Subsequently, Fredrickson assumed that decision-making processes would take different courses in the distinguished types of organizations. Decision-making in the centralist, simple structure will be more proactive and innovative, in the formalized machine bureaucracy more problem-linked and incremental, whereas in the complex professional bureaucracy it will be of a political nature. The same train of thought is found in Quinn et al. (1988), Butler (1991), and Pheysey (1993).

One of the primary organizational characteristics is the power constellation. Is power concentrated with one or a few players (dominant coalition) or is it distributed more evenly over the organization, e.g. as a result of the expertise of the employees? The authority commanded by management largely determines their room to manoeuvre, and thus the strategy to be followed. For their study, Horvath and McMillan (1979) selected three types of Mintzberg's power configurations (later elaborated in 1983): the bureaucracy, the autocracy, and the meritocracy. The similarity to the classification used by Fredrickson will be evident (see Table 14.6). However, some of the results were in contrast to the Fredrickson's expectations. In an autocratic organization they found a reactive pattern, with incomplete phasing and an informal approach, and not the proactive, rational pattern that Fredrickson expected. Horvath and McMillan found the latter pattern in a meritocracy; Fredrickson had expected a professional bureaucracy to show the most incremen-

TABLE 14.5

Typology of Grandori (1984).

	Conflict	Consequences	Alternatives	Problem	Past solution
Optimizing	No	Known	Complete analysis	Clear	Yes
Satisficing	Yes	Known	Incomplete	Clear	Yes
Incremental	Yes	Unknown	Incomplete	Clear	Yes
Cybernetic	Yes	Unknown	Incomplete	Unclear	Yes
Random	Yes	Unknown	Incomplete	Unclear	No

tal and politicized decision-making. In the bureaucratic configuration, where a reactive, standardised decision-making process was found, the results of Horvath and McMillan corresponded fairly well to Fredrickson's expectations.

Miller (1987) expanded on Fredrickson's work. In almost 100 small and medium-size companies, Miller researched the relation between organizational structure (formalization, integration, centralization, and complexity) and characteristics of decision-making processes (rationality, interaction, and assertiveness). Rationality here stands for the extent to which attention is paid during the decision-making process to an analysis of the problem and of alternatives and the extent to which there is explicit policy, an orientation to the future, and an active attitude towards the environment. Interaction stands for the extent to which decision-making is individual or by consensus and to the scope of negotiation. Assertiveness, finally, means whether behaviour is proactive and in how far risks are taken in decisions.

From Miller's study it appeared that formal integration (formalization and integration together turned out to form one structural factor) primarily went along with the rationality characteristics and to a lesser extent with interaction and assertiveness. The presence of "horizontal ties" (committees, project groups, and liaison officers) showed a particularly strong positive correlation with the rationality characteristics.

The research of Hickson et al. (1986) also indicated that the type of organization, in addition to the type of topic, partly determines the course of decision-making, although in a less consistent manner. The 30 organizations studied were classified on the dimensions of profit vs. non-profit, production vs. service, and private vs. state-owned company. Combinations thereof were also considered. The most remarkable finding is that production organizations in state hands exhibit the most sporadic processes, whereas private services (banks, insurance companies) exhibit the most fluid processes. Private producers (industry) and government services (hospitals, universities) occupy an intermediate position.

A last important factor at the level of the organization is the prevailing pattern of ideas and convictions (Schein, 1985; Schneider, 1990). This is viewed by the top as the organization's identity. Donaldson and Lorsch (1983) spoke of "belief systems". The most important question here is what the organization sees as its field of activity or its objective and what its strong points are (distinctive competence). In addition, ideas about what are acceptable risks and the importance attached to self-reliance make up an independent part of this "corporate belief system". This pattern of ideas and convictions "sets important limits on the strategic choices managers are willing to make", thus creating a certain stability and certainty. "Without these belief systems, managers would be

TABLE 14.6

Course of strategic decision-making depending on type of organization (after Fredrickson, 1986; and Horvath & McMillan, 1979).

Organizational type	Simple structure (Autocracy)	Machine bureaucracy	Professional bureaucracy (Meritocracy)
Central structural dimension	Centralization	Formalization	Complexity
Hypothesized course of decision-making process	• Proactive • Rational • Focus on "positive goals" • Fluid • Coherent whole	• Problem oriented • Standardized • Incremental • Detailed	• Negotiation • Parochial • Little integration

adrift in a turbulent sea, without charts." Fundamental changes in these more or less stable patterns occur if changes take place in the top of the organization (new top managers with fresh ideas) or during crises.

4.4   The environment

The type of organization is sometimes hard to separate from the nature of the environment. The pressure exerted on the organization from outside has important consequences for the internal power relations and—more in general—for the possibilities and limitations of the organization (Jemison, 1981; Mintzberg, 1983). The question of whether the external powers are spread or grouped is especially important to the autonomy of the organization. The market on which an organization concentrates, competitive relations, characteristics of products or services, and the technology are also strong determinants of the nature and the speed of decision-making (Hofer & Schendel, 1978; Miles & Snow, 1978; Porter, 1988).

The previously mentioned international study of 217 complex organizational decisions in England, (former) Yugoslavia, and the Netherlands (Heller et al., 1988) showed meta-power—that is, external influence on the decision-making process by external forces, e.g. by the parent company—to be one of the most important determinants of the structure of the process; another was the national legislation. A study of reallocation decisions in an international concern brought to light that decision-making at a plan level was almost entirely determined by prior negotiations between managers of various national organizations (Koopman, 1992). As a result, the leeway for consultation and negotiation with the local works council and trade unions was almost nil.

Based on a postal enquiry among 64 companies, Stein (1981a, b) studied the relationship between certain environmental characteristics and the course of organizational decision-making processes. The environmental characteristics used were volatility, complexity, change, competition and restrictiveness, the process characteristics explicitness of analysis, extensiveness of search process, flexibility, and political activity. Stein found relationships between complexity of the environment and explicitness of the analysis, between volatility and change in the environment and the extensiveness of the search process, and finally, between volatility of the environment, and the degree of political activity in the decision-making process.

Various authors (Toffler, 1985; Pettigrew, 1986) have emphasized the effect of a crisis situation on the manner of decision-making. Periods of relative calm and stability alternate with phases in which large changes take place. The latter may accompany a change in the top of the organization (Donaldson & Lorsch, 1983). Often, too, the need for change results from a shift in the environment, which confronts the organization with a new dominant problem. The external threat can become so great that management can push through changes for which insufficient legitimation would have been found during more stable periods.

Reviewing the main literature, we can agree with Janis' saying "We must acknowledge that at present we have no simple generalizations describing how major policy decisions are made. Nor do we have any valid theory that describes and accounts for linkages between procedures for arriving at policy decisions, and good versus poor outcomes, from which we could extract dependable prescriptions for improving the quality of policy-making in government, business, and public welfare organizations" (Janis, 1992, p.11). March had already come, in 1981, to a similar conclusion. Speaking on complex decision-making he asserts that "There are no clear universals". Individuals and groups in organizations often choose the first barely acceptable alternative that comes along rather than maximize, but not always. When major policy changes are needed, they frequently stick to obsolete policies by making only small incremental modifications, yet on occasion they make "heroic leaps". Sometimes they take account of a broad spectrum of objectives and long-term considerations when it seems required; other times they fail to do so. Certain of their new decisions reflect learning from past mistakes, others do not. And, at the level of the individual decision-maker, Abelson and Levi (1985) assert that "The human decision-maker has been variously seen as a corrigible rationalist, a bounded rationalist, an error-prone intuitive scientist, a slave to motivational forces, or as the butt of faulty normative models" (Abelson & Levi, 1985, p.233; Janis, 1992).

5 THE MANAGER IN DECISION-MAKING

In this section we want to look at the involvement of the individual manager in the decision-making process from her point of view. We have adopted the outline used by McCall and Kaplan (1985). We have drawn inspiration from the classic work of Janis and Mann (1977) on decision-making and extensions of this work from Janis on decision-making in groups, groupthink (1982), and the decision-making of individual policy-makers (1989). They stated that when managers must make important decisions, behavioural patterns on individual and group level become manifest that are comparable with reaction patterns in situations of extreme stress and conflict.

First, we want to sketch the nature of the work of the manager, and then to go into the factors that determine whether a manager labels an issue as a problem or an opportunity, or whether she finds it wiser to leave the matter for what it is. Once problems are identified, no hard-and-fast rule says that action will be taken. There are countless problems in organizations about which, for a variety of reasons, nothing is done. Factors that keep problems from becoming items for action or that encourage this process are thus our next point of attention. The phase of the actual decision-making has been sufficiently discussed in the previous sections. We conclude with a manager's involvement in the aftermath of a decision, in which reality is recreated. There are numerous emerging theories on organizing in which the focus is on the process of organizing, social construction of reality and meaning, and/or language creation that have been influencial in the description of the forcefield in which a manager makes decisions or tries to avoid them (Weick, 1979; Pfeffer, 1981; Tsoukas, 1994; Gergen, 1994; Shotter, 1993). Daft and Weick (1984) discuss organizations as interpretation systems, which either react on or create their own environ-

ment. Tsoukas (1994) speaks of the need to develop theories on how reality is constructed instead of theories that are reflections of reality. Winograd and Flores (1988) and Shotter (1993) argue that the concept of language as representing reality is being challenged more and more and that language can been seen as a vehicle for the construction of reality and to generate action. Gergen (1994) argues that the value of theories is the capacity to generate new ways of thinking and to facilitate action. It is not the predictive quality of a theory that counts but the "generative" capacity. Managers are not only problem-solvers and decision-makers but have an important role in the construction of meaning. The aspect of meaning creation becomes important in the process of problem creation and the aftermath of a decision process.

5.1 The nature of a work of a manager

One of the best-known studies of the nature of the work of a manager is that of Mintzberg (1973). This study altered the picture of the ruminating, policy-oriented manager who looks almost exclusively to the strategic issues touching the organization. Alongside the familiar typology of roles fulfilled by one manager, this study primarily showed how the nature of the work of a manager is very hectic and fragmentary. There is comparatively brief attention given to the matters on which a decision must be made. Mintzberg's characterization of the work of the manager was confirmed by several other studies (Morse & Wagner, 1978; Sayles, 1979; Stewart, 1982; Kotter, 1982; Carroll & Gillen, 1987; Luthans, Rosenkrantz, & Hennessey, 1985; Luthans, 1988; Yukl, 1994). Hunt (1991) approaches leadership as a multilevel activity in which the time span being addressed is regarded as a crucial variable.

In addition to the sheer amount of work, the unpredictability of the questions that come at a manager is another reason for an often fragmentary approach to matters. A manager's schedule is constantly being interrupted by all kinds of unexpected calamities, large and small. These disturbances of his schedule make the work highly disjointed, yielding a picture of chaos and a rushed manager.

Another outcome of research on what managers

do is their almost total reliance on oral communication. Even if written material is available, their appraisal of a situation is largely founded on an oral presentation or explanation. The importance of the factors of "ethos and pathos" to an oral presentation is well known from the communication literature (Ross, 1980). The factual quality of the claims and the substance of the arguments—logos—often carry less weight. If the sender of a message is of such importance (O'Reilly, 1983), what impact does this have on the manner and the quality of a manager's decision-making?

Every organization would rapidly grind to a halt if a manager could no longer rely on what he or she is told. The essence of cooperation lies in delegation to and trust in those with whom one works. Of course an organization employs some form of control, but most decisions are accepted in what Wrapp (1988) termed the "zone of indifference", the range within which organizational members perceive a decision as legitimate and accept it. As long as the decision does not concern a matter in which the manager has a strong personal involvement, he/she will rely on the judgment and the work of others. Because the level of trust within relations is so critical for managers in the process of decision-making, the process itself becomes dependent on the relational dynamics within the organization. Hirschhorn (1988) illustrates the impact of managers' intra-psychodynamics on their perception of others. The level of anxiety is a variable that strongly influences decision-making if we accept that anxiety is related to the level of defences, and defence mechanisms influence the perception of others. At this point it is sufficient to accept that complex decision-making is strongly influenced by the personality of the decision-maker and the psychodynamics within the relational network. It is regarded as "hot cognition" (Janis & Mann, 1977).

In brief, the work of a manager is characterized by a large amount of complexity and time pressure. The unpredictability of the pressure of a manager's work leads to interruptions in his schedule and so to fragmented attention to matters. The information on which a manager relies is nearly always oral. His relationship to the sender largely determines the credibility of the message. The process is highly dependent on the characteristics of the relationships and the personalities of those involved in the construction of reality and meaning. The term "management by walking around" might well be paraphrased as "management by running and talking around".

5.2   Problem identification and creation

In the ebb and flow of daily events, what determines whether a topic is recognized as a problem or an opportunity? When qualitative and quantitative norms can be given, they serve as a description of the target situation. Kepner and Tregoe (1981) designed a procedure for the systematic screening of the variables responsible for deviation from the norm. The model is primarily useful in production departments, although the authors had in mind a more universal application. In commercial departments, the market shares of the various products or the profit levels frequently serve as standards. Comparison with other companies and with the company's own aspirations on the basis of past experiences are the calibration points by which to assess whether the target level has been achieved.

When is a new opportunity identified? Leavitt (1986) distinguished three phases in the management process: "pathfinding", problem-solving, and implementation. According to Leavitt, pathfinding is often a neglected phase. Pathfinders have a sort of sixth sense when it comes to defining issues, and on the basis of all manner of vague information, they manage to create a meaningful Gestalt. In doing so, they let themselves be guided by their ideas and values; they develop their own vision. The result is a better equilibrium between qualitative and quantitative information, between intuition and facts (Morgan, 1986).

A person's cognitive frame or map of reality (Neisser, 1967) is decisive in the identification of chances. Using this filter, the manager selects things from "reality". Managers "enact" their own environment and interpret their enactment with their own cognitive causal maps (Argyris & Schön, 1978; Weick, 1979). A reactive manager will take a different attitude from a proactive manager. The latter is more open to developments, follows them, and influences them himself where he can (Weick, 1979; Vansina, 1986).

But the manager also has emotions (Kets de Vries & Miller, 1984; Morgan, 1986). Weick

(1985) stated: "As the field of organizational studies has become more cognitive, the power of its explanation has often been reduced. Efforts are now being made to remedy this problem by adding back in what we have neglected ... I want to discuss why we need to add emotion back in." In their treatment of decision-making, Janis and Mann (1977) spoke of "hot cognition". A manager is not a rational decision-maker who makes entirely disinterested decisions in the service of the general organizational goal. Her credibility and reputation are at stake. Consciously or intuitively, managers let issues go if the risks they entail for their own position and for the organization are too great. Janis (1989) speaks of variables that cluster within the domain of "egocentric constraints": desire for prestige, the need to cope with stress, to maintain self-esteem, and the desire to satisfy other emotional needs are examples of egocentric constraints. The literature in the field of "impression management" is interesting in this respect (Goffman, 1959; Tedeschi, 1982). Her aspiration level and the quality of her relationship with her immediate superior are particularly decisive in the question of how much information a manager will release when it poses a threat to her own reputation. Politically sensitive issues and ambiguously structured problems can long remain "unnoticed". March and Olson (1976) have argued that the condition of ambiguity is a more adequate description of organizational decision-making and learning processes then the assumed transparency of the rational models. They distinguish ambiguity of purpose (which are the goals we are striving to realize), ambiguity of power (what are the networks and coalitions with preferred outcomes?), ambiguity of experience (what really happened?), and ambiguity of success (did we reach the goals?).

Another essential aspect is how well informed a manager is. Colleagues and subordinates select the information they pass on to him carefully, thereby assessing what he wants to hear or can cope with. Information is withheld, filtered, or highlighted on the basis of such assumptions (Vansina, 1982; Argyris, 1985, 1992). A manager who wants to keep in touch with what is going on in the organization must actively seek information. Because he is often excluded from part of the informal circuit, he must develop a network of his own. The manager collects much information via personal relationships and loyalties, to get a picture of what is "really" the matter or to what reality the figures refer. Especially in complex problems, his data comes to him from many different points of view. Staff departments will often sketch an issue from an angle that throws their specialization into relief (Cooke & Slack, 1991). The manager must integrate this sort of piecemeal information from staff departments in order to obtain a good general view. A manager has to invest time and energy in building a network of trustees that can generate pieces of the organizational jigsaw. A manager actively constructs the jigsaw from the pieces, with the support of others and based on information largely obtained from others. If ambiguity is high, the jigsaw will allow different adequate solutions.

In considering her own power position, a manager will assess whether a topic important to her will receive sufficient support from colleagues and superiors. How much energy she puts into lobby activities will depend on her interest in getting something on "the agenda of the organization", on her estimate of the risks involved and the opportunities for herself and the organization as a whole (Janis, 1989). Before something is singled out as a problem, it is frequently explored; this helps to determine the timing and the force of the arguments. The willingness of a manager to take risks is therefore a product of her interaction with others, of the implicit rules of the game and the organizational culture.

So there are many factors that determine whether issues are acknowledged as problems. Even in situations in which the "facts" seem to speak loudly for themselves, teams of decision-makers are in a position to filter reality in such a way that the information is not observed or is disqualified—for example, to uphold harmonious internal relations and/or a collective fantasy (Bion, 1961; McCall & Kaplan, 1985; Hirschhorn, 1988; Janis, 1989).

5.3   From problems to action

But even the identification of a topic as a problem is no guarantee that something will be done about it. Every organization has countless accepted problems on which no action is taken. Managers' "capacity for beliefs, attitudes and concerns is larger than the capacity for action" (March & Olson, 1976, p.14). What determines whether a matter is tackled? If no immediate pressure is exerted on a manager, he will make his own selection of which matters to attend to and which to postpone.

An important factor here is whether a decision lies within the manager's realm of responsibility (McCall & Kaplan, 1985). If a matter lies in an area of overlapping responsibility of two or more managers, there is a good chance that no action will be taken. This is one reason why problems between departments in organizations with a highly functional structure can remain in existence for an irresponsible length of time. Swieringa and Wierdsma (1992) show that within bureaucratic organizations managers stay away from the problems resulting from the interdependencies between departments and avoid the "no-man's land" of unclear responsibilties at the interfaces between the departments. If departments or divisions have a high degree of autonomy, it may well result in numerous unsolved problems. Poor interfacing leads to a decreasing effectiveness of the organization as a whole (Brown, 1982; Swieringa & Wierdsma, 1992). A very comfortable position in the market (monopoly or market leadership), slow feedback from the environment (university or research department), or unclear feedback (welfare facilities) may allow such situations to remain in existence indefinitely.

But even without questions of competence, there is often a tendency to postpone things. The pressure of daily routine offers countless excuses. Routine problems take up so much of a manager's time that strategic matters scarcely get a chance. He never seems to manage to get his desk cleared so that he can really tackle a question. In addition, even management problems exhibit cases of spontaneous recovery. After a while, some problems seem to have vanished, or they have become someone else's problem in the meantime. After all, an organization is a system of mutual dependencies.

The risks in the decision-making process may be a deterrent, as we have already seen. Many a manager will refrain from taking steps if it means staking his reputation on a problem that is not clearly understood, while it is uncertain whether there is any regard for it in the organization (McCall & Kaplan, 1985; Janis, 1989). If a problem does seem to call for action, a lack of resources needed to achieve a solution can be an obstacle. New problems are often added to existing ones. Solutions to the extra problems must then be found in the reallocation of already scarce resources. Sometimes, instead of negotiating over resources, it is easier to pay a problem lip-service only, and to rationalize it later on.

Confidence that a better solution can be found and availability of sufficient time are of decisive importance. When confidence and time are lacking, it encourages defensive strategies. In addition to postponement, Janis and Mann (1977) named shrugging off responsibility and vindicating oneself ("bolstering"). In shrugging off responsibility, a person binds himself to someone else's decision without taking a critical look at the situation or the decision. "Tactics" in bolstering are: exaggerating the advantages, playing down the disadvantages, disowning one's own negative feelings, denying that action is needed, and minimizing one's responsibility for the decision (Janis & Mann, 1977; Janis, 1992). In such a situation, although information is sought, it is sought so selectively that one's own solution always comes out as the best.

Things are different if there is great pressure from the environment to take action. Then deadlines, crises or outside pressure can transcend a deadlock. Decisions emerge from making the most of opportunities, from solving problems or invoking a crisis. "An ignored opportunity can later emerge as a problem or even a crisis, and a manager may convert a crisis into a problem or a temporary solution, or he may use a crisis or problem situation as an opportunity to innovate" (Mintzberg et al., 1976).

5.4 In retrospect: Success or failure

Once a decision has been made, it is important to a manager to know how people look back on the decision-making process. In retrospect, the decision is placed in relation to its consequences. Seen in this light, the degree of success is a matter of interpretation by the parties involved. In view of the complexity of the decision-making process, there are but few uncontested successes. Managers operate in a field governed by the "law of inverse certainty": "The more important the management decision, the less precise the tools to deal with it ... and the longer it will take before anyone knows it was right" (Kanter, 1977). Factors contributing to this ambiguity are: the length of time between a decision and its consequences, the relationship between cause and effect, differences in being informed and involved in the decision-making, and the consequences for various persons and groups (McCall & Kaplan, 1985). Retrospective rationality was a term used by Weick (1979) to address this issue.

The amount of time that usually elapses between the decision itself and its consequences makes it difficult to point out what has led to what. In the course of time, views change on what the decision precisely was and who had the decisive voice; additional information becomes available that influences the retrospective point of view, or evaluation, of the consequences. March and Olson (1976) show that in this process trust and distrust linked with either a sense of integration or alienation with the organization influences the process of sense making.

In addition, developments take place in the periphery of the decision-making process that strengthen or weaken effects and that affect the decision-making process. The difficulty in linking the action of decision-makers to the results is a consequence of the ambiguity of the context in which several actors try to influence the course of action. "In this situation it is not clear what happened or why it happened. The individual tries to learn and to modify his behavior on the basis of this learning" (March & Olson, 1976, p.58). This makes it impossible to indicate exactly what the contribution of a decision was. Power of persuasion is much more helpful than allusion to the "facts" in placing the decision unambiguously in relation to its consequences. Because only a limited number of people in the organization are aware of all information that was taken into consideration in the decision-making, several versions of the story will circulate. Added to this is the fact that those who must live with the consequences of a decision are not those who were

involved in making it. This distance between decision-makers and "consequence bearers" is another factor strengthening the multiplicity of interpretations in the organization.

Since a manager's reputation depends on the view relevant others take of accomplished successes, this phase is crucial for her. Her "track record" has a bearing on her attractiveness as a leader and forms the basis for her credibility and influence (McCall & Kaplan, 1985; Janis, 1989). So she has every interest in remaining active in the aftermath. In order to actually score a success, she will have to air her views actively on what happened and acquire some acceptance for her point of view among the relevant persons. If a manager refrains from doing so, then she surrenders her influence on the "retrospective definition of reality". Because much rationality is defined in retrospect, the redefinition phase is an inevitable and normal part of the decision-making process. Decision-making is a very important process in which organizational actors construct, deconstruct and reconstruct reality or meaning in organizations. For managers this process is at the core of their existence. The ambiguity of the context, the lack of or uncertainty of information and political, relational, and cultural dimensions of the process make decision-making a process of "hot" cognition with a high impact on the manager's "track record" and reputation.

6 TOOLS IN DECISION-MAKING

In the previous sections, the development of decision-making theory from a normative to an empirical phase theory was described. The position was sketched of the individual manager who, in a dynamic and sometimes chaotic environment, must arrive at decisions. While briefly discussing a few applications of the decision-making theory, we want to go into two aspects in greater detail:

- recommendations with respect to decision-making in the context of organizational control;
- the influence of new technology on decision-making.

6.1 Recommendations with respect to decision-making

To guide them in their decision-making, many organizations still use old models based upon the following phases:

- identification of the problem;
- definition of the problem;
- analysis of the problem;
- formulation of alternatives;
- testing the alternatives against criteria and selection;
- implementation.

However, it is known from the literature that only a few decision-making processes actually run such a course. Of the many problems that a manager observes or has pointed out to him, only the problem that exceeds a certain threshold value as to urgency is actually tackled. In fact, only very serious problems or golden opportunities are immediately taken to hand. In such cases, the decision-making process takes place very rapidly, without observance of the phases of definition, analysis, formulation of alternatives, etc. The formal sequence of phases is only followed in decisions on somewhat less pressing problems, ones that have often been around for a long time. And here the danger is most imminent that the decision-making chain is interrupted by all manner of discussions and is never completed.

"Meta-decision-making" (see section 3) is therefore of great importance. Sometimes it is delegated by top management to a special functionary, the "decision controller". He decides on the design and execution of the decision-making process; he directs the process. He is not the one to decide on the topic in question, but he determines who will be involved, when, in what phases, and in what quality in the process. It means that, for serious problems, the decision controller must make sure that the phases are taken in a somewhat orderly fashion (phenomena such as "groupthink" form the greatest threat in a chaotic process) in order to keep the decision-making at the desired level of quality. For other types of problems, he must make sure that decision-making does not come standstill at the built-in decision-making milestones or through lack of attention on the part of management. Clear and specific deadlines and the explicit assignment of decisions to people and/or bodies can stop the process from foundering prematurely. Supervisory bodies such as boards of directors, the general management, and steering committees always ought to be have a part in this, or at least be highly involved in the selection of the decision controller.

Today's decision controller can avail herself of tools such as network planning, with which she can plan all influential factors in their overall relationship. Once the analysis phase has been completed, alternatives must be formulated. Experience has shown that people start by searching their memories for similar problem situations and first try out "old" solutions. Precisely this fact was the basis for the emergence of expert systems, by means of which new situations can be analyzed using old knowledge. In the phase of the formulation of alternatives, a decision controller has the most benefit from a well-organized experiential database.

Only when no single past solution proves to be satisfactory does one decide to design new solutions. Here, too, practice has shown that usually only one alternative is worked out and supported with much extra information, which in actual fact rules out the possibility of choice. A moot question is whether the future will bring a demand for various solutions in broad lines. For instance, De Boer and Vinke (1987) have suggested, for system-implementation situations, offering users various solutions or automation scenarios, each based on a different systems approach with different consequences for the user. In the automation world, it has so far been the practice to work out one design in depth, and then present it as *the* solution.

6.2 The influence of new technology on decision-making

Uncertainty, and the reduction of uncertainty, are central themes in decision-making. The rise of computer technology has made possible a better control of uncertainty, because more variables can be taken into consideration, consequences can be projected, and information can be collected faster and more accurately.

There are actually three areas in which computer technology in particular influences the practice of management:

- office automation;
- decision support systems (DSS);
- artificial intelligence (AI).

While office automation primarily affects the productivity and the efficiency of management, DSS and AI go further: They contribute to the problem identification, generate alternatives, and can set priorities. The value of these two techniques is that they improve information processing, and do not simply make it possible to process more information (Monger, 1987).

Decision support systems were first developed at the end of the 1960s thanks to the possibilities opened by the computer in the form of databases and direct access to information for purposes of manipulation. The object of DSS is defined by Keen and Morton (1978) as contributing to the effectiveness of semi-structured decision-making processes through analysis and simulation. Basically, this relates to quantitative decision-making processes such as production and stock planning, strategic planning, financial planning, and investment decisions.

If, as described by Mintzberg, bottle-necks in the current manner of decision-making lie in the phases of the generation of alternatives, the design and selection of solutions, then DS systems can offer support. The applications of DSS, however, are limited to situations in which a formal model (on which decision-making is based) can represent the decision-making process.

Artificial Intelligence goes one step further: It can also deal with conflicting or missing data. Artificial Intelligence is defined as that part of information science dealing with processes that produce intelligent action. Intelligent action refers to a purposeful decision arrived at through logical reasoning and founded on rules of experience (Magee, 1984). AI is composed of three subsystems: sensory systems, natural-language systems, and expert systems. The first type deals, for example, with interpreting and deriving as much information as possible from two-dimensional photos. Language systems are aimed at the interpretation of spoken language (Monger, 1987). Expert systems or knowledge systems are sometimes defined as programs to solve difficult problems that demand expertise. The influence of this form of AI on management will undoubtedly

be the greatest. Applications may be found in diagnosis, medical information systems, process control, planning, and industrial applications.

What effect will these new technologies have on management and decision-making? Monger (1987) described it in a number of questions:

- What evidence is there that information technology has improved the productivity of management?
- What potential do these new technologies have to redefine decision-making processes; will these techniques supplement or even replace traditional decision-making methods?
- What new options in doing business will arise as a result of these new techniques?

Brynjolfsson (1991), seeking a new theoretical basis for the new work in the information-processing role of the firm, asserts that "technological advances have reduced the costs of distributing decision-relevant information to the workforce. At the same time, the potential for more centralized decision-making has been limited by the bounded capacity of top management to assimilate more information, leading to an increase in the number of knowledge workers hired. The net result has been the decentralizing of decision-making authority."

Brynjolfsson (1991) believes it premature to assume that all investments in computers were unrational decisions, although there is plenty of literature showing a lack of convincing proof of substantial productivity improvement by information technology despite massive investment. Currently over 40% of new capital investment in the USA is spent on information technology (Brynjolfsson & Bimber, 1989). Brynjolfsson offers four explanations for the lack of convincing evidence: mismeasurement, time lags between introduction and results, mismanagement, and redistribution (meaning that although information is wider spread it has not led to higher productivity). But there is no conclusive evidence yet for any of these explanations.

The sector where one would expect the largest increase in productivity through the use of information technology is the services sector. With 75% of all jobs in the USA in the private economy (two-thirds are white-collar workers, of which some 45% are "knowledge workers"), that sector owns 85% of the total installed base of information technology. Roach (1991), in an article on the lagging efficiency in the service sector, states that the massive investments in technology have not improved productivity: In 1982, services in the USA invested $6000 in information technology for each white-collar worker. Since then the capital per white-collar worker has doubled, but the labour force and labour costs have remained the same.

The new communication and telecommunication techniques are another important development in this field. To a certain extent, such techniques make the physical workplace unimportant. Personal computers, linked to an electronic-mail system, and linked to the central database or the office automation network of the organization, make it possible to work at home or while away on a trip. The advantages of telecommunication are obvious: flexible working hours, less office space needed, opportunities for invalids and employees with household responsibilities, etc. A danger may perhaps be seen in the lessened personal contact.

Concisely, it may be stated that the figures published thus far on the improved efficiency expected of management as a result of automation are not very reliable, and that the speed with which these techniques are adopted by management is much slower than generally assumed.

Monger's second question was about the potential of the new techniques to redefine or to change the decision-making process. In 1955, Hurni predicted that computers would bring about decentralization, complexity, and growth of activities, thus invoking a great need for control. Although more communication and greater attention to the structuring of information would be needed, decision-making by management would not change in itself.

Brady (in 1967) expected that the influence of the computer would primarily be felt at the level of middle management. Only in 1971 did Gorry and Morton state that the influence of automation was related to the degree of structure in the decision-making process. The implication was that not all activities of middle management would be automated, but only those that were relatively well structured—which, as a matter of fact, may also be said of the activities of the top management. Later developments in the field of DSS and AI, as sketched earlier, have shown that emphasis in management activities will come to lie on the analysis and interpretation of information requiring great expertise in relation to the subject area. Middle management has indeed come under greater pressure. This is also the reason for the prediction that a growing number of companies with a basically horizontal structure will set up special units and temporary work groups to solve problems and to work markets.

The third question focused on new opportunities in "doing business". In other words, will competitive relations change as a result of these new techniques? Parsons (1983) reported a study which extended over a period of two years, in which he collected data from 12 different companies. He analyzed three aspects of the influence of automation: branch or sector, company, and strategy. According to his findings, changes at sector level were critical: Automation changed the rules for "economies of scale", entrance barriers, competition, and competitive relations. Larger companies, for instance, were in a position to expand their distribution from a regional to a national level. At a company level, examples were numerous: Strategic purchasing or supplier information entailed advantages, as did computer-aided manufacturing and robot techniques. Insurance companies were found to be directly dependent on their degree of automation. At a strategic level, he found companies to be most successful when they had information systems that most supported the company's strategy. Many sources (including Monger), however, come to the conclusion that the influence of automation and new techniques has so far been slight, because management has not yet really adopted them. Reasons vary from incomprehension to fear of the implications and the risks entailed.

6.3 In conclusion

In 1984 we stated: "Normative statements are not yet possible. On the basis of empirical research, a number of predictions can be made on what action will lead to what results under certain conditions.

But we have not yet been able to do much more than illustrate the complexity of the decision-making process and describe a few of its aspects and contexts" (Koopman, Brockhuysen, & Meijn, 1984).

In 1997 we observed that complex decision-making can be supported by technology. Experiences are recorded and can readily be consulted. The rationality of the decision-making process, which research has time and again shown to be limited, can thus again be enlarged. On the other hand, the limits of complexity seem to be expanding further and further in the direction of greater uncertainty. Globalization, growing competition and enormous international interdependencies, as shown by the stock exchange crash of 19 October 1987, or the present discussion on the influence of financial derivatives, for example, illustrate this point. The pressure on rationality in decision-making seems to remain present in many forms.

Leavitt (1986) criticized current management methods, which, in his view, place too much emphasis on problem-solving and quantitative analysis. Management, he said, should meet three requirements: vision, problem-solving, and implementation. This would seem to put complex decision-making in second place at the organizational level. Decision-making starts when there are matters to be decided. The finalization of decision-making processes is no guarantee that the right topics have been addressed. Vision and creativity are of growing importance, whereas decision-making theory seems to offer no tools for precisely these aspects.

A good illustration of this was given by Mintzberg and Waters (1982). They studied the strategy of Steinberg Inc. (principally a retail chain) between 1917 and 1974. The more this company grew, the greater became the necessity for formal planning. Entrepreneurial success, as it were, caused bureaucratic powers to develop that supplanted an entrepreneurial style. In this case, however, the founder continued to exert influence on essential moments of decisions. Mintzberg and Waters established that genuine strategic changes only occurred three times in a time span of more than 50 years. Strategy was thus not a continual concern of the top management. On the contrary, a

high frequency of strategic planning might well make management insensitive to the real issues. The approach taken in this case was comparable to the motion of a caterpillar. The organization expanded according to a certain strategy, and then took time to consolidate. One conclusion of the researchers was that organizations plan when they have a strategy, but that they do not plan to acquire a strategy. Planning imposes order on vision. Planning is apparently more a sort of programming for purposes of justification, implementation, and communication.

Porter (1987) published a study on the diversification strategy of 33 companies for the period from 1950–1986, which he analyzed based on the success of the diversification/takeover strategy. Each company embarked upon an average of 80 new but related fields and 27 entirely new fields. He observed that they disposed of an average of more than half of their takeovers in related fields and of over 60% in entirely new fields. For entirely unrelated activities, this figure was even higher than 70%.

The question is, of course, to what these results can be attributed. Porter formulated a number of criteria that a diversification strategy must meet before decisions are made on takeovers, joint ventures, or start-ups. As reasons for the failure of diversification strategies, he named: incomplete analysis of the branch of industry, insufficient awareness of the access barriers to another market or industry, and the impossibility to achieve certain synergetic effects by the company being taken over or by the buying company. In addition to insufficient analysis and the choice of a strategy on the basis of the improper criteria, Porter emphasized certain routines in decision-making that proved not to be successful. A preoccupation with growth in any way possible obstructs the company's healthy development. Entrepreneurs must have a clear vision of their entrepreneurial strategy and must verify their work on this basis. The results of Porter's study would then have been different.

What can be learned from this from a decision-making perspective? On the one hand, the element of vision comes forward in the literature as an important component of decision-making processes: "Intuition based on knowledge." Vision cannot be planned, not even in the resources in what is termed unstructured decision-making. On the other hand, expert systems help to record experience in one way or another, so that diagnostic and search activities can take place better and faster. The imperfections in human decision-making can be partially remedied by computer support. The stock exchange crash of 19 October 1987, however, also taught us a lesson: Decision-support systems can play a negative role when they are no longer used as decision support but as decision-takers. Recommendations to sell at a certain point were always put into practice at that occasion.

It would therefore seem that the role of rationality in decision-making processes will continue to be a modest one.

REFERENCES

Abelson, R.P., & Levi, A. (1985). Decision-making and decision theory. In G. Lindzey, & E. Aronson, (Eds.), *The handbook of social psychology* (Vol. 1). New York: Random House.

Allison, G.T. (1971). *Essence of decision: Explaining the Cuban missile crisis.* Boston: Little, Brown.

Andrews, K.R. (1980). *The concept of corporate strategy.* Homewood, IL: Irwin.

Ansoff, H.I. (1965). *Corporate strategy.* New York: McGraw-Hill.

Argyris, C. (1985). *Strategy change and defensive routines.* Boston: Pitman.

Argyris, C. (1992). *On organizational learning.* Cambridge, MA: Blackwell.

Argyris, C., & Schön, D.A. (1978). *Organizational learning: A theory of action perspective.* Reading, MA: Addison-Wesley.

Arnold, J.D. (1992), *The complete problem solver: A total system for competitive decision-making.* New York: Wiley.

Axelsson, R., & Rosenberg, L. (1979). Decision making and organizational turbulence. *Acta Sociologica, 22,* 45–62.

Bacharach, S.B., & Lawler, E.J. (1986). Power dependence and power paradoxes in bargaining. *Negotiation Journal, 2,* 167–174.

Beach, L.R. (1990). *Image theory: Decision making in personal and organizational contexts.* Chichester: Wiley.

Beach, L.R., & Mitchell, T.R. (1978). A contingency model for the selection of decision strategies. *Academy of Management Review, 3,* 439–444.

Bion, W.R., (1961). *Experiences in groups.* London: Tavistock Publications.

Bobbitt, H.R., & Ford, J.D. (1980). Decision maker choice as a determinant of organizational structure. *Academy of Management Journal, 5,* 13–23.

Boer, H. de, & Vinke R.H.W. (1987). *Taakkenmerken en computergebruik* [Task characteristics and use of computers]. Amsterdam: Sectie A&O-psychologie UvA.

Brady, H. (1967). Computer in top-level decision-making. *Harvard Business Review, 45* (July–August), 67–76.

Brim, O.G., Glass, D.C., Larvin D.E., & Goodman, N.E. (1962). *Personality and decision process.* Stanford, CA: Stanford University Press.

Brown, L.D. (1982). *Managing conflict at organizational interfaces.* Reading, MA: Addison-Wesley.

Brynjolfsson, E. (1991). *Information technology and the "New Managerial Work".* Cambridge, MA: Research paper MIT.

Brynjolfsson, E., & Bimber, B. (1989). *Information technology and the productivity paradox.* Cambridge, MA: MIT Laboratory for Computer Science.

Butler, R. (1991). *Designing organizations: A decision-making perspective.* London: Routledge.

Carroll, S.J., & Gillen, D.J. (1987). Are the classical management functions useful in describing managerial work? *Academy of Management Review, 12,* 38–51.

Child, J. (1972). Organization structure and strategies of control: A replication of the Aston study. *Administrative Science Quarterly, 17,* 163–177.

Clegg, S.R. (1987). The language of power and the power of language. *Organization Studies, 8,* 61–70.

Cohen, M.D., March, J.G., & Olsen, J.P., (1972) A garbage can model of organizational choice. *Administrative Science Quarterly, 17,* 1–25.

Cooke, S., & Slack, N. (1991). *Making management decisions* (2nd Edn). New York: Prentice-Hall.

Cyert, R.M., & March, J.G. (1963). *A behavioral theory of the firm.* Englewood Cliffs, NJ: Prentice-Hall.

Daft, R.L. & Weick, K.E. (1984). Toward a model of organizations as interpretation systems. *Academy of Management Review, 9,* 284–295.

Donaldson, G., & Lorsch, J.W. (1983). *Decision making at the top: the shaping of strategic direction.* New York: Basic Books.

Emerson, R.M. (1962). Power–dependence relations. *American Sociological Review, 27,* 31–41.

Enderud, H. (1980). Administrative leadership in organized anarchies. *International Journal of Management in Higher Education,* 235–253.

Etzioni, A. (1967). Mixed-scanning: A "third" approach to decision-making. *Public Administration Review, 27,* 385–392.

Fahey, L. (1981). On strategic management decision processes. *Strategic Management Journal, 2,* 43–60.

Fahey, L., & Naroyanan, V.K. (1983). The politics of strategic decision-making. In K.J. Albert (Ed.), *The strategic management handbook*. New York: McGraw-Hill.

Fredrickson, J.W. (1986). The strategic decision process and organizational structure. *Academy of Management Review, 11*, 280–297.

Fredrickson, J.W., & Mitchell, T.R. (1984). Strategic desicion processes: Comprehensiveness and performance in an industry with an unstable environment. *Academy of Management Journal, 27*, 399–423.

French, J.R.P., & Raven, B. (1959). The bases of social power. In D. Cartwright (Ed.), *Studies in social power*. Ann Arbor: Institute for Social Research, University of Michigan.

George, A.L. (1980). *Presidential decision-making in foreign policy: The effective use of information and advice*. Boulder, CO: Westview Press.

Gergen, K.J. (1994), *Towards transformation in social knowledge* (2nd Edn). London: Sage.

Gladstein, D., & Quinn, J.B. (1985), Making decisions and producing action. In J.M. Pennings & Associates (Eds.), *Organizational strategy and change*. San Francisco: Jossey-Bass.

Goffman, E. (1959). *The presentation of self in everyday life*. New York: Anchor.

Goodwin, P., & Wright, G. (1991), *Decision analysis for management judgment*. Chichester: Wiley.

Gorry G., & Morton, M.S.S. (1971). A framework for management information systems. *Sloan Management Review, 13*, 55–70.

Grandiori, A. (1984). A prescriptive contingency view of organizational decision-making. *Administrative Science Quarterly, 29*, 192–209.

Harrison, E.F. (1995). *The managerial decision-making process* (4th Edn). Boston: Houghton Mifflin.

Heller, F.A., Drenth, P.J.D., Koopman P.L., & Rus, V. (1988). *Decisions in organisations: A three-country comparative study*. London: Sage.

Hickson, D.J., Hinnings, C.R., Lee, A.C., Schneck, R.E., & Pennings, J.M. (1971). A strategic contingency theory of intra-organizational power. *Administrative Science Quarterly, 16*, 216–229.

Hickson, D.J., Butler, R.J., Cray, D., Mallory, G.R., & Wilson, D.C. (1986). *Top decisions: Strategic decision-making in organizations*. Oxford: Basil Blackwell.

Hill, C.W.L., & Jones, G.R. (1989). *Strategic management: An integrated approach*. Boston: Houghton Mifflin.

Hirschhorn, L. (1988). *The workplace within*. Cambridge, MA: MIT Press.

Hofer, C.W., & Schendel, D.E. (1978). *Strategy formulation: Analytical concepts*. St. Paul, MN: West.

Hogarth, R. (1987). *Judgement and choice* (2nd Edn). New York: Wiley.

Horvath, D., & McMillan, C.J. (1979). Strategic choice and the structure of decision processes. *International Studies of Management and Organization, 9*, 87–112.

Hosking, D.M., & Morley, I.E. (1991). *A social psychology of organizing*. New York: Harvester Wheatsheaf.

Howard, R.A. (1988). Decision analysis: Practice and promise. *Management Science, 34*, 679–695.

Hurni, M.L. (1955). Decision making in th age of automation. *Harvard Business Review, 33* (September–October), 49–58.

Hunt, J.G. (1991). *Leadership: A new synthesis*. London: Sage.

IDE-International Research Group (1993). *Industrial democracy in Europe revisited*. Oxford: Oxford University Press.

Janis, I.L. (1972). *Victims of groupthink*. Boston: Houghton Mifflin.

Janis, I.L. (1982). *Groupthink* (2nd Edn). Boston: Houghton Mifflin.

Janis, I.L (1989). *Crucial decisions: Leadership in policymaking and crisis management*. New York: Free Press.

Janis, I.L. (1992). Causes and consequences of defective policy-making: A new theoretical analysis. In F.A. Heller (Ed.), *Decision-making and leadership*. Cambridge: Cambridge University Press.

Janis, I.L., & Mann, L. (1977). *Decision making: A psychological analysis of conflict, choice and commitment*. New York: Free Press.

Jemison, D.B. (1981). Organizational versus environmental sources of influence in strategic decision-making. *Strategic Management Journal, 2*, 77–89.

Jongh, E.D.J. de (1987). *Commissarissen, directeuren, OR-leden: Verhoudingen en verwachtingen* [Directors, top-management, and members of works councils]. Leiden/Antwerpen: Stenfert Kroese.

Kahneman, D., & Tversky, A. (1984). Choices, values, and frames. *American Psychologist, 39*, 341–350.

Kayaalp, O. (1987). Towards a general theory of managerial decision: A critical appraisal. *SAM Advanced Management Journal, 52*, 36–42.

Kanter, R.M. (1977). *Men and women of the corporation*. New York: Basic Books.

Kanter, R.M. (1983). *The change masters; Innovation for productivity in the American corporation*. New York: Simon & Schuster.

Keen, G.W., & Morton, M.S.S. (1978). *Decision support systems*. Reading, MA: Addison-Wesley.

Kepner, C., & Tregoe, B.B. (1981). *The new rational manager*. New York: Princeton University Press.

Kets de Vries, M.F.R., & Miller, D. (1984). *The neurotic organization*. London: Jossey-Bass.

Kickert, W.J.M. (1979). Rationaliteit en structuur van organisatorische besluitvormingsprocessen [Rationality and structure of organizational decisions]. *Bestuurswetenschappen, 33*, 21–30.

Koopman, P.L. (1991). Between control and commitment: Management and change as the art of balancing. *Leadership and Organization Development Journal, 12, 5,* 3–7.

Koopman, P.L. (1992). Between economic-technical and socio-political rationality: Multilevel decision-making in a multinational organization. *The Irish Journal of Psychology, 13, 1,* 32–50.

Koopman, P.L., & Algera, J.A. (1989). Formalization and delegation: Two management dilemmas in automation design processes. In K. de Witte (Ed.), *The challenge of technological change for work and organisation: Tools and strategies for the nineties.* Leuven: Acco.

Koopman, P.L., Broekhuysen, J.W., & Meijn, O.M. (1984). Complex decision-making at the organizational level. In P.J.D. Drenth, H. Thierry, P.J. Willems, & C.J. de Wolff (Eds.), *Handbook of work and organizational psychology.* Chichester: Wiley.

Koopman, P.L., Drenth, P.J.D., Heller, F.A., & Rus, V. (1993). Participation in complex organizational decisions: A comparative study of the United Kindom, the Netherlands, and Yugoslavia, In E. Rosenstein & W.M. Lafferty (Eds.), *International handbook of participation in organizations* (Vol. 3, pp.113–133). Oxford: Oxford University Press.

Koopman, P.L., & Pool, J. (1990), Decision making in organizations. In C.L. Cooper & I.T. Robertson (Eds.), *International review of industrial and organizational psychology.* London: Wiley.

Koopman, P.L., & Pool, J. (1992). Management dilemmas in reorganization. *The European Work and Organizational Psychologist, 1, 4,* 225–244.

Kotter, J.P. (1982). *The general managers.* New York: Free Press.

Krogt, Th. van der, & Vroom, C. (1991). *Organisatie is beweging* [Organization is movement]. Culemborg: Lemma.

Lammers, C.J., & Széll, G. (1989). Concluding reflections organizational democracy: Taking stock. In C.J. Lammers, & G. Széll (Eds.), *International handbook of participation in organizations (Volume I).* Oxford: Oxford University Press.

Lawrence, P.R. (1985). In defense of planning as a rational approach. In J.M. Pennings & Associates (Eds.), *Organizational strategy and change.* San Francisco: Jossey-Bass.

Leavitt, H.J. (1986). *Corporate pathfinders.* Homewood, IL: Dow Jones-Irwin.

Lindblom, C.E. (1959). The science of "muddling through". *Public Administrative Review, 19,* 79–99.

Lindblom, C.E. (1980). *The policy-making process* (2nd edition). Englewood Cliffs, NJ: Prentice-Hall.

Luthans, F. (1988), Successful vs. effective managers. *The Academy of Management Executive, 2, 2,* 127–132.

Luthans, F., Rosenkrantz, S.A., & Hennessey, H.W. (1985). What do successful mannagers really do? An observational study of managerial activities. *Journal of Applied Behavioral Science, 21,* 255–270.

MacCrimmon, K.R. (1985), Understanding strategic decisions: Three systematic approaches. In J.M. Pennings & Associates (Eds.), *Organizational strategy and change.* San Francisco: Jossey-Bass.

Magee, J.F. (1984). What information technology has in store for managers. *Sloan Management Review, 26* (Winter), 17–31.

March, J.G. (1981). Decisions in organizations and theories of choice. In A.H. Van de Ven, & W.F. Joyce (Eds.), *Perspectives on organizational design and behavior.* New York: Wiley.

March, J.G. (Ed.)(1988). *Decisions and organizations.* Oxford: Basil Blackwell.

March, J.G. (1994). *A primer on decision-making: How decisions happen.* New York: Free Press.

March, J.G., & Olson, J.P. (1976). *Ambiguity and choice in organizations.* Bergen: Universiteitsforlaget.

March, J.G., & Simon, H.A. (1958). *Organizations.* New York: Wiley.

McCall, M.W., & Kaplan, R.E. (1985). *Whatever it takes: Decision-makers at work.* Englewood Cliffs, NJ: Prentice-Hall.

McMillan, C. (1980). Qualitative models of organizational decisionmaking. *Journal of General Management, 5,* 22–39.

Miles, R.E., & Snow, C.C. (1978). *Organizational strategy, structure and process.* New York: McGraw-Hill.

Miller, D. (1987). Strategy making and structure: Analysis and implications for performance. *Academy of Management Journal, 30,* 7–32.

Mintzberg, H. (1973). *The nature of managerial work.* New York: Harper & Row.

Mintzberg, H. (1979). *The structuring of organizations.* Englewood Cliffs, NJ: Prentice-Hall.

Mintzberg, H. (1983). *Power in and around organizations.* Englewood Cliffs, NJ: Prentice-Hall.

Mintzberg, H. (1994). *The rise and fall of strategic planning.* New York: Prentice-Hall.

Mintzberg, H., Raisinghani, D., & Théorêt, A. (1976). The structure of "unstructured" decision processes. *Administrative Science Quarterly, 21,* 246–275.

Mintzberg, H., & Waters, J.A. (1982). Tracking strategy in an entrepreneurial firm. *Academy of Management Journal, 3,* 465–499.

Monger, R.F. (1987). *Managerial decision-making with technology.* New York: Pergamon Press.

Morgan, G. (1986). *Images of organization.* London: Sage.

Morse, J.J., & Wagner, F.R. (1978). Measuring the process of managerial effectiveness. *Academy of Management Journal, 21, 1,* 23–35.

Neisser, U. (1967). *Cognitive psychology.* New York: Appleton-Century-Crofts.

Nutt, P.C. (1976). Models for decision-making in

organizations and some variables which stipulate optimal use. *Academy of Management Review, 1*, 84–98.

Nutt, P.C. (1984). Types of organizational decision processes. *Administrative Science Quarterly, 29*, 414–450.

O'Reilly, C.A. (1983). The use of information in organizational decision-making: A model and some propositions. In L.L. Cummings, & B.M. Shaw (Eds.), *Research in Organizational Behavior, 5*, (pp. 103–139). Greenwich, CT: JAI Press.

Parsons, G.L. (1983). Information technology: A new competitive weapon. *Sloan Management Review, 25* (Fall), 3–14.

Pearce, J.A., & Robinson, R.B. (1988), *Strategic management: Strategy formulation and interpretation* (3rd Edn). Homewood, IL: Irwin.

Pettigrew, A.M. (1972). Information control as a power-resource. *Sociology, 6*, 187–204.

Pettigrew, A.M. (1973). *The politics of organizational decision making*. London: Tavistock.

Pettigrew, A.M. (1986). Some limits of executive power in creating strategic change. In S. Srivastva (Ed.), *The functioning of executive power*. London: Jossey Bass.

Pfeffer, J. (1981). *Power in organisations*. Boston: Pitman.

Pfeffer, J., & Salancik, G.R. (1978). *The external control of organiztions*. New York: Harper and Row.

Pheffer, P. (1988). Management in symbolic action: Recreation and maintenance of of organizational paradigms. In L.L. Cummings, & B.M. Staw (Eds.), *Research in Organizational Behavior, Vol. 3* (pp. 1–53). Greenwich, CT: JAI Press.

Pheysey, D.C. (1993). *Organizational cultures: Types and transformations*. London: Routledge.

Pinfield, L.T. (1986). A field evaluation of perspectives on organizational decision-making. *Administrative Science Quarterly, 31*, 365–388.

Pool, J. (1990), *Sturing van strategische besluitvorming* [Steering of strategic decision-making]. Amsterdam: VU Publications.

Pool, J., & Koopman, P.L. (1992), Strategic decision-making in organizations: A research model and some initial findings. In D.M. Hosking, & N. Anderson (Eds.), *Organizational change and innovation*. London: Routledge.

Pool, J., & Koopman, P.L. (1993). Control options in managing strategic decision-making processes. *The European Work and Organizational Psychologist, 3*, 3, 285–296.

Poole, M. (1986). *Towards a new industrial democracy: Workers' participation in industry*. London: Routledge & Kegan Paul.

Porter, M.E. (1980). *Competitive strategy: Techniques for analyzing industries and competitors*. New York: Free Press.

Porter, M.E. (1987). From competitive advantage to corporate strategy. *Harvard Business Review, 65* (May–June), 43–59.

Porter, M.E. (1988). How competitive forces shape strategy. In J.B. Quinn, H. Mintzberg, & R.M. James (Eds.) *The strategy process: Concepts, contexts and cases*. London: Prentice-Hall.

Quinn, J.B. (1978). Strategic change: "Logical incrementalism". *Sloan Management Review, 20*, 7–21.

Quinn, J.B. (1980). *Strategies for change: Logical incrementalism*. Homewood, IL: Irwin.

Quinn, J.B. (1988). Managing strategies incrementally. In J.B. Quinn, H. Mintzberg, & R.M. James (Eds.), *The strategy process: Concepts, contexts, and cases*. London: Prentice-Hall.

Quinn, J.B., Mintzberg, H., & James, R.M. (Eds.) (1988) *The strategy process: Concepts, contexts and cases*. London: Prentice-Hall.

Quinn, R.E (1988). *Beyond rational management*. San Francisco: Jossey-Bass.

Roach, S.S. (1991). Services under siege: The restructuring imperative. *Harvard Business Review, 69*, 5, 82–91.

Ross, R.S. (1980). *Speech communication*. Englewood Cliffs, NJ: Prentice-Hall.

Rowe, A.J., & Boulgarides, J.D. (1992). *Managerial decision making*. New York: Macmillan.

Sayles, L. (1979). *Leadership*. New York: McGraw-Hill.

Schein, E. (1985), *Organizational culture and leadership*. San Francisco: Jossey-Bass.

Schneider, B. (Ed.)(1990). *Organizational climate and culture*. San Francisco: Jossey-Bass.

Schwenk, C.R. (1984). Cognitive simplification processes in strategic decision-making. *Strategic Management Journal, 5*, 111–128.

Schwenk, C.R. (1988). *The essence of strategic decision-making*. Lexington, MA: D.C. Heath & Co.

Sfez, L. (1978). Existe-t-il des decisions democratiques? *Dialectiques, 22*, 59–72.

Shotter, J. (1993). *Conversational realities*. London: Sage.

Shrivastava, P., & Grant, J.H. (1985). Empirically derived models of strategic decision-making processes. *Strategic Management Journal, 6*, 97–113.

Simon, H.A. (1947). *Administrative behavior*. New York: Free Press.

Simon, H.A. (1957). *Models of man*. New York: Wiley.

Simon, H.A. (1977). *The new science of management decision*. Englewood Cliffs, NJ: Prentice-Hall.

Starbuck, W.H. (1985), Acting first and thinking later: Theory versus reality in strategic change. In J.M. Pennings & Associates (Eds.), *Organizational strategy and change*. San Francisco: Jossey-Bass.

Stein, J. (1981a). Contextual factors in the selection of strategic decision methods. *Human Relations, 34*, 819–834.

Stein, J. (1981b). Strategic decision methods. *Human Relations, 34*, 917–933.

Stewart, R. (1982). A model for understanding managerial jobs and behavior. *Academy of Management Review, 7*, 7–13.

Swieringa, J., & Wierdsma, A. (1992). *Becoming a learning organization: Beyond the learning curve.* Reading, MA: Addison-Wesley.

Taylor, R.N. (1992). Strategic decision-making. In M.D. Dunnette, & L.M. Hough (Eds.), *Handbook of industrial and organizational psychology* (2nd Edn, Vol. 3). Palo Alto, CA: Consulting Psychologists Press.

Tedeschi, J.T. (Ed.) (1982). *Impression management: Theory and social psychological research.* New York: Academic Press.

Thompson, J.D. (1967). *Organizations in action.* New York: McGraw-Hill.

Thompson, J.D., & Tuden, A. (1959). Strategies, structures, and processes of organizational decision. In J.D. Thompson, P.B. Hammond, R.W. Hawkes, B.H. Junker, & A. Tuden (Eds.), *Comparative studies in administration.* Pittsburgh, PA: Pittsburgh University Press.

Toffler, A. (1985). *De flexibele organisatie* [The flexible organization]. Utrecht: Veen.

Tsoukas, H. (1994). *New thinking in organizational behaviour.* Oxford: Butterworth-Heinemann.

Tversky, A., & Kahneman, D. (1974). Judgement under uncertainty: Heuristics and biases. *Science, 185*, 1124–1131.

Vansina, L. (1982). Reorganiseren onder ongunstige economische omstandigheden [Reorganization under difficult economic conditions]. *Economische Sociaal Tijdschrift, 1*, 27–33, *3*, 275–287.

Vansina, L. (1986). Transformatiemanagement [Transformation management]. In H. Stufkes (Ed.) *Management voor nieuwe tijd: Transformatie in bedrijf en organisatie.* Rotterdam: Lemiscaat.

Vroom, V.H., & Yetton, P.W. (1973). *Leadership and decision-making.* Pittsburgh, PA: University of Pittsburgh Press.

Weick, K. (1979). *The social psychology of organizing.* Reading, MA: Addison-Wesley.

Weick, K. (1985). The emotions of organizing. *Academy of Management*, paper.

Wilson, D.C., Butler, R.J., Cray, D., Hickson, D.J., & Mallory, G.R. (1986). Breaking the bounds of organization in strategic decision-making. *Human Relations, 39*, 309–332.

Winograd, T., & Flores, F. (1988). *Understanding computers and cognition.* Norwood, NJ: Ablex Publications.

Witte, E. (1972). Field research on complex decision-making processes: The phase theorem. *International Studies of Management and Organization, 2*, 156–182.

Wrapp, H.E. (1988). Good managers don't make policy decisions. In J.B. Quinn, H. Mintzberg, & R.M. James (Eds.), *The strategy process: Concepts, contexts, and cases.* London: Prentice-Hall.

Winter, S.G. (1985), The case for "mechanistic" decision-making. In J.M. Pennings & Associates (Eds.), *Organizational strategy and change.* San Francisco: Jossey-Bass.

Yates, J.F. (1990). *Judgment and decision-making.* Englewood Cliffs, NJ: Prentice-Hall.

Yukl, G. (1994), *Leadership in organizations* (3rd Edn). Englewood Cliffs, NJ: Prentice-Hall.

15

Effective Communication within the Organization

Gaston de Cock, Karel de Witte and Stef van Nieuwkerke

1 INTRODUCTION

Communication can be defined as the sending and receiving of messages by means of symbols. This definition covers a very broad field, at micro-, meso-, and macro-level. In the chapter that follows, the emphasis is placed on the meso-level: the organization. Following a discussion of the communication process, communication is considered as an element within the organizational climate. Research (De Witte & De Cock, 1987) has shown that the form, content, and direction of communication varies according to the type of organizational climate. The different organizational climate types will be described, together with the means of communication associated with them. We shall then support this theory with research data before presenting some conclusions.

2 CONSTITUENT ELEMENTS OF THE COMMUNICATION PROCESS

From the—simplified—diagram presented in Figure 15.1, showing the different elements that make up the communication process, communication at first sight appears to be a linear system. During the discussion of the individual elements, however, it will become clear that communication—particularly within an organizational context—is in fact a circular process.

2.1 The sender-encoder

Communication cannot exist without a sender. There can also be no communication if the sender does not adequately encode his message so that it can be sent via a particular channel. This applies both for face-to-face interaction and for other

FIGURE 15.1

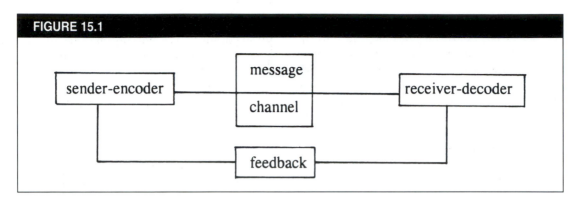

Communication diagram.

forms of communication such as letters, magazines, fax messages, and so on. For example, an information manager will encode his/her message in a different way when speaking to a senior manager than during a meeting with a team of programmers. If insufficient attention is paid during this encoding process to the receiver and/or if a form of language is used with which the receiver is insufficiently familiar, this will frequently lead to disruption of the communication process. Every sector of industry and commerce, every discipline—every individual, in fact— develop their own vocabulary; and, though this makes communication within that sector, discipline, or individual's own group easier, it also creates barriers for those outside the group (De Witte, 1981).

Sender and receiver do not communicate with each other directly, but via an intermediate process. This process uses a series of signs and symbols to represent the information or message that is to be communicated. The sender must thus ensure that his or her encoded message, once it has been decoded by the receiver, remains unchanged. This is only possible if the sender is able to "get under the skin" of the receiver and use signs and signals that have a meaning that is "shared" by both parties in the communication process. This term "shared meaning" is used by Weick (1987) to indicate that, in order for an organization to function well, the various members of that organization must jointly build up the meaning of words and practices used within it.

2.2 The message

The message is the stimulus sent by the sender to the receiver. The sender encodes the message using certain signals, so that it can be sent. The receiver then decodes these signals so that they convey a certain meaning.

As indicated already, an important precondition for effective communication is that sender and receiver have a series of shared experiences enabling them to allocate the same "shared meaning" to a given set of signals and symbols. However, as no two individuals ever have identical experiences, the language or system of symbols that they use will never have precisely the same meaning for both sender and receiver. Moreover, the meaning of signs and symbols can change for a single individual as a result of his or her own experiences. Many communication errors are due to incorrect interpretations of an encoded message.

Meaning is after all a relative concept, which is dependent on subjective interpretation. Berlo (1960) stated that "Meanings are in people, not in the message." As already indicated, we find the same ideas in the social constructivism of Weick (1987) and the kaleidoscope model based on it as devised by Bouwen and Salipante (1988).

The message dispatched by the sender may be a routine message or a unique message. Routine messages are commonly occurring messages, such as the canteen menu. Unique messages, on the other hand, occur much less frequently and for that specific are more susceptible to communication errors. These messages are frequently characterized by ambiguity, lack of time, and surprise. They often occur in the situation of innovation and/or where decisions and actions have to be taken rapidly. As a result, there are few if any shared experiences between sender and receiver, and this increases the chance that the interpretation of the signals will be influenced by personal emotions and assumptions.

With routine messages the chance that the communication act will fail is much smaller. These messages are more direct, logical, and contain few surprises. Sender and receiver have a whole series of shared experiences, so that adequate interpretation of the signs and signals is highly probable.

This distinction between routine and non-routine messages is of prime importance for the selection of the communication channel.

2.3 The channel
2.3.1 The different types of channel
The channel is the medium via which the message travels from sender to receiver. There are very many communication channels, and the sender is often free to choose which channel he wishes to use. A few obvious and frequently used channels are face-to-face interaction, telephone, email, letters, memos, fax messages, etc. However, not all channels provide the same information, or the same amount of information. The nature of the channel determines the quantity and the nature of the information which can pass along it, and thus influences the effectiveness of the communication. When choosing the channel, therefore, the desired objectives should be taken into account.

The various channels can be divided into two main categories, the *rich channels*, which permit direct feedback and where communication is circular in nature, and *poor channels*, where there is no possibility of direct feedback and communication is more linear. The rich channels can in turn be subdivided into channels where the sender is physically present during receipt of the message, and those where this is not the case.

Direct face-to-face interaction is the richest communication channel, because the sender is actually present and information can be processed via various physical senses. There is an oppor-

tunity for direct feedback, making this bidirectional channel ideal for in-depth and difficult discussions in which the emotional aspects of the message form an important part of the communication.

Interactive communication channels such as telephone, walkie-talkie, etc., have the advantage that they permit rapid feedback, though the receiver is not physically present here. Posture, eye contact, blushing, and innumerable other non-verbal signals therefore do not reach the receiver.

The "poor channels" can be subdivided into those where the message is directed personally to the receiver, and those where this is not the case. Personal letters, memos, reports, etc., are not directed at a wide audience by the sender, but at one individual receiver. The fax also belongs in this category. In the case of departmental memos, staff magazines, newspapers, magazines, radio, television, and other mass-communication media, this personal targeting is no longer present; these media are not aimed at one specific individual, but at a larger group of people or at a very wide audience.

Figure 15.2 shows the properties of the different categories in tabular form.

2.3.2 The choice of channel
The choice of channel plays an important role in the effectiveness of the communication process. Unfortunately, however, this choice is not always based on a logical decision. Earlier experiences, familiarity with a particular channel, and selective availability of certain channels are important factors.

However, some channels are more suitable than others for sending certain types of message. A distinction was made above between unique and routine messages, and between rich and poor communication channels. The most appropriate channel for unique communication is a rich channel such as face-to-face interaction. The poorer the channel, the greater the chance that errors will occur during interpretation of unique messages. A conflict between two managers, for example, is very difficult to resolve over the telephone; this is a situation that calls for the physical presence of both parties so that none of

FIGURE 15.2			
Very rich	Rich	Poor	Very poor
directed at one person	directed at one person	directed at one person	not directed at one person
feedback	feedback	no feedback	no feedback
receiver physically present	receiver not physically present	receiver not physically present	receiver not physically present

The various types of channel and their characteristics.

the non-verbal signals is missed. It is important when resolving such problems to be able to see whether one of the parties is angry, friendly, stubborn, tense, etc. If poorer communication channels are employed in such situations, many of the non-verbal, emotional signals are filtered out. This gives the impression that everything is under control, whereas this is not at all the case.

Routine messages often consist of statistical analyses, reports, conclusions, appointments, etc., in which emotional signals are superfluous and would tend to have a disruptive effect. Poorer communication channels such as letters, telephone, magazines, etc., are more suited to the sending of such messages. With routine messages of this nature, an excess of signs and signals such as occur during face-to-face communication would only cause confusion and lead to incorrect interpretations.

Figure 15.3 shows the interrelationship between message and channel.

2.3.3 *Development of new channels*

New channels are constantly being developed in order to optimize the effectiveness and efficiency of communication. Delays to urgent messages caused by sending through the post have become a thing of the past since the development of the fax, and email which can send a report or memo across the world in a matter of seconds. Efforts are also being made to reduce the need for managers to make time-consuming journeys by using "video conferencing". In addition, more and more use is being made of electronic communication and data-processing systems such as EDP (Electronic Data Processing) and MIS (Management Information Systems), which complement human communication and information-processing capacity and help accommodate its limitations.

However, it is not always easy to define what is the best way of using these new channels and systems; a great deal of comparative effectiveness research is needed in order to situate them within the framework of existing channels and to discover their strengths and weaknesses.

The increasing awareness of the need to use rich channels for unique messages has led to an attempt to enrich the purely verbal contact via the telephone by adding a visual component. This is "video conferencing", or "direct interactive audio-

FIGURE 15.3		
	Message	
rich channel	communication problem: too many signals	effective communication
poor channel	effective communication	communication problem: too few signals

What type of channel is most suited to what type of message? From Lengel and Daft (1988).

visual communication", which at first sight has much in common with direct face-to-face interaction.

Little research has been carried out into video conferencing, though a few researchers have studied its effect on the communication process within organizations (Romahn, Kellner, & Mühlbach, 1985; Schwarz & Tilse, 1980; Wabbels, 1986). To date, however, very little attention has been paid to the effectiveness of the use of this channel for various types of message, though comparative effectiveness research has been carried out in which video conferencing was compared with face-to-face interaction and telephoning. Field studies carried out by Antoni, Bungard, Schultz-Gambard, and Kattentidt (1987) revealed that during video conferencing around 70% of the subjects experience sound problems, whereas 85% have difficulties with eye contact. In a laboratory study (Antoni et al., 1987) the same authors found that, compared with face-to-face interaction, video conferencing gives a less positive perception of the interaction partners and is focused more on the problem than on the interaction. In addition, it was found that compromises are reached more quickly during video conferencing and that there is less subjective certainty in the perception of the other partners. Video conferencing also requires less time. Another study (Williams, 1987) found that the visual component does not add a great deal in comparison with normal interaction by telephone. This author concludes that face-to-face interaction is preferable to video conferencing for important and unique forms of communication.

One of the possible interpretations of the disaster some years ago involving the space shuttle "Challenger" is that the audio-visual communication system used by NASA inadequately communicated the non-verbal fear signals of the Morton-Thiokol engineers regarding the launching of the shuttle during bad weather (Weick, 1987). Because these emotional signals were filtered out, everything appeared in order, whereas in fact this was not the case at all.

In short, video conferencing can be situated at the same level as telephoning. In spite of the addition of the visual component, video confer-

ence does not succeed in reaching the level of face-to-face communication.

In the area of information processing, too, the explosion in the use of computers has led to the use of ever more advanced communication systems. As a result, an increasing amount of information is available to support the decision-making process within organizations. In small organizations the entire process of acquiring, processing, and selecting information is carried out by a manager, possibly with the assistance of a few rudimentary technological aids. In large-scale organizations, by contrast, the complexity both of the internal functioning of the organization and of its external environment is so great that the use of highly developed technology for the acquisition, processing, organization, and selection of information is necessary. In such cases we refer to the development of an information technology.

This information technology consists of two elements: electronic communication and human communication. The first of these incorporates both Electronic Data Processing (EDP) and Management Information Systems (MIS). Traditionally, these electronic and human communication forms are seen as each other's antithesis and as being mutually exclusive. Though supporters of EDP and MIS regard electronic communication as *the* solution to communication problems within organizations, critics see these systems rather as being responsible for the decline of the human aspect within the organization. According to them, the failure of most computer-controlled management communication is due to the associated reduction in the human element in that communication. Supporters of computer-controlled communication systems, on the other hand, are more inclined to attribute the problems arising from MIS and EDP to unwillingness and lack of understanding on the part of the employees.

Seen from the perspective of the communication system, such a division between these two forms of communication (and the flurry of arguments surrounding them) is not only undesirable, but actually harmful. Seen from this point of view, the two forms of communication are complementary processes, two equally valuable elements of the same phenomenon, namely communication within organizations, with the cognitive limitations of the human brain being supplemented by EDP and MIS. Efforts therefore need to be directed towards integrating the two forms of communication, each of which can make its own contribution to the optimum functioning of the organization. Little general research has been carried out into the demarcation of the territory for each of the communication forms. The correct application of each form depends on the specific nature of the organization.

2.4 The receiver

The receiver decodes the signals received and attaches a meaning to them. The receiver too, however, has his/her own background, own experiences, own place within the organization, and own vocabulary. If, as stated earlier, more than once, the sender fails to take account of these factors, the communication will frequently not be effective. This can be corrected where rich channels are used, in which the receiver has an opportunity to enhance the effectiveness of the communication through feedback. In the case of poor channels, however, where there is no possibility of direct feedback, improving the effectiveness of the communication is much more difficult.

2.5 Enhancing the effectiveness of the communication through feedback

2.5.1 The functions of feedback at individual level

A condition for good cooperation within an organization is good and, particularly, effective communication. Effective communication is only achieved when the receiver interprets the message in the same way as the sender intended. The receiver can only interpret the message correctly if he or she understands its content, i.e. is familiar with the signs used, attaches the same meaning as the sender to these signs, and understands how the message should be interpreted—what the intention of the sender is.

Watzlawick (1979) speaks here of the "report" and "command" aspects of communication. The report aspect of a message transmits information and is thus synonymous in human communication with the content of the message. It may cover anything that is communicable, irrespective of whether the information in question is true or untrue, correct or incorrect, or indeterminable. The command aspect, by contrast, refers to the way in which a message must be interpreted and thus, in the final analysis, to the relationship between the communicating individuals.

For example, the messages "It is important that you close the door behind you", and "Close the door" have approximately the same content (report aspect) but clearly define different relationships. However, relationships are seldom defined in a carefully considered way. As the relationship becomes more spontaneous and healthy, the relationship aspect in the communication process is pushed more and more into the background. Conversely, "unhealthy" relationships are characterized by a continual struggle concerning the nature of the relationship, whereas the content aspect of the communication becomes less and less important.

Feedback can serve to clarify the content, for example, when the receiver asks the meaning of a word, or to clarify the relationship between sender and receiver. These two roles of feedback are discussed in that which follows.

If someone is asked what they feel about the use of an overhead projector during the teaching of a course, though they do not know what an overhead projector is, the communication will be ineffective. A good response in such a case may be a request for an explanation. Explaining the meaning of the term "overhead projector" will make the question clearer and enable the person asked to give a more adequate response, and this in turn will enable the communication to proceed more smoothly. In this case we can say that feedback serves to clarify the content.

We should like at this juncture to attempt to clarify the meaning of giving feedback at relationship level using a model named after its devisers, Joseph Luft and Harry Ingham: the JOHARI-window (1970). This model, which has four parts, is shown schematically in Figure 15.4.

- The *free space* is the part of the personality that is known to both the person him/herself and to others. For example, an individual

FIGURE 15.4

	known to yourself	unknown to yourself
known to others	free space	blind spot
not known to others	hidden area	unknown self

The JOHARI-window.

knows that he or she has difficulty in putting thoughts into words, while others notice this in his/her unclear formulations.

- The *blind spot* is an area of behaviour patterns which are apparent to others but of which the individual is not aware. A person's voice, for example, may sometimes sound irritating to others, without the speaker being aware of this.
- The *hidden area* is the part of the personality that is known to the individual him/herself, but not to others. For example, an individual may have difficulty saying something positive about somebody else, though the other person is not aware of this.
- The *unknown self*, finally, is the area of the personality that is not known either to the individual or to other people. For example, neither the person nor other people know that the reason for his/her silence in groups is due to the fact that he or she was not allowed to speak at home as a child. This part therefore refers to the person's subconscious.

Providing feedback on the way participants per-

ceive each other in the communication situation and the reactions that this generates enlarges the "free space" of all concerned, in two ways. Firstly, receiving feedback about aspects of our behaviour of which we are not aware enlarges the "free space" and reduces the "blind spot". Secondly, feedback can also reduce the "hidden area". After all, the giving of feedback not only provides information about the person for whom the feedback is intended, but also about the person who provides the feedback. This is represented schematically in Figure 15.5.

De Cock (1976) reports how the JOHARI window provides a simple demonstration of the way in which feedback can enrich contacts. The "free space" is continually enlarged and the contact becomes deeper. The model also demonstrates how feedback from others is necessary in order to increase our self-knowledge, and how we can reveal ourselves to others through openness. Such contacts can be enriching both for the two partners concerned and for the organization to which they belong. Golembiewski and Carrigan (1970, 1973) point out that not every contact is automatically enriching for both partners. The

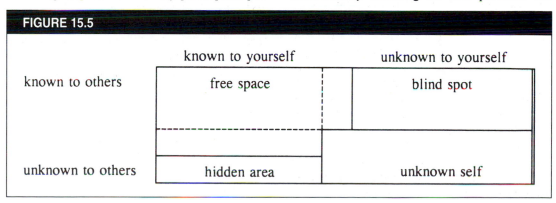

FIGURE 15.5

	known to yourself	unknown to yourself
known to others	free space	blind spot
unknown to others	hidden area	unknown self

The JOHARI-window, after use of feedback.

conditions for this are: safe atmosphere, trust, openness, and receptiveness.

2.5.2 The functions of feedback at organizational level

If the preceding basic conditions have not been met, the giving of feedback will be perceived as a loss of information and power, with the result that little or no feedback will be given thereafter. At organizational level this results in an inadequate flow of information, in turn causing developments to progress more slowly and with greater difficulty. We shall expand on this argument in more detail later.

In developing the feedback system it is important to take account of the link between information and power. In an organizational context, in particular, the possession of information means power. By passing on this information to others, the sender at the same time passes on this power. One-way traffic of this sort can be perceived as threatening by the sender, who may then be inclined to withhold his/her information. The simple feedback system, in which the receiver provides feedback on the information he or she has received, does not resolve this threat. A complete feedback cycle takes this into account by adding two new elements to the system, namely the giving and using of information. This feedback cycle, which is shown diagrammatically in Figure 15.6, makes it possible to discover communication difficulties.

Problems can manifest themselves in each of the four steps indicated in the figure. It is therefore important to analyse the potential problems in each step.

1. First it is necessary to examine whether the sender is actually giving information. It sometimes occurs that the sender uses lots of words, but deliberately keeps the message vague, ambiguous, unclear, and incomplete. This means that in fact no information is given and that the sender is not running the risk of giving away his/her power, which is linked to the information. In this case the reason for the breakdown in communication lies with the sender.

2. If information *is* given, it is important to ascertain whether the receiver is actually receiving the information. The receiver's receptiveness may be restricted by intellectual or emotional factors. He or she may not understand what the information is about, or may perceive the information as threatening and not admit it to his/her emotional world. The problem here lies with the receiver.

3. If the receiver receives the information he simultaneously receives the power linked to it. This can be perceived as very threatening by the sender, who may therefore shut off the information flow. In order to resolve this it is not enough for the receiver to provide feedback regarding the information received to the sender. It is more important that the receiver uses the information received and thus enriches it. In this way the receiver develops new information, together with the power that is attached to it.

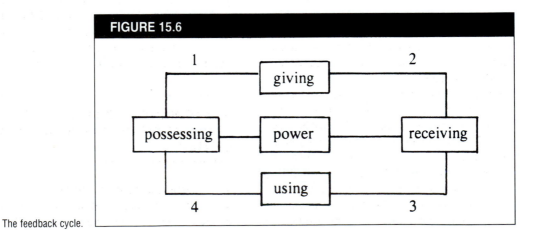

FIGURE 15.6

The feedback cycle.

4. Once the receiver has enriched the information received, the sender will expect to be provided with the new, enriched information. In this way the sender will see that the receiver is willing to enter into genuine cooperation.

This completes the circle and means that there has been an interchange of both information and power. This cycle could be termed a "participative feedback" system. If this can be achieved, the result will be fruitful cooperation within the organization.

3 THE ORGANIZATION BASED ON COMMUNICATION

Our society is made up of organizations, in which each of us spends a great portion of life—school, the company, the youth club, the sports club, and so on. The structure of an organization is very closely related to the forms of communication within it. As early as 1938, Barnard stated that: "In any exhaustive theory of organisation, communication should occupy a central place because the structure, extensiveness and scope of organisations are almost entirely determined by communication techniques." In 1957, Simon powerfully summarized the essence of Barnard's statement once again: "The question to be asked of any administrative process is: 'How does it influence the decisions of the individual?'. Without communication the answer must always be: 'It does not influence them at all!'" De Cock (1976a) defines an organization as "a whole of interdependent parts, in which each part has its own function geared to the objective of the whole, situated in a broader environment".

It is clear from these views of organizations that an organization cannot exist without communication. The objective of the whole must be clear to all the interdependent parts. These mutually independent parts must be coordinated in such a way that the objective of the whole can be achieved. Through communication, everyone knows his role, place, and task within the organization and the different parts of that organization are adequately coordinated. To use the words of Hicks (1972): "When communication stops, organized activity ceases to exist. Individual, uncoordinated activity returns."

There is a great difference, however, between communication within organizations and communication between individuals. Communication within organizations is determined by a series of factors that are different from those applying outside (Katz & Kahn, 1978). Studies carried out before 1966 were usually based on the assumption that communication was independent of the social structure within which it took place. The research methods used at that time were not suited to discovering the effects of social structure—mainly because most experiments and analyses were carried out on the basis of the individual as the central point or processing unit. But an atomistic approach such as this takes no account whatsoever of the relational structure of organizational communication. Communication within organizations is a bidirectional, transactional occurrence, rather than a unidirectional act as the majority of oversimplified communication models would have us believe (Rogers & Bhowmik, 1971).

Recent research and literature (Peters & Waterman, 1982; De Witte & De Cock, 1987), however, reveals that the social and relational structure of organizations is dependent on the organizational climate. This implies that communication, too, in terms of both form and content, is closely related to the organizational climate.

In the following section we shall first explain what we mean by "organizational climate" and the different types we identify. We shall then discuss the basic characteristics of each type and show how the form and content of communication varies according to the prevailing climate type.

4 COMMUNICATION FROM THE PERSPECTIVE OF ORGANIZATIONAL CLIMATE

4.1 Organizational climate

We define the organizational climate as "the collective perception of the relatively stable value orientations within the organization as a whole, which influences the behaviour of the members of that organization as a function of the organizational effectiveness and which is expressed descriptively by the members of the organization" (De Witte & De Cock, 1987). In other words, the organizational climate is the collective perception of the organization (See also Chapter 6 of this volume of the *Handbook*).

The relevance of the term "organizational climate" should no longer be questioned. There has been a sharp increase in the number of articles dealing with this topic in management journals in recent years, and the literature is describing more and more cases of failed "strategy implementations" because the climate needed for the strategy in question was not present within the organization. Experience and research have for some time bolstered the conviction of the importance of the organizational climate. Management methods such as concentration, quality circles, and management by objectives can only thrive in a certain organizational climate.

The model we have developed, and the measurement instrument based on it, the VOKIPO (Organizational Climate Index for Profit Organizations) (De Cock, Bouwen, De Witte & De Visch, 1984) enable a diagnosis to be made of the organizational climate. Based on our own research and data from other studies, we can distinguish between four basic types of climate. Two bipolar dimensions emerged from our study:

1. flexibility–control
2. individual-oriented–organization-oriented

Relating these two dimensions to each other produces four climate types:

1. supportive climate
2. innovative climate
3. respect for rules
4. goal-oriented information flows.

This is shown schematically in Figure 15.7.

4.2 The four organizational climate types and the associated method of communication

In this section we give a general description of the four types of organizational climate, focusing our attention particularly on the method of communication within each climate type.

Each climate has its own character. Just as the style of management varies in each of the four climate types, so each type has its own method of communication and its own consultative structures. The boundaries between the different climate types are not absolute; mixed climate forms—and mixed communication types—will in

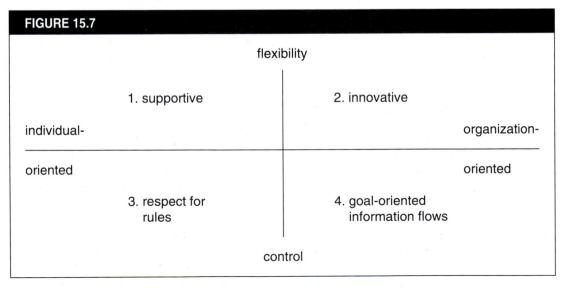

FIGURE 15.7

The four organizational climate types.

practice be encountered more often than the "pure" types.

A wide-ranging study carried out in a number of hospitals (De Witte, 1985) revealed that both the functioning and communication of the management and the use of consultative structures vary according to the predominant climate type.

As regards the functioning and communication of the management, the members of the management team were asked to note all their activities during a period of 14 days. The study concentrated mainly on the functioning and communication of the managers, with the chief aim of ascertaining whether any differences could be established in the activities of hospital managers as a function of the dominant organizational climate type. As regards the consultative structures, one of the most important problems within hospitals is coordination; this is achieved partly through information transfer, which itself is partially formalized in consultative structures. The hospitals were asked to make a list of all formal organizational consultative and information channels. As with the functioning of the managers, the aim was to examine the relationship between organizational climate and consultative structures.

The findings of this study, carried out in a specific type of organization, were confirmed in other studies (albeit less large in scale and not published) conducted both in manufacturing companies and service-providing organizations such as banks (Catteeuw, 1987).

4.2.1 Supportive climate

By a supportive climate we mean an organization focused on the individual, in which the flexibility is directed inwards. Decisions grow in informal contacts, and there is a tendency to postpone decisions that are necessary for the organization but that have a radical impact on the lives of those affected by them. Relational aspects prevail above task-oriented factors in conflicts. Attention for the personnel is reflected in well laid-out working areas and outside work activities. Newcomers need a good deal of time to get to grips with this informal structure and to acquire their own position within it. The style of leadership is focused on people and relationships. Individuals who attach importance to social contact and good relationships will feel most at home in such an organization. Characteristic of these organizations is the relative lack of structure. There is a danger that this climate type begins to take on more the character of a club than an organization. Human involvement is of central importance, but is focused more on the person as an individual than as a member of a group.

Hospitals where a predominantly supportive climate prevails are characterized by the high level of importance attached to informal and incidental contacts. Formal meetings take place only occasionally. Anyone can approach anyone else at any moment in order to make arrangements. Little information is put down on paper: Verbal notifications are sufficient. The direction of communication in contacts tends to be bottom-up, with the managers listening attentively to what is happening. Decisions are taken more on an individual basis than during meetings. Conflicts are first discussed with the individuals concerned, and only later in the group.

As regards the consultation process, it is difficult to speak of a formal consultative structure; information is passed on verbally and informally. Meetings also have a social function. In one of the hospitals studied it was found that a certain meeting was not achieving the intended objective. In spite of this, the management team hesitated to call off the meeting: In their opinion it was difficult to do away with this opportunity for people to meet. The powers and objectives of the meeting were unclear, and there was virtually no structured or systematic flow of information.

4.2.2 Innovative climate

Organizations that are focused on the objectives of the organization but whose flexibility is focused externally can be classified as the innovative climate type. These organizations are characterized by a decentralized and delegational way of working. There is little monitoring from above, but rather a belief that the members of the organization will dedicate themselves to achieving the organization's objectives. There is great pressure on those in the organization to respond rapidly to changes. The speed with which projects are launched means it is necessary now and then to ease off on the accelerator. Employees have a feeling of freedom and scope to develop their potential within the organization or department. The structure is a network; the influential power lies at the "nodes" and is based on know-how and skill. Conflicts are situations from which to learn and are to be solved in consultation.

The danger for this type of organization is a degeneration into chaos: A lot happens, but there is little control. The style of leadership is both task and relationship oriented. The personnel policy is geared towards achieving synergy, resulting in interaction between people and the organization.

In those hospitals that are characterized by a mainly innovative climate, the managers make a round of the hospital, recalling the idea of "management by wandering around" as coined by Peters and Waterman (1982). When problems have to be discussed, they are more inclined to visit the employee concerned than to summon him or her to their office. And yet this does not mean that managers get involved in the daily work; powers are delegated. There is a high level of flexibility regarding their presence in the hospital. A nursing manager, for example, may not arrive until the afternoon, but remains until late into the evening so as to be able to come into contact with the night staff. Communication, both in meetings and at individual level, criss-crosses the organization in all directions (with a view to fulfilling tasks). This communication is two-way. Important information is passed on verbally, discussed immediately, and confirmed later in writing. Conflicts are discussed immediately in a group context.

Discussions with external bodies are often conducted by different managers jointly. In other types of organizational climate, there is often only one manager directly involved in the discussions.

As regards the consultative structures, the composition of the meetings is more mixed and lateral than in the other climate types. By way of example, a particular hospital has a building committee, of which the nursing manager is also a member; in a "respect for rules" climate type, only the general and civil managers would sit on this committee. This lateral or mixed composition of the meetings is also found at the lower levels, where more doctors are involved in all manner of meetings. Powers are more delegated, enabling more decisions to be taken at lower levels. There is a matrix structure, a network of horizontal and vertical meetings. Task-oriented information is passed on via written information channels.

4.2.3 Respect for rules

An organization focused on the individual and on the control of individual behaviour is a climate type characterized by respect for rules. Order and systematic working are important in this climate. Balance is achieved by the development of a hierarchical structure. Authority is vested in established procedures and clearly defined powers. There is a strong degree of centralization.

The danger for such a climate type is ossification, whereby upholding rules and procedures is more important than the achievement of objectives. The style of leadership is procedure-oriented. Attempts are made to avoid conflicts through regulations. When new problems arise, new rules first have to be worked out to deal with them. The personnel policy protects the workers by establishing a set of rules. People with a strong need for security feel safe in such a climate.

Hospitals with a "respect for rules" climate type are largely characterized by a fixed division of daily tasks. Compared with the other organizational climate types, managers spend a lot of time alone in their own offices. Contacts take place within their own department. These contacts often consist of the passing on or requesting of information. If horizontal contacts are present they are either informative contacts or advisory formulations, which are later ratified or rejected by the management. In contrast to the three other climate types there are fewer contacts per day, but these contacts last longer. Problems are worked through logically and systematically. A great deal of information flows to the management, which makes the decisions. Management meetings therefore last longer (four to five hours per week) than in the other hospitals. This method of working means that the management is psychologically less accessible to the members of the organization. External discussions are conducted largely from the basis of the manager's own role within the organization.

As regards the consultative structures, meetings take place within a hierarchical structure that has much in common with the "linking pin" structure described by Likert (1967). This entails a vertical composition of the meetings, whereby each manager meets only with his own subordinates. There is a clear demarcation of authority, though decisions regarding implementation can be taken at lower level. New elements, decisions, and policy lines are referred to the management meeting. In terms of structure, there is strong centralization, Finally, guidelines are issued via a variety of information channels.

4.2.4 Goal-oriented information flow

An organization which is focused on the objectives of the organization and on the control of the means of achieving those objectives is characterized as a climate of goal-oriented information flow.

This organization attaches great importance to the objectives and to the means and power to realize them. The manager is the pivotal figure. Together with the staff, he or she aims to achieve maximum rationality, taking into account internal environmental factors and the members of the organization.

The style of leadership is predominantly task oriented. In conflict situations, the manager forces his/her solution through, and issues guidelines linked to the objectives. People are expected to adapt to the organization. Those who contribute to the achievement of the objectives are rewarded. People who seek recognition and power feel at home in this type of organization.

The danger for this type of climate is a narrow scope perspective; by being too strongly focused on the achievement of objectives, it is possible to lose sight of external factors.

Managers of hospitals of this type make contacts with a view to the achievement of the organizational objectives. To this end, they issue guidelines to subordinates; in contrast to the "respect for rules" climate type, a hierarchical level is often bypassed here. Managers often concern themselves with the everyday activities of the hospital, and have regular contact with family and patient groups.

As regards the consultative structures, there are lots of meetings, although it is difficult to determine the exact relationships between the different meetings. Some managers sit in on a number of different meetings, thus in effect issuing advice to themselves. The structures are not logically built up, though there is extensive written information. The consultative structure is focused, on the one hand, on the patient group, but, on the other hand, on the top echelons in the organization. In order to fathom the organizational structures it is necessary to understand the status of the people within the organization.

4.2.5 Conclusion

The descriptions above show clearly that there is a link between the type of organizational climate and the way in which managers spend their time. The way in which people communicate with each other and with their subordinates depends on the prevailing organizational climate. To date, analyses of the way in which managers spend their time have been performed on an individual basis, with no link being made with the organizational climate. Our study, however, shows that this is necessary for a thorough understanding of the functioning of managers.

The form of communication and the way in which information flows take place within the organization are also related to the organizational climate type. When setting up new consultative structures, therefore, an analysis should first be carried out of the prevailing organizational climate.

5 GENERAL CONCLUSIONS

Communication appears to be of vital importance for organizations. Indeed, without communication there can be no organization. The development of new information technologies creates new forms of communication. In order to assess the true value of these it will be necessary to carry out a good deal of comparative research. We have shown that the proper functioning of organizations demands a good deal of attention for feedback, in which the aspect of "power" should be central.

The form, content, and direction of the various forms and channels of communication are closely related to the prevailing organizational climate. When devising new consultative structures or changing existing forms of consultation, analysis of the prevailing and the required organizational climate is necessary.

In this chapter we have thrown some light on communication within organizations. We hope that we have provided a number of important frames of reference that will help to provide an insight into the effectiveness of this communication.

REFERENCES

Antoni, C., Bungard, W., Schultz-Gambard, J., & Kattentidt, H. (1987). *The impact of videoconferencing*. Paper presented at the Third West European Congress of work and organization, Leuven.

Barnard, C.I. (1966). *The functions of the executive* (17th Edn). Cambridge, MA: Harvard University Press.

Berlo, D.K. (1960). *The process of communication.* New York: Holt, Rinehart & Winston.

Bouwen, R., & Salipante, P. (1988). *A kaleidoscope model for conflict resolution.* Unpublished paper, K.U. Leuven.

Catteeuw, F. (1987). *Organisatieklimaat en personeelsbeleid in profit organisaties: Literatuurstudie en exploratief onderzoek.* [Organisational climate and Human Resources Management in profit organisations: a study of the literature and an exploratory research.] Unpublished dissertation. Faculty of Psychology and Educational Sciences, University of Leuven.

De Cock, G. (1976a). *Organisatiepsychologie, psychologie van organisaties in ontwikkeling.* [Organisational psychology: The psychology of organizations in development.] Leuven: Acco.

De Cock, G. (1976b). *Er hapert iets. Praktijk en theorie van organisatieontwikkeling.* [Something goes wrong: Practice and theory of organizational development]. Antwerp/Amsterdam: De Nederlandsche Boekhandel.

De Cock, G., Bouwen, R., De Witte, K., & De Visch, J. (1984, 1985, 1987). *Organisatieklimaat—en cultuur. Theorie en praktische toepassing van de organisatieklimaatindex voor profit organisaties (OKIPO) en de verkorte vorm (VOKIPO).* [Organizational climate and organizational culture: Theory and practical guidelines for the Index for Organizational Climate in Profit Organizations (OKIPO) and its short version (VOKIPO).] Leuven: Acco.

De Witte, K. (1981). Organigram en inspraak van het personeel [Organogram and concertation of the personnel]. In *Communicatie en informatie in verzorgingsinstellingen* (pp.125–135). Brussels: Licap s.v.

De Witte, K. (1985). *Organisatieklimaat in ziekenhuizen. Studie over het verband van het organisatieklimaat met het functioneren van de direkties en de overlegstrukturen.* [Organizational climate in hospitals: A study of the relation between organizational climate and the functioning of the directors and the consultative structures]. Unpublished doctoral thesis (Promoter Prof. G. de Cock), K.U. Leuven, Faculty of Psychology and Educational Sciences.

De Witte, K., & De Cock, G. (1987). Organisatieklimaat en samenwerking in de gezondheidszorg [Organizational climate and cooperation in health care organizations]. *Tijdschrift voor Geneeskunde 43*, 24.

Golembiewski, R., & Carrigan, S. (1970). Planned change in organisational style based on the laboratory approach. *Administrative Science Quarterly, 1,* 79–93.

Golembiewski, R., & Carrigan, S. (1973). Planned change through laboratory methods. *Training and Development Journal, 3*, 18–27.

Hicks, H.G. (1972). *The management of organisations: A systems and human resources approach.* New York: McGraw-Hill Book Company.

Katz, D., & Kahn, R.L. (1978). *The social psychology of organisations.* New York: John Wiley.

Lengel, R.H., & Daft, R.L. (1988). The selection of communication media as an executive skill. *The Academy of Management Executive, 2.*

Likert, R. (1967). *The human organisation.* New York: McGraw-Hill.

Luft, J. (1970). Group processes: An introduction to group dynamics. In R. Golembiewski & Blumberg (Eds.), *Sensitivity training and the laboratory approach.* New York: National Press.

Peters, T.J., & Waterman, R.H. (1982). *In search of Excellence.* New York: Harper & Row.

Rogers, E.M., & Bhowmik, D.K. (1971). Homophily—hetrophily: Relational concepts for communication research. *Public Opinion Quarterly, 34.*

Romahn, G., Kellner, B., & Mühlbach, L. (1985). Bildfernsprechkonferenz. Erste Erfahrungen mit einem Multipoint-Experimental system. *Netz Archive, 38, 10.*

Schwarz, E., & Tilse, V. (1980). Die Benutzerzufriedenheit mit 12 verschiedenen Videoconferenzsystemen und einer Audioconferenz im Vergleich zu normalen Konferenzen. *Netz Archiv, 5.*

Simon, H.A. (1957). *Administrative behavior* (2nd Edn). New York: Macmillan Company.

Wabbels, V. (1986). Praktische Erfahrungen mit Videokonferenzen. *Netz Archiv, 40, 1–2.*

Watzlawick, P. (1979). *Pragmatische aspecten der menselijke communicatie.* Deventer: Van Loghum Slaterus.

Weick, K.E. (1987). Organisational culture as source of high reliability. *California Management Review,* Winter.

Williams, E. (1987). Experimental comparison of face to face and mediated communication: A review. *Psychological Bulletin 84,5.*

16

Industrial Democratization and Industrial Relations

J.H. Erik Andriessen

1 INTRODUCTION

Workers' participation and codetermination within industrial organizations takes numerous forms. Large differences exist both among and within countries. The historical growth of these different forms has been culturally determined, within the wider context of general industrial relations. In the course of time, and under the influence of all kinds of circumstances, agreements and laws have emerged that regulate these industrial relations. In one country these may lead to a fairly uncomplicated structure: In the UK, industry is largely accustomed to the concept of union representation within the firm, the "shop steward". In other countries, such as the Netherlands, industrial democracy has adopted a wider variety of forms.

The terms "participation", "industrial democracy" and "codetermination" have so far been used as if they meant the same thing. They are not identical, but they do have the same core intention: They are all concerned with involving employees in their organization's decision-making processes.

The most common term is "participation". The literature apparently employs this term to mean both "present at" and "having influence on"; however, this can create confusion, and the two meanings are better segregated. One can "participate" in the labour market simply by having a job, but within the terms of this chapter participation is taken to mean taking a part in the decision-making process of an organization. This part may take many forms, in job consultations, in the corridors, in *ad hoc* committees, in a works council, or through union negotiations. Such forms of participation give employees a certain *voice* in organizational decision-making. Nevertheless, the term merely indicates the possibility of being present, of being able to say something or contribute something. However this does not automatically signify that employees thereby have a real *influence* on the decisions that are ultimately taken. This actual influence depends on numerous conditions, such as the availability of information and the possession of certain powers.

The concept of *industrial democratization* refers particularly, though not exclusively, to the development of institutionalized forms of consultation within work organizations. It is practically synonymous with the term "codetermination" as defined by Lammers (1965): *"forms of consultation, held on all sides to be legitimate, whereby subordinates influence the decisions taken by superiors"*. The term codetermination has the advantage of being less specifically associated with industrial enterprises; it is just as applicable to other work areas such as hospitals, governmental, and welfare organizations.

The term "industrial democracy", in particular, excited dispute during the 1960s and 1970s. Some held that the term only applied to situations where the workers constituted the highest authority in the enterprise (otherwise known as "workers' self-management"), as was then the case in (former) Yugoslavian workers' councils. This standpoint reflected the desire for complete equality of influence of all those involved in the decisions of work organizations. However, it is more fruitful to speak of a greater or lesser degree of participation, codetermination, and democracy, depending on the degree of involvement in decision-making. This degree of involvement varies; the formal steps of this "codetermination ladder" are often expressed as follows:

- the right to information;
- the right to advise;
- the right to an equal voice in consultations;
- the right of veto;
- the right to take independent decisions.

With regard to the question of the degree to which codetermination and influence are desirable in a given situation, this depends partly on the norms and values held by those involved and partly on practical experience.

In this introduction I have tried to make four issues clear:

1. There are many, very disparate forms of codetermination.
2. One must make a clear distinction between the formal aspects of codetermination and the actual influence.
3. In this document concepts such as industrial democracy and codetermination refer to the institutionalized (that is, the more formal) forms of worker involvement.

4. We are dealing with concepts and processes whose nature is dynamic and gradual: Codetermination is not a question of "all or nothing", but one of "here rather more, there rather less".

The goals, forms, and practices of codetermination will be discussed in the following paragraphs, preceded by an overview of Dutch industrial relations. This discussion is arranged according to the scheme set out in Figure 16.1.

After a review of the motives and values at stake in codetermination (section 2), the wider context of industrial relations is outlined (section 3). There follows a short overview of the various codetermination strategies and structures encountered in Europe (section 4). Sections 5 and 6 give closer attention to the forms predominating in the Netherlands. These first include works councils in the profit sector and analogous bodies, in government and the non-profit sectors. Union work in industry, and a number of specific forms of enterprise such as production cooperatives, are also considered. Sections 7 and 8 contain the results of national and international studies of the actual functioning and effects of representative bodies in particular. The

FIGURE 16.1

national culture
socio-economic system
(paragraph 3)

parties, visions,
industrial relations
(paragraph 2.3)

legislation, rights
structures
(paragraphs 4, 5, 6)

conditions
(paragraph 9)   functioning of the
codetermining body

effects
(paragraphs 7, 8)

Elements of the codetermination debate.

closing section concludes that a fairly stable trend towards further industrial democratization can be discerned. Although the influence of employees on affairs in companies cannot be called pervasive, representative bodies nevertheless play a substantial role, provided a number of conditions are met. One should neither lose sight of the wider context of European developments, the broader perspective of industrial relations in general, and the desire being shown by more professionally oriented employees for direct participation. When these developments are taken into account it becomes clear that future codetermination may well be an even more diverse undertaking than it is already. It also becomes apparent that commercial internationalization forms a threat to codetermination.

2 WHY CODETERMINATION?

2.1 Motives and aims

We may ask ourselves why codetermination is desirable or necessary in the first place. Do employees really want to be involved in everything? Does an enterprise do better with a works council than without? Discussions and conflicts related with codetermination reveal that different motives and aims are at work. Such motives and

aims are variously accorded to individual employees, to the management, or to the union movement: I speak here advisedly of "attributed" motives. Others sometimes expect individual employees to want this kind of influence and responsibility, when this enthusiasm is not always actually shared by the employees concerned. Managers are sometimes urged to believe that codetermination is constructive to the business, while the managers themselves are (rightly or wrongly) apprehensive. Table 16.1 lists six important motives.

Besides these six aims of democratization *per se*, other arguments may play a role in discussions on the justification for certain participatory procedures; for instance, management might support the idea of a works council because it expects it to neutralize the influence of trade unions.

1. *Improved business results due to the full employment of human resources and workforce motivation.* This motive is based on the idea that democratization can make a positive contribution towards the effectiveness and efficiency of the enterprise. According to this argument, participation leads to qualitatively better decision-making, because use is based on all the skills and knowledge available. Moreover, it is supposed that codetermination improves identification with the organization and increases confidence in its

---

TABLE 16.1

1. Motives to do with business administration
improved business results due to the full employment of available skills and the motivation of the workforce

2. Psychological motives
control of one's own situation; personal growth

3. Ethical motives
full human dignity; justice

4. Political motives
redistribution of power; defence of workers' interests

5. Sociological motives
the need for "countervailing power"

6. Societal motives
industrial democracy as a learning process for society

Motives for, and aims of, industrial democratization.

management, so that employees are better motivated and accept decisions more readily. Commitment and motivation, and the improved business results associated with them, are also the aims of financial participation amongst employees (see section 6.2).

2. *Control and development.* According to this argument, modern society is increasingly well educated and therefore emancipated. People increasingly want to direct their own destinies; they want to be responsible for their own situations and to have jobs that allow them to develop as individuals. According to the power–distance reduction theory (Mulder, 1977), people are inclined (by nature or as the result of circumstance) to strive for power. Humanistic psychology stresses the need to develop human qualities as far as possible. Such motives, incidentally, support the need for autonomy in particular, and for the ability to influence one's own work situation.

3. *Full human dignity.* This motive arises from the vision, particularly shared by Christians, that a mature human being is accountable for his or her actions. People should have a say on their situation, not so much because they want it, but because otherwise they cannot be responsible. This view sees co-responsibility, and the collective involvement of employees and employers, as of important value.

4. *Redistribution of power.* In this line of thought, democratization exists to serve not the interests of individual growth or organizational efficiency ("functional" democratization) but the fundamental redistribution of power within the enterprise ("structural" democratization). This redistribution means that the interests of the workers are brought more into balance with the interests of shareholders and of management. One consequence of this can also be that profits are divided differently. *In extremo* this can mean that workers, or their representatives, should exercise the highest authority: This is known as "workers' self-management".

5. *Countervailing power.* "Power corrupts; absolute power corrupts absolutely." In this view, organizations and society as a whole suffer if power is centralized and uncensured. It is therefore useful and beneficial for society and for institutions within that society if parties can oversee each other and, if necessary, reverse excessive imbalances of power. In other words, though this does not mean that employees should have a permanent say in all matters, in principle they should be able to mobilize enough power to provide a counterbalance.

6. *A school for society.* This motive is based on the hypothesis that employees confronted with disputes, negotiations, and the processes of democratic decision-making will learn from these experiences and be better equipped to exercise their civil rights elsewhere in society.

2.2 Basic perspectives on participation and organization

Closer examination reveals that these different motives are often based on different views about organization and society. An important distinction can be made between a vision in which an organization is seen as an integrated social *system*, and a vision that argues from the perspectives of the various *parties* to the organization. In the first, emphasis is laid on concepts such as integration and efficiency (see motive 1); much is made of *participation* in the sense of involvement and motivation, and much attention is paid to the question of whether democratization can be squared with efficiency and profitability. Such a vision is often referred to as a "*consultation model*" and in practice it gives rise to forms of direct and financial participation rather than to powerful roles for representative bodies.

In the second vision, it is the interests and aims of the *different individuals and groups* that comes to the fore. *Democratization* is the preferred term, and attention is focused on the opportunities for less empowered employees to give form to their own plans and aspirations. This approach also accords a degree of independent power to the various parties involved and brings a correspondingly higher likelihood of conflict. Within this vision, two models may be distinguished: the *codetermination model* and the *negotiation model* (see Teulings, 1987). In the codetermination model, employer and employees have their own interests but both are responsible for the satisfactory functioning of the organization (see motives 3 and 5). This implies both the right to a say in the organization's affairs and a certain loyalty to it. The codetermination model is often seen employed by internal consultation bodies such as works councils.

The negotiation model assumes, at least in principle, that the interests of employers and employees are at odds, and that these interests are embodied by the management and the unions. Negotiations allow the two parties to wrangle over the terms of effort and output. In principle, workers' representatives have no responsibility for the day-by-day affairs within the organization. Although the negotiation behaviour can be found in all forms of internal codetermination, English "shop stewards" and Dutch in-company trade-union representatives are typical instances of this model.

Arguably, motives 3 and 5 are the most important. Workers' codetermination is necessary in order that responsibility for what the enterprise actually does is shared and in order to reduce the risk of the abuse of power. This is not to say that the other motives are indefensible. Employees need sufficient leeway for the fulfilment of their interests, and in specific situations workers' participation can also be of benefit to the enterprise.

Even in situations where these two motives are absent, genuine codetermination remains important.

This section has already mentioned that one motive implies different forms and methods of codetermination than does another. In Figure 16.2, the motives that have been described and the main forms of participation are brought together. This is naturally no more than a schematic representation; in practice, aims and forms will also be aligned in other ways. In paragraph 4, the various structures will be examined in more detail.

3 INDUSTRIAL RELATIONS

3.1 Three models

In European industrial relations, three systems may be distinguished. First, the system of trade-union representatives called *"shop stewards"* found in England. The chief characteristic here is the negotiating method, in which collective bargaining takes place largely *within* companies. Collective labour agreements at sector level do exist, but these are primarily agreements on

---

FIGURE 16.2

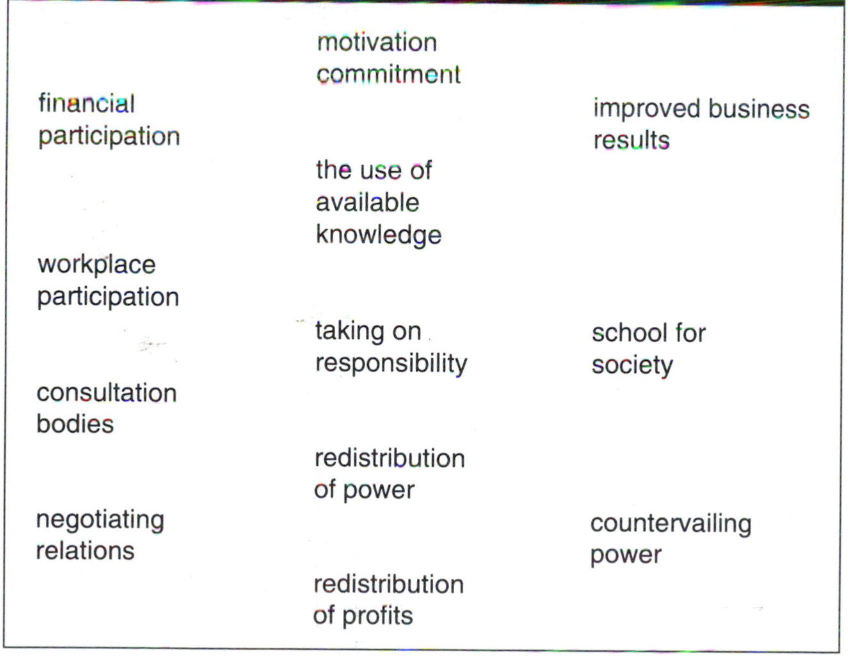

financial participation	motivation commitment	improved business results
	the use of available knowledge	
workplace participation		
	taking on responsibility	school for society
consultation bodies		
	redistribution of power	
negotiating relations		countervailing power
	redistribution of profits	

The main forms and intentions of workers' participation.

consultation procedures. Some companies have "consultative committees" but they have little influence.

Second, we have the *southern European system*, characterized less by a clear model than by rather confrontational relations. The trade unions are often divided and their actions frequently have a political character. Works councils are formally recognized, but in practice have little room to manoeuvre. There are large differences between sectors and between companies, depending on the strength of the trade union.

Third, there is the *northern European dual system*. Here the collective bargaining at the sector level is stressed. There is still plenty of room for codetermination at the level of the individual company, and this can take many different forms. Two subtypes of this system can be distinguished: one could be called the *dual model with union dominance* and is seen in Belgium, Denmark, and, to a lesser degree, Sweden, and elsewhere. Management and workers have equal representation on works councils, having little or no codetermination rights and a modest role exercised together (and in close consultation) with relatively strong union representation. Union membership is traditionally widespread in these countries. The second subtype, the *fully dual model*, can be seen in Germany and the Netherlands. An independent works council having considerable authority fulfils an autonomous role alongside a more detached and weaker trade-union movement with whom it has little (formal) relation. In these countries, the degree of unionization is generally limited.

In the Netherlands, as in Germany and Scandinavia, collective-bargaining agreements are governed by form part of national legislation. In England and the southern European countries, this is hardly ever, or never, the case (Jacobs, 1988). In these countries the observance of collective-bargaining agreements sometimes has to be enforced by resolute action. In the "northern" model, where the observance of collective-bargaining agreements can be judicially upheld, conflicts arising from them can first be fought in the courts. This has contributed to the fact that northern European countries enjoy a relatively low number of strikes.

3.2 Dutch industrial relations

Although the Dutch economy is to all intents and purposes a free-market economy, it nevertheless displays several aspects of planned as well as corporatist economies. In other words, labour-market legislation and wages policy originate on three levels at the same time:

1. on the free market, where the supply and demand of work lead to individual agreements;
2. in the many consultative organizations of employers' and employees' representatives;
3. via government legislation.

In the small-scale, proto-capitalist economies of previous centuries, the union movement in the present sense of the word did not exist. Working conditions were therefore largely settled between individual employees and employers. With the continuous growth in scale of industry, and the steadily weakening position of individual workers, a shift occurred towards labour agreements based on collective negotiations between employers and unions.

In the Netherlands collective-bargaining agreements, or CBAs, come in all shapes and sizes. When working conditions have been agreed for all enterprises at national level, this is termed a *Central Agreement*. There are also *Sector CBAs* and *Company CBAs*. Another category is formed by *Minimum CBAs* and *Standard CBAs*. The first list basic conditions, which must be met and may be exceeded. The Standard CBAs are binding. Most Sector CBAs have a minimum character, the Company CBAs are of the standard type. Finally there are the *Framework Collective Labour Agreements*, normally sector-level regulations having general rules that have to be completed or supplemented at company level.

Central government has played a growing role in this area, especially since the Second World War. In the 1950s and early 1960s this was expressed in the control of wages and prices. Government also played an active part in socio-economic discussions and in talks on collective labour agreements. A great deal of legislation was passed on the structure of enterprises and on the participatory rights of employees. Furthermore, various councils and committees were formed at national and industrial-sector level, in which employers and employees, occasionally supplemented by government representatives, could consult and regulate (see the following).

The Dutch system of industrial relations was, and to a degree still is, characterized by four concepts: denominational segregation, integration, centralization and consensus.

Denominational segregation

Like almost all other Dutch organizations, employers' and employees' organizations fell into groups according to their members' ideology: Roman Catholic, Protestant, and non-partisan. Besides this division there were other categories: trade organizations, professional associations, and a growing degree of organization in middle and upper management. In many companies, different employees are members of diverse unions.

Integration

Despite this diversity, in broad terms the different employees' organizations have had close agreement on socio-economic and political matters, as have the different employers' organizations. Moreover, employers and employees regularly met in all kinds of other ways; for instance, a cross-connection, the Convent of Social Christian Organizations, exists between Protestant employers and employees, and in many bodies and councils at national and sector level, such as the Labour Foundation, The Social and Economic Council, The Social Insurance Council, and the Sickness Funds Council, employers, employees, and government work closely and constructively together. Not for nothing it is said that the Netherlands has a "consultation economy".

The *Labour Foundation* was the fruit of regular contacts between employers' and employees' representatives during the war. The Foundation's directors are drawn from workers' unions (including traders' and agricultural organizations) and from traditional employers' organizations (including, from 1978 onwards, the Dutch trade-union federation of middle and higher management, the "*MHP*").

The *Social and Economic Council* has two functions: advising government on socio-econ-

omic measures and watching over certain sector organizations. The Council has 45 members: 15 are drawn from employers' organizations, 15 from employees' organizations, and 15 are so-called "crown members" representing government, drawn mostly from scientific circles.

The *Social Insurance Council* and the *Sickness Funds Council* keep an eye on the institutions that implement Dutch social-security legislation. The Social Security Council is a tripartite organization, while the Sickness Funds Council has representatives from these three bodies and also from the organizations, private and otherwise, that carry out health policy, from the sickness funds, and from organizations of those directly involved in healthcare provision.

Centralization

In the early 1980s the emphasis in industrial relations lay at national level. Right up to the 1970s, a yearly "central agreement" on general working conditions had been reached, and the sector CBAs had to stay within these lines. The employees' organizations and employers' organizations were, and are, rather centralized and hierarchical bodies. The government also played an important role in all sorts of areas.

Consensus

For the first 20 years after the war, the three "social partners"—employers, employees, and government—had compatible views on social and economic developments and on industrial relations.

Partly as the result of these four characteristics, we find that both employers and employees are concerned by problems of universal importance, such as income distribution, training, technological innovations, health, and social security. CBAs at sector and company level, too, include agreements on workplace democratization, training, and investment policy.

3.3 Developments

Each of the four characteristics described has undergone change over the past few decades because of socio-economic, technological, and political developments. The "harmony model" disintegrated at national level during the 1960s, and emphasis came to be laid on decision-making *within* the company. The unions then began to strengthen their positions within industrial sectors and within individual companies; they developed "*bedrijvenwerk*", union representation within companies (see section 5.3). Supported by the cultural developments of the 1960s, unions extended their influence and included more items of general interest (such as social security) on their agendas.

For the first half of the 1970s the unions retained their position, despite a deepening economic recession. They were supported by a progressive social-democratic government. However, by the end of the 1970s employers were improving their own organization. Partly as a result of escalating unemployment, employers grew stronger as employees grew weaker. The unions' weakened position was not the result of economic stagnation and unemployment alone; it also had to do with the composition of its members. The core of union membership consists of full-time, semi-skilled, middle-aged men. Two large groups of employees do not fall into this category, namely:

1. the *lowest segment* of the job market, that is, part-timers, temporary employees, home workers and so on;
2. the *new employees*, that is, professionals with advanced technical training.

Both groups are growing in size and neither is attracted to the union movement.

Around 1980 the unions developed new strategies in several areas, including technology policy and the reduction of the working week. In the former instance, this was an attempt to gain influence on company decisions on automation and new technologies. In 1982, the Labour Foundation succeeded in reaching a limited, general accord on the reduction of the working week to 38 hours. Nevertheless, working hours remained an issue, and the planned process of further reduction was brought to a standstill. One of the reasons for this was economic growth; for employers, this implied increased organizational problems in the use of a shortened working week; for employees, it meant that the threat of unemployment was falling. New calls were made for wage rises instead of reductions in working hours.

During the 1980s the position of employers was strengthened by the social revaluation of business. Government policy, too, was directed at reducing burdens on industry and at deregulating markets (that is, on less government interference). Finally, employers were improving their own internal discipline and collectively forming active strategies for establishing close contacts with government and the parties in office.

Clearly, denominational segregation was on the decline, but so too was the old consensus. Changes in the other two characteristics mentioned could also be seen: The new trend was for *decentralization* and *differentiation*. There was less central consultation on working conditions, and central agreements were correspondingly harder to reach. Negotiations took place more and more at the level of the industrial sector and the individual company. Moreover, there was a strong tendency to no longer settle issues of working conditions at national level but to differentiate, even within companies themselves. For instance, many different forms of employment contract appeared.

The Ministry of Social Services and Employment calculated that between 1974 and 1986 the number of general-sector CBAs stayed more or less the same but that the number of company CBAs rose by 30%.

Despite these changes, the Netherlands can still be said to have, compared with other countries, a "consultation economy". Considerable agreement still (or once again) exists on several main points of social and economic policy, such as the need for innovation, including technological innovation. The councils mentioned still form the framework for constructive cooperation between the "social partners". In the final section I shall examine the question of whether, given current European integration, this situation is likely to last for long.

4 STRATEGIES AND STRUCTURES OF CODETERMINATION

4.1 Forms of codetermination

In a previous section, three models of industrial democracy were distinguished: the consultation model, the codetermination model and the negotiation model. Each model gives its own form to the idea of participation:

1. In the *consultation model* the employer takes the initiative to consult employees, without being obliged to do so. In general, this sort of participation is not regarded as an example of formalized industrial democratization.

2. In the *codetermination model*, employees have the rights to obtain information, give advice, and exercise sanction, derived from statutory or other legislation. Specific bodies or jobs are created to administer these objectives.

3. In the *negotiation model*, trade-union representatives have the right to negotiate with employers' representatives on primary and secondary working conditions.

4. Besides these three models, which together form the foundation of a whole series of forms and structures of workers' participation, a fourth is sometimes described as another strategy for the involvement of employees: *financial participation*. This takes the form of profit-sharing schemes, employees' shares, and "buy-outs", this last being the situation in which employees collectively finance the rescue of a company threatened with collapse. In fact, workers' participation is seldom, or only indirectly, the intended aim of financial participation schemes (see section 6.2).

Figure 16.3 shows the various forms of participation, differentiated into the three models and according to the level in the company where a given form of participation is usually to be found.

The forms of participation shown in Figure 16.3 differ according to basic perspective and organizational level. They also vary along the dimensions personal/impersonal and direct/representative. Each of the bodies listed can finally be characterized by the following features:

a. *the nature and amount of the formal powers conferred*: Does participation apply only to (for example) personnel arrangements, or also to strategic company issues?

b. *the range of the powers conferred*: Are there rights to obtain information, to give advice, to sanction decisions, or to take independent decisions?

In a European study of employee involvement in technical innovation processes, this last basis for categorizing formal and informal consultation forms was applied (Cressey & Williams, 1991). The researchers subsequently encountered an enormous variety of information meetings, committees, project groups, organizations, agreements, and arrangements aimed at giving concrete form to employees' participation.

4.2 The big five

The five most common European participation structures at company level are the following.

Codetermination bodies

In these bodies elected representatives of the employees negotiate with company management. The best-known example is the works council, which can be found in many countries. But also, many committees with responsibilities for specific industrial issues, such as the Belgian Committees for Safety and Hygiene, belong in this category. Current Dutch works councils and German *"Betriebsraten"* do not at first sight look like codetermination bodies, given that they consist entirely of elected employee representatives. However, besides their own meetings these bodies also have consultation meetings with company management. Nevertheless, the committees and councils in this category differ widely in the way in which rights and powers are worked out.

Employee representatives on the boards of governors and directors

The best-known example of this is found in Germany, and particularly in the mining, iron, and steel industries. In these companies, the board of governors is composed half of shareholders' representatives and half of employees' representatives, with one neutral member. Besides such employee governors, the German system, known as *"Mitbestimmung"*, even includes employee directors as well as the aforementioned works council. In other German companies and in other countries the number of employee governors is

FIGURE 16.3

level	Consultation		Codetermination	Negotiation
Individual				
• personal	participatory leadership			
• impersonal	suggestion boxes			
Department				
• direct	job consultation Quality Circles			
• indirect	"SHW" committee			
Organization				
• direct	staff meeting			shop steward
• indirect		works council		in-company union work
			board members[a] directors[b] workers' council (former Yugoslavia) general meeting of producer cooperative staff	
Sector			Industry Board	union/CBA
National			National bi-party Advisory Commission on Social & Economic Affairs	the union movement

Forms of employee participation. NB: Participatory leadership, suggestion boxes, job consultation, and "Quality Circles" are not examined further in this chapter (see sections 3.1 and 3.3). "SHW" committee: Committee for Safety, Health, and Well-being. The other concepts are explained in the text.

[a] members of company board representing workers' interest
[b] members of company executive body representing workers' interest

quite small. In the Netherlands, the creation of such governors or directors is wholly disregarded by the law. However, a number of Dutch companies have initiated themselves the appointment of worker-related board members at their own instigation.

Workers' self-management

In 1948, Yugoslavia introduced the system of self-government as part of a national policy for preventing a Stalinist centralization of power. The workers' council has an important place in this system. Composed entirely of elected employee representatives, it forms the highest authority in the company. The management are engaged by the council and can also be fired by it. An executive committee, consisting of a small number of council members and the director, supervises the daily implementation of the decisions taken by the workers' council. With the fall of communism and the break-up of Yugoslavia, the workers' council will probably not last much longer.

Forms of workers' rule have also arisen in other countries outside Europe, such as in Libya, Algeria, and Peru. Most of these initiatives came about in the wake of revolutionary change. Most did not last long (for an overview see Monat, 1991). Another somewhat comparable form of organization is that of the workers' producer cooperative, discussed in section 6.1.

Union representation

Many countries are acquainted with some form or other of union representation in industry. The best-known example is that of the English "shop steward", a union representative elected by the union members in a given company, whose task is to negotiate the conditions of employment and to promote the employees' interests. In larger companies, many shop stewards can be found. This model is not based on the idea of consultation or collective decision-making, but on negotiation, even though in practice substantial understanding can exist between shop stewards and management. Similar specialties can be found in other countries; in Scandinavia they play a role alongside other consultative bodies.

Information procurement

Arrangements with regard to the procurement of information represent an important element both in and alongside all sorts of participation structures. Many countries have legal provisions allowing employers' representatives on works councils, unions, boards, and committees to obtain industrial information. There are also regulations covering the provision of information in general (Jain, 1979). The Dutch Works Council Act of 1979 names a number of specific issues for which regular reports must be submitted to works councils. Unions have increasingly stressed on the importance of extending such regulations.

4.3   Cultural variation

The various systems of industrial relations and forms of participation did not, of course, come out of the blue but reflect differences in national history and culture. Culture has to do with the values, norms, and concepts held by certain groups of people. Hofstede (1991) has endeavoured to establish a link between the results of his earlier research, on the values held by managers in different countries, and patterns of participation. In his view, value systems can be differentiated along a number of dimensions. The two most important are the "tolerance of power distance" and the "avoidance of uncertainty", that is, the inclination to arrange matters formally. According to Hofstede, in southern European countries the acceptance of large power differentials is widespread (allowing quite authoritarian relations within companies), as is the need to reduce uncertainty. This value system might explain why

it is that participation in company decisions is weak in these countries, with arrangements made only at higher, political levels.

In countries like Germany and the Netherlands the need to reduce uncertainty is less strong, though still present. Large power distances are, however, tolerated much less. This is reflected in a formally organized, strong participation structure. According to Hofstede, the UK belongs to those countries where the value system is characterized by a low tolerance for power distances and a weak avoidance of uncertainty. Participation is therefore hardly legislated at all, and in companies themselves is often informal. The last permutation of values, namely large power distances and weak uncertainty avoidance, Hofstede found in many Asian countries, where an organization is seen primarily as being a kind of extended family. Here, participation is politically chaotic and business life is marked by paternalistic relations.

This representation of Hofstede's work is too brief to do justice to his ideas on values and participation (see also Chapter 7 in this *Handbook*). Despite the criticism that excessive generalization is bound to attract, one cannot close one's eyes to the fact that strong national differences in value systems do exist and that these can influence industrial relations.

5   PARTICIPATION IN THE NETHERLANDS

Even before the Fist World War Dutch companies had bodies, known as "*kernen*" or cores, in which employees' representatives strove to promote their colleagues' interests. Nevertheless, the main pressure for workers' emancipation came from the trade unions. The organization of the union movement had come from outside the workplace, and was not manifested within the company, as was the case in the UK. Over the years the union movement acquired an important place in Dutch industrial relations.

After the Second World War, industrial relations were dominated by the rebuilding of society, and this was reflected in a number of new structures at different levels within industry, some laid down by statute. These new structures play an important role in the discussion of industrial democracy; they concern the board of governors, the works council, activities at shop-floor level such as in-company union work, job consultation and job design structuring (for the last two, see Chapter 13, Vol. 3 in this *Handbook*).

5.1 The board of governors

The Dutch Company Structure Act of 1971 made the institution of a board of governors a legal requirement for all large, public limited-liability companies (currently, those with more than 100 employees and more than 22.5 million Dutch form in capital assets). This law does not therefore apply to the large number of private limited companies in the Netherlands. The board exists to keep an eye on company policy. It is made up of people not employed by the company, generally leading figures from the worlds of banking, other industrial organizations, and science. The Company Structure Act widened the powers of the board to include the appointment and dismissal of management staff, and also gave it power of veto in extremely important company decisions (mergers, closure, mass redundancy, etc.). The interesting aspect of this with respect to industrial democracy is that the works council is entitled to propose candidates for board membership. The selection and appointment of new members is carried out by the board itself, but the works council has a right of veto if it considers that a candidate does not meet certain criteria.

5.2 The works council

The first Works Council Act ("*WOR*"), passed in 1950, required all enterprises with more than 25 employees to allow their employees to elect representatives. It stressed that the works council was a consultative body whose purpose was the common good of the enterprise. The primary tasks of the works council were to consult with management and to provide it with recommendations. In line with this philosophy, the rule was that the chairman's seat was to be filled by a member of the management.

Developments in industrial relations and in social-science research changed the conceptions of the role of the works council. This resulted in the 1971 Works Council Act, which accorded works councils two functions: collective consultation and the promotion of employees' interests. To make this role possible, the new Act gave works councils new powers and provisions:

- The employer must obtain the works council's approval on a large number of personnel policy decisions, such as pension schemes, appraisal systems, and working-hours schemes.
- The works council must be consulted on other important policy decisions.
- Duly elected works council members have the right to organize their own meetings and to invite external advisers.
- Works council members are protected against dismissal.

The debate did not come to an end with the introduction of this Act; on the contrary, it intensified, especially on the issue of the composition of a works council. Many, particularly in union circles, considered that members of the management did not belong in a works council and still less in its chairman's seat. A frequent criticism was that their experience and privileged access to information often meant that they dominated discussions. A more principled argument was that the works council, as a body primarily serving the interests of the employees, ought to be an independent employees' organization. The new, third Works Council Act passed in 1979 in part reflects this outlook; the new works council is indeed composed entirely of employees. However, the council is still seen as a body serving the whole company organization, and therefore retains the two functions accorded to it in 1971: collective consultation and promotion of employees' interests. Contacts with upper management are now prescribed: Consultative meetings with management are to be held at least six times a year, on the subjects on which the works council is entitled to advise or those for which its approval is required. The works council's powers were also increased, especially the number of decisions needing the council's approval.

Works councils gain rights and powers not only through these Acts, but also through CBAs and in-company regulations. As far as *legislation* is concerned, besides the Acts there exist a number of other important laws such as the aforementioned Company Structure Act and the Work Environment Act. The latter includes regulations on the role of the works council with regard to policy on working conditions and relations with the Labour Inspectorate. The second way in which powers can be extended to works councils is *through a CBA*. This occurs quite frequently and usually concerns the provision of information to works councils, the legal position of works council members, and especially the duty to consult the works council on certain matters. Finally, a third way of giving powers to works councils is by the creation of an official *company resolution*, after the works council itself has given its sanction. This third form does not appear often; at any rate, few have been officially declared. This should come as no surprise. First, employers seldom have anything to gain by simply giving their works councils more authority and power; second, the position of employees and their representatives in works councils is usually too weak to extract such powers; and third, the unions are ambivalent about the question of increasing works councils' powers.

In the Netherlands, then, a works council's authority is vested primarily in law, secondarily through CBAs, and very occasionally through company-specific measures. This situation is at least partly explained by the centralization of Dutch industrial relations. National legislation also has the advantages of upholding equality before the law, offering continuity, and providing appeal procedures and sanctions. Arrangements via CBAs and in-company agreements, on the other hand, have the advantage of being better attuned to specific situations in the sectors or companies of their application; they can also be set up more quickly.

5.3 In-company union work

Since the 1960s the unions have endeavoured to develop union work within companies. Union members in a company or part of a company elect or contact persons who, occasionally in collaboration with others, represents the union within the company. His job is to mobilize the union members, which can mean passing on complaints to the

union, initiating campaigns, organizing the rank-and-file for works council members or preparing CBA negotiations. The bond between these union representatives and works councils varies, from close cooperation to strained relations. The latter situation can develop, for instance, if the union fears that its position is weakened when the works council takes over particular tasks, or if the works council—in the eyes of employees and unions— takes too much of a "management" line.

In 1971 the first formal regulations with regard to in-company union work, in the Hoogovens steel company, were framed in a CBA. By 1974, 44 sector CBAs had similar provisions, and by 1981 this number had risen to 112. In practice, union work in certain industrial sectors is thriving; the Netherlands Trade Union Federation has about 8000 company executive members, of which 6000 also have seats on works councils.

5.4 Codetermination in small businesses

The Works Council Act applies principally to large organizations (those with over 100 employees). The regulations for medium-sized organizations (35–100 employees) differ in only a few details from those for the larger companies.

Codetermination in companies with fewer than 35 employees is subject to only a few regulations within the Works Council Act:

- The employer is obliged to call his employees together at least twice a year for a "personnel meeting".
- At these meetings he is obliged to give information on the general course of business and on the social policies being employed or proposed.
- He must give employees the opportunity to offer advice on decisions with important effects on jobs.

It was expected that these prescriptions for codetermination of those employed in small businesses would be meaningless. A study carried out in 1986 (Verstegen, Andriessen, & Dekkers, 1987) produced surprising results: 12.5% of these companies had a works council (often because they were the daughter company of a larger concern) and over 40% held personnel meetings more or less regularly. Over half of the employees questioned did not know, however, that these meetings were a legal requirement. Personnel meetings were more common in the business service and non-profit sectors, that is, in organizations employing well-trained employees, and they were seen by both employers and employees as playing a useful role in the circulation of information and the course of discussions on company affairs.

5.5   Codetermination in government

Dutch government organizations have long had consultations with civil-service unions, institutionalized in so-called "Special Committees". During the 1970s, about 400 "old-style civil-service committees" had been composed of civil servants who were union members. The role of these committees was to advise the head of the relevant civil-service department. The general trend at that time for the reduction of disputes between government organizations and private businesses resulted in a new ruling on codetermination in government: In 1982 the General Civil Service Regulations included prescriptions for the establishment of (new-style) civil-service committees (CSC) within government. This development also stimulated the creation of regulations for consultative committees at county and town-council level, so that by 1986 there were about 2000 consultative committees at government and town level in the Netherlands. In fact, each ministry can make independent decisions about the number of civil-service committees it holds and at what level in the organization, with the proviso that all the civil servants fall under one committee or another; the result is a wide range of practices, from ministries with a small number of CSCs at high level to others with many CSCs at lower levels. In all, there are about 800 CSCs. Research has also shown that CSCs show strong similarities with works councils, not just in terms of their formal regulations but also in terms of the main sticking points in their day-to-day functioning.

The establishment and objects of the CSCs and works council are strongly similar. Both are instituted as the representative bodies of all employees, by the minister and by the company respectively. In both cases, the objectives of the committee concern consultation and representation of employees' interests. With regard to *elections, composition, and term of office*, there are more similarities than dissimilarities.

As far as *working methods* are concerned, both organizations have internal meetings and both have discussion meetings with management. In companies, the chairmanship of such a meeting is decided by mutual agreement and is often performed by the employer and the works council chairman in turns. In CSCs, the chairman is the head of the department unless other arrangements are agreed. The CSCs' *facilities* are clearly inferior; there are fewer days off for training purposes and, on average, fewer hours in which to hold meetings.

As far as *the right to put forward initiatives* is concerned, the CSC is slightly better off. In certain circumstances the department head cannot simply lay such a proposal aside, while an employer can. More importantly, however, works councils have been given the right to advise on a large number of organizational, financial, and economic matters, whereas the CSC does not have this right. With regard to the *powers of sanction*, a direct comparison is harder to make. The CSC's authority depends on the authority held by its chairman, the head of the department. The CSC has the right to approve measures that the head of the department is empowered to administer. Strictly speaking, however, only the highest authority in each department, that is to say the minister, is responsible for all decisions. In practice, of course, managers at lower levels also have responsibilities, but these are not always clearly specified.

Finally, *employment protection and rights of appeal*. Redundancy-protection arrangements are not dissimilar. However, the appeal options for works councils are much better; first, because there are several appeal bodies to which they can go, allowing an appeal to a higher court if a lower court turns the appeal down, and second, because these bodies are independent of the company with which the works council is in dispute. A CSC can appeal only to its own minister, who then hears a so-called Advisory Council.

To sum up, then, we may conclude that few differences between works councils and CSCs with regard to establishment, composition, and working methods can be seen. The CSC's facilities are fewer, and their appeal options are less developed. In theory the CSC's powers are the greater, but in practice they are usually the smaller. In the judgment of CSC members, the most significant obstacles are formed by undefined powers, and inadequate provision of information. The question of powers has much to do with an important characteristic of civil-service work—the tension between politics and bureaucracy. On the one hand, one has "external democratization", the political accountability of the civil service to government in Parliament; on the other hand, one has "internal democratization", the right of civil servants to have a say in their own affairs. Civil servants are forbidden to influence decisions in a way that Parliament would not wish, and codetermination in government is therefore more narrowly defined than it is in the business world. In practice this is expressed by the indeterminate powers of the civil-service manager.

6 ALTERNATIVE FORMS OF ORGANIZATION

As is the case in other countries, the Netherlands also contains a small number of enterprises where workers' participation is arranged by other means. The best known is the "producer cooperative", a form of organization that already has a respectable record. More recent still are the "normal" businesses in which employers hold part of the shares. The third category is formed by a few, unique enterprises, which have developed their own far-reaching forms of employee participation. In the Netherlands these are represented by the Breman companies and by Endenburg. In all, these alternative forms of organization come about partly for reasons of ideology and partly out of financial and economic motives. Producer cooperatives and companies like Breman and Endenburg are motivated largely by the first motive, companies with shareholding employees largely by the second.

6.1 Producer cooperatives

There are two forms of producer cooperative. One is found in agriculture and its related sectors. Such a cooperative is actually an association, for example, of a number of farmers, who "own" a business (e.g. a milk factory) as would an ordinary company's shareholders. Employees in these companies are not members of the association, however, and do not therefore have a member's voice.

The second form is the so-called workers' producer cooperative. The central characteristics of a WPC are the following:

- Members of the cooperative society are also employees of the company; they manage the company, supplying both labour and capital;
- this management is carried out on the basis of decisions made by the so-called Members' General Meeting, in which every member has equal voting rights;
- the board of the society appoints and dismisses the management of the company, and also sees to it that the management carries out the policies decided by the General Meeting;
- the net profits are divided in just proportion.

Apart from this cooperative structure, normal company hierarchies exist: The management is the "boss" and the employees have to carry out management's orders.

In the second half of the last century, socialist views led to the establishment of tens of thousands of WPCs in Europe. England, especially, accounted for many thousands. By the 20th century, however, though the cooperative movement remained strong in Italy, France, and eastern Europe, most WPCs in England and the Netherlands had gone down without a trace. Nevertheless, in the 1970s and 1980s the number of WPCs rose once more (Russel, 1991). In 1975 there were at least 500 in France and 2600 in Italy. Many were inspired by the large group of WPCs around Mondragon, in north-western Spain, where in 1975 14,000 people were employed in a wide range of cooperative companies, such as a bank, a domestic appliance factory, insurance companies, farms and a technical college.

During the wave of democratization that swept

Europe in the 1960s and 1970s, many studies were made of Dutch WPCs. Researchers were interested in whether industrial relations in these companies were indeed more democratic than relations in companies having works councils, and whether they might approach the ideal of workers' self-management. It was also important to see how these companies fared, in financial and economic terms, in a predominantly capitalist economy.

The results of this research showed that the reality of WPCs was less utopian than some had allowed themselves to hope. In most WPCs by no means every employee was an association member. Company hierarchies appeared to operate here in much the same way as elsewhere. In practice, employees had less say in the company's business affairs than the prescribed company structure implied. Apart from the General Meeting, the cooperative structure has no institutionalized channels by which employees can genuinely influence the opinions and decisions that directly or indirectly affect their work. The structure does not automatically provide for works councils, job consultation, lobby contacts, training, or any of the forms of (and conditions for) employee participation. The development of these matters is just as much an issue in WPCs as it is in ordinary companies, and often just as troublesome.

The theory and practice of production cooperatives has been considerably substantiated over the past 20 years. It has become clear that this form of company organization is particularly viable in small or medium-sized labour-intensive enterprises in the business-service sector (Clarke, 1991). Here, the employers' production cooperative can indeed provide a vigorous example of industrial democratization.

6.2   Share ownership

Much attention has been paid recently to the company involvement of employees by means of financial participation. One form of this is *profit-sharing*. According to Voûte (1991), 14% of all Dutch large collective-bargaining agreements in 1988 included some form of profit-sharing. The institution of profit-sharing partly stems from employers' expectations that employees' motivation is thereby improved. Another reason for its

use is the idea that labour, too, has a right to part of the company's profits. However, profit-sharing schemes are not necessarily associated with codetermination.

In principle, another form of financial participation, employee *share ownership*, is indeed linked with codetermination. In the United States, many companies lavishly provide employees with shares; one such arrangement is known as the "Employee Stock Owner Plan", or ESOP. This is a structure in which a company pension fund invests in shares in the company itself. Russel (1989) reports that in 1986 there were already over 7000 ESOPs involving more than seven million workers. In a third of these cases employees had a majority shareholding.

Employers are often very enthusiastic about share ownership by their employees. This has several reasons, many to do with fiscal considerations: share endowments to employees are tax-deductible, and they can also form an effective defence against hostile takeovers. Finally, there is the conviction that financial involvement raises work motivation.

In the past, unions, employees, and government were not always equally enthusiastic about such plans. After all, employees risked losing not only their jobs but also their investments if the company did badly. However, in recent years many governments have created tax and other benefits to support them, in the belief that share participation raises industry's capital strength and can also save threatened industries from closure (Russel, 1991).

In the Netherlands, too, the 1970s and 1980s saw a rise in the number of companies whose employees owned a sizeable portion of the shares. The main reason for this was the struggle to refloat companies threatened with closure. An Employees' Participation Fund was set up to give shareholding employees financial support. Of course, it is a matter of enormous significance if one's own share investment means the difference between a job and no job. However, it is difficult to demonstrate that share ownership is a real work motivator in the long run. This is not to say that companies in which share ownership by employees did raise involvement and motivation cannot be found; they can (Voûte, 1991). Nevertheless, systematic studies have shown that such a link is by no means invariable (Rosen, Klein, & Young, 1985; Russel, 1991).

According to Voûte (1991), the stock exchange share prices of 10 Dutch companies whose employees own shares do much better than the 25 enterprises whose share prices together form the Dutch Stock Exchange Index (the EOE index). Further research will be needed to define the roles of employee share ownership and of other possible factors affecting business results.

Finally, as far as codetermination is concerned, shares are often held by a foundation and the influence employees can exert through this foundation, as shareholders, is slight (Russel, 1989).

6.3 Special companies
Endenburg
In the electrotechnical installation firm in Rotterdam, where he employs a couple of hundred staff, the entrepreneur Endenburg has established a codetermination system based on the principle of "sociocracy" (Endenburg, 1981). The first principle of this system is that decisions are taken on the basis of consent; consent exists where those involved have no objections to a given proposal. The sociocratic system is given form in a so-called "overlapping circle system". At every level in the organization, a circle is formed by a number of employees (e.g. a department), the head of the department, and an elected representative. The department head and the representative are members of the next circle above, and so on. Within each circle, decisions are made according to the consent principle. The system seems to work, but has been emulated little outside the Endenburg company.

Breman companies
The Breman companies, a group of technical installation firms in the east of the Netherlands, were born when Mr T. Breman, a bicycle repairman, started to broaden the scope of his concern. In 1972, the business by now encompassing a number of companies and several hundred employees, his five sons developed a special system in which the works council had as much say in business decisions as management. The last word on finance and investments, however, was retained by a holding company, Breman Management, led by the five brothers. In 1978, the structure was changed to bring finance under the control of Brebank BV, whose management, elected by both Breman employees and managers, also operates on the consent principle; all decisions must be unanimous.

A research study has shown that the works councils and work discussion groups in Breman companies lack adequate knowledge and are often brought into the actual decision-making process only at a late date. An attempt has been made to rectify this by means of an extensive educational and day-release programme. This appears to have been more successful in some companies than in others.

6.4 Conclusion
All the alternative forms of business organization that we have studied share the fundamental expectation that such organization will lead to increased employee motivation and identification with the company, whether or not this is the result of increased participation in company decision-making. This improved motivation, runs the argument, then leads to improved business results. In practice, these expectations are only partially fulfilled. Research on the distribution of power within producer cooperatives showed that this is similar to that in conventional businesses. Financial participation appears generally not to result in increased codetermination for employees. American employees' formal rights to a share in their companies sometimes do and sometimes do not lead to increased motivation (Rosen et al., 1985). A Dutch study of 19 companies with alternative organizational structures, carried out in the second half of the 1980s, showed that although employees were, on average, more motivated, this was not a sufficient guarantee of increased profitability (Voets, 1995). The 1980s can be characterized, for both industry and unions, as a period of withdrawal and concentration on core activities. The ideals of the previous years were gradually replaced by a more business-like attitude and a number of the companies concerned could no longer handle the competition.

These conclusions are in agreement with the results of a series of experiments with far-reaching employee codetermination that were carried out at the initiation of the Dutch Social and Economic Council (De Man, 1985). These included a number of cooperatives, Breman companies, and other companies such as the Dutch Post Office and a psychiatric hospital. The experiments were overtaken by socio-economic developments and provided only some more realistic insights into the nature of decision-making and company policy—at least for the often impassioned advocates of industrial democratization. In short, actual employee codetermination is not guaranteed by the formal structures of democratization. Neither employee codetermination nor financial participation are a guarantee of increased motivation, profitability, or business success. More conditions must be met if these goals are to be attained.

7   HOW WORKS COUNCILS WORK

7.1   Power and influence

Many studies have examined the way works councils work in practice, which difficulties appear and especially the degree to which they influence the course of events within the organization. Hövels and Nas (1976) carried out a study of about a hundred Dutch old-style works councils (where the employer is chairman). Data were drawn from the minutes of meetings and from interviews with key figures. The authors arrived at a four-fold categorization of works councils:

1. the dormant works council (about 20%), which did practically nothing;
2. the works council as agency of management (also about 20%), in which all activities (setting the agenda, discussions, etc.) were entirely dominated by the chairman;
3. the works council as agency of the employees (about 16%), in which members independently and unanimously confronted the management;
4. the works council as negotiating body (about 43%), in which elected members acted independently, while making deals with management—sometimes by accepting compromises, sometimes by negotiation.

The study results suggested that a considerable number of works councils had at least some degree of influence on company decision-making processes. Although no direct measurements of such influence were carried out, indirect indications led the researchers to conclude that in many instances *this influence was comparatively small.*

The results of the international comparative IDE project (Industrial Democracy in Europe) corroborate such scepticism about the influence of representative bodies (IDE Research Group, 1980). In this, the formal authority and actual influence of codetermination bodies was studied in a dozen European countries. To this end a list of questions was put to key figures in a large number of organizations, while simultaneously carrying out a survey of groups of employees in the same companies. The most important foundation of influence within the company turned out, as usual, to be the position on the hierarchical ladder, with representative bodies playing a limited role. Though there was *significant influence on personal matters*, the role of such bodies in important decisions on appointments, investments, reorganization, or alteration of the product lines was extremely small compared with the influence of lower and higher management.

The weak position of the average works council is further illustrated by the fact that compared with the influence of lower and higher management some decisions are never discussed by the works council at all—either because the works council refers them to other bodies (e.g., negotiations between unions and management) or because *management keep certain subjects off the agenda* (Hövels & Nas, 1976).

The IDE research project also found that *considerable differences exist in the nature and influence of different representative bodies*, both between different countries and between different companies in the same country. A very unexpected finding of the IDE research was the conclusion that differences in influence of representative bodies have more to do with *differences in legal powers* than with company attributes such as market independence, the type of production process, or organizational structure. However, also important in this respect is the *mobilization capability* of the body concerned, that is, the degree of involvement of the rank and file and of the union. There are, in fact, representative bodies (such as the Dutch works council) that succeed in influencing their employers' strategic decisions with the help of this wider support.

At the end of the 1980s the IDE research was repeated on a smaller scale (IDE Research Group, 1992). In most of the countries studied, employee participation was still rather limited, though on average the representative organizations had achieved a little more influence. The conclusions drawn by the first study were broadly confirmed.

According to research in the mid-1980s (Looise & De Lange, 1987) *bottlenecks* in the functioning of works councils are found, especially with regard to matters of the works councils' right to consultation; *information procurement was often late, sometimes too late,* and *works councils sometimes lacked the necessary expertise.* However, the works councils' sanctioning role was judged useful by both directors and works council members; this power appears to have been exercised mostly in personnel affairs.

Again it was also found that the functioning and the influence of works councils depended hardly at all on local factors like the scale or type of enterprise. Besides the active engagement of the works council itself, as already mentioned, according to this study it was a *constructive engagement on the part of the employer* that mattered. The many employers interviewed generally passed positive judgments on works councils. As reasons for this they mentioned the value of the works council to industrial relations within the company, in a kind of relief at the relatively limited consequences of the new Works Council Act to employers, and in the wide acceptance of works councils in society.

7.2 Influence or visibility

The above-mentioned research drew a distinction between the "quantitative" application of vested powers (the number of decisions in which the works council was involved) and the "qualitative" application (the decision-making phase at which the works council was involved). In this way, an important dilemma in works council tactics could be uncovered: a strategy aimed at high "quantitative" scores (that is, advising on large numbers of issues and frequently exercising sanction or veto) brings a works council into close contact with its constituency. However, the influence on decision-making is greater, though less visible, when a works council succeeds in being drawn into discussions at an early stage, thereby obtaining more real power to direct the course of decisions.

The *dilemma of industrial democracy* now becomes visible. Real influence on company business affairs is exercised invisibly, "in the corridors of power". When works councils and other employee representatives meet management in these corridors and real choices are discussed, the process is not clearly visible to the rest of the staff. Moreover, exercising influence on the first phases of a decision-making process makes it difficult to submit objections later on. In this way representatives can get themselves mired in a serious role conflict, especially if the final decisions reached are unattractive to the employees. It is the art of a good representative to *balance on this knife-edge between influence and visibility.*

This tension between "corridor involvement" and procedural transparency appears in more forms than one. Numerous studies agree that the satisfactory functioning of codetermination bodies depends on a certain degree of formalization and structuring in the whole organization. The exercise of power can only be monitored when the rules and processes of decision-making are clearly visible. A well-functioning works council needs clarity, with respect to responsibilities, powers, policy plans, and decision-making procedures within the company. However, in old-fashioned, paternalistic companies the structure and often the culture of formal procedure is absent. In this case, a business-like or forceful works council can have a hard time. The desire for formalization and structure can also collide with the business culture in flexible, organic companies such as high-tech and consultancy firms in which highly trained professionals are happier looking after their own "participation" interests than leaving it to a formal body.

7.3 Using the means of power

How does a works council get itself involved early on in the decision-making process? Is this predominantly a question of having a like-minded employer, or can something be done? Teulings (1987) undertook two studies of the tactical options for works councils. Attention was paid not to the formal authority but to the use of four "legitimate tools of power":

1. *boycott of consultation*, from the adjournment of negotiations to resignation from the works council;
2. forms of *disclosure*, for example via internal declarations or statements to the press;
3. calling in *third parties*, such as the board of governors or magistrates;
4. supporting *union actions*, such as demonstrative union meetings or interruptions of work.

Over two-thirds of the works councils appeared to have made use of one or more of these measures at least once. Their use actually grew between 1980 and 1984 (see Table 16.2), though the use of union-related measures decreased (see the first five measures in Table 16.2). It was agreed that more than half of these measures had real effects on company policy; the use of external specialists and other third parties, holding demonstrative meetings during the lunch break, and the involvement of the media were considered particularly effective.

In fact, all these pressure-increasing measures are needed to penetrate management decision-making processes. Teulings (1987) distinguishes between four phases in company decision-making, namely: Problem analysis, internal negotiations, formal decision-making, and operational implementation. He states that many works councils are involved only in the last two phases, whereas the actual direction of company policy is decided in the first two. However, inclusion in the first two phases requires a strong negotiating position, something that is achieved partly by means of legal pressure tactics.

A European study on the involvement of employees and their representatives in technological developments (Cressey & Williams, 1991) confirms this picture. They, too, distinguished four (slightly different) phases in the development of new technological systems: planning, selection, introduction, and evaluation. The degree of employee involvement in these four phases was marked by a *participation paradox*: involvement is limited in the beginning, when the options are

TABLE 16.2		
	1980	*1984*
Enlisting union officials	43%[*]	38%[*]
Supporting demonstrations	12%[*]	10%[*]
Supporting a short work stoppage	11%[*]	5%[*]
Articles in union papers	10%[*]	5%[*]
Supporting a strike	3%[*]	5%[*]
Calling on:		
– external consultants	26%[*]	34%[*]
• the board of governors	18%[*]	35%[*]
• the industry board	9%[*]	25%[*]
• Parliament	3%	12%
• magistrates	1%[*]	5%[*]
Strong opinion in company paper	33%[*]	64%[*]
Boycotting talks	39%[*]	30%[*]
Articles in national newspaper	10%[*]	10%[*]
Collective resignation from works council	4%[*]	10%

The use of legitimate power strategies by works councils. NB: The methods marked with an asterisk are considered particularly effective (Source: Teulings, 1987).

wide, and it grows during the later phases, when the die has already effectively been cast. The study included every kind of formal and informal channel of participation. Not only the participation of representative bodies but also the direct involvement of those operating the new technologies, was usually limited. Nevertheless, there were situations where considerable employee involvement in early decision-making stages did exist.

All these studies show that large differences exist in the degree to which employees' representatives develop successful strategies for acquiring a genuinely important role in company decisions. Works councils can be classified by the degree to which they employ their legally vested powers but also by the degree to which they use other power tactics. The one is in practice seldom related to the other, according to Teulings, which means that there are in fact *four types of works council* (see Figure 16.4). In particular, external assistance enables works councils to secure their rights. Besides union links and the mobilization of trade organizations, the consultative networks that link up with other works councils, commercial services (professional papers, advisory bureaux) and professional services (union offices, training institutes) are of importance. These external sources can help works councils to operate more professionally and thereby strengthen their negotiating position within the company.

7.4 Works councils and working conditions

Since the gradual introduction of the Dutch Working Environment Act during the 1980s, safety, health, and well-being issues have been climbing up works councils' agendas. According to Gevers (1987), in Europe there are three forms of institutionalized employee involvement in issues of safety and health at work (well-being, the third component of the Working Environment Act, is given no explicit attention in the laws of many of the other European countries):

1. general representative bodies such as works councils, sometimes supported by a health and safety committee;
2. a special company health and safety committee;
3. safety representatives.

Reubsaet (1988) studied some 30 more or less representative companies to assess the situation in the Netherlands. There are no safety representatives in the Netherlands, but the following four types of situation were encountered in about equal proportions:

- a separate company health, safety, and well-being ("*SHW*") committee;
- a works council SHW committee composed only of works council members;
- a works council SHW committee composed

		using power strategies	
		much	little
using formal authority	much	rational/ political works council	legalistic works council
	little	radical works council	ritualistic works council

FIGURE 16.4

Four types of works council.

of both works council members and non-members;

- a works council, which addressed health, safety, and well-being issues without setting up a specific committee.

In most cases, therefore, works councils are quite actively involved in SHW issues. An incidental conclusion was that the last group was the least effective, works council members having insufficient expertise in the area.

Article 16 of the Working Environment Act requires employers to organize talks at departmental level between workers and management on work-environment matters wherever such matters are of concern. Reubsaet's research (1988) showed that very few companies actually fulfilled this obligation, though health and safety issues were regularly to be found on the agendas of the work meetings held by many of the companies.

Decisions on health and safety issues can be strategic (for example, investing heavily in safety equipment) as well as operational (for example, revising prescriptions). Reubsaet's research also indicated that large variations existed in the degree to which works councils were involved in, and exerted an influence on, such decisions. This is to be expected, given the fact that the Work Environment Act was is still in its infancy, and that the role of works councils in its application has still to take its final form.

8   ATTITUDES OF EMPLOYEES

8.1   Codetermination and alienation

It has been suggested that the representative bodies supporting industrial democratization could help to reduce individual alienation. In the USA in 1973 a bill was proposed with the aim of solving the problem of alienation of American workers; one of its recommendations was that structures should be created that gave workers the greatest possible opportunity to have their say (Wall & Lischeron, 1977, p.2).

In fact, it remains open to question whether industrial democratization can overcome individual alienation. In the past, writers were optimistic about the positive effects of introducing participative structures (see, for instance, Blumberg, 1968). However, the supposed positive effects of participation on job satisfaction were principally related to participation in the immediate work situation (see also Koopman, Broekhuysen, & Wierdsma, Chapter 14 in this *Handbook*). Indirect participation seldom appears to be related to job satisfaction. Though most studies attest to a positive attitude towards representative bodies, they make it clear that these have little or no effect on overall job satisfaction.

We should not be too surprised. A relation between consultations (whether or not carried out by representative bodies) and individual job satisfaction will only exist when such consultations clearly pertain to issues important to the individual concerned. This would be the case, for instance, if the works council were to achieve a significant improvement in the job or in its pay; but such successes are unlikely to occur with any regularity. Works councils can influence company decisions in a wider sense, but this is often less conspicuous.

How much do employees really want to participate in company decision-making and how, in their terms, ought this to be organized? On the basis of the results of the IDE project (IDE Research Group, 1980) and others, the following conclusions can be drawn:

1. Employees are by and large much more interested in decisions influencing their own direct situation than in decisions on general company policy.
2. Higher-trained staff, often found in the service sector, have a strong preference for individual, direct involvement in decisions to do with their own work, whereas metal-workers and, especially, unskilled workers and union members prefer to see participation in these decisions take place through the mediation of representative bodies (given that their individual influence is very small).
3. Employees generally feel that their representatives have too little say in decisions on general policy.
4. Frequently, what is desired is not so much the right to ratify or block these decisions

but to have adequate information about them and the opportunity to discuss them.

5. Skilled employees, too, usually want to retain representative bodies, given the function they can fulfil in obtaining information and offering countervailing power in emergencies.

8.2 Works councils and employees

Employees' desire to retain organizations such as works councils is not necessarily associated with actual enthusiasm about their work. Complaints are often voiced (predominantly by works council members) that few employees have any interest in works council work, and in general there is little contact between works council members and other employees. This "constituency problem" has been noted in many studies.

With regard to the communications issue, there are no regulations at all prescribing the accountability of works council members to their constituents, nor to contacts between the two groups. Studies carried out by Hövels and Nas (1976) in businesses and by Lammers, Andriessen, Meys, and Meurs (1980) in hospitals have shown that not only are these contacts usually limited, but so also are the facilities and opportunities for the rank and file to become more involved. The larger the company, the higher the works council (as "group works council" or "central works council") is found in the company structure. Also, the earlier (and therefore more invisibly) the works council is involved in company decisions, the more severe this lack of contact and the greater the "psychological distance" between the works council and the employees becomes (Looise & De Lange, 1987). This is also illustrated by the fact that employees' enthusiasm about "employee board members" (as found in Germany and Scandinavia) is even less than that about works councils (Emery, Thorsrud, & Trist, 1969). The dilemma of influence and visibility in this respect has already been discussed.

Indeed, who are we justly to consider as the consituency? Formally, perhaps, all individual employees of the company. However, it is unreasonable to suppose that works council members sustain personal contact with every single employee. Teulings (1988) therefore puts forward

the recommendation that works councils set up networks sustaining a limited number of contacts with people seen as being "opinion-leaders". These would be known for the wide range of their contacts and for their ability to put other workers' experiences and feelings into words. The works councils would then agree to consult these people in certain circumstances.

8.3 Views of the members of representative bodies

In apparent contradiction to the conflicts between influence and visibility already described, it has been found that many works council members do indeed want to stay on. In the IDE project, 45% of the Dutch works council members interviewed declared their intention of standing for re-election, while only 15% of the other employees expressed this desire. This difference was also seen in other countries. A number of theories can be put forward to explain this. The "cognitive dissonance" theory accounts for the fact by suggesting that representatives overestimate the importance of their role and the scale of their influence because any more negative assessment would be at odds with the amount of energy they put into these functions. Mulder's (1977) "power–distance reduction" theory takes as given that the exercise of power is addictive; works council members, according to this theory, only want to stay on because they cannot bear to lose the possibility of influencing matters. A third factor could well be at work in those cases where it proves difficult to find new candidates. In such cases, an appeal to the existing occupant's sense of responsibility may well meet with success. Finally, membership of a representative body may well also represent the beginning, or indeed the continuation, of a career. In the larger Dutch companies especially, works council membership can be a stepping-stone towards a managerial function either within the company or within the union movement. Membership of a "central works council" (an umbrella organization covering the entire company) is often a part-time, and sometimes a full-time post, which can promote the professionalization of the job.

In fact, works council membership can bring disadvantages as well as advantages. A study of some 500 members of 54 works councils in all kinds of business sectors (Acampo, Kunst, Soeters, & Woltmeyer, 1987) revealed a mixed bag of pros and cons of works council work. Remarkably, about a quarter of those questioned saw works council membership as having adverse, or even very adverse, effects on their chances of promotion, while 12% expected favourable effects. The two groups, however, showed no differences in "objective career characteristics" (such as the number of promotions and the hierarchical level of their current post). This study could not, therefore, ascertain whether any real career benefits or disbenefits were associated with works council activities.

It was also found that the length of works council tenure was rising. Between 1978 and 1986 the percentage of works council members with more than three years of membership had risen from 30% to 54%. Over the same period the vacancy percentage had risen from 4.2% to 6.8%, and it was asserted that it was proving more difficult to find candidates. Relations, including those with the union, were generally considered good; negotiations with the employer were also considered reasonably fruitful.

8.4 Between the professions and the rank and file

The considerations and research results presented above can be integrated into a clear picture of the "area of tension" in which works councils carry out their activities.

The average worker is relatively uninterested in the functioning of the works council, partly because the issues that affect him or her most directly are raised so seldom. The average works council member finds it difficult to make strong contacts in the rank and file, and probably invests little energy in the matter, as he or she can well understand why this disinterest exists.

Once installed, works council members sense their activities as having important effects, and they attempt to fulfil their role to the best of their ability—not so much with regard to the rank and file but more with regard to their sparring partners, the employer and perhaps the union. A certain degree of "professionalization" of works council work then takes place, in the sense that a small group of employees perseveres, negotiates with

the employer and the union, and settles affairs skilfully. One could judge this kind of situation as not necessarily prejudicial to the satisfactory conduct of works council business; as I have said (see section 2.1), a professional works council offers useful "countervailing power" in the company's decision-making process. Nevertheless, this professionalization is accompanied by the risk that the works council thereby loses the ability to mobilize the rank and file in case of an emergency.

9 PERSPECTIVES

9.1 The preconditions for democratization

In my opinion, a substantial level of industrial democracy is both possible and necessary.

The view that a real degree of democratization in business life is necessary is a normative one, based on motives related to principles of countervailing power, shared interests, and individual accountability (see section 2.1). That a real form of codetermination is possible has been made clear with the help of the results of various studies. On balance, representative bodies have only little influence on the business affairs of a company, but examples do exist of situations where this influence can be considerable, provided certain preconditions are met.

The question is, of course, which conditions have to be met in order for industrial democracy to work. They have already been referred to implicitly in the preceding sections; they are briefly discussed here.

The first precondition is that the employees' representatives have a reasonably powerful position with respect to the employer. This position is related to the following four factors:

- enough formally invested powers;
- the ability to mobilize their constituents; that is to say, good contacts with the rank and file and/or with the union, so that legitimate pressure tactics can be employed;
- an external network of contacts, for example, with the press, political figures, and the board of governors, also in support of pressure tactics;

- job protection and an appeal court.

A second set of preconditions have to do with external conditions:

- a positive management attitude towards democratization;
- a visible power structure, i.e. a clear structuring of powers, authorities, and responsibilities within the organization;
- systematic consultation routines, so that involvement and participation is not an incidental, but a normal aspect of company affairs.

These conditions provide a solid starting-point from which to undertake discussions and negotiations with company management. The real work, of course, has yet to begin. The process consumes much energy and has occasional successes, but more often than not it is a frustrating and a thankless task.

As if this were not enough, the future of representative bodies is also in doubt. This has to do with three important issues:

- relations between in-company bodies (works councils) and trade unions;
- the room for employee participation in modern company life;
- the internationalization of business, in connection with developments in Europe and on the wider scene.

9.2 Works council or trade union?

The 1980s saw new arguments in the world of codetermination. The idea was strongly promoted that that works councils ought to take over the role in collective bargaining normally performed by the unions. Employees were considered to be quite emancipated and the union movement could not produce the manpower needed for such decentralized activities; they ought to produce some sort of framework agreement at sector level and then stand back, ready to assist if asked, while the works councils got on with negotiating working conditions with the employer. This view was supported by various employers' representatives, but others, including union representatives, were

vehemently against the idea. In their view, negotiations on working conditions could only be done properly by the unions; works councils were too closely connected to the company, they were probably reluctant to make their presence felt, and in any case they had little room for the defence of interests going beyond their own company.

Somewhere between these two views a third could be found: The idea that it was vital steadily to increase cooperation between works councils and unions on matters to do with working conditions. Works councils have a close understanding of the situation within a company, and will often have to safeguard the concrete implementation of agreements that a CBA can only describe in wider terms. The union, however, being independent of the employer, is much the stronger, and should therefore be the negotiating body.

Real life did not, and does not, accord perfectly with any one of these three standpoints. Centrifugal forces, such as a tendency towards decentralization in companies and in industrial relations, are increasing, whereas the linking forces of traditional labour relations are weakening. Increasingly, the future will see a patchwork of relations, schemes, and agreements.

Relations between the union movement and works councils have become increasingly tense. The 1980s saw a rising number of conflicts about working-hours arrangements; employers often declared that they preferred negotiating with the works council than with the unions, and works council complaints about lack of union support were growing. Looise (1988) saw the indeterminate task demarcation for both works councils and unions echoed in the lack of clear legal guidelines, as being an important source of this tension. The solution he proposed involved a strict separation of their tasks: The union would serve the collective and the individual interests within a company, whereas the works council would address itself to participating in the development of strategic company policy. This allocation of tasks would gradually take form, with union in-company work slowly being strengthened as the works council directed itself more and more towards company policy. In this view, unions would need more facilities to be able to work within companies, whereas works councils would have to be given additional powers in the decision-making process.

Teulings (1989) also detects tensions between works councils and unions, but in his view their origins lie in the fact that works councils are coming of age and refusing to allow anyone, whether employers, union, or government, to lay down the law. In fact, he considers these tensions evidence of a healthy spirit. If a works council is weak, let the union intervene; if the union is weak, let the works council assert itself. Wherever possible they should work closely and productively together, dividing responsibilities appropriately. This ideal does not exclude the possibility of legal directives, especially in situations—such as in many smaller businesses—where both union and works council have little influence.

9.3   Room for participation?

It is possible to hold the opinion, then, that works councils and unions can work together to fulfil their role—but has not this role been diminishing ever since the 1980s? The period since the late 1970s has been declared the age of "no-nonsense management" and the rehabilitation of free enterprise; in these terms, codetermination for employees is an ill-affordable luxury. Such opinions were heard on all sides, sometimes with regret and sometimes in relief.

This may have been true for other countries but in the Netherlands between 1975 and 1985 the role of discussions between representatives actually grew in importance (Looise, 1989). First, major legal provisions were introduced, namely the Works Council Act in 1979, a similar act for businesses having fewer than 100 personnel in 1982, new regulations for Works Councils in the Civil Service in 1982, the Codetermination in Education Act of 1982, and the Work Environment Act (introduced piecemeal, beginning in 1983). Second, the number of works councils, the various sectors rose from 4700 in 1977 to 22,000 in 1985, with 130,000 members in all. Finally, various studies have shown that the significance of these bodies has also grown. According to a research project carried out in the mid-1980s, the works council had become more active in setting the agenda and was more involved in all kinds of

company matters than had been the case 10 years previously. Moreover, compared with the IDE study (IDE Research Group, 1980), fewer differences in influence existed between the works council and the management or board of governors. The replication of the IDE research project in the second half of the 1980s also detected a small increase in works council influence (IDE Research Group, 1992).

It could be claimed that the coming into effect of the new laws during the 1980s was merely a time-lag effect; after all, they had already been set in motion in the early 1970s. Looise (1989), however, points out that the progress of new legislation can be stopped—witness the developments in union in-company work. No, there were evidently factors that genuinely stimulated the development of legislation and the growth of the activities of works councils and similar bodies, despite—or even, perhaps, because of—problems at the socio-economic level. A number of factors can be identified. First, the situation in which businesses operated was changed. Wanting to be able to react to very different circumstances in a flexible, decentralized way, company managers preferred negotiating with their own works council than with the unions. Second, both management and works council share a rational and professional attitude, considerable expertise, and an appreciation of the usefulness of skilled consultation. In modern, large industrial organizations it is ultimately more efficient to have a well-functioning and consequently successful negotiating body than a powerless and frustrated group of representatives who have little option but to be obstructive.

I would add a third factor: The role and influence of representative bodies being generally small, they offer no real threat to the status of management. Where attempts were made in the 1970s to introduce real and substantial industrial democracy, the experiences were rather disappointing.

9.4   Internationalization

Developments toward a single European market have been attended by discussions on codetermination arrangements in multinational companies. Many European countries now have far-reaching legal prescriptions for the participation of employees' representatives in national companies, but hardly any have been drawn up for multinationals. It might be supposed that the regular participatory procedures and bodies formulated at national level in the Dutch "negotiation economy" were impossible to bypass and that counterparts to these would be devised at European level. However, the "rise of the European lobby is overshadowing the stimulus given by the European Treaty to the more corporatist design of advisory procedures at EC level" (De Ru, 1991). The lobbying activities of such strong interest groups is unavoidable. Industrial democracy will have to be won from within the multinationals themselves.

A number of international concerns have set up a kind of internal "information council" in which information on company strategy is exchanged once or twice a year. In a small number of other cases, national works councils have themselves taken the initiative to consult each other. As yet, however, such initiatives are few in number and carry little weight. Insofar as European regulations are likely to come these are unlikely to be modelled on union representation as it exists in the UK, for example; the German and the Norwegian works council models are more likely candidates. For years there has been talk about provisions for a "Euro-works council". A bill has been drafted that would require multinational concerns with more than a thousand employees in all, and over two hundred employees in at least two member countries, to form a Euro-works council in order to inform and consult employees on decisions having international scope. The composition of such a Euro-works council ... may be negotiated at the level of the individual concern. Most EC countries support this proposal, but many multinationals, especially those with European employers are against it. Employers' resistance is probably related to a general antipathy towards anything that increases the influence of employees on company affairs, but research has made it clear that such influence, even in countries having far-reaching legislation, like the Netherlands, is minimal. The employers' contentions that the proposed European legislation is at odds with current trends towards decentralization and that it will encourage bureaucracy are probably better

founded. None the less it remains desirable to devise a form of codetermination at the international level; if it is not, the most important economic decisions will increasingly be taken without industrial-democratic sanction.

9.5 The future of employees' participation

We have seen that the role and influence of representative bodies, despite the economic stagnation of the 1980s, has not declined, and that here and there it appears to have grown stronger. Nevertheless, in the course of decades, *certain shifts can be detected in the strategies and forms employed by codetermination*. Some see in these developments the substitution of codetermination channels by something else: Up to the 1970s the unions were dominant; they gave way to works councils, and the future will see much more direct participation. Nevertheless, at sector and national level the unions have functions that a works council cannot perform, just as the works council of a company has functions that individual employees cannot perform. It would appear, rather, that in practice these different channels and forms are combined; indeed, that they presuppose each other's presence. Direct participation will indeed gain importance, especially among the more highly skilled employees, but should be supported by a works council, as the works council in its turn requires a union.

The Dutch developments that have been described here have also been seen in other countries. Lammers and Szell (1989) conclude that the expected decline in codetermination arrangements and practices has not taken place in the USA, France, Germany, Norway, or the Netherlands, at any rate. This finding has been supported by the results of an international comparative research project on representative bodies in many European countries (IDE Research Group, 1992).

Evidently, employee codetermination in industrial organizations has been subject to an underlying trend of stable, and even slowly increasing, operation, supported by the ordinances of national legislation, collective-bargaining agreements, or company rules. At national level, codetermination has achieved a definite standing in many societies.

At the international level, where future economic decisions will increasingly be made, this standing is still minimal. We have a long way to go before a solid countervailing power is established at that level.

REFERENCES

Acampo, J., Kunst, P.E.J., Soeters, J., & Woltmeyer, A. (1987). *OR-lidmaatschap, Loopbaan en verloop.* Maastricht: Rijksuniversiteit Limburg.

Blumberg, P. (1968). *Industrial democracy.* London: Constable.

Clarke, T. (1991). Producer cooperatives. In G. Szell (Ed.), *Concise encyclopedia of participation and co-management.* Berlin: De Gruyter.

Cressey, P., & Williams, R. (1991). *Participation in innovations. New technology and the role of employee participation.* Dublin: European Foundation for the improvement of living and working conditions.

Emery, F.E., Thorsrud, E., & Trist, E.L. (1969). *Form and context in industrial democracy.* Assen: Van Gorcum.

Endenburg, G. (1981). *Sociocratie.* Alphen aan den Rijn: Samsom.

Gevers, J.K.M. (1987). *Health and safety protection in industry: Participation and information of employers and workers.* Brussels: Europese Gemeenschap.

Hofstede, G. (1991). Nationale waarden in verband met medezeggenschap. Is een Europese medezeggenschapsregeling mogelijk? *M & O,* 459–473.

Hövels, B., & Nas, P. (1976). *Ondernemingsraden en medezeggenschap.* Nijmegen: Busser.

Hövels, B., & Nas, P. (1978). Ondernemingsraden: Enkele conclusies op grond van een onderzoek. *M & O, 32,* 330–347.

Huiskamp, M.J. (1983). De CAO-structuur in de Nederlandse industrie. *Economische Statistische Berichten,* 131–137, 154–158, 180–184.

IDE Research Group (1980). *Industrial democracy in Europe.* London: Oxford University Press.

IDE Research Group (1992). *Industrial democracy in Europe revisited.* London: Oxford University Press.

Jain, H.C. (1977). *Prerequisites for effective participation information and training.* Brussels: European Institute for Advanced Studies in Management.

Jacobs, A.T.J.M. (1988). Het Nederlandse CAO-recht, bezien door een Europese bril. *Sociaal Maandblad Arbeid, 43,* 244–254.

Lammers, C.J. (Ed.) (1965). *Medezeggenschap en overleg in het bedrijf.* Utrecht: Spectrum.

Lammers, C.J. (1980). *Organisaties vergelijkenderwijs.* Utrecht: Spectrum.

Lammers, C.J., Andriessen, J.H.T.H., Meys, A.A., & Meurs, P.L. (1980). Maakt de ondernemingsraad in het Nederlandse ziekenhuis een kans? *M & O,* 34.

Lammers, C.J., & Szell, G. (Eds.) (1989). *International handbook of participation in organizations.* Oxford: Oxford University Press.

Looise, J.C. (1988). *Werknemersvertegenwoordiging op de tweesprong.* Alphen aan den Rijn: Samson.

Looise, J.C. (1989). The recent growth in employee representation in the Netherlands: Defying the times? In C.J. Lammers & G Szell (Eds.), *International handbook of participation in organizations.* Oxford: Oxford University Press.

Looise, J.C., & Lange, F.G.M. de (1987). *Ondernemingsraden, bestuurders en besluitvorming.* Nijmegen: ITS.

Man, H. De (1985). *Medezeggenschap besluitvorming en organisatie.* Den Haag: COB/SER.

Monat, J. (1991). Workers participation. In G. Szell (Ed.), *Concise encyclopedia of participation and co-management.* Berlin: De Gruyter.

Mulder, M. (1977). *Omgaan met macht.* Amsterdam: Elsevier.

Reubsaet, T.J.M. (1988). *De ARBOwet in uitvoering.* Nijmegen: ITS.

Rosen, C.M., Klein, K.J., & Young, K.M. (1985). *Employee ownership in America.* Lexington, MA: Lexington Books.

Ru, H. De (1991). Vana overleg economic naar inspraak arena. *Beleid en Maatschappij, 6,* 196–302.

Russel, R. (1989). Taking stock of the ESOPs. In C.J. Lammers & G. Szell (Eds.), *International handbook of participation in organizations.* Oxford: Oxford University Press.

Russel, R. (1991). Producer co-operatives. In G. Szell (Ed.), *Concise encyclopedia of participation and co-management.* Berlin: De Gruyter.

Teulings, A.W.M. (1987). A political bargaining theory of codetermination. *Organization Studies, 87,* 1–23.

Teulings, A.W.M. (1988). Representing employee interests: Works councils and the rank and file. *Economic and Industrial Democracy, 9,* 1–11.

Teulings, A.W.M. (1989). Looise denkt de verkeerde kant op. *OR Informatie,* 14 juni.

Verstegen, R., Andriessen, J.H.T.H., & Dekkers, H. (1987). *Medezeggenschap in kleine ondernemingen (10–30 werknemers).* Tilburg: IVA.

Voets, H.J.L. (1995). *Success and enterprise.* Aldershot, UK: Avebury Press.

Voûte, A. (1991). *Aandelen voor werknemers. Motivatie door participatie.* Deventer: Kluwer.

Wall, T.D., & Lischeron, J.A. (1977). *Workers' participation.* London: McGraw-Hill.

17

Automation: Socio-organizational Aspects

Paul L. Koopman and Jen A. Algera

1 INTRODUCTION

In this chapter the concept of automation and its effects on the organization will be discussed. The past few decades have made it clear that automation has great influence on the manner in which goods or services are produced in organizations. The automation of both primary production processes and supporting processes such as administrative or logistic systems has major consequences for job content and for the organization of the work. The following topics will be treated: a brief description of the use of automation in work organizations; its consequences for the quality and the quantity of employment; the role of automation in strategic policy; the management of automation projects, and the personnel and organizational aspects of automation.

2 FORMS OF AUTOMATION

Although various definitions of the concept of automation can been given, it essentially involves the application of sophisticated technical resources in entirely or largely self-regulating processes or subprocesses, eliminating human intervention in the direct production process to an important extent. Supporting processes, such as administration and logistics, have also seen a genuine revolution in the use of automated information systems in recent years (Scott Morton, 1991). Often, a broad distinction is made between automation of production processes and office automation. In both cases computers take over information-processing and decision-making functions that were previously performed by human beings.

Large changes have taken place in the control of *industrial production* processes since the 1950s and 1960s (see, e.g., Algera, Reitsma, Scholtens, Vrins, & Wijnen, 1990). Developments in control engineering have led to remote operation from control rooms equipped with a large number of instruments and monitors. The help of the computer may be enlisted in various ways. In the first place, the computer can provide information on whether the raw materials and the installation meet the required specifications. If there are any deviations, the operator must adjust the procedure in order to achieve the desired final result. The second field in which the computer is applied is process control. Based upon process models, the computer uses feedback from the process to control its further course. In this application of computers the task of the operator shifts from operation to monitoring (see, e.g., Kragt, 1983). A third field in which the computer is enlisted is in monitoring warnings and alarms. The problem here is that the great variety and large number of signals and alarms can overload an operator with information, so that a vital alarm goes unnoticed. Computer-controlled support systems can play a role in structuring and conveying relevant process information to the operator.

In the 1970s, computer techniques gradually found applications in instrumentation systems. A familiar example is the TDC 2000 instrumentation system of Honeywell. Man-machine communication can now also take place via screens and keyboards instead of via conventional control panels. The chemical industry is a forerunner in the replacement of panel instrumentation by screen instrumentation (Kragt, 1992). One result of these technical developments is that fewer and fewer operators are needed to monitor the production process. Another result is that the nature of the work changes. Thanks to better control of the production process, an operator needs to intervene much less during "normal" operation. But when unexpected breakdowns occur, he may suddenly be required to perform a great many actions in quick succession. This combination of lengthy periods wherein no intervention is required and unexpected interventions sets high demands of design of the man–machine–interface, especially in the structuring of information.

In addition to the use of automation in the control of industrial production processes, a rapid increase of automated information and communication systems has been observed in *offices* in the past decades (Monger, 1987; Van Veen, 1993; Andriessen & Roe, 1994). Since the 1960s, human labour has increasingly been replaced by new information-processing technologies in the rapidly expanding service sector. In many organizations, the first step in office automation involved salary records. Later other office tasks, involving the processing and manipulation of data and information (usually relatively simple routine and repetitive tasks), were altered by automation.

Another development in office automation was the growth in the number of people involved. Initially, in the 1950s and 1960s, only automation experts were involved in the construction and use of automated systems. Professional knowledge of hardware and software was required to be able to deal with these systems. Spectacular developments in the field of hardware and software have considerably expanded the group of users. Thanks to cheaper hardware and the availability of user-friendly software, the computer has become an everyday tool for various types of office work in today's office. On the one hand, computers, and personal computers in particular, are used for traditional activities such as word processing. On the other hand, the development of sophisticated software has made possible a higher level of information processing as well as the generation of new information. A common problem this entails is the "transformation of data into information". Generally speaking, the use of automated information systems makes much more data available. Then the problem arises of how to process the data so as to produce information that can be of use to the organization as control information. Exploiting the possibilities of hardware and software can lead to the creation of new jobs in the organization—for example, "information managers" or "knowledge workers".

We now turn to a more detailed summary of the various forms of automation that are distinguished in the literature and in practice.

New forms of automation can be classified into categories of business operations: primary, secondary, and control processes in work organizations. The primary processes are those necessary for the manufacture of the key products, such as purchasing, sales, production, and physical distribution. The secondary processes involve supporting activities such as design, maintenance, bookkeeping, and records. Control processes are taken to be the activities that control or coordinate primary or secondary processes. They are distinguished into control processes at various levels of the organization: strategic (e.g. corporate planning, prognoses), tactical (e.g. capacity planning, production planning), and operational (e.g.

resource planning, production management). A publication in the mid-1980s (COB/SER, 1984) indicated five areas in which important developments have taken or will take place:

1. Computer Aided Engineering (CAE). The two most prominent new automation forms in this field are Computer Aided Design (CAD) and Computer Aided Process Planning (CAPP). These automation techniques use simulation and rotation to help obtain better insight into the design of manufacturing processes. They also speed up the design phase.

2. Computer Aided Manufacturing (CAM) in production. The CNC (Computer Numerical Controlled) machines are the most widely known example of this field of automation; they are primarily used in machine tools such as lathes, milling machines, and drills. Several such machines can be linked, and the feed motion of tools and semi-manufactures can be automatically controlled. At its most complete, when it integrates various functions in a single computer system, it is termed a Flexible Fabrication System (FFS). The primary advantages of such systems are that they allow a greater variety of treatments and products, quick switching, and better control of product quality.

3. Computer Aided Manufacturing (CAM) in assembly—in particular, the programmable robot. At present, programmable robots are chiefly used to join parts of a product, as by welding. This is a relatively recent application of automation to which much further refinement is needed—to the sensor systems, the control algorithms, the programmability, and the interfaces with other machines via the central computer.

4. Automation of the physical distribution. Emphasis here lies on stock control and production control. Familiar examples are automated warehouses, automatically guided transport vehicles, and computer reports when stock levels become critical. An important development in this field is the linking of physical distribution systems to more general production control systems.

5. Automation of control processes. These involve data processing, communication systems, and information systems at all three control levels (strategic, tactical, and operational). An important development in this field is Manufacturing Resource Planning (MRP), in which several elements have been combined with a view to optimal control and planning of the production process, so that materials and resources can be employed efficiently, ultimately to supply the products to the customer as planned. More and more information networks are also being set up between companies, to optimize the supply of products to customers and to minimize intermediate stocks. Co-makership between companies becomes a usual practice in trying to minimize losses in the whole chain of processes from raw materials to consumer.

All these types of automation are used in industrial production systems. Automation of control processes at the three control levels is also employed in administrative information systems, such as budgeting systems, personnel information systems, and management-accounting information systems.

Wentink and Zanders (1985) distinguished four types of office tasks: policy-making tasks, professional tasks, secretarial tasks, and administrative tasks. They differ from one another in the information subprocesses that make up the most important parts of the task. Examples of information subprocesses are: generating, handling, interpreting, recording, storing, retrieving, consulting, duplicating. Because they are of a more standardized and predictable nature, administrative and secretarial tasks are easier to automate than policy-making and professional tasks. The information subprocesses of interpretation and generation are among the main activities of the two latter types of tasks. This makes the application of computers more difficult, despite a growing interest in "expert systems". Expert systems aim at the representation of the knowledge of a human expert. Very few expert systems are in use as yet, although in principle many semi-structured decision problems could be approached with the help of expert systems

(Ballantine, 1988). If the user is unable to follow the decision-making process of the system, it is a considerable obstacle to the application of such systems. This is an essential condition: if the system is not able to explain its reasoning to the user, it will not be used. Another problem in the development of expert systems is specifying the knowledge. In other words, via what techniques can the knowledge be quantified? Methods have become available in recent years. Also in the field of management tasks automated information systems are being implemented, to support decision-making by managers. The adoption of these Executive Information Systems however is not so easy (see, e.g., Cullen, 1995).

The new communication technology also opens up other possibilities for the organization of the work, nowadays known under the term "telematics", described as a technology that integrates information, computer, and telecommunication technologies (Andriessen, 1994; Peiró & Prieto, 1994; Roe, 1994). One example of telework was described by Heller (1988), involving an initiative of the Rank Xerox company to offer a number of "professionals" a different type of employment contract in which they worked for the organization more as external consultants but were provided with a number of communication facilities. Teleworking has rapidly expanded in the 1990s.

3 SOCIETAL CONTEXT

The speed with which new technologies are implemented, or computers put to work in organizations, is also determined by the societal context. Government incentives or restraints can speed up or delay the application of new technologies. Conversely, automation also influences society, particularly the volume of employment and the quality of the work. This interaction seems to take place in different manners at different points in time. As to the influence of automation on society, and more specifically on the volume and quality of employment, Leyder (1979) distinguished a "first round" and a "second round". During the first round—up to the beginning of the 1970s—the implementation of automation was

fairly gradual. In this phase the use of computers was elitist: generally, only large organizations could afford to purchase computers (Nora & Minc, 1978). Another very important circumstance of the first round was that the implementation of automation took place in a period of economic growth. This meant that the heightened productivity led to an increase in Gross National Product, but not to increased unemployment at a national level. Naturally, certain positions became redundant, but on the other hand new jobs were created, while the service and government sectors, as growth sectors, compensated for the shedding of labour as a result of automation.

The "second round" is characterized by a number of fundamental technological socio-economic changes. Spectacular technological breakthroughs in the field of microelectronics have removed technical and economic obstacles to further automation. Thanks to microelectronics, it is possible to build very large-capacity computers for a very small price on a very small surface. This makes the computer almost universally applicable. The socio-economic context in which the "second round" is taking place differs fundamentally from that of the "first round". Economic growth collapsed during the second half of the 1970s, the profit-making capacity of business was eaten away and few new investments were made that could compensate for the loss of jobs. Now it is precisely the service sector, still a growth sector in the recent past, where labour-saving automation is expected to deal considerable blows to the volume of employment (Briefs, 1980).

Prognoses on the expected effect of automation on employment opportunity are highly divergent (Roe, 1989, 1991). Here it is important to make a distinction between short-term and long-term effects. The most pessimistic prognoses (Friedrichs & Schaff, 1982) assert that automation will ultimately make nearly all human work superfluous. Other authors state that actively exploiting the opportunities offered by microelectronics can lead to new employment. In the Netherlands, for example, a government advisory group advised in the early 1980s that, in general, it would not be a wise strategy to try to curb the use of microelectronics. The country's competitiveness would be adversely affected, implying a greater threat to employment than would the optimal utilization of the possibilities offered by this technological development.

After a long period of stagnation, economic growth again increased in the mid-1980s. Talk of restraints on the new technology, or even of creating an "automation tax", which was still heard in the late 1970s and early 1980s, has subsided. Partly against the background of European economic integration, interest in the development and implementation of new technologies has intensified, encouraged by national governments and by the European Community. A well-known example was ESPRIT (European Strategic Programme for Research and Development into Information Technology). In the mid-1990s the European Union still supports developments in information technology, to strengthen the competitive position of European countries against the USA and South East Asia. In the mid-1990s the discussion has concentrated on the issue of "jobless growth". This means that even in periods of economic growth the volume of employment would decrease.

We have seen great divergence in the prognoses on the effects of automation on the volume of employment. The same may be said of its expected effects on the quality of work life. The expectations of 100 Dutch experts garnered via the Delphi method in the 1980s are predominately positive. This is primarily true of physical working conditions; as to the content of the work, optimism is somewhat less strong, but still clearly present. Briefs (1980), Evans (1982), and Cressey (1989) expect job qualifications to "polarize". This is expected to lead to a relatively small elite of specialists on the one hand, who are continually obliged to increase their knowledge, with on the other hand a large mass of semi-skilled workers performing marginal routine tasks without deeper insight into the systems in which they function.

In discussing the effects of automation on quality of work life, one of the biggest impediments is that the concept is not sharply defined and therefore can easily be the source of misunderstandings (Evans, 1982). Improvements in the quality of work life emphasize very divergent matters such as physical working conditions, task content, and employee participation in the de-

cision-making processes of the organization. Automation may have a positive effect on one of these aspects, the elimination of dirty and hazardous work thanks to remote control, while at the same time negatively affecting another aspect, making the work monotonous by building decisions into the equipment (Roe, 1991; Sverko, 1991).

In the past, technological advances, such as the invention of the electromotor, greatly influenced the design of work tasks and the structure of the organizations in which the work took place. In a market economy, the choice of a technical system will generally be determined by economic criteria. This was confirmed by a study by the Dutch Socio-Economic Advisory Council (SER, 1982). According to this report, economic factors (lowering production costs, improving competitiveness) were the most important incentives to the continued implementation of microelectronics.

In discussing the influence of technology on the design of labour tasks and organizational structure, it is important to mention the classical notion of "technological determinism", which was formerly a popular concept in the literature. This idea rests upon three assumptions (Davis & Taylor, 1976). In the first place, it is assumed that the technology develops according to its own internal laws, independent of the social environment and the culture. In the second place, the concept assumes that, for an effective use to benefit society, the march of technology should not be obstructed by considerations other than those of the engineers and technicians who are directly involved in its development. In the third place, it is assumed that the structure of the organization is dictated by the technology. The third assumption in particular is important against the background of the question of how much latitude automation leaves in the job design and in the organizational structure to take into consideration the "quality" of the work in the design of systems.

In a comparative study of England and West Germany, Sorge, Hartmann, Warner, and Nicholas, (1982) investigated the use of computer numerical control (CNC) equipment (for example, in metal working). They observed an extreme degree of "malleability" in the CNC technology. This appeared from the fact that uses of CNC technology had been adapted to existing organizational structures and personnel-management strategies. For example, in smaller plants the programming function was much less concentrated in specialized departments remote from the work place than in larger companies. Differences between England and West Germany with respect to management, training, etc., also appeared to be unaffected by the introduction of CNC technology. The empirical findings of Sorge et al. (1982) illustrate that, even with a given technology, latitude certainly remains for organizational design. Other studies have confirmed this conclusion (Wilkinson, 1983; Buchanan & Boddy, 1986; Cressey, 1989). The impact of technology is contingent on the context; similar technologies have widely varying impacts in different circumstances (Osterman, 1991). In other words, new information technology only presents opportunities; other elements must be present to take full advantage of those opportunities (Yates & Benjamin, 1991).

"Technological determinism" has also been criticized from a more theoretical point of view (Berting, 1993). For instance, the classical socio-technical system approach regards production systems as consisting of two components, the technical system and the social system. The technical system comprises the installations, equipment, and procedures that are needed to transform "input" into products and services. The social system refers to the relationship among task performers and the technology, and among the task performers themselves. The socio-technical system approach assumes that quite some flexibility is possible in the design of an effective production system. The objectives of a system are best achieved not by optimizing the technical system and then adapting the social system, but by doing so simultaneously ("joint optimization" of the technical and the social components). Insufficient integration of the social and the technical aspects of a production system can lead to absenteeism, turnover, poor group cohesion, etc. An important tenet of socio-technical system design is to make units (individuals or groups) autonomous enough for self-regulation, so that the unit is in a position to solve any problems that occur.

In practice, task and organizational design still often take place from a technological point of view. In a survey, Clegg and Symon (1989) distinguished between the "technology-centred" and the "human-centred" approaches. The "technology-centred" approach, they observed, is still dominant in the design and implementation of new technology. They outlined a "human-centred" approach consisting of five elements and a checklist with questions for each of them.

- A philosophy: Is technology seen as a "tool"?
- Ownership: Who is responsible for the definition of system requirements?
- Goals: Have goals been defined in relation to task design and organizational structure?
- Method: Who is involved in the design process?
- Training: Are there plans for internal training courses aimed at a broad understanding of the new technology?

Clegg and Symon (1989) regarded these five elements as highly interdependent aspects that jointly determine whether a human-centred approach will be taken in a given situation. A number of the elements are more closely elaborated in the rest of this chapter.

4 AUTOMATION IN STRATEGIC POLICY

4.1 Corporate policy on technological innovation

How open are organizations to technological innovation? How can technological innovation processes be typified in general: As rational and analytical or more as political? To what extent is technological innovation a matter of systematic policy? Although the experiences differ from situation to situation and the research results are sometimes contradictory, a few trends can still be indicated.

An initial observation is that most organizations greatly underutilize the possibilities offered by the new technology. Child, Ganter, and Kieser (1987) referred to this as "organizational conservatism". It applies not only to the implementation of new technology, but also to the utilization of its increasing flexibility, which, at least theoretically, yields greater freedom in relation to the organizational design (Clegg, Kemp, & Wall, 1984; Warner, 1985; Ciborra & Lanzara, 1994). New developments in telematics, for example, make it possible to centralize in some respects while decentralizing in others, and thus to transcend the zero-sum nature of the centralization–decentralization balance (Keen, 1987; Robbins, 1990; Roe, 1991; Peiró & Prieto, 1994). According to Huppes (1985), the new information technology makes it possible to undo the division of labour inherited from our industrial past, and to switch from an industrial to a professional-technical organizational structure. Kern and Schumann (1985), too, envision no room in the key sectors of industry for unskilled personnel. In their view, important chances to improve productivity will often remain unused. Organizations seldom appear to make systematic use of such new chances. More often habits, procedures, and responsibilities are maintained as far as possible. Innovation is fine, but not too much at once.

Child et al. (1987) illustrated this with examples from hospital laboratories, retailing, and banking (see also Child & Loveridge, 1990). In hospitals, the performance of laboratory tests was not delegated to assistants, although the new automated system made it possible, and they could have been performed immediately. Instead, the custom was clung to that the "professionals" established the test outcome at the end of the day. In retailing and banks, different and more efficient manners of working, including delegation—made possible by the new technical possibilities—were fairly exceptional. For the banking world, this was confirmed by Hedberg's (1979) conclusions, on the basis of a study of automation in five banks in four European countries, that opportunities to revise the organizational structure and the individual tasks were practically ignored.

Of course there are also other examples. Algera et al. (1990) cited a good instance of organizational and task restructuring for the analysis of steel samples in the steel industry, induced by new technology. Thanks to the availability of new equipment for the analysis of steel samples, certain analyses could be performed by the personnel in the steel plant, instead of by the laboratory personnel as in the past.

Child et al. (1987) named eight sources of "organizational conservatism":

1. The status quo. Radical organizational changes are expensive; they demand much thought; they touch a large number of jobs and departments; they provide possibilities for conflicts and struggles for competence; they require additional retraining.

2. Key figures in the organization try to maintain or to improve their power position. This may cancel out opportunities to decentralize.

3. The organizational structure and culture generally have a long history, which affects the way in which organizational problems and the structural solutions to them are viewed.

4. The organization, its methods, and procedures are embedded in a society and a culture that have their own rules. Violation of these rules implies the risk of loss of legitimacy.

5. Hardware and software suppliers increasingly play into the resistance of organizations to implement large changes by making sure that new equipment and programs are compatible with existing organizational systems and methods. This is even more the case when the future users are also those who decide about the innovation (managers, specialists).

6. The manner in which a problem and potential solutions are defined partly depends on the analytical instruments available. More radical solutions are often omitted from a cost–benefit analysis because the expected advantages and disadvantages are so difficult to estimate. When it is difficult to demonstrate specific advantages of organizational innovation, it is tempting— and often also wise—to play safe and stick to existing practice.

7. Technological innovation with significant consequences for the job content of tasks are approached by bodies of personnel representatives with extra caution. Existing qualification systems and legal regulations are an added source of organizational conservatism here.

8. More in general, the formal participative procedures encourage a certain conservatism. In contrast to what is often claimed in the literature, that participation decreases resistance, it appears that trade unions and works councils are primarily out to defend existing jobs and qualifications.

In short, there are all kinds of factors that limit the openness of organizations to new technological possibilities. Countering the pressure from the market are people who defend established positions, who want to maintain existing procedures (Rammert, 1983) or who simply have no idea of the new possibilities (March & Olsen, 1976; Koopman & Pool, 1990). As a result, technological innovation is often a bit by bit and irregular process, and its pace is generally much slower than would be expedient, surely when management support systems are involved. An interesting hypothesis would be that the chance that an innovation be accepted and fully utilized increases as its effects on existing procedures decrease (Kimberly, 1987).

Of course the picture is sometimes quite different, depending in part on the policy of the organization and the type of innovation (Downs & Mohr, 1976; Pennings, 1987). According to Mohr (1987), there are two basic forms of technological innovation: "routine change" and "readaptation". Routine changes involve all kinds of lesser matters, such as replacing equipment, improvement and expansion of existing facilities, etc. This type of change is more or less "part of the game". Individual organizational members may pick up an idea from a neighbour or competitor and imitate it. Hobbyists bring in new machines and gradually manage to enthuse their environment. "Readaptation" is a much more drastic organizational innovation process in which important counterforces must be overcome. Long-standing and ingrained behaviour patterns and procedures can be changed only with great effort. This can only succeed if the advantages of changing, or the disadvantages of not changing, are extreme. This is also one of the reasons why such processes are often highly political in nature (Normann, 1971; Pettigrew, 1985; Hickson, Butler, Cray, Mallory, & Wilson, 1986). In the management literature the popularity of the Business Process Reengineering concept seems to illustrate that more drastic organization changes will dominate the scene in the late 1990s.

To what degree do automation processes take place on the basis of a systematic information and automation policy and what does this mean for the nature of the renewal process? Research results do not concur on this point. Asked in retrospect about their "strategy", most managers usually manage to paint a fairly rational picture (Kimberly, 1987). On the other hand, it is well known that much rationality only comes about in retrospect and that strategy takes shape gradually and along the way (Mintzberg, 1988; Quinn, 1988). Automation decisions, too, are often non-linear, tumultuous and unpredictable, following strict plans only to a degree. Intuition and political actions play a large role (Kimberly, 1987). So we must be cautious in our interpretations. Insofar as we do know something about management motives and strategy in automation, the following aspects are primarily important (Northcott & Rogers, 1982; Buchanan & Boddy, 1983; Child, 1987):

1. lowering costs;
2. increasing flexibility;
3. improving quality;
4. increasing control.

Blackler and Brown (1986) emphasized the importance of broad policy viewpoints in automation. These starting points determine whether automation is basically regarded as a technical issue or as a problem of personnel and organization. On this basis, they distinguished two poles in approach: the task and technology approach, and the organizational and user approach (Table 17.1).

The differences between these two approaches are not only related to the policy assumptions and the weight ascribed to the various goals, but also to the manner itself. The task and technology approach assumes that the goals of technological innovation have been formulated at an early stage and set down in detailed specifications. However, research has repeatedly shown that social-change processes seldom take place in this way (Lindblom, 1959; Herbst, 1974; Kling, 1983; Nutt, 1984; Quinn, 1988). Rather, it is the perceptions, motivation, expectations, and skills of people that develop gradually as organizations change. This

---

TABLE 17.1

Assumptions in automation (Blackler & Brown, 1986).

Task and technology approach	*Organizational and user approach*
Minimize personnel costs	Utilize personnel as well as possible
Pinpoint goals from the outset	Start with broad goals
Centralize coordination and control	Decentralization
Strong reliance on experts	Emphasis on user participation
Machines more important than people	People use machines
Task fragmentation	Meaningful tasks
Emphasis on what new systems can do	Emphasis on training

---

demands an evolutionary process in which there is room to learn (Floyd & Keil, 1983; Senge, 1990; Swieringa & Wierdsma, 1992; Van Offenbeek & Koopman, 1996a). We will come back to this in section 5.2.

4.2 System methods

What makes automation such a specific problem? According to Van Reeken (1986, p.6), first of all, Wildavsky's paradox: "The problem cannot be stated without knowing the solution." The solution must be developed by people (the designers) who must become acquainted with the problem and often with the organizational goals through people (the customers) who cannot state them, at least not yet or not adequately, and who often are not aware of the solution options. The communication between these two groups, in informal and colloquial language, is not unambiguous, accurate, and workable enough for the designer. If communication takes place in a formal language (method), then it is not comprehensible or controllable for the customer. Thus those who will have to work with the solution (the users), because they fear the consequences of the solution to be chosen, become unreliable discussion partners. Designers may be too quick to grasp. And finally, because development takes time, when the system is installed, the situation may differ from the situation when the specifications were formulated.

A familiar (and notorious) law in the automation world is "Golub's Law No 1": "No major computer project is ever installed on time, within budget, with the same staff that started it, nor does the project do what it is supposed to do." Pirow (1983) put this law to an empirical test by analyzing 536 computer projects on the criteria mentioned in Golub's Law (time, budget, etc.). From the available data, only 56 projects could be classified as "successful/profitable". These 56 successful projects included only 20 "major computer projects" (more than 100 man-months of work). Pirow (1983) ultimately concluded that only 2 of those 20 projects:

- had stayed within the anticipated budget;
- were completed within the set time;
- were judged by the users to be very successful.

Numerous other authors confirm that in automation, custom-made solutions are often sorely lacking, and that their time horizon and development costs often get entirely out of hand (see, e.g., Bubenko, 1986; Lyytinen, 1987; Van Offenbeek & Koopman, 1996a). But even if we assume that the situation is not always this bad, it is clear that system development is no simple matter. On the one hand, it demands intensive intellectual efforts; on the other hand, careful coordination. For the headwork, the designers by now have acquired a chock-full "tool-box", one that is still being supplemented almost daily. The methods based upon the tool-box principle are sometimes called "motoring methodologies" (Prakke, 1987), as opposed to "monitoring methodologies", which guide the organization through the various phases of system development, and sometimes also specify which actors should be involved in which activities. Bijvoet and Zomer (1996) termed the former "system development methodologies" and the latter "project control methodologies". We often see a combination of the two in practice, in which case they are sometimes referred to as "system methodologies" (Van Offenbeek & Koopman, 1996b). These are taken to be "a package of prescriptions for systematically controlling, performing and recording all activities that lead to the successful development and use of an automated information system" (Völlmar, 1985).

Why is the development of an information system so difficult and why is it currently the subject of such great interest? Bemelmans and De Boer (1986) mentioned four reasons. The first is the increasing awareness that the success of an information system is not primarily determined by its technical sophistication, but by the extent to which such a system actually meets the information needs of its users. This shifts the emphasis more to the "demand pull" rather than the "technology push". The second reason is an all-round endeavour for more integrated systems. This makes the development process more complex. The third reason has to do with the durability of an information system. The average life cycle of an administrative information system is currently around five years. As adaptation costs are particularly high, it is generally attempted to develop a system that will function as long as possible without necessitating too many revisions and adaptations. The fourth reason is a related one, involving the efficiency of the development process. It often happens that system wishes need retrospective adjustment, often because requirements were initially formulated unclearly or were wrongly interpreted by the designers. This is bound to cause communication problems during automation (see section 4.3). A good development method is conducive to bringing misunderstandings and design errors to light as early as possible.

What conditions must a development method satisfy? Bemelmans and De Boer (1986) named the following requirements (see also Blank & Krijger, 1982; Vandenbulcke, 1986; Olle et al., 1988):

- A method must be suitable as a means of communication between customers, users, designers, etc. In order to develop an effective system, a large amount of consensus will have to exist or be created.
- A method must be able to describe the various points of view that can be adopted in the development of an information system. A systelogic model goes into the "why" of the information, an infologic model sets down the "what", whereas a data model and a technical model specify the "how".
- A method must make it possible to indicate precisely what the object of study will be; in other words, it must be possible to strictly delineate the limits of a system.
- A method must be able to split a total system into convenient and practicable subsystems.
- A method must be able to build up design information step by step, working from general to detailed; this is known as the principle of step-by-step refinement.
- A method must be complete in the sense that it must describe both the manipulation processes and the relevant data.
- A method must yield the required documentation. This requirement has to do with the transferability of the development results and is of great importance with a view to efficient control and maintenance of the project.

Numerous phase models for the development of an information system are described in the literature (e.g. Gelper, 1986; Laagland & Schaddelee, 1986; Langerhorst, 1986; Ruys, 1986). Their object is to introduce clear checkpoints or milestones, at which the results thus far are evaluated and an assessment is made of how to proceed. For this reason, too, each phase must be wound up with thorough but easily readable documentation (see Table 17.2).

It is often difficult to pinpoint the beginning of an automation project. Sometimes it starts with a *preliminary study* of some company problem or other—for example, stock control, supply times, cost monitoring, or quality control. In other cases the first phase is part of the periodically formulated medium-range plans in which department

TABLE 17.2

A general phase model of automation projects (from Bemelmans & De Boer, 1986, p.11).

Phase	Goal and activites
Drawing up policy plan	The formulation of a long-term plan indicating when each project starts
Preliminary study	Short exploratory study of a particular system
Feasibility study	The object is more insight into what must be developed. Activities are the delineation of the system limits and an initial cost–benefit analysis
Logical or functional design	The object is a user-oriented blueprint of the future system: what will the new system look like, under what conditions must it function (response time, number of data, reliability, etc.)
Technical design	Formulation of detailed program descriptions and procedures to be performed by hand
Technical and organizational construction	Constructing and testing programs; setting up the organization to use the system
Conversion and implementation	Switch to the new system and completion of the documentation
System use and control	This phase follows the completion of the innovation project and is part of normal business operations

heads set down their wants in the way of technological innovation.

Their wants may be prompted by a perceived lack of efficiency in the work of the department (which may or may not be justified), by a feeling of tagging along behind others who have already automated, or by an attempt of the central management to make an "up-to-date" impression. Or the automation department, whose very existence is dependent on automation, may often take the initiative. In addition there may be pressure from suppliers of hardware and software: Automation in some units of the organization may prove to be inefficient unless other units are also automated, a computer of the following generation will increase the number of uses, etc. This, by the way, assumes that the company also invests in its employees, which is worthwhile, too, in the long run (Senker, 1985). A report by the Dutch Socio-Economic Advisory Council (SER, 1982), mentioned earlier,

shows that economic factors (lowering production costs, improving competitiveness) are the most important factors behind automation, followed by technical considerations in relation to production (better control of the production process, improved quality of products). In the third place come considerations of an internal organizational nature (improvement of the information flow and how the work is organized).

Some authors point out the danger of solution-oriented thinking during the preliminary study (Koopman & Pool, 1992). It can lead to over-emphasis of the informational aspects and to an incomplete diagnosis of the corporate problem (Mumford & Weir, 1979; Huber, 1980; Argelo, 1982; Vaas, 1988). Especially when the automation department is involved in the problem at a very early stage, there is a good chance that the corporate problem will be defined as an automation issue. In that case the direction for the solution has already been established before the problem has been sufficiently clarified.

The primary goal of the *feasibility study* is to investigate whether and in how far automation can be a solution to the company problem. Several solutions should be drafted, from which the best one will emerge. This solution must not only eliminate the corporate problem entirely or partly. It must also not be too contradictory to other policy criteria (often a solution to one problem creates another, larger problem). Automation often has unwanted side effects, and they must also be considered in appraising the proposed solution. An important question is who takes part in the discussion of the relevant policy criteria at this stage.

The final result of this phase is an automation plan or a recommendation that the problem can better be approached in another way. Any such plan should include the project structure. It is at this point that the actual project management starts. The previous phases largely take place within the normal routine. A general cost–benefit analysis and a schedule of the phases to follow are also part of the automation plan.

The object of the *logical or functional design* is to build further on the results of the feasibility study, to finalize the system requirements and to translate them into exact system specifications. These specifications relate the design of the entire system, including the specifications of the hardware and software, up to the point that programs and manual procedures can be set down. Specifications of the user–system interface must be tentatively tested for their usefulness. The test requirements for the acceptance test to be performed later should also be formulated. Consequences for the organization as a whole and for the personnel should be set down as well.

Most manuals emphasize the wisdom of first making an overall system design before working out parts in detail, this with a view to controlling costs. Elaboration of the technical details can only start on the basis of the progress report that terminates the functional design phase. One subject of this report is an estimate of the total project costs.

The *technical design* involves the elaboration and further detailing of the subsystems. In projects of limited scope, the distinction between functional and technical designs may become somewhat obscure. The technical design results in a concrete project proposal. This is the transition to the actual execution. The project proposal also contains the test criteria for the system and acceptance tests, the schedule for the execution phase and a more accurate cost–benefit analysis.

The object of the *construction phase* is first of all to convert the now complete design into tasks to be performed by hand and by computer programs. This is followed by the system test and the acceptance test. The former is a technical test of programs and the entire system. The latter is a test by the users based on requirements formulated earlier. Some manuals also mention the importance of instructing the users in this phase.

If the system meets the requirements, the next step can be *conversion* of data files and *implementation* of the new system. In contrast to the previous phases, activities in this phase have a direct influence on the functioning of the organization. Usually a fairly drastic reorganization will have to take place in the user departments. Depending on the circumstances, implementation can take place in three ways: switching all at once from the old to the new situation, phased transition, and shadow operation. In the last-mentioned case, the old and the new system are used simultaneously for some time. Finally, the new system is transferred to the user organization, the computer centre and the maintenance department. This is also the finalization of the project management.

During the *operational phase* there should be attention to the system use and control, and so to the effectiveness of the new system. In practice, a thorough evaluation is often neglected (Argelo, 1982). Such an evaluation should include the following questions: Have the system development goals been achieved? Have the bottlenecks that people perceived been eliminated? How do actual operating costs compare with the advance estimate? How great is the acceptance of the system by the user? Did the reorganization run smoothly? Are there unintended effects? Various checklists and evaluative questionnaires are available for this purpose (Bailey & Pearson, 1983;

Robinson, Fitter, Rector, Newton, & Sneath, 1991).

Can we tell whether some methods are more satisfactory than other methods? Of course, some methods emphasize different aspects from others. (For an international survey see Olle et al., 1988.) Some methods are more problem oriented (e.g. ISAC, MOS, SASO), others more solution oriented (e.g. IEM, JSD, NIAM, YOURDON). Some methods are exclusively geared to system development (e.g. NIAM, D2S2, PRISMA), others emphasize project management (e.g. METHOD/1, SDM, PARAET, PRODOSTA). One characteristic of the latter methods is that they take a linear approach with predictable steps. Other methods work with iterative procedures (e.g. USE, CIAM) or prototypes (see Boehm, 1986; Vonk, 1987) and/or strongly emphasize the importance of user participation (e.g. ETHICS, ISAC, PORGI, STTA, MAIA).

Things become more complicated, because developments in the field are fairly rapid. Methods fall into disuse; others are adapted by user organizations or evolve into new forms, perhaps in combination with other methods (e.g. ISES, which integrates MAIA, PRISMA, and PRODOSTA among others). The result is that almost no one has a commanding view of the field. Add to this the fact that nearly all potential informants are competitors, which will obviously influence their views. Authors show quite some reticence about making comparative evaluative statements in the literature. Van den Broek (1986) stated that it is near impossible to perform reliable measurements of the quality of a method. The weight to be attributed to the various criteria is debatable (e.g. the manageability, the transferability, and the flexibility of the new system), and there is no objective standard for the effectiveness of an information system; in fact, it is not truly possible to obtain reliable data on the influence of a method on the development process.

Van Rees (1986) also reached the conclusion that studying development methodologies along the lines of consumer research, with the object of selecting the best one, was not wise, because the person of the designer proved to be much more important for the final result than the method itself. Van Rees focused primarily on the thinking of the designer. According to this author, it is definitely not a process in which several different models (systological, infological, datalogical, and technological) develop alongside one other. The thought process of a designer can better be visualized as the growth, the crystallization, of one overall image of the ultimate situation. In the process the designer works from the general to the more detailed. He must set to work fairly intuitively; a method will never be able to prescribe at what point which aspect must be detailed. Alongside or, rather during, the steps from general to detailed, the thinking of a designer evolves from vague to precise. A strict distinction between goals and means cannot be maintained, neither in the thinking of the designer nor in the organization of the design process.

Designing can better be defined as the synchronization of goals and means. Sometimes the means have already been established, and the formulation of the goal is the primary problem. In other situations both goals and means must be chosen by the designer within very broadly sketched limits, or within bounds implicitly set by the situation. Every designer knows how roundabout the decision-making process on an information system can be. Van Rees (1986) concluded that the phases in the development process can only be set down in a very broad sense.

In short, the phasing and rational ordering of the decision-making process as recommended in the automation manuals is fundamentally different from the growth and learning process that those involved go through in their own thinking. Designing cannot be regarded as a one-off tour of the object model, information model, data model, and media model, in that order. It is more of a search and synchronization process, in which all models are continually being developed and synthesized. According to Van Rees, it is therefore wiser not to set down any standard phases at all and to place the responsibility for accomplishing and ordering the decision-making where it lies in practice, with the designer. However, this final bit of advice seems to us to bypass a crucial characteristic of most automation processes, which is the political aspect. In the following we will go into this.

4.3   Parties: Points of view and problems

Current methods scarcely take any account of political aspects that play a role in system development. Nevertheless, automation is not merely a technical matter. No adequate explanation can be given for the success or failure of automation projects if it is ignored that the relationships and processes in projects are closely interwoven with the relationships and processes that characterize the organization as a whole (Riesewijk & Warmerdam, 1988). Automation often has consequences for the quality of the work and for the control and coordination mechanisms in the organization (Leonova, 1991). So it is quite understandable that those directly involved watch developments warily and do not receive each proposal with unquestioning acceptance (Boonstra & Koopman, 1993). For this and other reasons, automation often acquires the nature of a complex decision-making and reorganization process, in which socio-organizational aspects play a role alongside technical aspects (Dekker & Slagmolen, 1984; Morssink & Kranendonk, 1987; Van Offenbeek & Koopman, 1996a). In addition to managers and designers, personnel representative bodies—works council, trade unions—also try to bring forward their standpoints (Cressey, 1989; Cressey & Williams, 1990). Incidentally, as we shall see later, the influence of personnel representative bodies has so far been very limited.

The following questions will be discussed:

- Broadly speaking, what parties can be distinguished?
- How do they stand with respect to one another and from what point of view do they regard the problem?
- What sources of power do parties have available to them in the achievement of their goals?

Most publications assume three key parties: management, system developers (or designers), and users (Argelo, 1982; Briefs, Ciborra, & Schneider, 1983). Sometimes various categories of users are distinguished. In 't Veld (1989) adopted Argelo's distinction of policy-making, functional, operational, and passive users. The operational user in particular is in direct contact with the new system (via keyboard and screen). His or her job can change considerably as a result of automation. As to management, we should first think of the corporate and departmental managers who must make available time, money, and manpower to make an automation project possible. After each phase, management assesses whether or not the project will be continued. The system developers or designers are technically skilled specialists; they include system analysts and programmers. Their specific expertise makes them indispensable to automation and they play a dominant role during a large part of the project.

In addition to these technical specialists, some publications (primarily those which take a socio-technical system approach) also ascribe a role to specialists in the field of social organization (Mumford, 1983; Reitsma, 1989; Van Eijnatten, Chapter 4 in this *Handbook*). This involves the foreseeable consequences of automation for task content and organizational structure. Finally, works councils and trade unions have made attempts to make technology agreements with management boards. These agreements cover such matters as: decision-making procedures, including the point at which trade unions and works council are informed, employment opportunity aspects, consequences for task content, education and retraining, terms of employment aspects, including pay scales, ergonomic aspects, and working conditions (Cressey, 1989).

How do the parties stand towards one another? Various authors frequently report great communication problems (Van Reeken, 1986) and biased images on all sides (Gingras & McLean, 1982). There are references to a semantic gap (De Brabander & Thiers, 1984) and to power differences, which some authors say are even purposely maintained (Argelo, 1982). So the parties differ in their points of view, in their interests, and in the possibilities they have to effectuate their interests.

The term "semantics" is a reference to more or less specialized "languages" for specific subjects. We may see these languages as intellectual resources or instruments with which persons or parties interpret "reality", so that it acquires a certain degree of orderliness, comprehensibility, and acceptability (Berger & Luckman, 1966; Luhmann, 1980; Riesewijk & Warmerdam, 1988). Specialized groups gradually develop semantics of their own; then they slip them into daily routine and try to use them to formulate and to enforce coherent interests. Communication between groups is only possible if their semantics overlap.

To what extent are certain semantics dominant in the key parties? And to what extent do persons or parties understand the dominant semantic categories of others and can they apply them? In Table 17.3 a distinction is made between automation semantics, control semantics, and work semantics. It is assumed that *information analysts and system developers* will largely allow themselves to be guided by automation semantics: It is the semantics of their profession. The system developer concentrates on the construction of elegant and rational information systems. He feels challenged by the construction problems and sees himself as the creator of complex, exciting systems (Riesewijk & Warmerdam, 1988, p.28). He views the managers and users who are involved in the development process first and foremost as sources of information, and treats them accordingly. His image of the other party is not seldom caricatural. Often the system developer sees the user as very naive, which leads to the tendency to design "idiot-proof systems". On the other hand, the ideal user resembles the designer's picture of himself. The view the developer takes of the user greatly differs from the image the user has of herself (Gingras & McLean, 1982).

Management approaches automation primarily from the semantics of control. From this point of view, it is primarily interested in aspects of effectiveness and efficiency. These might include: smaller stocks, faster operating, greater flexibility, improving product quality, and increasing productivity per employee (SER, 1982).

In practice, however, it is not uncommon for management to limit its interest to the economic aspects: What will it cost, what will it yield, and will the system be completed on time? Management shows less interest in the information-technical aspects. When confronted with the greatly superior knowledge that designers have in this field, and the technical jargon they employ, management (erroneously) tends to delegate a large part of its responsibility to this group. For instance, the project manager often comes from their side. Automation is viewed by management as a "technical" problem that needs an expert to solve it. Whether the expert has much experience with work coordination, planning, process supervision, and negotiating is a question that is often neglected. The responsible management does not utilize its opportunities to steer and control the process. The initial phases, in which the preliminary study and the feasibility study should take place, are often rushed through, which is highly detrimental to the quality and acceptance of the choice made (Vaas, 1988). In the later stages, management often limits its role to steering committee membership. Altogether, the role of management is much more modest and the role of the designers generally much more dominant than the manuals would lead one to believe (Argelo, 1982).

The involvement of the *users* is much slighter than most manuals prescribe (Vijlbrief, Algera, & Koopman, 1989). The users, like management, have to contend with their lack of expertise, technical and otherwise, especially in comparison with the designers. The specialists also sometimes carefully maintain this power distance by their use of jargon and by producing fairly incomprehensible documents (the so-called baseline documents). The manual used is not felt to be of any help at all by the users. Inexpertise, inhibitions, and inertia bring them to place all responsibility with the designers (Argelo, 1982).

We will come back to the consequences of such

TABLE 17.3

Dominant semantics	Key group	Dominant criteria
Automation semantics	Technical experts	Technical perfection
Control semantics	Management	Effectiveness, efficiency
Work semantics	Users	Quality of work life

Key groups and their dominant semantics.

limited participation by the users. Here we merely point out a problem. Automation often brings about great changes in task content and the working conditions of the users. It is perfectly understandable that they approach it from the point of view of work semantics. If the users cannot form an image of the consequences system development will have for the quantity and quality of their work, they are quite likely to fear the worst for their future. If, during the change process, management fails to build up support for the coming changes among those directly involved, one cannot count on a smooth introduction (Koopman, Drenth, Heller, & Rus, 1993; Heller, Drenth, Koopman, & Rus, 1988). What often happens in such a case is that a new information system is only partly used or even generally boycotted by the users (Eason, Damodaram, & Stewart, 1975). The greater effectiveness that the automation process was intended to achieve is entirely lost in this manner.

Fortunately, there is a growing awareness, even from a technical point of view, that automation without the active contribution of users is doomed to failure (Bemelmans, 1986; Blokdijk, 1986; McKersie & Walton, 1991). Various development methods have tried to profile themselves in this manner (e.g. USE, see Wasserman, 1979; ISAC, see Ruys, 1986; PRISMA, see Laagland & Schaddelee, 1986). But the extent to which user participation is felt to be functional varies quite a bit with the type of system and the type of situation/organization (McFarlan, 1981; Nicholas, 1985; Hirschheim & Klein, 1989; Koopman & Algera, 1989; Weitzel & Kerschberg, 1989; Ashmos, McDaniel, & Duchon, 1990; Van Offenbeek & Koopman, 1996a). Authors also differ considerably in their opinions of the form user participation should best take (see, e.g., Mumford & Henshall, 1979; Vaas, 1988). We will come back to both problems.

5 MANAGEMENT OF AUTOMATION PROJECTS

5.1 Automation projects in practice

When it comes to practice, to what extent do automation projects follow the blueprints and recommendations discussed earlier? How rational is the decision-making? What is the contribution of the various groups involved? How are automation projects evaluated on a number of success criteria? Research results on these questions are still fairly sporadic, and do not really give a consistent picture. It also partly depends on the type of automation, the type of informants, and the method of study used.

Much research has focused on the description and evaluation of one or a few cases (see, e.g., Heller, 1989; Ten Horn, 1991; Wilpert, 1991; Boonstra & Koopman, 1993; Holti, 1994; Rogard, 1994). One Dutch research project on the "success and failure of automation projects" (Riesewijk & Warmerdam, 1988) had a somewhat wider scope. It included a telephone inquiry among 274 user organizations (a sample that may be considered reasonably representative as to region, sector of industry, and company size in the Netherlands) and a written enquiry among 67 companies (a representative sample from the first group). The research focused primarily on socio-organizational aspects of administrative systems, both large scale and small scale. The inquiry was administered to the persons responsible for the automation projects, making it a good counterpart to most other evaluation studies, which primarily focused on users. The subjects discussed were: the project organization, the contributions of various groups, the primary bottlenecks and the relationship between project organization and project success.

As to the *project organization*, researchers found that matters such as planning, budget, etc. received fairly much attention, but that socio-organizational measures remained somewhat in the background. Most companies said that they worked on the basis of a specification of project goals and activities, and scheduled these activities in phases. A time schedule and a project budget were also commonly used. Two-thirds of the companies said they employed some form of user participation. The same number also said they worked with periodic reports and progress control. On the other hand, only one-third said that they worked with periodic cost–benefit analyses and that they had a personnel and organization plan. The conclusion of the authors was that the elements needed for good project organization were present in most cases, the periodic cost–benefit analysis and the personnel and organization plan being the exceptions. But the reader should remember that this reflected the opinions of those responsible for the project, which may increase the "retrospective rationality". This surmise is strengthened by the somewhat more mixed picture from other studies. For example, many projects have a fairly formalized start-up, but control of planning, costs, and quality demands is loosened more and more as the project progresses (Argelo, 1982; Algera, Koopman, & Vijlbrief, 1989).

And what about the *contribution of the various groups* during the automation process? A fairly large amount of influence was ascribed to external experts, as well as to departmental managers of the user organization. The greatest influence, however, the informants ascribed to internal experts, while the end users played a much smaller role in their view. This agrees with the findings of other studies (Hedberg, 1975; Child, 1987). Another confirmation of results found elsewhere was the slight amount of influence by the personnel department and the works council (see, e.g., Cressey & Williams, 1990; Boonstra & Koopman, 1993), if they were involved in the decision-making at all.

Where, according to Riesewijk and Warmerdam (1988), were the *primary bottle-necks*? Nearly half the companies said they had serious organizational problems while automating. An almost equally large group reported specification problems during system development. Around one-third of the companies experienced difficulties in the cooperation between the various groups during system development. A "mere" one-fifth of all companies reported social problems during system implementation. The research concluded that problems in project management and in communication between the parties carried the most weight. Technical problems and specifically personnel-related difficulties were perceived to a much smaller extent.

The finding of relatively few technical problems is in contrast to what many other researchers report (Bubenko, 1986; Lyytinen, 1987; Vonk, 1987). According to these studies, the technical aspects are at least part of the cause of many problems (Van Offenbeek & Koopman, 1996b). For example, development processes generally take a long time, years even, and much maintenance is required afterwards. The costs of maintenance, in comparison with those of the other phases of system development, are enormous. Another complaint involves the writing of applications. Here there is sometimes even a backlog of three or four years. The functional descriptions, another recurring problem, are often strung out in massive reports, which give the users absolutely no grasp of the matter. Naturally, such matters do not bring the hoped-for intensive involvement one step closer. Another oft-heard problem is that little attention is paid to the changing needs in an organization during the development, even though there are methods and techniques with which very flexible systems can be developed. Many suppliers who claim that they work with these methods and techniques turn out virtually to ignore them. A final complaint is that system development is still much too *ad hoc*. Often there is no information policy, or it is not geared to other aspects of corporate policy.

The fairly low percentage of specific personnel-related problems is in quite some contrast to what other studies have found on this point (Friedrichs & Schaff, 1982). To account for this, the researchers pointed out that many of the projects studied could be termed follow-up applications (such as a switch from batch processing to on-line systems; new systems for the integration of subprocesses). Such projects do not necessitate drastic restructuring; rather, they entail all kinds of unobtrusive reorganization. In fact, according to the researchers, this form of automation is currently dominant in business and industry, and its implications are far-reaching. In their view, serious conflicts with the shop-floor will become a thing of the past because no more large-scale reorganization and compulsory redundancies are to be expected. This will mean that attention will shift to departments above the actual production level. This may imply that the conflicts between the various management factions will become more important.

Finally, a remark on the *relationship between project organization and the chance of success*.

The aforementioned Dutch study (Riesewijk & Warmerdam, 1988) found a weak positive correlation between success and the existence of an automation plan, and regular and fixed management and user consultation. The formulation of project goals, phasing of activities, a time schedule, user participation, and reporting/progress control was of some significance for the successful execution of automation projects. A large amount of influence by external automation experts often appeared to have a negative effect.

5.2   Two basic strategies

More and more researchers have come to reject the idea of "technological determinism" on logical and empirical grounds (e.g. Cooley, 1980; Bessant & Dickson, 1981; Prakke, 1987). Rather, the introduction of a new technology in organizations is viewed as an adaptation process in which corporate political choices are made that are not without consequence for the various groups in the organization (Child, 1987). In addition, there is growing criticism in the literature of the idea that the classic/linear approach, the so-called waterfall approach, is the best or even the only approach (Blackler & Brown, 1986; Boehm, 1986; Van Reeken, 1986; Blackler, 1991). Various models of approaches are proposed instead; the chance of success of either type depends upon the context (Naumann, Davis, & McKeen, 1980; Pyborn, 1981; Shomenta, Kamp, Hanson, & Simpson, 1983; Episkopou & Wood-Harper, 1986; Van Reeken, 1986; Pennings, 1987; Van Offenbeek & Koopman, 1996a).

Koopman (1991) approached automation as a complex innovation and reorganization process. Other studies of reorganization processes have shown that the management responsible for the reorganization is faced with a number of options that often take the form of dilemmas (Koopman & Pool, 1991, 1992) The primary dilemmas are:

- How much openness to use in direction?
  (problem oriented vs. solution oriented)
- What process rationale will dominate?
  (socio-political vs. economic-technical rationale)
- How rigorous change?
  (gradual vs. integral)

- How much participation to allow?
  (bottom-up vs. top-down)
- How strongly structured and formalized?
  (broad vs. detailed decision-making design)
- How much delegation?
  (limited vs. broad mandate)
- How much time pressure and control?
  (clear deadlines and control vs. little pressure and control)
- How to deal with differences of opinion?
  (discuss openly vs. cover up or smooth).

Based upon these options, management has two basic "strategies" to choose from: a linear-integral approach and an incremental-iterative approach (see Table 17.4).

A linear-integral approach is solution oriented (the problem is known); any discussion is primarily about the means (discussion about the goals is unnecessary or impossible); the approach is integral and top-down, and is coordinated and controlled by the top. This is done on the basis of a detailed and formalized decision-making design, with precise norms and strict monitoring. There is little room for differences of opinion; if they do appear, there is a tendency to deny them or to cover them up.

The other extreme is an incremental-iterative approach, typifed by a problem orientation, and discussion first and foremost about goals. It is a gradual process in which ideas from below play an important role, and one that is controlled and monitored on the basis of a broad decision-making design, characterized by a large amount of flexibility and informal consultation. Regular consultation is held with the parties involved, which may lead to interim adjustments. Flexible norms make it possible to bridge any differences of opinion.

The design approach, as contrasted to the development approach (Boonstra & Koopman, 1993), is more or less along the same lines. Before turning to the arguments in favour of one approach or the other, we would now like to dwell briefly on the possibilities and limits of user participation.

5.3   User participation

As we have seen aready, one of the basic questions in the approach to automation projects is the desired amount of user participation. Several arguments in favour of user involvement in

TABLE 17.4

Two basic strategies in automation (Koopman, 1991)

Incremental – Iterative	Linear – Integral
Problem oriented	Solution oriented
Discussion on goals central	Discussion on means central
Gradual	Integral
Bottom-up	Top-down
Broad design (informal, flexible)	Detailed design (formalized)
Regular consultation with parties involved	Central coordination and control
Flexible norms, adjustment en route	Precise norms, strict control
Differences of opinion are discussed	Differences of opinion are denied/covered up

automation projects are mentioned in the literature (see e.g. Altman & Dull, 1988; Cressey, 1989; Cressey & Williams, 1990; Erez, 1993, 1994). First of all, in order for the new system to function well, it must be accepted by the users. Various studies have pointed out the relationship between user involvement in the preparation and the effectiveness of the new system after implemetation (Land, Mumford, & Hawgood, 1980; Oppelland & Kolf, 1980; Argelo, 1982; Eason, 1982), although such a relationship was not always demonstrated (Ives & Olsen, 1984; Algera et al., 1989).

A second argument for user participation is that the user often has specific knowledge and experience that can be of great significance to the project. Her motivation to make this knowledge available depends on the manner in which she is informed and consulted during the project, and on the expected consequences (Lawler & Rhode, 1976; Sääksjärvi, 1980). Of course, the position of the user varies greatly with her status and power position in the organization (Child, 1987).

Finally, user participation is sometimes advocated as a "strategy" in dealing with works council and trade unions (Levi & Williams, 1983; Blackler & Brown, 1986), sometimes against the background of legislation or collective agreements in which participation is set down as a right. The idea behind this is that it is better to hold constructive consultation with those involved than to risk being faced with unpredictable and destructive reactions.

There is a rapidly growing literature in which one or another form of user participation is propagated (e.g. Glasson, 1984; Hirschheim, 1985). On the other hand, research has brought to light more and more bottlenecks that limit the room for user participation. First of all we discuss the possibilities. Important questions here are: Is participation direct or indirect? In what phases of the project? On what secondary problems/activities does participation primarily focus?

Most authors agree that participation only makes sense if it takes place at a point when there is still something to decide (Edström, 1977; Cressey & Williams, 1990). This means that participation must not be limited to the implementation phase, actually a fairly common practice. User participation should primarily focus on the preparation and the design (Van Eijnatten, Chapter 4 in this *Handbook*). More specifically, users can be involved in: the definition of the problem, setting the goals and criteria, exploring alternatives, checking that the design meets the requirements, and evaluation of the system in practice (Mumford & Weir, 1979). In other words, user participation is possible from the preliminary study up to and including the functional design, and from the acceptance test up to and including the evaluation. The "technical phases" in between lend themselves less to user contributions.

There are various examples in the literature of an automation approach aimed at integral involvement of the "human factor" in the preparation and introduction of new systems (Land et al., 1980; Oppelland & Kolf, 1980; Schneiderman, 1980; Mumford, 1983; Vaas, 1988; Clegg & Symon, 1989). However, not all researchers have reported successes. For instance, Hedberg (1975) described two difficult situations in which user representatives often find themselves. The first he termed the "hostage situation". Because he has little knowledge of information technology, the user representative is extremely wary of asking "stupid questions". He does not take very active part in the discussion and runs no risks. The result is that he has scarcely any influence on events. The second situation goes by the name of the "indoctrination alternative". In this case the representative does start to ask "stupid questions". If the designers take them seriously, a learning process is set in motion, and communication between designers and user representatives thus improves. At the same time, however, a new problem emerges in the representative's contact with her constituency, which no longer recognizes itself in her language and her thinking.

In fact, these are problems that are typically encountered in other situations in which there is representative consultation, e.g. in the works council (IDE, 1993; Teulings, 1987). One party's knowledge is highly superior to that of the other. Sometimes this advantage is purposely maintained: The adage "knowledge is power" also applies here (Pfeffer, 1981). According to the research by Hedberg (1975) and Child (1987), the user—so much less expert—has but little to gain in this power game. These results are in line with the conclusions of Mulder (1971): When there are big differences in expertise, participation only leads to indoctrination. Child (1987) showed that the situation changed drastically when the users were professionals or managers.

Hedberg sought a way out of the dilemma of the hostage versus the indoctrination situation in influence via the "meta-system" in an organization. Because it is the embodiment of all kinds of unwritten rules and contingencies, the meta-

system exercises indirect control over decision-making processes (Kickert, 1979). Hedberg's argument is that, via the consultative organs available to them (works council, consultation with trade unions), employee representatives try to convert their interests and goals into guidelines, which are taken as a starting point in automation projects. Their influence is felt not during the project, but in advance, on the contingencies to which the designers must adhere. If employees effectively influence the contingencies, automation is said to be able to contribute to good relations and meaningful tasks (Briefs, 1975; Manor, 1975; Blackler & Brown, 1986).

Unfortunately, in practice, this often turns out not to be the case. For instance, Nygaard (1980), on the basis of research in the Scandinavian countries, concluded that advance influence (via the meta-sytem) is insufficient to get a grip on the course of the automation project. The formulation of demands in terms of abstract system characteristics apparently offers no guarantee of the desired result. The author's conclusion therefore was that user participation is necessary in all phases (but not in technical details). Some authors advocated a combination of direct and indirect participation, thus to integrate the strong points of both manners of working.

Taking everything into consideration, we should make a few critical remarks about the possibilities of user participation. First of all, its results, according to research, are not always unanimous (De Brabander & Thiers, 1984; Ives & Olsen, 1984; Algera et al., 1989). Although positive results are reported now and then, it seems they should be ascribed in part to methodological artefacts (Locke & Schweiger, 1979; Heller et al., 1988; Blackler & Brown, 1986). A second point of criticism comes primarily from the side of trade-union organizations. They are wary of participation for the sake of show and watchful for manipulation. In many cases, user participation is felt to be a mere cosmetic operation (Kelly, 1982; Mambray, Opperman, & Tepper, 1986, quoted by Blacker & Brown, 1986). Trade unions and works councils therefore often prefer to negotiate a technology agreement (Cressey, 1989).

Management may object to user participation on the grounds that it takes too much time, does not fit into the dominant organizational culture, increases the complexity of the development process, and disturbs the existing power balance in the organization (Hirschheim, 1983; Markus & Pfeffer, 1983; Robey & Markus, 1984).

Mambray et al. (1986) pointed out other circumstances that make user participation a nettlesome point. First of all, it is often difficult to make reliable predictions about the consequences of automation for the behaviour and the attitudes of those involved. In addition, it is not easy to reach consensus on the goals or on the results achieved. Furthermore, the authors pointed out the lopsided power relations between the participants. As also remarked by De Brabander and Thiers (1984), this does not improve communication. Mambray et al. even found a strong tendency of management to make a preliminary selection of topics. The matters selected were then represented in a good light. The users were usually poorly prepared and were primarily interested in short-term consequences. The latter was confirmed by Child (1987).

There are thus two difficulties with user participation that have to do with the nature of the technological developments. First of all, most people are quite unfamiliar with technological issues, so that they are often quite unable to form a picture of possible alternatives. This was discussed earlier. According to some authors (Riesewijk & Warmerdam, 1988) this problem might diminish in the future, as automation projects need replacing, systems become more flexible, and the users gain more experience. "End-user computing" will then take on true significance (Rokart & Flannery, 1983; Benson, 1983).

The second problem stems from the new possibilities of integration offered by the new technology. More and more different organizational functions are integrated, within branches, between branches and even across national borders (Andriessen & Roe, 1994). Good examples can be found in international transport, in retailing, and in banking (Child & Loveridge, 1990; Boonstra & Koopman, 1993).

Against this background it is difficult for personnel representatives to formulate a good answer to the plans of management. Scale enlargement and strengthening the uniformity in policy imply that little room remains for local decision-making (Koopman & Pool, 1991).

In brief, under what conditions does user participation "work"? Child (1988) made a few concrete remarks about this, based upon two international comparative studies in Europe. The first (*The Control of Frontiers*, Ruskin College, 1994) involved 20 cases in the manufacturing industry in Britain, West Germany, Italy, the Netherlands, and Sweden. The second ("Microelectronics in the Service Sector") involved 36 cases in banks, hospitals (laboratories), and retailing in Belgium, Britain, West Germany, Hungary, Italy, Sweden, Poland, (former) Yugoslavia and China (Child & Loveridge, 1990). His main conclusion was that, apart from Sweden and (former) Yugoslavia, no cases of serious user participation were encounted, a conclusion supported by the research by Cressey (1989). The primary obstacles to user participation were: information provided by management came too late; trade unions looked to procedures rather than substance; the design took place outside of the plant where the change was to be implemented; insufficient local time, information and expertise.

What factors are responsible for the differences between countries and organizations? Child (1988) first of all pointed to differences in national legislation and formal institutions. A role was also played by the attitudes and the policy of management—for example, as expressed in the information they gave, which was often limited and came too late. A third factor which Child felt was partly responsible for the low level of participation was trade-union policy and the low level of expertise among trade-union representatives. The attention of trade unions was usually trained on procedures and on the retention of formal rights rather than on questions relating to the fundamental design and the important system characteristics. Lastly, Child also pointed out the importance of cultural factors, both at a national and at an organizational level.

Finally, a brief remark on the differences between the various types of organizations. Certain banks gave personnel representatives an advance opportunity to view new installations in a trial set-up in another branch. The intention behind this was not so much to obtain input to prepare a decision, but rather to convince them of the correctness of a decision that had already been taken. In the larger banks the choice and development of new technology was primarily determined by the internal automation departments, in close cooperation with the suppliers. The primary influence in the hospitals rested with the medical specialists. In forming their opinions, they relied heavily on information from the suppliers, and generally did not involve their assistants, even though they would have to work with the equipment, in the preparation or the decision-making. In retailing, foremen, who were responsible for a smooth implementation, were not consulted at all. Conflicts and frustration were the understandable consequences (Child, 1988).

5.4   Towards a contingency approach to automation

The conclusion from the foregoing can only be that user participation is largely simply a matter of power relations. But there is another entirely different aspect in the opposition of linear-integral to incremental-iterative. It has to do with the amount of uncertainty—and thus the risk level—associated with the development of the new system.

Van Reeken (1986) distinguished between "technical risk" and "corporate risk". The first type is found on the supply side and is related to the technical complexity of the system. The second type is found on the demand side; it involves the amount of uncertainty in the company about the direction and specifications of the new system. Van Reeken (1986) states that the classic phased approach is still the best in technically complex projects with a low corporate risk. He compared it to architecture; the customer has an adequate view of what requirements the end product must meet. When the end result is not in such sharp focus, and hence the corporate risk is larger, an iterative approach with prototyping would be more appropriate. Here the metaphor of a sculpture is applicable: The goal is broadly known, but the design gradually comes about under way. If there is also a high technical risk, the situation becomes problematic: Then, according to Van Reeken, a careful step-by-step approach is required, the difference from the iterative approach being more a matter of gradation than of principle. If both the corporate and the technical risks are low, then buying a ready-made solution or a "Do It Yourself" approach would seem the most appropriate (see Figure 17.1).

Broadly speaking, we may state: The more unfamiliar and more complex the technology to be applied in comparison to the automation level of the organization, the more flexibility will be needed in the project control (Nicholas, 1985; Olle et al., 1988). So, in general, the development of "decision support systems" will demand more interaction of the users than "transaction processing systems" aimed at routine data processing (Bemelmans, 1984), because the predictability of how the latter will operate is much greater.

So the amount of structure in the system to be automated is of great importance: If tasks or information functions to be automated have little structure, one will sooner have recourse to a participative, incremental-iterative approach (Robey, 1977; Davis & Olson, 1985). But also the stability of the system to be automated is at issue:

		Corporate risk (demand side)	
		High	Low
Technical risk (supply side)	High	step-by-step approach	classical phased approach
	Low	iterative approach with prototyping	buy (DIY

FIGURE 17.1

Automation approach with given corporate risk and technical risk (Van Reeken, 1986).

When the organization or department that is the object of system development is fairly volatile, its information needs will not be very stable either. In that case ample flexibility of the system must be ensured (Robey, 1977; Van Offenbeek & Koopman, 1993).

One argument in favour of a linear-integral approach might be: interdependency with other fields of policy in the organization—as, for example, in the automation of mail sorting in the large postal offices. Demands of uniformity in customer treatment also sometimes demand an integral approach. A good example is the way in which banks' new counter terminals have been introduced in recent years. These examples have in common that one or two branches were used as test grounds. Once the system had overcome its growing pains, it became standard in all other branches. But by then there was no longer much leeway for participation by those directly involved (Dijksman, Elferen, & Rijmer, 1982).

The scale of the project is also important for other reasons. In our experience, intensive user participation as it is proposed, e.g. in Mumford's (1983) ETHICS procedure, is really only practicable: (1) in relatively small-scale projects; (2) in which knowledge of users is indispensable for good results; (3) in an organization in which uniformity of design is not a requirement; and (4) there is a certain consensus on the goals of the project (Algera et al., 1989). The importance of this final point must not be underestimated. If the introduction of the new system has important negative consequences for some organization members, participation rapidly degenerates into a sort of ritual, and it may even backfire (Kelly, 1982; Kraft, 1979).

Whether or not to utilize potential variety and leeway in the organization for a more open consultation strategy is partly a question of policy and organizational culture (Mantelaers, 1988). Is personnel strategy primarily aimed at greater involvement or at greater control (Koopman, 1991)? Is automation viewed as a new way to make better use of human capacities or more as a way to become less dependent on the "labour factor" (Sanders, 1985; Blackler & Brown, 1986; Watson, 1986; Walton, 1985)?

Recognized expertise or other power sources of organizational members can be an important argument in this respect. So, too, the attitude of personnel representatives in works councils and trade unions (Child, 1987). If the parties are truly autonomous opponents—for example, in an interorganizational innovation process—one may be obliged to adopt an incremental-iterative strategy.

Finally, there are a number of external circumstances that exert some pressure in the direction of one or approach the other. Here we have in mind the amount of time pressure, the extent to which external forces—e.g. the corporate management—make their influence felt on the organization (Mintzberg, 1983), the extent to which legislation dictates and the *Zeitgeist* within which the organization must operate. As far as the last factor goes, there is a marked difference between the 1970s, the 1980s, and the 1990s. This has its effects on management style and organizational culture.

6 THE ROLE OF THE WORK AND ORGANIZATIONAL PSYCHOLOGIST

If the work and organizational psychologist wants to be treated as a serious partner in automation projects, (s)he will need to make a distinct and unique contribution. This obviously requires a thorough understanding of the matter: knowledge of the manner in which the input (resources, clients) of the organization or a part of it are converted into output (products, services). Research (Algera et al., 1989) has shown that the functional design phase generally makes high requirements of users as to abstract thinking and imagination. The work and organizational psychologist who understands the administrative or production process might play a supporting role here in the articulation and translation of wishes of the users. In doing so, (s)he would, at least in this phase, also be able to act as a catalyst for user participation. The work and organizational psychologist also has his/her own expertise to contribute to organizational and task design. This would comprise knowledge of various organizational models, the effects of different job characteristics on the perception and the performance of task performers, the feasibility of setting up semi-autonomous groups, job rotation, etc.

Any such functional contribution by the work and organizational psychologist is partly dependent on prevailing views in the organization of the design of production processes (see, e.g., Clegg, 1988). In some organizations the responsibility for product quality and quantity lies as much as possible with the operator. This means, for instance, that the operator rights as many malfunctions as possible on his own. In other organizations the operator traditionally stops the production process as soon as something goes wrong, at which point others, perhaps superiors or maintenance engineers, decide what action should be taken.

Such different approaches to the control of production have important consequences for organizational and task structure. This was clearly illustrated in the publication by Wall, Burner, Clegg, and Kemp (1983). These authors distinguished two determinants of job design, "technical choice" and "social choice" (see also Clegg, 1984). The former has to do with the physical lay-out and the nature of the equipment and determines "task(s) performance characteristics" (cycle time, pace, required mental and motory skills, etc.). The latter refers to the control philosophy of management and is decisive for "task(s) management" (the control of daily routine on the shop-floor).

"Task(s) performance characteristics" and "task(s) management" together form the task structure. The postulate of Wall et al. (1983) is that, even with extremely limited options as to technology, the autonomy of the operator on the shop-floor is greatly influenced by the control philosophy.

The work and organizational psychologist can make a specific contribution in two areas:

1. the performance of the system (optimizing the man–machine interface);
2. the quality of the work.

6.1 Optimizing the man–machine interface

Ergonomy in particular has done much research of the fine-tuning of the man–machine interface with a view to the performance of the total system (Frese, 1989; Johansson, 1989). Recent developments in the field of automation tend more and more towards interactive interfaces. In this context, Card, Moran, and Newell (1983) stated that there is a big difference between interactive and non-interactive systems. In other words, communicating with machines is a different matter from operating machines. Interactive interfaces bring about a sort of dialogue between man and computer. There is much ergonomic knowledge and insight in the perceptive and psychomotor aspects (design and positioning of screen, shape and size of letters, etc.) but much less insight into the cognitive aspects (the exchange of information) of interactive interfaces. Via software, the computer performs "cognitive" tasks such as interpretation, problem-solving, and deciding. This makes the dialogue between man and computer an interaction between two "cognitive" systems. This interaction has become the subject of research in recent years ("software psychology"). Optimizing the man–machine interface in interactive systems is sometimes referred to as "cognitive systems engineering" (Hollnagel & Woods, 1983). In some cases, optimizing the allication of tasks may mean suboptimization of fulfilment of subtasks/routines by the computer. This point of view embraces the development of an integral task structure for the man–computer system (see also Eason & Harker, 1994).

The cognitive-systems approach stems from cognitive psychology, in which man is regarded as an information-processing system with a perceptual, a cognitive, and a motory system (see also Card et al., 1983). This approach generally distinguishes three different levels of information processing (Rasmussen, 1983):

1. Skill-based: This level refers to non-conscious (automated) human actions such as the operation of a keyboard.
2. Rule-based: This level refers to more or less conscious decisions that take place according to fixed rules. Important here are the observation and diagnosis of stimuli, as in controlling production processes according to what has been stated in the manual.
3. Knowledge-based: Conscious information processing in which the individual develops

a purposive strategy that precedes her actions.

These three levels differ in the mental capacity (attention) required to perform them. In fact, the three levels are not distinct and separate, but are continually alternated in task performance. Experience causes the level of information processing to become lower; in other words, actions that are at first consciously controlled take place more or less automatically after much practice (compare a beginner and an experienced typist). However, not all tasks or task elements should ultimately be able to be performed at a skill-based level, as Card et al. (1983) rightly observed after their study of word-processing systems. If the information-processing level is too low in relation to the capacities of the task performer, motivational and concentration problems can result.

6.2 Promoting the quality of the work

In addition to attention to system performance, work and organizational psychology should surely also attach importance to the acceptance of the system in the sense of the quality of the work. The concept of quality of the work is an all-embracing concept covering many aspects such as task content, working conditions, work and labour relations, and terms of employment.

Since automation often goes hand in hand with cutbacks among personnel, employee attention is primarily focused on job security. As long as the organization does not propose solutions on this point that are acceptable to the employees, user participation that focuses on the content of the future work would not seem the most urgent matter.

As to task content, a number of specific job characteristics known from the literature are generally considered relevant in connection with the quality of the work (see Chapter 6, Vol. 3, this *Handbook*). There is no reason why these same job characteristics would not be important in automated systems. On the other hand, it is not possible to set down general norms, not only because there are different groups of system users with divergent qualifications, but also because individual differences may exist within a user group in the assessment of the same "objective" job characteristics.

A number of job characteristics are listed in the following, with an indication of their specific significance in automated systems (see also Vijlbrief et al., 1985; Roe, 1988; Algera, Chapter 6, Vol. 3, this *Handbook*). In practice, such a list of job characteristics could serve as a checklist for discussions with the designers. Job characteristics that may be considered relevant from this point of view include:

1. Feedback on the effects of the actions of the task performer. This job characteristic is important, both to promote the performance of the system and to bring about feelings of competence in the system user. Two aspects are of prime importance: In the first place, the speed with which feedback takes place; and in the second place, the question of whether the system provides "diagnostic" feedback, on the basis of which the user can improve his task performance.

2. Time pressure. A remarkable sort of time pressure can occur in interactive computer use when the system responds too slowly. Too long a response time arouses much irritation in users. Users begin to complain that their "thoughts started to stray".

3. Seriousness of the mistakes that can be made. This characteristic is often an indication of the extent to which a task is critical for the organization (cf. "task significance", Hackman & Oldham, 1980) and thus may be motivational. Automated systems are usually constructed so as to limit the chance of making mistakes as well as their seriousness. Furthermore, automated systems often make it theoretically possible to trace any mistakes made by a task performer. This brings up the question of who in the organization has access to such information. The answer to this question is closely related to the choices that the organization makes in assigning responsibilities, as was discussed earlier.

4. Vigilance. Interactive computer use requires a large degree of alertness and concentration. Interruptions by telephone calls or by colleagues are perceived as most disturbing, because they interfere with a sequence of actions.

5. Being able to decide about work pace, order of activities, and method of working. These, often related, task characteristics refer to the autonomy of the task performer. Automated systems sometimes force the user to follow certain prescribed actions. On the other hand, there are systems that can be operated by sporadic users using fixed routines, while daily users get answers to their questions in a more or less individualized manner via all kinds of shortcuts.

6. Social contacts. In the literature a distinction is made between the contacts that are necessary for task performance and opportunities for social contacts apart from the actual work. Using automated administrative systems, the necessity for social contacts seems to decrease because the task performer can request all kinds of data from the databank and no longer needs to make the rounds of other departments. On the other hand, automation and remote control also create the possibility to concentrate a number of operator functions in a central control room, so that previously isolated operators have more opportunities for social contact.

7. Task identity. This characteristic has to do with the question of whether a task constitutes an entity with a beginning and an end, so that the contribution of the task to the larger whole of the total product can become manifest. From this point of view, tasks should not be too much split into individually performed subtasks, so that the contribution of the task performer is no longer recognizable. This is, in other words, the "transformational value" (Cooper, 1973), the contribution to the total task.

Finally, it should be remarked that these aspects need not necessarily be combined in one and the same person in order to be effective from a socio-organizational point of view. Reitsma's (1989) findings illustrate that, in the design of technologically sophisticated (automated) systems, a team of different specialists concentrating both on system performance and on the quality of work can make a meaningful contribution in a socio-organizational respect.

REFERENCES

Algera, J.A., & Koopman, P.L. (1989). Coping with new technology: Central issues in perspective. *Applied Psychology: An International Review, 38,* 1–13.

Algera, J.A., Koopman, P.L., & Vijlbrief, H.P.J. (1989). Management strategies in introducing computer-based information systems. *Applied Psychology: An International Review, 38,* 87–103.

Algera, J.A., Reitsma, W.D., Scholtens, S., Vrins, A.A.C., & Wijnen, C.J.D. (1990). Ingredients of ergonomic intervention: How to get ergonomics applied. *Ergonomics, 5,* 557–578.

Altman, N., & Dull, K. (1988). *Participation in technological change: Company strategies and participation.* Dublin: European Foundation for the Improvement of Living and Working Conditions.

Andriessen, J.H.T.H. (1994). Conditions for successful adoption and implementation of telematics in user organizations. In J.H.T.H. Andriessen, & R.A. Roe (Eds.), *Telematics and work.* Hove: Lawrence Erlbaum.

Andriessen, J.H.T.H., & Roe, R.A. (1994). *Telematics and work.* Hove: Lawrence Erlbaum.

Argelo, S.M. (1982). Valkuilen bij automatiseringsprojecten [Pitfalls in automatization]. *Informatie, 24,* 133–144.

Ashmos, D.P., McDaniel, R.R., & Duchon, D. (1990). Differences in perception of strategic decision-making processes: The case of physicians and administraters. *The Journal of Applied Behavioral Science, 26,* 201–218.

Bailey, J.E., & Pearson, S.W. (1983). Development of a tool for measuring and analysing computer user satisfaction. *Management Service, 29,* 530–545.

Ballantine, M. (1988). The potential of decision support and expert systems. In V. de Keyser et al. (Eds.), *The meaning of work and technological options* (pp. 111–129). Chichester: Wiley.

Bemelmans, T.M.A. (1986). Ontwikkelingsmethoden voor informatiesystemen: Onopgeloste problemen [Development methods for information systems]. In *Methodieken voor informatiesysteemontwikkeling* [Methods for system development]. NGI-rapport 3a. Amsterdam: De Cirkel.

Bemelmans, T.M.A. (1984). *Bestuurlijke informatiesystemen en automatisering.* [Information systems and automation]. Leiden/Antwerpen: Stenfert Kroese.

Bemelmans, T.M.A., & Boer, J.G. de (1986). Het ontwikkelen van informatiesystemen [Development of information systems]. In *Methodieken voor informatiesysteemontwikkeling* [Methods for system development]. NGI-rapport 3a. Amsterdam: De Cirkel.

Benson, D.H. (1983). A field study of end user

computing: Findings and issues. *MIS Quarterly, 7*, 35–45.

Berger, P., & Luckman, T. (1966). *The social construction of reality*. London: Penguin Press.

Berting, J. (1993). Organization studies and the ideology of technological determinism. In S.M. Lindenberg & H. Schreuder (Eds.), *Interdisciplinary perspectives on organization studies*. Oxford: Pergamon Press.

Bessant, J., & Dickson, K. (1981). *Issues in the adoption of micro-electronics*. London: Frances Pinter.

Bijvoet, L.C.L., & Zomer, (1996). Toepassingsgebieden voor methoden voor IS-ontwikkeling. *Informatie, 28*, 280–288.

Blackler, F. (1991). Technological choice and organizational cultures. Applying Unger's theory of social construction. In R.A. Roe, M. Antalovits, & E. Dienes, (Eds.), *Proceedings of the workshop on technological change process and its impact on work*. Budapest: Füti Nyomdaüzem.

Blackler, F., & Brown, C. (1986). Alternative models to guide the design and introduction of the new information technologies into work organizations. *Journal of Occupational Psychology, 59*, 287–313.

Blank, J., & Krijger, M.J. (1982). *Evaluation of methods and technics for the analysis, design and implementation of information systems*. Den Haag: Academic Press.

Blokdijk, A. (1986). Systeemontwikkelingsmethodiek SASO [System development method SASO]. In *Methodieken voor informatiesysteemontwikkeling* [Methods for system development]. NGI-rapport 3a. Amsterdam: De Cirkel.

Boehm, B.W. (1986). A spiral model of software development and enhancement. *ACM Sigsoft Software Engineering Notes, 11, 4*, 14–24.

Boonstra, J.J., & Koopman, P.L. (1993). *Strategies for organizational and technological innovations: Experiences in Dutch retailing*. Paper at International Work Conference of the Active Society with Action Research. Helsinki, Finland, 25–27 August.

Brabander, B. de, & Thiers, G. (1984). Successful information system development in relation to situational factors wich affect effective communication between MIS-users and EDP-specialists. *Management Science, 30*, 137–155.

Briefs, U. (1975). The role of information processing systems in employee participation in managerial decision making. In E. Mumford & H. Sackman (Eds.), *Human choice and computers*. Amsterdam: North-Holland.

Briefs, U. (1980). The effects of computerisation on human work. In A. Mowshowitz (Ed.), *Human choice and computers, 2*. Amsterdam: North-Holland.

Briefs, U., Ciborra, C., & Schneider, L. (1983). *System design for, with and by the users*. Amsterdam: North-Holland.

Broek, J.G.A. van den (1986). Het evalueren van methoden voor systeemontwikkeling [Evaluating methods for system development]. In *Methodieken voor informatiesysteemontwikkeling* [Methods for system development]. NGI-rapport 3a. Amsterdam: De Cirkel.

Bubenko, J.A. (1986). Information system methodologies: A research view. In T.W. Olle, H.G. Sol, & A.A. Verrijn-Stuart (Eds.), *Information systems design methodologies: Improving the practice*. Amsterdam: North-Holland.

Buchanan, D.A., & Boddy, D. (1983). *Organizations in the computer age: Technological imperatives and strategic choice*. Aldershot: Gower.

Buchanan, D.A., & Boddy, D. (1986). *Organizations in the computer age: Technological imperatives and strategic choice*. Oxford: Blackwell.

Card, S.K., Moran, T.P., & Newell, A. (1983). *The psychology of human-computer interaction*. Hillsdale, NJ: Lawrence Erlbaum Associates Inc.

Child, J. (1987). Managerial strategies, new technology, and the labor process. In J.M. Pennings & A. Buitendam (Eds.), *New technology as organizational innovation: The development and diffusion of microelectronics*. Cambridge, MA: Ballinger.

Child, J. (1988). *Participation in the introduction of new technology into organisations*. Aston: Aston University, Work Organisation Research Centre.

Child, J., Ganter, H.D., & Kieser, A. (1987). Technological innovation and organizational conservatism. In J.M. Pennings & A. Buitendam (Eds.), *New technology as organizational innovation: The development and diffusion of microelectronics*. Cambridge, MA: Ballinger.

Child, J., & Loveridge, R. (1990). *Information technology in European services: Towards a microelectronic future*. Oxford: Basil Blackwell.

Ciborra, C.U., & Lanzara, G.F. (1994). Designing networks in action: Formative contexts and reflective intervention. In J.H.T.H. Andriessen, & R.A. Roe, (Eds.), *Telematics and work*. Hove: Lawrence Erlbaum Associates Ltd.

Clegg, C. (1984). The derivation of job designs. *Journal of Occupational Behavior, 5*, 131–146.

Clegg, C. (1988). Appropriate technology for manufacturing: Some management issues. *Applied Ergonomics, 19, 1*, 25–34.

Clegg, C.W., Kemp, N.J., & Wall, T.D. (1984). New technology: Choice, control and skills. In G. van der Veer, M.J. Tauber, T.R. Green, & P. Gorny (Eds.), *Readings in cognitive ergonomics: Mind and computers*. Berlin: Springer-Verlag.

Clegg, C., & Symon, G. (1989). *A review of human-centered manufacturing technology and a framework for its design and evaluation*. Sheffield: Memo NO 1036.

COB/SER (1984). *Flexibele automatisering*. [Flexible automation]. Den Haag: Ministerie van Onderwijs en Wetenschappen.

Cooley, M. (1980). *Architect or bee? The human/*

technology relationship. Slough: Langley Technical Services.

Cooper, R. (1973). Task characteristics and intrinsic motivation. *Human Relations, 26*, 387–413.

Cressey, P. (1985). *The role of the parties concerned by the introduction of new technology*. Dublin: European Foundation of the Improvement of Living and Working Conditions.

Cressey, P. (1989). *Trends in employee participation and new technology*. Glasgow: University of Glasgow.

Cressey, P., & Williams, R. (1990). *Participation in change: New technology and the role of employee involvement*. Dublin: European Foundation for the Improvement of Living and Working Conditions.

Cullen, R. (1995). *Eis meer dan gegevens! Onderzoek naar computerondersteuning voor algemeen management*. [Executive Information Support Systems: Research into computer support for general management]. Eindhoven: Technische Universiteit, Academisch Proefschrift.

Davis, G.B., & Olson, M.H. (1985). *Management information systems: Conceptual foundations and development*. New York: McGraw-Hill.

Davis, L.E., & Taylor, J.C. (1976). Technology, organization and job structure. In R. Dubin (Ed.), *Handbook of work, organization and society*. Chicago: Rand McNally.

Dekker, J., & Slagmolen, G. (1984). *Flexibele automatisering: Kansen op beter werk*. Den Haag: COB/SER.

Dijksman, P., Elferen, J.L.M., & Rijmer, F.E. (1982). Automatisering bij de post [Automation in the post office]. In H.J.G. Verhallen (Ed.), *Automatisering: De sociale dimensie* [Automation: The social dimension]. Alphen aan de Rijn: Samsom.

Downs, G.W., & Mohr, L.B. (1976). Conceptual issues in the study of innovation. *Administrative Science Quarterly, 21*, 700–714.

Eason, K. (1982). The process of introducing new technology. *Behaviour and Information Technology, 1*, 197–199.

Eason, K.D., Damodaran, L., & Stewart, T.F.M. (1975). Interface problems in man–computer interaction. In E. Mumford & H. Sackman (Eds.), *Human choice and computers*. Amsterdam: North-Holland.

Eason, K., & Harker, S. (1994). Tele-informatic systems to meet organizational requirements. In J.H.T.H. Andriessen, & R.A. Roe (Eds.), *Telematics and work*. Hove: Lawrence Erlbaum.

Edström, A. (1977). User influence and the succes of management information systems projects: A contingency approach. *Human Relations, 30*, 589–607.

Episkopou, D.M., & Wood-Harper, A.T. (1986). Towards a framework to choose appropriate IS approaches. *The Computer Journal, 29*, 222–228.

Erez, M. (1993). Participation in goal-setting: A motivational approach. In W.M. Lafferty, & E. Rosenstein (Eds.), *International handbook of participation in organizations (Volume III)*. Oxford: Oxford University Press.

Erez, M. (1994). Towards a model of cross-cultural industrial and orgasnizational psychology. In H.C. Triandis, M.D. Dunnette, & M.H. Leaetta (Eds.), *Handbook of industrial and organizational psychology* (2nd Edn, Vol. 4). Palo Alto, CA: Consulting Psychologists Press.

Evans, J. (1982). Arbeitsnehmer und Arbeitsplatz. In G. Friedrichs, & A. Schaff (Eds.), *Auf Gedeih und Verderb: Mikroelektronik und Gesellschaft*. Vienna: Europaverlag.

Floyd, C., & Keil, R. (1983). Adapting software development for systems design with users. In U. Briefs, C. Ciborra, & L. Schneider (Eds.), *Systems design: By, for and with users*. Amsterdam: North-Holland.

Frese, M. (1989). Human computer interaction within an industrial psychology framework. *Applied Psychology: An International Review, 38*, 29–44.

Friedrichs, G., & Schaff, A. (Eds.) (1982). *Microelectronics and society*. Oxford: Pergamon Press.

Gelper, R.P.E. (1986). Method/1. In *Methodieken voor informatiesysteemontwikkeling* [Methods for system development]. NGI-rapport 3a. Amsterdam: De Cirkel.

Gingras, B.C., & McLean, E.R. (1982). *Designers and users of information systems: A study in differing profiles*. Proceedings of Third International Congress of Information Systems. Ann Arbor, 13–15 December.

Glasson, B.C. (1984). *Guidelines for user participation in the system development process*. Proceedings of Interact "84", IFIP Conference on Human–Computer Interaction. London, 4–7 September.

Hackman, J.R., & Oldham, G.R. (1980). *Work redesign*. Reading, MA: Addison-Wesley.

Hedberg, B. (1975). Computer systems to support industrial democracy. In E. Mumford & H. Sackman (Eds.), *Human choice and computers*. Amsterdam: North-Holland.

Hedberg, B. (1979). Design process in the five banks. In N. Bjorn-Anderson et al. (Eds.), *The impact of systems change in organizations*. Alphen: Sijthof and Noordhof.

Heller, F.A. (1988). The impact of technology on the social meaning of work: A sociotechnical system's perspective. In V. de Keyser, T. Quale, B. Wilpert, & S.A. Ruiz Quintanilla (Eds.), *The meaning of work and technological options*, (pp. 111–129). Chichester: Wiley.

Heller, F.A. (1989). On humanising technology. *Applied Psychology: An International Review, 38*, 15–28.

Heller, F.A., Drenth, P.J.D., Koopman, P.L., & Rus, V. (1988). *Decisions in organizations: A three-country comparative study*. London: Sage.

Herbst, P.G. (1974). *Sociotechnical design*. London: Tavistock.

Hickson, D.J., Butler, R.J., Cray, D., Mallory, G.R., & Wilson, D.C. (1986). *Top decisions: Strategic decision-making in organizations.* Oxford: Basil Blackwell.

Hirschheim, R.A. (1983). Assessing participative systems design: Some conclusions from an explorative study. *Information & Management, 6,* 317–327.

Hirschheim, R.A. (1985). User experience with and assessment of participative systems design. *MIS Quarterly,* December, 295–304.

Hirschheim, R.A., & Klein, H.K. (1989). Four paradigms of information system development. *Communication of the ACM, 32,* 1199–1216.

Hollnagel, E., & Woods, D.D. (1983). Cognitive systems engineering: New wine in new bottles. *International Journal of Man-Machine Studies, 18,* 583–600.

Holti, R. (1994). Telematics, work places and homes: The evolving picture of teleworking. In J.H.T.H. Andriessen, & R.A. Roe (Eds.), *Telematics and work.* Hove: Lawrence Erlbaum.

Horn, L.A. ten (1991). VDU's in newspaper editing: Introduction policy, task distribution and quality of work. In R.A. Roe, M. Antalovits, & E. Dienes (Eds.), *Proceedings of the workshop on technological change process and its impact on work.* Budapest: Füti Nyomdaüzem.

Huber, G.P. (1980). *Managerial decision making.* Glenview, IL: Scott, Foresman and Company.

Huppes, T. (1985). *Een nieuw ambachtelijk elan: Arbeid en management in het informatietijdperk.* Leiden/Antwerpen: Stenfert Kroese.

IDE-International Research Group (1993). *Industrial democracy in Europe revisited.* Oxford: Oxford University Press.

Ives, B., & Olson, M.H. (1984). User involvement and MIS success: A review of research. *Management Science, 30,* 586–603.

Johansson, G. (1989). Stress, autonomy, and the maintenance of skill in supervisory control of automated systems. *Applied Psychology: An International Review, 38,* 45–56.

Keen, P.G.W. (1987). Telecommunications and organizational choice. *Communication Research, 14,* 588–606.

Kelly, J. (1982). Useful work and useless toil. *Marxism Today, 26,* 8, 12–17

Kern, H., & Schumann, M. (1985). *Das Ende der Arbeitsteilung? Rationaliserung in der industrellen Produktion.* Munich: Beck.

Kickert, W.J.M. (1979). *Organizational decision making: A systems-theoretical approach.* Amsterdam: North-Holland.

Kimberly, J.R. (1987). Organizational and contextual influences on the diffusion of technological innovation. In J.M. Pennings & A. Buitendam (Eds.), *New technology as organizational innovation: The development and diffusion of microelectronics.* Cambridge, MA: Ballinger.

Kling, R. (1983). Social goals in planning and development. In H. Otway & M. Peltu (Eds.), *New office technologies: Human and organizational aspects.* London: Francis Pinter.

Koopman, P.L. (1990). New information technology and organizational decision making. *The Irish Journal of Psychology, 11, 2,* 186–210.

Koopman, P.L. (1991). Between control and commitment: Management and change as the art of balancing. *Leadership and Organization Development Journal, 12, 5,* 3–7.

Koopman, P.L. (1992). Between economic-technical and socio-political rationality: Multilevel decision making in a multinational organization. *The Irish Journal of Psychology, 13, 1,* 32–50.

Koopman, P.L., & Algera, J.A. (1989). Formalization and delegation: Two management dilemmas in automation design processes. In K. de Witte, (Ed.), *The challenge of technological change for work and organisation: Tools and strategies for the 1990s.* Leuven: Acco.

Koopman, P.L., Drenth, P.J.D., Heller, F.A., & Rus, V. (1993). Participation in complex organizational decisions: A comparative study of the United Kindom, the Netherlands, and Yugoslavia, In E. Rosenstein & W.M. Lafferty (Eds.), *International handbook of participation in organizations* (Vol. 3), pp.113–133). Oxford: Oxford University Press.

Koopman, P.L., & Pool, J. (1990). Decision making in organizations. In C.L. Cooper & I.T. Robertson (Eds.), *International review of industrial and organizational psychology.* London: Wiley.

Koopman, P.L., & Pool, J. (1991). Organizational decision making: models, contingencies and strategies. In J. Rasmussen, B. Brehmer, & J. Leplat (Eds.), *Modelling distributed decision making:* (pp. 19–46). London, Wiley.

Koopman, P.L., & Pool, J. (1992). Management dilemmas in reorganization. *The European Work and Organizational Psychologist, 1, 4,* 225–244.

Kraft, P. (1979). Challenging the Mumford democrats at Derby works. *Computing Europe, 17,* August.

Kragt, H. (1983). *Operator tasks and annunciator systems; studies in the process industry.* Eindhoven: Technische Universiteit.

Kragt, H. (Ed.), (1992). *Enhancing industrial performance: Experiences with integrating the human factor.* Basingstoke: Taylor & Francis.

Laagland, P.T.M., & Schaddelee, C. (1986). PRISMA: Een methode voor informatiesysteemplanning en systeemontwikkeling [PRISMA: A method for planning and development of information systems]. In *Methodieken voor informatiesysteemontwikkeling* [Methods for system development]. NGI-rapport 3a. Amsterdam: De Cirkel.

Land, F., Mumford, E., & Hawgood, J. (1980). Training the system analyst of the 1980s: Four analytical procedures to assign the design process. In H.C. Lucas, F.F. Land, T. Lincoln, & K. Supper (Eds.),

The information systems environment. Amsterdam: North-Holland.

Langerhorst, R.P. (1986). SDM vernieuwd [SDM renewed]. *Informatie, 28,* 478–481.

Lawler, E.E., & Rhode, J.G. (1976). *Information and control in organizations.* Pacific Palisades: Goodyear.

Leonova, A.B. (1991). Psychological means of control and prevention of industrial stress at computerized working places. In R.A. Roe, M. Antalovits, & E. Dienes (Eds.), *Proceedings of the Workshop on Technological change process and its impact on work.* Budapest: Füti Nyomdaüzem.

Levi, H., & Williams, R. (1983). User involvement and industrial democracy. In U. Briefs, C. Ciborra, & L. Schneider (Eds.), *System design: By, for and with users.* Amsterdam: North-Holland.

Leyder, R. (1979). De computer, de werkgelegenheid en de crisis: een beschavingszorg? [The computer, employment, and the crisis]. *Informatie, 21, 7/8,* 308–426.

Lindblom, C.E. (1959). The science of "muddling through". *Public Administrative Review, 19,* 79–99.

Locke, E.A., & Schweiger, D.M. (1979). Participation in decision making: One more look. *Research in Organizational Behaviour, 1,* 265–339.

Luhmann, N. (1980). *Gesellschaftsstruktur und Semantik.* Frankfurt am Main: Suhrkamp.

Lyytinen, K. (1987). Different perspectives on information systems: Problems and solutions. *AMC Computing Surveys, 19,* 5–46.

Mambray, P., Opperman, R., & Tepper, A. (1986). *Experiences in participative systems design.* Bonn: Gesellschaft für Mathematik und Datenverarbeitung.

Manor, Y. (1975). The contribution of computers to participatory democracy. In E. Mumford & H. Sackman (Eds.), *Human choice and computers.* Amsterdam: North-Holland.

Mantelaers, P.A.H.M. (1988). *Systeemontwikkeling.* Delft: Technical University.

March, J.G., & Olsen, J.P. (1976). *Ambiguity and choice in organizations.* Bergen (Norway): Universitetsforlaget.

Markus, M.L., & Pfeffer, J. (1983). Power and the design and implementation of accounting and control systems. *Accounting, Organizations and Society, 8,* 205–218.

McFarlan, F.W. (1981). Portfolio approach to information systems. *Harvard Business Review, 59,* 5, 142–150.

McKersie, R.B., & Walton, R.E. (1991). Organizational change. In M.S. Scott Morton (Ed.), *The corporation of the 1990s: Information technology and organizational transformation.* New York: Oxford University Press.

Mintzberg, H. (1983). *Power in and around organizations.* Englewood Cliffs, NJ, Prentice-Hall.

Mintzberg, H. (1988) Opening up the definition of strategy. In J.B. Quinn, H. Mintzberg, & R.M. James

(Eds.), *The strategy process: Concepts, contexts and cases.* London: Prentice-Hall.

Mohr, L.B. (1987). Innovation theory: An assessment from the vantage point of the new electronic technology in organizations. In J.M. Pennings & A. Buitendam (Eds.), *New technology as organizational innovation: The development and diffusion of microelectronics.* Cambridge, MA: Ballinger.

Monger, R.F. (1987). *Managerial decision making with technology.* New York: Pergamonn Press.

Morssink, P.B., & Kranendonk, A. (1987). *De voorkant van het automatiseren* [The frontside of automation]. Leiden: Stenfert Kroese.

Mulder, M. (1971). Power equalization through participation? *Administrative Science Quarterly, 16,* 31–38.

Mumford, E. (1983). Participative systems design: Practice and theory. *Journal of Occupational Behaviour, 4,* 47–57.

Mumford, E., & Henshall, D. (1979). *A participative approach to computersystems design.* London: Associated Business Press.

Mumford, E., & Weir, M. (1979). *Computer systems in work design: The ETHICS method.* London: Associated Business Press.

Naumann, J.D., Davis, G.B., & McKeen, J.D. (1980). Determining information requirements: A contingency method for selection of a requirements assurance strategy. *The Journal of Systems and Software, 1,* 273–281.

Nicholas, J.M. (1985). User involvement: What kind, how much and when? *Journal of Systems Management, 36,* 23–27.

Nora, S., & Minc, A. (1978). *L'information de la société.* Paris: La Documentation Française.

Normann, R. (1971). Organizational innovativeness: Product variation and reorientation. *Administrative Science Quarterly, 16,* 203–215.

Northcott, J., & Rogers, P. (1982). *Microelectronics in industry: Survey statistics.* London: Policy Studies Institute.

Nutt, P.C. (1984). Types of organizational decision processes. *Administrative Science Quarterly, 29,* 414–450.

Nygaard, K. (1980). Workers participation in system development. In A. Mowshowitz (Ed.), *Human choice and computers, 2.* Amsterdam: North-Holland.

Offenbeek, M.A.G. (1992). Van methode naar scenario's [From methods to scenarios]. Amsterdam: Thesis Free University.

Offenbeek, M.A.G. van, & Koopman, P.L. (1996a). Interaction and decision making in project teams. In M. West (Ed.), *Handbook of work group psychology.* Chichester: Wiley.

Offenbeek, M.A.G. van, & Koopman, P.L. (1996b). Scenarios for system development: Matching context and strategy. *Behaviour & Information Technology, 15,* 250–265.

Olle, T.W., Hagelstein, J., MacDonald, I.G., Rolland,

C., Sol, H.G., Assche, F.J.M. von, & Verrijn-Stuart, A.A. (1988). *Information systems methodologies: A framework for understanding.* Wokingham (England): Addison-Wesley.

Oppelland, H.J., & Kolf, F. (1980). Participative development of information systems: Methodological aspects and empirical experiences. In H.C. Lucas, F.F. Land, T. Lincoln, & K. Supper (Eds.), *The information systems environment.* Amsterdam: North-Holland.

Osterman, P. (1991). The impact of IT on jobs and skills. In M.S. Scott Morton (Ed.), *The corporation of the 1990s: Information technology and organizational transformation.* New York: Oxford University Press.

Peiró, J.M., & Prieto, P. (1994). Telematics and organizational structure and processes: An overview. In J.H.T.H. Andriessen, & R.A. Roe (Eds.), *Telematics and work.* Hove: Lawrence Erlbaum.

Pennings, J.M. (1987). On the nature of new technology as organizational innovation. In J.M. Pennings & A. Buitendam (Eds.), *New technology as organizational innovation: The development and diffusion of microelectronics.* Cambridge, MA: Ballinger.

Pettigrew, A. (1985). *The awaking giant.* Oxford: Blackwell.

Pfeffer, J. (1981). *Power in organizations.* Boston: Pitman.

Pirow, C. (1983). Why systems don't provide solutions. *Systems, Objectives, Solutions, 3,* 89–94.

Prakke, F. (Ed.) (1987). *Human factors in system design: Methodology and cases in factory automation.* Apeldoorn, Netherlands: TNO.

Pyborn, P.J. (1981). *Information systems planning: A contingency perspective.* Boston, MA: MBA dissertation Harvard University.

Quinn, J.B. (1988) Managing strategies incrementally. In J.B. Quinn, H. Mintzberg, & R.M. James (Eds.), *The strategy process: Concepts, contexts, and cases.* Englewood Cliffs, NJ: Prentice-Hall.

Rammert, W. (1983). *Soziale Dynamik der technische Entwicklung.* Opladen: Westdeutsche Verlag.

Rammert, W. (1985). *Soziale Dynamik der technische Entwicklung.* Opladen: Westdeutscher Verlag.

Rasmussen, J. (1983). Skills, rules and knowledge: Signals, signs and symbols, and other distincions in human performance models. *IEEE Transactions on Systems, Man, Cybernetics, 13,* 257–266.

Reeken, A.J. van (1986). *Naar een andere aanpak in de systemering [To a different approach in automation].* Paper at Conference on Technology, Labour and Economics, Maastricht, 23–24 October.

Rees, A.J. van (1986). De methode doet het niet [The method does not work]. In *Methodieken voor informatiesysteemontwikkeling* [Methods for system development]. NGI-rapport 3a. Amsterdam: De Cirkel.

Reitsma, W.D. (1989). Personele gevolgen van technologische innovatie [Personnel consequences of technological innovation]. In A. Simonse, W. Kerkhoff & A. Rip (Eds.), *Technology assessment in ondernemingen* [Technology assessment in organizations]. Deventer: Kluwer.

Riesewijk, B., & Warmerdam, J. (1988). *Het slagen en falen van automatiseringsprojecten* [Success and failure of automation]. Nijmegen: Instituut voor Toegepast Sociaal-Wetenschappelijk Onderzoek.

Robbins, S.P. (1990). *Organization theory: Structure, design, and applications* (3rd Edn). Englewood Cliffs, NJ: Prentice-Hall.

Robey, D. (1977). Computers and management structure: Some empirical findings re-examined. *Human Relations, 30,* 963–976.

Robey, D., & Markus, M.L. (1984). Rituals in information system design. *MIS Quarterly, 8,* 5–15.

Robinson, D.N., Fitter, M.J., Rector, A., Newton, P., & Sneath, E. (1991). Supportive assessment: An evaluation methodology for the development of medical information systems. In R.A. Roe, M. Antalovits, & E. Dienes (Eds.), *Proceedings of the workshop on technological change process and its impact on work.* Budapest: Füti Nyomdaüzem.

Roe, R.A. (1988). Acting systems design: An action theoretical approach to the design of man-computer sytems. In V. de Keyser, T. Qvale, B. Wilpert, & S.A. Ruiz Quintanilla (Eds.), *The meaning of work and technological options* (pp.111–129). Chichester: Wiley.

Roe, R.A. (1989). New technology and work. In B.J. Fallon, H.P. Pfister, & J. Brebner (Eds.), *Advances in industrial and organizational psychology.* Amsterdam: Elsevier Science Publications.

Roe, R.A. (1991). Technological change process and its impact on work: Conclusions and perspective. In R.A. Roe, M. Antalovits, & E. Dienes (Eds.), *Proceedings of the Workshop on Technological change process and its impact on work.* Budapest: Füti Nyomdaüzem.

Roe, R.A. (1994). Reflections on telematics and work: Conceptual and methodological issues. In J.H.T.H. Andriessen, & R.A. Roe (Eds.), *Telematics and work.* Hove: Lawrence Erlbaum.

Rogard, V. (1994). Experimentation with eletronic mail in the banking sector: A case study. In J.H.T.H. Andriessen, & R.A. Roe (Eds.), *Telematics and work.* Hove: Lawrence Erlbaum.

Rokart, J.F., & Flannery, L.S. (1983). The management of end user computing. *Communications of the ACM, 26,* 776–783.

Ruskin College (1994). *The control of frontiers: Workers and new technology: Disclosure and use of company information.* Oxford: Ruskin College.

Ruys, H.D. (1986). De ISAC-methodiek. In *Methodieken voor informatiesysteemontwikkeling* [Methods for system development]. NGI-rapport 3a. Amsterdam: De Cirkel.

Sääksjärvi, M. (1980). Framework for participative systems long range planning. In H.C. Lucas, F.F.

Land, T. Lincoln, & K. Supper (Eds.), *The information systems environment.* Amsterdam: North-Holland.

Sanders, A. (1985). *Automatiseren of werken.* Eindhoven: Technical University.

Schneiderman, B. (1980). *Software psychology: Human factors in computer and information systems.* Cambridge, MA: Winthrop.

Scott Morton, M.S. (Ed.) (1991). *The corporation of the 1990s: Information technology and organizational transformation.* New York: Oxford University Press.

Senge, P.M. (1990). *The fifth discipline: The art and practice of the learning organization.* New York: Doubleday Currency.

Senker, P. (1985). Training for automation. In M. Warner (Ed.), *Microprocessors, manpower and society.* Aldershot: Gower.

SER (1982). *Rapport werkgelegenheidseffecten micro-electronica* [Report employment consequences of micro-electronics]. Den Haag: Sociaal-Economische Raad.

Shenkar, O. (1988). Robotics: A challenge for occupational psychology. *Journal of Occupational Psychology, 61,* 103–112.

Shomenta, J., Kamp, G., Hanson, B., & Simpson, B. (1983). The application approach work-sheet: An evaluative tool for matching new development methods with appropriate applications. *MIS Quarterly,* December, 1–10.

Sorge, A., Hartmann, G., Warner, M., & Nicholas, I. (1982). *Mikroelektronik und Arbeit in der Industrie.* Frankfurt/New York: Campus Verlag.

Sverko, B. (1991). New technologies and the content of work. In R.A. Roe, M. Antalovits, & E. Dienes (Eds.), *Proceedings of the Workshop on Technological change process and its impact on work.* Budapest: Füti Nyomdaüzem.

Swieringa. J., & Wierdsma, A.F.M. (1992). *Becoming a learning organization.* Berkshire: Addison-Wesley.

Teulings, A.W.M. (1987). A political bargaining theory of co-determination: An empirical test for the Dutch system of organizational democracy. *Organizational Studies, 8,* 1–24.

Vaas, S. (1988). *A model approach towards industrial automation.* Ppaer at International Conference on "Joint design of technology organization and people's growth", Venice.

Vandenbulcke, J. (1986). Systeemmethoden. In *Methoden voor informatieontwikkeling* [Methods for system development]. NGI-rapport 3A. Amsterdam: De Cirkel.

Veen, J.M. van (1993). *Toy or tool? Electronic mail as*

an organizational medium. Dissertation. Amsterdam: Free University.

Veld, J. In 't (1989). *Manager en informatie: Informatiesystemen met of zonder computer.* Amsterdam: Elsevier.

Vijlbrief, H.P.J., Algera, J.A., & Koopman, P.L. (1985). *Management of automation projects.* Paper at Second West-European Conference on the Psychology of Work and Organization, Aachen.

Völlmar, H. (1985). *De organisatie-aspecten van de automatisering* [Organizational aspects of automation]. Leiden: Stenfert Kroese.

Vonk, R. (1987). *Prototyping van informatiesystemen.* Den Haag: Academic Service.

Wall, T.D., Burner, B., Clegg, C.W., & Kemp, N.J. (1983) *New technology, old jobs?* Paper at First North-West European Conference on the Psychology of Work and Organization, Nijmegen.

Walton, R.E. (1985). From control to commitment: Transforming work force management in the United States. In K.B. Clark, R.H. Hayes, & C. Lorenz (Eds.), *The uneasy alliance.* Boston: Harvard Business School Press.

Warner, M. (1985). *Microelectronics, technological change and industrialized economies: An overview.* Henley: Management College.

Wasserman, A.I. (1979). USE: A methodology for the design and development of interactive information systems. In H.J. Schneider (Ed.), *Formal models and practical tools for information systems design.* Amsterdam: North-Holland.

Watson, T.J. (1986). *Management, organization and employment strategy: New directions in theory and practice.* London: Routledge & Kegan Paul.

Weitzel, J.R., & Kerschberg, L. (1989). Developing knowledge-based systems: Reorganizing the system development life cycle. *Communications of the ACM, 32,* 482–488.

Wentink, A., & Zanders, H. (1985). *Kantoren in actie* [Offices in action]. Deventer: Kluwer.

Wilkinson, B. (1983). *The shopfloor politics of new technology.* Aldershot: Gower.

Wilpert, B. (1991). Decision making, interest and influence patterns in introducing new technologies. In R.A. Roe, M. Antalovits, & E. Dienes (Eds.), *Proceedings of the Workshop on Technological change process and its impact on work.* Budapest: Füti Nyomdaükem.

Yates, J., & Benjamin, R.I. (1991). The past and present as a window on the future. In M.S. Scott Morton (Ed.), *The corporation of the 1990s: Information technology and organizational transformation.* New York: Oxford University Press.

18

Transformation to a Market Economy: The Case of Poland

Stanisława Borkowska and Jolanta Kulpińska

1 CHARACTERISTICS OF TRANSFORMATION–THE STARTING POINT

Poland, like the other central European countries was placed under the Soviet influence after the end of the Second World War, although it was one of the victorious Allies. Besides, the war deprived it of one-third of its territory. These facts, along with a political system imposed by another country that benefited from Poland's territory, had to have some effect on people's attitudes and expectations towards work also, as it was a common feeling that some part of any work done was not to the benefit of the country. However, in the late 1940s, the attitude of reluctance, a kind of opportunism, also at work, was not commonly shared (reconstruction of the country, social promotion of millions of people due to the elimination of illiteracy, distribution of land among the landless peasants or petty farmers as the result of the so-called "land reform", nationalisation of landed estates, etc.).

Intensifying Stalinism in the 1950s brought about a change in social attitudes, behaviour, and expectations. A feeling of the inefficiency of real socialism was spreading, combined with dissatisfaction with the low living standards and Poland's political position in the world, placed, to some extent, on the outskirts of the main stream of civilization. This was linked with the feeling of lack of real independence

Despite similarity between the systems, the Polish case significantly differs from other central European countries. Its main features were: strong position of the Catholic Church, considered as an institution representing the core of Polish nature and national continuity; Catholicism constituted a kind of antithesis of communism, although some party members were often practising Catholics, maintaining private farming. The bright side of the latter was that it gave much better output than in other central European countries. However, it continued to be underinvested and scattered because of the state's economic policy. These two features, as well as the size of the country (population of 38 million and an area several times greater than of any other central European country except the USSR) and almost complete ethnic homogeneity meant that the USSR's control over Poland was more difficult to exercise and consequently weaker than that observed in the other real-socialism countries.

Dissatisfaction with the political system was expressed in outbursts of social unrest, more frequent in Poland than in the other countries of the Soviet zone, and the attempts at economic and even social reforms undertaken occasionally from 1956. The reforms faced political barriers lifted only in 1989 as the consequence of the so-called "Round Table". Nevertheless, a day before the political switch over Poland was one of the leaders among the central European economies regarding the economic and social reforms. For instance, Poland was the first among the real-socialism countries to establish a Court of State, Constitutional Court, and an Ombudsman. Also, Polish political opposition was the strongest. In terms of economic reforms one needs to take note of activities aimed at the free running of economic activities, a liberal legal framework for establishing joint ventures and foreign companies, the breaking down of the state monopoly of purchasing agricultural products and the state's monopoly of supplying and selling, the large independence of enterprises in setting their wage policy on the basis of the company agreements and taking advantage of the point method of job evaluation, the start of the banking reforms, etc. Hungary, however, outpaced Poland in two issues, very important for efficient functioning of economy: Earlier, in 1988, it had introduced the tax on personal income and VAT.

So, the strong will to act as well as political and economic preparation of the transformation to the market economy meant that this process was first started in Poland.

Still, the economic background to the initial reforms was not completely favourable. Firstly, Poland suffered from the greatest debt compared with its possibilities of repayment. Secondly, discipline in economy was much lower in Poland, i.e. the disequilibrium was higher than in the other central European countries: high inflation, severe shortages in the market, queuing people, monetary chaos. Thirdly, compared with the other post-socialist countries (excluding Albania and Romania in the later years) the degree of mobilization of employees and the intensity of their social and wage claims were extremely high. These were the means for forcing political changes.

Implementation of the transformation process needs prior introduction of a package of political changes, i.e. the constitution of the state. In Poland, these changes are not complete and they are often delayed in relation to the economic ones, which must influence their course.

From the point of view of work and organizational psychology, evaluation of the process of economic transformation in Poland needs earlier characterizing of its social and cultural background and the process itself.

2 GOALS, WAYS, AND BARRIERS IN THE TRANSFORMATIONS

The term "transformation to a market economy" only defines a general direction of the changes. These directions gained full social approval, as they were identified with the future welfare characteristic of Western countries. It also meant rejection of alien domination and the unwanted Soviet system. However, the model of this economy was unclear—social-market economy or neoliberal?

The Polish–German treaty mentioned the social-market economy. This model was also supported by the Prime Minister of the first government, but then the same government followed the neoliberal policy by introducing the so-called "Balcerowicz plan" based on monetary ideas. After eight years this problem remains open although the last two governments have also declared implementation of the model of a social-market economy.

Given the not very clear direction of the transformation, it is difficult to expect a clear definition of its long-term objectives, as well as of its conditions and methods of execution. In political terms, an especially important issue is to answer the question: parliamentary democracy or strong presidential power, unity of the state and

Church or their autonomy, industrial democracy or administrative and legislative model of regulations of labour relations? On the other hand, in social and economic terms, the highest uncertainty is associated with the question of social insurance and privatization.

In other words, as the society is unaware of what is ahead of it, when it may happen, and what the cost is going to be, why should it give its support? This is one of the principal causes of political instability.

Since the very beginning, however, the goals and necessary short-term activities that condition the transformation into a market economy have been obvious. These goals are economic stabilization and construction of the private sector. They were distinctly defined in the Balcerowicz programme (named after the vice Prime Minister responsible for carrying out this programme).

The Balcerowicz programme assumed that economic stabilization would be reached during 1990 by:

- balancing the budget;
- radical suppression of inflation to a one per cent monthly rate by the end of 1990 (see Table 18.1);
- consolidation of the zloty and providing for its internal convertibility.

To execute these tasks, a shock therapy was applied, quite rightly as it seems, or, to be more precise, a demand shock, a drastic drop in household's incomes, producing a collapse in the demand for commodities and services. This had to lead to a decrease in the output and deterioration in the financial standing of companies.

This choice—different from the other central European countries (excluding East Germany)—continues to be controversial. Arguments for and against are pronounced. At least two arguments advocated it for the stabilization of the economy:

- At the moment of the political switch over inflation in Poland was higher than in the other central European countries. In the first half of 1989, it amounted to 160% and in the second half—mainly due to the liberalization of the farming products' and foodstuff's prices and

elimination of subsidies to agriculture—reached the level of 2000% (PTE, 1991). Suppression of hyper-inflation requires radical and not gradually implemented actions.

- The painful operations of lowering the standard of living are easier to carry out when enthusiastic support is being given to reforms and immense social trust is being placed in the authorities. Therefore, one should have taken advantage of the moment, considering that no enthusiasm is forever (Dabrowski, 1992).

On the other hand, psychological and social aspects spoke against the shock therapy.

1. At the starting point of building a new system, Polish society, like those of the other central European countries, was relatively poor. Yet, it enjoyed social security, i.e. stability of employment, social insurance, and social welfare, free medical care and free education, as well as a number of other social benefits such as state subsidies to medicines, railway tickets, coach tickets and municipal transport, etc.

2. The post-socialist societies were brought up to be egalitarian. This is both in property terms as well as in professional and social achievements. Therefore, these societies generally do not accept polarization of wealth. Egalitarianism, including levelling of wages, was the direct way to uniformity of structural and instrumental solutions applied nation-wide. Hence, these societies were unprepared for decentralization and differentiation.

3. The central European countries are characterized by relatively high qualifications and ambitions. Considering their long period of a relative poverty and the sharp contrast with the standard of living in the neighbouring Western countries, they demand the swiftest possible improvement of their material position, and their working and living conditions. It is quite clear that a comparison of the present position of the central European countries with the situation of West Germany or other west European countries soon after the Second World War cannot be justified. It should be added that at the start of the reconstruction, expectation of a fast rise in the standard of living was perhaps excessive because of the trust in the new authorities elected from the "Solidarity" trade union and the faith in their reliability

and professionalism. In these circumstances disappointment appears deeper and continuous, adding to more profound passiveness and distrust.

Therefore, the main objective was to cushion the impact of the shock so that its social costs were not too high and long lasting, to give society the time and opportunity to adapt to new requirements. In other words, suppression of inflation should not bring about too deep a recession, since this would cause a return of inflation, further deterioration of the standard of living, high unemployment, and delay in privatization.

On the other hand, in the period of the structural transformations, including privatization, the shock approach was unjustified, owing to the complexity of the changes needed, and insufficient domestic capital to privatize the extensive state-owned sector (84% of industrial output in 1989 came from this sector). Consequently, unlike in the former GDR, the path of gradual privatization was chosen in line with the general neoliberal strategy in Poland. First to be privatized were trade and services (almost 100%) and the best manufacturing companies. Because of the shortage of capital, privatization of the manufacturing sector is carried out mainly by liquidation. According to the data available at the end of 1993, over half (56%) of the state-owned companies entered into the process of privatization (Sytuacja, 1994, p.57). Unfortunately, the most monopolized and unprofitable industries were not included in the restructuring (mining, metallurgy, fuels, energy, and shipbuilding). They are a considerable burden for the whole economy, thereby delaying its transformation. Powerful trade unions in these industries and the threat of social tensions have made the state protect them. This is reflected in tax exemptions, suspended tax payments, or lifting duty to pay social-insurance contributions.

Privatization was assumed to be a way to increase economic efficiency. Therefore, it should convey significant and required change in the level and structure of employment, management techniques and production, etc. This, however, did not happen. Excessive politicization meant that privatization became, in a sense, an objective in itself. Budget revenues from the private sector are insignificant and statistical indices of this sector's

efficiency of management are worse than in the state-owned sector (Sytuacja, 1994, p.47). The "propensity" to invest, however, is higher.

Tending to accelerate the processes of privatization, the state implements a restrictive financial and fiscal policy with respect to the state-owned companies. Still, in 1992, the burden of taxation exceeded their gross financial result by almost 20% and a year later made up 90.8% of this result. This fact, combined with a high interest rate and maintained fixed and overestimated dollar exchange rate, explains the deep drop of investment in the sector of the state-owned companies.

On the other hand, the activities accelerating privatization were accompanied by a "slowdown" policy, probably as an unintended side-effect of the implemented programme of economic stabilization. A symptom of this policy was the aforementioned protection of monopolistic organizations. It was also applied by means of a tax on over standard wages (the so-called "popivek"). This was to be paid by these state-owned companies that exceeded the allowed standard increase in average wages. It encouraged them to keep low-paid employees (that is, with low skills or productivity) instead of employing highly qualified persons able to accelerate the development of the company, but paid accordingly, i.e. above the average. Consequently, "popivek" added to the reduction of the rate of growth of unemployment. However, because it arrested an increase in wages it has remained a tool rejected by the trade unions and an object of economic and socio-political controversy.

As we can see, the process of restructuring is characterized by internal inconsistencies. Measures were not taken towards adjustment of education and human attitudes and behaviour to the market economy. Its course is rather slow, with a focus on privatization. It also produces distrust in the authorities and many disputes originating in the suspicions that persons constituting governmental bodies trade in public assets to gain personal profits (with the major target being here the Ministry of Transformation of Ownership). On the other hand, the trade unions have attempted to include in the privatization agreements such items as guarantees of maintaining the current level of employment for several years, current social benefits, components of wages, and even indexation linked to the increase in wages, as well as levels of wages comparable with those in corresponding industries of the EU countries. Further, they have pressed on granting the employees participation shares of high value (free or at very preferential prices) in the assets of the privatized companies.

Unlike with the restructuring, the assumptions of the stabilization strategy, and more precisely the demand shock, were actually overrun many times (Table 18.1). Here social costs turned out to be much higher and persistent.

The greatest success of stabilization was the consolidation of the currency and the introduction of internal convertibility of the zloty. Owing to this, the currency black market was wound up. Inflation has been suppressed to a great extent, but nevertheless is still high (Biuletyn, 1996):

1st half	1989—160%
2nd half	1990—2000%
	1990—585%
	1991—70.3%
	1992—43%
	1993—35.3%
	1994—32.2% (forecasted)

A surplus in the commodities and services appeared in the market accompanied by a shortage of money, queues became history. Also, the plan to balance the state budget deficit was more than reached in the first year of the reconstruction by applying the demand shock. Nevertheless, a budget deficit appeared in the next years, deeper than in 1989. The major reason for this failure was the above-mentioned restrictive financial policy towards the sector of the state-owned enterprises, which were the major source of the budget's incomes.

Apart from the external factors (collapse of markets of the former USSR and the central European countries, war in the Middle East, restrictions on exports to Western countries), implementation of the stabilisation programme brought about a deep recession (Tables 18.2 and 18.3).

In the years 1989–91 the GDP per capita fell by over one-fifth, production by over one-third and productivity by 26% (Table 18.3). Unemployment emerged (unknown in Poland still in 1989) and its rate in the first year of stabilizing the economy already amounted to 6.3%. Only (compared with assumptions) in the second half of 1992 (or perhaps already?) did the first symptoms of arrested recessionary trends became visible and a year later economic growth appeared. It intensified in 1994 (Hume I., 1994). GDP per capita grew by 5.8%, inflation declined, industrial output and productivity also grew (Tables 18.2 and 18.3).

Poland left crisis behind as the first country of central Europe. Still in 1993, GDP per capita in the group of these countries dropped by 9%, whereas in Poland it grew by 4% and in Czech Republic by 1%. In 1994, further improvement of these results against the countries and the region was anticipated (Figures 18.1 and 18.2).

It cannot be questioned that economic successes

TABLE 18.1		
Specification	*Assumptions*	*Results*
Rate of inflation (GPI) %	20.0	90.0
Production of the socialized industry	−5.0	−25.0
National income distributed	−3.1	−19.0
Trade balance:		
Billions US dollars	−0,8	+2.2
Billions Rbl	+0.5	+6.6

Polish stabilization programme: Assumptions and results, 1990.

Note:
In the second letter of intent to IMF, the following rates of inflation were assumed for the last three months of 1990, respectively: 1.5%, 1.0%, and 2.0% monthly, i.e. 20% yearly on average. Real inflation amounted to 5.5% monthly on average.

Source: Data from GUS, Rocznik Statystyczny (1991), Warsaw (1992).

Comparison of basic economic values in 1993 (1989 = 100%).

TABLE 18.2

Economic values	1993
1. Employed in national economy (annual average)	87
2. GDP produced	86
3. Incomes from sale of production and services:	
—in industry	74
—in agriculture	86
4. Prices of industrial production	1817
5. Retail prices of consumer goods and services (CPI)	2260
6. Investment outlays	87
7. Average net real wage	72
8. Average net real old age pension	88
9. Flats put to use	57

Source: Elaborated on the basis of: *Socio-economic situation in 1993*, Central Planning Office, Warsaw, 1994, pp.28–29.

were achieved, although with much delay compared with the forecast, but in advance of the other countries going through the transformation period.

A part of the economic effects of transformation directly influence society. This is the area where successes are really few.

2 BASIC ECONOMIC EFFECTS OF TRANSFORMATION AFFECTING SOCIETY

Among others, these effects mainly comprise:

- on the positive side: liquidation of queues and thus higher comfort of living;
- on the negative side, as the population views it: spreading poverty zone, wealth inequalities, high unemployment, feeling of social insecurity, and unreformd administrative and legislative labour relations.

Excessive politicization of economic decisions and the unclear situation of the state-owned companies (and thus their employees) also gave birth to some symptoms of social disintegration, frequent replacement of the managing staff in the state administration and companies and, consequently, a questioning of their authority, short-term decisions, and insufficient professionalism.

Although the need for stronger finance, banking, marketing, and accounting is perceived because of the adaptation of the economy to the market-economy logic, the role of Human Resources Management is still underestimated, as well as the need for qualitative restructuring of labour resources.

2.1 Impoverishment of society

The basic source of population's income is wages, remuneration, and then company and supra-company social benefits.

In the post-war period, the model of low wages and full employment dominated in the central European countries. At the same time, owing to ideological and partially to practical reasons (industrialization), higher wages were enjoyed in the material-production sphere, particularly in heavy industry, building, and transportation. Blue-collar workers were relatively better paid. On the other hand, workers in the so-called budgetary sphere—education, science, healthcare, culture—and the executive staff in enterprises were definitely and permanently underpaid. For example, in 1988, the earnings of directors were still on average only twice as high as the earnings of the workers subject to them (Borkowska, 1992), but the wages of directors in the budgetary sphere were lower than the wages of workers in the material-production sphere.

Low wages are a social problem because of the

TABLE 18.3

Basic economic value (%).

Specification	1990	1991	1992	1993	1994
1. Employment (previous year = 100)	95.8	94.1	95.8	97.6	99.8
2. Labour productivity (previous year = 100)	94.2	97.8	105.0	104.0	104.1
3. Rate of unemployment (end of period)	6.3	11.8	14.3	16.4	16.0
4. Investment outlays (previous year = 100)	89.9	95.9	100.7	102.2	106.0
5. Average annual price index of:					
• consumer goods and services	685.8	170.3	143.0	135.3	132.2
• industrial production	722.4	148.1	128.5	131.9	125.3
6. Budget deficit a percentage of GDP	0.4	−3.8	−6.0	−2.8	−2.8
7. Estimates of the percentage of the population living in poverty*	39.7	38.8	42.5	—	—

* 45% of the 1989 average wage (*Public policy and social conditions. Central and Eastern Europe in transition*, Regional Monitoring Report No. 1, 1993).

rising costs of living, a drop in the demand constraining the possibilities of recovering from recession, the insufficient supply of domestic capital that could be used for privatization and the development of small business, intensifying poverty and the strong contrast to such rich neighbours (Table 18.4) as Germany, the Scandinavian countries, as well as the better financial standing of the Czecho-Slovak and Hungarian populations. This contrast is growing more acute considering Poland's association with the European Community. It may provoke the emergence of social tensions.

Another feature of wages was their "levelling", i.e. narrow spreads reflecting job and performance evaluation.

The relatively low average wages in the period of less than 10 years were reduced twice by about a quarter; once in 1982, i.e. under the martial law, and for the second time in 1990 as an element of the stabilization programme being implemented. The level of real wages of 1980 was reconstructed only at the end of 1989, then it dropped again by as much as 28% in the period 1989–93. Hence, the already relatively low wages experienced a deep and long-lasting reduction. According to the World Bank experts, they account for as much as 60% of the poverty, whereas unemployment accounts for only 35% (Analiza, 1994, p.5).

Wages growth is forecasted within the next four years, but relatively low compared to the growth of GDP, Consumer Price Index or labour pro-

FIGURE 18.1

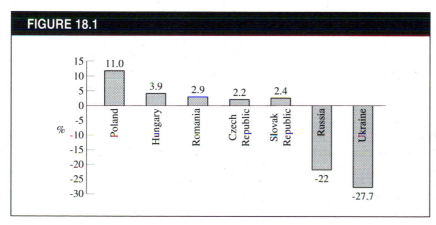

Rate of changes in industrial output in 1994.

Source: Data from Wstępna, Centralny Urząd Planowania (Central Planning Office), Warsaw (1995).

Growth of GDP in 1994.

Source: Data from Informacja o sytuacji społeczno-ekonomicznej kraju w I kwartale 1997. GUS (Information on socio-economic situation in the 1st Quarter 1997, Central Statistical Office), Warsaw (1997).

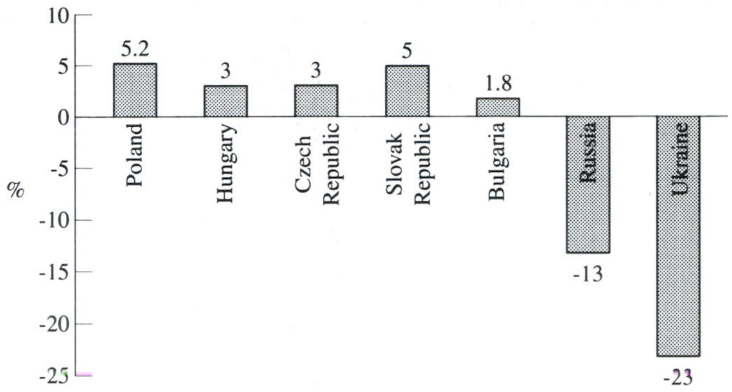

FIGURE 18.2

ductivity. According to the "Strategy for Poland", relevant economic ratios worked out by the government are to evolve as follows (Kołodko, 1993):

the year 1997 (forecast)

1993 = 100

average wage in the national economy in fixed prices	110.8%
average old age and disability pension	112.5%
productivity of labour in fixed prices	117.5%
GDP	121.8%
investments	132.4%
CPI	121.4%
rate of unemployment	14.7%

(in reality, in the first half of 1997, the rate of unemployment was 11.6%).

Even though wages in Poland do not make the major sources of inflation (the present inflation is cost-push and not demand-pull), the restrictive wages policy is still applied in the public sector by using the above-mentioned "popivek" for fear of the return of inflation.

The generally drastic decline of real wages was not distributed evenly. It affected the budgetary-sector employees the most strongly, especially those in education and medical service with, at the same time, a considerable increase in wages of the state-administration employees and those in juris-diction. In the manufacturing sector, the highest increase in wages took place in companies operating within large monopolistic organizations (Informacja, 1994, p.52), despite their being the least profitable and subject to deep restructuring (e.g. the mining industry, fuels-energy, tobacco, and telecommunications).

2.2 Supra-company social benefits

The decline of wages is accompanied by a reduction of social benefits and commercialization of social services (see Table 18.5).

These benefits were rather extensive and supplemented low wages. For example, pensioners, medical personnel, railway workers, military personnel, police forces, and war veterans took advantage of free medicines, others paid only 33% of the medicine's price. Almost all the groups (except for the medical personnel and railway workers, although the latter and their families paid only 20% of railway fare) enjoyed free public transport. Half-fare tickets were used by pupils, students, teachers, etc. In total, about 10 million people took advantage of free or half-price railway tickets and about 4.7 million people of bus tickets. The majority of them were deprived of these privileges as a logical consequence of the introduced market rules. Because of the budget deficit also, pensions for two million people and many other social benefits rendered by the state, for instance family allowances for the unemployed, were lowered. Also, the access to them was largely restricted.

The ratio of an average pension to average wage

TABLE 18.4

Daily income in US$, 1992–1993.

	Poverty line	Lowest old age pension	Unemployment benefit	Minimum wage	Average home manufacturing wage	Ratio of minimum wage: poverty line
France	7	17		33	47	4.7
USA	<10		21	26	65	3.0
UK	5	6	9	32	47	8.4
Sweden	8	19	56		63	
West Germany	9				82	
Portugal	3	3	8	8.5	18	3
Poland	2	2	2.5	3	7	1.5

Note:

Poverty line per head in a four-member family. The real poverty line in the USA is lower: US$10 per person a day is the federal level (for calculations), not used by all states in payments. In the case of Poland and Portugal, this is the lowest old age pension (not guaranteed). Unemployment benefits in the UK and Poland are levelled. In the case of USA, average unemployment benefit (however granted for 9 months, compared with 12 in other countries), for Sweden average benefit for 1989. For minimum wages, the hourly rates were converted to monthly amounts (for 22 working days) and then divided by 30. For Poland the data are as at the end of 1993.

Source: Analiza (1994, p. 18).

has been declining. For example, it dropped from 65.3% in 1991 to 64.0% in 1994 (Biuletyn, 1996).

Social prices were abandoned, e.g. for books, rentals, public utilities, etc. and this produced their radical price increase. Because of the budget deficit, public expenditures on schools and hospitals were reduced. Out of necessity, but informally, pupils' parents, in the case of schools, and patients, in the case of hospitals, have to participate in the costs of maintaining these institutions, although formally, their services are free (see Table 18.5).

2.3 Company social benefits

Drastic deterioration of the financial condition of the state-owned companies and institutions made them narrow, to some extent, the range and size of their present and rather extensive non-wage benefits rendered to the employees, for example, reimbursement of the recreation costs of employees and their children. These benefits varied across industries and companies. Their highest share could be found in the public services and the mining industry.

Despite the drastic restrictions imposed on the social benefits, these continue to be—in the view of the World Bank (Analiza, 1994)—relatively high compared with the other European countries with "typical" market economies. In Poland in 1992, they made up about 19% of the GDP, whereas in Spain and Portugal only 11% and 13%, respectively, "although the GDP per capita in these countries is two and three times higher". The question that can be posed here is "despite" or rather "because" of the ratio? It is commonly known that the lower the GDP per capita and the poorer the society, the higher the share of the relatively low benefits per capita in the GDP.

If we compare the proportion of these expenditures with those occurring in central Europe, then we shall see that it is lower by one-third than in Hungary, the Czech Republic, and the Slovak Republic (Public, 1993, p.76). Of course, we can view this phenomenon as an irrational social policy, but that is a separate problem.

The part of the population living off agriculture also experienced a drastic reduction of their real incomes.

Following the decline of all three categories of real incomes (i.e. wages, supra-company, and

TABLE 18.5

Average differences between the regional values of the national average for selected variables and countries, 1989–1992.

	Year	Rate of unemployment	Rate of social assistance	Rate of crime	Total consumer expenditure per capita	Share of household expenditure on:		
						Health[a]	Education[b]	Rentals, water charges and . . .
Bulgaria	1989	—	0.29	---	--	0.77	----	3.53
	1990	0.38	0.21	--	0.7	—	--	—
	1991	1.16	4.64	----	38.1	—	—	—
	1992		7.08	---	6.9	1.19	—	5.07
	1993	—	—	—	--	--	—	—
Hungary	1989	0.20	3.39	284.4	--	1.39	0.88	11.42
	1990	0.45	4.01	583.7	---	—	--	—
	1991	1.53	5.18	652.9	17.4	1.53	1.15	14.36
	1992	2.90	--	638.7	-	—	--	--
	1993	---	---	---		—	—	—
Czech Republic	1989	---	1.50	420.7	—	0.33	0.29	8.41
	1990	0.10	1.11	968.9	0.3	—	—	---
	1991	1.50	1.30	1091.1	−27.0	—	—	—
	1992	1.08	—	--	9.3	0.63	0.67	11.69
	1993	—	—	—	--	---	---	---
Poland	1989	1.26	--	263.0	—	2.55	0.60	3.45
	1990	2.33	---	527.3	22.2	—	—	—
	1991	2.69	—	458.9	4.1	—	---	—
	1992	—	---	693.8	3.0	5.25	1.54	12.98
	1993							

Note:
The natural increase is equal to the difference between the crude birth-rate (CBR) and the crude death rate (CDR) per 1,000 persons; [a] all households; [b] active households

Source: Based on *Public policy and social conditions, Central and Eastern Europe in transition*, Regional Monitoring Report, No. 4, (1993) pp.14, 22, 29.

company benefits), the poverty zone spread. Poverty, as we know, has not received a clear definition. Even the measures of so-called "objective poverty" (i.e. according to the statistical data) are varied. Hence, any unquestionable estimation of its range in Poland is not possible. Taking 45% of the average wage of 1989 as the poverty line, we see that as much as 42.5% (Table 18.3) of the population entered the poverty zone in 1992. A similar outcome can be obtained by taking as the poverty line the social minimum for a household with a single old-age pensioner (Informacja, 1994, p.55).

The assessment of poverty in Poland presented by the World Bank, applying much more severe criteria, is quite different. These are expenditures per adult in a household (children are treated as "half" of an adult) being lower than the highest old-age pension (Table 18.4). The poverty index is only 14.4%. What is more, in the Bank's opinion, this poverty is rather narrow, since expenditures of the poor are only by 12–15% lower than the lowest old-age pension (Analiza, 1994). When interpreting such an established poverty index, at least two factors need to be considered:

● in 1993 the lowest old age in pension in Poland was only 52% of the social minimum in a household with a single old-age pensioner;
● the general price increase index was used in the calculation and not the index of price changes for the basic consumer products that prevail in the

spending of the poor people measured by the first two mentioned criteria.

The threat of poverty is growing from year to year. It is highest in households of old-age pensioners, the unemployed, and farmers (Panek, 1994, p.4), and in the case of families with three and more children.

The individual fear of poverty turns out to be much stronger than is shown by the objective indices. This can be caused by frequent changes of prices and the lack of security of employment and social benefits, but also by the unfavourable arrangement of many social indices (Table 18.5), such as increasing number of crimes, shortened duration of life, etc. The appearance of homeless people and beggars cannot be questioned, either. For many post-war generations it is a new phenomenon. Charity activities start to flourish, almost non-existent until recently (excluding Western assistance during the martial law), under the system of common social insurance.

2.4 Labour market and unemployment

Transformation of the system combined with the growing world competition resulted in the need to face several major challenges linked with labour. These include:

● reduction of excessive unemployment and deep transformation of the structure of the labour market in terms of skills and occupations, sectors and industries, and sectors of proprietorship; this also means the need to stimulate increase in the mobility of the labour resources;
● increase in productivity and improvement of labour and production quality, allowing for the ecological requirements;
● reduction of the costs of labour in relation to the productivity and quality and, at the same time, growth of the motivating role of wages;
● curbing inflation.

This seemingly complex and difficult set of tasks poses the problem of accurate choice of strategies ensuring their accomplishment. When estimating them, we need to take into account the opening possibilities of free flows of labour resources within Europe resulting from the treaty on associ-

ation signed by Poland. Another factor to be considered is the forecasted high increase in population at production age. It is foreseen that by the year 2010 the increase in population will amount in Poland to 3.5 million, that is, 54% of the total increase in Europe (The sex and age distribution of population, 1991). At the same time, the European Union will experience a decline of population at production age. This especially concerns the neighbours of Poland: Germany and Sweden). The choice of strategies is determined by two key issues. The first and elementary one is the choice between an integrated macro-employment policy and the labour market policy that aims at: (1) reduction of unemployment (the employment objective); (2) improved functioning of the labour market by means of labour agencies, occupational guidance and better information supporting occupational and geographical mobility of employees (structural objective); (3) social protection of persons affected by unemployment.

In other words, the point is to solve the dilemma irrespective of whether state interventionism is indispensable or whether the state's role should be limited to facilitating the smooth course of the market regulation of labour issues? This dilemma reflects the old argument between Keynesianism (demand economy) and neoliberalism (supply economy). Alternative application of these two theories proved fallible. Convincing evidence is provided by the German economy, where Keynesianism was applied in the years 1968–74 and the supply economy in the 1980s. None of these strategies turned out to be effective. It is everyday life that imposes a pragmatic approach, combining elements of both Keynesianism and neoliberalism, while at the same time indicating the need for an active employment policy, especially in education, as well as for complementary development of labour-market policy. The latter cannot replace employment policy.

Another problem is the shape of the model of labour relations (LR) and more accurately, the labour-market control model. Here we have to handle the problem of two models. The negotiatory (consultative) or the administrative and legislative model. If negotiatory, then we have to decide whether a corporatist one (centralized), close to the west European solutions or a decentralized one, based on company collective agreements? The answer to the first part of the question is quite simple: Practice proved the inefficiency of a one-sided administrative and legislative regulation of labour problems.

Two different labour-market strategies can be distinguished. First, the neoliberal one, was in force in the years 1990–93 and was a sort of a by-product of the strategy aiming at stabilization and privatization.

The elementary features of the neoliberal Polish labour-market strategy can be summarized as follows:

1. lack of integrated employment policy at the macro level and belief in the efficiency of the "invisible hand of the market";

2. reduction of the rates of growth of unemployment by means of the so-called "popivek", by suspension of the restructuring of employment in the public sector which was mentioned before;

3. domination of the passive measures counteracting unemployment;

4. development of social-welfare and non-governmental charity actions. The spending on social welfare between 1992 and 1993 in real terms was five times higher than in 1985 (Analiza, 1994, p.16).

Let us have a look at the effects of the applied strategy in terms of employment, unemployment, wages, and productivity.

2.5 Level and structure of employment

In central Europe the constitutional principle of full employment was in force. Its execution led to partially social employment, that is, hidden unemployment. This was accompanied by a steady, although illusory, shortage of employees, which enabled them to press on increases in wages. For example, in 1988 as many as 251 job offers fell per one man and 31 per one woman. At the end of 1989, relevant numbers were as follows: 53 and 10 (*Statistical yearbook*, 1991, p.139).

Deep economic recession resulted in a drop of employment between 1989 and 1993 by almost 20% and the number of employees by almost 14%. Despite this, hidden unemployment estimated at

1.5 million people continues (Kabaj, 1995, p.90) as the fruit of a much deeper drop in production than employment.

Essential changes took place in the structure of employment by sectors of proprietorship. Employment declined mainly in the state-owned companies and some sectors of public services, namely in physical culture and sports (by about 45%) and science and technological progress (by about 40%!). On the other hand, growth took place mainly in the private sector, finance and insurance, regardless of the type of proprietorship, and in the state administration (by about 40%!). In June 1994 the share of the employed in the private sector amounted to 53.6% (Kwartalna, 1994). However, this sector absorbed only 30% of the decline in employment in the public sector.

Some changes took place in the sector-industry structure of the employed. Namely, compared with 1989, the percentage of the employed in the No. II sector (industry and construction) declined, whereas it grew considerably in the No. III sector (Table 18.6). In the last year employment in agriculture also dropped, which resulted from liquidation of the state farms. Therefore, the initiated changes aim at still higher compatibility with the EU structures. However, they are still insufficient.

● Despite transformations that took several years, the branch structure of industry was still close to the structure of the early 1970s (Kabaj, 1995b). It is characterized by a high share (about 56%) of industries producing raw materials. Employment even grew in such unprofitable industries as mining (considering drop of production and increase in wages), metallurgy and power.

An inevitable fall of some traditional manufacturing industries and companies, and development of others, will require shifts of the labour resources. Shifts between regions and countries should be anticipated. The processes of reallocation of human resources are only at their initial stage. It can be expected that they will face two main barriers: psychological and residential (deep shortage of dwellings or funds for their purchase).

● The market economy requires new qualifications and skills and makes permanent upgrading

TABLE 18.6			
Sector	1989	1992	1994 (February)
I Agriculture and forestry	29.3	29.5	24.6
II Industry and construction	35.3	32.1	31.7
III Services	35.4	38.4	43.7

Structure of employment by sectors as on 31 December 1992.

Source: *GUS statistical yearbook (1993) and Quarterly information on economic activity of population*, Labour Market Monitoring (1994).

and extending present qualifications necessary. On the other hand, the uncertainty of employment combined with the technological and organizational changes makes natural the need for single or multiple changes of occupation or employer. Industriousness and hunger for success have become the driving forces. So, changes in the structure of qualifications and occupations of employees are also necessary. Yet, they have not become a part of the neoliberal labour-market strategy .

● The appearance of the private sector outside agriculture produced new forms of employment radically suppressing the feeling of security, but, on the other hand, often allowing the avoidance of tax liabilities by the employees and employers. The common phenomenon is a job contract for a period of under one month to avoid paying contributions to social insurance. Overtime is also reduced. In the state-owned companies overtime is not necessary considering the recession; it occurs in the private sector but is not recorded. The working conditions also deteriorate. In the private sector this is mainly due to the weakness or lack of the trade unions that could protect the interests of employees.

2.6 Unemployment

This economic phenomenon is an inseparable component of the market economy. Its novelty meant that society was not psychologically prepared to face it, the labour infrastructure was not adequate, and, finally, the state had insufficient measures to counteract unemployment.

In the years 1990–94 a fast-growing unemployment appeared, despite the declining rate of inflation and wages. In 1994 it affected almost 2.8 million people and its rate was 16% (Figure 18.3) of the economically active population.

Therefore, the unique drop in wages does not affect its rate. In some regions of Poland almost every third person at the age of economic activity remains jobless. The Polish unemployed have faint opportunities of finding jobs, for example in

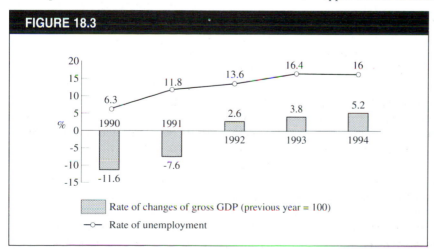

FIGURE 18.3

Rate of changes of gross GDP (previous year = 100)

—○— Rate of unemployment

Rate of changes of gross GDP and unemployment rate.

1994, 112.6 people exist per one job vacancy. One should notice, however, that the dynamics of the growth of unemployment is declining. At the same time, the high open unemployment is accompanied by the hidden one, that is, being in excess compared with the productivity of labour. Its size is estimated at about one million persons.

Unemployment in Poland affected mainly relatively well-educated and young people. It is best reflected in the fact that almost 70% of the unemployed are people with education higher than primary, and as much as 63% of the unemployed are below 34 years of age. Despite the comparative novelty of unemployment in Poland, a very large part of it (almost 45%) is chronic, which weakens the pressure on reduction in wages. It should also be added that more than half of the unemployed (51.7%) is not authorized to receive sick benefit; this means that they are forced to use social assistance (Informacja, 1994, p.64).

The unemployment that emerged is a consequence of economic recession and especially the erroneous exchange rate and tariffs policy, as well as investment and liquidation policies. Experts of the World Bank estimate the drop in competitiveness of the Polish companies to be at about 30% (UNDP Polska, 1995). This means that the structural unemployment only will appear (Kabaj, 1995, p.25)).

Undoubtedly, unemployment added to better discipline at work (Smuga, 1995), but also produced frustration and a sense of social degradation among the unemployed.

2.7 Passive character of the labour-market policy

A natural consequence of the supply (liberal) policy was domination of the passive, over active, labour-market policy. It was to cushion the effects of the rapid increase in unemployment caused mainly by the economic recession, but also by excessive liberalism.

The rudimentary features of the policy are as follows:

● Shortage of measures for combating unemployment and improper use of those available. This is very well illustrated by comparing the average annual expenditures per unemployed person in Poland and the Western countries.

When, for example, in Sweden, Switzerland, and Denmark about US$30,000 were spent in 1991 per unemployed person, in Poland US$770. What is more, the Labour Fund meant to combat unemployment showed falling dynamics in the years 1990–93.

● Spending the lion's share of the scarce resources on the passive forms of counteracting unemployment, mainly benefits. In 1992 only 4.7% of them were allocated to the active forms and one year later 11.1%, i.e. some 0.22% of the GDP. Despite the necessary qualitative restructuring of employment, training was provided to only 2.8% of the unemployed (18% in OECD, including the Netherlands 25%, Austria 27%, Norway 87%, and Sweden 110%.

● Reducing the range of unemployment by early retirement. In the years 1990–92 only the number of old-age and disability pensioners grew by over 1,668,000 people. The rapid increase in old-age pensions and higher unemployment benefits turned out to be a great burden for the state budget.

The failure of the internally inconsistent neoliberal employment policy made the state change it in favour of:

● integrated active employment policy combined with a complementary labour-market policy;

● increase in the resources allocated to programmes combating unemployment;

● stressing active forms of combating unemployment that lead to domination of labour and training over unemployment. We call this strategy pragmatic. Its pillars are optimization of the economic relations with other countries, stimulation of investments, acceleration of the rate of reforms in the education system, and arresting further increase in wages, so that the growth rate of productivity is almost three times higher than the rate of growth of wages.

Since implementation of this strategy is only commencing any evaluation of it would be premature.

2.8 Labour productivity and wages

The fall in employment is accompanied by a less than proportional drop of productivity (Table 18.3) and a much deeper fall in real wages. The growth of the GDP in 1993 by 4% was entirely the product of the increase in the productivity of labour. In 1994, productivity grew by 4.1% (Informaja, 1994, p.69).

Within the wages policy several interesting phenomena can be observed:

- high absolute and relative elasticity of wages in the first stage of transformation: This elasticity faces changes in their low level, impossible to keep in the long run;
- significant weakening of the motivating function of wages in the first years of transformations in relation to the costs of living. Wage relation to productivity (30%) was similar to that in the EU (33%);
- gradual increase in wage differentiation during the last several years, reflected in:
  spreading span between wages of blue-collar workers and salaries of white-collar workers;
  increasing differentiation of salaries in the blue-collar workers' group;
  higher differentiation of wages in the private than in the public sector;
- gradual simplification of the internal structure of wages (reduction of the number of their components and tighter link with labour),
- further administrative arrest on the increase in wages in the public sector to protect from the increase in inflation.

To maintain low wages for a longer period of time is risky both from the psycho-social and economic points of view, although some advantages cannot be denied. Because of the psycho-social reasons, low wages and high inflation must be of some influence on the material position of households and their attitude to transformation. Wages, with their currently low level, when confronted with the appearance of not always honestly gained wealth, become the major source of collective disputes and social unrest. They also stimulate the propensity to immigrate.

Economically, wages restrict the possibility of effective motivating as well as qualitative and quantitative restructuring of employment. This is all the more difficult with continuing high inflation, making living costs the major determinant of the increase in wages.

Low wages, as was pointed out by the entrepreneurs, are the main obstacle in the growth of the effective demand (Kabaj, 1995) necessary to speed up economic growth. On the other hand, low wages, to some extent and temporarily, provide an opportunity for increasing the competitiveness of the Polish economy. Partly because the total labour costs dropped less than wages, owing to the fast increase in the non-wage costs such as taxes ("popivek"), social contributions to the Labour Fund designed to combat unemployment, etc. Let us note that in 1991 the cost of one hour of labour in Poland was 8.3 times lower than in Germany and Sweden. Between 1992 and 1993 the average daily pay in Poland was 11.7 times lower than in Germany and 9 times lower than in Sweden (see Table 18.4), the GDP per capita was 12.7 times lower than in each of these countries, and only 6.3 times lower if the purchase power of money is allowed for (Rocznik, 1994, p.220).

2.9 Industrial relations

Solving difficult problems is more effective when efforts are integrated and cooperation between all interested parties is effected. This view and the logic of democracy mean that an immanent feature of market economies are consultations on industrial relations, involving all agents of the labour market in solving the problems of labour and wages. In Poland, as in the other central European countries, the system of public, administrative regulation of the rate of wage increases, combating unemployment, and social policy continues to dominate. It is a relic of the past system; combined with poor communication, it has an impact on the inefficiency of problem-solving. This happened because actually none of the parties (government, employers, employees) is prepared to use consultative industrial relations and they are generally not perceived by politicians as an integral part of the democratic system. Still, it is for the first time in the history of Poland that legal grounds have been created that enable employers' organizations to act as a party to collective bargaining and enter into collective agreements. However, the organizations are still very weak and are no match for the strong trade unions.

Let us explain that until now collective agreements in the real-socialism countries were concluded between headquarters of the trade unions and governmental bodies. The present three major headquarters of trade unions do not cooperate mainly due to political reasons. Therefore, they do not make a joint representation either to the employers or to the government. Moreover, they behave as political parties or their instrument rather than as trade unions protecting employees' interests. Last but not least, trade unions mainly present their own claims. Cooperation between labour and management in seeking possibilities for improving productivity and expanding to protect jobs and increase wages has not yet evolved.

On the other hand, the government, partly out of fear that consultative, partner-type labour relations may result in increases in inflation, and partly due to the belief in its omnipotence, maintains the traditional, administrative model of these relations. It is characteristic that from 1948 real negotiatory labour relations have not earned approval from the authorities. In the 1980s, in the period of reformation of the economy, company wage systems were introduced as a kind of experiment to avoid rigid centralized collective labour agreements. Companies that reported their will to implement company wage systems were granted freedom in their wage policy and the opportunity to adjust this policy to their financial condition. Agreements on wages were special collective agreements limited to problems of wages and company specific. Soon, almost 90% of the state-owned companies put them into action. Traditional branch collective agreements focused on social issues and working conditions. As the level of social benefits was frozen by the law, so the collective agreements actually remained dead. This situation continued because legal grounds for entering collective agreements, suited to the logic of market conditions, became available only from 1 January 1995.

Meanwhile, the company collective agreements, even extended with the social issues,

cannot by assumption regulate problems at the supra-company level, such as unemployment and the rate of growth of wages at the macro-level, or coordinate attempts of various labour market agents in this area. Because of this, a Tripartite Social and Economic Committee was established at the macro-level in 1993. So Poland, like the other central European countries, has taken the direction of neocorporatism.

The efficiency of the consultative industrial relations depends on the will to compromise and the learnt art of negotiation. The western European countries have formed their skills over many years; Poland has taken only the first step.

Economic crisis, problems accompanying privatisation and political volatility undermined trust in the authorities and added to the fall of authority. Social costs of transformation turned out to be much higher than assumed. In these circumstances, the question concerning the model of the market economy, the method and conditions of constructing it was posed openly. Without a clear answer, the society will not be willing to support undefined transformation any longer. It wishes to control its course.

The crisis produced also apathy and frustration among a part of the society, being reflected, among other ways, in the low turnout during the election and the victory of the left wing (post-communists and the rural party), both in the parliamentary election in 1993 and in that for the local authorities. Why?

3   INTERPRETATIONS

3.1   New social order and its perception

In the 20th century Polish people have undertaken three attempts to build a new political and economic system; after the First World War the major objective was to reconstruct the state and integrate the nation and society after the years of alien occupation; after the Second World War a new socialist (communist) society—within new borders—was to emerge; in 1989 the society rejected this experiment in favour of a transformation to a democratic system, based on market-economy rules. This process of transformation is equally experimental—never have such fundamental changes been implemented anywhere, when the objectives are only outlined and the ways to achieve them more the result of various political and economic circumstances than planned activities. Examples of the developed countries, where the currently functioning solutions result from historical experiences, were not sufficient, it was not always rational to implement changes by turning down ways offered by the past period, it is also rather difficult to reach back for the still older solutions from before the Second World War. Hence, only the general objective: "to go back to normality" has been formulated, or more specifically—to reform institutions and economic rules so that the economy could function according to market principles and to reform institutions and organization of the state according to the principles of the parliamentary democracy and respect for citizens' rights. Therefore, changes were viewed as a passage from the monocentric order to a society similar to those in the developed Western countries. It turned out promptly that the period of transition can be long lasting, during which hybrid solutions inherited from the past system, from relations with the surrounding as well as from external and internal factors, will coexist. So, it is advisable to use the term transformation rather than transition, when we have to face many various changes, the meaning and outcome of which are a combination of spontaneous and single activities (see Kwaśniewicz, 1992; Rychard & Federowicz, 1994).

This is not only the problem of how to define the behaviour of the processes occurring as each of the terms is related with different methods of interpretation. In particular, a lack of clarity or hybridism of solutions is stressed. Moreover, we have here an example of varied and occasional methods of interpreting the changes developing in the research. Thus, approaches to their description and analyses are subject to permanent variations resulting from the accumulation of experiences and the gaining of new knowledge. Looking back at the five years of the transformation, some of its characteristic features can be pinpointed.

The transformation bases in the top-to-bottom method of introducing changes and the main force driving them is the state. This is followed by defining, at least temporarily, some strategy and activities aimed mainly at the institutional and legal changes. Despite the initial opinions, changes of institutions cannot be a mere filling in the gap that emerged after the former system had collapsed (Stark 1992), or a transferring of institutions known elsewhere (see the situation in former East Germany), but an organic contact between the new rules and social habits. A regular characteristic of the transformation is recession, with its high social costs. The symptoms and effects of recession and unemployment have particular qualities that lead us to call them the transformation recession (unemployment) (Kornai 1990). The political chaos, the core of which is formation or evolution of parties and political movements, cannot be underestimated. The programmes of these parties are rather blurred, which produces problems with choosing the parties by their potential supporters. Usually, two programmes are confronted: liberal and socio democrat. Somewhere between them, the Christian-democratic or national-Catholic groups are located, as well as those formed on a different base—rural groups. This breakdown does not fully reflect the positions and programmes of the groupings of Polish parties in the parliament and outside of it. The situation is affected by the political role and tradition of the trade union NSZZ, "Solidarity", the disintegration of the citizens' committees that played the conclusive role in the elections of 1989 and ceased to exist in 1990, and changes in the left-wing parties, including the post-communist ones. The political chaos supports low understanding of the situation and intentions of politicians, which further produces low attendance at elections and feelings of helplessness—alienation (Korzeniewski 1993). On the other hand, we face politicization of other activities and institutions—trade unions (and more broadly, the industrial relations) and the state-owned companies. This is especially well seen in the struggle for power in companies and for the strategy of restructuring.

The institutional gap and institutional changes, leading to construction of new laws and new patterns of behaviour, encounter old habits and old rules, which, even though not always accepted and observed, were forming human behaviour. This produces a growing sense of uncertainty and even fear. This uncertainty and lower feeling of security is considered to be the characteristic feature of the post-industrial societies based on the capitalist market economy. In our case the uncertainty is quite special, which is associated with the very speed and mystery of the changes.

Apart from the really experienced costs of the changes, this uncertainty produces dissatisfaction with the course of the transformation and claims submitted to the government viewed as being responsible for the hardship of the changes. A question arises, how it was possible that the communist system collapsed and then the post-communist parties gained large support in the democratic election (Poland—1993, Hungary—1994).

The change of the political system in Poland in 1989 was not surprising. It was preceded by a period when the communist authorities searched for a way to reform the Polish economy, to make it more efficient and competitive to meet the social needs and challenges of the world economy. The factors to put under control were the structural crisis of the central planning economy, the administration–party command system as well as the shortage of resources. On the other hand, the authorities attempted to legitimize the system in society. At the same time, society, or its socially more active parts, sought ways to overthrow or "domesticate" the increasingly disapproved political regime. Sociological investigations, especially those of the 1980s, show the course of this process. Following E. Wnuk-Lipiñski, the shortest definition would be that a contradiction of values and interests was revealed in the society. The major social groups were unable to satisfy their economic and social needs; but the regime did not tolerate articulation of these needs (interests) or their institutionalization. Thus, blocking the pronouncement of interests led to the exposure of the conflict of values (such as freedom, citizenship, subjectivity, dignity). The conflict of values and interests was reflected in the duality of the social life: public and private, in the split into "us" and "them" (the authorities). Finally, all this resulted in the rejection of the system at the same moment as an opportunity appeared (Adamski, 1993). This

rejection of the socialist system made up the major, if not a single, premise of the transformation, which lacked institutional and programmatic preparation. It seemed that changing the political authorities and taking the most important decisions concerning the system would automatically affect institutions and social consciousness. It was expected that the rejection of the old regime would be equivalent to an approval of the new order, in which citizens' rights were guaranteed, but social security was not granted.

The complexity and internal contradictions of the top-and-bottom changes result, among other things, from the introduction of liberal market rules into the old structure of the economy, when the new elements of social structure, characteristic of the market economy, confront the old structure of occupations and classes, and the mentality of people formed in the former system (despite all the resistance and mutinies) faces the pattern of mentality based on entrepreneurship and individual responsiblity (Wnuk-Lipiñski, in Adamski, 1993).

3.2   Socialist mentality

In the first period (1989–90) the hardship of adaptation, symptoms of passive expectation of the success of transformation were explained just as the result of the impact of socialist mentality. It was supposed to be characterized by the following features: passive expectation of benefits and claims submited to the state, in other words, a lack of self-sufficiency and initiative, susceptibility to external factors; collectivist inclinations and no sense of personal responsibility; collectivism, but, at the same time, a feeling that uncontrolled social activities are useless. In its extreme form, it was referred to as the mentality of "homo sovieticus" (Tischner, 1993, after Zinoviev).

The socialist mentality was assumed to be a product of the system's impact, with its political care, educational patterns, and egalitarianism. Symptoms of this mentality could be found in the dissatisfaction with the course of the transformation, strikes of workers and teachers, behaviour at elections. It was an important element of the resistance against the changes. It is interesting that Jan Szczepañski (Szczepañski, 1993) considered failures of the educational system to be one of the sources of the breakdown of the socialist system, that is, unformed collectivist attitudes and subordination to the political authorities. Perhaps both views are justified. Another version stresses not so much the mentality mismatching new conditions as the developed patterns of social behaviour being not necessarily conscious habits. This stand is presented by Marody (Marody, 1991), who points to the inherent needs of the society and the sense of life, personal and social. They were not satisfactorily met under the socialist system and other ways to satisfy them have not been formed under the new system. Hence, the feeling of fear and threat that affects attitudes and opinions (Świda-Ziemba, 1994).

3.3 Cognitive shock

In the opinion of the social psychologists, the source of fears and frustration could be the so-called "cognitive shock" associated with a dramatic change. People experience cognitive difficulties with understanding the sense of the changes, purposefulness of solutions, especially the long-term ones, and calculation of personal benefits and costs. Therefore, they are rather self-restrained in approaching the changes. If the cognitive difficulties are too heavy and people stop to understand their own position, then we face "learnt helplessness". This feature, according to Kofta and Sedek (1989), is characteristic of the period of transformation. It accompanies frustration resulting from the "great expectations" associated with breaking down communism and the opening to the West. It was hoped that in a short time Western wealth would also be enjoyed by the central European countries and that the new authorities can introduce the new longed-for social order (based on freedom, sovereignty, and democracy). However, the transformation, recession, and political chaos have brought disappointment and distrust in the new leading elite.

Lower levels of education sharply co-occur with the cognitive shock, learnt helplessness, and disappointment due to the hardships. In these groups, one can find a higher propensity to authoritarianism, also regarding the political order.

3.4 Mentality and the directions of changes

Reykowski reproduces the popular "romantic" concept of transformation. This assumed that the approval of the new order results, based on centre-rightist ideology, individualism, democracy, and independence, results from the social rejection of the communist rules, collectivism, authoritarianism, and authority imposed by an alien country. According to this psychologist, this romantic and naive vision of conscience unveiled scratches and contradictions within four years . The situation is that approval of privatization and full freedom of the private sector in the formation of prices is declining, whereas it is growing regarding the protection of jobs and, at the same time, the differentiation of incomes (depending on qualifications and productivity). The state is obligated to the provision of social security. This leftist inclination is accompanied by traditional, national-communitarian, and religious values, characteristic of the right wing (Reykowski 1993). In this author's opinion also the collectivist (and demanding) attitudes and authoritarianism seem to be stronger than expected. Thus, we deal with gaps between the level of social consciousness and the direction of changes taken by the system. This can produce various reactions: apathy or political isolation (e.g. alienation, absenteeism during elections) if the citizens decide that the mechanism of democracy is not useful to articulate their needs or to form the political representation to express opinions described here (Reykowski, 1993, pp.39–46).

Apparently, both these reactions can be found in Poland and the results of the 1993 elections reflected the discussed attitudes. They are rooted not only in the inherited mentality (socialist or not) but also, or perhaps mainly, in the estimated high personal and social costs, as well as crystallized group interests.

In section 1, the scale and range of the transformation costs, mainly due to the unemployment and poverty, have been presented. Undoubtedly, the costs are a source of dissatisfaction and disappointment with the process of transformation. The wrongful policy of the authorities originating from "Solidarity" has been blamed for this and it has been expected that the coalition of the leftist parties will carry out reforms guaranteeing social security.

3.5   The winners—the losers

The transformation of the system has its winners and losers. At the beginning, the latter are more numerous when costs and sacrifices as well as individual reactions and views are looked at. In particular, the group of losers includes workers of the manufacturing industries who lost their privileged economic and social position and farmers whose small farms cannot adapt to the market needs. The losers are these groups who are threatened by a particularly high risk of losing a job, impoverishment, and with no career opportunities.

The winners are those who can trace chances in the new environment and are both qualified and industrious.

The transformation of the system changes the social structure and brings new rules of its formation. The present structure is amorphic and subject to different rules and the aforementioned crystallization of groups and interests is multi-directional. Mainly the traditional social classes are changing—the working class, farmers, and intelligentsia. New ones emerge, above all private entrepreneurs; also managers in the state-owned companies enjoy more independence and higher position in terms of incomes. They constitute (beside other specialists) a "new middle class" representing those who benefited from the transformation. Unfortunately, at the other end, the unemployed are among those who lost the most. This group is also new on the social scene, and its behaviour is mainly determined by the uncertainty of the future and its position on the peripheries of society (Dziecielska-Machnikowska, 1994).

The major factor influencing the economic and social position and mentality is the level of education. Educated people pronounce their pro-reform attitudes, individualist, and anti-authoritarian inclinations the most strongly. This is especially visible with young people.

One can hope that the economic growth and more concerned social policy will also favour increasing satisfaction with the process of change.

3.6   Anomie and everyday life

From the psychological point of view, however, such emotional reactions as the feeling of threat and frustration rank first (Koralewicz & Ziołkowski, 1991). These seem to be predominating over the sense of freedom and independence. This is undoubtedly connected with the nature of the institutional changes and structural threats, which account for the high social and psychical costs of transformations. A common change of the rules of functioning gives rise to uncertainty and a collapse of standards and norms, that is anomie (in Durkheim's sense) (Szafraniec 1991). This could be also observed under real socialism, but today its character is different. In the past, dimorphism could be observed, dualism of norms governing the public and private life, elements of social vacuum, i.e. weak identification with institutions (see Nowak, 1979, 1984). Today we can observe incoherence of axiological choices, owing, for example, to the religious requirements and everyday lack of sense and helplessness, lack of prospects for an individual success and its translation into collective, political, alienation. Maybe, it is a democratic utopia to expect political participation from most citizens. Perhaps the most important thing is building a society through everyday, routine ties and activities subordinated to "normal" desire to survive and succeed?

In relation to the "real-socialism" period, explanations of the systemic and social character seemed to be the most adequate also in the case of an analysis of behaviours and attitudes on the micro-scale, because of the authoritarian character of the system with its political control over any aspects of the social life. According to some researchers (e.g. Rychard, 1993) such a macro-social approach does not allow us to understand the dynamics of the transformation process, changes of habits and mentality take place, after all, in various dimensions of the social life. Apart from the macro-social dimension seen in its political, economic, institutional, and structural categories, attention should be paid to everything that happens within families, local groups, and occupational circles (Szczepañski, 1989). A macro-social dimension, changes in the forms of daily life are more visible the faster autonomization proceeds in relation to economic policy, consumption, and everyday life (see, Jawiowska & Kempny, 1994). This autonomization of segments of social life differs from the previous dualism, although similar elements can be found there at the present time. Among other things, its expression shows an ambiguity of success criteria (material versus meritocratic). The absence of commonly accepted moral authorities can be clearly felt. The example can be the Catholic Church losing its previously highest position among the integrative institutions.

The four-year period of changes has been a challenge for the social sciences. The Polish and foreign literature on the subject have been growing rapidly, continuously bringing new data and newer and newer attempts at interpretation. As regards studies on particular problems, cases, or spheres of social life, researchers can make reference to different detailed theories, but a new approach is still needed to explicate global processes. It appears especially interesting to refer to the theory of modernization and dependent growth formulated for the developing countries (Staniszkis, 1991; Szczepański, 1992). They point, among other things, at the importance of configuration of social factors—the so-called "modernisation" potential for the process of transformations. Very interesting also are the deliberations of economists and sociologists on the significance of the so-called "invisible" factors, i.e. social and cultural factors for the effectiveness of development processes (Doeringer et al., 1990; Porter, 1990).

This approach is all the more important as the project of economic reforms has been making insignificant allowances for socio-cultural factors all the time. They are only mentioned in the political aspect, taking into consideration the political consequences of citizens' dissatisfaction, the threat of populism, etc., but not as an important long-term modernization potential.

On the macro- and mezzo-social scales, a reference could be made to the institutional approach integrating different social disciplines and stressing the role of social actors playing in the frame of approved norms and regulations. The theory of innovations particularly regarding motivations of innovators and a socio-technique of introducing technological-organizational innovations is also referred to (Górniak, 1992;

Ratajczak, 1993). If motivation to succeed leads to enterpreneurship then psychical costs of change may produce resistance and tensions—this makes a conclusion and a warning, one of many.

As has already been mentioned, various symptoms of social resistance were approached with some surprise. Their sources were sought in the conservative mentality developed by the former system. However, explanations as to the "old" mentality cannot satisfy, especially when the institutional and structural tensions are analyzed, and crystallization of the conflict of interests characteristic of the present situation and the transformation period in general (Hausner, 1994). Some approaches integrating the macro- and micro-social factors seem to be necessary as well as pointing at the dynamics of the interrelationships (Mokrzycki, 1991; Szczepański, 1993; Sztompka, 1994). Evaluations reaching into the psychological concept of frustration and "learnt helplessness" by socio-psychologists are referring to the cognitive and humanist social psychology (see Reykowski, 1993). These concepts are accompanied by activistic theories referring to the subjective inspirations of both individuals and groups, which make up the social tissue, while tensions in this process are explained in terms of the theory of anomie (Szafraniec, 1991). The depreciation and ambiguity of norms and values is "normal" during the period of changes and fundamental transformation. The success of innovations is followed by adaptation and learning new patterns of behaviour. The tensions accompanying it would find their solutions in the negotiatory procedures of democracy.

4 CONCLUSIONS

In the preceding sections certain psycho-social problems of the transformation in Poland have been presented. Our analysis was based almost solely on the latest publications of Polish sociologists and psychologists. The question arising here is whether the picture emerging from this analysis is typically Polish or whether it resembles a picture that could be outlined by a Hungarian or a Czech author? Undoubtedly, a particularly Polish feature is the role of the trade union and workers' council, as well as a propensity to go on strike, meaning an industrial conflict, and special institutions of industrial relations. Maybe the course and character of recession and the resulting unemployment are different. It seems, however, that many problems and social reactions are similar in different countries of central Europe. These include, in particular, institutional changes, on the one hand, and the problems of facing the new reality, on the other. Besides, everywhere human helplessness collides with the readiness to change in hope of better.

REFERENCES

Adamski, W. (Ed.) (1993). *Societal Conflict and Systemic Change. The Case of Poland 1980–1992.* Warsaw: IFiS Publications.

Analiza i oceny sfery ubóstwa w Polsce. (1994). *Raport Bankuswiatowego* (Analysis and evaluation of the poverty zone in Poland). The World Bank Report. Warsaw.

Biuletyn Statystyczny GUS (Central Statistic Office Statistical Bulletin), 1996, 12.

Borkowska, S. (1992). Wage determinants in a transforming economy. In *Wages and labour relations.* Budapest: European Committee for Work and Pay.

Dabrowski, M. (1992). Pierwsze pólrocze przebra¿eñ w Rosji (First six months of transformation in Russia), *"Rzeczpospolita"—Ekonomia V*, 252.

Doeringer P., et al. (1990). *Invisible factors in local economic development.* Oxford: Oxford University Press.

Dziecielska-Machnikowska, S. (1994). *Co myśla łódzcy bezrobotni?* (What do the unemployed of Lodz think?). Institute of Sociology, University of Lodz (a research report).

Górniak, J. (1992). *Innowacyjno ść organizacji gospodarczych* (Innovations in economic organizations). Doctoral thesis, Institute of Sociology, UJ, Cracow.

Hausner, J. (1994). Reprezentacja interesów w społeczeństwach socjalistycznych i postsocjalistycznych (Representation of interests in the socialist and post socialist societies). In J. Hausner & P. Marciniak (Eds.), *Od socjologicznego korporacjonizmu do . . . ?* (From sociological corporatism to . . . ?). Studies In the System of Interests' Representation, vol. 2, Warsaw: Foundation of "Polish Labour".

Hume, I. (1994). Jak to było mozliwe? (How was it possible?). *Rzeczpospolita—Rynki, 103.*

Informacja o przebiegu procesów społecznogospodarczych w I pó roczu 1994 wraz z prognoza do końca (1994). (Information on the course of the socio-

economic processes in the first half of 1994 with the forecast until the end of 1994). Warsaw: Central Planning Office.

Jawiowska, A., & Kempny, M. (Eds.) (1994). *Cultural dilemmas of postcommunist societies.* Warsaw: IFIS Publishers.

Kabaj, M. (1995a). Labour market policies and programmes for counteracting unemployment in Poland. In M. Simai (Ed.), *Global employment. An international investigation into the future of work, Vol. 2.* London and New Jersey: Zed Books Ltd.

Kabaj, M. (1995b). *Programme for the promotion of productive employment and reducing unemployment.* Warsaw: Institute of Labour & Social Studies and Ministry of Labour and Social Policy.

Kofta, M., & Sedek, G. (1989). Learned helplessness: Affective or cognitive disturbance. In C. Spielberger, I. Sarason, & J. Stredan (Eds.), *Stress and Anxiety* (Vol. 12), Washington, DC: Hemisphere.

Kołodko, G.W. (1993). *Strategia dla Polski* (Strategy for Poland). Warsaw: Poltext.

Koralewicz, J., & Ziółkowski, M. (1991). *Mentalno ść Polaków* (Mentality of the Polish people). Warsaw: Institute of Psychology, PAN.

Kornai, J. (1990). *The road to a free economy. Shifting from the socialist system. The example of Hungary.* New York/London: W.W. Norton

Korzeniewski, K. (1993). Alienacja polityczna a uczestnictwo polityczne w warunkach transformacji systemu (Political alienation and political participation in the period of system transformation). In J. Reykowski (Ed.), *Wartosci i postawy Polaków a zmiany systemowe. Szkice z psychologii społecznej.* Warsaw: Publishing House of the Institute of Psychology, PAN.

Kwartalna informacja o aktywno ciśekonomicznej ludności. Monitoring rynku pracy. (1994). (Quarterly information about economic activity of population. Labour market monitoring). Warsaw: GUS.

Kwaśniewicz, W. (1992). Planned social change versus spontaneous processes. *The Polish Sociological Bulletin, 2.*

Marody, M. (Ed.). (1990). *Co nam zostało z tych lat. Społeczeństwo polskie u progu zmiany systemowej* (What have we kept from years gone? The Polish society at the gate of the systemic change). London: "Aneks".

Mokrzycki, E. (1991). Dziedzictwo realnego socjalizmu, interesy grupowe i poszukiwanie nowej utopii (Legacy of the Real Socialism, group interests and searching for new utopia). In *Breakthrough and challenge, diary of the 8th All Polish Sociologists Meeting.* Warsaw: Toruñ, UMK.

Nowak, S. (1979). Przekonania i odczucia współ czesnych (Beliefs and feelings of the contemporaries). In *Polaków portret własny* (The portrait of Poles painted by themselves). Cracow: Wydawnictwo Literackie.

Nowak, S. (Ed.). (1984). *Społeczeństwo polskie czasu*

kryzysu (The Polish society in the period of crisis). Warsaw: Institute of Sociology, UW.

North, D. (1990). *Institutions, institutional change and economic performance.* Cambridge.

Panek, T. (1994). Sfera ubóstwa w Polsce w latach 1990–1992 (Poverty zone in Poland between 1990–1992). *Wiadomości Statystyczne, 5.*

Porter, M.E. (1990). *The competitive advantages of nations.* London: Macmillan Press.

PTE (Polskie Towarzystwo Ekonomiczne [Polish Economic Society]). (1991). *Drogi wyjścia z polskiego kryzysu gospodarczego* (Ways of overcoming Polish economic crisis). Warsaw: PTE.

Public policy and social conditions. Central and eastern European in transition. (1993). Regional Monitoring, Report 1993, no 1.

Ratajczak, Z. (Ed.). (1993). *Zmiany społeczne. Zagrozenia i wyzwania dla jednostki* (Psychological changes. Threats and challenges for an individual). Warsaw: Institute of Psychology, PAN.

Reykowski, J. (Ed.). (1993). *Wartości i postawy Polaków a zmiany systemowe. Szkice z psychologii społecznej* (Values and attitudes of Poles versus the systemic changes. Sketches from the political psychology). Warsaw. Publishing House of the Institute of Psychology, PAN.

Rychard, A. (1993). *Reforms, adaptation and breakthrough. The sources of and limits to institutional changes in Poland.* Warsaw: IFiS Publishers.

Rychard, A., & Federowicz, M. (Eds). (1994). *Spo eczeństwo w transformacji. Expertyzy i Studia* (Society in transformation. Surveys and studies). Warsaw: IFiS PAN.

Sachs, K. (1991). Przeciw dogmatowi własnosci (Against the dogma of ownership). *Zycie Gospodarcze, 18.*

The sex and age distribution of population; The 1990 revision of the United Nations global population estimates and projections. (1991). New York: United Nations Population Studies, No 122. Department of International Economic and Social Affairs.

Staniszkis, J. (1991). *The dynamics of the breakthrough in eastern Europe. The Polish experience.* Berkeley: University of California Press.

Smuga, T. (1995). Gospodarowanie zasobami pracy (Human resources management). *Gospodarka Narodowa* (National Economy) 8–9.

Stark, D. (1992). Path dependence and privatisation, strategies in east-central Europe, *East European Politics and Societies, 6, 1,* Winter.

Statistical Yearbook (1991). Rocznik statystyczny GUS. Warsaw: Central Statistical Office.

Statistical Yearbook (1994). Rocznik statystyczny GUS. Warsaw: Central Statistical Office.

Sytuacja społeczno-gospodarcza w 1993. (Social and Economic Situation in 1993). Warsaw: Central Planning Office.

Szafraniec, K. (1991). *Człowiek wobec zmian społecznych* (An individual facing social changes). Toruń: University of Nicolaus Copernicus Publications.

Szczepański, J. (1989). *Polska wobec wyzwań przyszłości* (Poland and the challenges of the future). Warsaw: Institute of Physical Economy, UW.

Szczepański, J. (1993). *Polskie losy* (Polish paths). Warsaw: Polska Oficyna Wydawnicza, "BGW".

Szczepański, Ś. (1992). *Pokusy nowoczesno ci—polskie dylematy rozwojowe* (Temptation of modernity—Polish development dilemmas). Katowice—Cracow.

Sztompka, P. (1994). Teorie zmian społecznych a doświadczenia polskiej transformacji (Theories of social changes and the experiences of the Polish transformation). *Sociological Studies, 1.*

Świda-Ziemba, H. (1994). Mentalno ść postkomunistyczna (The post communist mentality). *Kultura i Społeczeństwo, 1.*

Tischner, J. (1992). *Etyka "Solidarności". Homo Sovieticus* (The ethics of "Solidarity". Homo Sovieticus)

UNDP Polska 95 (1995). *Raport o rozwoju spolecznym* (Report on social development). Warsaw: Split Trading.

Wnuk-Lipiński, E. (1993). *Rozpad połowiczny. Szkice z socjologii transformacji ustrojowej* (Semi-decomposition. Sketches from the sociology of the system transformation). Warsaw: Institute of Political Studies, PAN.

Yearbook of labour statistics. (1991). ILO. Geneva.

Zalozenia polityki przemysłowej, Ministerstwo Przemysłu i Handlu (Assumptions in the industrial policy. Ministry of Industry and Trade). (1992). Warsaw.

Author Index

Subject Index